Understanding Object-Oriented Programming with JAVA

Updated Edition

Understanding Object-Oriented Programming with JAVA

Updated Edition

Timothy Budd

Oregon State University

 ADDISON-WESLEY

An imprint of Addison Wesley Longman, Inc.

Reading, Massachusetts · Menlo Park, California · New York · Harlow, England
Don Mills, Ontario · Sydney · Mexico City · Madrid · Amsterdam

Senior Acquisitions Editor: Susan Hartman
Cover Designer: Lynne Reed
Project Manager: Brooke D. Albright
Compositor: Windfall Software, Paul C. Anagnostopoulos
Manufacturing Coordinator: Timothy McDonald
Cover Illustrator: Susan Cyr

Access the latest information about Addison-Wesley titles from our World Wide Web site:
http://www.awlonline.com

Java is a trademark of Sun Microsystems, Inc.

Many of the designations used by manufacturers and sellers to distinguish their products are claimed as trademarks. Where those designations appear in this book, and the publisher was aware of a trademark claim, the designations have been printed in initial caps or in all caps.

The programs and the applications presented in this book have been included for their instructional value. They have been tested with care but are not guaranteed for any particular purpose. Neither the publisher or the author offers any warranties or representations, nor do they accept any liabilities with respect to the programs or applications.

This book was typeset in ZzTEX on a PC. The fonts used were Sabon, Univers, MathTime, and Bell Centennial. It was printed on New Era Matte.

Library of Congress Cataloging-in-Publication Data

Budd, Timothy.
    Understanding object-oriented programming with Java / by Timothy
Budd. — Updated ed.
        p.   cm.
    Includes bibliographical references and index.
    ISBN 0-201-61273-9
    1. Object-oriented programming (Computer science)   I. Title.
QA76.64.B835   2000
005.13′3—dc21   99-32136
                                                                CIP

2 3 4 5 6 7 8 9 10   MA   03020100

Preface

There are many books on Java that teach you *how* to use the language, but few books that teach you *why* the language works in the way that it does.

Many books help you learn the mechanics of Java programming; few books teach you the deeper issues that lie behind the programming syntax. The goal of this book is to give you a fuller, more complete understanding of the philosophy behind Java, not just the mechanics of the language.

These principles and practices are illustrated throughout the book with extensive examples from the Java standard library. Here you can learn, for example, the many design patterns that are found in the AWT, the multitude of purposes for which inheritance is used in the standard classes, and why there are 22 different types of input/output file streams. Here you can discover why the lack of an ordered container class in the standard library is not a simple omission but is instead a reflection of a fundamental and deep property of the Java language.

In short, this book should not be considered a reference manual for the Java language, but rather a tool for understanding the Java philosophy.

STRUCTURE OF THE BOOK

The book is structured in five major sections:

Part 1 is a general, language-independent introduction to the ideas that lie at the heart of the Java world. The first major object-oriented concepts–those of classes, encapsulation, behavior, and responsibilities–will be introduced in this part and reinforced in Part 2. Chapter 1 presents the idea that the solution to a problem can be structured as interactions among a community of agents. Chapter 2 presents a brief history of the development of Java, and can be omitted at the instructor's discretion. However, Chapter 3, on design, should in no way be avoided. In fact, I strongly encourage students to conduct at least one, if not several, design exercises using CRC cards, similar to the one presented here, even before they start to learn aspects of the Java programming language.

Part 2 introduces Java through several graduated example programs (paradigms, in the original sense of the word). These examples lead students through successive steps in learning the Java language, introducing new features as they are required for specific applications. This is not a systematic introduction to all of the Java language, but rather provides examples designed to motivate the need for mechanisms discussed in other parts of the text.

Part 3 discusses inheritance, the next major object-oriented concept that the student must master after learning about classes and objects. Inheritance is a technique that is superficially obvious, but that possesses many subtle aspects that can trap the unwary programmer. The introduction of inheritance into a programming language has an impact on almost every other aspect of the language. For this reason, students familiar with conventional non-object-oriented languages should pay careful attention to this part of the book.

Part 4 discusses polymorphism, which is often an even subtler concept for the student to understand than inheritance. As the mechanism through which much of the power and applicability of object-oriented techniques is manifest, polymorphism is found in Java in many ways, as shown by the extensive examples studied in this part of the book.

Part 5 discusses features of the Java world that are important for the student to understand but not particularly notable for their object-oriented features. These items are separated from the remainder of the text so that they do not interrupt the flow of the narrative developed earlier in the book. However, the features discussed are not as difficult as their late placement in the book might indicate. At the instructor's discretion, these features can be omitted altogether, or introduced in parallel with earlier material.

OBTAINING THE SOURCE

Source code for the case studies presented in the book can be accessed via the mechanism of anonymous ftp from the machine `ftp.cs.orst.edu`, in the directory `/pub/budd/java`. This directory is also used to maintain a number of other items, such as an errata list. This information can also be accessed via the World Wide Web, from my personal home pages at `http://www.cs.orst.edu/ ~budd/`. Requests for further information can be forwarded to the electronic mail address `budd@cs.orst.edu`, or to Professor Timothy A. Budd, Department of Computer Science, Oregon State University, Corvallis, Oregon, 97331.

ACKNOWLEDGMENTS

Invaluable advice was provided by the reviewers who examined an early draft of the book. These included Richard Anderson, University of Washington; Richard Carver, George Mason University; Deborah Frincke, University of Idaho; Matt Greenwood, Bell Laboratories; David Riley, University of Wisconsin–La Crosse; and J. Richard Rinewalt, Texas Christian University.

I would like to thank my editors at Addison-Wesley, Susan Hartman and Deborah Lafferty, who patiently and quietly suffered through countless delays and postponements. It is my sincere hope that they, as well as the reader, will find the result to have been worth the wait.

ACKNOWLEDGMENTS FOR THE REVISION

A number of people have been very helpful in bringing about this update of the original manuscript. The impetus for the revision came from Ray Weedon and Pete Thomas of the Open University in the United Kingdom, who wanted to adopt the book for a course they were developing but first wanted to see "just a few changes." Ray and Pete have worked closely with me during the revision process, but the blame for any remaining errors should rest on my shoulders, not theirs.

The process of revision also gave me the opportunity to correct a number of small errors or omissions that had been reported in the first printing. Many of these were first noticed and brought to my attention by alert readers. In particular, I would like to thank Walter Beck, University of Nothern Iowa; Andrew Black, Oregon Graduate Institute; Thomas Gross, Carnegie-Mellon University; Jon Heggland, Forsvarets Forskningsinstitutt, Norway; Mattias Karlström, student at the Royal Institute of Technology, Stockholm; Thomas Larsson, Mälardalen University, Sweden; Mark Morrissey, Oregon Graduate Institute; Eyal Shifroni, Center for Educational Technology, Israel; Neal Smith, Oregon State University; and John Trono, St. Michael's College, Vermont.

Susan Hartman has once again been my able and talented editor at Addison-Wesley, assisted this time by Lisa Kalner. Paul Anagnostopoulos of Windfall Software was in charge of converting my original manuscript into a more pleasing format. He has been most patient in helping me understand the process of that conversion and how I could most easily make the new material blend in with the old. As always, I have found it a pleasure to work with the entire editorial and production staff at Addison-Wesley.

Contents

II UNDERSTANDING PARADIGMS   51

4 A Paradigm   53

5 Ball Worlds   67

         A.3.1   Literal   387
         A.3.2   Variable   388
         A.3.3   Data Field and Method Access   389
         A.3.4   Operators   389
         A.3.5   Object Creation   390
         A.3.6   Arrays   390

  B   Packages in the Java API   393

       Glossary   395
       Bibliography   409
       Index   413

Understanding Object-Oriented Programming with JAVA

Updated Edition

I

Understanding the
Object-Oriented Worldview

1 Object-Oriented Thinking

This is a book about object-oriented programming. In particular, this is a book that explores the principal ideas of object-oriented programming in the context of the Java programming language. Object-oriented programming has been a hot topic for over a decade, and more recently Java has become the commonly perceived embodiment of object-oriented ideas. This book will help you *understand* Java. It makes no pretensions to being a language reference manual; there are many other books that fall into that category. But knowing the syntax for a language should not be confused with understanding why the language has been developed in the way it has, why certain things are done the way they are, or why Java programs look the way they do. This book explores the *why*'s.

Object-oriented programming is frequently referred to as a new programming *paradigm*. The word "paradigm" originally meant example, or model. For example, a paradigm sentence would help you remember how to conjugate a verb in a foreign language. More generally, a model is an example that helps you understand how the world works. For example, the Newtonian model of physics explains why apples fall to the ground. In computer science, a paradigm explains how the elements that go into making a computer program are organized and how they interact with one another. For this reason the first step in understanding Java is appreciating the object-oriented worldview.

1.1 A WAY OF VIEWING THE WORLD

To illustrate the major ideas in object-oriented programming, let us consider how we might go about handling a real-world situation and then ask how we could make the computer more closely model the techniques employed. Suppose I wish to send flowers to a friend who lives in a city many miles away. Let me call my friend Sally. Because of the distance, there is no possibility of my picking

3

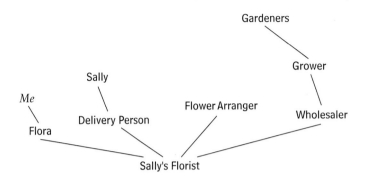

Figure 1.1   The community of agents helping me.

the flowers and carrying them to Sally's door myself. Nevertheless, sending her the flowers is an easy enough task; I merely go down to Flora, my local florist, tell her the variety and quantity of flowers I wish to send and Sally's address, and I can be assured the flowers will be delivered expediently and automatically.

1.1.1 *Agents and Communities*

At the risk of belaboring a point, let me emphasize that the mechanism I used to solve my problem was to find an appropriate *agent* (namely, Flora) and to pass to her a *message* containing my request. It is the *responsibility* of Flora to satisfy my request. There is some *method*—some algorithm or set of operations—used by Flora to do this. I do not need to know the particular method she will use to satisfy my request; indeed, often I do not want to know the details. This information is usually *hidden* from my inspection.

If I investigated, however, I might discover that Flora delivers a slightly different message to another florist in my friend's city. That florist, in turn, perhaps has a subordinate who makes the floral arrangement. The florist then passes the flowers, along with yet another message, to a delivery person, and so on. Earlier, the florist in Sally's city had obtained her flowers from a flower wholesaler who, in turn, had interactions with the flower growers, each of whom had to manage a team of gardeners.

So, our first observation of object-oriented problem solving is that the solution to my problem required the help of many other individuals (Figure 1.1). Without their help, my problem could not be easily solved. We phrase this in a general fashion as the following:

> An object-oriented program is structured as a *community* of interacting agents, called *objects*. Each object has a role to play. Each object provides a service, or performs an action, that is used by other members of the community.

1.1.2 *Messages and Methods*

The chain reaction that ultimately resulted in the solution to my program began with my request to Flora. This request led to other requests, which led to still more requests, until my flowers ultimately reached my friend. We see, therefore, that members of this community interact with one another by making requests. So, our next principle of object-oriented problem solving is the vehicle by which activities are initiated:

> Action is initiated in object-oriented programming by the transmission of a *message* to an agent (an *object*) responsible for the action. The message encodes the request for an action and is accompanied by any additional information (arguments) needed to carry out the request. The *receiver* is the object to whom the message is sent. If the receiver accepts the message, it accepts the responsibility to carry out the indicated action. In response to a message, the receiver will perform some *method* to satisfy the request.

We have noted the important principle of *information hiding* in regard to message passing—that is, the client sending the request need not know the actual means by which the request will be honored. Another all too human principle is implicit in message passing. If there is a task to perform, the first thought of the client is to find somebody else he or she can ask to do the work. This second reaction often becomes atrophied in many programmers with extensive experience in conventional techniques. Frequently, a difficult hurdle to overcome is the programmer's belief that he or she must write everything and not use the services of others. An important part of object-oriented programming is the development of reusable components, and an important first step in the use of reusable components is a willingness to trust software written by others.

Information hiding is also an important aspect of programming in conventional languages. In what sense is a message different from, say, a procedure call? In both cases, there is a set of well-defined steps that will be initiated following the request. But, there are two important distinctions.

The first is that a message has a designated *receiver*; the receiver is some object to which the message is sent. In a procedure call, there is no designated receiver.

The second is that the *interpretation* of the message (that is, the method used to respond to the message) is dependent on the receiver and can vary with different receivers. I can give a message to my wife Elizabeth, for example, and she will understand it and a satisfactory outcome will be produced (that is, flowers will be delivered to my friend). However, the method Elizabeth uses to satisfy the request (in all likelihood, simply passing the request on to Flora) will be different from that used by Flora in response to the same request. If I ask Kenneth, my dentist, to send flowers to my friend, he may not have a method for solving that problem. If he understands the request at all, he will probably issue an appropriate error diagnostic.

Let us move our discussion back to the level of computers and programs. There, the distinction between message passing and procedure calling is that message passing has a designated receiver, and the interpretation—the selection of a method to execute in response to the message—may vary with different receivers. Usually, the specific receiver for any given message will not be known until run time, so the determination of which method to invoke cannot be made until then. Thus, we say there is late *binding* between the message (function or procedure name) and the code fragment (method) used to respond to the message. This situation is in contrast to the very early (compile-time or link-time) binding of name to code fragment in conventional procedure calls.

1.1.3   *Responsibilities*

A fundamental concept in object-oriented programming is to describe behavior in terms of *responsibilities*. My request for action indicates only the desired outcome (flowers for my friend). Flora is free to pursue any technique that achieves the desired objective and is not hampered by interference on my part.

By discussing a problem in terms of responsibilities, we increase the level of abstraction. This permits greater *independence* between objects, a critical factor in solving complex problems. The entire collection of responsibilities associated with an object is often termed the *protocol*.

A traditional program often operates by acting *on* data structures, for example changing fields in an array or record. In contrast, an object-oriented program *requests* data structures (that is, objects) to perform a service. This difference between viewing software in traditional, structured terms and viewing it from an object-oriented perspective can be summarized by a twist on a well-known quote:

> Ask not what you can do *to* your data structures, but what your data structures can do *for* you.

1.1.4   *Classes and Instances*

Although I have only dealt with Flora a few times, I have a rough idea of the behavior I can expect when I walk into her shop and present my request. I am able to make certain assumptions because I have information about florists in general, and I expect that Flora, being an instance of this category, will fit the general pattern. We can use the term Florist to represent the category (or *class*) of all florists. Let us incorporate these notions into our next principle of object-oriented programming:

> All objects are *instances* of a *class*. The method invoked by an object in response to a message is determined by the class of the receiver. All objects of a given class use the same method in response to similar messages.

1.1.5   *Class Hierarchies—Inheritance*

I have more information about Flora—not necessarily because she is a florist but because she is a shopkeeper. I know, for example, that I probably will be asked for money as part of the transaction, and that in return for payment I will be given a receipt. These actions are true of grocers, stationers, and other shopkeepers. Since the category Florist is a more specialized form of the category Shopkeeper, any knowledge I have of Shopkeepers is also true of Florists and hence of Flora.

One way to think about how I have organized my knowledge of Flora is in terms of a hierarchy of categories (see Figure 1.2). Flora is a Florist, but Florist is a specialized form of Shopkeeper. Furthermore, a Shopkeeper is also a Human; so I know, for example, that Flora is probably bipedal. A Human is a Mammal (therefore they nurse their young and have hair), and a Mammal is an Animal (therefore it breathes oxygen), and an Animal is a Material Object (therefore it has mass and weight). Thus, quite a lot of knowledge that I have that is applicable to Flora is not directly associated with her, or even with her category Florist.

The principle that knowledge of a more general category is also applicable to a more specific category is called *inheritance*. We say that the class Florist will inherit attributes of the class (or category) Shopkeeper.

Another graphical technique is often used to illustrate this relationship, particularly when there are many individuals with differing lineages. This technique

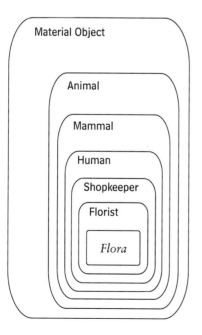

Figure 1.2   The categories surrounding Flora.

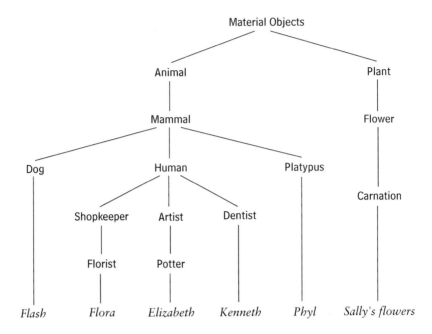

Figure 1.3 A class hierarchy for various material objects.

shows classes listed in a hierarchical treelike structure, with more abstract classes (such as Material Object or Animal) listed near the top of the tree, and more specific classes, and finally individuals, listed near the bottom. Figure 1.3 shows this class hierarchy for Flora. This same hierarchy also includes Elizabeth, my dog Flash, Phyl the platypus who lives at the zoo, and the flowers I am sending to my friend.

Information that I possess about Flora because she is an instance of class Human is also applicable to my wife Elizabeth. Information that I have about her because she is a Mammal is applicable to Flash as well. Information about all members of Material Object is equally applicable to Flora and to her flowers. We capture this in the idea of inheritance:

> Classes can be organized into a hierarchical *inheritance* structure. A *child class* (or *subclass*) will inherit attributes from a *parent class* higher in the tree. An *abstract parent class* is a class (such as Mammal) for which there are no direct instances; it is used only to create subclasses.

1.1.6 *Method Binding, Overriding, and Exceptions*

Phyl the platypus presents a problem for our simple organizing structure. I know that mammals give birth to live offspring, and Phyl is certainly a Mammal, yet

Phyl (or rather his mate Phyllis) lays eggs. To accommodate this variation, we need to find a technique to encode *exceptions* to a general rule.

We do this by decreeing that information contained in a subclass can *override* information inherited from a parent class. Most often, implementations of this approach take the form of a method in a subclass having the same name as a method in the parent class, combined with a rule stating how to conduct the search for a method to match a specific message:

> The search for a method to invoke in response to a given message begins with the *class* of the receiver. If no appropriate method is found, the search is conducted in the *parent class* of this class. The search continues up the parent class chain until either a method is found or the parent class chain is exhausted. In the former case, the method is executed; in the latter case, an error message is issued. If methods with the same name can be found higher in the class hierarchy, the method executed is said to *override* the inherited behavior.

Even if the compiler cannot determine which method will be invoked at run time, in many object-oriented languages, such as Java, it can determine whether there will be an appropriate method and issue an error message as a compile-time error diagnostic rather than as a run-time message.

That my wife Elizabeth and my florist Flora will respond to my message by different methods is an example of one form of *polymorphism*, an important aspect of object-oriented programming discussed in Chapter 12. As explained, that I do not, and need not, know exactly what method Flora will use to honor my message is an example of *information hiding*.

1.1.7   *Summary of Object-Oriented Concepts*

Alan Kay, considered by some to be the father of object-oriented programming (OOP), identified the following characteristics as fundamental to OOP [Kay 1993]:

1. Everything is an *object*.

2. Computation is performed by objects communicating with each other, requesting that other objects perform actions. Objects communicate by sending and receiving *messages*. A message is a request for action bundled with whatever arguments may be necessary to complete the task.

3. Each object has its own *memory*, which consists of other objects.

4. Every object is an *instance* of a *class*. A class simply represents a grouping of similar objects, such as integers or lists.

5. The class is the repository for *behavior* associated with an object. That is, all objects that are instances of the same class can perform the same actions.

6. Classes are organized into a singly rooted tree structure, called the *inheritance hierarchy*. Memory and behavior associated with instances of a class are automatically available to any class associated with a descendant in this tree structure.

1.2   COMPUTATION AS SIMULATION

The view of programming represented by the example of sending flowers to my friend is very different from the conventional conception of a computer. The traditional model describing the behavior of a computer executing a program is a *process-state* or *pigeonhole* model. In this view, the computer is a data manager, following some pattern of instructions, wandering through memory, pulling values out of various slots (memory addresses), transforming them in some manner, and pushing the results back into other slots (see Figure 1.4). By examining the values in the slots, we can determine the state of the machine or the results produced by a computation. Although this model may be a more or less accurate picture of what takes place inside a computer, it does little to help us understand how to solve problems using the computer, and it is certainly not the way most people (pigeon handlers and postal workers excepted) go about solving problems.

In contrast, in the object-oriented framework we never mention memory addresses, variables, assignments, or any of the conventional programming terms. Instead, we speak of objects, messages, and responsibility for some action. In Dan Ingalls's memorable phrase:

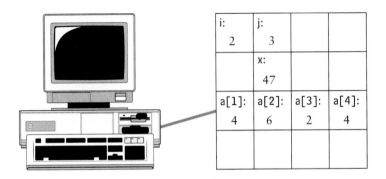

Figure 1.4   Visualization of imperative programming.

> Instead of a bit-grinding processor . . . plundering data structures, we have
> a universe of well-behaved objects that courteously ask each other to carry
> out their various desires. [Ingalls 1981]

Another author has described object-oriented programming as "animistic":
a process of creating a host of helpers that form a community and assist the
programmer in the solution of a problem (see the *Actor Language Manual*)
[Actor 1987].

This view of programming as creating a "universe" is in many ways similar
to a style of computer simulation called "discrete event-driven simulation." In
brief, in a discrete event-driven simulation the user creates computer models of
the various elements of the simulation, describes how they will interact with
one another, and sets them moving. This is almost identical to the average
object-oriented program, in which the user describes what the various entities
in the universe for the program are, and how they will interact, and finally sets
them in motion. Thus, in object-oriented programming, we have the view that
computation is simulation [Kay 1977].

1.2.1   *The Power of Metaphor*

An easily overlooked benefit to the use of object-oriented techniques is the power
of *metaphor*. When programmers think about problems in terms of behaviors
and responsibilities of objects, they bring with them a wealth of intuition, ideas,
and understanding from their everyday experience. When solutions to problems
are envisioned as pigeonholes, mailboxes, or slots containing values, there is
little in the programmer's background to provide insight into how problems
should be structured.

Although anthropomorphic descriptions such as the quote by Ingalls may
strike some people as odd, in fact they reflect the great expositive power of
metaphor. Journalists make use of metaphor every day, as in the following
description of object-oriented programming from *Newsweek:*

> Unlike the usual programming method—writing software one line at a
> time—NeXT's "object-oriented" system offers larger building blocks that
> developers can quickly assemble the way a kid builds faces on Mr. Potato
> Head.

Possibly it is this power of metaphor, more than any other feature, that is
responsible for the frequent observation that it is often easier to teach object-
oriented programming concepts to computer novices than to computer professionals. Novice users quickly adapt the metaphors with which they are already
comfortable from their everyday life, whereas seasoned computer professionals
are blinded by an adherence to more traditional ways of viewing computation.

As you start to examine the Java programs presented in the book, as well as
create your own Java programs, you may find it useful to envision the process

of programming as like the task of "training" a universe of agents to interact smoothly with each other, each providing a certain small and well-defined service to the others, each contributing to the effective execution of the whole. Think about how you have organized communities of individuals, such as a club or committee. Each member of the group is given certain responsibilities, and the achievement of the goals for the organization depends upon each member fulfilling his or her role.

1.3   CHAPTER SUMMARY

- Object-oriented programming is not simply a few new features added to programming languages. Rather, it is a new way of *thinking* about the process of decomposing problems and developing programming solutions.

- Object-oriented programming views a program as a collection of loosely connected agents, termed *objects*. Each object is responsible for specific tasks. It is by the interaction of objects that computation proceeds. In a certain sense, therefore, programming is nothing more or less than the simulation of a model universe.

- An object is an encapsulation of *state* (data values) and *behavior* (operations). Thus, an object is in many ways similar to a module or an abstract data type.

- The behavior of objects is dictated by the object *class*. Every object is an instance of some class. All instances of the same class will behave in a similar fashion (that is, invoke the same method) in response to a similar request.

- An object will exhibit its behavior by invoking a method (similar to executing a procedure) in response to a message. The interpretation of the message (that is, the specific method used) is decided by the object and may differ from one class of objects to another.

- Objects and classes extend the concept of abstract data types by adding the notion of *inheritance*. Classes can be organized into a hierarchical inheritance tree. Data and behavior associated with classes higher in the tree can also be accessed and used by classes lower in the tree. Such classes are said to inherit their behavior from the parent classes.

- Designing an object-oriented program is like organizing a community of individuals. Each member of the community is given certain responsibilities. The achievement of the goals for the community as a whole comes about through the work of each member, and the interactions of members with each other.

- By reducing the interdependency among software components, object-oriented programming permits the development of reusable software systems. Such components can be created and tested as independent units, in isolation from other portions of a software application.

- Reusable software components permit the programmer to deal with problems on a higher level of abstraction. We can define and manipulate objects simply in terms of the messages they understand and a description of the tasks they perform, ignoring implementation details.

FURTHER READING

I said at the beginning of the chapter that this is not a reference manual. The reference manual written by the developers of the language, James Gosling, Billy Joy, and Guy Steele is [Gosling, Joy, and Steele 1996]. But perhaps even more useful for most programmers is the annotated description of the Java class library presented by Patrick Chan and Rosanna Lee [Chan 1996]. Information on the internal workings of the Java system is presented by Tim Lindholm and Frank Yellin [Lindholm and Yellin 1997].

I noted earlier that many consider Alan Kay to be the father of object-oriented programming. Like most simple assertions, this one is only somewhat supportable. Kay himself [Kay 1993] traces much of the influence on his development of Smalltalk to the earlier computer programming language Simula, developed in Scandinavia in the early 1960s by Ole-Johan Dahl and Kristen Nygaard [Dahl and Nygaard 1966]. A more accurate history would be that most of the principles of object-oriented programming were fully worked out by the developers of Simula, but that these would have been largely ignored by the profession had they not been rediscovered by Kay in the creation of the Smalltalk programming language. I will discuss the history of OOP in more detail in the next chapter.

Like most terms that have found their way into the popular jargon, *object-oriented* is used more often than it is defined. Thus, the question "What is object-oriented programming?" is surprisingly difficult to answer. Bjarne Stroustrup has quipped that many arguments appear to boil down to the following syllogism:

- X is good.

- Object-oriented is good.

- *Ergo*, X is object-oriented [Stroustrup 1988].

Roger King argued [Kim and Lochovsky 1989], that his cat is object-oriented. After all, a cat exhibits characteristic behavior, responds to messages, is heir to a long tradition of inherited responses, and manages its own quite independent internal state.

Many authors have tried to provide a precise description of the properties a programming language must possess to be called *object-oriented*. I myself have written an earlier book [Budd 1997] that tries to explain object-oriented concepts in a language-independent fashion. See also, for example, the analysis by Josephine Micallef [1998], or Peter Wegner [1986]. Wegner distinguishes *object-based* languages, which support only abstraction (such as Ada), from *object-oriented* languages, which must also support inheritance.

Other authors—notably Brad Cox [1990]—define the term much more broadly. To Cox, object-oriented programming represents the *objective* of programming by assembling solutions from collections of off-the-shelf subcomponents, rather than any particular *technology* we may use to achieve this objective. Rather than drawing lines that are divisive, we should embrace any and all means that show promise in leading to a new software industrial revolution. Cox's book on OOP [Cox 1986], although written early in the development of object-oriented programming and now somewhat dated in details, is nevertheless one of the most readable manifestos of the object-oriented movement.

STUDY QUESTIONS

1. What is the original meaning of the word *paradigm*?

2. How do objects interact with one another?

3. How are messages different from procedure calls?

4. What is the name applied to an algorithm an object uses to respond to a request?

5. Why does the object-oriented approach naturally imply a high degree of information hiding?

6. What is a class? How are classes linked to behavior?

7. What is a class inheritance hierarchy? How is it linked to classes and behavior?

8. What does it mean for one method to override another method from a parent class?

9. What are the basic elements of the process-state model of computation?

10. How does the object-oriented model of computation differ from the process-state model?

11. In what way is an object-oriented program like a simulation?

EXERCISES

1. In an object-oriented inheritance hierarchy, each level is a more specialized form of the preceding level. Give an example of a hierarchy found in everyday life that has this property. Some types of hierarchy found in everyday

life are not inheritance hierarchies. Give an example of a hierarchy that is not an inheritance hierarchy.

2. Look up the definition of *paradigm* in at least three dictionaries. Relate these definitions to computer programming languages.

3. Take a real-world problem, like the task of sending flowers described earlier, and describe its solution in terms of agents (objects) and responsibilities.

4. Consider an object in the real world, such as a pet. Describe some of the classes, or categories, to which the object belongs. Can you organize these categories into an inheritance hierarchy? What knowledge concerning the object is represented in each category?

5. If you are familiar with two or more distinct computer programming languages, give an example of a problem showing how one language would direct the programmer to one type of solution, and a different language would encourage an alternative solution.

6. Argue either for or against the position that computing is basically simulation. (You may want to read the article by Alan Kay in *Scientific American* [Kay 1977].)

2
A Brief History of Object-Oriented Programming

It is commonly thought that object-oriented programming (OOP) is a relatively recent phenomenon in computer science. To the contrary in fact, almost all the major concepts we now associate with object-oriented programs, such as objects, classes, and inheritance hierarchies, were developed in the 1960s as part of a language called Simula, designed by researchers at the Norwegian Computing Center. Simula, as the name suggests, was a language inspired by problems involving the simulation of real-life systems. However the importance of these constructs, even to the developers of Simula, was only slowly recognized [Nygaard and Dahl 1981].

In the 1970s, Alan Kay organized a research group at Xerox PARC (the Palo Alto Research Center). With great prescience, Kay predicted the coming revolution in personal computing that was to develop nearly a decade later (see, for example, his 1977 article in *Scientific American* [Kay 1977]). Kay was concerned with discovering a programming language that would be understandable to people who were not computer professionals, to ordinary people with no prior training in computer use.[1] He found in the notion of classes and computing as simulation a metaphor that could easily be understood by novice users, as he then demonstrated by a series of experiments conducted at PARC using children as programmers. The programming language developed by his group was named Smalltalk. This language evolved through several revisions during

---

[1] I have always found it ironic that Kay missed an important point. He thought that to *use* a computer one would be required to *program* a computer. Although he correctly predicted in 1977 the coming trend in hardware, few could have predicted at that time the rapid development of general purpose computer applications that was to accompany, perhaps even drive, the introduction of personal computers. Nowadays the vast majority of people who use personal computers have no idea how to program.

the decade. A widely read 1981 issue of *Byte* magazine, in which the remark by Ingalls quoted in the first chapter appears, did much to popularize the concepts developed by Kay and his team at Xerox.

Roughly contemporaneous with Kay's work was another project being conducted on the other side of the country. Bjarne Stroustrup, a researcher at Bell Laboratories who had learned Simula while completing his doctorate at Cambridge University in England, was developing an extension to the C language that would facilitate the creation of objects and classes [Stroustrup 1982]. This was eventually to evolve into the language C++ [Stroustrup 1994].

With the dissemination of information on these and similar projects, an explosion of research in object-oriented programming techniques began. By the time of the first major conference on object-oriented programming, in 1986, there were literally dozens of new programming languages vying for acceptance. These included Eiffel [Meyer 1988], Objective-C [Cox 1986], Actor, Object Pascal, and various Lisp dialects.

In the decade since the 1986 OOPSLA conference, object-oriented programming has moved from being revolutionary to being mainstream, and in the process has transformed a major portion of the field of computer science as a whole.

2.1   THE HISTORY OF JAVA

The language we now call Java was originally named Oak, and was developed in 1991 by a computer scientist at Sun Microsystems named James Gosling. Oak's intended purpose was as a language for use in embedded consumer electronic applications, such as VCRs. Although this intended use might at first seem to be only a bit of historical computer trivia, in fact it was important in determining the characteristics of the language we see today.

In designing Oak, Gosling envisioned a world where many electronic devices, such as your telephone, your VCR, your television, and your computer, would all be connected together over a vast computer network. Such applications would generally possess embedded computer processors, which would control the essential running of the component. (Although we have not yet reached the point where telephones are routinely connected to the Internet, the part about electronic devices having embedded processors is now almost universally true.)

Several characteristics of embedded systems make them different from the average general purpose computer. Two of the most important features are size and reliability. Generally, the processors that run in embedded systems are very small, possessing only meager amounts of memory. Thus, a programming language designed for an embedded system must be able to be translated into a very concise encoding. An even more important aspect is reliability. When a program fails on a typical general purpose computer, the user is annoyed, but even in the worst case the user can generally recover and continue the program by rebooting the computer. The annoyance is greater if, for example, the software controlling a telephone fails. For this reason embedded systems should almost never fail, and should respond as gracefully as possible to exceptional and erroneous conditions.

Many features of Java reflect this original mindset. The language itself is small and simple, and can be translated into a very compact internal representation. Programming constructs, such as pointers or the goto statement, which experience had shown to be a source of many programming errors, were simply eliminated from the language. A powerful concept called exception handling was borrowed from earlier languages but greatly extended and intimately tied into the other aspects of the language. This *exception-handling* facility meant that any programmer writing in Java would be forced to deal with the possibilities of how programs could fail in unpredictable ways, and create code to handle the unexpected in a (hopefully) graceful fashion.

For a number of reasons, Java (or Oak) as a language for embedded consumer electronics did not materialize. But as interest in embedded systems at Sun was starting to wane, the phenomenon known as the World Wide Web was just beginning. The Web was originally developed in the early 1990s by a small group of scientists at a research lab in Switzerland as a means of quickly communicating research results to a physically far-flung set of colleagues. It was quickly realized, however, that the framework provided by the Web was applicable to a wide range of information. First, scientists in all disciplines started using the Web, and eventually the ideas found their way into the mainstream. Now, almost every organization, large or small, must have a Web page. Similarly, almost every advertisement in print or television contains an obligatory Web address (the universal resource locator, or URL).

To understand how Java fits into the World Wide Web, and to grasp the importance of Internet computing, one must first understand a little about the concept of clients and servers, and the difference between server-side computing and client-side computing.

2.2   CLIENT-SIDE COMPUTING

Although Java is a general purpose programming language that can be used to create almost any type of computer program, much of the excitement surrounding Java has been generated by its employment as a language for creating programs intended for execution across the Internet. To understand the process of programming for the Web, one must first understand a few basic characteristics of the Internet in general. The Internet is a classic example of a *client/server* system. A person using the Internet works at his or her own computer, which runs an Internet-aware application, such as a Web browser (Figure 2.1). This is

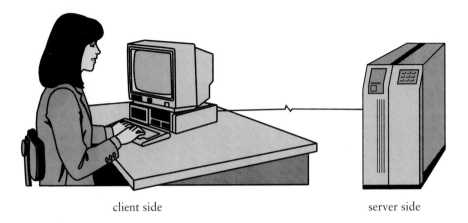

client side   server side

Figure 2.1   Client and server-side computing.

called the *client* system. The client application communicates over the Internet with another computer, perhaps one physically very far away. For example, a Web browser might request the information on a Web page stored on a distant computer. The second computer, the *server* computer, transmits the contents of the Web page to the client application. The client computer then determines how to display this information to the user.

From the beginning of the Web, it has been possible to add dynamic behavior to Web pages by executing programs. However, in the past these programs executed on the server computer. The client transmitted a request, and the server responded by executing a program, and transmitting the result. Many Web-based forms are still implemented in this fashion. Such an arrangement is sometimes termed *CGI–bin* processing, after the directory where executable programs are conventionally located on the server computer.

Several problems occur with this arrangement. For one, transmission times are often slow, causing a noticeable delay between the moment when the client asks that a program be executed and the time the results are returned. In addition, server programs often deal with many clients at once (perhaps hundreds or thousands), further reducing performance. In contrast, the client machines are often lightly loaded personal machines. Frequently the client machine is executing little more than the single Internet application.

The key idea of *client-side* computing is that rather than executing the program on the server side and transmitting the result, the server will transmit the *program* to the client. The client will then execute the program locally. Not only is the program then run on a less heavily loaded system, but the only delay is the time to transmit the program. Once the program starts executing, any interactions between the user and the program take place locally, and do not need to cross the Internet.

2.2.1 *Bytecode Interpreters and Just-In-Time Compilers*

Of course, many difficulties must be overcome for this process to succeed. The first is that the client computer must be able to execute the program. Often the server and client machines will be different types of computers. Indeed, the client may not even know what type of machine the server is using. Thus, the traditional concept of computer programs being translated into machine code for a specific machine will not work in this environment; machine code that executes well on the server computer may not work at all for the client computer.

Instead, Java is translated into a device-independent *bytecode*. This bytecode (so-called because most instructions are one or two bytes long), is like a machine language for an imaginary machine, a Java-specific machine, or *virtual machine*. Each computer that runs Java programs then processes these bytecodes into a form that works correctly on the current system.

There are several ways this can be done. The easiest scheme is to have an *interpreter* that reads and executes bytecodes one by one as they are needed. Better performance can be obtained by using a *just-in-time (JIT) compiler*. This system takes the Java bytecodes and translates them into the machine code native to the client system. These programs then run as fast as any compiled program created specifically for the client computer.

2.2.2 *Security Issues*

Another problem that must be overcome for client-side computing to be widely accepted is the issue of security. A program running on a server machine can do very little damage to a client machine; the server simply does not have access to memory or to files to which damage could be done. But a program running on the client side could, in theory, have full access to the client computer resources. There is great potential for such a program to do significant damage, such as erasing files from a hard drive.

Java programs get around this problem by using a *security manager*. The security manager is provided by the client, and limits the actions that can be performed by the Java program provided by the server. For example, most security managers will not allow a Java program to access the file system or to transmit information across the Internet to machines other than the client or server processors. Thus, the potential damage that a Java program can cause is very limited.

Despite the use of a security manager, the issue of security remains one of the more controversial aspects of Java programming. In fact, the security manager is only part of a multilayer approach to providing security for client machines that run Java programs. Despite these, the short history of experiences with computer viruses and other attacks should caution us that a truly malicious programmer can probably still find weaknesses to exploit. However, the use of techniques such as the security manager has made the task of the malicious programmer greatly more difficult.

2.2.3 *Specialization of Interfaces*

Yet another issue arises due to the fact that the client and server systems can be entirely different types of computers. As anybody who has tried to write a graphical program in another language for multiple platforms has discovered, the sequences of commands needed to perform graphical operations, such as placing a window on the display, varies greatly from one machine to another. As will be explained in Section 15.11, the solution to this problem requires a careful coordination between the client and server computers, with portions of a Java program originating on one machine, and other parts coming from the second.

The server program is structured in terms of generic classes, such as Window and Button. These classes are the same regardless of the type of system on which the Java program is run. But when executed, the first task these components perform is to create a *peer* component. The peer component originates on the client system and is not part of the server program. Thus, a button running on a PC will create a PC-Button peer, while the same program running on a Macintosh will create a Mac-Button peer. All the device-specific aspects of drawing the image on the local computer system are held in the peer class, and not in the generic button class.

2.3   THE WHITE PAPER DESCRIPTION

In one of the first papers published by Sun Microsystems that dealt with Java, the language was described in the following fashion:

> Java: A simple, object-oriented, network-savvy, interpreted, robust, secure, architecture neutral, portable, high-performance, multithreaded, dynamic language.

The tongue-in-cheek description is intentionally reminiscent of the hyperbole-laden and buzzword-heavy descriptions characteristic of advertising copy. Nevertheless, each phrase had been carefully selected, and in total, they accurately sum up the language.

2.3.1 *Java Is Simple*

Although much of the syntax of Java is based on the earlier object-oriented language C++, the Java language is considerably simpler than C++. Many keywords have been eliminated, there is no preprocessor, there are far fewer special cases, and the language is augmented with a much larger library of high-level development tools. Confusing features such as operator overloading have been eliminated, as have independent functions, global variables, the `goto` statement, structures, and pointers.

One of the more notable omissions from Java is the latter, the concept of the pointer. In many other languages there is a distinction between a *value* and a *pointer to a value*. Values are static, fixed-size entities. Pointers are dynamic quantities that are filled at run time. As explained in Chapter 11, there are important reasons why an object-oriented language should make heavy use of pointers. Java does so, but hides this fact from the programmer. As far as the programmer is concerned, there are no pointers, although in truth this illusion is only possible because almost everything is internally a pointer. However, the elimination of this construct removes an entire class of common programming errors, making it greatly easier to construct reliable and correct programs.

2.3.2 *Java Is Object-Oriented*

The language Java is founded upon the object-oriented principles described in Chapter 1. The only unit of programming is the class description. Unlike other languages, Java has no functions and no variables that can exist outside of class boundaries. Thus, all Java programs must be built out of objects. Other languages, notably C++ and Object Pascal, have tried to combine object-oriented features on top of an existing, non–object-oriented language. The unfortunate consequence of such a design is that programmers can continue working in their old, non–object-oriented fashion. By forcing all programs into an object-oriented structure, the many benefits of object-oriented design (an emphasis on encapsulation, an orientation toward reusability) are much more easily realized.

2.3.3 *Java Is Network Savvy*

From the start, Java was designed with the Internet in mind. Although it is possible to construct Java programs that do not deal with the Internet (indeed, most of the programs in this book will not), the language provides a rich set of tools for programming across a network. The Java standard library provides a plethora of classes for describing universal resource locators (URLs), for making connections between client and server computers (see Chapter 21), and for execution in controlled environments such as a World Wide Web browser.

2.3.4 *Java Is Interpreted*

Java was designed for a multicomputer execution environment. From the first, it was intended that the computer a program was developed on might not be the same as the computer on which it is stored, which might again be different from the computer on which it is finally executed. Thus, the traditional model where a program is translated by a *compiler* into the machine language for a particular machine will not work for Java; the machine language for the system on which the program is developed will probably not work for the machine on which the program is eventually executed.

Java systems initially got around this problem by using an *interpreter*. Java programs were compiled into an assembly language for an imaginary machine, called the *virtual machine*. These assembly language instructions, called *byte-codes*, could be stored on any type of machine. Any machine that supported Java programs would provide a simulator, an *interpreter*, that would read the bytecode values and execute them. In this fashion, any type of computer could be used as a Java virtual machine.

However, interpreters have one serious disadvantage over conventional systems. They are generally much slower in execution. Recent innovations in the Java world have advanced upon this idea of interpreters, and largely eliminated this performance penalty. A *just-in-time (JIT) compiler* is a system that reads the machine-independent bytecode representation of a Java program, and immediately prior to execution translates the bytecode representation into actual machine instructions for the system on which the Java program is being run. Because Java programs then execute as machine instructions, they can be almost as fast as programs compiled in more conventional languages for the specific hardware platform, and still retain the portability of the virtual machine.

2.3.5   *Java Is Robust*

The Java language and associated libraries are designed to be graceful in the presence of hardware and software errors. An example of this is the extensive use of *exception handling*. Statements that can potentially receive an error, such as a file operation that could attempt to read from a nonexistent source, will generate an exception instead of performing an erroneous operation. The semantics of the language insist that the programmer *must* deal with this possibility any time a file operation is intended. Thus, programmers are forced into thinking about potential sources of error, and their programs are therefore much more robust in the presence of error-producing conditions.

Another feature that makes Java programs more robust is automatic memory management, or garbage collection. Programmers writing in languages that use manual memory management, for example C++, frequently forget to release memory resources once they are finished with them. Long-running programs therefore slowly increase their memory requirements, until they catastrophically fail. The Java run-time system instead automatically detects and recovers memory that is no longer being used by the currently running program. This both simplifies the programmer's task and makes programs more reliable.

2.3.6   *Java Is Secure*

By eliminating pointers, the Java language removes what is perhaps the most common source of programming errors, inadvertently overwriting memory locations that are being addressed by pointers with improperly set values. The Java language also insists that array index values are checked for validity before they are referenced and that all variables must be assigned a value before being used.

But the Java language is just the first layer in a multilevel security system. Bytecodes themselves (which may or may not have been produced by a Java compiler) are examined before they are executed by the Java interpreter. This check determines that bytecodes are free of a number of common errors, for example that they do not access classes incorrectly, overflow or underflow the operand stack, or use illegal data conversions.

Finally, as we will discuss in Chapter 21, many of the applications envisioned for Java involve programs that are stored on one computer but executed on another. Typically, the computer on which the Java program will execute is a user's personal computer. Few users would trust Java if it were possible that programs brought over a network could possibly cause damage, such as erasing a hard drive or removing a file. For this reason, the designers of Java purposely created a programming environment where programs are severely restricted in the type of operations they can perform. Because of these restrictions, users can be largely assured that when they execute a program brought over the network, their local computer is safe from tampering.

2.3.7   *Java Is Architecture Neutral*

Because Java bytecodes do not correspond to any particular machine, they work with all machines. A Java program is the same whether it runs on a PC, a Macintosh, or a Unix system. This is very different from conventional languages. Although C++ is a standard language, and therefore should be the same on all machines, the libraries needed to perform activities such as placing a window on a display, or responding to a button press, differ considerably from one platform to another. This is why it is very difficult to, for example, move programs designed for the PC onto a Macintosh, or vice versa. But Java hides these application-specific details under a layer of abstraction in the standard Java library. Thus, from the programmer's point of view, all machines look the same.

2.3.8   *Java Is Portable*

Because the Java library hides architecture-specific concepts, and because bytecodes are the same regardless of the machine on which they are generated, Java programs possess an unparalleled degree of portability. Indeed, the exact same program can be compiled on one system, then executed on many different types of systems.

2.3.9 *Java Is High-Performance*

Although the initial implementations of Java bytecode interpreters exacted a heavy performance penalty, the technology of Java execution has rapidly evolved since the language was introduced. Systems such as just-in-time compilers now allow platform-independent Java programs to be executed with nearly the same run-time performance as conventional compiled languages.

2.3.10 *Java Is Multithreaded*

Java is one of the first languages to be designed explicitly for the possibility of multiple threads of execution running in one program. As shown in Chapter 20, not only is it easy to set up such multitasking, but the coordination of these parallel processes is also relatively simple.

2.3.11 *Java Is Dynamic*

Finally, because Java programs move across the Internet and execute on the user's local computer, they permit a degree of dynamic behavior impossible in older style systems.

2.4 CHAPTER SUMMARY

Although much of the excitement of Java stems from its use in developing Web-based application programs, or *applets*, the Java language itself is a general purpose programming language suitable for any task that can be solved using a computer. For most of this book we will deal with more general application programs. We will return to a discussion of Web-based programming and applets in Chapter 21.

The intent of this book is to discuss the principles of object-oriented programming, and in particular, the way that object-oriented concepts are manifest in the Java programming language. Nevertheless, an understanding of Java is not possible without an appreciation of the history and intent of the language. In this chapter we have examined how the Java language was developed and the original purpose for the language. The characteristics required for this original purpose, namely a small language with a high degree of reliability, turn out also to be desirable characteristics for any programming language. Thus, the Java language has potential uses that far exceed the original designers' intent.

STUDY QUESTIONS

1. What was the name of the first object-oriented language? In what country was it developed?

2. What problem was the research group founded by Alan Kay concerned with when they developed the language Smalltalk?

3. What was the original name given to the Java language?

4. What was the original intended use of Java programs?

5. What are some characteristics of embedded systems?

6. What is the difference between server-side computing (also known as CGI-bin processing) and client-side computing?

7. What is a bytecode interpreter?

8. What is a just-in-time compiler?

EXERCISES

1. Read Alan Kay's 1977 paper in *Scientific American*. List the issues that Kay thought would be important when truly personal computers attained widespread use. In hindsight, in what ways were his predictions correct, and in what ways did his predictions miss the mark?

2. Try to identify all the embedded computer processors found in a typical home.

3 ■ Object-Oriented Design

A superficial description of the distinction between an object-oriented language, such as Java, and a conventional programming language, such as Pascal, might concentrate on syntactic differences. In this area, discussion would center on topics such as classes, inheritance, message passing, and methods. But such an analysis would miss the most important point of object-oriented programming, which has nothing to do with syntax.

Working in an object-oriented language (that is, one that supports inheritance, message passing, and classes) is neither a necessary nor sufficient condition for doing object-oriented programming. As emphasized in Chapter 1, an object-oriented program is like a community of interacting individuals, each having assigned responsibilities, working together toward the attainment of a common goal. As in real life, a major aspect in the design of such a community is determining the specific responsibilities for each member. To this end, practitioners of object-oriented design have developed a design technique driven by the specification and delegation of responsibilities. Rebecca Wirfs-Brock and Brian Wilkerson have called this technique *responsibility-driven design* [Wirfs-Brock 1989, 1990].

3.1 RESPONSIBILITY IMPLIES NONINTERFERENCE

As anyone can attest who can remember being a child, or who has raised children, responsibility is a sword that cuts both ways. When you make an object (be it a child or a software system) responsible for specific actions, you expect a certain behavior, at least when the rules are observed. But just as important, responsibility implies a degree of independence or noninterference. If you tell a child that she is responsible for cleaning her room, you do not normally stand over her and watch while that task is being performed—that is not the nature of responsibility. Instead, you expect that, having issued a directive in the correct fashion, the desired outcome will be produced.

Similarly, in the floral delivery example from Chapter 1, I give the request to deliver flowers to my florist without stopping to think about how my request will be serviced. Flora, having taken on the responsibility for this service, is free to operate without interference on my part.

The difference between conventional programming and object-oriented programming is in many ways the difference between actively supervising a child while she performs a task, and delegating to the child responsibility for that performance. Conventional programming proceeds largely by doing something *to* something else—modifying a record or updating an array, for example. Thus, one portion of code in a software system is often intimately tied, by control and data connections, to many other sections of the system. Such dependencies can come about through the use of global variables, through use of pointer values, or simply through inappropriate use of and dependence on implementation details of other portions of code. A responsibility-driven design attempts to cut these links, or at least make them as unobtrusive as possible.

This notion might at first seem no more subtle than the notions of information hiding and modularity, which are important to programming even in conventional languages. But responsibility-driven design elevates information hiding from a technique to an art. The principle of information hiding becomes vitally important when one moves from programming in the small to programming in the large.

One of the major benefits of object-oriented programming is reaped when software subsystems are reused from one project to the next. For example, a simulation system might work for both a simulation of balls on a billiards table and a simulation of fish in a fish tank. This ability to reuse code implies that the software can have almost no domain-specific components; it must totally delegate responsibility for domain-specific behavior to application-specific portions of the system. The ability to create such reusable code is not one that is easily learned—it requires experience, careful examination of case studies (paradigms, in the original sense of the word), and use of a programming language in which such delegation is natural and easy to express. In subsequent chapters, we will look at several such examples.

3.2 PROGRAMMING IN THE SMALL AND IN THE LARGE

The difference between the development of individual projects and of more sizable software systems is often described as programming in the small versus programming in the large. *Programming in the small* characterizes projects with the following attributes:

- Code is developed by a single programmer, or perhaps by a very small collection of programmers. A single individual can understand all aspects of a project, from top to bottom, beginning to end.

- The major problem in the software development process is the design and development of algorithms for dealing with the problem at hand.

Programming in the large, on the other hand, characterizes software projects with features such as the following:

- The software system is developed by a large team of programmers. Individuals involved in the specification or design of the system may differ from those involved in the coding of individual components, who may differ as well from those involved in the integration of various components in the final product. No single individual can be considered responsible for the entire project or even necessarily understand all aspects of the project.

- The major problem in the software development process is the management of details and the communication of information between diverse portions of the project.

While the beginning student will usually be acquainted with programming in the small, aspects of many object-oriented languages are best understood as responses to the problems encountered while programming in the large. Thus, some appreciation of the difficulties involved in developing large systems is a helpful prerequisite to understanding OOP.

3.3 WHY BEGIN WITH BEHAVIOR?

Why begin the design process with an analysis of behavior? The simple answer is that the behavior of a system is usually understood long before any other aspect.

Earlier software development techniques concentrated on ideas such as characterizing the basic data structures or the overall sequence of function calls, often within the creation of a formal specification of the desired application. But structural elements of the application can be identified only after a considerable amount of problem analysis. Similarly, a formal specification often ended up as a document understood by neither programmer nor client. But *behavior* is something that can be described almost from the moment an idea is conceived, and (often unlike a formal specification) can be described in terms meaningful to both the programmers and the client.

The following case study illustrates the application of responsibility-driven design (RDD).

3.4   A CASE STUDY IN RDD

Imagine you are the chief software architect in a major computer firm. One day your boss walks into your office with an idea that, it is hoped, will be the next major success in your product line. Your assignment is to develop the Interactive Intelligent Kitchen Helper (IIKH) (Figure 3.1). The task given to your software team is stated in very few words, written on what appears to be the back of a slightly used paper napkin, in handwriting that appears to be your boss's.

3.4.1   *The Interactive Intelligent Kitchen Helper*

Briefly, the Interactive Intelligent Kitchen Helper is a PC-based application that will replace the index-card system of recipes found in the average kitchen. But more than simply maintaining a database of recipes, the kitchen helper assists in the planning of meals for an extended period, say a week. The user of the IIKH can sit down at a terminal, browse the database of recipes, and interactively create a series of menus. The IIKH will automatically scale the recipes to any number of servings and will print out menus for the entire week, for a particular day, or for a particular meal. And it will print an integrated grocery list of all the items needed for the recipes for the entire period.

As is usually true with the initial descriptions of most software systems, the specification for the IIKH is highly ambiguous on a number of important

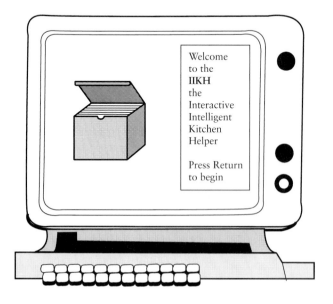

Figure 3.1   View of the Interactive Intelligent Kitchen Helper.

points. It is also true that, in all likelihood, the eventual design and development of the software system to support the IIKH will require the efforts of several programmers working together. Thus, the initial goal of the software team must be to clarify the ambiguities in the description and to outline how the project can be divided into components to be assigned for development to individual team members.

The cornerstone of object-oriented programming is to characterize software in terms of *behavior*, that is, actions to be performed. We will see this repeated on many levels in the development of the IIKH. Initially, the team will try to characterize, at a very high level of abstraction, the behavior of the entire application. This then leads to a description of the behavior of various software subsystems. Only when all behavior has been identified and described will the software design team proceed to the coding step. In the next several sections, we will trace the tasks the software design team will perform in producing this application.

3.4.2   *Working With Components*

The first task is to refine the specification. As already noted, initial specifications are almost always ambiguous and unclear on anything except the most general points. There are several goals for this step. One objective is to get a better handle on the "look and feel" of the eventual product. This information can then be carried back to the client (in this case, your boss) to see if it is in agreement with the original conception. It is likely, perhaps inevitable, that the specifications for the final application will change during the creation of the software system, and it is important that the design be developed to easily accommodate change and that potential changes be noted as early as possible. (See Section 3.6.2, "Preparing for Change.") Equally important, at this point very high-level decisions can be made concerning the structure of the eventual software system. In particular, the activities to be performed can be mapped onto components.

3.4.3   *Identification of Components*

The engineering of a complex physical system, such as a building or an automobile engine, is simplified by dividing the design into smaller units. So, too, the engineering of software is simplified by the identification and development of software components. A *component* is simply an abstract entity that can perform tasks—that is, fulfill some responsibilities. At this point, it is not necessary to know exactly the eventual representation for a component or how a component will perform a task. A component may ultimately be turned into a function, a structure or class, or a collection of other components (a *pattern*). At this level of development, just two characteristics are important:

- A component must have a small, well-defined set of responsibilities.

- A component should interact with other components as little as possible.

We will shortly discuss the reasoning behind the second characteristic. For the moment, we are simply concerned with the identification of component responsibilities.

3.5 CRC CARDS—RECORDING RESPONSIBILITY

In order to discover components and their responsibilities, the programming team walks through scenarios. That is, the team acts out the running of the application just as if it already possessed a working system. Every activity that must take place is identified and assigned to some component as a responsibility. (See Figure 3.2.)

As part of this process, it is often useful to represent components using small index cards. On the face of the card the programming team writes the name of the software component, the responsibilities of the component, and the names of other components with which the component must interact. Such cards are sometimes known as CRC (component, responsibility, collaborator) cards [Beck and Cunningham 1989], [Bellin and Simone 1997], and are associated with each software component. As responsibilities for the component are discovered, they are recorded on the face of the CRC card.

3.5.1 *Giving Components a Physical Representation*

While working through scenarios, it is useful to assign CRC cards to different members of the design team. The member holding the card representing a component records the responsibilities of the associated software component, and

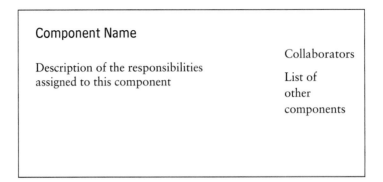

Figure 3.2 A component, responsibility, collaborator (CRC) card.

acts as the "surrogate" for the software during the scenario simulation. He or she describes the activities of the software system, passing "control" to another member when the software system requires the services of another component.

An advantage of CRC cards is that index cards are widely available, inexpensive, and erasable. This encourages experimentation, since alternative designs can be tried, explored, or abandoned with little investment. The physical separation of the cards encourages an intuitive understanding of the importance of the logical separation of the various components, helping to emphasize the cohesion and coupling (described shortly). The constraints of an index card are also a good measure of approximate complexity–a component that is expected to perform more tasks than can fit easily in the space of a card is probably too complex, and the team should find a simpler solution, perhaps by moving some responsibilities elsewhere to divide a task between two or more new components.

3.5.2 *The What/Who Cycle*

As noted at the beginning of this discussion, the identification of components takes place during the process of imagining the execution of a working system. Often this proceeds as a cycle of what/who questions. First, the programming team identifies *what* activity needs to be performed next. This is immediately followed by answering the question of *who* performs the action. In this manner, designing a software system is much like organizing a collection of people, such as a club. Any activity that is to be performed must be assigned as a responsibility to some component.

We know, from real life, that if any action is to take place, there must be an agent assigned to perform it. Just as in the running of a club, any action to be performed must be assigned to some individual; in organizing an object-oriented program, all actions must be the responsibility of some component. The secret to good object-oriented design is to first establish an agent for each action.

3.5.3 *Documentation*

At this point the development of documentation should begin. Two documents should be essential parts of any software system: the user manual and the system design documentation. Work on both of these can commence even before the first line of code has been written.

The user manual describes the interaction with the system from the user's point of view; it is an excellent means of verifying that the development team's conception of the application matches the client's. Since the decisions made in creating the scenarios will closely match the decisions the user will be required to make in the eventual application, the development of the user manual naturally dovetails with the process of walking through scenarios.

Before any actual code has been written, the mindset of the software team is most similar to that of the eventual users. Thus, it is at this point that the developers can most easily anticipate the sort of questions to which a novice user will need answers.

The second essential document is the design documentation. Because the design documentation records the major decisions made during software design, it should thus be produced when these decisions are fresh in the minds of the creators, and not after the fact when many of the relevant details will have been forgotten. It is often far easier to write a general global description of the software system early in the development. Too soon, the focus will move to the level of individual components or modules. And although it is also important to document the module level, too much concern with the details of each module will make it difficult for subsequent software maintainers to form an initial picture of the larger structure.

CRC cards are one aspect of the design documentation, but they do not reflect *all* important decisions. Arguments for and against any major design alternatives should be recorded, as well as factors that influenced the final decisions. A log or diary of the project schedule should be maintained. Both the user manual and the design documents are refined and evolve over time in exactly the same way the software is refined and evolves.

3.6   COMPONENTS AND BEHAVIOR

To return to the Interactive Kitchen Helper application, the IIKH, the team decides that when the system begins, the user will be presented with an attractive informative window (shown in Figure 3.1). The responsibility for displaying this window is assigned to a component called the Greeter. In some as yet unspecified manner (perhaps by pull-down menus, button or key presses, or use of a pressure-sensitive screen), the user can select one of several actions. Initially, the team identifies just five actions:

1. Casually browse the database of existing recipes, but without reference to any particular meal plan.

2. Add a new recipe to the database.

3. Edit or annotate an existing recipe.

4. Review an existing plan for several meals.

5. Create a new plan of meals.

These activities seem to divide themselves naturally into two groups. The first three are associated with the recipe database; the latter two are associated with menu plans. As a result, the team next decides to create components corresponding to these two responsibilities. Continuing with the scenario, the

```
┌─────────────────────────────────────────────────────────────┐
│                                                               │
│   Greeter                                                     │
│                                              Collaborators    │
│   Display informative initial message                         │
│                                              Database Manager  │
│   Offer user choice of options               Plan Manager     │
│   Pass control to either                                      │
│       Recipe Database Manager                                 │
│       Plan Manager for processing                             │
│                                                               │
│                                                               │
└─────────────────────────────────────────────────────────────┘
```

Figure 3.3   CRC card for the Greeter.

team elects to ignore the meal plan management for the moment and move on to refine the activities of the Recipe Database component. Figure 3.3 shows the initial CRC card representation of the Greeter.

Broadly speaking, the responsibility of the recipe database component is simply to maintain a collection of recipes. We have already identified three elements of this task: The recipe component database must facilitate browsing the library of existing recipes, editing the recipes, and including new recipes in the database.

3.6.1   *Postponing Decisions*

A number of decisions must eventually be made concerning how best to let the user browse the database. For example, should the user first be presented with a list of categories, such as "Soups," "Salads," "Main Courses," and "Desserts"? Alternatively, should the user be able to describe keywords to narrow a search, perhaps by providing a list of ingredients, and then see all the recipes that contain those items ("Almonds, Strawberries, Cheese"), or a list of previously inserted keywords ("Bob's favorite cake")? Should scroll bars be used or simulated thumbholes in a virtual book? These choices are fun to think about, but the important point is that such decisions do not need to be made at this point (see next section). Since they affect only a single component and do not affect the functioning of any other system, all that is necessary to continue the scenario is to assert that by some means the user can select a specific recipe.

3.6.2   *Preparing for Change*

It has been said that all that is constant in life is the inevitability of change. The same is true of software. No matter how carefully one tries to develop the initial specification and design of a software system, it is almost certain that changes in the user's needs or requirements will, sometime during the life of the system, force changes to be made in the software. Programmers and software designers need to anticipate this and plan accordingly.

- The primary objective is that changes should affect as few components as possible. Even major changes in the appearance or functioning of an application should be possible with alterations to only one or two sections of code.

- Try to predict the most likely sources of change and isolate the effects of such changes to as few software components as possible. The most likely sources of change are interfaces, communication formats, and output formats.

- Try to isolate and reduce the dependency of software on hardware. For example, the interface for recipe browsing in our application may depend in part on the hardware on which the system is running. Future releases may be ported to different platforms. A good design will anticipate this change.

- Reducing coupling between software components will reduce the dependence of one upon another and increase the likelihood that one can be changed with minimal effect on the other.

- In the design documentation, maintain careful records of the design process and the discussions surrounding all major decisions. It is almost certain that the team responsible for maintaining the software and designing future releases will be at least partially different from the team producing the initial release. The design documentation will allow future teams to know the important factors behind a decision and help them avoid spending time discussing issues that have already been resolved.

3.6.3 *Continuing the Scenario*

Each recipe will be identified with a specific recipe component. Once a recipe is selected, control is passed to the associated recipe object. A recipe must contain certain information. Basically, it consists of a list of ingredients and the steps needed to transform the ingredients into the final product. In our scenario, the recipe component must also perform other activities. For example, it will display the recipe interactively on the terminal screen. The user may be given the ability to annotate or change either the list of ingredients or the instruction portion. Alternatively, the user may request a printed copy of the recipe. All of these actions are the responsibility of the Recipe component. (For the moment, we will continue to describe the Recipe in singular form. During design we can think of this as a prototypical recipe that stands in place of a multitude of actual recipes. We will later return to a discussion of singular versus multiple components.)

Having outlined the actions that must take place to permit the user to browse the database, we return to the recipe database manager and pretend the user has indicated a desire to add a new recipe. The Database Manager somehow decides in which category to place the new recipe (again, the details of how this is done are unimportant for our development at this point), requests the name of the new recipe, and then creates a new recipe component, permitting the user to edit this new blank entry. Thus, the responsibilities of performing this new task are a subset of those we already identified in permitting users to edit existing recipes.

Having explored the browsing and creation of new recipes, we return to the Greeter and investigate the development of daily menu plans, which is the Plan Manager's task. In some way (again, the details are unimportant here) the user can save existing plans. Thus, the Plan Manager can either be started by retrieving an already developed plan or by creating a new plan. In the latter case, the user is prompted for a list of dates for the plan. Each date is associated with a separate Date component. The user can select a specific date for further investigation, in which case control is passed to the corresponding Date component. Another activity of the Plan Manager is printing out the recipes for the planning period. Finally, the user can instruct the Plan Manager to produce a grocery list for the period.

The Date component maintains a collection of meals as well as any other annotations provided by the user (birthdays, anniversaries, and other reminders). It prints information on the display concerning the specified date. By some means (again unspecified), the user can indicate a desire to print all the information concerning a specific date or choose to explore in more detail a specific meal. In the latter case, control is passed to a Meal component.

The Meal component maintains a collection of augmented recipes, where the augmentation refers to the user's desire to double, triple, or otherwise increase a recipe. The Meal component displays information about the meal. The user can add or remove recipes from the meal, or can instruct that information about the meal be printed. In order to discover new recipes, the user must be permitted at this point to browse the recipe database. Thus, the Meal component must interact with the recipe database component. The design team will continue in this fashion, investigating every possible scenario.

The major category of scenarios we have not developed here is exceptional cases. For example, what happens if a user selects a number of keywords for a recipe and no matching recipe is found? How can the user cancel an activity, such as entering a new recipe, if he or she decides not to continue? Each possibility must be explored, and the responsibilities for handling the situation assigned to one or more components.

Having walked through the various scenarios, the software design team eventually decides that all activities can be adequately handled by six components (Figure 3.4). The Greeter needs to communicate only with the Plan Manager and the Recipe Database components. The Plan Manager needs to communicate only

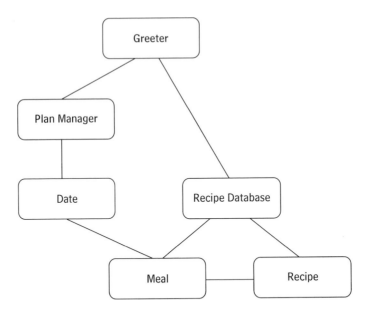

Figure 3.4   Communication among the six components in the IIKH.

with the Date component; and the Date agent, only with the Meal component. The Meal component communicates with the Recipe Database and, through this agent, with individual recipes.

3.6.4   *Interaction Diagrams*

While a description such as that shown in Figure 3.4 may describe the static relationships between components, it is not very good for describing their dynamic interactions during the execution of a scenario. A better tool for this purpose is an *interaction diagram*. Figure 3.5 shows the beginning of an interaction diagram for the Interactive Kitchen Helper. In the diagram, time moves forward from the top to the bottom. Each component is represented by a labeled vertical line. A component sending a message to another component is represented by a horizontal arrow from one line to another. Similarly, a component returning control and perhaps a result value back to the caller is represented by an arrow. (Some authors use two different arrow forms, such as a solid line to represent message passing and a dashed line to represent returning control.) The commentary on the right-hand side of the figure explains more fully the interaction taking place.

With a time axis, the interaction diagram is able to describe better the sequencing of events during a scenario. For this reason, interaction diagrams can be a useful documentation tool for complex software systems.

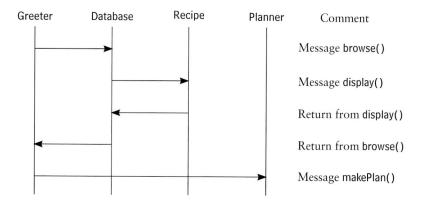

Greeter   Database   Recipe   Planner   Comment

Message browse( )

Message display( )

Return from display( )

Return from browse( )

Message makePlan( )

Figure 3.5 An example interaction diagram.

3.7 SOFTWARE COMPONENTS

In this section we will explore a software component in more detail. As is true of all but the most trivial ideas, there are many aspects to this seemingly simple concept.

3.7.1 *Behavior and State*

We have already seen how components are characterized by their behavior, that is, by what they can do. But components may also hold certain information. Let us take as our prototypical component a Recipe structure from the IIKH. One way to view such a component is as a pair consisting of *behavior* and *state*.

- The *behavior* of a component is the set of actions it can perform. The complete description of all the behavior for a component is sometimes called the *protocol*. For the Recipe component this includes activities such as editing the preparation instructions, displaying the recipe on a terminal screen, or printing a copy of the recipe.

- The *state* of a component represents all the information held within it. For our Recipe component the state includes the ingredients and preparation instructions. Notice that the state is not static and can change over time. For example, by editing a recipe (a behavior) the user can make changes to the preparation instructions (part of the state).

It is not necessary that all components maintain state information. For example, it is possible that the Greeter component will not have any state since it does not need to remember any information during the course of execution. However, most components will consist of a combination of behavior and state.

3.7.2   *Instances and Classes*

The separation of state and behavior permits us to clarify a point we avoided in our earlier discussion. Note that in the real application there will probably be many different recipes. However, all of these recipes will *perform* in the same manner. That is, the behavior of each recipe is the same; it is only the state—the individual lists of ingredients and instructions for preparation—that differs between individual recipes. In the early stages of development our interest is in characterizing the behavior common to all recipes; the details particular to any one recipe are unimportant.

The term *class* is used to describe a set of objects with similar behavior. We will see in later chapters that a class is also used as a syntactic mechanism in Java. An individual representative of a class is known as an *instance*. Note that behavior is associated with a class, not with an individual. That is, all instances of a class will respond to the same instructions and perform in a similar manner. On the other hand, state is a property of an individual. We see this in the various instances of the class Recipe. They can all perform the same actions (editing, displaying, printing) but use different data values.

3.7.3   *Coupling and Cohesion*

Two important concepts in the design of software components are coupling and cohesion. *Cohesion* is the degree to which the responsibilities of a single component form a meaningful unit. High cohesion is achieved by associating in a single component tasks that are related in some manner. Probably the most frequent way in which tasks are related is through the necessity to access a common data area. This is the overriding theme that joins, for example, the various responsibilities of the Recipe component.

Coupling, on the other hand, describes the relationship between software components. In general, it is desirable to reduce the amount of coupling as much as possible, since connections between software components inhibit ease of development, modification, or reuse.

In particular, coupling is increased when one software component must access data values—the state—held by another component. Such situations should almost always be avoided in favor of moving a task into the list of responsibilities of the component that holds the necessary data. For example, one might conceivably first assign responsibility for editing a recipe to the Recipe Database component, since it is while performing tasks associated with this component that the need to edit a recipe first occurs. But if we did so, the Recipe Database agent would need the ability to directly manipulate the state (the internal data values representing the list of ingredients and the preparation instructions) of an individual recipe. It is better to avoid this tight connection by moving the responsibility for editing to the recipe itself.

3.7.4 *Interface and Implementation: Parnas's Principles*

The emphasis on characterizing a software component by its behavior has one extremely important consequence. It is possible for one programmer to know how to *use* a component developed by another programmer, without needing to know how the component is *implemented*. For example, suppose each of the six components in the IIKH is assigned to a different programmer. The programmer developing the Meal component needs to allow the IIKH user to browse the database of recipes and select a single recipe for inclusion in the meal. To do this, the Meal component can simply invoke the browse behavior associated with the Recipe Database component, which is defined to return an individual Recipe. This description is valid regardless of the particular implementation used by the Recipe Database component to perform the actual browsing action.

The purposeful omission of implementation details behind a simple interface is known as *information hiding*. We say the component *encapsulates* the behavior, showing only how the component can be used, not the detailed actions it performs. This naturally leads to two different views of a software system. The interface view is the face seen by other programmers. It describes *what* a software component can perform. The implementation view is the face seen by the programmer working on a particular component. It describes *how* a component goes about completing a task.

The separation of interface and implementation is perhaps *the* most important concept in software engineering. Yet it is difficult for students to understand, or to motivate. Information hiding is largely meaningful only in the context of multiperson programming projects. In such efforts, the limiting factor is often not the amount of coding involved, but the amount of communication required among the various programmers and among their respective software systems. As will be described shortly, software components are often developed in parallel by different programmers, and in isolation from one another.

There is also an increasing emphasis on the reuse of general purpose software components in multiple projects. For this to be successful, there must be minimal and well-understood interconnections between the various portions of the system. These ideas were captured by computer scientist David Parnas in a pair of rules, known as *Parnas's principles*:

- The developer of a software component must provide the intended user with all the information needed to make effective use of the services provided by the component, and should provide *no* other information.

- The developer of a software component must be provided with all the information necessary to carry out the given responsibilities assigned to the component, and should be provided with *no* other information.

A consequence of the separation of interface from implementation is that a programmer can experiment with several different implementations of the same structure without affecting other software components.

3.8   FORMALIZING THE INTERFACE

We continue with the description of the IIKH development. In the next several steps the descriptions of the components will be refined. The first step in this process is to formalize the patterns and channels of communication.

A decision should be made as to the general structure that will be used to implement each component. A component with only one behavior and no internal state may be made into a function—for example, a component that simply takes a string of text and translates all capital letters to lowercase. Components with many tasks are probably more easily implemented as classes. Names are given to each of the responsibilities identified on the CRC card for each component, and these will eventually be mapped onto procedure names. Along with the names, the types of any arguments to be passed to the procedure are identified. Next, the information maintained within the component itself should be described. All information must be accounted for. If a component requires some data to perform a specific task, the source of the data, either through argument or global value, or maintained internally by the component, must be clearly identified.

3.8.1   *Coming Up with Names*

Careful thought should be given to the names associated with various activities. Shakespeare has Juliet claiming that a name change does not alter the object being described, but certainly not all names will conjure up the same mental images in the listener.[1] As government bureaucrats have long known, obscure and idiomatic names can make even the simplest operation sound intimidating. The selection of useful names is extremely important, as names create the vocabulary with which the eventual design will be formulated. Names should be internally consistent, meaningful, preferably short, and evocative in the context of the problem. Often a considerable amount of time is spent finding just the right set of terms to describe the tasks performed and the objects manipulated. Far from being a barren and useless exercise, proper naming early in the design process greatly simplifies and facilitates later steps.

The following general guidelines have been suggested [Keller 1990]:

---

[1] "What's in a name? That which we call a rose, by any other name would smell as sweet; So Romeo would, were he not Romeo call'd, retain that dear perfection which he owes without that title." *Romeo and Juliet*, Act II, Scene 2.

- Use pronounceable names. As a rule of thumb, if you cannot read a name out loud, it is not a good one.

- Use capitalization (or underscores) to mark the beginning of a new word within a name, such as "CardReader" or "Card_reader," rather than the less readable "cardreader."

- Examine abbreviations carefully. An abbreviation that is clear to one person may be confusing to the next. Is a "TermProcess" a terminal process, something that terminates processes, or a process associated with a terminal?

- Avoid names with several interpretations. Does the empty function tell whether something is empty, or empty the values from the object?

- Avoid digits within a name. They are easy to misread as letters (0 as O, 1 as l, 2 as Z, 5 as S).

- Name functions and variables that yield Boolean values so they describe clearly the interpretation of a true or false value. For example, "PrinterIsReady" clearly indicates that a true value means the printer is working, whereas "PrinterStatus" is much less precise.

- Take extra care in the selection of names for operations that are costly and infrequently used. Doing so can avoid errors caused by using the wrong function.

Once names have been developed for each activity, the CRC cards for each component are redrawn, with the name and formal arguments of the function used to elicit each behavior identified. An example of a CRC card for the Date is shown in Figure 3.6. What is not yet specified is how each component will perform the associated tasks.

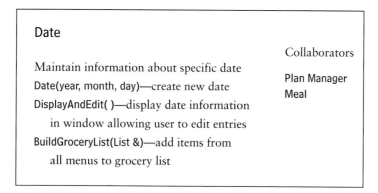

Date

Maintain information about specific date
Date(year, month, day)—create new date
DisplayAndEdit( )—display date information
    in window allowing user to edit entries
BuildGroceryList(List &)—add items from
    all menus to grocery list

Collaborators

Plan Manager
Meal

Figure 3.6 Revised CRC card for the Date component.

Once more, scenarios or role playing should be carried out at a more detailed level to ensure that all activities are accounted for and that all necessary information is maintained and made available to the responsible components.

3.9   DESIGNING THE REPRESENTATION

At this point, if not before, the design team can be divided into groups, each responsible for one or more software components. The task now is to transform the description of a component into a software system implementation. The major portion of this process is designing the data structures that will be used by each subsystem to maintain the state information required to fulfill the assigned responsibilities.

It is here that the classic data structures of computer science come into play. The selection of data structures is an important task, central to the software design process. Once they have been chosen, the code used by a component in the fulfillment of a responsibility is often almost self-evident. But data structures must be carefully matched to the task at hand. A wrong choice can result in complex and inefficient programs, while an intelligent choice can result in just the opposite.

It is also at this point that descriptions of behavior must be transformed into algorithms. These descriptions should then be matched against the expectations of each component listed as a collaborator, to ensure that expectations are fulfilled and necessary data items are available to carry out each process.

3.10   IMPLEMENTING COMPONENTS

Once the design of each software subsystem is laid out, the next step is to implement each component's desired behavior. If the previous steps were correctly addressed, each responsibility or behavior will be characterized by a short description. The task at this step is to implement the desired activities in a computer language. In a later section we will describe some of the more common heuristics used in this process.

If they were not determined earlier (say, as part of the specification of the system), then decisions can now be made on issues that are entirely self-contained within a single component. A decision we saw in our example problem was how best to let the user browse the database of recipes.

As multiperson programming projects become the norm, it becomes increasingly rare that any one programmer will work on all aspects of a system. More often, the skills a programmer will need to master are understanding how one section of code fits into a larger framework and working well with other members of a team. Often, in the implementation of one component it will

become clear that certain information or actions might be assigned to yet another component that will act "behind the scene," with little or no visibility
to users of the software abstraction. Such components are sometimes known
as *facilitators*. We will see examples of facilitators in some of the later case
studies.

An important part of analysis and coding at this point is characterizing and
documenting the necessary preconditions a software component requires to
complete a task, and verifying that the software component will perform correctly when presented with legal input values. This is establishing the correctness
aspect of the algorithms used in the implementation of a component.

3.11   INTEGRATION OF COMPONENTS

Once software subsystems have been individually designed and tested, they can
be integrated into the final product. This is often not a single step, but part of
a larger process. Starting from a simple base, elements are slowly added to the
system and tested, using *stubs*—simple dummy routines with no behavior or
with very limited behavior—for the as yet unimplemented parts.

For example, in the development of the IIKH, it would be reasonable to start
integration with the Greeter component. To test the Greeter in isolation, stubs
are written for the Recipe Database manager and the daily Plan manager. These
stubs need not do any more than print an informative message and return. With
these, the component development team can test various aspects of the Greeter
system (for example, that button presses elicit the correct response). Testing of
an individual component is often referred to as *unit testing*.

Next, one or the other of the stubs can be replaced by more complete code.
For example, the team might decide to replace the stub for the Recipe Database
component with the actual system, maintaining the stub for the other portion.
Further testing can be performed until it appears that the system is working as
desired. (This is sometimes referred to as *integration testing*.)

The application is finally complete when all stubs have been replaced with
working components. The ability to test components in isolation is greatly facili-
tated by the conscious design goal of reducing connections between components,
since this reduces the need for extensive stubbing.

During integration it is not uncommon for an error to be manifested in one
software system, and yet to be caused by a coding mistake in another system.
Thus, testing during integration can involve the discovery of errors, which
then results in changes to some of the components. Following these changes,
the components should once again be tested in isolation before an attempt
to reintegrate the software, once more, into the larger system. Reexecuting
previously developed test cases following a change to a software component is
sometimes referred to as *regression testing*.

3.12 MAINTENANCE AND EVOLUTION

It is tempting to think that once a working version of an application has been delivered, the task of the software development team is finished. Unfortunately, that is almost never true. The term *software maintenance* describes activities subsequent to the delivery of the initial working version of a software system. A wide variety of activities fall into this category.

- Errors, or *bugs*, can be discovered in the delivered product. These must be corrected, either in *patches* to existing releases or in subsequent releases.

- Requirements may change, perhaps as a result of government regulations or standardization among similar products.

- Hardware may change. For example, the system may be moved to different platforms, or input devices, such as a pen-based system or a pressure-sensitive touch screen, may become available. Output technology may change—for example, from a text-based system to a graphical window-based arrangement.

- User expectations may change. Users may expect greater functionality, lower cost, and easier use. This can occur as a result of competition with similar products.

- Better documentation may be requested by users.

A good design recognizes the inevitability of changes and plans an accommodation for them from the very beginning.

3.13 CHAPTER SUMMARY

Object-oriented programming begins with object-oriented analysis and design. Object-oriented design is characterized by an emphasis on responsibility, rather than on structure. Responsibility and behavior are attributes that can be discovered for a software system well before any other features can be identified. By systematically tracing the behavior of a system, the design of the software elements flows naturally from the general specification.

A key tool in the characterization of behavior is the idea of scenarios. Developers trace through the execution of an imaginary system, identifying actions that need to be performed, and more importantly assigning the responsibilities for these actions to individual software components. A useful tool in this activity is the CRC card, which is an index card that records the responsibilities of a software system. As design evolves, the descriptions of the actions of each component can be rewritten in more precise formats.

Developing a working software system involves many steps, frequently termed the software life cycle. Design and implementation are the first major steps. Implementation can be broken into the identification of components, development and testing of components in isolation, integration of components into larger units, and finally testing of the completed application. The life of a software system does not, however, halt with the first completed applications. Errors are uncovered, requirements change, and hardware modifications can all cause changes in the software system. The management of these changes that come after the first release is known as software maintenance.

STUDY QUESTIONS

1. What is the key idea driving object-oriented design?

2. How is the idea of responsibility tied to information hiding?

3. What are some of the characteristics of programming in the small?

4. How does programming in the large differ from programming in the small?

5. Why is information hiding an important aspect of programming in the large?

6. Why should the design of a software system begin with the characterization of behavior?

7. What is a scenario? How does a scenario help the identification of behaviors?

8. What do the three fields of a CRC card represent?

9. What are some of the advantages of using a physical index card to represent a CRC card?

10. What is the what/who cycle?

11. Why should the user manual be written before actual coding of an application is begun?

12. What are the most common sources of change in the requirements for an application over time? How can some of the difficulties inherent in change be mitigated?

13. What information is being conveyed by an interaction diagram?

14. Describe in your own words the following aspects of software components:

    (a) Behavior and state

    (b) Instances and classes

    (c) Coupling and cohesion

    (d) Interface and implementation

15. What are Parnas's principles of information hiding?

16. What are some guidelines to follow in the selection of names for components, arguments, behaviors, and so on?

17. After design, what are the later stages of the software life cycle?

18. What is software maintenance?

EXERCISES

1. Finish the development of CRC cards for the IIKH.

2. Having done Exercise 1, give a complete interaction diagram for one scenario use of the IIKH.

3. Describe the responsibilities of an organization that includes at least six types of members. Examples of such organizations are a school (students, teachers, principal, janitor), a business (secretary, president, worker), and a club (president, vice-president, member). For each member type, describe the responsibilities and the collaborators.

4. Create a scenario for the organization you described in Exercise 3 using an interaction diagram.

5. For a common game such as solitaire or twenty-one, describe a software system that will interact with the user as an opposing player. Example components include the deck and the discard pile.

6. Describe the software system to control an automated teller machine (ATM). Give interaction diagrams for various scenarios that describe the most common uses of the machine.

7. Consider a large program with which you are familiar (not necessarily object-oriented), and examine the names of variables and functions. Which names do you think are particularly apt? Why? Which names do you think might have been badly selected?

II

Understanding Paradigms

4 ∎ A Paradigm

As we noted in Chapter 1, to a medieval scholar a *paradigm* was an example sentence, one that could be used as a model or as an aid in learning a language. You are learning a new language, the programming language Java. This book will introduce Java by means of many small paradigms, or example code fragments. You as the reader should examine these programs carefully, paying close attention to those features that are new or different in comparison to earlier programs. Learning to view programs as a form of literature, that is, learning how to read programs as well as to write them, is a skill well worth an investment in time.

Our first paradigm is shown in Figure 4.1. Line numbers have been provided in comments along the right side. Like all comments, these are mainly intended to help the human reader, and are not actually part of the program. While exceedingly short and largely lacking in interesting functionality (the program prints one line of output and exits), this program nevertheless exhibits characteristics found in all Java programs, and is therefore a good place to begin our explorations. In the remainder of this chapter we will analyze the features of this program from several different perspectives.

```
import java.lang.*;                                      // 1

public class FirstProgram {                              // 2

   public static void main ( String [ ] args ) {         // 3
      System.out.println( "My first Java program!" );    // 4
   }                                                      // 5
}                                                         // 6
```

Figure 4.1 A simple Java program.

4.1 PROGRAM STRUCTURE

The first step is to understand the structure of a Java program. As noted in Chapter 1, the Java universe is a community populated by *objects*, and by little else (for more on the types of values found in the Java world, see the next section). Objects are all instances of *classes*, and thus the overall structure of a Java program is simply a series of class descriptions. In our example program there is a single class, named FirstProgram. The name of the class (given on line number 2) is important in several respects. First, it will be the handle we use to create instances of the class. Of more pragmatic concern in running your first program, it is also the name used to create the file in which the executable version of the class will be stored. On most systems this file will be named FirstProgram.class. To execute the program, this would be the file you hand to the Java interpreter.

Figure 4.2 shows the commands used to compile and execute this first program on a computer running the Unix operating system. The text of the program is stored in a file named FirstProgram.java. The command javac, the Java compiler, analyzes this program, creating the file FirstProgram.class to hold the executable version of the program. The command ls lists the contents of the directory, showing these two files. The command java, the Java bytecode interpeter, is used to execute the program. The output of the program is shown immediately after this command.

The names of the applications used to compile and execute a Java program, the steps needed to invoke these applications, and the location of the output are all features that differ greatly between platforms. We will not discuss these further here, concentrating instead on the features of the Java programming language, which will be the same on all platforms.

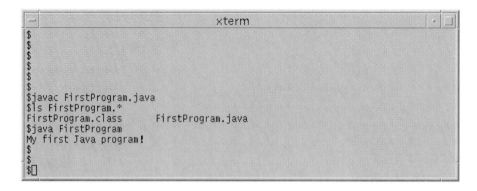

Figure 4.2 Compiling and executing a Java program.

A class consists of a class *header* and a class *body*. The header is found on line 2, and provides the name of the class. The keyword class indicates (both to the compiler, and to you as a program reader) that this is a new class description, and that the text following the class keyword should be taken to be the class name.

```
public class FirstProgram {                                    // 2
    .
    .
    .
}                                                              // 6
```

The class body begins with the curly brace at the end of line 2 and terminates with the matching curly brace on line 6. The Java language places few restrictions on the use of spaces in programs, and the placement of elements such as curly braces relative to the rest of the line is largely a matter of personal taste—and consequently the subject of a great deal of heated debate. I personally like to place the starting brace on the same line as the unit it is grouping, with the closing brace on a line all by itself. I deviate from this only when an entire statement group can be placed on a line by itself. Others prefer to place both braces on separate lines, as in the following:

```
public class FirstProgram
{
    public static void main ( String [ ] args )
    {
        System.out.println( "My first Java program!");
    }
}
```

Find a style that seems comfortable to you personally, and use it consistently.

Within the body of a class are found a series of *members*. A member can be either a *data field*, or a *method*. The former characterize the internal data being held by an object, while the latter define the behaviors an instance of the class can perform.

In our initial program there are no data fields, and only one method. This method is named main, which *must* be the name used in describing the first method that will be invoked when execution commences.

Like a class, a method consists of two parts; a method *header* and a method *body*. All method headers have the same form, which can be described as a sequence of zero or more modifiers, a return type, a name, and a list of arguments. Thus, a prototypical method has the following form:

```
modifiers return-type method-name ( arguments ) {
    sequence-of-statements
}
```

The method header for main is given on line number 3 of the example program. It includes two modifiers, public and static. The first, as indicated earlier, will be subsequently discussed in Section 4.4, while the latter is described in Section 4.5. The return type for this method is void, which will be introduced in Section 4.3. The remaining parts are the name of the method (main) and the list of arguments to the method. The initial method for execution always takes a single argument, which is an array of string values. More will be said about Java types, such as the types shown in the argument declaration, in Section 4.3.

```
public static void main ( String [ ] args ) {              // 3
     .
     .
     .
}                                                          // 5
```

The method body begins with the curly brace on line 3, and ends with the corresponding curly brace on line 5. Method bodies must always be properly nested within a class description.

Within a method body are a series of statements that indicate the actions to be executed when an instance of the given class is asked to perform the indicated method. In our sample program, there is one action, which is to print a single line of output. We will discuss this statement in more detail in the next section.

4.2 THE CONNECTION TO THE JAVA WORLD

A Java program is never entirely self-contained but must instead execute in the "universe" provided by the Java run-time system. We see this characteristic exhibited in two ways in our sample program. The first connection to the Java world is created by the import statement in line 1.

```
import java.lang.*;                                        // 1
```

This statement makes a portion (or *package*) of the Java library (usually referred to as the Java Application Programming Interface, or API) visible to the class description that follows it. The Java API is both powerful and exceedingly large. Because of its size, the API is arranged in packages of related classes that are only made available when the user explicitly requests them. The import statement in line 1 above requests that a package of the Java API (in this case java.lang) should be treated as part of this program.

The package java.lang has been selected because it is where the class System is defined.[1] Among the data members held by System is one named out that holds various features associated with output. Among the behaviors provided by out is

---

[1] Technically, importing java.lang is not required since it is automatically available to all Java programs. It has been included in this first program to illustrate the process of importing a package.

the method println, which takes as argument a text string, and uses the argument to print a single line of output on a standard output area (often called the *output console*).

```
System.out.println( "My first Java program!" );                 // 4
```

The data member out is declared as a static variable of the class System. You have already met a static method in line 3 of FirstProgram. An important property of static variables (or class variables as they are sometimes called) is that they can be accessed from anywhere in a program by prefixing them with the name of their class, provided of course that they are public and that their class is part of the program. Line 4 shows how FirstProgram accesses the variable out by prefixing it with its class name System. Another useful class is Math. The Math class has public static methods for performing a variety of useful mathematical operations. We will encounter several other static values in later case studies.

4.3 TYPES

In addition to a variety of useful objects, the initial Java world contains the descriptions for a large collection of useful *types*, called *primitive data types*, that programmers can employ in their own code. The most basic types are integers and real (or floating-point) values. Integer variables are declared using the keyword int, as in the following assignment, which both declares a new integer variable and initializes it with a value.

```
int newVar = 42;
```

Such variables could be declared either as data members within a class or as local variables within a method. Floating-point values are declared using either the primitive data type float or the type double. Another basic type is boolean. A Boolean value is either true or false. Boolean values are produced by the relational operators (less-than, written <; less-than-or-equal, written <=; and so on) as well as the logical operators (and, written &&; or, written ||; and the like)[2]. The most common use for Boolean values is in the test portion of an if or a while statement.

The keyword void is used as a type mainly to describe methods that do not, in fact, return any value. We see this in our example program, as the return type for the method main:

---

[2] Two other operators, & and |, can be used in place of && and ||. For boolean values, they produce exactly the same result as && and || but evaluate their result in a slightly different manner. Both will evaluate their left argument before the right. If the value of the result can be determined by the left argument alone, the doubled operators will ignore, and not evaluate, their right argument. This is sometimes called *short circuit evaluation*. The single character operators also have a different meaning altogether when used with integers.

```
public static void main ( String [ ] args ) {                    // 3
```

The argument list for this method also illustrates another useful type provided by the Java language, the type String. A literal value, for example like "Fred Smith" below, has the type String.

```
String name = "Fred Smith";
```

Notice that the types int, float, double, and boolean all begin with lowercase letters, while the type String, as well as the majority of other types provided by the Java library, begin with an uppercase letter. The reason for this is that the primitive data types (int and the like) are technically not objects, while all other values are objects. That is, there is no class definition that corresponds to int, while there *is* a class description that defines the characteristics of the String data type. This is a minor distinction that in rare situations is important, and one we will return to in a later chapter.

An *array* in Java is rather different from arrays in many other languages. One difference is that the array type declaration does not specify the number of elements, or extent, of the array. We see this in our sample program in line 3:

```
public static void main ( String [ ] args ) {                    // 3
```

The parameter value for this method is named args, and is an array of string values. The square brackets in the declaration give us the clue that the value is an array; however, they do not specify the size of the array. The size will have been set when the array was created (we will see examples in later chapters). Methods provided by the class Array can be used to access information about the array. For example, consider the following program, which is only slightly more complicated than the first example:

```
import java.lang.*;

public class SecondProgram {

    public static void main ( String [ ] args ) {
        if (args.length > 0)
            System.out.println("Hello " + args[0]);
        else
            System.out.println( "Hello  everybody!");
    }
}
```

Here, the data member length is being used to determine the number of values held by the array named args. If the user entered a command line argument, such as the string "Fred", the output would be "hello Fred".[3]

If the size of the array args is larger than zero (that is, if there are array elements) then the subscript operator is used to access the first element. The set of legal index values for an array in Java begins with zero, and extends to the value one smaller than the number of elements in the array.

Finally, this example shows the use of the + operator with a string value. When at least one argument to the "addition" operator is a String, the other argument is automatically converted into a string, and the operation of string catenation is performed. The result will be a new string value in which the left argument is immediately followed by the right argument. This feature is often used to format output. For example, suppose x is an integer variable; we could display the value of x by means of the following statement:

```
System.out.println("The value of x is " + x);
```

There are other interesting features of both strings and the array data type in Java that we will discuss in subsequent chapters.

4.4 ACCESS MODIFIERS

The modifier public appears twice in our example program, first in line 2 and then again in line 3.

```
public class FirstProgram {                              // 2
    public static void main ( String [ ] args ) {        // 3
```

This modifier is one of a trio that are used to control the *accessibility* of names. The other possibilities are protected and private. By controlling access we mean that these modifiers control which objects in a program can make use of a name, and in which portions of a program that name can appear.

Recall once again our intuitive description of an object-oriented program as a community populated by many agents, or objects, that interact with one another in order to achieve some desired objective. Each object has a role to play, and that role is defined by the data values it holds and the services it can provide to the other objects in the universe.

Those features that are public are the aspects of an object that another object can see; the outward appearance of the object. Any feature that another object might want to use should be declared as public.

---

[3] Exactly how command-line arguments are entered differs depending upon which platform you are executing your Java programs. Consult a reference manual for further information.

```
class BankAccount {

   private int accountBalance = 0;

   public void deposit (int amount) {
      accountBalance = accountBalance + amount;
   }

   public void withdrawal (int amount) {
      accountBalance = accountBalance - amount;
   }
}
```

Figure 4.3   A data member being hidden using the keyword private.

The use of the public modifier in front of the class keyword in our first program indicates that the entire class description is public; it is visible to the program loader that gets an application ready for execution.

```
public class FirstProgram {                                    // 2
```

Similarly, the keyword used in front of the method named main indicates that the method is visible outside of the class. This means that the program loader not only can see the class FirstProgram, but also can see the method inside of the class. This is important; otherwise the program loader would not be able to execute the method.

```
public static void main ( String [ ] args ) {                 // 3
```

Frequently a programmer desires that features of a class, or entire classes themselves, be "hidden" from other classes. This means that other objects in the program universe cannot "see" these features, and since they cannot be seen, they cannot be manipulated.

Data members are most commonly hidden. An object might want to hold a data value and not let the value be seen by other objects. It can do this by using the keyword private. For example, the class description shown in Figure 4.3 is a simple model of a bank account. The bank account object holds an "internal" piece of information, which represents the account balance. Because the variable holding this value is declared private, other objects in the program universe are not allowed to directly examine or modify the account balance. There are, however, two methods that are declared public. These allow deposits or withdrawals to be made from the bank account object. Thus, other objects in the simulation can indirectly modify the value of the balance (by performing a deposit or a withdrawal) even though they cannot directly set the account balance.

Private features (both data members and methods) can only be accessed within the bounds of a class description. A third possibility, termed protected, comes into play when inheritance is used as a technique to create new types of objects out of an existing, older class description. A protected member is one that is still inaccessible to other objects but that *is* accessible within the bounds of any subclass (or derived class). We will see examples of this in subsequent chapters.

4.5   LIFETIME MODIFIERS

Another important keyword in our first program is the term static, which appears preceding the method main. Like the accessibility keywords, the keyword static can be applied both to data fields and to methods.

```
public static void main ( String [ ] args ) {                    // 3
```

There are two ways to envision the effect that static has on the member it modifies. One way is to imagine that static members are shared by all instances of a class. That is, no matter how many similar objects are created, only one manifestation of a static member will be created. This one member will be shared by all the instances of the class.

Because a static member is shared by all instances, it is not *part* of any one instance. In this sense, it can be imagined to be outside of all instances. (Although accessibility modifiers can still be applied, a private but static data member is outside of all objects but can only be accessed from inside the class definition.) Since a static data member is outside of the object definitions, it also exists no matter how many instances of a class have been created. In particular, a static member exists even if *no instances of a class have yet been created*!

It is for this reason that the main method in any program must be declared to be static. The main method must exist, even before any instances of the class have been created. The program loader selects this static method (which must also be public) and runs it. If it were not declared static, it would be necessary to first create an instance of the class before executing the method.

Also, as described in Section 4.2, static (or class) members that are public have another very useful purpose; they can be accessed from anywhere within the program by prefixing them with their class name, as for example System.out.

4.6   CHAPTER SUMMARY

The first *paradigm*, or example program, we have examined will print a single line of output and halt. Although trivial in purpose, the structure of this program is similar to every Java program we will subsequently encounter. Thus, a good appreciation of this simple example is a necessary prerequisite to understanding the remainder of this book:

```
import java.lang.*;

public class FirstProgram {

    public static void main (String [ ] args ) {
        System.out.println ( "My first Java program!" );
    }
}
```

- The import statement connects *this* Java program to the initial Java universe; it indicates which portions of the Java run-time system will be used by this program.

- A Java program is a sequence of class descriptions.

- Each class description consists of a class heading and a class body.

- The class heading consists of modifiers, the keyword class, and a class name.

- A class body is a sequence of members.

- A member is either a data member or a method.

- A method consists of a method heading and a method body.

- A method heading consists of modifiers, the method name, and the argument list.

- A method body is a sequence of statements.

- The modifier public indicates attributes (entire classes, or members within a class) that can be accessed and used by other objects.

- The modifier static indicates attributes (data members of methods) that are shared by all instances of a class. Such members exist even when no instances of the class have yet been created.

- The method main must be declared as both public and static, since it must be visible to the program loader and must exist even before instances of the class have been created.

CROSS REFERENCES

Other, more extensive paradigms will be introduced in the remaining chapters in this part of the book. The keyword protected, discussed briefly in Section 4.4, becomes important when *inheritance* is used to create new classes. Inheritance will be investigated more fully beginning in Chapter 8. The class String and related facilities will be explored in Chapter 17.

STUDY QUESTIONS

1. What is the original meaning of the word *paradigm?*

2. What is the overall structure of a Java program?

3. What are the two major parts of a class description?

4. How is the body of a class delineated?

5. What are the two types of members that can be found within a class body?

6. What is the connection between a class name and the file it is stored in?

7. What is a method?

8. What are the parts of a method header?

9. What operation is performed by System.out.println?

10. What is the purpose of an import statement?

11. What is the type void mainly used for?

12. What does the difference in case in the initial letter of the types int and String indicate?

13. How in Java does one determine the number of elements held by an array?

14. What is the meaning of the + operator when one of the arguments is a String?

15. What are the three access modifier keywords? What does each of them signify?

16. When applied to a data member, what does the modifier static signify?

EXERCISES

1. Add a member method named display to the class description shown in Figure 4.3. When invoked, this method should print the current account balance.

2. The looping statement in Java uses the for keyword, and consists of three parts. The first part is an initialization statement, which can also be used to declare the loop variable. The second part is a test for termination; the loop will execute as long as the expression returns true. The final part is

the increment, which is a statement that is evaluated to update the loop variable.

Consider the following main program. Describe the effect produced by the program when it is executed with three command-line arguments.

```
public static void main ( String [ ] args ) {
    for (int i = 0; i < args.length; i = i + 1)
        System.out.println(args[i]);
}
```

3. Now consider the following, slightly more complex program:

```
public static void main ( String [ ] args ) {
    for (int i = 0; i < args.length; i = i + 1)
        for (int j = 0; j <= i; j = j + 1)
            System.out.println(args[i]);
}
```

Describe the pattern of the output when the program is executed with three command-line arguments.

4. Consider the following main program:

```
public static void main ( String [ ] args ) {
    String result = "";
    for (int i = args.length - 1; i >= 0; i = i - 1)
        result = result + " " + args[i];
    System.out.println(result);
}
```

What does this method do? What will be the result printed given the arguments Sam saw Sarah said Sally ?

5. Another useful method provided by the class String is the substring operation. This takes an integer argument, and returns the portion of the string that remains following the given index position. For example, if word is a variable containing the string "unhappy", then word.substring(2) is the string "happy".

This operation is used in the following program. What will the output be given the command-line argument Sally?

```
static public void main ( String [ ] args ) {
    String name = args[0];
    String shortName = name.substring(1);
    System.out.println(name + "," + name + ", bo-B" + shortName);
    System.out.println("Banana-fana Fo-F" + shortName);
```

```
        System.out.println("Fee, Fie, mo-M" + shortName);
        System.out.println(name + "!");
    }
```

6. By placing the code shown in the previous question inside a loop, write a program that will take any number of command-line arguments, and write one verse of the name game for each.

5   Ball Worlds

In the intuitive description of object-oriented programming presented in Chapter 1, an object-oriented program was described as a universe of interacting agents. However, in our first example Java program, in Chapter 4, we did not actually create any new objects, but only used the static method named main in the program class.

Our second program is slightly more complex in structure, although hardly more complicated in functionality. It places a graphical window on the user's screen, draws a ball that bounces around the window for a few moments, and then halts. The result is the screen shown as Figure 5.1.

Our second example program, or paradigm, is constructed out of two classes. The first of these appears in Figure 5.2. Again, we have added line numbers for the purposes of reference; however, these are not part of the actual program.[1] The reader should compare this program to the example program described in the previous chapter, noting both the similarities and differences. Like the previous program, this program imports (on line 1) information from the Java library. Like the earlier program, execution will begin in the method named main (lines 3–6), which is declared as static, void, and public. Like all main programs, this method must take as argument an array of string values, which are, in this case, being ignored.

---

[1] In order to draw more attention to the Java code itself, the programs presented in this text have purposely been written using very few comments. In practice, comments would usually be used to describe each method in a class.

Figure 5.1   Ball World screen.

This program also incorporates a number of new features. These are summarized by the following list, and will be the subject of more detailed discussion in subsequent sections.

- The class defines a number of private internal variable data fields, some of which are constant, some of which are initialized but not constant, and some of which are not initialized. These data fields will be described in detail in Section 5.1.

- The main() method creates an instance of the class BallWorld. This object is initialized by means of a constructor. A *constructor* is a method that automatically ties together the actions of object *creation* and object *initialization*. Constructors will be introduced in Section 5.2.

- The class is declared as an *extension* of an existing Java class named Frame. This technique is called *inheritance*, and is the principal means in object-oriented languages for constructing new software abstractions that are variations on existing data types. Inheritance will be introduced in Section 5.3 and will be more extensively studied beginning in Chapter 8.

- The output displayed in a window by this program is created using some of the graphics primitives provided by the Java run-time library. These graphics operators are explained in Section 5.4.

```
import java.awt.*;                                          // 1

public class BallWorld extends Frame {                      // 2

  public static void main (String [ ] args) {               // 3
     BallWorld world = new BallWorld (Color.red);           // 4
     world.show ( );                                        // 5
  }                                                         // 6

  private static final int FrameWidth = 600;                // 7
  private static final int FrameHeight = 400;               // 8
  private Ball aBall;                                       // 9
  private int counter = 0;                                  // 10

  private BallWorld (Color ballColor) {// constructor for new window // 11
        // resize our frame, initialize title               // 12
     setSize (FrameWidth, FrameHeight);                     // 13
     setTitle ("Ball World");                               // 14

        // initialize aBall data field                      // 15
     aBall = new Ball (10, 15, 5);                          // 16
     aBall.setColor (ballColor);                            // 17
     aBall.setMotion (3.0, 6.0);                            // 18
  }                                                         // 19

  public void paint (Graphics g) {                          // 20
        // first, draw the ball                             // 21
     aBall.paint (g);                                       // 22
        // then move it slightly                            // 23
     aBall.move( );                                         // 24
     if ((aBall.x( ) < 0) || (aBall.x( ) > FrameWidth))     // 25
        aBall.setMotion (-aBall.xMotion( ), aBall.yMotion( )); // 26
     if ((aBall.y( ) < 0) || (aBall.y( ) > FrameHeight))    // 27
        aBall.setMotion (aBall.xMotion( ), -aBall.yMotion( )); // 28
        // finally, redraw the frame                        // 29
     counter = counter + 1;                                 // 30
     if (counter < 2000) repaint( );                        // 31
     else System.exit(0);                                   // 32
  }                                                         // 33
}                                                           // 34
```

Figure 5.2   Class description for Ball World.

5.1   DATA FIELDS

We have seen in the previous chapter (Section 4.4) how data fields can be declared within a class and how they can be initialized. The example program here includes features we have not seen in our previous programs in the four data fields declared on lines 7–10:

```
public static final int FrameWidth = 600;              // 7
public static final int FrameHeight = 400;             // 8
private Ball aBall;                                    // 9
private int counter = 0;                               // 10
```

Recall that the keyword public means that the variables being declared can be accessed (that is, used directly) anywhere in a Java program, while those that are declared as private can be used only within the bounds of the class description in which the declaration appears. Recall also that the keyword static means that there is one instance of the data field, shared by all instances of the class. The modifier keyword final means that this is the last time when an object is changed. It is here applied to a variable declaration; we will, in later chapters, see how the modifier can also be applied to a method definition. When used with a variable declaration, the declaration must also include an initialization, as shown here.

Data fields that are declared static and final behave as constants, because they exist in only one place and cannot change value. The identifier of such a data field is sometimes called a symbolic name. Because they cannot be modified, there is less reason to encapsulate a static final variable by declaring it private. Thus, such values are often made public, as shown here. The particular symbolic values being defined in this program represent the height and width of the window in which the application will eventually produce its output. Symbolic constants are useful in programs for a number of different reasons:

- By being defined in only one place, they make it easy to change subsequently, should circumstances require. For example, changing the height and or width of the window merely requires editing the file to change the values being used to initialize these symbolic constants, rather than hunting down all locations in the code where the quantities are used.

- When subsequently used elsewhere in the program, the symbolic name helps document the purpose of the constant values.

The counter data field is an integer value, initialized to zero:

```
private int counter = 0;                               // 10
```

Because the field is declared private, we know it can be used only within the bounds of the class definition. Because it was not declared static, we know that each instance of the class will hold its own different value. Because it was not declared final we know that the value being assigned is simply the initial value the variable will hold, but that it could subsequently be reassigned. We will see how this variable is used in the discussion of the graphical aspects of the current program.

```
private Ball aBall;                                              // 9
```

The final data field is declared as an instance of class Ball, which is the second class used in the creation of our example program. A ball is an abstraction that represents a bouncing ball. It is represented by a colored circle that can move around the display surface. The class Ball will be described in Section 5.5. How this field is initialized is described in the next section.

5.2 CONSTRUCTORS

As noted at the beginning of the chapter, one of the major topics of this chapter is the creation of new objects. This occurs in two places in the program shown in Figure 5.2. The first is in the main program, which creates an instance of the class BallWorld.

```
BallWorld world = new BallWorld (Color.red);                    // 4
```

The new operator is always used to create a new object. In this case, it is being used to create an instance of BallWorld, which (the next section shows) is the name given to the window in which the program will display its output. The new operator is followed by a class name, indicating the type of object being created. A parenthesized list then gives any arguments needed in the *initialization* of the object.

Object *creation* and object *initialization* are intimately tied in concept, and it is important that a programming language also bring these concepts together. Without support from the programming language, two types of errors can easily occur:

- An object is created, but it is used before it is initialized.

- An object is created and is initialized several times before it is used.

The language Java uses a concept called a *constructor* to guarantee that objects are placed into a proper initial state the moment they are created. A constructor bears a strong resemblance to a method; however, the name of the constructor matches the name of the class in which it appears, the constructor does not specify a return type, and the user will never (indeed, can never) directly execute the constructor. Like a method, though, a constructor can have arguments, and the body of the constructor consists of a sequence of statements. In our example program the constructor occurs in lines 11–19:

```
    private BallWorld (Color ballColor) {// constructor for new window 11
        // resize our frame, initialize title                    // 12
    setSize (FrameWidth, FrameHeight);                           // 13
    setTitle ("Ball World");                                     // 14

        // initialize aBall data field                           // 15
    aBall = new Ball (10, 15, 5);                                // 16
    aBall.setColor (ballColor);                                  // 17
    aBall.setMotion (3.0, 6.0);                                  // 18
}                                                                // 19
```

When an object is created (via the new operator), the first method invoked using the newly created object is the constructor method. The arguments passed to the constructor are the arguments supplied in the new expression.

In this particular case, the argument represents a color. The class Color is part of the Java run-time library. The value red is simply a constant (a value declared both as static and final) in the class description of Color.

```
BallWorld world = new BallWorld (Color.red);                    // 4
```

The corresponding parameter value in the constructor method is named ball-Color (see line 11). The constructor method must ensure that the instance of the class BallWorld is properly initialized. As noted earlier, the BallWorld represents the window in which the output will be displayed. The first two statements in the constructor set some of the attributes for this window; namely, the size and the title.

Line 16 of the constructor again uses the new operator to create and initialize a new object. In this case the object is an instance of the class Ball. Not only will memory for this object be created by the new statement, but also the arguments will be matched by a corresponding constructor in the class Ball, which will then be invoked to initialize the newly created ball:

```
public class Ball { // a generic round colored object that moves
    .
    .
    .
    public Ball (int x, int y, int r) { // ball with given center
                                        // and radius
        .
        .
        .
    }
}
```

The complete class description for Ball will be shown in Figure 5.3. Not all aspects of a Ball are set by the constructor. The final two statements in the

```
public class Ball { // a generic round colored object that moves
   protected Rectangle location; // position on graphic surface
   protected double dx, dy; // x and y components of motion vector
   protected Color color;   // color of ball

   public Ball (int x, int y, int r) { // ball with given center and radius
      location = new Rectangle(x-r, y-r, 2*r, 2*r);
      dx = 0; dy = 0; // initially no motion
      color = Color.blue;
   }

      // methods that set attributes
   public void setColor (Color newColor) { color = newColor; }

   public void setMotion (double ndx, double ndy) { dx = ndx; dy = ndy; }

      // methods that access attributes of ball
   public int radius () { return location.width / 2; }

   public int x () { return location.x + radius(); }

   public int y () { return location.y + radius(); }

   public double xMotion () { return dx; }

   public double yMotion () { return dy; }

   public Rectangle region () { return location; }

      // methods that change attributes of ball
   public void moveTo (int x, int y) { location.setLocation (x, y); }

   public void move () { location.translate ((int) dx, (int) dy); }

   public void paint (Graphics g) {
      g.setColor (color);
      g.fillOval
         (location.x, location.y, location.width, location.height);
   }
}
```

Figure 5.3 Implementation of the class Ball.

constructor for BallWorld set the color of the ball, and set the direction of motion for the ball. These attributes will be discussed in more detail in Section 5.5.

5.2.1 *Constructing the Application*

It is perhaps helpful at this point to say a word about the role and positioning of the main method. As you learned in Chapter 4, this method is invoked when execution of the program begins. This is possible because it is declared as static and therefore exists before any objects of its class exist. Consequently, an object of class BallWorld need not already exist in order to invoke the main() method.

Because it exists, in a sense, outside of all objects of the class, the main procedure can be used to create an instance of the class. This accounts for what might seem the strange phenomenon of main being a method in the BallWorld class, but at the same time being used to create a BallWorld object.

Some developers believe that it is less confusing to place the main method for a program into a class of its own, and to use this additional class merely to create an instance of the application class (in this case BallWorld), and then send it an appropriate message to begin the application. The code for such a class might look as follows:

```
public class BallWorldProgram {

    public static void main(String [ ] args) {
        BallWorld world = new BallWorld(Color.red);
        world.show();
    }
}
```

A disadvantage of this approach is that it creates two classes which, on many platforms, must reside in two separate files. Since this is in many ways just as cumbersome as the approach we have taken, and in most cases results in a longer program, we have adopted the style of incorporating the main method into the application class itself.

5.3 INHERITANCE

The most important feature of this program is the use of *inheritance* (sometimes also called *extension*). As noted earlier, the ball world is a rectangular window in which the action of the program (the bouncing ball) is displayed. The code needed to display and manipulate a window in a modern graphical user interface is exceedingly complex, in part because of the fact that the user can indicate actions such as moving, resizing, or iconifying the window. As a consequence, recent languages attempt to provide a means of reusing existing code so that the programmer need only be concerned with those features of the application that distinguish the program from other window applications.

The programming language Java uses the class Frame to represent a generic window. By saying that the class BallWorld extends the class Frame, we indicate that our new class, BallWorld, is a type of frame, but a more specialized type with a single purpose. The class Frame defines code to perform actions such as resizing the window, arranging for the window to be displayed on the workstation screen, and so on. By extending the class Frame, our new class *inherits* this functionality, which means the abilities are made available to the new class, and do not need to be rewritten anew.

```
public class BallWorld extends Frame {                              // 2
```

By executing the example program, the reader can verify that the window exhibits the functionality we expect of graphical windows—the ability to move, resize, and iconify, even though the program does not explicitly define any code to support these behaviors. (The reader might also note some expected behaviors that are not provided. For example, the handling of menu items and the close or quit box. A later chapter will describe how these features can be provided.)

We can observe the use of inheritance in the variety of methods that are invoked in our example program, but are not defined by the class BallWorld. These methods are instead inherited from the *parent class* Frame. Two examples are the methods setSize and setTitle invoked in the BallWorld constructor. These methods set the dimensions (in pixels) and title value for the window, respectively.

```
private BallWorld (Color ballColor) {// constructor for new window 11
        // resize our frame, initialize title                       // 12
    setSize (FrameWidth, FrameHeight);                              // 13
    setTitle ("Ball World");                                        // 14
        .
        .
        .
}                                                                   // 19
```

Another example is the method show, which is invoked in the static method main after the instance of BallWorld has been created. The show method arranges for the window to appear on the display surface, and then for the surface of the window to be drawn.

```
public static void main (String [ ] args) {                        // 3
    BallWorld world = new BallWorld (Color.red);                    // 4
    world.show ();                                                  // 5
}                                                                   // 6
```

5.4   THE JAVA GRAPHICS MODEL

Graphics in Java is provided as part of the Abstract Windowing Toolkit (AWT). The Java AWT is an example of a software *framework*. The idea of a framework is to provide the structure of a program but no application-specific details. The overall control, the flow of execution, is provided by the framework and therefore does not need to be rewritten for each new program. Thus, the programmer does not "see" the majority of the program code.

This is illustrated by the actions that occur subsequent to the program issuing the show method that is inherited from the class Frame. The window in which the action will take place is created, and the image of the window must be rendered (drawn on the screen). To do so, the show method invokes a method named paint, passing as argument a *graphics object*.

The programmer defines the appearance of the window by providing an implementation of the method paint. The graphics object passed as argument provides the ability to draw a host of items, such as lines and polygons as well as text. In our example program we use the paint method for two purposes. The only image in the window itself is the bouncing ball. The image of the ball is produced by invoking the paint method in the class Ball (see Figure 5.3). The second purpose of the paint method is to provide a simple means of updating the location for the ball. The ball is moved slightly, checking to see if the resulting new location is outside the bounds of the window. If it is outside the window the direction of the ball is reflected. Finally, invoking the repaint method (also inherited from Frame) indicates to the framework that the window should be redrawn, and the cycle continues.[2] A counter is used to prevent the program from running indefinitely, invoking the method System.exit after a certain number of iterations. (Later programs will use other techniques to halt the program.)

```
public void paint (Graphics g) {                              // 20
    // first, draw the ball                                   // 21
    aBall.paint (g);                                          // 22
    // then move it slightly                                  // 23
    aBall.move ( );                                           // 24
    if ((aBall.x( ) < 0) || (aBall.x( ) > FrameWidth))        // 25
        aBall.setMotion (-aBall.xMotion( ), aBall.yMotion( )); // 26
    if ((aBall.y( ) < 0) || (aBall.y( ) > FrameHeight))       // 27
        aBall.setMotion (aBall.xMotion( ), -aBall.yMotion( )); // 28
    // finally, redraw the frame                              // 29
    counter = counter + 1;                                    // 30
```

---

[2] Some readers might object that the control of the animation has little to do with the rendering of the image on the window and thus does not belong in the paint routine. While there is merit to this argument, this is also the simplest way to make primitive animations. Later chapters present more robust ways to control animations.

```
     if (counter < 2000) repaint( );                    // 31
     else System.exit(0);                               // 32
   }                                                    // 33
```

Note that the programmer calls the inherited method named repaint, which in turn will clear what has been drawn in the window and will eventually result in the paint method being invoked. The programmer does not directly call the paint method for the class.

In later examples we will investigate more of the abilities of the graphics objects provided by the Java library.

5.5   THE CLASS Ball

We will use a ball, that is, a round colored object that moves, in a number of our subsequent example programs. It is therefore useful to define the behavior of a Ball in a general fashion so that it can be used in a variety of ways. The description of class Ball is placed in its own file (Ball.java) and is linked together with the BallWorld class to create the executable program.

A Ball (Figure 5.3) maintains four data fields. The location of the ball is represented by a Rectangle, a general purpose class provided in the Java run-time library. Two floating-point values represent the horizontal and vertical components of the direction of motion for the ball. Finally, the color of the ball is represented by an instance of class Color, a Java library class we have previously encountered.

These four data fields are declared as protected. This allows classes within the same package, as well as any subsequent child classes we might create, to have access to the data fields, without exposing the data to modification by other objects. It is good practice to declare data fields protected, rather than private, even if you do not anticipate extending the class to make new classes.

The constructor for the class Ball records the location by creating a new instance of class Rectangle. Note that the three integer arguments passed as arguments to the constructor represent the center location of the ball and the radius: A simple calculation is used to convert these to the corner of the rectangle and the extent. The constructor also provides default values for color (blue) and motion. As we have seen in our example program, these can be redefined by invoking the method setColor and setMotion.

A number of methods are used to access some of the attributes of a ball. Attributes that can be obtained in this fashion include the radius, the x and y coordinate of the center of the ball, the horizontal and vertical directions of motion, and the region occupied by the ball. Methods that allow access to a data field in a class are termed *accessor methods*. The use of accessor methods is strongly encouraged in preference to making the data fields themselves public, as an accessor method only permits the value to be *read*, and not modified. This ensures that any modification to a data field will be mediated by the proper method, such as through the methods setMotion or moveTo.

Some of the methods use operations provided by the class Rectangle. A rectangle can provide a width (used in method radius), the location of the upper corner (used in methods x and y), can move to a new position (used in method moveTo), and can transliterate on the two-dimensional surface (used in the method move).

Finally, the method paint uses two operations that are provided by the class Graphics in the Java library. These are the methods to set the current color for rendering graphics (setColor) and to display a painted oval at a given location on the window (fillOval).

5.6 MULTIPLE OBJECTS OF THE SAME CLASS

Every instance of a class maintains its own internal data fields. We can illustrate this by making variations on our sample program. The simplest change is to modify the main routine to create two independent windows. Each window will have a different ball, each window can be independently moved or resized.

```
public static void main (String [ ] args) {
        // create first window with red ball
    BallWorld world = new BallWorld (Color.red);
    world.show( );
        // now create a second window with yellow ball
    BallWorld world2 = new BallWorld (Color.yellow);
    world2.show( );
}
```

The reader should try making this change, and observe the result. Note how one window is bouncing a red ball and the second is bouncing a yellow ball. This indicates that each instance of class BallWorld must be maintaining its own Ball value, given that a ball cannot be both red and yellow at the same time.

A second variation illustrates even more dramatically the independence of different objects, even when they derive from the same class. The class MultiBallWorld (Figure 5.4) is similar to our initial program except that it creates a collection of balls rather than just a single ball. Only the lines that have changed are included, and those that are elided are the same as the earlier program. The new program declares an array of Balls, rather than just a single ball. Note the syntax used to declare an array. As noted in the previous chapter, arrays in Java are different from arrays in most other languages. Even though the array is declared, space is still not set aside for the array elements. Instead, the array itself must be created (again with a new command):

```
ballArray = new Ball [ BallArraySize ];
```

```
public class MultiBallWorld extends Frame {

   .
   .
   .
   private Ball [ ] ballArray;
   private static final int BallArraySize = 10;

   private MultiBallWorld (Color ballColor) {
      .
      .
      .
         // initialize object data field
      ballArray = new Ball [ BallArraySize ];
      for (int i = 0; i < BallArraySize; i++) {
         ballArray[i] = new Ball(10, 15, 5);
         ballArray[i].setColor (ballColor);
         ballArray[i].setMotion (3.0+i, 6.0-i);
      }
   }

   public void paint (Graphics g) {
      for (int i = 0; i < BallArraySize; i++) {
         ballArray[i].paint (g);
            // then move it slightly
         ballArray[i].move ( );
         if ((ballArray[i].x( ) < 0) ||
               (ballArray[i].x( ) > FrameWidth))
            ballArray[i].setMotion
               (-ballArray[i].xMotion( ), ballArray[i].yMotion( ));
         if ((ballArray[i].y( ) < 0) ||
               (ballArray[i].y( ) > FrameHeight))
            ballArray[i].setMotion
               (ballArray[i].xMotion( ), -ballArray[i].yMotion( ));
      }
      .
      .
      .
   }
}
```

Figure 5.4   Class description for Multiple Ball World.

Note how the size of the array is specified by a symbolic constant, defined earlier in the program. Even then, however, the array elements cannot be accessed. Instead, each array element must be individually created, once more using a new operation:

```
for (int i = 0; i < BallArraySize; i++) {
    ballArray[i] = new Ball(10, 15, 5);
    ballArray[i].setColor (ballColor);
    ballArray[i].setMotion (3.0+i, 6.0-i);
}
```

Each ball is created, then initialized with the given color, and set in motion. We have used the loop index variable to change the direction of motion slightly, so that each ball will initially move in a different direction. The ++ operator, which we have not used previously, is a shorthand way of writing i = i + 1.

When the program is executed, ten different balls will be created. Each ball will maintain its own location and direction. As each ball is asked to paint, it will display its value on the window. Each ball will then move, independently of all other balls.

5.7   CHAPTER SUMMARY

The two major themes introduced in this chapter have been the creation of new objects using the operator new, and the definition of new classes using *inheritance* to extend an existing class. Topics discussed in this chapter include the following:

- Data fields that are declared final cannot be subsequently redefined. A static and final value is the technique normally used to create a symbolic constant.

- New objects are always created using the operator new.

- When a new object is created, the *constructor* for the class of the object is automatically invoked as part of the creation process. The constructor should guarantee the object is properly initialized.

- A constructor is a method that has the same name as the class in which it is defined.

- Any arguments used by the constructor must appear in the new statement that creates the corresponding object.

- Classes can be defined using *inheritance*. Such classes extend the functionality of an existing class. Any public or protected data fields or methods defined in the parent class become part of the new class.

- The class Frame can be used to create simple Java windows. This class can be extended to define application-specific windows.

- The *framework* provided by the Java AWT displays a frame (a window) when the frame object is given the message show. To create the image shown in the window the message paint is used. The programmer can define this method to produce application-specific pictures.

- The paint method is given as argument an instance of the library class Graphics. This object can be used to create a variety of graphical images.

- The class Rectangle (used in our class Ball) is a library class that represents a rectangular region on the two-dimensional window surface. The class provides a large amount of useful functionality.

- Multiple instances of the same class each maintain their own separate data fields. This was illustrated by creating multiple independent Ball objects, which move independently of each other.

Cross References

We will use the Ball class in case studies in Chapters 6–8 and 20. The topic of inheritance is simple to explain but has many subtle points that can easily trap the unwary. We will examine inheritance in detail in Chapters 8 through 11. The AWT will be examined in more detail in Chapter 13.

Study Questions

1. How would you change the color of the ball in our example application to yellow?

2. How would you change the size of the application window to 500 by 300 pixels?

3. What does the modifier keyword final mean when applied in a data field declaration?

4. Why do symbolic constants make it easier to read and maintain programs?

5. What two actions are tied together by the concept of a constructor?

6. What types of errors does the use of constructors prevent?

7. What does it mean to say that a new class inherits from an existing class?

8. What methods inherited from class Frame are used in our example application?

9. What methods provided by our example program are invoked by the code inherited from class Frame?

10. What abstraction does the Java library class Rectangle represent?

11. What are some reasons that data fields should be declared as private or protected, and access provided only through public methods?

12. In Java, what are the steps involved in creating an array of objects?

EXERCISES

1. The method Math.random returns a random floating-point value between 0 and 1.0. Using this method, modify the example program shown in Figure 5.2 so that the ball will initially move in a random direction.

2. Modify the MultiBallWorld so that the colors of the various balls created are selected randomly from the values red, blue and yellow. (*Hint*: Call Math.random( ) and test the resulting value for various ranges, selecting red if the value is in one range, blue if it is in another, and so on.)

3. Modify the MultiBallWorld so that it will produce balls of different radiuses, as well as different colors.

4. Rather than testing whether or not a ball has hit the wall in our main program, we could have used inheritance to provide a specialized form of Ball. Create a class BoundedBall that inherits from class Ball. The constructor for this class should provide the height and width of the window, which should subsequently be maintained as data fields in the class. Rewrite the move method so that if the ball moves outside the bounds, it automatically reverses direction. Finally, rewrite the BallWorld class to use an instance of BoundedBall, rather than an ordinary Ball, and eliminate the bounds test in the main program.

5. Our Ball abstraction is not as simple as it could have been. Separate the Ball class into two separate classes. The first, the new class Ball, knows only a location, its size, and how to paint itself. The second class, MovableBall, extends the class Ball and adds all behavior related to motion, such as the data fields dx and dy, the methods setMotion and move, and so on. Rewrite the MultiBallWorld to use instances of class MovableBall.

6

A Cannon Game

In this chapter we will examine an implementation of a classic "shooting cannon" game. In this simple game, there is a cannon on the left portion of the user's window, and a target on the right portion, as shown in Figure 6.1. The user can control the angle of elevation for the cannon and fire a cannonball. The objective of the game is, of course, to hit the target.

As with all the case studies, our objective is not so much the cannon application itself, which is only moderately interesting, but the use of a simple program to illustrate a number of different features of the Java language. In particular, in this chapter we will examine the features of the Java library that simplify the creation of a graphical user interface (GUI). We will develop two variations on this game:

- The first version is the simplest. The user enters the angle of the cannon from the command argument line, the cannon fires once, and the program halts.

Figure 6.1 A window of the Cannon Game.

■ In the second version, we improve user interaction, by providing both a slider with which the angle of the cannon can be changed, and a button to fire the cannon. Thus, multiple attempts to hit the target can be made during one execution of the program.

6.1   THE SIMPLE CANNON GAME

The principal class for our cannon application is shown in Figure 6.2. The main method is similar to those described in the previous chapters. The universe for our application is termed CannonGame. An instance of this class is created, then passed the message show. The message show causes the window in which the application is played to be displayed.

In our first version of the Cannon Game, the angle for the cannon is read from the command-line argument. The first string in the command-line argument list is assumed to be an integer value, representing the angle (in degrees) for the cannon to be set prior to launch of the cannonball. This value is converted by a method from the Java library class Integer, and passed as argument to the constructor for the cannon world. There, the method intValue() is used to convert an Integer into an int. We will return to a discussion of the relationship between these two data types in Section 6.1.2.

The cannon world is declared to be a type of Frame, which you will recall from the preceding chapter is how Java declares a new type of window. The class description defines two public constant values (declared as static final, see Section 5.1) that describe the height and width of the window that represents the cannon application. In addition, three new data fields are declared. These are the angle of the cannon, a message that will be displayed in the middle of the playing window, and a cannonball. The latter is an instance of class CannonBall, which will be described shortly.

The constructor for the class CannonGame resizes the window frame to the declared bounds, and sets the window title. The argument value is converted from the type Integer to the built-in type int using the method intValue. The string representing the message is set to a value that will, when printed, indicate the current angle of the cannon. Finally, the cannonball is created using the angle to determine the initial direction of movement. There are two other methods defined in this class. The method dy is used in the display method and will be described shortly. The remaining method paints the window area.

Rendering pictures is complicated by the fact that Java, like almost all windowing systems, uses a coordinate system that is "upside down." As shown in Figure 6.3, the upper left corner of a window is the 0,0 coordinate, with x values increasing as they move right, and y values increasing as they move *down*. However, most people prefer to think in a coordinate system where the 0,0 location is the bottom left corner, and y values increase as they move *up* as depicted in Figure 6.4.

```
class CannonGame extends Frame {

   public static void main (String [ ] args) {
      CannonGame world = new CannonGame (Integer.valueOf(args[0]));
      world.show ();
   }

   public static final int FrameWidth = 600;
   public static final int FrameHeight = 400;

      // data fields
   private int angle = 45;
   private String message = "";
   private CannonBall cannonBall = null;
   private static final int barrelLength = 30;
   private static final int barrelWidth = 10;

      // constructor
   public CannonGame (Integer theta) {

      setSize (FrameWidth, FrameHeight);
      setTitle ("Cannon Game");

         // set the local variables
      angle = theta.intValue( );
      message = "Angle = " + angle;

         // create the cannon ball
      double radianAngle = angle * Math.PI / 180.0;
      double sinAngle = Math.sin(radianAngle);
      double cosAngle = Math.cos(radianAngle);
      double initialVelocity = 12;
      cannonBall = new CannonBall (    // calculations determine end of cannon
         20 + (int) (barrelLength * cosAngle),
         dy(5+(int) (barrelLength * sinAngle)),
         5, initialVelocity * cosAngle, -initialVelocity * sinAngle);
   }

   public int dy (int y) { return FrameHeight - y; }

   public void paint (Graphics g) { ... }
}
```

Figure 6.2   Description of the principal class for the Cannon Game.

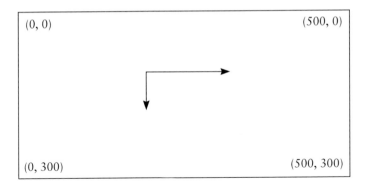

Figure 6.3 The "upside down" coordinate system of Java and other windowing software.

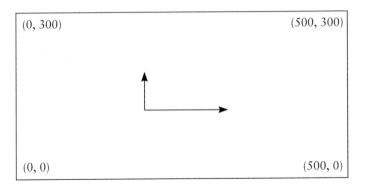

Figure 6.4 Coordinate system as most people think of it.

One way to handle this is to perform a coordinate transformation as the very last operation before any drawing command. This is the task of the method dy, shown in Figure 6.2. By subtracting a value from the maximum window size, we can take a value in the more natural coordinate system, and convert it into a value in the upside-down coordinate system. An advantage of the method dy is that it is self-inverting; applying the function twice returns the original value. We will use this observation by expressing all our drawing operations in the zero-centered form while allowing the ball itself to work in the Java window coordinates.

The method to draw the elements in the Cannon Game world is shown in Figure 6.5. Recall from the previous chapter that drawing is performed by the method paint, which will be invoked implicitly when the application is rendered, and can be requested explicitly by invoking the method repaint. Also recall that

```
public void paint (Graphics g) {
   int x = 20; // location of cannon
   int y = 5;
   double radianAngle = angle * Math.PI / 180.0;
   int lv = (int) (barrelLength * Math.sin(radianAngle));
   int lh = (int) (barrelLength * Math.cos(radianAngle));
   int sv = (int) (barrelWidth * Math.sin(radianAngle + Math.PI/2));
   int sh = (int) (barrelWidth * Math.cos(radianAngle + Math.PI/2));
      // draw cannon
   g.setColor(Color.green);
   g.drawLine(x, dy(y), x+lh, dy(y+lv));
   g.drawLine(x+lh, dy(y+lv), x+lh+sh, dy(y+lv+sv));
   g.drawLine(x+lh+sh, dy(y+lv+sv), x+sh, dy(y+sv));
   g.drawLine(x+sh, dy(y+sv), x, dy(y));
   g.drawOval(x-8, dy(y+10), 12, 12);
      // draw target
   g.setColor(Color.red);
   g.fillRoundRect(FrameWidth-100, dy(12), 50, 10, 6, 6);
      // draw cannon ball
   if (cannonBall != null) {
      cannonBall.move();
      cannonBall.paint(g);
      if (dy(cannonBall.y()) > 0)
         repaint();
      else {
         int targetX = FrameWidth - 100;
         if ((cannonBall.x() > targetX) &&
               (cannonBall.x() < (targetX + 50)))
            message = "You Hit It!";
         else
            message = "Missed!";
         cannonBall = null;
         }
      }
      // draw message
   g.drawString(message, FrameWidth/2, FrameHeight/2);
}
```

Figure 6.5   The paint method for the Cannon Game application.

drawing commands are provided by the library class Graphics, an instance of which is supplied to the paint method. The cannon itself is represented by a rectangle, 10 pixels by 30, with a circular wheel. A bit of simple math is used to tilt the cannon to the appropriate angle. One complicating factor is that the application is representing angles in degrees using an integer value, while the sine and cosine functions in the Math library require a double-precision floating-point value in radians. A simple algorithm is used to convert between the two. The target is represented by a red rectangle. If a cannonball exists, it is asked to move itself, paint itself at the transformed location, and if not at the final target, schedule the picture for another repainting.[1] Finally, the message is printed in the middle of the playing area.

6.1.1   *Balls That Respond to Gravity*

The class Ball was introduced in Chapter 5. A Ball, you will recall, possessed a radius, a location, a color, and a direction. The latter was represented by a pair of values, representing the extent of motion in the *x* coordinate and the extent of motion in the *y* coordinate.

A CannonBall is built using inheritance as an extension of class Ball. This means that a CannonBall has all the properties of a Ball and also includes new properties or alters existing properties. In this case, a CannonBall changes the move method, simulating the effect of gravity by reducing the change in the vertical direction by a small amount each update cycle.

```
public class CannonBall extends Ball {

    public CannonBall (int sx, int sy, int r, double dx, double dy)
    {
        super (sx, sy, r);
        setMotion (dx, dy);
    }

    public static final double GravityEffect = 0.3;

    public void move () {
        dy = dy + GravityEffect;
        super.move( );  // update the ball position
    }
}
```

---

[1] Please remember that we are using the paint method in this manner merely as a simple means of animation. Later chapters will demonstrate how to move the control over the animation out of the paint routine.

We have not yet encountered the pseudovariable super, shown here in both methods. When a method *overrides* (that is, replaces) a similarly named method in the parent class, a technique must be provided to indicate that the method should invoke the method inherited from the parent class. The method cannot simply be named, as the name in the child class and the parent class are the same. Thus, for example, if one was to try to invoke the move method in class Ball by simply executing the method move, the result would be an infinite series of recursive method calls; which is not the outcome we wish.

The pseudovariable super is used to represent the receiver but is viewed as an instance of the parent class, not the current class. Thus, by invoking super.move( ), the method move is asking that the move method from the parent class be executed, and not the version overridden by the class CannonBall.

Similarly, the use of the name super as a method in a constructor is used to indicate that the constructor for the parent class should be invoked, using the arguments shown. Note how the class CannonBall is invoked with a slightly different set of arguments than were used for the class Ball.

6.1.2 *Integers and* ints

As noted in Section 4.3 of Chapter 4, integer values are not actually *objects*, in the technical sense of the world. Thus, integers do not have classes, there are no methods associated with integers, and so on. For each of the nonclass primitive types, the Java library defines a "wrapper" class that can be used as an object. For integers this wrapper class is named Integer. The class Integer provides a number of useful operations. The one we utilize in our example program is the ability to take a String (the command-line argument), and convert it into a numeric value. To do this, a string is passed as argument to the message valueOf:

```
CannonGame world = new CannonGame (Integer.valueOf(args[0]));
```

The result produced by the message valueOf is a new instance of class Integer, initialized to the indicated value. The conversion from Integer to int is performed using the message intValue:

```
angle = theta.intValue( );
```

6.2 ADDING USER INTERACTION

The user interaction in our first application was very primitive. The user could select one angle, run the program, and see the result. In our second variation, we improve user interaction by providing the ability to dynamically set the angle of the cannon, and fire several times during one execution.

The conventional way to set a varying quantity, such as the angle of the cannon, is with a scroll bar. The normal way to indicate that an action should

Figure 6.6   A screen of the revised game, renamed CannonWorld.

commence, such as the cannon should be fired, is with a button. In our revised game we will incorporate both these items, placing the button on the top of the screen, and the scroll bar to the right of the playing area, as shown in Figure 6.6.

The program for the revised game, now named CannonWorld, is shown in Figure 6.7. One feature to note is that we must now import the Java library java.awt.event.*, in order to include the definitions of the event-handling routines for the Java system. This is in addition to the java.awt.* library we have been including from the start. Although in code length the amount of change from the first version of our program is relatively small, a number of important features distinguish this program. We will explore these in the following sections.

6.2.1   Inner Classes

One of the more notable features of the program in Figure 6.7 is the declaration of two new classes *within* the application class itself. A class declared in such a fashion is known as an *inner class*. Modifiers used in declaring an inner class match the meanings we have previously described for data fields and methods; thus, an inner class that is declared as private (such as shown here) can only be used within the outer class in which it is defined.

```
class CannonWorld extends Frame {
    .
    .
    .

    private class FireButtonListener implements ActionListener {
        .
        .
        .
    }
```

```
private class ScrollBarListener implements AdjustmentListener {
   .
   .
   .
}

   .
   .
   .
}
```

Inner classes are allowed to access their surrounding environment. That is, methods in an inner class can use data fields declared in the surrounding outer class, as well as invoke methods from the surrounding context. We see this in the method defined in class ScrollBarListener, which modifies both the data fields angle and message.

6.2.2 *Interfaces*

Both the inner classes created in this example use the keyword implements in their header. The *implementation* of an *interface* is yet another program-structuring mechanism, one that can be understood by comparison to the technique of *inheritance* we have been using previously.

An interface in Java is a description of *behavior*. It is written in a fashion that appears similar to a class definition; however, there are no implementations (method bodies) associated with methods, and the only data fields permitted must be declared static. An interface for ActionListener, used in our sample program, might be written as follows:

```
interface ActionListener {
   public void actionPerformed (ActionEvent);
}
```

The Java library, particularly in those sections that relate to the handling of events (such as pressing buttons or moving sliders), makes extensive use of interfaces. When a class is declared as implementing an interface, it is a guarantee (one that is checked by the compiler) that the class must provide a certain behavior. In this case, an assertion that a class is an ActionListener means that the class must provide a method named actionPerformed.

The reader should consider carefully the difference between this and inheritance. Using inheritance, methods and data fields that are declared in the parent class may be used in the child class. Thus, the child class inherits the *structure* of the parent, as well as being able to mimic the parent behavior. Using an interface, on the other hand, there is no implementation of the methods in the "parent interface" at all. Instead, the parent simply defines the names of the methods, which *must* then be implemented in the child class. In this manner a

```
import java.awt.event.*; // import the event interface

class CannonWorld extends Frame {
   .
   .
   private String message = "Angle: " + angle;
   private CannonBall cannonBall = null;
   private Scrollbar slider;

   private class FireButtonListener implements ActionListener {
      public void actionPerformed (ActionEvent e) {
         double radianAngle = angle * Math.PI / 180.0;
         double sinAngle = Math.sin(radianAngle);
         double cosAngle = Math.cos(radianAngle);
         // create the cannon ball
         cannonBall = new CannonBall (
            20 + (int) (barrelLength * cosAngle),
            dy(5+(int) (barrelLength * sinAngle)),
            5, 12 * cosAngle, -12 * sinAngle);
         repaint( );
      }
   }

   private class ScrollBarListener implements AdjustmentListener {
      public void adjustmentValueChanged (AdjustmentEvent e) {
         angle = slider.getValue( );
         message = "Angle: " + angle;
         repaint( );
      }
   }

   public CannonWorld ( ) {
      setSize (FrameWidth, FrameHeight);
      setTitle ("Cannon Game");
         // add the scroll bar and button
      Button fire = new Button("fire");
      fire.addActionListener(new FireButtonListener( ));
      add ("North", fire);
      slider = new Scrollbar(Scrollbar.VERTICAL, angle, 5, 0, 90);
      slider.addAdjustmentListener(new ScrollBarListener( ));
      add ("East", slider);
   }
}
```

Figure 6.7   Revised program renamed CannonWorld with button and slider.

child class inherits a specification of methods from an interface, but no structure, no data fields, and no member functions.

Despite the fact that methods of an interface have no implementation, an interface can be used as a type name in an argument declared in a method header. The matching parameter value must then be an instance of a class that implements the interface. In our example program, the addActionListener method in class Button expects an argument that implements the ActionListener interface, and the addAdjustmentListener method in class ScrollBar expects an argument that implements the AdjustmentListener interface.

6.2.3 *The Java Event Model*

Modern graphical user interfaces are structured around the concept of events. An *event* is an action, such as the user clicking the mouse on a button, selecting a menu item, pressing a key, or inserting a disk into a drive. The program responds to an event by performing certain actions. Thus, such interfaces are said to be *event-driven*.

The Java event model is based on the concept of listeners. A *listener* is an object whose sole purpose is to sit and wait for an event to occur. When the event does occur, the listener goes into action and performs the appropriate behavior.

Our sample program uses two listeners. The first is waiting for the button to be pressed. The class Button is one of many graphical elements provided by the Java library. The string argument passed to the constructor for the class is the text that will appear on the face of the button. A listener for a button must implement the interface ActionListener. The listener in our sample program is declared as an instance of the inner class FireButtonListener, and is attached to a newly created button by the following code:

```
Button fire = new Button("fire");
fire.addActionListener(new FireButtonListener());
```

When the button is pressed, the message actionPerformed will be passed to the listener. In this case, this message will be handled by the one method in the class body:

```
private class FireButtonListener implements ActionListener {
    public void actionPerformed (ActionEvent e) {
        // convert angle in degrees to radians
        double radianAngle = angle * Math.PI / 180.0;
        double sinAngle = Math.sin(radianAngle);
        double cosAngle = Math.cos(radianAngle);
        // create the cannon ball
        cannonBall = new CannonBall ( // calculations to find end of
                                      // cannon
            20 + (int) (barrelLength * cosAngle),
```

```
            dy(5+(int) (barrelLength * sinAngle)),
            5, 12 * cosAngle, -12 * sinAngle);
        repaint( );
        }
    }
```

The argument of type ActionEvent which is passed to the method actionPer-formed describes details of the event with more precision. However, the value is ignored, since in this case there is only one event a button can perform that is of any interest, namely the event that occurs when it is pressed. The action when this occurs is to convert the angle of elevation for the cannon into radians, create a new cannonball for firing, and schedule the window for repainting.

The slider that is used to control the elevation of the cannon is created in a similar fashion. The constructor for class ScrollBar takes as argument an indication whether the slidebar is horizontal or vertical, an initial value, and the range of accepted values. The constructor for our application creates both a new slider and a new listener:

```
// create a vertical scroll bar, limits zero and 90, step size 5
// initial value set by value in variable angle
slider = new Scrollbar(Scrollbar.VERTICAL, angle, 5, 0, 90);
slider.addAdjustmentListener(new ScrollBarListener( ));
```

The listener must implement the AdjustmentListener interface. When the slider is moved, the listener is given the message adjustmentValueChanged. Note that, unlike the situation involving the button, the slide bar must be made available to the listener, so that the current value of the slide bar can be determined (using the message getValue). It is for this reason that the slide bar is saved in a data field, but the button need not be. Once the value of the slide bar has been determined, the angle and message can be changed, and the window scheduled for repainting.

```
    private class ScrollBarListener implements AdjustmentListener {
        public void adjustmentValueChanged (AdjustmentEvent e) {
            angle = slider.getValue( );
            message = "Angle: " + angle;
            repaint( );
            }
    }
```

6.2.4   Window Layout

Part of every Java program is a *layout manager*. The layout manager controls the placement of graphical items in a Java program. By using sophisticated layout managers the programmer can have a great deal of control over the appearance of a Java window. For simple programs, however, we can use the default layout manager, which permits values to be placed on the four sides of the screen. These four portions of the screen are identified as North (the top), East (the right), West (the left), and South (the bottom). The constructor for our application places the button on the top of the window, and the slider on the right hand side.

```
public CannonWorld ( ) {
    .
    .
    .
        // add the scroll bar
        Button fire = new Button("fire");
        fire.addActionListener(new FireButtonListener( ));
    add ("North", fire);
        slider = new ScrollBar(Scrollbar.VERTICAL, angle, 5, 0, 90);
        slider.addAdjustmentListener(new ScrollBarListener( ));
    add ("East", slider);
}
```

In later chapters we will explore a variety of other layout managers.

6.3 CHAPTER SUMMARY

This chapter has once again made use of a relatively simple application as a vehicle to introduce a number of new concepts. The following list summarizes some of the ideas introduced in this chapter:

- The class Integer, which is a wrapper class that can hold an integer value. Instances of this class are objects, unlike normal integer values, which are not objects. The class Integer provides some useful functionality, such as the ability to parse a string value that holds the textual representation of an integer quantity.

- The use of inheritance in the construction of the class CannonBall, so that the majority of the behavior for the ball is inherited from the parent class Ball.

- The pseudovariable super, which when used as a value inside a method refers to the parent class from which the current class inherits.

- The idea of an *inner class*, which is a class definition nested within another class definition. Inner classes are allowed full access to the data values and methods provided by surrounding classes.

- The idea of an *interface*, which is a means to ensure that classes satisfy certain behavior. An interface defines the names and arguments for member functions but does not provide an implementation. A class that declares itself as implementing an interface must then provide an implementation for these operations. A method can insist that an argument implement certain functionality, by declaring the argument using the interface as a type.

- The Java event model, in which *listener* objects are attached to event producing objects, such as buttons. When an event occurs, the listener is notified and then performs whatever action is appropriate.

- The graphical component classes Button and Slider, which simplify the creation of graphical features in a user interface.

- The idea of a window layout manager. In our application program we used the default layout manager, which is an instance of the class BorderLayout.

Note that as our application has become more complex, we have moved closer to the idea that an object-oriented program is a "community" of agents that interact to produce the desired behavior. Instances of the following categories of objects are all used in this example program:

- The class CannonWorld, which inherits from the class Frame provided by the Java library.

- The class CannonBall, built as an extension of the earlier class Ball developed in Chapter 5.

- The class Integer, used here for its ability to translate a number in text into a numeric quantity.

- The graphical component classes Button and ScrollBar, and their listener classes FireButtonListener and ScrollBarListener, the latter two constructed as inner classes within our application class.

- Instances of the class ActionEvent and AdjustmentEvent, which are created when an event occurs and carry information to the event listener.

- The layout manager, an instance of class BorderLayout.

CROSS REFERENCES

Wrapper classes, such as Integer and Double, will be explained in more detail in Chapter 19. The distinction between inheritance and implementation, and the uses of each, will be a topic addressed in Chapter 10. Window layouts, layout managers, graphical components, and other features of the AWT will be examined in more detail in Chapter 13.

STUDY QUESTIONS

1. What is the parent class for class CannonGame?

2. In the first cannon game, how is the angle of the cannon determined?

3. What transformation is performed by the member function dy?

4. What is the difference in behavior between a Ball and a CannonBall?

5. How is the pseudovariable super used in a method? What effect does it have in a message expression?

6. What is the difference between the types Integer and int?

7. What is an inner class?

8. What is an interface?

9. What would an interface for the class CannonBall look like?

10. What does it mean to say that a class implements an interface?

11. What does it mean to say that a program is event-driven?

12. What is an event listener?

13. What is a window layout manager?

14. In Figure 6.7, although both the fire button and the slider are graphical components, one is declared as a member data field and the other a local variable. Explain why. Could they both have been declared as member data fields? As local variables?

EXERCISES

1. Change the CannonGame so that the message being displayed provides not only the angle of the cannon, but also the current position of the cannonball. This value should change as the cannonball moves through the air.

2. Modify the class CannonBall so that the ball is colored blue when the ball is moving upward, and colored red when the ball is descending. Will this change have any impact on the rest of the program?

3. Modify the CannonWorld program so that it maintains both a count of the number of balls fired and the number of times the target was hit. Display both of these values in the message area, as well as the angle of the cannon.

4. On some platforms it may be difficult to halt the cannon application once it has finished. Add a button labeled "Quit" to the bottom (south) part

of the application window. When pressed, this button should execute the method System.exit(0).

5. Create a simple program that draws a window with a colored ball in the center. Place a button at the top of the window. When the user presses the button, the color of the ball will change from red to yellow, or from yellow to green, or from green to red.

6. Create a simple program that draws a window with a colored ball in the center. Place a slider on the right side of the window. As the user moves the slider, move the ball up and down the window.

7. The constructor for class Color can also take three integer arguments, which represent the saturation values for red, blue, and green. The arguments must be integers between 0 and 255. Create a simple program that draws a window with a colored ball in the center. Place sliders on three sides. As the user moves the sliders, the saturation values change for one of these arguments, and the ball changes color.

7 Pinball Game Construction Kit

In this chapter we will expand on the techniques introduced in the Cannon Game of Chapter 6, creating an entirely different type of interactive application. Along the way, we will use the development of this program to discuss standard data structures, event handling, inheritance, exceptions, interfaces, and multiple threads of control.

The application we will develop, the Pinball Construction Kit, simulates a pinball game. Users can fire a ball from the small square in the right corner of the bottom of the screen. (See Figure 7.1.) Balls rise, then encounter a variety of different types of targets as they fall back to the ground. The user scores points that depend upon the type and number of targets encountered as the ball descends. The objective of the game is to score as many points as possible.

As we did with the cannonball application in Chapter 6, we will develop this program in a sequence of stages, each stage emphasizing a small number of new programming concepts. The intent is simply to introduce these concepts in the context of a relatively simple and easy to understand program. Many of the major ideas introduced here will be discussed in more detail in later chapters.

7.1 FIRST VERSION OF GAME

Our first version (Figure 7.2) is in many ways the same as the cannonball application from Chapter 6, but with a number of new features. Because we will later be creating objects that will need to communicate with the window object, the variable world is declared as a public static value, rather than as a local variable to the main method. Balls are "fired" from a square box labelled with a red circle that appears at the bottom right corner of the window. A notable difference between this version and the cannonball application of Chapter 6 is the mechanism for placing a new ball into motion. Whereas in the earlier

99

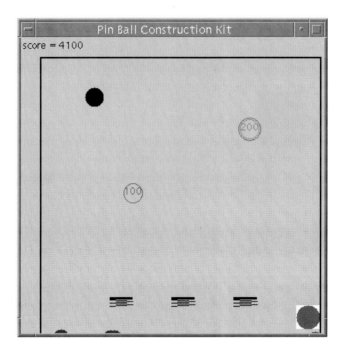

Figure 7.1   The Pinball Application

program firing was tied to a button, in this version we will trap mouse activities in a more general routine. Two other notable changes are that the pinball game allows several balls to be in the air at once (the Cannon Game fired only a single ball), and we will finally move the control over the animation out of the paint routine, by introducing the concept of multiple threads of execution. Each of these ideas will be explored in more detail in the following sections.

The class PinBall (Figure 7.3) is almost identical to the class CannonBall described in Chapter 6 (Section 6.1.1), except that the initial direction is slightly to the left of vertical, and includes a small random number perturbation so as to be less predicatable.

7.1.1   *Collection Classes*

Unlike the Cannon Game described in the previous chapter, the pinball game allows several balls to be moving at one time. Every time the user clicks on the "fire" button, a new ball is placed in motion, even if earlier balls have not yet ceased moving.

To manage this, we need a data structure that can hold a collection of values. The one collection data structure we have seen up to now is the array (see Section 5.6). However, the array is limited by the fact that when we allocate

```
import java.awt.*;
import java.awt.event.*;
import java.util.Vector;

public class PinBallGame extends Frame {

   public static void main (String [ ] args) {
      world = new PinBallGame( );
      world.show( );
   }

   public static final int FrameWidth = 400;
   public static final int FrameHeight = 400;
   public static PinBallGame world;
   private Vector balls;

   public PinBallGame ( ) {
      setTitle ("PinBall Construction Kit");
      setSize (FrameWidth, FrameHeight);

      balls = new Vector( );
      addMouseListener (new MouseKeeper( ));
   }

   private class MouseKeeper extends MouseAdapter { ... }

   private class PinBallThread extends Thread { ... }

   public void paint (Graphics g) { // fire button is 30 by 30
      g.setColor (Color.white); // white rectangle
      g.fillRect (FrameWidth-40, FrameHeight-40, 30, 30);
      g.setColor (Color.red); // with red button
      g.fillOval (FrameWidth-40, FrameHeight-40, 30, 30);
        // draw balls
      for (int i = 0; i < balls.size( ); i++) {
         PinBall aBall = (PinBall) balls.elementAt(i);
         aBall.paint(g);
         }
      }
}
```

Figure 7.2   First version of PinBallGame class.

```
public class PinBall extends Ball {

   public PinBall (int sx, int sy)
   {
      super(sx, sy, 10);
         // start out moving (roughly) vertically
      setMotion (-2 + Math.random()/4, -15);
   }

   private static final double gravityEffect = 0.3;

   public void move ()
   {
      dy = dy + gravityEffect; // effect of gravity
      super.move();    // update the ball position
   }
}
```

Figure 7.3 The class PinBall.

a new array object we must state the number of elements the array will hold. In the present case, we cannot make any such estimate since we do not know how many times the user will hit the "fire" button.

Fortunately, the Java library provides a number of other data structures we can employ. One of the simplest ones is a Vector. A vector is, like an array, an indexed data structure; meaning that each element has a position in the collection, and elements are accessed by requesting the value at a given position. However, unlike an array, a vector can dynamically grow as new values are inserted into the collection.

To use a vector, the programmer must first import the vector class definition from the standard library:

```
import java.util.Vector;
```

The vector is declared by simply providing a name:

```
private Vector balls;
```

Note, in particular, that unlike an array, it is not necessary to state the type of values that a Vector will hold. For technical reasons having to do with their internal structure, a vector is restricted to holding only objects. Thus, for example, one cannot create a vector of integer values (ints) but one *can* create a vector of instances of class Integer. This is one reason for the existence of "wrapper" classes, such as Integer and Float.

Just as an array in Java separates the declaration of the array name and the allocation of space for the array, the space for a Vector must be similarly created and assigned. In our example program this occurs in the constructor for the class PinBallGame. Note that no fixed limit is set for the space:

```
balls = new Vector( );
```

Although we have not seen it yet, a new element will be inserted into the vector by the method addElement:

```
balls.addElement (newBall);
```

The number of values stored in a Vector can be determined by invoking the method size.

```
for (int i = 0; i < balls.size( ); i++)
```

Finally, values are accessed in a vector using the method elementAt. Like an array, the set of legal index values ranges from zero to one less than the number of elements in the collection. The compiler only knows that the accessed element is a value of type object; it must be *cast* to the appropriate type before it can be used. Here we cast the value into the type PinBall. A run-time check is performed to ensure that the conversion is actually valid:

```
PinBall aBall = (PinBall) balls.elementAt (i);
```

The reader should note how the paint method in Figure 7.2 cycles over the collection of balls, asking each to paint itself.

7.1.2   *Mouse Listeners*

As noted in Chapter 6, the Java event model is based around the concept of *listeners*; objects that wait and "listen" for an event to take place, and then respond appropriately. The earlier examples showed how to create a listener by defining a class that implements the corresponding *interface* for the event in question.

Mouse events are treated in a similar fashion; however, there are five different mouse-related events that could potentially be of interest. Thus, the interface for a MouseListener has the following structure:

```
public interface MouseListener {
    public void mouseClicked (MouseEvent e);
    public void mouseEntered (MouseEvent e);
    public void mouseExited (MouseEvent e);
    public void mousePressed (MouseEvent e);
    public void mouseReleased (MouseEvent e);
}
```

Often a programmer is interested in only one or two of these five events. However, to implement an interface the Java language insists that the programmer provide a definition for all operations. To simplify such cases, the Java library provides a simple class named MouseAdapter. The class MouseAdapter implements the MouseListener interface but uses an empty method for each method. That is, a MouseAdapter does nothing in response to any mouse event. However, the programmer can write a new class that *inherits* from MouseAdapter, and overrides (or redefines) the methods of interest.

That is what we do in the example program. An inner class defines a MouseListener by extending MouseAdapter. An instance of this class is created, and passed as an argument to the method addMouseListener, which is inherited from class Frame.

```
addMouseListener (new MouseKeeper( ));
```

The class MouseKeeper inherits all five methods defined by MouseAdapter and redefines only one. The other four messages will be handled by the methods inherited from the parent class, which will do nothing.

```
private class MouseKeeper extends MouseAdapter {

    public void mousePressed (MouseEvent e) {
        int x = e.getX( ); // get coordinates where
        int y = e.getY( ); // mouse was pressed
            // only handle mouse event in the fire region
        if ((x > FrameWidth - 40) && (y > FrameHeight - 40)) {
            PinBall newBall = new PinBall(x, y);
            balls.addElement (newBall);
            Thread newThread = new PinBallThread (newBall);
            newThread.start( );
        }
    }
}
```

The argument passed to each method in the MouseListener interface is a value of type MouseEvent. The mouse event encodes certain information relating to the type of event that occurred. In our case, the most important information is the position (or coordinate) of the mouse at the moment the button was pressed. This information can be derived from the mouse event object using the methods getX and getY. With these values, a new ball is created, added to the list of balls, and placed into motion.

7.1.3 *Multiple Threads of Execution*

The structure of the Cannon Game application (Figure 6.7) was clouded by the fact that we used the paint routine to control the animation. During each painting cycle the ball would be moved a little, and the window would be scheduled for another repainting. From a logical point of view, the animation task has little to do with repainting the screen image. Thus combining these two tasks makes the structure of the program unnecessarily difficult to understand.

In every Java program there must be one principal process that is listening for mouse clicks, repainting the window, and performing other administrative tasks. In the Cannon Game, we abused this process by slipping in control of the animation as tasks to be performed while the process was also carrying out its regular duties. A more straightforward solution is to separate these two tasks, leaving the listening for mouse clicks task to one process, and creating a separate process for the control and movement of the pinballs.

A *thread* represents a separate task being executed by the computer. One can think of a computer processor as being similar to a person reading the text of a Java program and completing the associated actions one statement at a time. With this image in mind, you can think of a program with two threads as being like two people reading the *same* program, but working independently of each other. Each may be operating in a different part of the program, executing different instructions, despite the fact that they are working at the same time. Occasionally the two may meet in the same area, or at least exchange information with each other; but in other respects, they are independent.

In our pinball program we will create a separate thread for each ball. The thread will be responsible for controlling the motion of the ball, and the interaction with other balls (and eventually, with targets). In Java a thread is created by making a class that is a subclass of the class Thread.[1] The inner class PinBallThread is shown below:

```
public class PinBallGame {
     .
     .
     .

   private class PinBallThread extends Thread {
      private Ball theBall;

      public PinBallThread (Ball aBall)
         { theBall = aBall; }

      public void run () {
         while (theBall.y( ) < FrameHeight) {
            theBall.move ( );
               // more actions here later
            repaint ( );
```

---

[1] This is not the only way. In Chapter 20 we will describe an alternative way to create a thread.

```
            try {
                sleep(10);
            } catch (InterruptedException e) { System.exit(0); }
        }
    }
}
        .
        .
        .
}
```

The constructor for the thread is given the ball it will be controlling. The actions for a new thread are those provided by the method named run. In this case the actions of a pinball thread will be to move the ball slightly, schedule the window for repainting, then sleep for 10 milliseconds. The latter action is performed by the method sleep inherited from class Thread, and is designed to keep the simulation from moving too quickly. We will subsequently add more work to the loop controlling the life of a PinBall.

When the programmer hits the fire button, a new PinBall is created, and a new instance of the class PinBallThread is created to manage the new ball. The method start, inherited from class Thread, arranges the thread for execution, and begins processing.

```
PinBall newBall = new PinBall(x, y);
balls.addElement (newBall);
Thread newThread = new PinBallThread (newBall);
newThread.start();
```

Note carefully that to start a thread the programmer should execute the inherited method start. This, in turn, will eventually execute the method run that the programmer provides. You should never directly execute the run method; as there are a number of actions that the Thread manager must perform before the actions of a new thread can be initiated.

7.1.4 *Exception Handling*

The sleep command is the first occasion we have encountered where a method can potentially throw an *exception*. An exception is an error condition, which can be caught and handled so as to recover from the error in a systematic fashion. Methods that can potentially "throw" exceptions must declare so in their heading, in a manner to be described in a later chapter. Any use of such a method must either occur inside a method that itself declares that it can throw an exception, or within a try statement, as shown here:

```
try {
    sleep(10);
} catch (InterruptedException e) { System.exit(0); }
```

In this case, the potential source of exception is the fact that a thread could be interrupted while it is sleeping, for example (on some operating systems) by the user entering the "interrupt" key while the program is running. If such a condition occurs, the sleep statement will be halted before it can complete, and control will transfer to the statement in the closing block (that is, the code between the curly brackets) of the catch statement whose argument matches the type of exception raised by the interrupt. In this case, we will terminate the program by invoking the method System.exit. In subsequent programs we will encounter many more statements that can throw a variety of different exceptional conditions.

7.2 ADDING TARGETS: INHERITANCE AND INTERFACES

To provide realism and interest to our pinball game, we need to add targets for the ball to encounter on its way down the playing surface. As in real pinball games, we will want to include a variety of different types of targets. Some targets simply add values to the score, some move the ball in a new direction, and some swallow the ball, removing it from play. In order to simplify the program, we will want to maintain all the different types of targets in a single data structure, a vector.

7.2.1 *The* Pinball Target *Interface*

Because we want to process targets uniformly, for example in a loop that asks whether a ball has hit any target, we need all the targets to have a uniform interface. However, the various different types of targets will be represented internally by different data structures. Thus, we do not want to use *inheritance*, such as we have been doing with the different forms of Ball up to this point. Inheritance is a mechanism for sharing *structure*; a PinBall, for example, is simply a type of Ball that has the same structure and behavior as a Ball, adding a few new features (such as being able to run as a separate thread), but maintaining all the characteristics of the original. There is little in the way of common structure between a Peg (a target that when hit by a ball scores a number of points and moves the ball in a new direction) and a Wall (a target that when struck simply reflects the motion of the ball).

What is needed in this case is the ability to state that the two concepts (Peg and Wall, in this case), share the same *behavior*, although they have nothing in common in *structure*. As we saw in our earlier case study, in Java this is accomplished by describing the common behavior as an interface, and declaring that both objects implement the same interface. An interface for our pinball targets can be described as follows:

```
interface PinBallTarget {
    public boolean intersects (Ball aBall);
```

Figure 7.4   Graphical representation of a spring.

```
    public void moveTo (int x, int y);
    public void paint (Graphics g);
    public void hitBy (Ball aBall);
}
```

The interface in this case is declaring that there are four characteristics of interest in a pinball target. Each target can tell if it has been hit by a ball; that is, if it intersects the region occupied by a ball. Each target can be moved to a specific point on the playing surface, each can paint itself, and each provides some response when it has been hit by a given ball. However, the means by which each of these behaviors will be achieved is left unspecified, and different targets are free to *implement* the interface in different fashions.

An examination of a few different targets will help illustrate the point. Our first type of target will be a Spring. When hit by a falling ball, a Spring rebounds the ball back into the playing area, moving it upward where we hope it will encounter further targets. A spring is represented graphically by a small horizontal box, and a series of zigzag lines, as in Figure 7.4.

The class description for Spring is shown in Figure 7.5. Note how the class Spring must explicitly state that it implements the PinBallTarget interface, and must provide a specific meaning for each of the four elements of that interface. In this case, we will state that a spring intersects a ball if the rectangle surrounding the ball intersects with the rectangle representing the spring platform. When the spring is hit by the ball, it reverses the vertical direction of movement for the ball. (In actual fact, it simply guarantees the ball is moving upward. In rare situations, a spring could possibly be hit from below, although we don't expect this to be the norm.) It then gives the ball a slight boost in the vertical direction.

One slight element of interest has been added to the drawing of the Spring object. We have provided two different graphical representations for the Spring object, selected by an integer variable named state. Normally, a spring will be held in state 1. When struck, the value of state is changed to 2, and the *next* time the spring is redrawn it will present an alternative image, one in which the spring has been elongated. Drawing this second image changes the state back to state 1, and a subsequent redraw will display the original. The effect is a simple form of animation, where a moving spring will appear to stretch momentarily, then return to a ready state.

```
class Spring implements PinBallTarget {
   private Rectangle pad;
   private int state = 1;

   public Spring (int x, int y)
      { pad = new Rectangle (x, y, 30, 3); }

   public void moveTo (int x, int y)
      { pad.setLocation (x, y); }

   public void paint (Graphics g) {
      int x = pad.x; int y = pad.y;
      g.setColor(Color.black);
      if (state == 1) { // draw compressed spring
         g.fillRect(x, y, pad.width, pad.height);
         g.drawLine(x, y+3, x+30, y+5);
         g.drawLine(x+30, y+5, x, y+7);
         g.drawLine(x, y+7, x+30, y+9);
         g.drawLine(x+30, y+9, x, y+11);
         }
      else {   // draw extended spring
         g.fillRect(x, y-8, pad.width, pad.height);
         g.drawLine(x, y+5, x+30, y-1);
         g.drawLine(x+30, y-1, x, y+3);
         g.drawLine(x, y+3, x+30, y+7);
         g.drawLine(x+30, y+7, x, y+11);
         state = 1;
      }
   }


   public boolean intersects (Ball aBall)
      { return pad.intersects(aBall.location); }

   public void hitBy (Ball aBall) {
      // make sure we are moving up
      if (aBall.dy > 0) aBall.dy = - aBall.dy;
         // give the ball a little boost
      aBall.dy = aBall.dy - 0.5;
      state = 2;
   }
}
```

Figure 7.5   Definition for class Spring.

```
class Wall implements PinBallTarget {
   public Rectangle location;

   public Wall (int x, int y, int width, int height)
      { location = new Rectangle(x, y, width, height); }

   public void moveTo (int x, int y)
      { location.setLocation (x, y); }

   public void paint (Graphics g) {
      g.setColor(Color.black);
      g.fillRect(location.x, location.y,
         location.width, location.height);
   }

   public boolean intersects (Ball aBall)
      { return location.intersects(aBall.location); }

   public void hitBy (Ball aBall) {
      if ((aBall.y() < location.y)
         || (aBall.y() > (location.y + location.height)))
            aBall.dy = - aBall.dy;
      else
         aBall.dx = - aBall.dx;
   }
}
```

Figure 7.6 Definition of class Wall.

A second type of target is a Wall. A Wall (Figure 7.6) is a rectangular region. A ball intersects a wall if their regions overlap, and if so, the ball is simply reflected back, in effect bouncing off the wall. The bounce is either along the horizontal or along the vertical direction, depending upon which side of the wall has been hit.

The advantage of declaring these two different structures as both implementing an interface is that an interface name can be used as a *type*. That is, we can declare a variable as holding a value of type PinBallTarget. In much the same way that a variable declared as maintaining a value of type Ball could, in fact, be holding a cannonball, a pinball, or any other value derived from a class that extends the original class Ball, a variable declared as maintaining a PinBallTarget could, in fact, be holding either a Spring, a Wall, or any of the other varieties of target to be described subsequently. (This is one aspect of *polymorphism*, a topic we will return to in more detail in Chapter 12.) We will shortly make use of this

```
class Hole extends Ball implements PinBallTarget {

   public Hole (int x, int y) {
      super (x, y, 12);
      setColor (Color.black);
   }

   public boolean intersects (Ball aBall)
      { return location.intersects(aBall.location); }

   public void hitBy (Ball aBall) {
         // move ball totally off frame
      aBall.moveTo (0, PinBallGame.FrameHeight + 30);
         // stop motion of ball
      aBall.setMotion(0, 0);
   }
}
```

Figure 7.7 Definition of class Hole.

property, by storing all the targets in our game in a single data structure, and testing the motion of the ball against the location of each target in turn.

Consider now a third type of target, a Hole. A Hole (Figure 7.7) consumes any ball it comes in contact with, removing the ball from the playing surface. A Hole is represented by a circular colored image, just like a ball. A Hole has a location on the playing surface, just like a Ball. In fact, because a hole is *structurally* similar to a Ball, we can use inheritance to simplify the implementation of the Hole abstraction.

This illustrates the important difference between the use of inheritance and the use of interfaces. The mechanism of inheritance should be used when two (or more) concepts have a *structural* relationship. Note that with objects, a structural relationship almost always implies at least some behavioral relationship. In contrast, the interface mechanism should be used with two (or more) concepts having a *behavioral* relationship but no structural relationship. We will explore these ideas in more detail in Chapter 8.

Note how a Hole uses both inheritance and an interface. The hole *inherits* much of its behavior from the class Ball, including the methods paint and moveTo. The Hole declares that it implements the PinBallTarget interface, and to do so must provide a method to see if the hole has intersected with a ball, and the actions to be performed when such an event occurs. In the case of a hole, the ball is moved clear off the playing surface, and motion of the ball is halted. Eventually the ball will note that its location exceeds the window size, and the thread controlling the ball will halt.

```
class ScorePad extends Hole {
   protected int value;

   public ScorePad (int x, int y, int v) {
      super (x, y);
      value = v;
      setColor (Color.red);
   }

   public void hitBy (Ball aBall)
      { PinBallGame.world.addScore(value); }

   public void paint (Graphics g) {
      g.setColor (color);
      g.drawOval (location.x, location.y,
         location.width, location.height);
      String s = "" + value;
      g.drawString(s, location.x, y( )+2);
   }
}
```

Figure 7.8 Definition of the class ScorePad.

A class that inherits from an existing class that implements an interface must of necessity also implement the interface. We will use this property in defining the next two types of targets in our pinball game. A ScorePad is, like a hole, represented by a circular region. When struck by a ball, the score pad has no effect on the ball (the ball simply moves over it); however, the score pad adds a certain amount to the player's score. The particular amount to add is defined as part of the state for the score object.

Note how the ScorePad class (Figure 7.8) inherits the intersects behavior from class Hole and the moveTo behavior from class Ball, but overrides the paint and hitBy methods that would otherwise be inherited from class Hole. The first now draws a colored circle with the scoring amount in the middle, while the latter adds the given value to the player score.

Because a ScorePad inherits from class Hole, which implements the PinBallTarget interface, the class ScorePad is also said to implement the interface. This means, for example, that a ScorePad could be assigned to a variable that was declared to be a PinBallTarget.

7.2.2 *Adding a Label to Our Pinball Game*

In the revised version of our program we will add a new graphical element, a textual label in a banner across the top of the window. This is accomplished

```
public class PinBallGame extends Frame {

    private int score;
    private Label scoreLabel;

    public PinBallGame () {
        .
        .
        .
      score = 0;
      scoreLabel = new Label ("Score = 0");
      add ("North", scoreLabel);
        .
        .
        .
    }

    synchronized public void addScore (int v) {
      score = score + v;
      scoreLabel.setText ("Score = " + score);
      }
    .
    .
    .
}
```

Figure 7.9 Adding labels to our pinball game.

by declaring a new Label, and adding it in the "North" part of the window (Figure 7.9). As the user scores new points, the text of the label is updated. Note that a ScorePad refers back to the application object through the variable world.

A feature of the addScore method deserves note. In the revised form of the pinball game application class, the method addScore is declared as synchronized. Recall that balls move independently of each other, and so in theory, two balls could roll over two different score pads at much the same time. Two attempts could then be made to update the player score at once. The resulting actions could easily be unpredictable, and almost certainly wrong. By declaring the method that updates the score value as synchronized, the Java language will guarantee that two threads cannot be executing this method at once. If a thread tries to execute a synchronized method that is currently being executed by another thread, the second thread is suspended until the first thread exits the synchronized routine. Synchronization and threads will be discussed in more detail in Chapter 20.

A Peg is similar to a ScorePad, but it sticks up above the playing surface. Thus, when a Peg is struck, it deflects the ball off in a new direction, depending upon the angle of the ball and the point at which it encounters the peg. (The algorithm used in Figure 7.10 is not exactly correct as far as actual physics is concerned, but it does have the advantage of being easy to compute.) The ball is

```
class Peg extends ScorePad {
   private int state = 1;

   public Peg (int x, int y, int v)
      { super(x, y, v); }

   public void paint (Graphics g) {
      super.paint(g);
      if (state == 2) { // draw expanded circle
         g.drawOval(location.x-3, location.y-3,
            location.width+6, location.height+6);
         state = 1;
         }
      else
         g.drawOval(location.x-2, location.y-2,
            location.width+4, location.height+4);
   }

   public void hitBy (Ball aBall) {
      super.hitBy (aBall); // update the score
      aBall.setMotion (-aBall.dy, -aBall.dx); // update direction
      while (intersects(aBall)) // move out of range
         aBall.move( );
      state = 2; // next draw will expand circle
   }
}
```

Figure 7.10 Definition of the class Peg.

then updated until it no longer intersects with the peg, thereby avoiding having the method executed multiple times for a single encounter. We have once again added a simple animation to the class Peg, so that the first time a peg is redrawn after it has been struck, the circle surrounding the peg will appear to enlarge and then return to a normal size.

To create the second version of our game (Figure 7.11), we simply create a Vector of targets, along with the vector of balls. We initialize the targets in the constructor for the game, including placing walls on the sides and top of the playing area, to reflect wayward balls. The user fires balls as before, which then proceed to interact with the various targets as the balls move down the playing surface. Each time a ball moves, a loop is executed to determine if the new location of the ball has struck a target. If so, the target is informed, and the location of the ball potentially updated. Finally, the entire screen is repainted, which involves repainting both the targets and the collection of balls.

```
public class PinBallGame extends Frame {
   private Vector targets;

   public PinBallGame ( ) {
      .
      .
      .

         // create the targets
      targets = new Vector( );
      targets.addElement(new Wall(30, 50, 2, 350));
      targets.addElement(new Wall(30, 50, 360, 2));
      targets.addElement(new Wall(390, 50, 2, 380));
      targets.addElement(new Hole(100, 100));
      targets.addElement(new ScorePad(150, 220, 100));
      targets.addElement(new Peg(300, 140, 200));
      targets.addElement(new Spring(120, 350));
   }

   private class PinBallThread extends Thread {
      .
      .
      .
      public void run ( ) {
         while (theBall.y( ) < FrameHeight) {
            theBall.move ( );
               // see if we ran into anything
            for (int j = 0; j < targets.size( ); j++) {
               PinBallTarget target =
                  (PinBallTarget) targets.elementAt(j);
               if (target.intersects(theBall)) target.hitBy(theBall);
               }
            .
            .
            .

         }
      }
   }

   public void paint (Graphics g) {
      .
      .
      .
      for (int j = 0; j < targets.size( ); j++) { // draw targets
         PinBallTarget target = (PinBallTarget) targets.elementAt(j);
         target.paint(g);
         }
      }
}
```

Figure 7.11 Addition of targets to the class PinBallGame.

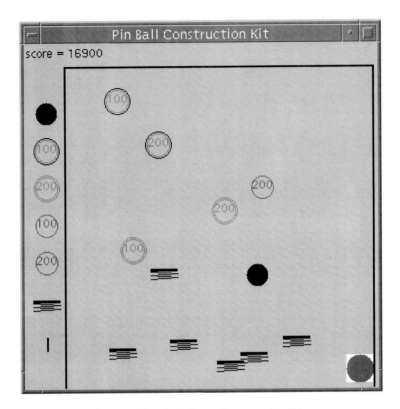

Figure 7.12   The revised Pinball Game Construction Kit.

7.3   PINBALL GAME CONSTRUCTION KIT: MOUSE EVENTS RECONSIDERED

Although the second version of the pinball game is certainly more interesting than the first, it is still limited by the fact that the layout of the various targets is determined by the original programmer. To create a different layout, the program must be changed and then recompiled and executed. In our final version, we will show how this limitation can be overcome, by providing a *pallet* of target elements from which the *user* can select, dynamically constructing the pinball game while the program is executing.

In appearance, our revised game will move the playing area slightly to the right, placing a sequence of potential target components along a strip in the far left. (See Figure 7.12.) The user can click the mouse down in one of these alternatives, then slide the mouse (still down) over into the playing area. When the user releases the mouse, the selected target element will be installed into the new location.

```
private class MouseKeeper extends MouseAdapter {
   private PinBallTarget element;

   public void mousePressed (MouseEvent e) {
      element = null;
      int x = e.getX( );
      int y = e.getY( );
      if ((x > FrameWidth-40) && (y > FrameHeight -40)) {
         PinBall newBall = new PinBall(x, y);
         balls.addElement (newBall);
         Thread newThread = new PinBallThread (newBall);
         newThread.start( );
      }
      if (x < 40) { // each target occupies a 40 by 40 pixel box
         switch (y / 40) {
            case 2: element = new Hole(0, 0); break;
            case 3: element = new Peg(0, 0, 100); break;
            case 4: element = new Peg(0, 0, 200); break;
            case 5: element = new ScorePad(0, 0, 100); break;
            case 6: element = new ScorePad(0, 0, 200); break;
            case 7: element = new Spring(0, 0); break;
            case 8: element = new Wall(0, 0, 2, 15); break;
         }
      }
   }

   public void mouseReleased (MouseEvent e) {
      int x = e.getX( ); // only perform release action if mouse is
      int y = e.getY( ); // released on playing surface
      if ((element != null) && (x > 50)){
         element.moveTo(x, y);
         targets.addElement (element);
         repaint( );
      }
   }
}
```

Figure 7.13   Capturing both mouse presses and releases.

   The effect is produced by overriding both the mousePressed and the mouseReleased methods inherited from the mouse adapter (Figure 7.13). The two methods communicate with each other by means of a variable named element. The
mousePressed method creates a potential target, determined by the coordinates
of the point at which the mouse goes down. Note that we have not eliminated

the original use of the mousePressed method, simply added a new condition. The MouseReleased method checks the location of the release, and if it is in the playing area and if a target item was previously selected (*both* conditions must be true), then it adds a new target to the game.

Other changes needed to provide our final version of the Pinball Construction Kit simply involve repositioning the left wall, and drawing the images of the selection pallet.

7.4   CHAPTER SUMMARY

In this chapter the development of an example program has once again served as a vehicle to introduce a number of features of the Java programming language. Introduced in this chapter were the following features:

- The use of collection classes, in particular the collection class Vector. We will discuss collection classes in more detail in Chapter 19.

- An expanded discussion of the Java listener event model (started in Chapter 6), focusing on how to create objects that will listen for mouse events.

- The concept of a program having multiple threads of execution. While the main thread of our program listens for events and paints the windows, each ball in the simulation is being controlled by an independent routine.

- Our first example of a statement that could potentially produce an *exception*, and the way the Java language permits the programmer to specify what actions to take when an exception occurs.

- More on interfaces, contrasting the use of the interface mechanism with the use of inheritance.

- One aspect of the important concept of *polymorphism*. A variable declared as an instance of a parent class (such as Ball) can, in fact, be holding a value derived from a child class (such as PinBall). Similarly, a variable declared as an interface value (such as PinBallTarget) can, in fact, hold any object that implements that interface (such as Peg). This property allows us to create arrays of different objects, such as an array of pinball targets, and process them in a uniform fashion.

CROSS REFERENCES

The distinction between interfaces and inheritances is explored in more detail in Chapter 8. Collection classes will be investigated in detail in Chapter 19. Chapter 13 presents a more systematic investigation of the services provided by the AWT. Chapter 20 explores the multithreading features of Java.

Study Questions

1. Why must the variable world be declared static?

2. In what ways is a Vector object similar to an array? In what ways is it different?

3. What method is used to determine the number of elements held in a Vector? What method is used to access the values? What method is used to insert a new value into the collection?

4. What is the relationship between MouseAdapter and MouseListener? In what ways are they different?

5. What is a *thread*? What are the tasks assigned to the different threads in our application?

6. How is a thread started? How does the programmer specify the actions a thread should perform?

7. What is an exception?

8. What action is performed by the method System.exit? Under what circumstances in our program will this method be called?

9. When should two software components be tied together through the use of inheritance rather than a common interface?

10. What type of objects can be held by a variable declared using the interface PinBallTarget?

11. In what ways does the class Hole modify the behavior inherited from class Ball?

12. What is a Label? How is a label attached to a window? What methods are used to change the text of a label?

13. What does it mean to say that a method is *synchronized*?

Exercises

1. The class Peg inherits from ScorePad, which in turn inherits from Hole, which in turn inherits from Ball. For each of these classes, describe all the methods defined in the class or inherited from parent classes, and for each of the latter indicate in which parent class the method definition occurs.

2. The pinball game as presented allows the user an unlimited number of balls. Change the program to fire only a fixed number of balls, disallowing firing once the supply is exhausted. Change the display at the top of the

screen so that it will indicate the number of remaining balls, as well as the score.

3. Add a "reset" button to the bottom of the screen. When pressed, the reset button sets the score back to zero and, if you implemented the suggestion in the previous question, resets the number of balls in play.

4. On some platforms it may be difficult to halt the PinBall application once it has finished. Add a button labeled "Quit" to the bottom (south) part of the application window. When pressed, this button should execute the method System.exit(0).

5. In the final program, the items on the pallet are still stored in the targets vector, so that they will be checked for a hit, even though they can never be hit by a ball. A better solution would have been to create a new vector pallet that will hold these items, redrawing both the pallet and the targets on a repaint, but only if a target in the targets vector is hit by a ball. Modify the program in this fashion.

6. Currently balls do not test to see if they intersect with other balls. We could support this modification by making PinBall implement the PinBallTarget interface, and adding balls to the list of targets as well as the list of balls. Describe what changes would need to be added to modify the program in this fashion.

7. Another change could allow the programmer to reposition items even after they have been placed in the playing area. If a mouse click occurs on the playing surface over a target, select the target and move it to the location given by the associated mouse up. Be careful that you don't end up placing the element in the target vector twice.

8. Create a program that opens a window, listens for mouse clicks, and when a mouse is released, displays the distance (in pixel units) between the location the mouse was pressed and the location it was released.

9. Write a program that places a red circle in the middle of the window. The circle should change color to blue when the mouse enters the window, then return to red when the mouse leaves the window. When the mouse is clicked inside the window, the circle should change color to green and remain green for 1000 milliseconds, before returning to blue. Finally, if the mouse is clicked within the bounds of the circle and released outside the circle, the circle should be moved so as to be centered on the location of the mouse release.

10. Develop a "paddle" target object. When the user clicks the mouse over the paddle, the paddle should move back and forth (perhaps only once). If a paddle encounters a ball, the ball is reflected off the paddle.

III

Understanding Inheritance

8 Understanding Inheritance

The first step in learning object-oriented programming is understanding the basic philosophy of organizing a computer program as the interaction of loosely coupled software components. This idea was the central lesson in the case studies presented in the first part of the book. The next step in learning object-oriented programming is organizing classes into a hierarchical structure based on the concept of inheritance. By *inheritance*, we mean the property that instances of a child class (or subclass) can access both data and behavior (methods) associated with a parent class (or superclass).

Although in Java the term *inheritance* is correctly applied only to the creation of new classes using subclassing (the extends keyword), there are numerous correspondences between subclassification and the designation that classes satisfy an interface (the implements keyword). The latter is sometimes termed "inheritance of specification," contrasted with the "inheritance of code" provided by subclassification. In this chapter we will use the word in a general fashion, meaning both mechanisms.

Although the intuitive meaning of inheritance is clear, and we have used inheritance in many of our earlier case studies, and the mechanics of using inheritance are relatively simple, there are nevertheless subtle features involved in the use of inheritance in Java. In this and subsequent chapters we will explore some of these issues.

8.1 AN INTUITIVE DESCRIPTION OF INHERITANCE

Let us return to Flora the florist from the first chapter. There is a certain behavior we expect florists to perform, not because they are florists but simply because they are shopkeepers. For example, we expect Flora to request money for the transaction and in turn give us a receipt. These activities are not unique to florists, but are common to bakers, grocers, stationers, car dealers, and other merchants. It is as though we have associated certain behavior with the general category Shopkeeper, and as Florists are a specialized form of shopkeepers, the behavior is automatically identified with the subclass.

In programming languages, inheritance means that the behavior and data associated with child classes are always an *extension* (that is, a larger set) of the properties associated with parent classes. A child class will be given all the properties of the parent class, and may in addition define new properties. On the other hand, since a child class is a more specialized (or restricted) form of the parent class, it is also, in a certain sense, a *contraction* of the parent type. For example, the Java library Frame represents any type of window, but a PinBallGame frame is restricted to a single type of game. This tension between inheritance as expansion and inheritance as contraction is a source for much of the power inherent in the technique, but at the same time it causes much confusion as to its proper employment. We will see this when we examine a few of the uses of inheritance in a subsequent section.

Inheritance is always transitive, so that a class can inherit features from superclasses many levels away. That is, if class Dog is a subclass of class Mammal, and class Mammal is a subclass of class Animal, then Dog will inherit attributes both from Mammal and from Animal.

A complicating factor in our intuitive description of inheritance is the fact that subclasses can *override* behavior inherited from parent classes. For example, the class Platypus overrides the reproduction behavior inherited from class Mammal, since platypuses lay eggs. The mechanics of overriding is treated briefly in this chapter and in more detail in Chapter 11.

8.2 THE BASE CLASS OBJECT

In Java all classes use inheritance. Unless specified otherwise, all classes are derived from a single root class, named Object. If no parent class is explicitly provided, the class Object is implicitly assumed. Thus, the class declaration for FirstProgram (Chapter 4, Figure 4.1) is the same as the following:

```
class FirstProgram extends Object {
    // ...
    };
```

The class Object provides minimal functionality guaranteed to be common to all objects. These include the following methods:

equals (Object obj)   Determine whether the argument object is the same as the receiver. This method is often overridden to change the equality test for different classes.

getClass ()   Returns the class of the receiver, an object of type Class (see Section 15.5).

hashCode() Returns a hash value for this object (see Section 19.7). This method should also be overridden when the equals method is changed.

toString() Converts object into a string value. This method is also often overridden.

8.3 SUBCLASS, SUBTYPE, AND SUBSTITUTABILITY

The concept of *substitutability* is fundamental to many of the most powerful software development techniques in object-oriented programming. The idea of substitutability is that the type given in a declaration of a variable does not have to match the type associated with a value the variable is holding. Note that this is never true in conventional programming languages but is a common occurrence in object-oriented programs.

We have seen several examples of substitutability in our earlier case studies. In the Pin Ball Game program described in Chapter 7, the variable target was declared as a PinBallTarget, but in fact held a variety of different types of values that were created using implementations of PinBallTarget. (These target values were held in the vector named targets.)

```
PinBallTarget target = (PinBallTarget) targets.elementAt(j);
```

Substitutability can also occur through the use of interfaces. An example is the instance of the class FireButtonListener created in the Cannon Game (Chapter 6). The class from which this value was defined was declared as implementing the interface ActionListener. Because it implements the ActionListener interface, we can use this value as a parameter to a method (in this case, addActionListener) that expects an ActionListener value.

```
class CannonWorld extends Frame {
   .
   .
   .
   private class FireButtonListener implements ActionListener {
      public void actionPerformed (ActionEvent e) {
         .
         .
         .
      }
   }

   public CannonWorld () {
      .
      .
      .
      fire.addActionListener(new FireButtonListener());
   }
}
```

Because Object is a parent class to all objects, a variable declared using this type can hold any nonprimitive value. The collection class Vector makes use of this property, holding its values in an array of Object values. Because the array is declared as Object, any object value can be stored in a Vector.

When new classes are constructed using inheritance from existing classes, the argument used to justify the validity of substitutability is as follows:

- Instances of the subclass must possess all data fields associated with the parent class.

- Instances of the subclass must implement, through inheritance at least (if not explicitly overridden) all functionality defined for the parent class. (They can also define new functionality, but that is unimportant for the argument.)

- Thus, an instance of a child class can mimic the behavior of the parent class and should be *indistinguishable* from an instance of the parent class if substituted in a similar situation.

We will see later in this chapter, when we examine the various ways in which inheritance can be used, that this is not always a valid argument. Thus, not all subclasses formed using inheritance are candidates for substitution.

The term *subtype* is used to describe the relationship between types that explicitly recognizes the principle of substitution. That is, a type B is considered to be a subtype of A if two conditions hold. The first is that an instance of B can legally be assigned to a variable declared as type A. And the second is that this value can then be used by the variable with no observable change in behavior.

The term *subclass* refers merely to the mechanics of constructing a new class using inheritance, and is easy to recognize from the source description of a program by the presence of the keyword extends. The *subtype* relationship is more abstract, and is only loosely documented directly by the program source. In the majority of situations a subclass is also a subtype. However, later in this chapter we will discover ways in which subclasses can be formed that are not subtypes. In addition, subtypes can be formed using interfaces, linking types that have no inheritance relationship whatsoever. So it is important to understand both the similarities and the differences between these two concepts.

8.4   FORMS OF INHERITANCE

Inheritance is employed in a surprising variety of ways. Presented in this section are a few of its more common uses. Note that the following list represents general abstract categories and is not intended to be exhaustive. Furthermore, it sometimes happens that two or more descriptions are applicable to a single situation, because some methods in a single class use inheritance in one way while others use it in another. In the following list, pay attention to which uses of inheritance support the subtyping relationship and which do not.

8.4.1 *Inheritance for Specialization*

Probably the most common use of inheritance and subclassification is for specialization. In this form, the new class is a specialized variety of the parent class but it satisfies the specifications of the parent in all relevant respects. Thus, this form always creates a subtype, and the principle of substitutability is explicitly upheld. Along with the following category (subclassification for specification) this is the most ideal form of inheritance, and something that a good design should strive for.

The creation of application window classes using inheritance from the Java library class Frame is an example of subclassification for specialization. The following is from the PinBallGame program in Chapter 7.

```
public class PinBallGame extends Frame {
    .
    .
    .
}
```

To run such an application, an instance of PinBallGame is first created. Various methods inherited from class Frame, such as setSize, setTitle, and show, are then invoked. These methods do not realize they are manipulating an instance of PinBallGame, but instead act as if they were operating on an instance of Frame. The actions they perform would be the same for any instance of class Frame.

Where application-specific behavior is necessary, for example, in repainting the window, a method is invoked that is overridden by the application class. For example, the method in the parent class will invoke the method paint. Although the parent class Frame possesses a method of this name, the parent method is not the one executed. Instead, the method defined in the child class is executed.

We say that subclassification for specialization occurs in this example because the child class (in this example, PinBallGame) satisfies all the properties that we expect of the parent class (Frame). In addition, the new class overrides one or more methods, specializing them with application-specific behavior.

8.4.2 *Inheritance for Specification*

Another frequent use for inheritance is to guarantee that classes maintain a certain common interface—that is, they implement methods having the same headings. The parent class can be a combination of implemented operations and operations that are deferred to the child classes. Often, there is no interface change of any sort between the parent class and the child class—the child merely implements the methods described, but not implemented, in the parent.

This is actually a special case of subclassification for specialization, except that the subclasses are not refinements of an existing type but rather realizations of an incomplete abstract specification. That is, the parent class defines the operation but has no implementation. It is only the child class that provides an implementation. In such cases the parent class is sometimes known as an *abstract specification class*.

There are two different mechanisms provided by the Java language to support the idea of inheritance of specification. The most obvious technique is the use of interfaces. We have seen examples of this in the way that events are handled by the Java library. For instance, the characteristics needed for an ActionListener (the object type that responds to button presses) can be described by a single method, and the implementation of that method cannot be predicted, since it differs from one application to another. Thus, an interface is used to describe only the necessary requirements, and no actual behavior is inherited by a subclass that implements the behavior.

```
interface ActionListener {
    public void actionPerformed (ActionEvent e);
    }
```

When a button is created, an associated listener class is defined. The listener class provides the specific behavior for the method in the context of the current application.

```
class CannonWorld extends Frame {
    .
    .
    .
        // a fire button listener implements the action listener interface
    private class FireButtonListener implements ActionListener {
        public void actionPerformed (ActionEvent e) {
        ... // action to perform in response to button press
        }
    }
}
```

Subclassification for specification can also take place with inheritance of classes formed using extension. One way to guarantee that a subclass must be constructed is to use the keyword abstract. A class declared as abstract must be subclassed; it is not possible to create an instance of such a class using the operator new. In addition, individual methods can also be declared as abstract, and they, too, must be overridden before instances can be constructed.

An example abstract class in the Java library is Number, a parent class for the numeric wrapper classes Integer, Long, Double, and so on. The class description is as follows:

```
public abstract class Number {

    public abstract int intValue( );

    public abstract long longValue( );

    public abstract float floatValue( );

    public abstract double doubleValue( );

    public byte byteValue( )
        { return (byte) intValue( ); }

    public short shortValue( )
        { return (short) intValue( ); }
}
```

Subclasses of Number must override the methods intValue, longValue, floatValue, and doubleValue. Notice that not all methods in an abstract class must themselves be declared abstract. Subclasses of Number need not override byteValue or shortValue, as these methods are provided with an implementation that can be inherited without change.

In general, subclassification for specification can be recognized when the parent class does not implement actual behavior but merely provides the headings for methods that must be implemented in child classes.

8.4.3   *Inheritance for Construction*

A class can often inherit almost all of its desired functionality from a parent class, perhaps changing only the names of the methods used to interface to the class, or modifying the arguments. This may be true even if the new class and the parent class fail to share any relationship as abstract concepts.

An example of subclassification for construction occurred in the pinball game application described in Chapter 7. In that program, the class Hole was declared as a subclass of Ball. There is no logical relationship between the concepts of a Ball and a Hole, but from a practical point of view much of the behavior needed for the Hole abstraction matches the behavior of the class Ball. Thus, using inheritance in this situation reduces the amount of work necessary to develop the class Hole.

```
class Hole extends Ball implements PinBallTarget {

    public Hole (int x, int y) {
        super (x, y, 12);
        setColor (Color.black);
    }
```

```
        public boolean intersects (Ball aBall)
            { return location.intersects(aBall.location); }

        public void hitBy (Ball aBall) {
                // move ball totally off frame
            aBall.moveTo (0, PinBallGame.FrameHeight + 30);
                // stop motion of ball
            aBall.setMotion(0, 0);
        }
    }
```

Another example of inheritance for construction occurs in the Java library. There, the class Stack is constructed using inheritance from the class Vector:

```
class Stack extends Vector {

    public Object push(Object item)
        { addElement(item); return item; }

    public boolean empty ( )
        { return isEmpty( ); }

    public synchronized Object pop( ) {
        Object obj = peek( );
        removeElementAt(size( ) - 1);
        return obj;
    }

    public synchronized Object peek( )
        { return elementAt(size( ) - 1); }
    }
```

As abstractions, the concept of the stack and the concept of a vector have little in common; however, from a pragmatic point of view using the Vector class as a parent greatly simplifies the implementation of the stack.

Inheritance for construction is sometimes frowned upon, since it often directly breaks the principle of substitutability (forming subclasses that are not subtypes). On the other hand, because it is often a fast and easy route to developing new data abstractions, it is nevertheless widely used. See Chapter 10 for a more detailed discussion of the construction of the Stack abstraction.

8.4.4 *Inheritance for Extension*

Subclassification for extension occurs when a child class only adds new behavior
to the parent class and does not modify or alter any of the inherited attributes.
An example of inheritance for extension in the Java library is the class Properties, which inherits from class HashTable. A hash table is a dictionary structure
(see Section 19.7). A dictionary stores a collection of key/value pairs and allows
the user to retrieve the value associated with a given key. Properties represent
information concerning the current execution environment. Examples of properties are the name of the user running the Java program, the version of the
Java interpreter being used, the name of the operating system under which the
Java program is running, and so on. The class Properties uses the parent class,
HashTable, to store and retrieve the actual property name/value pairs. In addition, the class defines a few methods specific to the task of managing properties,
such as reading or writing properties to or from a file.

```
class Properties extends Hashtable {
    .
    .
    .

    public synchronized void load(InputStream in) throws
        IOException { ... }

    public synchronized void save(OutputStream out, String header)
        { ... }

    public String getProperty(String key) { ... }

    public Enumeration propertyNames() { ... }

    public void list(PrintStream out) { ... }
}
```

As the functionality of the parent remains available and untouched, subclassification for extension does not contravene the principle of substitutability, and
so such subclasses are always subtypes.

8.4.5 *Inheritance for Limitation*

Subclassification for limitation occurs when the behavior of the subclass is
smaller or more restrictive than the behavior of the parent class. Like subclassification for extension, subclassification for limitation occurs most frequently
when a programmer is building on a base of existing classes that should not,
or cannot, be modified.

Although there are no examples of subclassification for limitation in the Java library, we could imagine the following. Suppose you wanted to create the class Set, in a fashion similar to the way the class Stack is subclassed from Vector. Say you also wanted to *ensure* that only Set operations were used on the set, and not vector operations. One way to accomplish this would be to override the undesired methods, so that if they were executed they would produce obviously incorrect results, or print a message indicating they should not be used.[1]

```
class Set extends Vector {
    // methods addElement, removeElement, contains
    // isEmpty and size
    // are all inherited from vector

    public int indexOf (Object obj)
        { System.out.println("Do not use Set.indexOf"); return 0; }

    public Object elementAt (int index)
        { return null; }
}
```

In theory an alternative would be to have the undesired methods throw an exception. However, the Java compiler does not permit subclasses to override a method and introduce new exceptions that are not already declared in the parent class.

Subclassification for limitation is characterized by the presence of techniques that take a previously permitted method and make it illegal. Because subclassification for limitation is an explicit contravention of the principle of substitutability, and because it builds subclasses that are not subtypes, it should be avoided whenever possible.

8.4.6 *Inheritance for Combination*

When discussing abstract concepts, it is common to form a new abstraction by combining features of two or more abstractions. A teaching assistant, for example, may have characteristics of both a teacher and a student, and can therefore logically behave as both. The ability of a class to inherit from two or more parent classes is known as *multiple inheritance*.

Although the Java language does not permit a subclass to be formed by inheritance from more than one parent class, several approximations to the concept are possible. For example, it is common for a new class to both extend an existing class and implement an interface. We saw this in the example of

---

[1] In actuality, the methods indexOf and elementAt are declared as final in class Vector, so this example will not compile. But it does illustrate the concept.

the class Hole that both extended class Ball and implemented the interface for PinBallTarget.

```
class Hole extends Ball implements PinBallTarget {
    .
    .
    .
}
```

It is also possible for classes to implement more than one interface, and thus be viewed as a combination of the two categories. Many examples occur in the input/output sections of the Java library. A RandomAccessFile, for example, implements both the DataInput and DataOutput protocols.

8.4.7 *Summary of the Forms of Inheritance*

We can summarize the various forms of inheritance by the following list:

Specialization   The child class is a special case of the parent class; in other words, the child class is a subtype of the parent class.

Specification   The parent class defines behavior that is implemented in the child class but not in the parent class.

Construction   The child class makes use of the behavior provided by the parent class but is not a subtype of the parent class.

Extension   The child class adds new functionality to the parent class, but does not change any inherited behavior.

Limitation   The child class restricts the use of some of the behavior inherited from the parent class.

Combination   The child class inherits features from more than one parent class. Although multiple inheritance is not supported directly by Java, it can be simulated in part by classes that use both inheritance and implementation of an interface, or implement two or more interfaces.

The Java language implicitly assumes that subclasses are also subtypes. This means that an instance of a subclass can be assigned to a variable declared as the parent class type. Methods in the child class that have the same name as those in the parent class override the inherited behavior. We have seen that this assumption that subclasses are subtypes is not always valid, and creating subclasses that are not subtypes is a possible source of program error.

8.5   MODIFIERS AND INHERITANCE

The language Java provides several modifiers that can be used to alter aspects of the inheritance process. For example, in the case studies in earlier chapters, we made extensive use of the visibility (or access control) modifiers public, protected, and private.

- A public feature (data field or method) can be accessed outside the class definition. A public class can be accessed outside the package in which it is declared.

- A protected feature can be accessed only within the class definition in which it appears, within other classes in the same package, or within the definition of subclasses.

- A private feature can be accessed only within the class definition in which it appears.

The earlier case studies illustrated how both methods and data fields can be declared as static. A static field is shared by all instances of a class. A static method can be invoked even when no instance of the class has been created. Static data fields and methods are inherited in the same manner as nonstatic items, except that static methods cannot be overridden.

Both methods and classes can be declared to be abstract. An abstract class cannot be instanciated. That is, it is not legal to create an instance of an abstraction class using the operator new. Such a class can only be used as a parent class, to create a new type of object. Similarly, an abstract method must be overridden by a subclass.

An alternative modifier, final, is the opposite of abstract. When applied to a class, the keyword indicates that the class *cannot* be subclassified. Similarly, when applied to a method, the keyword indicates that the method cannot be overridden. Thus, the user is guaranteed that the behavior of the class will be as defined and not modified by a later subclass.

```
final class newClass extends oldClass {
    .
    .
    .
}
```

We have seen that program constants are generally defined by variables that are both static and final:

```
class CannonGame extends Frame {
    .
    .
    .
    public static final int FrameWidth = 600;
```

```
    public static final int FrameHeight = 400;
        .
        .
        .
}
```

Optimizing compilers can sometimes make use of the fact that a data field, class, or method is declared as final and can thus generate better code than would otherwise be possible.

8.6 PROGRAMMING AS A MULTIPERSON ACTIVITY

When programs are constructed out of reusable, off-the-shelf components, programming moves from an individual activity (one programmer and the computer) to a community effort. A programmer may operate both as the *developer* of new abstractions and as the *user* of a software system created by an earlier programmer. The reader should not confuse the term *user* when applied to a programmer with the same term denoting the application end-user. Similarly, we will often speak of the organization of several objects by describing a *client* object that is requesting the services of a *provider*. Again, the client in this case is likely a programmer (or the code being developed by a programmer) making use of the services developed by an earlier programmer. This should not be confused with the idea of *client/server* computing, as described in Chapter 2.

8.7 THE BENEFITS OF INHERITANCE

In this section we will describe some of the many important benefits of the proper use of inheritance.

8.7.1 *Software Reusability*

When behavior is inherited from another class, the code that provides that behavior does not have to be rewritten. This may seem obvious, but the implications are important. Many programmers spend much of their time rewriting code they have written many times before—for example, to search for a pattern in a string or to insert a new element into a table. With object-oriented techniques, these functions can be written once and reused.

8.7.2 *Increased Reliability*

Code that is executed frequently tends to have fewer bugs than code that is executed infrequently. When the same components are used in two or more applications, the code will be exercised more than code that is developed for a single application. Thus, bugs in such code tend to be discovered more quickly, and latter applications gain the benefit of using components that are more error free. Similarly, the costs of maintenance of shared components can be split among many projects.

8.7.3   *Code Sharing*

Code sharing can occur on several levels with object-oriented techniques. On one level, many users or projects can use the same classes. (Brad Cox [1986] calls these software-ICs, in analogy to the integrated circuits used in hardware design.) Another form of sharing occurs when two or more classes developed by a single programmer as part of a project inherit from a single parent class. For example, a Set and an Array may both be considered a form of Collection. When this happens, two or more types of objects will share the code that they inherit. This code needs to be written only once and will contribute only once to the size of the resulting program.

8.7.4   *Consistency of Interface*

When two or more classes inherit from the same superclass, we are assured that the behavior they inherit will be the same in all cases. Thus, it is easier to guarantee that interfaces to similar objects are in fact similar and that the user is not presented with a confusing collection of objects that are almost the same but behave, and are interacted with, very differently.

8.7.5   *Software Components*

Inheritance enables programmers to construct reusable software components. The goal is to permit the development of new and novel applications that nevertheless require little or no actual coding. The Java library offers a rich collection of software components for use in the development of applications.

8.7.6   *Rapid Prototyping*

When a software system is constructed largely out of reusable components, developers can concentrate their time on understanding the new and unusual portion of the system. Thus, software systems can be generated more quickly and easily, leading to a style of programming known as *rapid prototyping* or *exploratory programming*. A prototype system is developed, users experiment with it, a second system is produced that is based on experience with the first, further experimentation takes place, and so on for several iterations. Such programming is particularly useful in situations where the goals and requirements of the system are only vaguely understood when the project begins.

8.7.7 *Polymorphism and Frameworks*

Software produced conventionally is generally written from the bottom up, although it may be *designed* from the top down. That is, the lower-level routines are written, and on top of these, slightly higher abstractions are produced, and on top of these even more abstract elements are generated. This process is like building a wall, where every brick must be laid on top of an already laid brick.

Normally, code portability decreases as one moves up the levels of abstraction. That is, the lowest-level routines may be used in several different projects, and perhaps even the next level of abstraction may be reused, but the higher-level routines are intimately tied to a particular application. The lower-level pieces can be carried to a new system and generally make sense standing on their own; the higher-level components generally make sense (because of declarations or data dependencies) only when they are built on top of specific lower-level units.

Polymorphism in programming languages permits the programmer to generate high-level reusable components that can be tailored to fit different applications by changes in their low-level parts. The Java AWT is an example of a large software framework that relies on inheritance and substitutability for its operation.

8.7.8 *Information Hiding*

A programmer who reuses a software component needs only to understand the nature of the component and its interface. It is not necessary for the programmer to have detailed information concerning matters such as the techniques used to implement the component. Thus, the interconnectedness between software systems is reduced. As mentioned earlier in this book, the interconnected nature of conventional software is one of the principal causes of software complexity.

8.8 THE COSTS OF INHERITANCE

Although the benefits of inheritance in object-oriented programming are great, almost nothing is without cost of one sort or another. For this reason, we must consider the cost of object-oriented programming techniques, and in particular the cost of inheritance.

8.8.1 *Execution Speed*

It is seldom possible for general purpose software tools to be as fast as carefully handcrafted systems. Thus, inherited methods, which must deal with arbitrary subclasses, are often slower than specialized code.

Yet, concern about efficiency is often misplaced.[2] First, the difference in speed or complexity is often small. Second, the reduction in execution speed may be balanced by an increase in the speed of software development. Finally, most programmers actually have little idea of how execution time is being used in their programs. It is far better to develop a working system, monitor it to discover where execution time is being used, and improve those sections, than to spend an inordinate amount of time worrying about efficiency early in a project.

8.8.2   *Program Size*

The use of any software library frequently imposes a size penalty not imposed by systems constructed for a specific project. Although this expense may be substantial, as memory costs decrease, the size of programs becomes less important. Containing development costs and producing high-quality and error-free code rapidly are now more important than limiting the size of programs.

8.8.3   *Message-Passing Overhead*

Much has been made of the fact that passing messages is by nature a more costly operation than simply invoking procedures. As with overall execution speed, however, overconcern about the cost of message passing is frequently penny wise and pound foolish. For one thing, the increased cost is often marginal—perhaps two or three additional assembly-language instructions and a total time penalty of 10 percent. This increased cost, like others, must be weighed against the many benefits of the object-oriented technique.

8.8.4   *Program Complexity*

Although object-oriented programming is often touted as a solution to software complexity, in fact, overuse of inheritance can often simply replace one form of complexity with another. Understanding the control flow of a program that uses inheritance may require several multiple scans up and down the inheritance graph. This is what is known as the *yo-yo* problem, which we will discuss in more detail in a later chapter.

8.9   Chapter Summary

Inheritance is a mechanism for relating a new software abstraction being developed to an older, existing abstraction. By stating that the new component

---

[2] The following quote from an article by Bill Wulf is an apt remark on the importance of efficiency: "More computing sins are committed in the name of efficiency (without necessarily achieving it) than for any other single reason—including blind stupidity" [Wulf 1972/1979].

inherits (or *extends*) the older abstraction, the programmer means that all the public and protected properties of the original class are also now part of the new abstraction. In addition, the new class can add new data fields and behavior, and can override methods that are inherited from the original class. Interfaces are a closely related mechanism, which tie the concrete realization of behavior to an abstract description.

All classes in Java use inheritance. If their inheritance is not explicitly stated, classes are assumed to inherit from the fundamental root class Object.

Inheritance is tied to the principle of substitutability. A variable that is declared as one class can be assigned a value that is created from a child class. A similar mechanism also works with interfaces. A class that can be used in lieu of another class is said to be a *subtype*. Java implicitly assumes that all subclasses are subtypes. However, this need not be true (a subclass can override a method in an incompatible fashion, for example). Subtypes can also be constructed from interfaces, avoiding subclasses altogether.

There are many different types of inheritance, used for different purposes. Variations include specialization, specification, construction, extension, limitation, and combination.

A variety of modifiers alter the meaning of inheritance. A private feature is not inherited by subclasses. A static feature (data field or method) is shared by all instances. An abstract method must be overridden. A final feature (data field or method) cannot be overridden.

STUDY QUESTIONS

1. Give an intuitive description of inheritance.

2. What does it mean for a method to override an inherited method?

3. What is the name of the root class for all objects in Java?

4. What behavior is provided by the root class in Java?

5. What does it mean to say that child classes are substitutable for parent classes in Java?

6. What is the difference between a subclass and a subtype?

7. What are the characteristics of inheritance for specialization?

8. What are the characteristics of inheritance for specification? How does this differ from inheritance for specialization?

9. What is the difference between an abstract class and an interface?

10. What are the characteristics of inheritance for construction? Why is construction not generally considered to be a good use of inheritance?

11. What are the characteristics of inheritance for extension?

12. What are the characteristics of inheritance for limitation? Why is limitation not generally considered to be a good use of inheritance?

13. Why would it not make sense for a method in Java to be declared both abstract and final?

14. What are some of the benefits of developing classes using inheritance, rather than developing each new class from scratch?

15. What are some of the costs of using inheritance for software development?

EXERCISES

1. Suppose you were required to program a project in a non-object-oriented language, such as Pascal or C. How would you simulate the notion of classes and methods? How would you simulate inheritance? Could you support multiple inheritance? Explain your answer.

2. We noted that the execution overhead associated with message passing is typically greater than the overhead associated with a conventional procedure call. How might you measure these overheads? For a language that supports both classes and procedures (such as C++ or Object Pascal), devise an experiment to determine the actual performance penalty of message passing.

3. Consider the three geometric concepts of a line (infinite in both directions), a ray (fixed at a point, infinite in one direction), and a segment (a portion of a line with fixed end points). How might you structure classes representing these three concepts in an inheritance hierarchy? Would your answer differ if you concentrated more on the data representation or more on the behavior? Characterize the type of inheritance you would use. Explain the reasoning behind your design.

4. Why is the example used in the following explanation not a valid illustration of inheritance?

> Perhaps the most powerful concept in object-oriented programming systems is inheritance. Objects can be created by inheriting the properties of other objects, thus removing the need to write any code whatsoever! Suppose, for example, a program is to process complex numbers consisting of real and imaginary parts. In a complex number, the real and imaginary parts behave like real numbers, so all of the operations (+, −, /, *, sqrt, sin, cos, etc.) can be inherited from the class of objects called REAL, instead of having to be written in code. This has a major impact on programmer productivity.

9 A Case Study: Solitaire

A program for playing the card game *Solitaire* will illustrate the utility and power of inheritance and overriding. A major part of the game of Solitaire is moving cards from one pile of cards to another. There are a number of different types of card piles, each having some features in common with the others, while other features are unique. A parent class can therefore be used to capture the common elements, while inheritance and overriding can be used to produce specialized types of piles. The development of this program will illustrate how inheritance can be used to simplify the creation of these components and ensure that they can all be manipulated in a similar fashion.

9.1 THE CLASS Card

To create a card game, we first need to define a class to represent a playing card. Each instance of class Card (Figure 9.1) maintains a suit value and a rank. To prevent modification of these values, the instance variables maintaining them are declared private and access is mediated through *accessor methods*. The value of the suit and rank fields are set by the constructor for the class. Integer constant values (in Java defined by the use of final static constants) are defined for the height and width of the card as well as for the suits. Another method permits the user to determine the color of the card. The Java library class Color is used to represent the color abstraction. The Color class defines constants for various colors. The values Color.red, Color.black, Color.yellow, and Color.blue are used in the Solitaire program.

There are important reasons that data values representing suit and rank should be returned through an accessor method, as opposed to defining the data fields s and r as public and allowing direct access to the data values. One of the most important is that access through a method ensures that the rank and

```
import java.awt.*;

public class Card {
      // public constants for card width and suits
   public final static int width = 50;
   public final static int height = 70;
   public final static int heart = 0;
   public final static int spade = 1;
   public final static int diamond = 2;
   public final static int club = 3;
      // internal data fields for rank and suit
   private boolean faceup;
   private int r;
   private int s;

      // constructor
   Card (int sv, int rv) { s = sv; r = rv; faceup = false; }

      // access attributes of card
   public final int rank () { return r; }

   public final int suit() { return s; }

   public final boolean faceUp() { return faceup; }

   public final void flip() { faceup = ! faceup; }

   public final Color color() {
      if (faceUp())
         if (suit() == heart || suit() == diamond)
            return Color.red;
         else
            return Color.black;
      return Color.yellow;
      }

   public void draw (Graphics g, int x, int y) { ... }
}
```

Figure 9.1   Description of the class Card.

suit characteristics of a card can be read but not altered once the card has been created.

Note that many of the methods in the Card abstraction have been declared as final. This modifier serves two important purposes. First, it is a documentation aid, signaling to the reader of the listing that the methods cannot be overridden by subclasses. Second, in some situations the Java compiler can optimize the invocation of final methods, creating faster code than could be generated for the execution of non-final methods.

The only other actions a card can perform, besides setting and returning the state of the card, are to flip over and to display itself. The method flip() is a one-line function that simply reverses the value held by an instance variable. The drawing method is more complex, making use of the drawing facilities provided by the Java standard application library. As seen in the earlier case studies, the application library provides a data type called Graphics that provides a variety of methods for drawing lines and common shapes, as well as for coloring. An argument of this type is passed to the draw method, as are the integer coordinates representing the upper left corner of the card.

The card images are simple line drawings, as shown in Figure 9.3. Diamonds and hearts are drawn in red, spades and clubs in black. The hash marks on the back are drawn in yellow. A portion of the method for drawing a playing card is shown in Figure 9.2.

The most important feature of the playing-card abstraction is the manner in which each card is responsible for maintaining within itself all card-related information and behaviors. The card knows both its value and how to draw itself. In this manner the information is encapsulated and isolated from the application using the playing card. If, for example, one were to move the program to a new platform using different graphics facilities, only the draw method within the class itself would need to be altered.

9.2   THE GAME

The version of Solitaire we will describe is known as Klondike. The countless variations on this game make it probably the most common version of Solitaire; so much so that when you say "Solitaire," most people think of Klondike. The version we will use is that described in [Morehead and Mott-Smith 1949]; in the exercises we will explore some of the common variations.

The layout of the game is shown in Figure 9.4. A single standard pack of 52 cards is used. The *tableau*, or playing table, consists of 28 cards in 7 piles. the first pile has 1 card, the second 2, and so on up to 7. The top card of each pile is initially face up; all other cards are face down.

The suit piles (sometimes called *foundations*) are built up from aces to kings in suits. They are constructed above the tableau as the cards become available. The object of the game is to build all 52 cards into the suit piles.

```
public class Card {
    .
    .
    .
  public void    draw (Graphics g, int x, int y) {
     String names[] = {"A", "2", "3", "4", "5", "6",
         "7", "8", "9", "10", "J", "Q", "K"};
       // clear rectangle, draw border
     g.clearRect(x, y, width, height);
     g.setColor(Color.blue);
     g.drawRect(x, y, width, height);
       // draw body of card
     g.setColor(color());
     if (faceUp()) {
        g.drawString(names[rank()], x+3, y+15);
        if (suit() == heart) {
           g.drawLine(x+25, y+30, x+35, y+20);
           g.drawLine(x+35, y+20, x+45, y+30);
           g.drawLine(x+45, y+30, x+25, y+60);
           g.drawLine(x+25, y+60, x+5, y+30);
           g.drawLine(x+5, y+30, x+15, y+20);
           g.drawLine(x+15, y+20, x+25, y+30);
           }
        else if (suit() == spade) { ... }
        else if (suit() == diamond) { ... }
        else if (suit() == club) {
           g.drawOval(x+20, y+25, 10, 10);
           g.drawOval(x+25, y+35, 10, 10);
           g.drawOval(x+15, y+35, 10, 10);
           g.drawLine(x+23, y+45, x+20, y+55);
           g.drawLine(x+20, y+55, x+30, y+55);
           g.drawLine(x+30, y+55, x+27, y+45);
           }
        }
     else { // face down
        g.drawLine(x+15, y+5, x+15, y+65);
        g.drawLine(x+35, y+5, x+35, y+65);
        g.drawLine(x+5, y+20, x+45, y+20);
        g.drawLine(x+5, y+35, x+45, y+35);
        g.drawLine(x+5, y+50, x+45, y+50);
        }
     }
}
```

Figure 9.2   Method to draw a playing card.

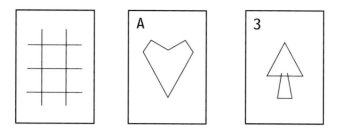

Figure 9.3   Card images for Solitaire.

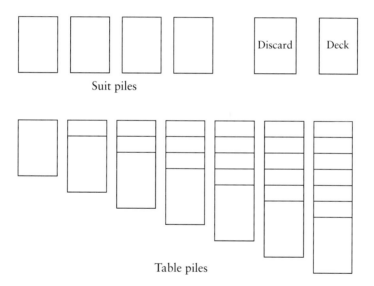

Figure 9.4   Layout for the Solitaire game.

The cards that are not part of the tableau are initially all in the *deck*. Cards in the deck are face down, and are drawn one by one from the deck and placed, face up, on the *discard pile*. From there, they can be moved onto either a tableau pile or a foundation. Cards are drawn from the deck until the pile is empty; at this point, the game is over if no further moves can be made.

Cards can be placed on a tableau pile only on a card of next-higher rank and opposite color. They can be placed on a foundation only if they are the same suit and next higher card or if the foundation is empty and the card is an ace. Spaces in the tableau that arise during play can be filled only by kings.

The topmost card of each tableau pile and the topmost card of the discard pile are always available for play. The only time more than one card is moved is when an entire collection of face-up cards from a tableau (called a *build*) is moved to another tableau pile. This can be done if the bottommost card of the build can be legally played on the topmost card of the destination. Our initial game will not support the transfer of a build, but we will discuss this as a possible extension. The topmost card of a tableau is always face up. If a card is moved from a tableau, leaving a face-down card on the top, the latter card can be turned face up.

From this short description, it is clear that the game of Solitaire mostly involves manipulating piles of cards. Each type of pile has many features in common with the others and a few aspects unique to the particular type. In the next section, we will investigate in detail how inheritance can be used in such circumstances to simplify the implementation of the various card piles by providing a common base for the generic actions and permitting this base to be redefined when necessary.

9.3   CARD PILES—INHERITANCE IN ACTION

Much of the behavior we associate with a card pile is common to each variety of pile in the game. For example, each pile maintains a collection of the cards in the pile (held in a Stack), and the operations of inserting and deleting elements from this collection are common. Other operations are given default behavior in the class CardPile, but they are sometimes overridden in the various subclasses. The class CardPile is shown in Figure 9.5.

Each card pile maintains the coordinate location for the upper left corner of the pile, as well as a Stack. The stack is used to hold the cards in the pile. All three of these values are set by the constructor for the class. The data fields are declared as protected and thus accessible to member functions associated with this class, with other classes in the same package, and to member functions associated with subclasses.

The three methods top( ), pop( ), and isEmpty( ) manipulate the list of cards, using methods provided by the Stack utility class. Note that these three methods have been declared final, and can not therefore be overridden in subclasses.

The topmost card in a pile is returned by the method top( ). This card will be the last card in the underlying container. Note that the method peek( ) provided by the Stack class returns a value declared as Object. This result must be cast to a Card value before it can be returned as the result.

The method pop( ) uses the similarly named operation provided by the underlying stack. The stack method generates an exception if an attempt is made to remove an element from an empty stack. The pop( ) method in the class CardPile catches the exception and returns a null value in this situation.

The five operations that are not declared final are common to the abstract notion of our card piles, but they differ in details in each case. For example, the method canTake(Card) asks whether it is legal to place a card on the given pile.

```java
import java.util.Stack;
import java.util.EmptyStackException;

public class CardPile {
   protected int x; // coordinates of the card pile
   protected int y;
   protected Stack thePile; // the collection of cards

   CardPile (int x1, int y1) { x = x1; y = y1; thePile = new Stack(); }

   public final Card top() { return (Card) thePile.peek(); }

   public final boolean isEmpty() { return thePile.empty(); }

   public final Card pop() {
      try {
         return (Card) thePile.pop();
         } catch (EmptyStackException e) { return null; }
      }

      // the following are sometimes overridden
   public boolean includes (int tx, int ty) {
      return x <= tx && tx <= x + Card.width &&
         y <= ty && ty <= y + Card.height;
      }

   public void select (int tx, int ty) { }

   public void addCard (Card aCard)  { thePile.push(aCard); }

   public void display (Graphics g) {
      g.setColor(Color.blue);
      if (isEmpty()) g.drawRect(x, y, Card.width, Card.height);
      else top().draw(g, x, y);
      }

   public boolean canTake (Card aCard) { return false; }
}
```

Figure 9.5   Description of the class CardPile.

A card can be added to a foundation pile, for instance, only if it is an ace and the foundation is empty, or if the card is of the same suit as the current topmost card in the pile and has the next-higher value. A card can be added to a tableau pile, on the other hand, only if the pile is empty and the card is a king, or if it is of the opposite color as the current topmost card in the pile and has the next lower value.

The actions of the five non-final methods defined in CardPile can be characterized as follows:

includes Determines if the coordinates given as arguments are contained within the boundaries of the pile. The default action simply tests the topmost card; this is overridden in the tableau piles to test all card values.

canTake Tells whether a pile can take a specific card. Only the tableau and suit piles can take cards, so the default action is simply to return no; this is overridden in the two classes mentioned.

addCard Adds a card to the card list. It is redefined in the discard pile class to ensure that the card is face up.

display Displays the card deck. The default method merely displays the topmost card of the pile, but it is overridden in the tableau class to display a column of cards. The top half of each hidden card is displayed. So that the playing surface area is conserved, only the topmost and bottommost face-up cards are displayed (this permits us to give definite bounds to the playing surface).

select Performs an action in response to a mouse click. It is invoked when the user selects a pile by clicking the mouse in the portion of the playing field covered by the pile. The default action does nothing, but it is overridden by the table, deck, and discard piles to play the topmost card, if possible.

Table 9.1 illustrates the important benefits of inheritance. Given five operations and five classes, there are 25 potential methods we might have had to

Table 9.1 The benefits of inheritance.

	CardPile	SuitPile	DeckPile	DiscardPile	TableauPile
includes	×				×
canTake	×	×			×
addCard	×			×	
display	×				×
select	×		×	×	×

```
class SuitPile extends CardPile {

    SuitPile (int x, int y) { super(x, y); }

    public boolean canTake (Card aCard) {
        if (isEmpty())
            return aCard.rank() == 0;
        Card topCard = top();
        return (aCard.suit() == topCard.suit()) &&
            (aCard.rank() == 1 + topCard.rank());
    }
}
```

Figure 9.6   The class SuitPile.

define. By making use of inheritance we need to implement only 13. Furthermore, we are guaranteed that each pile will respond in the same way to similar requests.

9.3.1   *The Suit Piles*

We will examine each of the subclasses of CardPile in detail, pointing out various uses of object-oriented features as they are encountered. The simplest subclass is the class SuitPile, shown in Figure 9.6, which represents the pile of cards at the top of the playing surface, the pile being built up in suit from ace to king.

The class SuitPile defines only two methods. The constructor for the class takes two integer arguments and does nothing more than invoke the constructor for the parent class CardPile. Note the use of the keyword super to indicate the parent class. The method canTake determines whether or not a card can be placed on the pile. A card is legal if the pile is empty and the card is an ace (that is, has rank zero) or if the card is the same suit as the topmost card in the pile and of the next higher rank (for example, a three of spades can only be played on a two of spades).

All other behavior of the suit pile is the same as that of our generic card pile. When selected, a suit pile does nothing. When a card is added, it is simply inserted into the collection of cards. To display the pile only the topmost card is drawn.

9.3.2   *The Deck Pile*

The DeckPile (Figure 9.7) maintains the original deck of cards. It differs from the generic card pile in two ways. When constructed, rather than creating an empty pile of cards, it creates the complete deck of 52 cards, inserting them in order into the collection. Once all the cards have been created, the collection

```
class DeckPile extends CardPile {

    DeckPile (int x, int y) {
        // first initialize parent
        super(x, y);
        // then create the new deck
        // first put them into a local pile
        for (int i = 0;  i < 4;  i++)
            for (int j = 0;  j <= 12;  j++)
                addCard(new Card(i, j));

        // then shuffle the cards
        Random generator = new Random( );
        for (int i = 0;  i < 52;  i++) {
            int j = Math.abs(generator.nextInt( )) % 52;
            // swap the two card values
            Object temp = thePile.elementAt(i);
            thePile.setElementAt(thePile.elementAt(j), i);
            thePile.setElementAt(temp, j);
            }
        }

    public void select(int tx, int ty) {
        if (isEmpty( ))
            return;
        Solitare.discardPile.addCard(pop( ));
        }
    }
```

Figure 9.7   The class DeckPile.

is then shuffled. To do this, a *random number generator* is first created. This generator is provided by the Java utility class Random. A loop then examines each card in turn, exchanging the card with another randomly selected card. To produce the index of the latter card, the random number generator first produces a randomly selected integer value (using by the method nextInt). Since this value could potentially be negative, the math library function abs is called to make it positive. The modular division operation is finally used to produce a randomly selected integer value between 0 and 51.

A subtle feature to note is that we are here performing a random access to the elements of a Stack. The conventional view of a stack does not allow access to any but the topmost element. However, in the Java library the Stack container is constructed using inheritance from the Vector class. Thus, any legal operation on a Vector, such as the method elementAt( ), can also be applied to a Stack.

The method select is invoked when the mouse button is used to select the card deck. If the deck is empty, it does nothing. Otherwise, the topmost card is removed from the deck and added to the discard pile.

Java does not have global variables. Where a value is shared between multiple instances of similar classes, such as the various piles used in our Solitaire game, an instance variable can be declared static. As noted in Chapter 4, one copy of a static variable is created and shared among all instances. In the present program, static variables will be used to maintain all the various card piles. These will be held in an instance of class Solitaire, described subsequently. To access these values we use a complete qualified name, which includes the name of the class as well as the name of the variable. This is shown in the select method in Figure 9.7, which refers to the variable Solitare.discardPile to access the discard pile.

9.3.3 *The Discard Pile*

The class DiscardPile (Figure 9.8) is interesting in that it exhibits two very different forms of inheritance. The select method *overrides* or *replaces* the default behavior provided by class CardPile, replacing it with code that when invoked (when the mouse is pressed over the card pile), checks to see if the topmost card can be played on any suit pile or, alternatively, on any tableau pile. If the card cannot be played, it is kept in the discard pile.

The method addCard is a different sort of overriding. Here the behavior is a *refinement* of the default behavior in the parent class. That is, the behavior of the parent class is completely executed, and, in addition, new behavior is added. In this case, the new behavior ensures that when a card is placed on the discard pile it is always face up. After satisfying this condition, the code in the parent class is invoked to add the card to the pile by passing the message to the pseudovariable named super.

Another form of refinement occurs in the constructors for the various subclasses. Each must invoke the constructor for the parent class to guarantee that the parent is properly initialized before the constructor performs its own actions. The parent constructor is invoked by the pseudovariable super being used as a method inside the constructor for the child class. Chapter 12 has much more about the distinction between replacement and refinement in overriding.

9.3.4 *The Tableau Piles*

The most complex of the subclasses of CardPile is that used to hold a tableau, or table pile. It is shown in Figures 9.9 and 9.10. Table piles differ from the generic card pile in the following ways:

```
class DiscardPile extends CardPile {

  DiscardPile (int x, int y) { super (x, y); }

  public void addCard (Card aCard) {
    if (! aCard.faceUp( ))
      aCard.flip( );
    super.addCard(aCard);
    }

  public void select (int tx, int ty) {
    if (isEmpty( ))
      return;
    Card topCard = pop( );
    for (int i = 0; i < 4; i++)
      if (Solitare.suitPile[i].canTake(topCard)) {
        Solitare.suitPile[i].addCard(topCard);
        return;
        }
    for (int i = 0; i < 7; i++)
      if (Solitare.tableau[i].canTake(topCard)) {
        Solitare.tableau[i].addCard(topCard);
        return;
        }
    // nobody can use it, put it back on our list
    addCard(topCard);
    }
}
```

Figure 9.8   The class DiscardPile.

- When initialized (by the constructor), the table pile removes a certain number of cards from the deck, placing them in its pile. The number of cards so removed is determined by an additional argument to the constructor. The topmost card of this pile is then displayed face up.

- A card can be added to the pile (method canTake) only if the pile is empty and the card is a king, or if the card is the opposite color from that of the current topmost card and one smaller in rank.

- When a mouse press is tested to determine if it covers this pile (method includes) only the left, right, and top bounds are checked; the bottom bound is not tested since the pile may be of variable length.

```
class TablePile extends CardPile {

    TablePile (int x, int y, int c) {
            // initialize the parent class
        super(x, y);
            // then initialize our pile of cards
        for (int i = 0; i < c; i++) {
            addCard(Solitare.deckPile.pop( ));
            }
            // flip topmost card face up
        top( ).flip( );
        }

    public boolean canTake (Card aCard) {
        if (isEmpty( ))
            return aCard.rank( ) == 12;
        Card topCard = top( );
        return (aCard.color( ) != topCard.color( )) &&
            (aCard.rank( ) == topCard.rank( ) - 1);
        }

    public boolean includes (int tx, int ty) {
            // don't test bottom of card
        return x <= tx && tx <= x + Card.width &&
            y <= ty;
        }

    public void display (Graphics g) {
        int localy = y;
        for (Enumeration e = thePile.elements( ); e.hasMoreElements( ); ) {
            Card aCard = (Card) e.nextElement( );
            aCard.draw (g, x, localy);
            localy += 35;
            }
        }
        .
        .
        .
}
```

Figure 9.9   The class TablePile, part 1.

```
class TablePile extends CardPile {
    .
    .
    .

    public void select (int tx, int ty) {
        if (isEmpty( ))
            return;

            // if face down, then flip
        Card topCard = top( );
        if (! topCard.faceUp( )) {
            topCard.flip( );
            return;
            }

            // else see if any suit pile can take card
        topCard = pop( );
        for (int i = 0; i < 4; i++)
            if (Solitare.suitPile[i].canTake(topCard)) {
                Solitare.suitPile[i].addCard(topCard);
                return;
                }
            // else see if any other table pile can take card
        for (int i = 0; i < 7; i++)
            if (Solitare.tableau[i].canTake(topCard)) {
                Solitare.tableau[i].addCard(topCard);
                return;
                }
            // else put it back on our pile
        addCard(topCard);
        }
}
```

Figure 9.10   The class TablePile, part 2.

- When the pile is selected, the topmost card is flipped if it is face down. If it is face up, an attempt is made to move the card first to any available suit pile, and then to any available table pile. Only if no pile can take the card is it left in place.

- To display the pile, each card in the pile is drawn in turn, each moving down slightly. To access the individual elements of the stack, an Enumeration is created. Enumeration objects are provided by all the containers in the Java library; they allow the programmer to easily loop over the elements in the container.

9.4 THE APPLICATION CLASS

Figure 9.11 shows the central class for the Solitaire application. As in our earlier case studies, the control is initially given to the static method named main, which creates an instance of the application class. The constructor for the application

```
public class Solitare {
   static public DeckPile deckPile;
   static public DiscardPile discardPile;
   static public TablePile tableau [ ];
   static public SuitPile suitPile [ ];
   static public CardPile allPiles [ ];
   private Frame window;

   static public void main (String [ ] args) {
      Solitare world = new Solitare( );
      }

   public Solitare ( ) {
      window = new SolitareFrame( );
      init( );
      window.show( );
      }

   public void init ( ) {
         // first allocate the arrays
      allPiles = new CardPile[13];
      suitPile = new SuitPile[4];
      tableau = new TablePile[7];
         // then fill them in
      allPiles[0] = deckPile = new DeckPile(335, 30);
      allPiles[1] = discardPile = new DiscardPile(268, 30);
      for (int i = 0; i < 4; i++)
         allPiles[2+i] = suitPile[i] =
            new SuitPile(15 + (Card.width+10) * i, 30);
      for (int i = 0; i < 7; i++)
         allPiles[6+i] = tableau[i] =
            new TablePile(15+(Card.width+5)*i, Card.height+35, i+1);
      }

   private class SolitareFrame extends Frame { ... }
}
```

Figure 9.11   The class Solitaire.

creates a window for the application, by constructing an instance of a nested class SolitareFrame that inherits from the library class Frame. After invoking the init method, which performs the application initialization, the window is given the message show, which will cause it to display itself.

As noted earlier, the variables maintaining the different piles, which are shared in common between all classes, are declared as static data fields in this class. These data fields are initialized in the method name init.

Arrays in Java are somewhat different from arrays in most computer languages. Java distinguishes the three activities of array declaration, array allocation, and assignment to an array location. Note that the declaration statements indicate only that the named objects are an array and not that they have any specific bound. One of the first steps in the initialization routine is to allocate space for the three arrays (the suit piles, the tableau, and the array allPiles we will discuss shortly). The new command allocates space for the arrays, but does not assign any values to the array elements.

The next step is to create the deck pile. Recall that the constructor for this class creates and shuffles the entire deck of 52 cards. The discard pile is similarly constructed. A loop then creates and initializes the four suit piles, and a second loop creates and initializes the tableau piles. Recall that as part of the initialization of the tableau, cards are removed from the deck and inserted in the tableau pile.

The inner class SolitareFrame, used to manage the application window, is shown in Figure 9.12. In addition to the cards, a button will be placed at the bottom of the window. Listeners are created both for mouse events (see Chapter 7) and for the button. When pressed, the button will invoke the button listener method. This method will reinitialize the game, then repaint the window. Similarly, when the mouse listener is invoked (in response to a mouse press) the collection of card piles will be examined, and the appropriate pile will be displayed.

9.5   PLAYING THE POLYMORPHIC GAME

Both the mouse listener and the repaint method for the application window make use of the array allPiles. This array is used to represent all 13 card piles. Note that as each pile is created it is also assigned a location in this array, as well as in the appropriate static variable. We will use this array to illustrate yet another aspect of inheritance. The principle of substitutability is used here: The array allPiles is declared as an array of CardPile, but in fact is maintaining a variety of card piles.

This array of all piles is used in situations where it is not important to distinguish between various types of card piles; for example, in the repaint method. To repaint the display, each different card pile is simply asked to display itself. Similarly, when the mouse is pressed, each pile is queried to see

```
private class SolitareFrame extends Frame {

   private class RestartButtonListener implements ActionListener {
      public void actionPerformed (ActionEvent e) {
         init( );
         repaint( );
         }
      }

   private class MouseKeeper extends MouseAdapter {
      public void mousePressed (MouseEvent e) {
         int x = e.getX( );
         int y = e.getY( );
         for (int i = 0; i < 13; i++)
            if (allPiles[i].includes(x, y)) {
               allPiles[i].select(x, y);
               repaint( );
               }
         }
      }

   public SolitareFrame( ) { // constructor for window
      setSize(600, 500);
      setTitle("Solitaire Game");
      addMouseListener (new MouseKeeper( ));
      Button restartButton = new Button("New Game");
      restartButton.addActionListener(new RestartButtonListener( ));
      add("South", restartButton);
      }

   public void paint(Graphics g) {
      for (int i = 0; i < 13; i++)
         allPiles[i].display(g);
      }
   }
```

Figure 9.12   The inner class SolitareFrame.

if it contains the given position. If the pile does contain the given position, the pile is selected. Remember, of the piles being queried here, seven are tableau piles, four are foundations, and the remaining are the discard pile and the deck. Furthermore, the actual code executed in response to the invocation of the includes and select routines may be different in each call, depending upon the type of pile being manipulated. In other object-oriented languages, such methods are often described as *virtual*.

The use of a variable declared as an instance of the parent class holding a value from a subclass is one aspect of *polymorphism*, a topic we will return to in more detail in a subsequent chapter.

9.6   BUILDING A MORE COMPLETE GAME

The Solitaire game described here is minimal and exceedingly hard to win. A more realistic game would include at least a few of the following variations:

- The method select in class TablePile would be extended to recognize builds. That is, if the topmost card could not be played, the bottommost face-up card in the pile should be tested against each tableau pile; if it could be played, the entire collection of face-up cards should be moved.

- Our game halts after one series of moves through the deck. An alternative would be that when the user selected the empty deck pile (by clicking the mouse in the area covered by the deck pile) the discard pile would be reshuffled and copied back into the deck, allowing execution to continue.

Various other alternatives are described in the exercises.

9.7   CHAPTER SUMMARY

The Solitaire program in this chapter is used as a case study to present many of the features and benefits of inheritance. The various different types of card piles found in the game can all be specialized from one common parent class. This parent class provides default behavior, which can be overridden when a pile requires more specialized code. In the program presented here, the default behavior is overridden less than half the time.

The following are some of the aspects of inheritance discussed in this chapter:

- By creating a common parent class, default behavior can be shared among several different software components.

- Methods can be declared as final, in which case they cannot be overridden in subclasses. (As noted in the previous chapter, methods can also be declared as abstract, in which case they *must* be overridden in subclasses.)

- Overriding methods can be divided into those that *replace* the code inherited from the parent, and those that *refine* the parent code. In the former case only the child code is executed, while in the latter both the child and the parent code is executed. In Java refinement is specified by explicitly executing the parent method, using the pseudovariable super.

- Inheritance is tied to polymorphism through the concept of substitutability. An instance of a child class can be assigned to a variable that is declared as a parent class type. Using this idea, we can create a variable (or, in this case, an array of values) that maintains any type of card pile.

- When an overridden method is applied to a polymorphic variable, the code executed is determined by the value the variable currently holds, not the declared type of the variable. Such methods are sometimes described as *virtual*.

STUDY QUESTIONS

1. What data values are maintained by class Card? What behaviors can a card perform? (That is, what methods are implemented by the class Card?)

2. Explain why the suit and rank data fields are declared private.

3. What is a default constructor? What is a copy constructor?

4. What is an accessor method? What is the advantage of using an accessor methods as opposed to direct access to a data member?

5. What are the 13 different card piles that are used in the Solitaire game?

6. What does it mean when a method is declared final?

7. Describe the five non-final methods implemented in class CardPile and over-ridden in at least one child class.

8. How does the use of inheritance reduce the amount of code that would otherwise be necessary to implement the various types of card piles?

9. Explain the difference between overriding used for replacement and over-riding used for refinement. Find another example of each in the methods associated with class CardPile and its various subclasses.

10. Explain how polymorphism is exhibited in the Solitaire game application.

EXERCISES

1. The Solitaire game has been designed to be as simple as possible. A few features are somewhat annoying, but they can be easily remedied with more coding. These include the following:

   (a) The topmost card of a tableau pile should not be moved to another tableau pile if there is another face-up card below it.

   (b) An entire build should not be moved if the bottommost card is a king and there are no remaining face-down cards.

For each, describe what methods need to be changed, and give the code for the updated routine.

2. The following are common variations of Klondike. For each, describe which portions of the Solitaire program need to be altered to incorporate the change.

   (a) If the user clicks on an empty deck pile, the discard pile is moved (perhaps with shuffling) back to the deck pile. Thus, the user can traverse the deck pile repeatedly.

   (b) Cards can be moved from the suit pile back into the tableau pile.

   (c) Cards are drawn from the deck three at a time and placed on the discard pile in reverse order. As before, only the topmost card of the discard pile is available for playing. If fewer than three cards remain in the deck pile, all the remaining cards (as many as that may be) are moved to the discard pile. (In practice, this variation is often accompanied by variation (a), permitting multiple passes through the deck.)

   (d) The same as variation (c), but any of the three selected cards can be played. (This requires a slight change to the layout as well as an extensive change to the discard pile class.)

   (e) Any royalty card, not simply a king, can be moved onto an empty tableau pile.

3. The game Thumb and Pouch is similar to Klondike except that a card may be built on any card of next-higher rank, of any suit but its own. Thus, a nine of spades can be played on a ten of clubs, but not on a ten of spades. This variation greatly improves the chances of winning. (According to Morehead and Mott-Smith [1949], the chances of winning Klondike are 1 in 30, whereas the chances of winning Thumb and Pouch are 1 in 4.) What portions of the program need to be changed to accommodate this variation?

4. The game Whitehead is superficially similar to Klondike, in the sense that it uses the same layout. However, it uses different rules for when a card can be played in the tableau:

   (a) A card can be moved onto another face-up card in the tableau only if it has the *same* color and is one smaller in rank. For example, a five of spades can be played on either a six of clubs or a six of spades, but not on a six of diamonds or a six of hearts.

   (b) A build can only be moved if all cards in the build are of the same suit.

   What portions of the program need to be changed to accommodate this variation?

10 Mechanisms for Software Reuse

Object-oriented programming has been billed as the technology that will finally permit software to be constructed from general purpose reusable components. Writers such as Brad Cox have even gone so far as to describe object orientation as heralding the "industrial revolution" in software development [Cox 1986]. While reality may not quite match the expectations of OOP pioneers, it *is* true that object-oriented programming makes possible a level of software reuse that is orders of magnitude more powerful than that permitted by previous software construction techniques. In this chapter, we will investigate the two most common mechanisms for software reuse, which are known as *inheritance* and *composition*.

Inheritance in Java is made more flexible by the presence of two different mechanisms, interfaces and subclassification. In addition to contrasting inheritance and composition, we will contrast inheritance performed using subclassification and inheritance performed using interfaces, and relate all to the concept of substitutability.

10.1 SUBSTITUTABILITY

The concept of substitutability is fundamental to many of the most powerful software development techniques in object-oriented programming. You will recall that substitutability referred to the situation that occurs when a *variable* declared as one type is used to hold a *value* derived from another type.

In Java, substitutability can occur either through the use of classes and inheritance, or through the use of interfaces. Examples of both occurred in the case studies in earlier chapters. In the PinBall Game program described in Chapter 7, the variable targets was declared a PinBallTarget, but in fact it held a variety of different types of values that were created using implementations of PinBallTarget. In the Solitaire program from Chapter 9, the variable allPiles was declared as holding a CardPile, but in fact it held values that were subclasses of CardPile, such as DeckPile and DiscardPile as follows:

```
public class Solitare {
    static public CardPile allPiles [ ];

    public void init ( ) {
        .
        .

        allPiles = new CardPile[13];
        // then fill them in
        allPiles[0] = new DeckPile(335, 30);
        allPiles[1] = new DiscardPile(268, 30);
    }
    .
    .
    .

}
```

We have also seen examples of substitutability arising through interfaces. An example is the instance of the class FireButtonListener created in the Cannon Game (Chapter 6). The class from which this value was defined was declared as implementing the interface ActionListener. Because it implements the ActionListener interface, we can use this value as a parameter to a method (in this case, addActionListener) that expects an ActionListener value.

```
class CannonWorld extends Frame {
    .
    .

    private class FireButtonListener implements ActionListener {
        public void actionPerformed (ActionEvent e) {
            .
            .
            .
        }
    }

    public CannonWorld ( ) {
        .
        .

        fire.addActionListener(new FireButtonListener( ));
    }
}
```

We will return to the distinction between inheritance of classes and inheritance of interfaces in Section 10.1.2.

10.1.1 *The* Is-a *Rule and the* Has-a *Rule*

A commonly employed rule of thumb that can be used to understand when inheritance is an appropriate software technique is known colloquially as *is-a* and *has-a* (or *part-of*) relationship.

The *is-a* relationship holds between two concepts when the first is a specialized instance of the second. That is, for all practical purposes the behavior and data associated with the more specific idea form a subset of the behavior and data associated with the more abstract idea. For example, all the examples of inheritance described in the early chapters satisfy the *is-a* relationship (a Florist *is-a* Shopkeeper, a Dog *is-a* Mammal, a PinBall *is-a* Ball, and so on). The relationship derives its name from a simple rule of thumb that tests the relationship. To determine if concept X is a specialized instance of concept Y, simply form the English sentence "*An* X *is a* Y". If the assertion "sounds correct," that is, if it seems to match your everyday experience, you may judge that X and Y have the *is-a* relationship.

The *has-a* relationship, on the other hand, holds when the second concept is a component of the first but the two are not in any sense the same thing, no matter how abstract the generality. For example, a Car *has-a* Engine, although clearly it is not the case that a Car *is-a* Engine or that an Engine *is-a* Car. A Car, however, *is-a* Vehicle, which in turn *is-a* MeansOfTransportation. Once again, the test for the *has-a* relationship is to simply form the English sentence "*An* X *has a* Y", and let common sense tell you whether the result sounds reasonable.

Most of the time, the distinction is clear-cut. But, sometimes it may be subtle or may depend on circumstances. In Section 10.2 we will use one such indefinite case to illustrate the two software development techniques that are naturally tied to these two relationships.

10.1.2 *Inheritance of Code and Inheritance of Behavior*

There are at least two different ways in which a concept can satisfy the *is-a* relationship with another concept, and these are reflected in two different mechanisms in the Java language. Inheritance is the mechanism of choice when two concepts share a *structure* or *code* relationship with each other, while an interface is the more appropriate technique when two concepts share the *specification of behavior,* but no actual code.

This can be illustrated with examples from the Java run-time library. The class Frame, from which most Java windows inherit, provides a great deal of code, in the form of methods that are inherited and used without being overridden. Thus, inheritance using the extends modifier in the class heading is the appropriate mechanism to use in this situation.

```
    // a cannon game is a type of Frame
public class CannonGame extends Frame {
    .
    .
    .
}
```

On the other hand, the characteristics needed for an ActionListener (the object type that responds to button presses) can be described by a single method, and the implementation of that method cannot be predicted, since it differs from one application to another. Thus, an interface is used to describe only the necessary requirements, and no actual behavior is inherited by a subclass that implements the behavior.

```
class CannonWorld extends Frame {
    .
    .
    .

        // a fire button listener implements the action listener interface
    private class FireButtonListener implements ActionListener {
        public void actionPerformed (ActionEvent e) {
            .
            .
            .
        }
    }
}
```

In general, the class-subclass relationship should be used whenever a subclass can usefully inherit code, data values, or behavior from the parent class. The interface mechanism should be used when the child class inherits only the specification of the expected behavior, but no actual code.

10.2 COMPOSITION AND INHERITANCE DESCRIBED

Two different techniques for software reuse are *composition* and *inheritance*. Although uses of inheritance were explicitly noted in earlier chapters, and composition was used in several places as well, this was not pointed out. One way to view these two different mechanisms is as manifestations of the *has-a* rule and the *is-a* rule, respectively.

Although in most situations the distinction between *is-a* and *has-a* is clear-cut, it does happen occasionally that it can be difficult to determine which mechanism is most appropriate to use in a particular situation. By examining one such indefinite case, we can more easily point out the differences between the use of inheritance and the use of composition. The example we will use is taken from the Java library and concerns the development of a Stack abstraction from an existing Vector data type.

The Vector data type is described in detail in Chapter 19. While abstractly a vector is most commonly thought of as an indexed collection, the Java implementation also permits values to be added or removed from the end of the collection, growing and shrinking the container as necessary. The methods of interest for this discussion can be described as follows:

```
class Vector {
    // see if collection is empty
  public boolean isEmpty () { ... }

    // return size of collection
  public int size () { ... }

    // add element to end of collection
  public void addElement (Object value) { ... }

    // return last element in collection
  public Object lastElement () { ... }

    // remove element at given index
  public Object removeElementAt (int index) { ... }

    .
    .
    .

}
```

A *stack* is an abstract data type that allows elements to be added or removed from one end only. If you think about a stack of dishes sitting on a counter, you can get a good intuitive image. It is easy to access the topmost dish, or to place a new dish on the top. It is much more difficult to access any dish other than the topmost dish. In fact, it might be that the only way to do this is to remove dishes one by one until you reach the dish you want.

The Stack abstractions defined here will be slightly simpler than the version provided by the Java library. In particular, the library abstraction will generate an exception if an attempt is made to access or remove an element from an empty stack, a condition we will ignore. The Java library stack routine names the empty test method *empty*, instead of the method isEmpty from class Vector, and finally the Stack abstraction provides a method to search the stack to determine if it includes a given element. We will not describe this method here.

10.2.1   *Using Composition*

We will first investigate how the stack abstraction can be formed with composition. Recall from our earlier discussion that an object is simply an encapsulation of data values and behavior. When composition is employed to reuse an existing data abstraction in the development of a new data type, a portion of the state of the new data structure is simply an instance of the existing structure. This is illustrated in Figure 10.1, where the data type Stack contains a private instance field named theData, which is declared to be of type Vector.

Because the Vector abstraction is stored as part of the data area for our stack, it must be initialized in the constructor. The constructor for class Stack allocates space for the vector, giving a value to the variable theData.

Operations that manipulate the new structure are implemented by making use of the existing operations provided for the earlier data type. For example, the implementation of the empty operation for our stack data structure simply invokes the method already defined for vectors. The peek operation is known by a different name, but the task is already provided by the lastElement operation in the Vector class. Similarly, the push operation is simply performed by executing an addElement on the vector.

```
class Stack {
    private Vector theData;

    public Stack ()
        { theData = new Vector( ); }

    public boolean empty ()
        { return theData.isEmpty( ); }

    public Object push (Object item)
        { theData.addElement (item); return item; }

    public Object peek ()
        { return theData.lastElement(); }

    public Object pop () {
        Object result = theData.lastElement( );
        theData.removeElementAt(theData.size( )-1);
        return result;
        }
}
```

Figure 10.1   A stack created using composition.

The only operation that is slightly more complex is popping an element from the stack. This involves using two methods provided by the Vector class, namely obtaining the topmost element and removing it from the collection. Notice that to remove the element we must first determine its index position, then remove the element by naming its position.

The important point to emphasize is the fact that composition provides a way to leverage off an existing software component in the creation of a new application. By use of the existing Vector class, we have already addressed the majority of the difficult work in managing the data values for our new component.

But composition makes no explicit or implicit claims about substitutability. When formed in this fashion, the data types Stack and Vector are entirely distinct and neither can be substituted in situations where the other is required.

10.2.2   *Using Inheritance*

An entirely different mechanism for software reuse in object-oriented programming is the concept of inheritance, with which a new class can be declared a *subclass*, or *child class*, of an existing class. In this way, all data areas and methods associated with the original class are automatically associated with the new data abstraction. The new class can, in addition, define new data values or new methods; it can also *override* methods in the original class, simply by defining new methods with the same names as those of methods that appear in the parent class.

These possibilities are illustrated in the class description shown in Figure 10.2, which implements a different version of the Stack abstraction. By naming the class Vector in the class heading, we indicate that our Stack abstraction is an extension, or a refinement, of the existing class Vector. Thus, all data fields and operations associated with vectors are immediately applicable to stacks as well.

The most obvious features of this class in comparison to the earlier are the items that are missing. There are no local data fields. There is no constructor, since no local data values need be initialized. The method isEmpty need not be provided, since the method is inherited already from the parent class Vector.

Compare this method with the earlier version, shown in Figure 10.1. Both techniques are powerful mechanisms for code reuse, but unlike composition, inheritance carries an implicit assumption that subclasses are, in fact, subtypes. This means that instances of the new abstraction should react similarly to instances of the parent class.

In fact, the version using inheritance provides more useful functionality than the version using composition. For example, the method size in the Vector class yields the number of elements stored in a vector. With the version of the Stack formed using inheritance we get this method automatically for free, while the composition version needs to explicitly add a new operation if we want to include this new ability. Similarly, the ability to access intermediate values directly

```
class Stack extends Vector {

    public Object push (Object item)
       { addElement (item); return item; }

    public Object peek ()
       { return elementAt(size( ) - 1); }

    public Object pop ( ) {
       Object obj = peek( );
       removeElementAt(size( )-1);
       return obj;
    }
}
```

Figure 10.2   A stack created using inheritance.

using an index is in this version possible with a stack, but not permitted in the abstraction created using composition.

10.3 COMPOSITION AND INHERITANCE CONTRASTED

Having illustrated two mechanisms for software reuse, and having seen that they are both applicable to the implementation of stacks, we can comment on some of the advantages and disadvantages of the two approaches.

- Inheritance carries with it an implicit, if not explicit, assumption of substitutability. That is, classes formed by inheritance are assumed to be subtypes of the parent class, and therefore candidates for values to be used when an instance of the parent class is expected. No such assumption of substitutability is associated with the use of composition.

- Composition is the simpler of the two techniques. Its advantage is that it more clearly indicates exactly what operations can be performed on a particular data structure. Looking at the declaration for the Stack data abstraction, it is clear that the only operations provided for the data type are the test for emptiness, push, peek, and pop. This is true regardless of what operations are defined for vectors.

- In inheritance the operations of the new data abstraction are a superset of the operations of the original data structure on which the new object is built. Thus, to know exactly what operations are legal for the new structure, the programmer must examine the declaration for the original. An examination of the Stack declaration, for example, does not immediately indicate that the size method can be legally applied to stacks. It is only by examination of the declaration for the earlier Vector data abstraction that the entire set of legal operations can be ascertained.

The difficulty that occurs when, to understand a class constructed using inheritance, the programmer must frequently flip back and forth between two (or more) class declarations has been labeled the "yo-yo" problem by Taenzer, Ganti, and Podar [Taenzer 1989].

- The brevity of data abstractions constructed with inheritance is, in another light, an advantage. Using inheritance it is not necessary to write any code to access the functionality provided by the class on which the new structure is built. For this reason, implementations using inheritance are almost always, as in the present case, considerably shorter in code than are implementations constructed with composition, and they often provide greater functionality. For example, the inheritance implementation makes available not only the size test for stacks but also the index-related operations (inserting, modifying, or removing elements by giving their index locations).

- Inheritance does not prevent users from manipulating the new structure using methods from the parent class, even if these are not appropriate. For example, when we use inheritance to derive the class Stack from the class Vector, nothing prevents users from adding new elements to the stack using the inherited method insertElementAt, and thereby placing elements in locations other than the top of the stack.

- In composition the fact that the class Vector is used as the storage mechanism for our stack is merely an implementation detail. With this technique it would be easy to reimplement the class to make use of a different technique (such as a linked list), with minimal impact on the users of the Stack abstraction. If users counted on the fact that a Stack is merely a specialized form of Vector, such changes would be more difficult to implement.

- A component constructed using inheritance has access to fields and methods in the parent class that have been declared as protected. A component constructed using composition can only access the public portions of the included component.

- Inheritance may allow us to use the new abstraction as an argument in an existing *polymorphic* method. We will investigate this possibility in more detail in Chapter 12. Because composition does not imply substitutability, it usually precludes polymorphism.

- Understandability and maintainability are difficult to judge. Inheritance has the advantage of brevity of code but not of protocol. Composition code, although longer, is the only code that another programmer must understand to use the abstraction. A programmer faced with understanding the inheritance version needs to ask whether any behavior inherited from the parent class was necessary for proper utilization of the new class, and would thus have to understand both classes.

- Data structures implemented through inheritance tend to have a very small advantage in execution time over those constructed with composition, since one additional method call is avoided (although optimization techniques, such as inline functions, can in theory be used to eliminate much of this overhead).

Of the two possible implementation techniques, can we say which is better in this case? One answer involves the substitution principle. Ask yourself whether, in an application that expected to use a Vector data abstraction, it is correct to substitute instead an instance of class Stack.

The bottom line is that the two techniques are very useful, and an object-oriented programmer should be familiar with both of them.

10.4   COMBINING INHERITANCE AND COMPOSITION

The Java input/output system, which we will investigate in more detail in Chapter 14, provides an interesting illustration of the way in which inheritance and composition can interact with each other, and the particular problems each mechanism is designed to solve.

To begin with, there is an abstract concept, and several concrete realizations of the concept. For the file input system the abstract concept is the idea of reading a stream of bytes in sequence, one after the other. This idea is embodied in the class InputStream, which defines a number of methods for reading byte values. The concrete realizations differ in the source of the data values. Values can come from an array of bytes being held in memory, from an external file, or from another process that is generating values as needed. There is a different subclass of InputStream for each of these, as shown in Figure 10.3.

Because each of these is declared as a subclass of InputStream, they can be substituted for a value of type InputStream. In this fashion methods can be written to process a stream of byte values, without regard to where the values originate (whether in memory, or from an external file, or from another process).

However, there is an additional source of variation among input streams. Or rather, there is additional functionality that is sometimes required when using an input stream. Furthermore, this functionality is independent of the source for the byte values. One example is the ability to keep track of line numbers, so that the programmer can determine on which line of the input the current byte originates. Another useful function is the ability to buffer input so as to have the possibility of rereading recently referenced bytes once again.

These features are provided by defining a subclass of InputStream, named FilterInputStream. Thus, using the principle of substitutability, a FilterInputStream

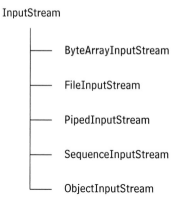

InputStream

— ByteArrayInputStream

— FileInputStream

— PipedInputStream

— SequenceInputStream

— ObjectInputStream

Figure 10.3   Subclasses of InputStream.

can be used in places where an InputStream is expected. On the other hand, a FilterInputStream holds as a component another instance of InputStream, which is used as the source for data values. Thus, the class InputStream is both parent and component to FilterInputStream. As requests for values are received, the FilterInputStream will access the InputStream it holds to get the values it needs, performing whatever additional actions are required (for example, counting newline characters in order to keep track of the current line number).

```
class FilterInputStream extends InputStream {

    protected InputStream in;
    .
    .
    .
}
```

Because the component held by the FilterInputStream can be any type of InputStream, this additional functionality can be used to augment any type of InputStream, regardless of where the byte values originate. This idea of *filters* (sometimes called *wrappers* in other object-oriented literature) can be quite powerful when there are orthogonal sources of variation. Here the two reasons of variation are (1) the source of the input values and (2) the additional functionality that may or may not be needed in any particular application.

10.5   NOVEL FORMS OF SOFTWARE REUSE

There are several novel ways in which composition, or inheritance, or both, are used to achieve different effects.

```
class Frog {
   private FrogBehavior behavior;

   public Frog () {
      behavior = new TadpoleBehavior( );
      }

   public grow () { // see if behavior should change
      if (behavior.growUp( ))
         behavior = new AdultFrogBehavior( );
      behavior.grow( ); // behavior does actual work
      behavior.swim( );
      }
}
```

Figure 10.4   Class Frog holds dynamically changing behavior component.

10.5.1   Dynamic Composition

One advantage of composition over inheritance concerns the delay in binding time. With inheritance, the link between child class and parent class is established at compile time and cannot later be modified. With composition, the link between the new abstraction and the older abstraction is created at run time, and is therefore much weaker, since it can also be changed at run time. This is sometimes called *dynamic composition.*

To illustrate, imagine a class that is simulating the behavior of a Frog. Although the frog interface can be fixed throughout its life, the actual actions it performs might be very different when the frog is a tadpole or when it is an adult. One way to model this is to create a class Frog (Figure 10.4) that uses composition to hold a value of type FrogBehavior. The Frog class is largely a facade, invoking the FrogBehavior object to do the majority of the real work.

The novel idea is that the variable holding the instance of FrogBehavior can actually be polymorphic. There might be more than one class that implements the FrogBehavior specification, such as TadpoleBehavior and AdultFrogBehavior. Figure 10.5 illustrates these classes. The parent class FrogBehavior is here declared *abstract,* which means that it *must* be overridden before any instances can be created. As the frog "grows," it can dynamically change behavior by reassigning the value behavior to a different value (for example, moving from a TadpoleBehavior to an AdultFrogBehavior). The user of the Frog abstraction need not know about this change, or even be aware when it occurs.

Dynamic composition is a useful technique if the behavior of an object varies dramatically according to some internal concept of "state," and the change in state occurs infrequently.

```
abstract class FrogBehavior {
   public boolean growUp () { return false; }

   public void grow ();

   public void swim ();
}

class TadpoleBehavior extends FrogBehavior {
   private int age = 0;

   public boolean growUp () { if (++age > 24) return true; }

   public void grow () { ... }

   public void swim () { ... }
}

class AdultFrogBehavior extends FrogBehavior {

   public void grow () { ... }

   public void swim () { ... }
}
```

Figure 10.5   Class FrogBehavior can dynamically change

10.5.2   *Inheritance of Inner Classes*

We have seen another combination of inheritance and composition in some
of the case studies presented in earlier chapters. For example, the "listener"
classes that responded to events were constructed using inheritance, but were
themselves components in the application class. The following is a skeleton of
the class PinBallGame from Chapter 7.

```
public class PinBallGame extends Frame {
   .
   .
   .
   private class MouseKeeper extends MouseAdapter { ... }

   private class PinBallThread extends Thread { ... }
}
```

The classes MouseKeeper and PinBallThread are each constructed using inheritance. Each is then used to create a new component, which will be held as part of the state of the pinball game. When used in this fashion, inner classes combine aspects of both inheritance and composition.

10.5.3 *Unnamed Classes*

In several of the earlier case studies we have seen situations where inheritance is used to override an existing class, yet only one instance of the new class is created. An alternative to naming the new class and then creating an instance of the named class is to use a class definition expression. Such an expression places the entire class definition inside the instance creation expression.

An example where this could be used is in the definition of an event listener. For example, the Cannon Game described in Chapter 6 contained the following code:

```
class CannonWorld extends Frame {
    .
    .
    .

    private class FireButtonListener implements ActionListener {
        public void actionPerformed (ActionEvent e) {
            .
            .
            .
        }
    }

    public CannonWorld ( ) {
        fire.addActionListener(new FireButtonListener( ));
        .
        .
        .
    }
}
```

Note how the constructor for the class CannonWorld creates an instance of the inner class FireButtonListener. This is the only instance of this class created. An alternative way to achieve the same effect would be as follows:

```
class CannonWorld extends Frame {
    .
    .
    .

    public CannonWorld ( ) {
        fire.addActionListener(new ActionListener( ) {
```

```
public void actionPerformed (ActionEvent e) {
    .
    .
    .
}
});
.
.
.
}
}
```

Notice that in this example the object being created is declared only as being an instance of ActionListener. However, a class definition follows immediately the ending parenthesis, indicating that a new and *unnamed* class is being defined. This class definition would have exactly the same form as before, ending with a closing curly brace. The parenthesis that follows this curly brace ends the argument list for the addActionListener call. (The reader should carefully match curly braces and parenthesis to see how this takes place.) An unnamed class is also sometimes known as an *anonymous class*.

An advantage to the use of the class definition expression in this situation is that it avoids the need to introduce a new class name (in this case, the inner class name FireButtonListener). A disadvantage is that such expressions tend to be difficult to read, since the entire class definition must be wrapped up as an expression, and the close of the expressions occurs after the end of the class definition.

10.6   CHAPTER SUMMARY

The two most common techniques for reusing software abstractions are inheritance and composition. Both are valuable techniques, and a good object-oriented system will usually have many examples of each.

A good rule of thumb for deciding when to use inheritance is the *is-a* rule. Form the sentence "An X is a Y", and if it sounds right to your ear, then the two concepts X and Y can probably be related using inheritance. The corresponding rule for composition is the *has-a* rule.

The decision whether to use inheritance or not is not always clear. By examining one borderline case, one can more easily see some of the advantages and disadvantages of the two software structuring techniques.

The idea of *filters*, found in the portion of the Java library used for input and output, is an interesting technique that combines features of both inheritance and composition.

Study Questions

1. Explain in your own words the principle of substitutability.

2. What is the *is-a* rule? What is the *has-a* rule? How are these two rules related to inheritance and composition?

3. How are interfaces and inheritance related?

4. What are some of the advantages of composition over inheritance?

5. What are some of the advantages of using inheritance that are not available when composition is used?

6. How does a FilterStream combine inheritance and composition?

Exercises

1. A set is simply an unorganized collection of values. Describe how one could use a Vector to implement a set. Would inheritance or composition be the more appropriate mechanism in this case?

2. Modify the Stack data abstractions given in this chapter so that they will throw a EmptyStackException if an attempt is made to read or remove a value from an empty stack.

3. Modify each of the Stack data abstractions given in this chapter so that when given the message size they will return the number of elements they hold.

4. Give some rules for deciding when it is appropriate to use inheritance and when it is appropriate to use composition.

11 Implications of Inheritance

The decision to support inheritance and the principle of substitutability in a language sets off a series of chain reactions that end up impacting almost every aspect of a programming language. In this chapter, we will illustrate this point by considering some of the implications of the decision to support in a natural fashion the idea of the polymorphic variable.

The links between inheritance and other language features can be summarized as follows:

- In order to make the most effective use of object-oriented techniques, the language must support the polymorphic variable. A polymorphic variable is a variable that is declared as one type but actually maintains either a value of that type or a value derived from a subtype of the declared type.

- Because at compile time we cannot determine the amount of memory that will be required to hold the value assigned to a polymorphic variable, all objects must reside on the heap, rather than on the stack.

- Because values reside in heaps, the most natural interpretation of assignment and parameter passing uses reference semantics, rather than copy semantics.

- Similarly, the most natural interpretation of equality testing is to test object identity. However, since often the programmer requires a different meaning for equality, two different operators are necessary.

- Because values reside on the heap, there must be some memory management mechanism. Because assignment is by reference semantics, it is difficult for the programmer to determine when a value is no longer being used. Therefore a garbage collection system is necessary to recover unused memory.

Each of these points will be more fully developed in the following sections.

11.1   THE POLYMORPHIC VARIABLE

As we will see in Chapter 12, a great deal of the power of the object-oriented features of Java comes through the use of a *polymorphic variable*. A polymorphic variable is declared as maintaining a value of one type but in fact holds a value from another type. We have seen many such examples in the sample

```java
class Shape {
   protected int x;
   protected int y;

   public Shape (int ix, int iy)
      { x = ix; y = iy; }

   public String describe ()
      { return "unknown shape"; }
}

class Square extends Shape {
   protected int side;

   public Square (int ix, int iy, int is)
      { super(ix, iy); side = is; }

   public String describe ()
      { return "square with side " + side; }
}

class Circle extends Shape {
   protected int radius;

   public Circle (int ix, int iy, int ir)
      { super(ix, iy); radius = ir; }

   public String describe ()
      { return "circle with radius " + radius; }
}
```

Figure 11.1 Shape classes and a polymorphic variable.

programs presented in Part 1. For instance, much of the standard user interface code thinks only that an application is an instance of class Frame, when in fact each program we created used inheritance to create a new type of application. Similarly, in the Pin Ball Game Construction Kit program (Chapter 7) a variable was declared as holding a value of type PinBallTarget, when in fact it would hold a Hole or a ScorePad.

Figure 11.1 provides a class hierarchy consisting of three classes, Shape and two subclasses Circle and Square. In the small test program shown below the variable named form is declared as type Shape, then assigned a value of type Circle. As expected, when the method describe() is invoked, the method that is executed is the method in class Circle, not the method inherited from class Shape. We will use this example class in the subsequent discussion in this chapter.

```
class ShapeTest {
    static public void main (String [ ] args) {
        Shape form = new Circle (10, 10, 5);
        System.out.println("form is " + form.describe());
        form = new Square (15, 20, 10);
        System.out.println("form is " + form.describe());
    }
}
```

11.2 MEMORY LAYOUT

Before we can observe the impact of the polymorphic variable on memory management, it is first necessary to review how variables are normally represented in memory in most programming languages. From the point of view of the memory manager, there are two major categories of memory values. These are *stack-based* memory locations, and *heap-based* memory values.

Stack-based memory locations are tied to method entry and exit. When a method is started, space is allocated on a run-time stack for local variables. These values exist as long as the method is executing, and are erased, and the memory recovered, when the method exits. Figure 11.2 shows, for example, a snapshot of the run-time stack for the following simple recursive algorithm:

```
class FacTest {
    static public void main (String [ ] args) {
        int f = factorial(3);
        System.out.println("Factorial of 3 is " + f);
    }

    static public int factorial (int n) {
        int c = n - 1;
        int r;
```

0	n: 1	third activation record
4	r: 1	
8	c: 0	
0	n: 2	second activation record
4	r: ?	
8	c: 1	
0	n: 3	first activation record
4	r: ?	
8	c: 2	

Figure 11.2   A snapshot of the activation frame stack.

```
if (c > 0)
    r = n * factorial(c);
else
    r = 1;
return r;
}

}
```

The snapshot is taken after the method has recursed three times, just as the innermost method is starting to return. The data values for three methods are shown. In the innermost method the variable r has been assigned the value 1, while for the two pending methods the value of r has yet to be determined.

There are a number of advantages of stack-based memory allocation. All local variables can be allocated or deallocated as a block, for example, instead of one by one. This block is commonly called an *activation record*. Internally, variables can be described by their numeric offset within the activation record, rather than by their symbolic address. These numeric offsets have been noted in Figure 11.2. Most machines are much more efficient at dealing with numeric offsets than with symbolic names. Notice that each new activation record creates a new set of offsets, so that the offset is always relative to the activation frame in which a variable appears.

Stack-based allocation has one serious disadvantage: These numeric offsets associated with variables must be determined at compile time, not at run time. In order to do this, the compiler must know the amount of memory to assign to each variable. In Figure 11.2, the compiler only knows that variable c can be found at address 8 because it knows that variable r, which starts at location 4, requires only four bytes.

But, this is exactly the information we do not know for a polymorphic variable. The storage requirements for a polymorphic variable value are determined when the value is created at run time, and can even change during the course of execution. Recall the classes shown in Figure 11.1, and the memory requirements for the method main in the sample program described earlier. Here the variable form, which is declared as holding a Shape, can at one moment be holding a circle, at another a square, and so on. Both the subclasses add more data fields that are not found as part of the parent class. Thus the translator cannot know at compile time exactly how much memory will be required to hold the variable form.

In Java the solution to this problem is that objects are not stored on the activation record stack but are instead stored on the *heap*. A heap is an alternative memory-management system, one that is not tied to method entry and exit. Instead, memory is allocated on the heap when explicitly requested (to create a new object, using the new operator) and is freed, and recycled, when no longer needed. At run time, when the memory is requested, the Java system knows precisely how much memory is required to hold a value. In this fashion the Java language avoids the need to predict, at compile time, the amount of memory that will be needed at run time.

The code generated by the compiler, however, must still be able to access variables through numeric offsets, even though the actual heap addresses will not be known until run time. The solution to this dilemma is to use one level of indirection. Local variables are represented on the stack as pointer values. The size of a pointer is known at compile time and is independent of the size of the object it points to. This pointer field is filled when an object is created.

It is said that the programming language Java has no pointers. This is true as far as the language the programmer sees is concerned. But ironically, this is only possible because *all* object values are, in fact, represented internally by pointers.

11.2.1   *An Alternative Technique*

It should be noted that the solution to this problem selected by the designers of Java is not the only possibility. This can be illustrated by considering the language C++, which uses an entirely different approach. C++ treats assignment of *variables* and assignment of *pointers* very differently.

The designers of C++ elected to store variable values on the stack. Thus, the memory allocated to a variable of type Shape is only large enough to hold a value of type Shape, not the additional fields added by the subclass Circle. During the process of assignment these extra fields are simply sliced off and discarded. Of course, the resulting value is then no longer a Circle. For this reason, when we try to execute a member function, such as the describe method, the code executed will be that associated with class Shape, not the value associated with class Circle, as in Java. The programmer who uses both C++ and Java should be aware of this subtle, but nevertheless important difference.

11.3 ASSIGNMENT

In Section 11.2 we saw why values in Java are most naturally maintained on the heap, rather than being held in the activation record stack. Because to the compiler the underlying "value" of a variable is simply a pointer into the heap, the most natural semantics for assignment simply copy this pointer value. In this manner, the right and left sides of an assignment statement end up referring to the same object. This is often termed *reference* semantics (sometimes also called *pointer* semantics). The consequences of this interpretation of assignment are subtle but are, again, a key point for Java programmers to remember. Suppose we create a simple class Box as follows:

```
public class Box {
    private int value;

    public Box () { value = 0; }
    public void setValue (int v) { value = v; }
    public int getValue () { return value; }
}
```

Now imagine that we create a new box, assign it to a variable x, and set the internal value to 7. We then assign the box held by x to another variable, named y. Since both x and y now hold non-null values of type Box, the programmer might assume that they are distinct. But, in fact, they are exactly the same box, as can be verified by changing the value held in the y box and printing the value held by the x box:

```
public class BoxTest {
    static public void main (String [ ] args) {

        Box x = new Box();
        x.setValue (7);      // set value of x

        Box y = x;      // assign y the same value as x
        y.setValue (11);      // change value of y

        System.out.println("contents of x " + x.getValue());
        System.out.println("contents of y " + y.getValue());
    }
}
```

The key observation is that the two variables, although assigned separate locations on the activation record stack, nevertheless point to the same location on the heap, as shown in Figure 11.3.

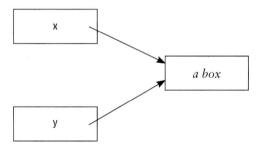

Figure 11.3 Two variables pointing to the same location.

11.3.1 *Clones*

If the desired effect of an assignment is indeed a copy, then the programmer must indicate this. One way would be to explicitly create a new value, copying the internal contents from the existing value:

```
// create new box with same value as x
Box y = new Box ( );
y.setValue(x.getValue( ));
```

If making copies is a common operation, it might be better to provide a method in the original class:

```
public class Box {
    .
    .
    .
    public Box copy( ) { // make copy of box
        Box b = new Box( );
        b.setValue (getValue( ));
        return b;
    }
    .
    .
    .
}
```

A copy of a box is then created by invoking the copy( ) method:

```
// create new box with same value as x
Box y = x.copy( );
```

There is no general mechanism in Java to copy an arbitrary object; however, the base class Object does provide a protected method named clone( ) that creates a bitwise copy of the receiver, as well as an interface Cloneable that represents objects that can be cloned. Several methods in the Java library require that arguments be values that are cloneable.

To create a class that is cloneable, the programmer must not only override the clone method to make it public but also explicitly indicate that the result satisfies the Cloneable interface. The following, for example, shows how to create a cloneable box.

```
public class Box implements Cloneable {
   private int value;

   public Box () { value = 0; }
   public void setValue (int v) { value = v; }
   public int getValue () { return value; }

   public Object clone () {
      Box b = new Box();
      b.setValue (getValue());
      return b;
   }
}
```

The clone method is declared as yielding a result of type Object. This property cannot be modified when the method is overridden. As a consequence, the result of cloning a value must be cast to the actual type before it can be assigned to a variable.

```
public class BoxTest {
   static public void main (String [ ] args) {

      Box x = new Box();
      x.setValue (7);

      Box y = (Box) x.clone(); // assign copy of x to y

      y.setValue (11); // change value of x

      System.out.println("contents of x " + x.getValue());
      System.out.println("contents of y " + y.getValue());
   }
}
```

As always, subtleties can trap the unwary programmer. Consider the object that is being held by our box. Imagine, instead of simply an integer, that it is something more complex, such as a Shape. Should a clone also clone this value, or just copy it? A copy results in two distinct boxes, but ones that share a common value. This is called a *shallow copy* (Figure 11.4).

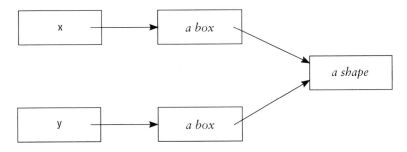

Figure 11.4   A shallow copy.

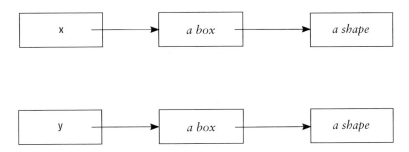

Figure 11.5   A deep copy.

Cloning the contents of the box (which must therefore be itself a type that is cloneable) results in two box values that are not only themselves distinct, but that point to values that are also distinct. This is termed a *deep copy* (Figure 11.5).

Whether a copy should be shallow or deep is something that must be determined by the programmer when overriding the clone interface.

11.3.2   *Parameters as a Form of Assignment*

Note that passing a variable as an argument to a member function can be considered to be a form of assignment, in that parameter passing, like assignment, results in the same value being accessible through two different names. Thus, the issues raised in Section 11.3 regarding assignment apply equally to parameter values. Consider the method sneaky in the following example, which modifies the value held in a box that is passed through a parameter value.

```
public class BoxTest {
    static public void main (String [ ] args) {
```

```
Box x = new Box( );
x.setValue (7);

sneaky (x);

System.out.println("contents of x " + x.getValue( ));
}


static void sneaky (Box y) {
    y.setValue (11); // change value of parameter
    }
}
```

A programmer who passes a box to this method, as shown in the main method, could subsequently see the resulting change in a local variable. In this example, the local variable x, has its value initially set to 7. The class sneaky(x) changes the value to 11, which is then printed out.

A Java programmer should always keep in mind that when a value is passed to a method, a certain degree of control over the variable is lost. In particular, the method is free to invoke any method applicable to the parameter type, which could result in the state of the variable being changed, as in this example.

11.4   EQUALITY TEST

For basic data types the concept of equality is relatively simple. The value 7 should clearly be equivalent to $3 + 4$, for example, because we think of integers as being unique entities—there is one and only one 7 value. This is true even when there are two syntactic representations for the same quantity, for example the ASCII value of the letter a is 141, and thus '\141' is the same as 'a'.

The situation becomes slightly more complicated when the two values being defined are not the same type. For example, should the value 2 (an integer constant) be considered equal to 2.0 (a floating-point constant)? The Java language says that the two values are equivalent in this case, since the integer value can be *converted* into a floating-point value, and the two floating values compared. Thus, all the following expressions will yield a true result.

```
7 == (3 + 4)
'a' == '\141'
2 == 2.0
```

When the concept of equality testing is expanded to include objects, the most natural interpretation becomes less obvious. In Section 11.3 it was argued that because objects are internally represented by pointers, the natural interpretation of assignment uses reference semantics. One interpretation of equality testing follows the same reasoning. That is, two objects can be considered equal if they are identically the same. This form of equality testing is often termed "testing object *identity*," and is the interpretation provided by the operator == and its inverse, the operator ! =. This can cause certain anomalies. For example, although 7 is equal to 3 + 4, the following code fragment will nevertheless show that an Integer value 7 is a distinct object from a different Integer object, even if it has the same value:

```
Integer x = new Integer(7);
Integer y = new Integer(3 + 4);
if (x == y)
    System.out.println("equivalent");
else
    System.out.println("not equivalent");
```

The Java compiler does apply type checking rules to the two arguments, which will help detect many programming errors. For example, although a numeric value can be compared to another numeric, a numeric cannot be compared to a different type of object (for example, a String). Two object values can be compared if they are the same type, or if the class of one can be converted into the class of the second. For example, a variable that was declared to be an instance of class Shape could be compared with a variable of type Circle, since a Circle would be converted into a Shape. A particular instance of the conversion rule is one of the more frequent uses of the == operator; namely, any object can be compared to the constant null, since the value null can be assigned to any object type.

Often object identity is not the relation one would like to test, and instead one is interested in object *equality*. This is provided by the method equals, which is defined by the base class Object and redefined by a number of classes. The following, for example, would return true using the equals method but would not be true using the == operator:

```
String a = new String("abc");
String b = new String("abc");
Integer c = new Integer(7);
Integer d = new Integer(3 + 4);
if (a.equals(b))
    System.out.println("strings are equal");
if (c.equals(d))
    System.out.println("integers are equal");
```

Because the equals method is defined in class Object, it can be used with any object type. However, for the same reason, the argument is declared only as type Object. This means that any two objects can be compared for equality, even if there is no possible way for either to be assigned to the other:

```
if (a.equals(c)) // can never be true
    System.out.println("string equal to integer");
```

The developer of a class is free to override the equals operator and thereby allow comparison between objects of the same class. Since the argument is an Object it must first be tested to ensure it is the correct type. By convention, the value false is returned in cases where the type is not correct. The following, for example, would be how one could define a method to compare two instances of class Circle (Figure 11.1).

```
class Circle extends Shape {
    .
    :
    .

    public boolean equals (Object arg) {
        if (arg instanceof Circle) {
            // convert argument to circle
            Circle argc = (Circle) arg;
            if (radius == argc.radius)
                return true;   // just test radius
        }
        return false; // return false otherwise
    }
}
```

Because the type of the argument is not necessarily the same as the type of the receiver, unusual situations can occur if the programmer is not careful. For example, suppose we defined equals in class Shape from Figure 11.1 to test equality of the x and y values, but forgot to also override the method in class Square. It could happen in this situation that if we tried to compare a square and a circle, the comparison would be true one way and false the other.

```
Square s = new Square(10, 10, 5);
Circle c = new Circle(10, 10, 5);
if (s.equals(c)) // true, since method in shape is used
    System.out.println("square equal to circle");
if (c.equals(s)) // false, since method in circle is used
    System.out.println("circle equal to square");
```

When overriding the equals method the programmer should be careful to avoid this problem and should ensure that the resulting methods are both symmetric (if x is equal to y, then y is equal to x) and transitive (if x is equal to y and y is equal to z, then x is equal to z).

A good rule of thumb is to use == when testing numeric quantities, and when testing an object against the constant null. In all other situations the method equals should be used.

11.5 GARBAGE COLLECTION

In Section 11.2 it was argued that support for polymorphic variables naturally implies that values are allocated to the heap, rather than to the stack. Memory of any type is always a finite resource, which must be managed if a program is to avoid running out of storage. In order to prevent this problem, both stack-based and heap-based memory is recycled, with new memory requests being assigned the same locations as previous memory values that are no longer being used.

Unlike stack-based memory allocation, heap-based memory management is not tied to method activation, and is thus not automatically recovered when a method returns. This means an alternative mechanism must be introduced.

Two different approaches to the recovery of heap-based memory values are found in programming languages. In languages such as Object Pascal or C++, it is up to the programmer to explicitly indicate when a memory value is no longer being used and can therefore be reused to satisfy new memory requests. In Object Pascal, for example, this is accomplished by means of the statement dispose:

```
var
    aShape : Shape;
begin
    new (aShape); (* allocate a new shape *)
    .
    .
    .
    dispose (aShape); (* free memory used by variable *)
end.
```

In such languages, if an object is to be freed, it must be "owned" by some variable (the variable that will be the target for the free request). But Java values are simply references, and are shared equally by all variables that refer to the same value. If a programmer assigns a value to another variable, or passes the value as an argument, the programmer may no longer be aware of how many references a value might have.

Leaving to the programmer the responsibility for freeing memory in this situation exposes a program to a number of common errors, such as freeing the same memory location twice. Even more commonly, programmers avoid committing this error by simply never freeing memory, causing long-running programs to slowly degrade as they consume more and more memory resources.

For these reasons, the designers of Java elected a different approach. Rather than having the programmer indicate when a value is no longer needed, a run-time system is provided that periodically searches the memory being used by a program to discover which heap values are being accessed and, more importantly, which heap values are no longer being referenced by any variable and can therefore be recovered and recycled. This mechanism is known as the *garbage collection* system.

The use of a garbage collection system in Java is a compromise. The task of garbage collection does exact a toll in execution time. However, in return a garbage collection system greatly simplifies the programming process and eliminates several categories of common programming errors. For most programs, the improvements in reliability are well worth the execution time overhead.

11.6   Chapter Summary

The idea of a polymorphic variable is an extremely powerful concept, one we will explore in detail in later chapters. However, the decision to support the concept of a polymorphic variable raises a number of subtle and difficult issues in other aspects of the language. In this chapter we have investigated some of these, showing how inheritance alters the way the language must handle storage management, the concept of assignment, and the testing of two values for equality.

Study Questions

1. What is a polymorphic variable?

2. Given the class definitions shown in Figure 11.1, which of the following statements are legitimate in Java and why?

   ```
   Shape s = new Square(6, 8, 3);
   Circle c = new Square(10, 12, 4);
   ```

3. From the language implementation point of view, what are the two major categories of memory values?

4. How does the idea of a polymorphic variable conflict with the ability to determine memory requirements at compile time?

5. What does it mean to say that Java uses reference semantics for assignment of object values?

6. What does it mean to say that Java uses copy semantics for assignment of primitive data values?

7. What must a programmer do to create a class that supports the Cloneable interface?

8. What is the difference between a deep and shallow copy?

9. In what way is passing a parameter similar to assignment?

10. What is the difference between the == operator and the equals( ) method?

11. What task is being performed by the garbage collection system in the Java run-time library?

12. What are some advantages of a language that uses garbage collection? What are some disadvantages?

EXERCISES

1. Rewrite the Shape classes shown in Figure 11.1 so that they support the Cloneable interface.

2. Rewrite the class Box so that it also has a data field that refers to a Shape object. It should be cloneable in such a way that a deep-copy is created.

3. Rewrite the class Box so that it supports the equals method.

4. Rewrite the Shape classes so that they support the equals method.

5. The concepts of shallow and deep copy have a correspondance with the equals( ) method. Explain the ideas of shallow equals and deep equals, and give an implementation of each.

IV

Understanding Polymorphism

12 Polymorphism

The term *polymorphic* has Greek roots and means roughly "many forms." (*poly* = many, *morphos* = form. Morphos is related to the Greek god Morphus, who could appear to sleeping individuals in any form he wished and hence was truly polymorphic.) In biology, a polymorphic species is one, such as *Homo sapiens*, that is characterized by the occurrence of different forms or color types in individual organisms or among organisms. In chemistry, a polymorphic compound is one that can crystallize in at least two distinct forms, such as carbon, which can crystallize both as graphite and as diamond.

12.1 VARIETIES OF POLYMORPHISM

In object-oriented languages, polymorphism is a natural result of the *is-a* relationship and of the mechanisms of message passing, inheritance, and the concept of substitutability. One of the great strengths of the OOP approach is that these devices can be combined in a variety of ways, yielding a number of techniques for code sharing and reuse.

Pure polymorphism occurs when a single function can be applied to arguments of a variety of types. In pure polymorphism, there is one function (the code body) and a number of interpretations (different meanings). The other extreme occurs when we have a number of different functions (code bodies) all denoted by the same name—a situation known as *overloading* or sometimes *ad hoc polymorphism*. Between these two extremes are *overriding* and *deferred methods*.[1]

---

[1] Note that there is little agreement regarding terminology in the programming language community. In [Horowitz 1984], [Marcotty and Ledgard 1987], [MacLennan 1987], and [Pinson and Wiener 1988] for example, *polymorphism* is defined in a manner roughly equivalent to what we are here calling *overloading*. In [Sethi 1989] and [Meyer 1988] and in the functional programming languages community (such as [Wikström 1987] and [Milner, Tofte, and Harper 1990]), the term is reserved for what we are calling *pure polymorphism*. Other authors use the term for one, two, or all of the mechanisms described in this chapter. Two complete, but technically daunting, analyses are [Cardelli and Wegner 1985] and [Danforth and Tomlinson 1988].

12.2 POLYMORPHIC VARIABLES

With the exception of overloading, polymorphism in object-oriented languages is made possible only by the existence of *polymorphic variables* and the idea of substitutability. A polymorphic variable is one with many faces; that is, it can hold values of different types. Polymorphic variables embody the principle of substitutability. In other words, although there is an expected type for any variable, the actual type can be from any value that is a subtype of the expected type.

In dynamically bound languages (such as Smalltalk), all variables are potentially polymorphic—any variable can hold values of any type. In these languages the desired type is defined by a set of expected behaviors. For example, an algorithm may make use of an array value, expecting the subscripting operations to be defined for a certain variable; any type that defines the appropriate behavior is suitable. Thus, the user could define his or her own type of array (for example, a sparse array) and, if the array operations were implemented using the same names, use this new type with an existing algorithm.

In statically typed languages, such as Java, the situation is slightly more complex. Polymorphism occurs in Java through the difference between the declared (static) class of a variable and the actual (dynamic) class of the value the variable contains.

A good example of a polymorphic variable is the array allPiles in the Solitaire game presented in Chapter 9. The array was declared as maintaining a value of type CardPile, but in fact it maintains values from each of the different subclasses of the parent class. A message presented to a value from this array, such as display in the example code shown below, executes the method associated with the dynamic type of the variable and not that of the static class.

```
public class Solitaire {
    .
    .
    .
    static CardPile allPiles [ ];
    .
    .
    .

    public void paint(Graphics g) {
        for (int i = 0; i < 13; i++)
            allPiles[i].display(g);
    }
    .
    .
    .
}
```

12.3   OVERLOADING

We say a method name is *overloaded* if two or more function bodies are associated with it. Note that overloading is a necessary part of overriding, described in the next section, but the two terms are not identical and overloading can occur without overriding.

In overloading, it is the method *name* that is polymorphic—it has many forms. Another way to think of overloading and polymorphism is that there is a single abstract function that takes various types of arguments; the actual code executed depends on the arguments given. The fact that the compiler can often determine the correct method at compile time (in a strongly typed language) and the fact that it can therefore generate only a single code sequence are simply optimizations.

12.3.1   *Overloading Messages in Real Life*

In Chapter 1 we saw an example in which overloading occurred without overriding, when I wanted to surprise my friend with flowers for her birthday. One possible solution was to send the message sendFlowersTo to my local florist; another was to give the *same* message to my wife. Both my florist and my wife (an instance of class Spouse) would have understood the message, and both would have acted on it to produce a similar result. In a certain sense, I could have thought of sendFlowersTo as being one method understood by both my wife and my florist, but each would have used a different algorithm to respond to my request.

Note, in particular, that there was no inheritance involved in this example. The first common superclass for my wife and my florist was the category Human. But certainly the behavior sendFlowersTo was not associated with all humans. My dentist, for example, who is also a human, would have been very puzzled by the message.

12.3.2   *Overloading and Coercion*

As an example more closely tied to programming languages, suppose a programmer is developing a library of classes representing common data structures. A number of data structures can be used to maintain a collection of elements (sets, bags, dictionaries, arrays, and priority queues, for example), and these might all define a method, add, to insert a new element into the collection.

This situation—in which two totally separate functions are used to provide semantically similar actions for different data types—occurs frequently in all programming languages, not simply in object-oriented languages. Perhaps the most common example is the overloading of the addition operator, +. The code generated by a compiler for an integer addition is often radically different from the code generated for a floating-point addition, yet programmers tend to think of the operations as a single entity, the "addition" function.

In this example it is important to point out that overloading may not be the only activity taking place. A semantically separate operation, *coercion*, is also usually associated with arithmetic operations. It occurs when a value of one type is converted into one of a different type. If mixed-type arithmetic is permitted, the addition of two values may be interpreted in a number of different ways:

- There may be four different functions, corresponding to integer + integer, integer + real, real + integer, and real + real. In this case, there is overloading but no coercion.

- There may be two different functions for integer + integer and real + real. In integer + real and real + integer, the integer value is coerced by being changed into a real value. In this situation there is a combination of overloading and coercion.

- There may be only one function, for real + real addition. All arguments are coerced into being real. In this case there is coercion only, with no overloading.

12.3.3   *Overloading from Separate Classes*

Two different forms of overloading can be distinguished. One form occurs when the same method name is found in two or more classes that are not linked by inheritance. The second form occurs when two or more methods with the same name are found within one class definition. The latter form will be described in the next section.

A good example of overloading of the first type is the method isEmpty. This method is used to determine if an object is empty; however, the exact meaning of empty will differ depending upon circumstances. The message is understood by the classes Vector, Hashtable, and Rectangle. The first two are collection classes, and the message returns true when there are no elements in the collection. In the class Rectangle the message returns true if either the height or width of a rectangle is zero, and thus the rectangle has no area.

```
Rectangle r1 = new Rectangle ();
if (r1.isEmpty()) ...
```

Overloading Does Not Imply Similarity

There is nothing intrinsic to overloading that requires the methods associated with an overloaded name to have any semantic similarity. Consider a program that plays a card game, such as the Solitaire game we examined in Chapter 9. The method draw was used to draw the image of a card on the screen. In another application we might also have included a draw method for the pack of cards, that is, to draw a single card from the top of the deck. This draw method is not even remotely similar in semantics to the draw method for the single card, and yet they share the same name.

Note that this overloading of a single name with independent and unrelated meanings should *not* necessarily be considered bad style, and generally it will not contribute to confusion. In fact, the selection of short, clear, and meaningful names such as add, draw, and so on, contributes to ease of understanding and correct use of object-oriented components. It is far simpler to remember that you can add an element to a set than to recall that to do so requires invoking the addNewElement method, or, worse, that it requires calling the routine Set_Module_Addition_Method.

All object-oriented languages permit the occurrence of methods with similar names in unrelated classes. In this case the resolution of overloaded names is determined by observation of the class of the receiver for the message. Nevertheless, this does not mean that functions or methods can be written that take arbitrary arguments. The statically typed nature of Java still requires specific declarations of all names.

12.3.4   *Parametric Overloading*

Another style of overloading, in which procedures (or functions or methods) in the same context are allowed to share a name and are disambiguated by the number and type of arguments supplied, is called *parametric overloading*; it occurs in Java as well as in some imperative languages (such as Ada) and many functional languages. Parametric overloading is most often found in constructor methods. A new Rectangle, for example, can be created either with no arguments (generating a rectangle with size zero and northwest corner 0,0), with two integer arguments (a width and height), with four integer arguments (width, height, northwest corner), with a Point (the northwest corner, size is zero), with a Dimension (height and width, corner 0,0), or with both a Point and a Dimension.

```
Rectangle r1 = new Rectangle ();
Rectangle r2 = new Rectangle (6, 7);
Rectangle r3 = new Rectangle (10, 10, 6, 7);
Point p1 = new Point (10, 10);
Dimension d1 = new Dimension (6, 7);
Rectangle r4 = new Rectangle (p1);
Rectangle r5 = new Rectangle (d1);
Rectangle r6 = new Rectangle (p1, d1);
```

There are six different constructor methods in this class, all with the same name. The compiler decides which method to execute based on the number and type of arguments used with the method call.

Overloading is a necessary prerequisite to the other forms of polymorphism we will consider: overriding, deferred methods, and pure polymorphism. It is also often useful in reducing the "conceptual space," that is, in reducing the amount of information that the programmer must remember. Often, this reduction in programmer-memory space is just as significant as the reduction in computer-memory space permitted by code sharing.

12.4   OVERRIDING

In Chapter 8 we described the mechanics of overriding, so it is not necessary to repeat that discussion here. Recall, however, the following essential elements of the technique. In one class (typically an abstract superclass), a general method is defined for a particular message that is inherited and used by subclasses. In at least one subclass, however, a method with the same name is defined that hides access to the general method for instances of this class (or, in the case of refinement, subsumes access to the general method). We say the second method *overrides* the first.

Overriding is often transparent to the user of a class, and, as with overloading, frequently the two methods are thought of semantically as a single entity.

12.4.1   *Replacement and Refinement*

In Chapter 9 it was briefly noted that overriding can occur in two different forms. A method can *replace* the method in the parent class, in which case the code in the parent is not executed at all. Alternatively, the code from the child can be used to form a *refinement*, which combines the code from the parent and the child classes.

Normally, overridden methods use replacement semantics. If a refinement is desired, it can be constructed by explicitly invoking the parent method as a function. This is accomplished by using the pseudovariable super as the receiver in a message-passing expression. An example from the Solitaire program described in Chapter 9 showed this:

```
class DiscardPile extends CardPile {

   public void addCard (Card aCard) {
      if (! aCard.faceUp( ))
         aCard.flip( );
      super.addCard(aCard);
      }

   }
```

Constructors, on the other hand, *always* use refinement semantics. A constructor for a child class will always invoke the constructor for the parent class. This invocation will take place *before* the code for the constructor is executed. If

the constructor for the parent class requires arguments, the pseudovariable super
is used as if it were a method:

```
class DeckPile extends CardPile {

    DeckPile (int x, int y) {
            // first initialize parent
        super(x, y);
            // then create the new deck
            // first put them into a local pile
        for (int i = 0; i < 4; i++)
            for (int j = 0; j <= 12; j++)
                addCard(new Card(i, j));

            // then shuffle the cards
        Random generator = new Random( );
        for (int i = 0; i < 52; i++) {
            int j = Math.abs(generator.nextInt( )) % 52;
                // swap the two card values
            Object temp = thePile.elementAt(i);
            thePile.setElementAt(thePile.elementAt(j), i);
            thePile.setElementAt(temp, j);
        }
    }

}
```

When used in this fashion, the call on the parent constructor must be the first
statement executed. If no call on super is made explicitly and there exist two or
more overloaded forms of the constructor, the constructor with no arguments
(sometimes called the *default* constructor) will be the form used.

12.5 ABSTRACT METHODS

A method that is declared as *abstract* can be thought of as defining a method
that is *deferred*; it is specified in the parent class but must be implemented in a
descendent class. Interfaces can also be viewed as a method for defining deferred
classes. Both can be considered to be a generalization of overriding. In both
cases, the behavior described in a parent class is modified by the child class. In
an abstract method, however, the behavior in the parent class is essentially null,
a place holder, and *all* useful activity is defined as part of the code provided by
the child class.

One advantage of abstract methods is conceptual, in that their use allows
the programmer to think of an activity as associated with an abstraction at a

higher level than may actually be the case. For example, in a collection of classes representing geometric shapes, we can define a method to draw the shape in each of the subclasses Circle, Square, and Triangle. We could have defined a similar method in the parent class Shape, but such a method cannot, in actuality, produce any useful behavior since the class Shape does not have sufficient information to draw the shape in question. Nevertheless, the mere presence of this method permits the user to associate the concept *draw* with the single class Shape, and not with the three separate concepts Square, Triangle, and Circle.

There is a second, more practical reason for using abstract methods. In statically typed object-oriented languages, such as Java, a programmer is permitted to send a message to an object only if the compiler can determine that there is in fact a corresponding method that matches the message selector. Suppose the programmer wishes to define a polymorphic variable of class Shape that will, at various times, contain instances of each of the different shapes. Such an assignment is possible, according to our rule of substitutability; nevertheless, the compiler will permit the message draw to be used with this variable only if it can ensure that the message will be understood by any value that may be associated with the variable. Assigning a method to the class Shape effectively provides this assurance, even when the method in class Shape is never actually executed.

12.6   PURE POLYMORPHISM

Many authors reserve the term *polymorphism* (or *pure polymorphism*) for situations where one method can be used with a variety of arguments, and the term *overloading* for situations where multiple methods are all denoted by a single name.[2] Such facilities are not restricted to object-oriented languages. In Lisp or ML, for example, it is easy to write functions that manipulate lists of arbitrary elements; such functions are polymorphic, because the type of the argument is not known at the time the function is defined. The ability to form polymorphic functions is one of the most powerful techniques in object-oriented programming. It permits code to be written once, at a high level of abstraction, and to be tailored as necessary to fit a variety of situations. Usually, the programmer accomplishes this tailoring by sending further messages to the receiver for the method. These subsequent messages often are not associated with the class at the level of the polymorphic method, but rather are deferred methods defined in the lower classes.

---

[2] The extreme cases may be easy to recognize, but discovering the line that separates overloading from polymorphism can be difficult. In both Java and ML a programmer can define a number of functions, each having the same name, but which take different arguments. Is it overloading in Java because the various functions sharing the same name are not defined in one location, whereas in ML-style polymorphism they must all be bundled together under a single heading?

An example of pure polymorphism is the method valueOf, found in the class String. This method is used to generate a textual description of an object, and has roughly the following definition:

```
public class String {

    public static String valueOf (Object obj)
    {
        if (obj == null)
            return "null";
        return obj.toString();
    }
}
```

The method toString is defined in class Object and redefined in a large number of different subclasses. Each of these definitions of toString will have a slightly different effect; a Double will produce a textual representation of its numeric value, a Color will generate a string that describes the red, green, and blue values in the color, a Button will create a string representing the class name followed by a hexadecimal number that represents the location of the object in memory, and so on.

Because these various versions of toString produce a variety of different effects, the method valueOf will similarly produce a number of different results. This variety of effects is achieved despite the fact that there is only one definition of method valueOf.

The important defining characteristic of pure polymorphism, as opposed to overloading and overriding, is that there is one function with the given name, used with a variety of different arguments. Almost always, as in this case, the body of such an algorithm will make use of other forms of polymorphism, such as a polymorphic variable used as an argument, which in turn invokes an overridden method.

12.7 EFFICIENCY AND POLYMORPHISM

An essential point to note is that programming always involves compromises. In particular, programming with polymorphism involves compromises among ease of development and use, readability, and efficiency. In large part, efficiency has been already considered and dismissed; however, it would be remiss not to admit that it is an issue, however slight.

A method, such as the valueOf method described in the last section, that does not know the type of its arguments can seldom be as efficient as a method that has more complete information. Nevertheless, the advantages of rapid development and consistent application behavior and the possibilities of code reuse usually more than make up for any small losses in efficiency.

12.8 CHAPTER SUMMARY

Polymorphism is an umbrella term used to describe a variety of different mechanisms found in programming languages. In object-oriented languages the most important forms of polymorphism are tied to the polymorphic variable—a variable that can hold many different types of values. For example, overloading occurs when two or more functions share the same name. If these methods happen to be found in classes that have a parent class/child class relationship, then it is called overriding. If an overridden method is used with a polymorphic variable, then the particular method executed will be determined by the run-time value of the variable, not the compile-time declaration for the variable.

Other forms of polymorphism include overloading from independent classes, parametric overloading (overloading that is disambiguated by the types of arguments used in a function call), and abstract methods.

Note that the use of polymorphism tends to optimize program development time and reliability, at the cost of run-time efficiency. For most programs, the benefits far exceed the costs.

FURTHER READING

In the interests of completeness, it should be mentioned that there is at least one important style of polymorphism, found in other computer languages, that is not found in Java. A *generic* (sometimes called a template) is a technique that allows a class description to be parameterized with a type. In C++, for example, one could declare a class as follows:

```
template <class T> class box {
public:
    box (T init) { value = init; }
    T getValue( ) { return value; }
private
    T value;
};
```

The result is a "box of T", and not simply a box. To create such a value, one must also specify a type for the parameter value T:

```
box<int> aBox(5); // create a box with an integer
box<Shape> aBox(aCircle); // create a box with a circle
```

One important place where this mechanism is useful is in the creation of collection classes (see Chapter 19). A language with generics, for example, would allow one to declare a vector *of Cards*, rather than (as in Java) simply a vector of objects. The compiler can then verify that the collection contains only the indicated type of values. More importantly, the compiler can avoid the cast necessary in Java when an object is removed from a container.

A discussion of generics in relation to other forms of polymorphism can be found in [Budd 1997].

STUDY QUESTIONS

1. What does the term *polymorphic* mean in common usage?

2. What is a polymorphic variable?

3. How is the characterization of polymorphic variables different in dynamically typed languages than in statically typed languages?

4. What does it mean to say that a method name is overloaded?

5. What does it mean to say that a value has been coerced to a different type?

6. What is parametric overloading?

7. What is overriding, and how is it different from overloading?

8. What is the difference between overriding using replacement and overriding using refinement?

9. What is the default semantics for overriding for methods? For constructors?

10. What is an abstract method?

11. How is an abstract method denoted?

12. What characterizes pure polymorphism?

13. Why should a programmer not be overly concerned with the loss of efficiency due to the use of polymorphic programming techniques?

EXERCISES

1. Describe the various types of polymorphism found in the PinBall Game application presented in Chapter 7.

2. Describe the various types of polymorphism found in the Solitaire application presented in Chapter 9.

13 The AWT

Java's Abstract Windowing Toolkit, or AWT, is the portion of the Java run-time library that is involved with creating, displaying, and facilitating user interaction with window objects. The AWT is an example of a software *framework*. A framework is a way of structuring generic solutions to a common problem, using polymorphism as a means of creating specialized solutions for each new application. Thus, examining the AWT will illustrate how polymorphism is used in a powerful and dynamic fashion in the language Java.

13.1 THE AWT CLASS HIERARCHY

From the very first, we have said that class Frame represents the Java notion of an application window, a two-dimensional graphical surface that is shown on the display device and through which the user interacts with a computer program. All our applications have been formed by inheriting from Frame, overriding various methods, such as the paint method for repainting the window. In actuality, much of the behavior provided by class Frame is inherited from parent classes (see Figure 13.1). Examining each of these abstractions in turn will help illustrate the functioning of the Java windowing system, as well as illustrate the power of inheritance as a mechanism for code reuse and sharing.

The class Object is the parent class of all classes in Java. It provides the ability to compare two objects for equality, compute a hash value for an object, and determine the class of an object. Methods defined in class Object include the following:

equals (anObject)	Return true if object is equal to argument
getClass ( )	Return the class of an object
hashCode ( )	Return a hash value for an object
toString ( )	Return a string representation of an object

207

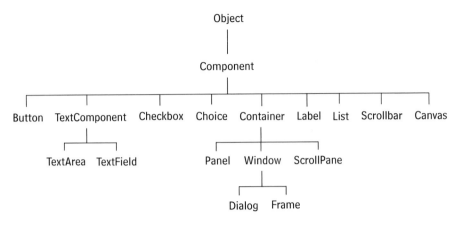

Figure 13.1 The AWT class hierarchy.

A Component is something that can be displayed on a two-dimensional screen and with which the user can interact. Attributes of a component include a size, a location, foreground and background colors, whether or not it is visible, and a set of listeners for events. Methods defined in class Component include the following:

setEnabled(boolean)	Enable/disable a component
setLocation(int,int), getLocation( )	Set and get component location
setSize(int,int), getSize( )	Set and get size of component
setVisible(boolean)	Show or hide the component
setForeground(Color), getForegound( )	Set and get foreground colors
setBackground(Color), getBackground( )	Set and get background colors
setFont(Font), getFont( )	Set and get font
repaint(Graphics)	Schedule component for repainting
paint(Graphics)	Repaint component appearance
addMouseListener(MouseListener)	Add a mouse listener for component
addKeyListener(KeyListener)	Add a keypress listener for component

Besides frames, other types of components include buttons, checkboxes, scroll bars, and text areas.

A Container is a type of component that can nest other components within it. A container is the way that complex graphical interfaces are constructed. A

Frame is a type of Container, so it can hold objects such as buttons and scroll bars. When more complicated interfaces are necessary, a Panel (another type of container) can be constructed, which might hold, for example, a collection of buttons. Since this Panel is both a Container and a Component, it can be inserted into the Frame. A container maintains a list of the components it manipulates, as well as a layout manager to determine how the components should be displayed. Methods defined in class Container include the following:

setLayout (LayoutManager)	Set layout manager for display
add (Component), remove (Component)	Add or remove component from display

A Window is a type of Container. A window is a two-dimensional drawing surface that can be displayed on an output device. A window can be stacked on top of other windows and can be moved either to the front or back of the visible windows. Methods defined in class Window include the following:

show( )	Make the window visible
toFront( )	Move window to front
toBack( )	Move window to back

Finally, a Frame is a type of window with a title bar, a menu bar, a border, a cursor, and other properties. Methods defined in class Frame include:

setTitle(String), getTitle( )	Set or get title
setCursor(int)	Set cursor
setResizable( )	Make the window resizable
setMenuBar(MenuBar)	Set menu bar for window

If we consider a typical application, such as the CannonWorld application of Chapter 6, we see that it uses methods from a number of different levels of the class hierarchy:

setTitle(String)	Inherited from class Frame
setSize(int, int)	Inherited from class Component
show( )	Inherited from class Window
repaint( )	Inherited from class Component
paint( )	Inherited from Component, overridden in application class

The power of the AWT, indeed the power of any framework, comes through the use of a polymorphic variable. When the method show in class Window is invoked, it calls the method setVisible in class Component. This method calls

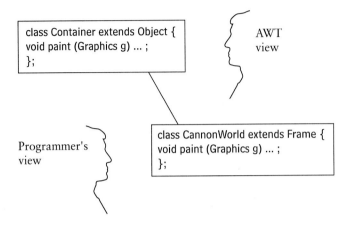

```
class Container extends Object {
void paint (Graphics g) ... ;
};
```

AWT
view

Programmer's
view

```
class CannonWorld extends Frame {
void paint (Graphics g) ... ;
};
```

Figure 13.2   Two views of a component.

repaint, which in turn calls paint. The code for the algorithm used by setVisible and repaint resides in class Component. When it is being executed, the framework "thinks" that it is dealing only with an instance of Component. However, in actuality the method paint that is being executed is the version that has been overridden in the application class. Thus, there are two views of the method being executed, as described in Figure 13.2.

The code in the parent classes (Component, Container, Window, and Frame) can all be written without reference to any particular application. Thus, this code can be easily carried from one application to the next. To specialize the design framework to a new application it is only necessary to override the appropriate methods (such as paint or event listeners) to define application-specific behavior. Thus, the combination of inheritance, overriding, and polymorphism permits design and software reuse on a grand scale.

13.2   THE LAYOUT MANAGER

The idea of a layout manager, which is the technique used by the AWT to assign the locations of components within a container, is an excellent illustration of the combination of polymorphic techniques of composition and inheritance. The layout manager is charged with assigning positions on the surface of a container to the complements held in that container. There are a variety of standard layout managers, each of which will place components in slightly different ways. The programmer developing a graphical user interface creates an instance of a layout manager and hands it to a container. Generally, the task of creation is the only direct interaction the programmer will have with the layout manager, as thereafter all commands will be handled by the container itself.

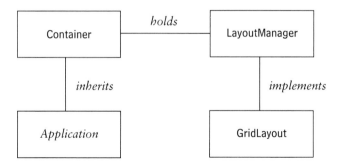

Figure 13.3   Relationships between Layout Manager Components

The connections between the application class, the container, and the layout manager illustrate yet again the many ways that inheritance, composition, and interfaces can be combined (Figure 13.3). The application class may inherit from the container (as is usually the case when an application is formed using inheritance from class Frame) or it may hold the container as a component. The container itself, however, holds the layout manager as a data field, as part of the internal state of the container. But in actual fact, the variable that holds the layout manager is polymorphic. While the Container thinks that it is maintaining a value of type LayoutManager, in fact it will be holding a value from some other type, such as GridLayout, that is implementing the LayoutManager interface.

There are three different mechanisms at work here: inheritance, composition, and implementation of an interface. Each is serving a slightly different purpose. Inheritance is the *is-a* relation that links the application class to the parent window class. This allows the code written in the AWT class Window to perform application-specific actions, by invoking methods in the application class that override methods in the parent class (paint( ), for example). The fact that composition is used to link the container with the layout manager makes the link between these two items very dynamic—the programmer can easily change the type of layout manager being employed by a container. This dynamic behavior is very difficult to achieve using inheritance alone, since the inheritance relationship between a parent and child is established at compile time. Finally, the fact that LayoutManager is simply an interface; and as well as the fact that various different classes of objects implement this interface, means that the programmer is free to develop alternative layout managers using a wide variety of techniques. (This freedom would be much more constrained if, for example, LayoutManager was a class that alternative layout managers needed to extend.)

13.2.1   *Layout Manager Types*

There are five standard types of layout managers: BorderLayout, GridLayout, Card-Layout, FlowLayout, and GridBagLayout. The BorderLayout manager can manage no

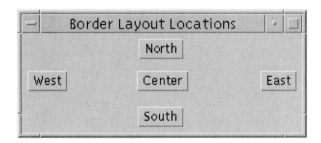

Figure 13.4   Locations recognized by Border Layout Manager.

more than five different components. This is the default layout manager for applications constructed by subclassing from Frame. The five locations are shown in Figure 13.4. They correspond to the left and right, top and bottom, and center of the display. Not all five locations need be filled. If a location is not used, the space is allocated to the remaining components.

When a border layout manager is employed, the first argument in the add method is used to specify which position a component is filling in a collection:

```
add("North", new Button("quit"));
add("Center", colorField);
```

The next most common type of layout is the GridLayout. The manager for this layout creates a rectangular array of components, each occupying the same size portion of the screen. Using arguments with the constructor, the programmer specifies the number of rows and the number of columns in the grid. Two additional integer arguments can be used to specify a horizontal and vertical space between the components. An example of a panel formatted using a GridLayout is shown in Figure 13.12. The section of code for that application that creates the layout manager is as follows:

```
Panel p = new Panel( );
   // make a 4 by 4 grid,
   // with 3 pixels between each element
p.setLayout (new GridLayout(4, 4, 3, 3));

p.add (new ColorButton(Color.black, "black"));
p.add (new ColorButton(Color.blue, "blue"));
```

A FlowLayout manager places components in rows left to right, top to bottom. Unlike the layout created by a GridLayout manager, the components managed by a flow layout manager need not all have the same size. When a component cannot be completely placed on a row without truncation, a new row is created. The flow manager is the default layout manager for the class Panel (as opposed to Frame, where the default manager is a BorderLayout).

A CardLayout manager stacks components vertically. Only one component is visible at any one time. The components managed by a card layout manager can be named (using the string argument to the add method). Subsequently, a named component can be made the visible component. This is one of the few instances where the programmer would have direct interaction with the layout manager.

```
CardLayout lm = new CardLayout( );
Panel p = new Panel (lm);
p.add ("One", new Label ("Number One"));
p.add ("Two", new Label ("Number Two"));
p.add ("Three", new Label ("Number Three"));
  .
  .
  .
lm.show (p, "Two"); // show component "Two"
```

The most general type of layout manager is the GridBagLayout manager. This manager allows the programmer to create a nonuniform grid of squares, and place components in various positions within each square. However, the details of the use of this manager are complex and will not be described here.

13.3 USER INTERFACE COMPONENTS

The variety of user interface components in the Java AWT library are again a good illustration of the power of polymorphism provided both through inheritance and interfaces. With the exception of menu bars, all the user interface components are subclasses of the parent class Component (Figure 13.1). Containers assume only that the elements they will hold are instances of class Component. In fact, the values they maintain are polymorphic and represent more specialized values, such as buttons or scroll bars. Thus, the design of the user interface construction system depends upon the mechanisms of inheritance, polymorphism, and substitutability.

13.3.1 *Labels*

The simplest type of user interface component is a Label. A label has only the text it will display. It will display as much of the text as it can in the area it is given.

```
Label lab = new Label("score: 0 to 0");
add ("South", lab); // put label on bottom of window
```

Unlike other components, a label does not respond to any type of event, such as a mouse click or a key press. However, the text of the label can be changed using the method setText(String), and the current text of a label can be retrieved using getText( ).

13.3.2 *Button*

A Button is a labeled component, usually represented by a rounded box, that can respond to user interaction. As we have seen in earlier programs, interaction with a button is achieved by attaching an ActionListener object to the button. The ActionListener object is then notified when the button is pressed.

```
Button b = new Button ("do it!");
b.addActionListener (new DoIt( ));
    .
    .
    .
private class DoIt implements ActionListener {
   public void actionPerformed (ActionEvent e) {
      // whatever DoIt does
         .
         .
         .
   }
}
```

A useful technique is to combine the button object and the button listener in one new class. This new class both subclasses from the original Button class and implements the ActionListener interface. For example, in the case study presented in Section 13.5, we create a set of buttons for different colors. Each button holds a color value, and when pressed it invokes a method using the color as argument. This class is written as follows:

```
private class ColorButton
      extends Button implements ActionListener {
   private Color ourColor;

   public ColorButton (Color c, String name) {
      super (name); // create the button
      ourColor = c; // save the color value
      addActionListener (this); // add ourselves as listener
   }

   public void actionPerformed (ActionEvent e) {
         // set color for middle panel
      setFromColor (ourColor);
   }
}
```

Notice how the object registers itself as a listener for button actions. The pseudovariable this is used when an object needs to denote itself. When pressed, the button will invoke the method actionPerformed, which will then invoke the method setFromColor that is found in the surrounding class.

We can even take this technique one step further, and define a generic ButtonAdapter class that is both a button and a listener. The actions of the listener will be encapsulated by an abstract method, which must be implemented by a subclass:

```
abstract class ButtonAdapter
     extends Button implements ActionListener {
  public ButtonAdapter (String name) {
    super (name);
    addActionListener (this);
  }

  public void actionPerformed (ActionEvent e) { pressed(); }

  public abstract void pressed ();
}
```

To create a button using this abstraction, the programmer must create a subclass and override the method pressed. This, however, can be done easily using a class definition expression (see Section 10.5.3). The following, for example, creates a button that when pressed will halt the application.

```
Panel p = new Panel();

p.add (new ButtonAdapter("Quit"){
   public void pressed () { System.exit(0); }});
```

13.3.3 *Canvas*

A Canvas is a simple type of component, having only a size and the ability to be a target for drawing operations. Among other uses, the class Canvas is often subclassified to form new types of components. An illustration of one use of a Canvas occurs in the discussion of the class ScrollPane (Section 13.4.1).

13.3.4 *Scroll Bars*

A ScrollBar is a slider, used to specify integer values over a wide range. Scroll bars can be displayed in either a horizontal or a vertical direction. The maximum and minimum values can be specified, as well as the line increment (the amount the scroll bar will move when it is touched in the ends), and the page increment (the amount it will move when it is touched in the background area between the slider and the end). Like a button, interaction is provided for a scroll bar by defining a listener that will be notified when the scroll bar is modified.

The case study at the end of this chapter uses a technique similar to the one described earlier in the section on buttons. Figure 13.12 offers a a snapshot of this application, which includes three vertical scroll bars. The class ColorBar represents a scroll bar for maintaining colors. The constructor for the class creates a vertical scroll bar with an initial value of 40 and a range between 0 and 255. The background color for the scroll bar is set using a given argument. Finally, the object itself is made a listener for scroll bar events. When the scroll bar is changed, the method adjustmentValueChanged will be executed. Typically, within this method the current value of the scroll bar would be accessed using getValue(). In this particular application, a bank of three scroll bars will be created, and the value of all three will be recovered in a shared method named setFromBar.

```
private class ColorBar
      extends Scrollbar implements AdjustmentListener {
   public ColorBar (Color c) {
      super (Scrollbar.VERTICAL, 40, 0, 0, 255);
      setBackground (c);
      addAdjustmentListener (this);
   }

   public void adjustmentValueChanged (AdjustmentEvent e) {
      // method setFromBar will get scroll bar
      // value using getValue();
      setFromBar ();
   }
}
```

13.3.5   Text Components

A text component is used to display editable text. There are two varieties of text components, TextField and TextArea. The first is a fixed-size block, while the second uses scroll bars to display a larger block of text, not all of which might be viewable at any one time. Figure 13.5 illustrates these two types of items.

The text in a text component can be set or accessed by the program using the methods setText(String) and getText(). Additional text can be added to the text area using the method append(String). Various other methods can be used to indicate whether or not the text is editable and to select a subportion of the text. A TextListener can be attached to a text component. The listener must implement the TextListener interface:

```
interface TextListener extends EventListener {
   public void textValueChanged (TextEvent e);
   }
```

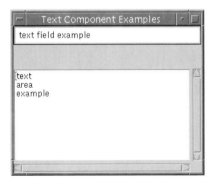

Figure 13.5   A window with two text components.

Figure 13.6   A window with a checkbox.

13.3.6   *Checkbox*

A Checkbox is a component that maintains and displays a labeled binary state. The state described by a checkbox can be either on or off. The current state of the checkbox can be set or tested by the programmer. A checkbox is typically used in an application to indicate a binary (on/off, yes/no) choice (see Figure 13.6).

Both the label and the state of the checkbox can be set by the programmer, using the methods getLabel, setLabel, getState, and setState. Changing the state of a checkbox creates an ItemEvent, that is registered with any ItemListener objects. The following simple application illustrates the use of these methods:

```
class CheckTest extends Frame {
   private Checkbox cb = new Checkbox ("the checkbox is off");

   public static void main (String [ ] args)
      { CheckTest world = new CheckTest( ); world.show( ); }

   public CheckTest ( ) {
      setTitle("Check box example"); setSize(300, 70);
      cb.addItemListener (new CheckListener( ));
      add ("Center", cb);
      }
```

```
    private class CheckListener implements ItemListener {

        public void itemStateChanged (ItemEvent e) {
            if (cb.getState( ))
                cb.setLabel ("The checkbox is on");
            else cb.setLabel ("The checkbox is off");
        }
    }
}
```

13.3.7   *Checkbox Groups, Choices, and Lists*

Three types of interface components are typically employed to allow the user to select one item from a large number of possibilities. The first is a group of connected checkboxes with the property that only one can be set at any one time. Such a collection is sometimes called a *radio button* group, since their behavior is similar to the way buttons in car radios work. The second form is termed a Choice. A Choice object displays only one selection, but when the user clicks the mouse in the selection area, a pop-up menu appears that allows the choice to be changed to a different selection. A third possibility is termed a List. A List is similar to a Choice, however several possibilities out of the range can be displayed at one time.

Figure 13.7 illustrates all three possibilities. The code to produce this example is shown in Figure 13.8.

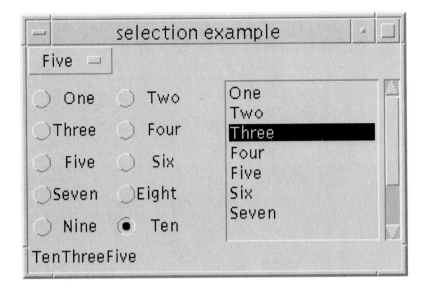

Figure 13.7   Three selection possibilities: radio button Checkbox group, Choice object, and a List.

```
class ChoiceTest extends Frame {
    public static void main (String [ ] args)
        { ChoiceTest world = new ChoiceTest( ); world.show( ); }

    private String [ ] choices = {"One", "Two", "Three", "Four",
        "Five", "Six", "Seven", "Eight", "Nine", "Ten"};
    private Label display = new Label( );
    private Choice theChoice = new Choice( );
    private List theList = new List( );
    private CheckboxGroup theGroup = new CheckboxGroup( );
    private ItemListener theListener = new ChoiceListener( );

    public ChoiceTest ( ) {
        setTitle ("selection example ");
        setSize (300, 300);
        for (int i = 0; i < 10; i++) {
            theChoice.addItem (choices[i]);
            theList.addItem (choices[i]);
        }
        theChoice.addItemListener (theListener);
        theList.addItemListener (theListener);
        add ("West", makeCheckBoxes( )); add ("North", theChoice);
        add ("East", theList); add ("South", display);
    }

    private class ChoiceListener implements ItemListener {
        public void itemStateChanged (ItemEvent e) {
            display.setText (theGroup.getSelectedCheckboxGroup( ).getLabel( )
                + theList.getSelectedItem( ) + theChoice.getSelectedItem( ));
        }
    }

    private Panel makeCheckBoxes( ) {
        Panel p = new Panel (new GridLayout(5,2));
        for (int i = 0; i < 10; i++) {
            Checkbox cb = new Checkbox(choices[i], theGroup, false);
            cb.addItemListener (theListener); p.add (cb); }
        return p;
    }
}
```

Figure 13.8   Alternative ways to display choices.

A Checkbox group should be used when the number of alternatives is small. A choice or a list should be used if the number of alternatives is five or more. A choice takes up less space in the display, but makes it more difficult to view all the alternatives.

To create a Choice or a List object, the programmer specifies each alternative using the method addItem. An ItemListener can be attached to the object. When a selection is made, the listener will be informed using the method item-StateChanged. The text of the selected item can be recovered using the method getSelectedItem.

To structure a group of checkboxes as a group, the programmer first creates a CheckboxGroup. This value is then passed as an argument to each created checkbox, along with a third argument that indicates whether or not the checkbox should be initially active. If more than one button is made active (as here) only the last button will remain active. The current checkbox can be accessed using the method getSelectedCheckbox.

As a checkbox group is constructed out of several components, it is almost always laid out on a Panel. The Panel is then placed as a single element in the original layout. This is shown in Figure 13.8. Here a 5 by 2 grid is used as layout for the 10 checkboxes.

13.4   PANELS

A Panel is a Container that acts like a Component. A panel represents a rectangular region of the display. Each panel holds its own layout manager, which can differ from the layout manager for the application display. Items can be inserted into the panel. The panel, as a single unit, is then inserted into the application display.

The use of a panel is illustrated by the application described in Figure 13.8. Here the method makeCheckBoxes creates a panel to hold the 10 checkboxes that make up the checkbox group. This panel is structured, using a GridLayout as a 5 by 2 element matrix. This group of 10 components can then be treated as a single element, and is placed on the left side of the application layout.

More examples of the use of panels will be provided by the application that will be described in the next section. A snapshot of the window for this application is shown in Figure 13.12. The three scroll bars on the left are placed on a panel. This panel is laid out using a BorderLayout manager. The method to create and return this panel is described as follows:

```
private Panel makeScrollBars ( ) {
    Panel p = new Panel( );
    p.setLayout (new BorderLayout( ));
    p.add("West", redBar);
    p.add("Center", greenBar);
```

```
      p.add("East", blueBar);
      return p;
   }
```

The panel returned as the result of this method is then placed on the left side of the application window.

13.4.1 ScrollPane

A ScrollPane is in many ways similar to a Panel. Like a panel, it can hold another component. (See Figure 13.9.) However, a ScrollPane can only hold one component, and it does not have a layout manager. If the size of the component being held is larger than the size of the ScrollPane itself, scroll bars will be automatically generated to allow the user to move the underlying component.

We illustrate the use of a ScrollPane with a simple test program, shown in Figure 13.10. The application window in this program will be set to 300 by 300 pixels, but a scroll pane is created that holds a canvas that has been sized to 1000 by 1000 pixels. Scroll bars will therefore be added automatically that allow the user to see portions of the underlying canvas. As mouse events are detected by the canvas, points will be added to a Polygon. To paint the application window, the canvas simply draws the polygon values.

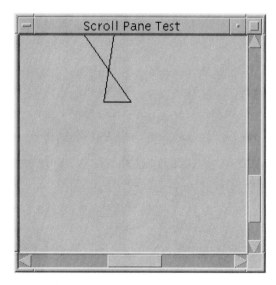

Figure 13.9 A ScrollPane test.

```
class BigCanvas extends Frame {
   public static void main ( String [ ] args) {
      BigCanvas world = new BigCanvas( );
      world.show( );
   }

   private Polygon poly = new Polygon( );
   private Canvas cv = new Canvas( );

   public BigCanvas( ) {
      setSize (300, 300);
      setTitle ("Scroll Pane Test");
         // make canvas larger than window
      cv.setSize (1000, 1000);
      cv.addMouseListener (new MouseKeeper( ));
         // make scroll pane to manage canvas
      ScrollPane sp = new ScrollPane( );
      sp.add(cv);
      add("Center", sp);
   }

   public void paint (Graphics g) {
         // redraw canvas
      Graphics gr = cv.getGraphics( );
      gr.drawPolygon (poly);
   }

   private class MouseKeeper extends MouseAdapter {
      public void mousePressed (MouseEvent e) {
         poly.addPoint (e.getX( ), e.getY( ));
         repaint( );
      }
   }
}
```

Figure 13.10   Test program for scrollpanes.

13.5 CASE STUDY: A COLOR DISPLAY

A simple test program will illustrate how panels and layout managers are used in developing user interfaces. The application will also illustrate the use of scroll bars and the use of methods provided by the class Color. Finally, we can also use this program to illustrate how nested classes can be employed to combine the actions of creating a new graphical component (such as a button or a slider) and listening for actions relating to the component.

The class ColorTest (Fig. 13.11) creates a window to display color values. The window (Fig. 13.12) is divided into four regions. The regions are managed by the default layout manager for class Frame, which is a value of type BorderLayout.

```
class ColorTest extends Frame {
    static public void main (String [ ] args)
        { ColorTest world = new ColorTest( ); world.show( ); }

    private TextField colorDescription = new TextField( );
    private Panel colorField = new Panel( );
    private Color current = Color.black;
    private Scrollbar redBar = new ColorBar(Color.red);
    private Scrollbar greenBar = new ColorBar(Color.green);
    private Scrollbar blueBar = new ColorBar(Color.blue);

    public ColorTest( ) {
        setTitle ("color test"); setSize (400, 600);
        add("North", colorDescription);
        add("East", makeColorButtons( ));
        add("Center", colorField);
        add("West", makeScrollBars( ));
        setFromColor (current);
    }

    private void setFromColor (Color c) {
        current = c; colorField.setBackground (current);
        redBar.setValue(c.getRed( )); greenBar.setValue(c.getGreen( ));
        blueBar.setValue(c.getBlue( ));
        colorDescription.setText(c.toString( ));
    }

    private void setFromBar ( ) {
        int r = redBar.getValue( ); int g = greenBar.getValue( );
        int b = blueBar.getValue( ); setFromColor (new Color(r, g, b));
    }

    private Panel makeColorButtons ( ) { ... }
    private Panel makeScrollBars ( ) { ... }
private class BrightenButton extends Button implements ActionListener ...
private class ColorButton extends Button implements ActionListener ...
private class ColorBar extends Scrollbar implements AdjustmentListener ...
}
```

Figure 13.11   The class ColorTest.

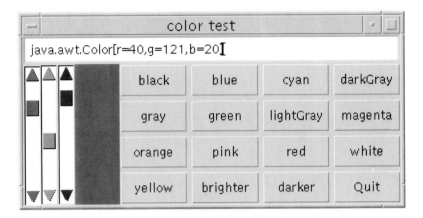

Figure 13.12 Snapshot of ColorTest application.

At the top (the "north" side) is a text region, a component of type TextField, that describes the current color. To the left (the "west" region) is a trio of sliders that can be used to set the red, green, and blue values. To the right (the "east" region) is a 4 by 4 bank of 16 buttons. These are constructed on a Panel that is organized by a GridLayout manager. Thirteen of the buttons represent the predefined color values. Two more represent the actions of making a color brighter and darker. The final button will halt the application. Finally, in the middle will be a square panel that represents the specified color.

The class ColorTest holds six data fields. The first represents the text field at the top of the page. The second represents the color panel in the center. The third represents the current color of this center panel. The remaining three represent the three scrollbars that will be placed in the panel on the left.

The three sliders make use of the class ColorBar described earlier in Section 13.3.4. The argument used with the constructor for each class is the color to be used in painting the buttons and background for the scroll bar. You will recall that when adjusted, the scroll bar will invoke its listener, which will execute the method adjustmentValueChanged. This method will then execute the method setFromBar.

A method makeScrollBars, used to create the panel that holds the three scroll bars, was described earlier in Section 13.4.

The idea of combining inheritance and implementation of an interface is used in creating the buttons that represent the 13 predefined colors. Each instance of ColorButton, shown earlier in Section 13.3.2, both extends the class Button and implements the ActionListener interface. When the button is pressed, the method setFromColor will be used to set the color of the middle panel using the color stored in the button.

The class BrightenButton is slightly more complex. An index value is stored with the button. This value indicates whether the button represents the "brighten" button or the "darken" button. When pressed, the current color is modified by the appropriate method, and the new value used to set the current color.

```
private class BrightenButton
        extends Button implements ActionListener {
    private int index;
    public BrightenButton (int i) {
        super ( i == 0 ? "brighter" : "darker");
        index = i;
        addActionListener(this);
    }

    public void actionPerformed (ActionEvent e) {
        if (index == 0)
            setFromColor (current.brighter( ));
        else
            setFromColor (current.darker( ));
    }
}
```

A panel is used to hold the 16 button values. In this case the layout is described by a 4 by 4 grid pattern. Thirteen represent the predefined buttons. Two represent the brighter and darker buttons. And the final creates a button that when pressed exits the application.

```
private Panel makeColorButtons ( ) {
    Panel p = new Panel( );
    p.setLayout (new GridLayout(4,4,3,3));
    p.add (new ColorButton(Color.black, "black"));
    p.add (new ColorButton(Color.blue, "blue"));
    p.add (new ColorButton(Color.cyan, "cyan"));
    p.add (new ColorButton(Color.darkGray, "darkGray"));
    p.add (new ColorButton(Color.gray, "gray"));
    p.add (new ColorButton(Color.green, "green"));
    p.add (new ColorButton(Color.lightGray, "lightGray"));
    p.add (new ColorButton(Color.magenta, "magenta"));
    p.add (new ColorButton(Color.orange, "orange"));
    p.add (new ColorButton(Color.pink, "pink"));
    p.add (new ColorButton(Color.red, "red"));
    p.add (new ColorButton(Color.white, "white"));
    p.add (new ColorButton(Color.yellow, "yellow"));
    p.add (new BrightenButton(0));
    p.add (new BrightenButton(1));
```

```
    p.add (new ButtonAdapter("Quit"){
       public void pressed( ) { System.exit(0); }});
    return p;
}
```

13.6 DIALOGS

A Dialog is a special purpose window that is displayed for a short period of time during the course of execution, disappearing thereafter. Dialogs are often used to notify the user of certain events, or to ask simple questions. A dialog must always be attached to an instance of Frame, and disappears automatically when the frame is hidden (such as when the application halts).

Dialog windows can be modal or nonmodal. A modal dialog demands a response from the user, and it prevents the user from performing any further action until the dialog is dismissed. A nonmodal dialog, sometimes called a modeless dialog, can be ignored by the user. The processing of actions for a nonmodal dialog is often placed in a separate Thread (see Chapter 20), so that the actions produced by the dialog will not disrupt the continuing processing of the rest of the application. Whether or not a dialog is modal is determined when the dialog is created. The two arguments used in the constructor for the dialog are the application Frame and a Boolean value that is true if the dialog is modal.

```
// create a new nonmodal dialog in current application
Dialog dig = new Dialog (this, false);
```

Because a Dialog is a type of Window, graphical components can be placed in the dialog area, just as in a Frame or Panel. The default layout manager for a dialog is BorderLayout, the same as with Frame.

The most common methods used with a dialog are not actually defined in the class Dialog but are inherited from parent classes. These include the following:

setSize(int, int)	Set window size
show( )	Display window
setVisible(false)	Remove window from display
setTitle(String), getTitle( )	Set or get title of window

For modal dialogs, the show method does not return until the dialog is dismissed. Such dialogs must therefore invoke the setVisible(false) method sometime during their processing.

13.6.1 Example Program for Dialogs

An example program will illustrate the creation and manipulation of dialogs. The application shown in Figure 13.14, on page 228, creates a window with

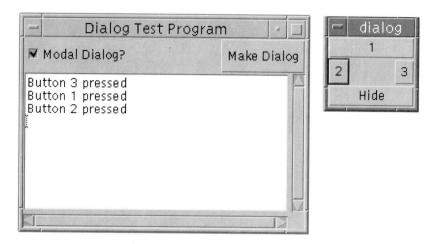

Figure 13.13   Dialog example window.

a checkbox, a button, and a text area. The application window, as well as an example dialog box window, is shown in Figure 13.13. The checkbox allows the user to specify whether a modal or modeless dialog box should be created. The button creates the dialog, while the text area records button presses performed by the dialog.

The method makeDialog creates the dialog box. The size of the box is set at 100 by 100 pixels, and four buttons are placed on the box. Three buttons simply type text into the display when pressed, while the last button will hide the dialog. For a modal dialog, hiding the dialog is the same as dismissing the dialog box, and it returns control to the method that created the dialog.

13.7   THE MENU BAR

Although a menu bar is a graphical component, it is not declared as a subclass of Component. This is because platforms differ in how they handle menu bars, so the implementation must be more constrained. Both menu bars and menus act like containers. A menu bar contains a series of menus, and each menu contains a series of menu items.

An instance of *MenuBar* can be attached to a Frame using the method set-MenuBar:

```
          .
          .
          .
MenuBar bar = new MenuBar( );
setMenuBar (bar);
          .
          .
          .
```

```
class DialogTest extends Frame {
   static public void main (String [ ] args)
      { DialogTest world = new DialogTest( ); world.show( ); }

   private TextArea display = new TextArea( );
   private Checkbox cb = new Checkbox("Modal Dialog?");

   public DialogTest( ) {
      setTitle ("Dialog Test Program");
      setSize (300, 220);

      add ("West", cb);
      add ("East", new Makebutton( ));
      add ("South", display);
   }

   private class Makebutton extends ButtonAdapter {
      public Makebutton ( ) { super ("Make Dialog"); }
      public void pressed ( ) { makeDialog (cb.getState( )); }
   }

   private void makeDialog (boolean modalFlag) {
      Dialog dlg = new Dialog (this, modalFlag);
      dlg.setSize (100, 100);
      dlg.add ("North", new CountButton(1));
      dlg.add ("West", new CountButton(2));
      dlg.add ("East", new CountButton(3));
      dlg.add ("South", new ButtonAdapter("Hide") {
         public void pressed ( ) { dlg.setVisible(false); }});
      dlg.show( );
   }

   private class CountButton extends ButtonAdapter {
      public CountButton (int val) { super ("" + val); }
      public void pressed ( ) {
         display.append("Button " + getLabel( ) + " pressed\n");}
   }
}
```

Figure 13.14   Example program for creating dialogs.

Individual menus are named, and are placed on the menu bar using the method add:

```
        .
        .
        .
Menu helpMenu = new Menu ("Help");
bar.add (helpMenu);
        .
        .
        .
```

Menu items are created using the class MenuItem. Each menu item maintains a list of ActionListener objects, the same class used to handle Button events. The listeners will be notified when the menu item is selected.

```
        .
        .
        .
MenuItem quitItem = new MenuItem ("Quit");
quitItem.addActionListener (new QuitListener( ));
helpMenu.add (quitItem);
        .
        .
        .
```

A number of techniques can be used to create special purpose menus, such as tear-off menus, cascading menus, and so on. However, these will not be described here.

13.7.1 *A Quit Menu Facility*

On many platforms it is sometimes difficult to stop a running Java application. For this reason, it is useful to define a general purpose "Quit" menu bar facility. The class QuitItem (Figure 13.15) creates a listener that will halt the running application when the associated menu item is selected. By overloading the constructor, we make it trivial to add this functionality to any application.

The constructor for QuitItem can be given a MenuItem as argument. In this case it merely attaches itself as a listener to the menu item. Alternatively, it can be given a Menu, in which case it creates a menu item labeled "Quit." Or it can be given a MenuBar, in which case it creates a new menu labeled "Quit" that contains only the quit menu item. Finally, the constructor can be given an application as argument, in which case it creates a new menu bar containing only the one menu that contains only the single quit item. Using the application

```
class QuitItem implements ActionListener {

  public QuitItem (Frame application) {
      MenuBar mBar = new MenuBar( );
      application.setMenuBar (mBar);
      Menu menu = new Menu("Quit");
      mBar.add (menu);
      MenuItem mItem = new MenuItem("Quit");
      mItem.addActionListener (this);
      menu.add (mItem);
  }

   public QuitItem (MenuBar mBar) {
      Menu menu = new Menu("Quit");
      mBar.add (menu);
      MenuItem mItem = new MenuItem("Quit");
      mItem.addActionListener (this);
      menu.add (mItem);
  }

   public QuitItem (Menu menu) {
      MenuItem mItem = new MenuItem("Quit");
      mItem.addActionListener (this);
      menu.add (mItem);
  }

   public QuitItem (MenuItem mItem)
      { mItem.addActionListener (this); }

   public void actionPerformed (ActionEvent e)
       { System.exit(0); }
}
```

Figure 13.15   A general purpose QuitItem class.

constructor, a quit menu selection can be added to an application by placing
only a single line in the constructor for the application:

```
class ColorTest extends Frame {
   .
   .
   public ColorTest ( ) {
      .
      .
```

```
            // add quit menu item to application
        new QuitItem (this);
            .
            .
            .
        }
    }
```

13.8 CHAPTER SUMMARY

The Abstract Windowing Toolkit, or AWT, is the portion of the Java library used for the creation of graphical user interfaces. The design of the AWT is an excellent illustration of the power of object-oriented techniques. In this chapter we have described the various AWT components, and the way in which they are used to develop user interfaces.

STUDY QUESTIONS

1. What do the letters *AWT* stand for?

2. What is a Component object in the Java AWT?

3. What are the parent classes of class Frame?

4. In what AWT class is the method setBackground defined?

5. How is a container different from other types of components?

6. What is the difference between a frame, a window, and a container?

7. Explain why in a framework there are two views of an overridden method, such as paint.

8. What is the task performed by the layout manager?

9. Explain how the three mechanisms of inheritance, composition, and implementation of an interface are all involved in the task of attaching a layout manager to a container.

10. What are the five different layout manager types? Which managers use the one argument add method, and which use the method in which the first argument is a String value and the second a component?

11. What two roles are being combined in a ButtonAdapter?

12. Show how the class ColorButton could have been written using a ButtonAdapter.

13. What is the difference between a TextArea and a TextField?

14. What are the three different types of components that allow the user to select one item out of many possibilities?

15. What is a Panel?

16. What are the 13 predefined values provided by class Color?

17. What do the three numerical values that define a color represent?

18. In what ways is a MenuBar similar to a Component? In what ways is it different?

EXERCISES

1. Add a menu bar to the Solitaire program described in Chapter 9. Then, add two menu items, one to quit the application, and one to reset the application for a new game.

2. Write code to create a panel having a 2 by 2 grid layout with 3 pixels horizontal space and 5 pixels vertical space between components. Place buttons labelled "one" to "four" in the panels of the grid. Place this panel in the center of your frame.

3. After placing the panel from the last question into the center portion of a window, add a small text box at the top. As each button is pressed, display the button number in the text box.

4. Using a text box and a grid of buttons, create a simple calculator application. Buttons correspond to digits and the four arithmetic functions +, −, *, and /, as well as the equals sign.

14 Input and Output Streams

At first glance, the input/output facilities in Java seem to present a confusing profusion of alternatives. At the highest level, there is the distinction between the *stream* classes, used to manipulate binary 8-bit quantities, and the *reader/writer* classes, used to manipulate string and 16-bit Unicode character values. Underneath each of these major categories are a plethora of subclasses. In all, over 40 classes are used to provide input and output. However, standing behind this multitude is an elegant logical structure that makes efficient and effective use of inheritance, composition, and polymorphism. Understanding how to manipulate the network and file facilities provided by Java will be much easier once you appreciate the structure and purpose of the I/O classes.

14.1 STREAMS VERSUS READERS AND WRITERS

The term *stream* conjures up an image of a narrow conduit through which values must pass. And indeed, at the lowest level, a stream is a device for transmitting or retrieving 8-bit (or *byte*) values. Note the emphasis on the action of reading or writing, as opposed to the data itself. A *file* is a collection of items stored on an external device, such as a floppy disk or CD-ROM. The Java object through which the file is accessed—for instance, a FileStream—provides the means to access the data values in the file but does not actually hold the file contents. And although we emphasize that at the lowest levels streams are always pipelines for transmitting 8-bit values, we also note that much of the functionality provided by the various different stream abstractions is intended to permit the programmer to think in terms of higher level units—for example, transmitting strings or integers or object values, instead of their 8-bit internal representation. For example, a method such as readInt() (found in class DataInputStream) will process four 8-bit values in the process of reading a single 32-bit integer.

233

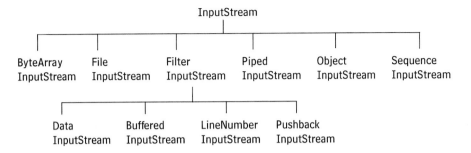

Figure 14.1   Subclasses of InputStream.

Next note that there are two independent and largely parallel systems involved in I/O. The hierarchy rooted in the two classes InputStream and Output-Stream are used to read and write 8-bit quantities. Most networking software and file systems are still based around the 8-bit unit, and for the time being these classes will therefore be the ones most commonly used. The alternative hierarchy is rooted in two different classes, Reader and Writer. These abstractions are used to read and write 16-bit Unicode character values.

Figure 14.1 gives the hierarchy of classes that descend from InputStream. (Figure 14.3 will later show a similar hierarchy for the class Reader.) The majority of this chapter will discuss the stream abstractions, as they will likely be the more commonly used for the near future (until 16-bit characters become more of the norm). However, we will briefly discuss the reader/writer classes in Section 14.7, and will use them in the networking examples presented in Chapter 22.

14.2   INPUT STREAMS

The class InputStream is an abstract class, parent to 10 subclasses in the Java library. Each class implements roughly the same behavior. This input stream protocol can be described as follows:

```
abstract class InputStream {

    // read a single byte from the input
    int read( ) throws IOException;

    // read an array of values from the input
    int read (byte [ ] buffer) throws IOException;

    // skip the indicated number of values from input
    long skip (long n) throws IOException;

    // determine number of bytes readable without blocking
```

```
int available( ) throws IOException;

    // close this input stream
void close( ) throws IOException;
}
```

An IOException will be generated if a file cannot be opened, or if an interrupt is encountered while reading from a pipe, or in other exceptional conditions.

The differences among the variety of input stream classes can best be understood by dividing them into two major categories. The first are classes tied to a *physical* input source. These read values from a byte array, a file, or a pipe. The second are those input streams that are *virtual*, depending upon another input stream for the actual reading operations but extending the functionality of the input stream in some fashion. For example, a PushbackInputStream reads values from another input stream but also allows the program to "unread" characters, "pushing them back" into the input stream. In reality the pushed back characters are stored in a local buffer within the PushbackInputStream. When a subsequent read operation is performed, the characters will be read first from the local buffer, before once again reading from the underlying input stream once the buffer is emptied.

14.2.1   *Physical Input Streams*

There are three input stream classes that read from actual data areas. These are distinguished by their names and the arguments used in their constructors. A ByteArrayInputStream, for example, must be given an array of byte values as an argument. A FileInputStream requires either a file or a file name, and so on.

```
    // constructors for various input streams
ByteArrayInputStream (byte [ ] buffer);
ByteArrayInputStream (byte [ ] buffer, int offset, int count);
FileInputStream (File f);
FileInputStream (String fileName);
PipedInputStream (PipedOutputStream p);
```

Note that for simple reading and writing, a FileInputStream or FileOutputStream can be manipulated without first creating a File object. Generally, a File object is necessary only if one is doing operations to the file itself, such as renaming or removing the file. Another reason for creating a File object would be to test whether a file is readable or writable before beginning a sequence of input/output operations.

14.2.2   *Virtual Input Streams*

The classes SequenceInputStream, ObjectInputStream, and the three subclasses of FilterInputStream can be thought of as *virtual* input classes. None of these actually read characters from any input area, but instead they rely on one or more underlying input streams for their data source. Each adds useful functionality as values are passed through the class.

For example, a SequenceInputStream takes a sequence of two or more input streams, and logically places them end to end. When one input stream is exhausted, the next stream in sequence is started without interruption or any action on the user's part. The underlying streams can be specified either as two arguments to the constructor (if there are only two input streams to be catenated) or as an enumeration to an underlying collection of input streams (if there are more than two input streams).

```
InputStream f1 = new FileInputStream ("file1.text");
InputStream f2 = new FileInputStream ("file2.text");
InputStream f3 = new SequenceInputStream (f1, f2);
      // f3 now represents the catenation of file1 and file2
Vector fv = new Vector ( );
fv.addElement (f1); fv.addElement (f2);
InputStream f4 = new SequenceInputStream (fv.elements( ));
      // f4 also now represents the same catenation
```

The structure of the class SequenceInputStream is an example of the *composite* design pattern (see Section 15.2).

The class ObjectInputStream is used to provide *serialization*, the ability to convert an object value into a representation that can be transmitted as a sequence of 8-bit values. These values are themselves written to or read from an underlying stream, typically a file stream although any type of stream abstraction will work. We will discuss this class in more detail in Section 14.5.

As noted in Chapter 10, the subclasses of FilterInputStream represent an interesting combination of the object-oriented mechanisms of inheritance and composition, characteristic of the *wrapper* design pattern (see Section 15.9). Because each class inherits from InputStream, they can be used in all situations where an input stream is expected. But each also holds as a component an underlying input stream, used to read the actual character values. One way to envision these classes is as an adapter, or filter, that sits between the client (the code making the request for values) and the physical input stream producing the values.

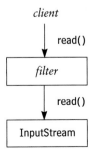

Because they support the interface common to all input streams, such filters can be easily added or removed as needed.

The PushbackInputStream allows a single character to be unread. A value pushed back into the input stream will subsequently be returned as the result of the next read operation. This facility is useful when scanning textual input. Imagine, for example, reading the textual representation of a numeric value, such as 456. It is only *after* the first nondigit character is read that one knows that all of the digits of the number have been seen. But the last character, the nondigit, should not be considered part of the number. Thus, this value is "pushed back" into the input, to be read again later.

The PushbackInputStream allows only a single character to be reprocessed. The BufferedInputStream is a more general facility, allowing the input operations to be backed up over a larger range. A BufferedInputStream reads values from the underlying input stream in large blocks, which for external devices such as a file is much more efficient than reading values byte-by-byte. The BufferedInputStream then responds to the read operation by returning characters from its internal buffer, refilling the buffer with new values if necessary. The method mark( ) tells the stream to mark a location in this internal buffer. A subsequent reset( ) then resets the input back to the marked location. All characters between the mark and the reset will then be read again. Although declared only as an instance of InputStream, on most systems the standard input stream System.in is *implemented* by an instance of a buffered input stream. Thus, on most platforms, characters cannot be read from this input stream until an entire line of text has been entered.

The input filter that adds the most additional functionality is the class DataInputStream. In this class, methods are provided to read bytes from the source and return them as a primitive data type. To read an int, for example, will require reading four characters from the underlying input stream. In response to a call on readInt, the four-byte values are read in and combined together to form the new integer value, which is then returned as the result of the call on readInt. Similar methods are provided for each of the primitive data types.

```
class DataInputStream extends FilterInputStream
    implements DataInput {
  .
  .
  .
  public boolean readBoolean ( ) throws IOException

  public byte readByte ( ) throws IOException

  public char readChar ( ) throws IOException

  public double readDouble ( ) throws IOException
```

```
    public int readInt () throws IOException

    public int readLong () throws IOException

    public short readShort () throws IOException

    public int readUnsignedByte () throws IOException

    public int readUnsignedShort () throws IOException
}
```

Note that these methods read a binary representation, not a textual representation of the values. Most generally, the input stream being processed will have been produced using a DataOutputStream. The DataInput interface is also used by the class RandomAccessFile.

14.3   STREAM TOKENIZER

Although not specifically an InputStream, the class StreamTokenizer provides a useful mechanism for breaking a textual file into a sequence of tokens. The stream tokenizer recognizes words (sequences of letters separated by nonletter characters) and numbers (sequences of digit characters), and it can even be set up to recognize comments or convert all tokens to lowercase. Each token returned is characterized by a token type, which is either one of several symbol constants defined in the class or the integer value of the last character read. The following program illustrates several of the methods provided by this class:

```
class TokenTest {
    public static void main (String [ ] args) {
        StreamTokenizer tok = new StreamTokenizer (System.in);
        try {
        while (tok.nextToken( ) != tok.TT_EOF) {
            switch (tok.ttype) { // ttype is token type
                case tok.TT_NUMBER: // nval is numeric value
                    System.out.println("number " + tok.nval);
                    break;
                case tok.TT_EOL:
                    System.out.println("end of line");
                    break;
                case tok.TT_WORD: // sval is text value
                    System.out.println("word " + tok.sval);
                    break;
```

```
                  default:
                     System.out.println("token " + (char) tok.ttype);
                     break;
               }
            }
         } catch (IOException e) { }
      }
   }
```

Giving this program the input "23-skidoo, kid!" yields the output:

```
number 23.0
token -
word skidoo
token ,
word kid
token !
```

The class StringTokenizer (Section 17.8.3) provides a similar facility for breaking apart a string value.

14.4   OUTPUT STREAMS

Although not as extensive as the input stream classes, the subclasses of OutputStream (Figure 14.2) also exhibit the same interesting use of polymorphism, composition, and inheritance. Like InputStream, the abstract parent class OutputStream defines minimal functionality:

```
abstract class OutputStream {
      // write a single byte value
      public abstract void write (int b) throws IOException
```

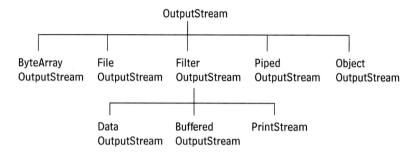

Figure 14.2   Subclasses of OutputStream.

```
        // write an array of byte values
    public void write (byte [ ] buffer) throws IOException

        // flush all output from buffers
    public void flush () throws IOException

        // close stream
    public void close () throws IOException
}
```

The OutputStream abstraction views writing as a task performed one character at a time. However, for many devices (files or networks, for example), such character-by-character processing can be very inefficient. For this reason many subclasses of OutputStream will *buffer* their values, collecting characters in an internal data area until a sufficiently large number of values have been generated, and then writing them out in one step. For the most part this buffering is transparent to the programmer and is of little concern. Occasionally, however, the buffering process is undesirable. We will see an example in Chapter 22, where input and output streams are used to conduct a dialog between two computers. One computer will send a question along an output stream and then wait for the response to arrive in an input stream. Here it is necessary that an output operation be performed, even if the internal buffers have not yet been filled, since the response will not be generated until the computer at the other end of the network receives the question. It is for this reason that the OutputStream abstraction provides the method flush. Issuing a flush will force the completion of all pending output operations, even if internally maintained buffers have not been completely filled. Closing a stream will automatically flush all pending operations.

As we did with input streams, we can divide the description of output streams into two major categories: (1) those classes that characterize the physical location of the output and (2) those classes that add more behavior to an output stream.

In the first group are the three classes: (1) ByteArrayOutputStream, (2) FileOutputStream, and (3) PipedOutputStream. The first writes values into an in-memory byte array, the second on to an external file, and the third on to a pipe (see Section 14.6).

The second category is represented by the class ObjectOutputStream and by the class FilterOutputStream and its subclasses. Just as FilterInputStream provided an orthogonal way of adding additional functionality to an input stream regardless of the physical source of the data, a filtered output stream adds new functionality to an output operation. Whereas a filtered input stream generally performs new operations after reading from the underlying stream, a filtered output stream generally performs some task *before* sending the values (which are perhaps transformed) to the underlying output stream. There are three subclasses of FilterOutputStream: (1) BufferedOutputStream, (2) DataOutputStream, and (3) PrintStream.

A BufferedOutputStream maintains an internal buffer of values that have been output. Rather than writing bytes one by one, values are written to the underlying output stream only when the buffer becomes full or when the output is flushed. This is useful if writing an individual byte to the output stream involves a high overhead that can be amortized if many characters are written at once.

A DataOutputStream is the output equivalent of DataInputStream. This class adds methods to write the binary values for each of the primitive data types. The output will be read subsequently by a DataInputStream. A program in Section 14.6 will illustrate the use of a DataOutputStream.

A PrintStream is similar but generates a textual representation rather than a binary representation. The methods print( ) and println( ) are overloaded with functions specific to each of the primitive data types. Typically, a print stream is used to generate output that will be read by human users, as opposed to processing by another program. Both the streams System.out and System.err are instances of PrintStream.

```
class PrintStream extends FilterOutputStream  {
    .
    .
    .

    // print textual representation of primitive value
    public void print (boolean bool)
    public void print (int inum)
    public void print (float fnum)
    public void print (double dnum)
    public void print (String str)
    public void print (Object obj) { print (obj.toString( )); }
    .
    .
    .

}
```

The implementation of the method print( ) when used with an object as argument is an example of pure polymorphism combined with an abstract, or deferred method. Because all objects are subclasses of Object, any value can be used as argument with this method. When executed, the method uses the function toString( ) to convert the object into a string representation. The implementation of this method in class Object simply returns the name of the class of the receiver. However, this method is overridden in many classes to provide more meaningful output. The function executed will be determined by the dynamic, run-time type of the argument, not by the static type Object. In this fashion, whatever text the programmer has provided using the toString( ) method will be the output produced.

The stream accessed through System.out will likely continue to be an instance of PrintStream, since so much existing Java code depends upon this feature. However, the creation of new data streams using PrintStream is being discouraged, in favor of the more general PrintWriter facility that provides similar functionality and also supports 16-bit Unicode character values. We will discuss the writer classes in Section 14.7.

The class ObjectOutputStream is used to provide object serialization, a topic we will discuss in the next section.

14.5 OBJECT SERIALIZATION

The class ObjectOutputStream is designed for writing object values to a stream in a form that allows them to be easily read back in using an ObjectInputStream. This process of converting an object into a representation that can be accommodated in 8-bit units is termed *object serialization*. The concept of object serialization is essential to almost all network programming, as it is the process that allows arguments to be passed along a network to an application running on another machine. It is also the key to providing object *persistence*, the ability to save an object's state across program invocations.

A serialized object can be stored in an 8-bit form—for example, on a file—and yet be read back and restored to its exact representation. This process is not as easy as it seems. For example, objects almost always have internal state that must also be restored. Worse yet, the same object may be referenced two or more times within an object. When restored, these common references must also be restored to a single value. Fortunately, the classes ObjectOutputStream and ObjectInputStream and the Serializable interface hide most of these details from the programmer.

A few simple classes will illustrate the difficulties of object serialization, and the use of the serialization abstractions. Imagine a class Pair that holds two object values, and a class Holder that maintains a single value:

```
import java.io.Serializable;

class Pair implements Serializable {
    public Object first;
    public Object second;
}

class Holder implements Serializable {
    public Object value;
}
```

Using these, we construct an instance of class Pair in which each field is a Holder, and in which the two holder objects point to the same value, say the current date:

```
import java.util.Date;

Date today = new Date();
Holder a = new Holder();
a.value = today;
Holder b = new Holder();
b.value = today;
Pair c = new Pair();
c.first = a;
c.second = b;
```

We can visualize the value of c as a diamond; each of its two child fields eventually pointing to the same value:

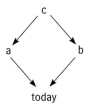

To save the current value we create an ObjectOutputStream. Note that an object output stream must be built on top of another stream that is used for the actual values. In this case we use a file stream:

```
try {
        // Open output stream
    FileOutputStream f = new FileOutputStream("saveState");
    ObjectOutputStream s = new ObjectOutputStream(f);
        // Write string, followed by representation of object
    s.writeObject("The Value of c is");
    s.writeObject(c);
    s.flush();
} catch (IOException e) {
    System.out.println("received error " + e);
}
```

The end result is that the state of the variable c, along with an identifying string, will have been been saved in the file. This value can be read, generally in another program, as follows:

```
try {
        // Open input stream
    FileInputStream f = new FileInputStream("saveState");
    ObjectInputStream s = new ObjectInputStream(f);
        // Read string, then representation of object
    String tag = (String) s.readObject();
    Pair c = (Pair) s.readObject();
} catch (IOException e) {
    System.out.println("received IO exception " + e);
} catch (ClassNotFoundException e) {
    System.out.println("received class exception " + e);
}
```

Note that it is necessary to cast the value returned by the readObject method to the correct type, and that the readObject method declares the ClassNotFoundException which must be handled. The following test will ensure that, as we hope, only one copy of the Date object will be found in the restored state:

```
Holder a = (Holder) c.first;
Holder b = (Holder) c.second;
if (a.value == b.value)
    System.out.println("its the same object");
```

Note that to make an object serializable requires almost no effort whatsoever. All we have done is to indicate that the new classes will satisfy the Serializable interface. Because the interface is empty and it defines no additional behavior, this is very easy to do. This is all that is needed for the vast majority of situations. More complex actions may be necessary if, for instance, only a portion of an object's state is to be saved on the output stream.

14.6   PIPED INPUT AND OUTPUT

In some types of applications a common situation is for one portion of a program to be producing values that are being consumed by a different portion of the same program. Such an arrangement is called a *producer/consumer* relationship. Java provides an elegant way of organizing this type of program, through the use of multiple threads of execution and pipes. The producer and consumer each run in their own thread of execution, communicating through a pipe.

A *pipe* is a buffered data area that is used for both reading and writing. A pipe can hold only a limited number of values. Either reading from or writing to a pipe can cause a thread to be temporarily suspended. A write will be suspended if the current pipe buffer is full, whereas a read operation will be suspended if the buffer is empty. In both cases, execution will continue when the condition is resolved—for example, when a subsequent read frees up space in the buffer, or a subsequent write adds a new element.

Each pipe is manifested by a matched pair of stream pointers, a PipedOutput-Stream and a PipedInputStream. The second value created (either input or output pipe) is passed the first value as an argument, and the connection is thereby made between the two:

```
PipedInputStream in = new PipedInputStream( );
PipedOutputStream out = new PipedOutputStream (in);
```

Values can subsequently be written to the piped output stream as if it were any other type of output stream, and these values can then be read, in the same order they were inserted, from the corresponding input stream.

We can illustrate the use of pipes by means of a program designed to find all the integers smaller than 100,000 that are both prime numbers and Fibonacci numbers. A prime number, you will recall, is a value with no divisors other than 1 and itself. A Fibonacci number is defined by the recurrence relation $f_0 = 0$, $f_1 = 1$, $f_n = f_{n-2} + f_{n-1}$. [1]

A separate thread of control (see Chapter 20) is created to generate both sequences of numbers. The thread, in fact, need not even know that it is dealing with a pipe. The Fibonacci thread simply creates a sequence of values and writes them to an output stream. Using a DataOutputStream makes it easier to write integer values. Although it looks as if the thread produces all the values at once, a print( ) statement placed inside the loop will demonstrate that this is not so, and that production of values will be delayed until they are required.

```
class FibMaker extends Thread {
    private DataOutputStream out;

    public FibMaker (DataOutputStream o) { out = o; }

    public void run ( ) {
        int n = 0;
        int m = 1;
        try {
            out.writeInt (m);
```

---

[1] Tradition has it that Fibonacci numbers describe the population growth of rabbits. Rabbits take two years to mature. Once mature, they give birth each year to a single offspring. Thus, each new year the number of rabbits is the number of rabbits in the previous year plus the number of mature rabbits in the previous year, each of which has given birth. Hardly realistic, but the sequence of numbers produced by this relation has some fascinating properties.

```
        while (m < 100000) {
            int newValue = n + m;
            n = m;
            m = newValue;
            System.out.println("writing new Fibonacci " + newValue);
            out.writeInt (newValue);
            }
        out.close( );
        } catch (IOException e) { return; }
    }
}
```

A similar thread creates prime numbers:

```
class PrimeMaker extends Thread {
    private DataOutputStream out;

    public PrimeMaker (DataOutputStream o) { out = o; }

    public void run ( ) {
        int newValue = 1;
        try {
            while (newValue < 100000) {
                newValue = newValue + 1;
                boolean isPrime = true;
                for (int i = 2; i * i <= newValue; i++)
                    if (newValue % i == 0) {
                        isPrime = false; break; // no use checking further
                        }
                if (isPrime) {
                    System.out.println("writing new prime " + newValue);
                    out.writeInt (newValue);
                    }
                }
            out.close( );
            } catch (IOException e) { return; }
        }
}
```

The main program shows how these are connected. The thread for each generator and for the pipes as well is created in the methods makeFibs( ) and makePrimes( ). Note how all the pipe mechanism is encapsulated in these two routines, and the remainder of the program simply views input as coming from

a DataInputStream. The main program simply reads values as long as they are
available, comparing them and outputting those that match.

```
class PipeTest {
   static public void main (String [ ] args)
      { PipeTest world = new PipeTest(System.out); }

   private PipeTest (PrintStream out) {
      DataInputStream fibs = makeFibs( );
      DataInputStream primes = makePrimes( );
      try {
         int x = fibs.readInt( );
         int y = primes.readInt( );
         while (x < 100000) {
            if (x == y) {
               out.println ("integer " + x + " is both fib
                  and prime");
               x = fibs.readInt( );
               y = primes.readInt( );
               }
            else if (x < y)
               x = fibs.readInt( );
            else
               y = primes.readInt( );
            }
         } catch (IOException e) { System.exit(0); }
      }

   private DataInputStream makeFibs ( ) {
      try {    // create the Fibonacci number generator
         PipedInputStream in = new PipedInputStream( );
         PipedOutputStream out = new PipedOutputStream (in);
         Thread fibThread = new FibMaker
            (new DataOutputStream(out));
         fibThread.start( );
         return new DataInputStream (in);
         } catch (IOException e) { return null; }
      }

   private DataInputStream makePrimes ( ) {
      try {    // create the prime number generator
         PipedInputStream in = new PipedInputStream( );
         PipedOutputStream out = new PipedOutputStream (in);
```

```
        Thread primeThread = new PrimeMaker
            (new DataOutputStream(out));
        primeThread.start();
        return new DataInputStream (in);
        } catch (IOException e) { return null; }
    }
}
```

An examination of the output will show that values are being generated on demand, rather than being all computed at once.

```
writing new Fibonacci 1
writing new Fibonacci 2
writing new prime 2
writing new prime 3
writing new prime 5
writing new prime 7
writing new Fibonacci 3
writing new Fibonacci 5
writing new prime 11
writing new prime 13
writing new prime 17
writing new Fibonacci 8
writing new Fibonacci 13
writing new Fibonacci 21
integer 2 is both fib and prime
integer 3 is both fib and prime
integer 5 is both fib and prime
integer 13 is both fib and prime
writing new Fibonacci 34
    .
    .
    .
writing new prime 19
writing new prime 23
    .
    .
    .
writing new prime 31
writing new Fibonacci 233
    .
    .
    .
integer 89 is both fib and prime
    .
    .
    .
integer 233 is both fib and prime
```

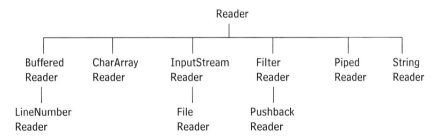

Figure 14.3   Subclasses of Reader.

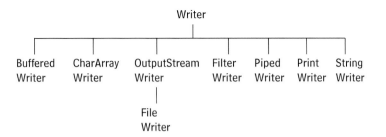

Figure 14.4   Subclasses of Writer.

14.7   READERS AND WRITERS

The class hierarchies rooted at Reader and Writer largely mirror the functionality provided by the classes InputStream and OutputStream and their dependents. However, readers and writers manipulate 16-bit Unicode character values, rather than 8-bit bytes. The class hierarchy for readers is shown in Figure 14.3, and for writers in Figure 14.4.

As with input streams, we can divide the various types of readers into those that directly manipulate a data area (CharArrayReader, StringReader, FileReader) and those that add functionality to data being generated by another reader (BufferedReader, LineNumberReader, FilterReader).

Readers and writers are useful whenever the input or output values are purely textual, as opposed to binary data such as colors or images. For example, the class BufferedReader provides a method readLine, which yields a line of text stored in a value of type String. We use this facility in a case study discussed in Chapter 19 (see Figure 19.2). The application in this example generates a concordance, a table of words and the lines on which they appear. The heart of the algorithm that generates the concordance is a loop that reads the input line by line:

```
public void readLines (BufferedReader input) throws IOException
{
    .
    .
    .
    for (int line = 1; true; line++) {
        String text = input.readLine();
        if (text == null)
            return; // a null value signals end of input
        .
        .
        .
    }
}
```

The class BufferedReader is a filter, which must be built on top of another reader. To use the above code with text drawn from a file, for example, one would first create a FileReader, and then use the file reader to construct the BufferedReader:

```
try {
    FileReader f = new FileReader("filename");
    BufferedReader input = new BufferedReader(f);
    .
    .
    .
} catch (FileNotFoundException e) { ... }
```

A reader can also be built on top of an InputStream using an instance of InputStreamReader, a class that acts as a filter for input streams. Similarly, writers can be directed to any type of output stream by means of an OutputStreamWriter. An *encoding algorithm* is used to translate between the 16-bit Unicode character representation and the 8-bit byte representation used by streams and low-level devices (such as files). There are a large number of encoding algorithms provided by the standard library to support the various foreign alphabets that can be represented by the Unicode character set. The programmer can specify one of these encodings when creating a reader. The following, for example, could be used to read lines from a file that contained cyrillic characters:

```
    // first get access to the file
FileInputStream f = new FileInputStream("fileName");
    // then convert bytes to characters
InputStreamReader r = new InputStreamReader(f, "MacCyrillic");
    // then buffer the input
BufferedReader input = new BufferedReader(r);

    // now read text line by line
String text = input.readLine();
```

```
while (text != null) {
    .
    .
    .
    text = input.readLine();
}
```

Many of the output stream writers will buffer their values internally. In situations where this is undesirable the flush method can be used to force the processing of all pending characters.

14.8 CHAPTER SUMMARY

Although the number of different classes can initially make the input/output facilities of Java seem confusing, the structure of these classes is very simple and a good illustration of the use of inheritance and polymorphism.

Input and output can be divided into the *stream* abstractions, which read and write 8-bit values, and the *reader/writer* classes, which manipulate 16-bit Unicode character values.

Input streams can be divided into those based on a physical input source (reading input from a file, for example), and those based on adding new functionality to a logical input stream. An example of the latter is the class PushbackInputStream, which adds the ability to unread already processed characters, returning them once more in response to a subsequent read operation. The design of the subclasses of FilterInputStream combines both the techniques of inheritance and composition.

Although not specifically an input stream, the class StreamTokenizer provides a way to break a stream into individual tokens. A similar facility for strings will be described in Chapter 17.

Object serialization is the process of encoding an object's state into a form that can be represented as a series of 8-bit values. This serialized form can then be transferred across a network, or stored on a permanent storage device to provide object *persistence*.

Like input streams, the various subclasses of output streams differ in the physical location to which the output is directed. Although the output stream abstraction describes writing only a single character value, many subclasses will maintain values in an internal buffer and only perform a physical output operation when the buffer is full, or when the user explicitly requests, using the method flush, that the output be processed. Closing a stream will automatically flush all pending operations.

Pipes provide a mechanism for structuring programs that include both the production and consumption of a given resource. The producer writes values to the pipe, while the consumer reads values. The pipe facility will automatically suspend either the producer or the consumer tasks if values are not available or the pipe buffer becomes full.

The reader/writer abstractions provide the ability to work with character and string data types that may contain extended Unicode character values. The translation betweeen 16-bit Unicode characters and an 8-bit physical representation is handled automatically behind the scenes. Readers and writers should be used whenever input or output values are entirely textual.

STUDY QUESTIONS

1. What is the difference between the *stream* class hierarchies and the *Reader/Writer* hierarchies?

2. Describe the methods that are common to all subclasses of InputStream.

3. What are the different types of physical locations from which an input stream can read?

4. Describe how a FilterInputStream combines both inheritance and composition.

5. What is the difference between the InputStream class and the DataInputStream class?

6. What does it mean to say that a PushBackInputStream permits a character to be unread?

7. What task is performed by a StreamTokenizer?

8. What is the purpose of the method flush in both output stream and writer abstractions?

9. Describe the different targets to which an output stream can write.

10. What is object serialization? How is the concept linked to network computing? How is the concept linked to persistence?

11. In what ways is a pipe different from a file? In what ways are they the same?

12. How are readers and writers linked to streams?

13. What task is performed by a byte encoding algorithm?

EXERCISES

1. Create a new subclass of FilterInputStream that reads values from an input stream and converts all uppercase characters to lowercase. How would you test your program?

2. Using BufferedReader.readLine( ) and a StringTokenizer, write an application that will count and display the number of lines, words, and characters in a file. The name of the file should be taken from the argument list for the application.

3. Write the class description for a new class SequenceOutputStream, which is the output analog to SequenceInputStream. The constructor for this class will take two output streams as arguments. Each write to the SequenceOutputStream will thereafter be translated into a write on each of the argument streams.

4. Extend the class you developed in the preceding exercise so that the constructor can take an enumeration of output streams as an argument.

5. Write a subclass of FilterInputStream that looks for positive integer digit characters, such as "4231", and replaces them with the textual equivalent, in this example the words "four thousand two hundred and thirty one". Do this in several steps:

   (a) Convert the input stream into a PushbackInputStream.

   (b) As long as the source input stream is not a digit character, return it.

   (c) When a digit character is encountered, read the number until the end of digit is found.

   (d) Push the terminating nondigit character back into the input.

   (e) Translate the number into its textual equivalent, stored in a String. Create an InputStream to read characters from this string.

   (f) For subsequent requests, read from the string buffer input stream until no further characters remain, then revert to reading from the original push back input stream.

15 Design Patterns

Like most complex structures, good computer programs are often formed by imitating the structure of older, similar programs that have already proven successful. A *design pattern* is an attempt to capture and formalize this process of imitation. The basic idea is to characterize the features of a proven solution to a small problem, summarizing the essential elements and omitting the unnecessary detail. A catalog of design patterns is a fascinating illustration of the myriad ways that software can be structured so as to address different problems. Later, patterns can give insight into how to approach new problems that are similar to those situations described by the pattern.

This chapter will introduce the idea of design patterns by describing several found in the Java library. The terminology used in describing the patterns is adapted from the book *Design Patterns: Elements of Reusable Object-Oriented Software*, by Erich Gamma, Richard Helm, Ralph Johnson, and John Vlissides [1995]. This was one of the first books to describe the concept of design patterns and provide a systematic cataloging of patterns. Many more patterns than are described in the present chapter can be found in this book, as well as in the recent literature on design patterns.

The format used in describing each pattern is to first characterize the problem the pattern is addressing, then to summarize the essential features of the solution. In some cases this is followed by a discussion of some of the context for the problem or of alternative design possibilities. This is followed by a more detailed description of the pattern as it is manifested in the Java Library. Finally, a sentence or two summarizes the situations where the pattern is applicable.

15.1 ADAPTER

Problem: How do you use an object that provides appropriate behavior but uses a different interface than is required in some situation?

Figure 15.1   The adapter pattern.

Solution: Define an *adapter* class that acts as an intermediary (Figure 15.1). The adapter does little work itself but merely translates commands from one form into the other.

Discussion: International travelers frequently overcome the problem of differing electrical plug and voltage standards by using adapters for their appliances. These adapters are connectors that allow an electrical appliance with a plug for one type of outlet to be plugged into a different type of electrical outlet. Like an electrical adapter, a software adapter uses the functionality of an existing class, and maps it to a new interface.

Example: In Section 10.2 we discussed two different techniques for creating a Stack abstraction using the facilities provided by the class Vector. One approach used inheritance, having the class Stack inherit from Vector. The second approach used composition, having Stack maintain a data field of type Vector. Both these techniques are forms of adaptors. In both cases the majority of the effort is being provided by the Vector, and the Stack is solely used to change the Vector interface.

Another example is provided by the classes InputStreamReader and Output-StreamWriter discussed in Chapter 14. Here again it is the underlying stream abstractions that are doing the actual work, and the InputStreamReader and OutputStreamWriter classes merely provide the mechanism for changing the *input/output* stream interfaces into the required *reader/writer* interfaces.

An adapter can be used whenever there is the need for a change in interface, but no, or very little, additional behavior beyond that provided by the worker.

15.2   COMPOSITE

Problem: How do you permit the creation of complex objects using only simple parts?

Solution: Provide a small collection of simple components, but also allow these components to be nested arbitrarily. The resulting composite objects allow individual objects and compositions of objects to be treated uniformly. Frequently, an interesting feature of the *composition* pattern is the merging of the *is-a* relation with the *has-a* relation.

Example: A good example of composition in the Java library is the creation of design layouts through the interaction of Components and Containers. Only five simple types of layouts are provided by the standard library, and of these five only two, border layouts and grid layouts, are commonly used. Each item

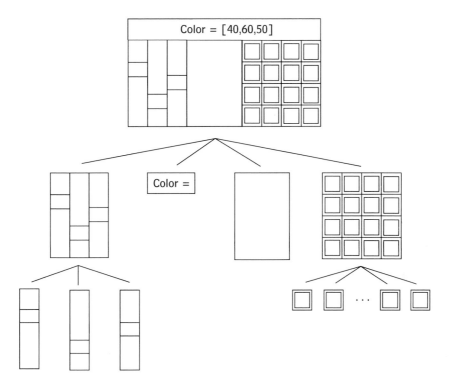

Figure 15.2   An example of a Composite.

in a layout is a Component. Composition occurs because Containers are also Components. A container holds its own layout, which is again one of only a few simple varieties. Yet the container is treated as a unit in the original layout.

The structure of a composite object is often described in a treelike format. Consider, for example, Figure 15.2, the layout of the window shown in Figure 13.12 of Chapter 13. At the application level there are four elements to the layout. These are a text area, a simple blank panel, and two panels that hold composite objects. One of these composite panels holds three scroll bars, while the second is holding a grid of 16 buttons.

By nesting panels one within another, arbitrarily complex layouts can be created. Another example of composition is the class SequenceInputStream, which is used to catenate two or more input streams so that they appear to be a single input source (see Section 14.2.2). A SequenceInputStream *is-a* InputStream (meaning it extends the class InputStream). But a SequenceInputStream also *has-a* InputStream as part of its internal state. By combining inheritance and composition, the class permits multiple sequences of input sources to be treated as a single unit.

This pattern is useful whenever it is necessary to build complex structures out of a few simple elements. Note that the merging of the *is-a* and *has-a* relations is characteristic of the *wrapper* pattern (Section 15.9), although wrappers can be constructed that are not composites.

15.3   STRATEGY

Problem: How do you allow the algorithm that is used to solve a particular problem to be easily and dynamically changed by the client?

Solution: Define a family of algorithms with a similar interface. Each algorithm provides a different strategy for solving the problem at hand. Encapsulate each algorithm, and let the client select the strategy to be used in any situation.

Discussion: If a complex algorithm is embedded in a larger application, it may be difficult to extract the algorithm and replace it with another, alternative version. If several alternative algorithms are included in the same object, both the complexity and the code of the resulting object may be increased unnecessarily. Separating problem and solution makes it easier for the client to select the solution (strategy algorithm) appropriate for any particular situation.

Example: An example of the use of the strategy pattern is the creation of layout managers in the AWT. Rather than coding in the component library the details of how items are laid out on the screen, these decisions are left to the layout manager. An interface for LayoutManager is defined, and five standard layout managers are provided. The ambitious programmer is even allowed, should he or she choose, to define a new object that satisfies the LayoutManager interface. (See Figure 15.3.)

The activities of the design component (such as a Panel or a Window) are independent of the particular layout manager that is being used. This both simplifies the container component and permits a much greater degree of flexibility in the

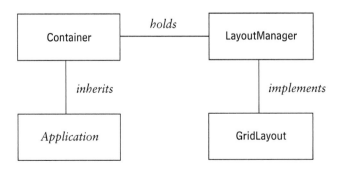

Figure 15.3   An example of the strategy pattern.

structure of the resulting layout than would be possible if layout decisions were an intrinsic part of the container.

The strategy pattern is useful whenever it is necessary to provide a set of alternative solutions to a problem and the algorithms used to address the problem can be encapsulated with a simple interface.

15.4 OBSERVER

Problem: How do you allow two or more independent and loosely coupled objects to change in synchrony with each other?

Solution: Maintain a list of objects that are tied, or dependent, on another object. When the target object changes, the dependents, or observers, are notified that they should update themselves.

Discussion: It is easy to maintain tightly coupled objects in synchrony. For example, if a new class is defined as a subclass of an existing parent class, modifications of the parent that are made via method invocations can be monitored by simply overriding the methods. It is much more difficult to keep objects in step with one another when links are formed and broken dynamically at run time, or when no obvious class relationship exists between the separate elements.

Example: There are two good examples of the use of the observer pattern in the Java library. The first we have seen in many earlier case studies, such as the Cannon World examined in Chapter 6. Each of the user interface components that permits interaction, such as buttons, scroll bars, and checkboxes, maintains a collection of *listener* objects. This list is dynamic; listeners for any component can be easily added or removed at run time. Furthermore, the structure of the listeners is not specified, they are only required to satisfy the necessary interface. When the component changes state (the button is pressed, the slider moved, the checkbox changed), each of the listeners is notified that a change has occurred. It is up to the listener to decide what action should be taken as a result of the change.

The idea behind listeners is also found in a more general facility that can be used by programmers for situations that do not involve user interaction. The library class `Observable` represents objects that can be "observed," the equivalent of the components in the AWT mechanism. Programmers can either subclass a new class from `Observable`, or simply create an `Observable` field within a class. Other objects can implement the `Observer` interface. These correspond to "listener" objects. An instance of `Observer` registers itself with the object being observed.

At any time, the `Observable` object can indicate that it has changed, by invoking the message `notifyObservers()`. An optional argument can be passed along with this message. Each observer is passed the message `update(Observable, Object)`, where the first argument is the `Observable` that has changed, and the second is the optional argument provided by the notification. The observer takes whatever action is necessary to bring the state into synchrony with the observed object.

The *observer* pattern is applicable whenever two or more objects must be loosely coupled but must still maintain synchronization in some aspect of their behavior or state.

15.5 FLYWEIGHT

Problem: How can one reduce the storage costs associated with a large number of objects that have a similar state?

Solution: Share state in common with similar objects, thereby reducing the storage required by any single object.

Example: With the exception of primitive values, all objects in Java are an instance of some class. With each class it is necessary to associate certain information. Examples of information are the name of the class (a String), and the description of the interface for the class. If this information were duplicated in each object, the memory costs would be prohibitive. Instead, this information is defined once by an object of type Class, and each instance of the class points to this object.

The objects that share the information are known as *flyweights*, since their memory requirements are reduced (often dramatically) by moving part of their state to the shared value. The flyweight pattern can be used whenever there are a large number of objects that share a significant common internal state.

15.6 ABSTRACT FACTORY

Problem: How to provide a mechanism for creating instances of families of related objects without specifying their concrete representations.

Solution: Provide a method that returns a new value that is characterized only by an interface or parent class, not by the actual type produced.

Discussion: There are several instances where the value returned by a method in the standard library is characterized by either an abstract class or an interface. Clearly the actual value being returned is a different type, but normally the client using the method is not concerned with the actual type, but only the behavior described by the characterizing attributes.

Example: Two examples out of the many found in the Java library will be described. Each of the collection classes Vector, Hashtable, and Dictionary define a method named elements( ) that is described as returning a value of type Enumeration. As Enumeration is only an interface, not a class, the value returned is clearly formed as an instance of some other class. Almost always, the client has no interest in the actual type being yielded by elements( ) and is only interested in the behavior common to all values that satisfy the Enumeration interface.

A similar situation occurs with the classes Font and FontMetrics. The class Font-Metrics is used to describe the characteristics of a Font, such as the height and width of characters, the distance characters extend above or below the baseline, and so on. A FontMetrics is an abstract class, one that cannot be instanciated directly by the programmer using the new command. Instead, a value of type FontMetric is returned by a Graphics object in response to the message getFontMetrics. Clearly, the graphics object is returning a value derived from a subclass of FontMetric, but the particular value returned is normally of no concern to the client.

A similar facility is used by class Applet, which can return an AppletContext that describes the current execution environment.

The abstract factory pattern should be used whenever the type of the actual value to be created cannot be predicted in advance and therefore must be determined dynamically.

15.7   FACTORY METHOD

Problem: You have a method that returns a newly created object, but you want subclasses to have the ability to return different types of objects.

Solution: Allow the subclass to override the creation method and return a different type of object.

Discussion: This pattern is very similar to the abstract factory but is specialized for the situation where new abstractions are formed using inheritance.

Example: The method clone( ) is a good example of a factory method. This method returns a copy of an object, provided the object supports the Cloneable interface. The default method in class Object raises an exception, indicating that the cloneable interface is not supported. Subclasses that wish to permit clones must override this method and return a different type of value.

Note that the value returned by a factory method must be the same for all classes. For the Cloneable interface this type is Object. Any class that permits cloning will still return a value of type Object in response to the message clone( ). This value must then be cast to the appropriate type.

The factory method pattern is useful when there is a hierarchy of abstractions formed using inheritance, and part of the behavior of these abstractions is the creation of new objects.

15.8   ITERATOR

Problem: How to provide a way to access elements of an aggregate object sequentially without exposing the underlying representation.

Solution: Provide a mediator object for the sole purpose of sequential access. This mediator can be aware of the representation of the aggregate although the client using the object need not be aware of these details.

Example: The Enumeration interface for container access actually addresses two related problems. It provides a uniform means of accessing elements from many different types of containers and it hides the details of the underlying container representation. It is the second aspect that makes the Enumeration a good example of the iterator pattern.

Consider, for example, an enumeration that is generating elements from a Hashtable. Internally, a hash table is implemented as an array, each element of the array being a list. Values that hash into the same locations are found on the same list. (See Figure 15.4.)

The programmer who uses a hash table and wishes to iterate over the values should not be concerned with the representation, such as moving from one list to the next when the elements in one hash location have been exhausted. The hash table enumeration hides these difficulties behind a simple interface. The programmer sees only the two methods hasMoreElements() and nextElement(). With these, a loop can be written that does not even hint at the complex actions needed to access the underlying elements.

```
HashTable htab = new HashTable( );
  .
  .
  .
for (Enumeration e = htab.elements( ); e.hasMoreElements( ); ) {
   Object val = e.nextElement( );
     .
     .
     .
   }
```

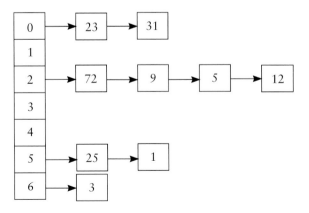

Figure 15.4   Internal representation of a hash table.

The fact that the method elements returns a value that is not directly an Enumeration, but is rather a value from another class that implements the Enumeration interface, is an example of the *abstract factory* pattern (Section 15.6).

The iterator pattern is useful whenever an aggregate object is created that can hold an arbitrary number of values, and it is necessary to provide access to values without exposing the underlying representation.

15.9 DECORATOR (FILTER OR WRAPPER)

Problem: How can you attach additional responsibilities to an object dynamically?

Solution: By combining the *is-a* and *has-a* relations, create an object that wraps around an existing value, adding new behavior without changing the interface.

Discussion: Inheritance is one technique for providing new functionality to an existing abstraction. But inheritance is rather heavyhanded, and is often not flexible enough to accommodate situations that must dynamically change during the course of execution. A decorator wraps around an existing object and satisfies the same requirements (for example, is subclassed from the same parent class or implements the same interface). The wrapper delegates much of the responsibility to the original but occasionally adds new functionality. (See Figure 15.5.)

Example: The class InputStream provides a way to read bytes from an input device, such as a file. The class BufferedInputStream is a subclass of InputStream, adding the ability to buffer the input so that it can be reset to an earlier point and values can be reread two or more times. Furthermore, a BufferedInputStream can take an InputStream as an argument in its constructor.

Because a BufferedInputStream both *is* an InputStream and *has* an input stream as part of its data, it can be easily wrapped around an existing input stream. Due to inheritance and substitutability, the BufferedInputStream can be used where the original InputStream was expected. Because it holds the original input stream, any

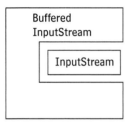

Figure 15.5   Buffered InputStream as an example of the wrapper or filter pattern.

actions unrelated to the buffering activities are simply passed on to the original stream.

A decorator, or wrapper class, is often a flexible alternative to the use of subclassing. Functionality can be added or removed simply by adding or deleting wrappers around an object.

15.10 PROXY

Problem: How do you hide details such as transmission protocols to remote objects?

Solution: Provide a proxy that acts as a surrogate or placeholder for another object.

Discussion: A proxy is an object that stands in place of another. The first object receives requests for the second, and generally forwards the requests to the second, after processing them in some fashion. (See Figure 15.6.)

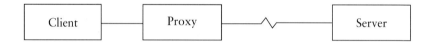

Figure 15.6 The proxy pattern.

Example: An example proxy in the Java Library is the Remote Method Invocation (RMI) system. RMI is a mechanism that can be used to coordinate Java programs running on two or more machines. RMI creates a proxy object that runs on the same machine as the client. When the client invokes a method on the proxy, the proxy transmits the method across the network to the server on another machine. The server handles the request, then transmits the result back to the proxy. The proxy hands the result back to the client. In this fashion, the details of transmission over the network are handled by the proxy and the server, and are hidden from the client.

15.11 BRIDGE

Problem: How to decouple an abstraction from its implementation so that the latter can vary independently.

Solution: Remove implementation details from the abstraction, placing them instead in an object that is held as a component in the abstraction.

Example: Most of the component classes in the AWT make use of the *bridge* pattern. Fundamentally, this is because the actions necessary to implement a graphical component vary in great detail from one platform to another. For example, the actions needed to display a window are different depending upon whether the underlying display is X-Windows/Motif, Windows-95, or the Macintosh. Rather than placing platform specific details in the class Window, instead each window maintains a component of type WindowPeer. The interface Window-Peer has different implementations, depending upon the platform on which the application is being executed. This separation allows a Java program that depends only on the class Window to be executed in any environment for which there is a corresponding peer.

The bridge pattern is in many ways similar to the strategy pattern described earlier. Differences are that bridges are almost always hidden from the client (for example, the average Java programmer is generally unaware of the existence of the peer classes), and are generally dictated by environmental issues rather than reflecting design decisions.

15.12 CHAPTER SUMMARY

An emerging new area of study in object-oriented languages is the concept of design patterns. A design pattern captures the salient characteristics of a solution to a commonly observed problem, hiding details that are particular to any one situation. By examining design patterns, programmers learn about techniques that have proven to be useful in previous problems, and are therefore likely to be useful in new situations.

FURTHER READING

The most important reference for design patterns is the 1995 book of the same name by Gamma, Helm, Johnson, and Vlissides (commonly known as the Gang of Four, or GOF). Another recent book on patterns is by Richard Gabriel [1996].

STUDY QUESTIONS

1. In what ways is an adapter similar to a proxy? In what ways are they different?

2. What does the link between an Adapter and a Worker represent? Composition or Inheritance?

3. In what way is the composition design pattern similar to the idea of composition examined in Chapter 10?

4. Explain how the Composite pattern works in the AWT, and explain how this relies on both inheritance and composition.

5. In what ways is a strategy design pattern similar to a bridge pattern? In what ways are they different?

6. In what ways is an iterator similar to an adapter?

EXERCISE

1. What design pattern is exhibited by the class PrintStream (see Section 14.4)? Explain your answer.

V

Understanding the Java World

16 Exception Handling

From the start, Java was designed with the understanding that errors occur, that unexpected events happen, and that programmers should always be prepared for the worst. Part of this outlook is the inclusion in the language of a simple yet powerful mechanism for handling *exceptions*.

An exception is an event that occurs during the execution of a program that disrupts the flow of instructions and prevents the program from continuing along its normal course. An example that is easy to understand is the exception that occurs when a file cannot be opened. The programmer developing a file-processing application starts out with a structure that perhaps looks something like the following:

```
ask the user for the name of a file
open the file
read the contents
do something with the contents
close the file
```

The programmer probably develops the application using some simple test cases and might not even think about the possibility that the file cannot be opened. What happens if the user enters incorrect values, a name that is not a valid file name? In most languages, the likely answer is that the program will fail in totally unexpected and inexplicable ways.

In Java, the programmer cannot simply forget to think about this possibility, because the language will not allow the programmer to write a statement that opens a file without providing the code that will be executed should a failure occur. The file-opening method is declared as a function that can potentially "throw an exception", and the compiler will refuse to recognize any use of the method that does not handle the exception.

As we saw earlier in the case study described in Chapter 7, a method that can potentially raise an exception must be invoked within the framework of a *try/catch* block. This is written as a nested statement following the keyword try, and an associated set of statements following the keyword catch:

```
try {
    File fd = new File(filename);
} catch (FileOpenFailed e) {
    System.err.println("Cannot open file " + filename);
}
```

The exception mechanism is in fact dealing with an actual object, which is an instance of class Throwable. When an error occurs, the value of this object is assigned to the variable e in the statements shown above.

Multiple statements can be nested within the try block. In fact, often almost the entire application will be held within a surrounding block.

```
try {
    File fd = new File(filename);
    processFile (fd);
    fd.close( );
} catch (FileOpenFailed e) {
    System.err.println("Cannot open file " + filename);
}
```

Multiple exceptions can also be tested, by writing a series of catch clauses

```
try {
    File fd = new File(filename);
    processFile (fd);
    fd.close( );
} catch (FileNotFoundException e) {
    System.err.println("Cannot find file " + filename);
} catch (FileOpenFailed e) {
    System.err.println("Cannot open file " + filename);
}
```

Exceptions are a useful programming construct because the location where an error is detected is usually not the place where the appropriate solution is known. For example, suppose you are the programmer developing the file-processing library routines. That is, you are the person developing the code for the class File. Certainly you are aware of the fact that the string passed to the constructor for your class might not represent a valid file name. But what should you do in this situation? Without knowledge of the surrounding application, there is no good answer.

One common solution is to return a special value, such as the value null, when a command cannot be processed. But constructors are not permitted to return a null value, furthermore there might be multiple reasons for a failure. Does a null value returned by a file open operation mean the file does not exist, or that it exists but cannot be read? Finally, what if a null value is perfectly legal? How would one indicate an error in that case?

The exception mechanism not only gives the programmer who detects the message the ability to return precise information, it also places responsibility for dealing with the error on the shoulders of the programmer, who knows the appropriate action to take.

16.1 INFORMATION TRANSMITTED TO THE CATCH BLOCK

You will note that a catch block looks something like a method declaration. Like a method heading, the catch block defines a *variable* that is given a value when the exception is handled. Each of the various exceptional conditions is in fact a class name, a subclass of Throwable. The variable that is thrown often contains useful information pertaining to the exception, such as the name of the file that cannot be opened, or the value of an illegal array index. If the exception is converted to a String value, as in many of the examples shown in this chapter, then this information will be printed.

The class Throwable also defines several methods. One of the most useful is a method that will print a stack trace, which describes the sequence of method calls up to the point where the exception occurred. The following shows how this could be used:

```
try {
   File fileOne = new File (fileName);
   processfile (fileOne);
   fileOne.close( );
} catch (FileNotFoundException e) {
   System.error.println("Cannot find file " + e);
   e.printStackTrace( );
}
```

16.2 CATCHING MULTIPLE ERRORS

There need not be a one-to-one correspondence between methods that can throw an exception and the try block that handles the error. The Java language only requires that the statement that can throw the exception must be handled somewhere. For example, if two or more files are being opened, they can be surrounded by a single try/catch statement. An error opening either file will be handled in the same way.

```
try {
   File fileOne = new File (filenameOne);
   File fileTwo = new File (filenameTwo);
   processFile (fileOne, fileTwo);
   fileOne.close();
   fileTwo.close();
} catch (FileNotFoundException e) {
   System.err.println("Cannot find file " + e);
} catch (FileOpenFailed e) {
   System.err.println("Cannot open file " + e);
}
```

16.3 THE FINALLY CLAUSE

The try/catch statement permits an optional last clause, labeled finally. Statements contained in the finally block will be executed, regardless of whether or not an exception is raised. Consider, for example, the following:

```
try {
   System.out.println("start");
   File fileOne = new File (filenameOne);
   System.out.println("open worked");
} catch (FileNotFoundException e) {
   System.out.println("not found error");
} catch (FileOpenFailed e) {
   System.out.println("open error");
} finally {
   System.out.println("all done");
}
```

One possible sequence of output is *start-open worked-all done*. Another sequence, should it happen that the file name is not valid, is *start-not found error-all done*. Yet another might be *start-open error-all done*. The key feature to note in all of these is that it is not possible to execute the try/catch statement without executing the finally block. This is true even if a return statement is executed inside the body of the try/catch statement!

16.4 TERMINATION OR RESUMPTIVE MODELS

When an exception is thrown, control transfers directly to the catch block that handles the error. Unless the programmer explicitly reinvokes the same method, control will not return to the point at which the error occurred. This is sometimes referred to as the *termination model* of exception handling. There exist other programming languages that permit control to be returned to the point of error. Such languages are said to use the *resumptive model* of exception handling.

16.5 EXCEPTIONS THROWN IN THE STANDARD LIBRARY

Exceptions come in several varieties, which are all subclasses of the class Throwable. The two major subclasses of Throwable are Error and Exception. Some of the more common exceptions are described in Figure 16.1.

The subclasses of Error represent "hard" failures, such as the virtual machine detecting an error in the bytecode representation. Processing will immediately halt once such an error is detected. Fortunately, it is unlikely that a typical Java program will ever see or throw such an error.

```
Throwable
   Error
      LinkageError
         IncompatibleClassChangeError
            InstantiationError
      VirtualMachineError
         InternalError
         OutOfMemoryError
         StackOverflowError
   Exception
      IllegalAccessException
      IOException
         EOFException
         FileNotFoundException
         InterruptedIOException
         MalformedURLException
      RuntimeException
         ArithmeticException
         ClassCastException
         EmptyStackException
         IndexOutOfBoundsException
            ArrayIndexOutOfBoundsException
            StringIndexOutOfBoundsException
         NegativeArraySizeException
         NullPointerException
         SecurityException
```

Figure 16.1 Some of the exceptions issued in the standard library.

Most programmers will write code to throw and catch objects that derive from the class Exception. Once again, these can be divided into categories, the two most important being RuntimeException and IOException.

The subclasses of RuntimeException represent conditions that arise within the Java virtual machine itself during the processing of the bytecodes that represent a program. Examples include the use of a variable that has not been initialized (NullPointerException), an improper cast conversion, or an arithmetic operation that overflows. Because the source for such an error could potentially be almost any Java statement, the compiler does not insist that the programmer test for or catch these errors. (Think about what a program would look like if every variable reference needed to be surrounded by a try statement to detect null value possibilities.)

The subclasses of IOException represent errors that can occur during the processing of input and output statements. Examples include not being able to open files, attempting to read past the end of a file, or attempting to access information across the network using a badly formed URL.

16.6   THROWING EXCEPTIONS

A method that will in some situations throw an exception must declare so in the method heading. For example, suppose one is developing a stack abstraction (see Chapter 19) making use of an array. Popping from an empty stack might be a condition that would trigger an exception. To throw an exception, a new value is created (using the new operator). This value must be a subclass of Throwable.

```
class Stack {
   private int index;
   private Vector values;
      .
      .
      .

   Object pop( ) throws Exception {
      if (index < 0)
         throw new Exception("pop on empty stack");
      Object result = values.elementAt(index);
      index--;
      return result;
   }
}
```

It is possible to convey more precise information by first creating a subclass of Exception, then throwing an instance of this class. The class Exception has two constructor forms, and subclasses generally follow the same pattern.

```
class StackUnderflowException extends Exception {
   StackUnderflowException ( ) { super( ); }
```

```
        StackUnderflowException (String gripe) { super(gripe); }
    }

    class Stack {
        private int index;
        private Vector values;
          .
          .
          .

        Object pop() throws StackUnderflowException {
            if (index < 0)
                throw new StackUnderflowException();
            Object result = values.elementAt(index);
            index--;
            return result;
        }
    }
```

A child class that overrides a method inherited from a parent class is not permitted to introduce new exceptions that were not already declared in the parent.

16.7   PASSING ON EXCEPTIONS

Occasionally it is useful for a method not to handle an exceptional condition and simply to pass the exception back to the caller. This can be accomplished by simply adding the exception type to the method header. An example occurs in the concordance program examined in Chapter 19.

```
class Concordance {

    public void readLines (DataInputStream input) throws IOException {
        String delims = " \t\n.,!?;:";
        for (int line = 1; true; line++ ) {
            String text = input.readLine();
            if (text == null) return;
            text = text.toLowerCase();
            Enumeration e = new StringTokenizer(text, delims);
            while (e.hasMoreElements())
                enterWord ((String) e.nextElement(), new Integer(line));
        }
    }
      .
      .
      .
}
```

Here the IOException could be thrown by the method readLine. However, the method readLines really had no better way of dealing with this particular error than did the readLine method itself. Thus, the error is simply passed back to the caller of readLines, who could take the appropriate action. We will see further examples of this usage in the client-server programs in Chapter 22.

16.8   CHAPTER SUMMARY

The exception-handling mechanism in Java is a powerful technique for increasing the reliability and robustness of Java programs. Exceptions handle unexpected conditions that can disrupt the normal flow of control in the execution of a program. By properly declaring and catching exceptions, programmers are provided with a way to recover gracefully from potentially error-producing situations.

STUDY QUESTIONS

1. What is an exception?

2. Before exceptions were part of programming languages, a common technique used to indicate errors was to have a function return a special value, such as a null pointer. How is the exception mechanism an improvement over this technique?

3. In what ways is a catch clause similar to a method heading? In what ways is it different?

4. What is the difference between the termination and resumptive models of exception handling?

5. What is the difference between exceptions formed as subclasses of Error, and those that are subclasses of Exception?

EXERCISES

1. Modify the Stack data abstractions given in Chapter 10 so that they will throw an EmptyStackException if an attempt is made to read or remove a value from an empty stack.

17 Utility Classes

The Java library provides a number of small utility classes that are useful in a wide variety of situations. In this chapter we will consider several of these, including Point, Dimension, Date, Math, Random, Toolkit, and the data field named System. In addition, we will consider strings and their related classes.

17.1 POINT

A Point represents a location in two-dimensional space. The point is described by a pair of integer values, called the x and y values. Points are used in conjunction with a number of the AWT painting operations and with layout managers. An important feature to remember is that in the AWT coordinate system, the y coordinates increase as locations move downward, rather than decreasing as is true in classical geometry.

The following summarizes the characteristics of the class Point:

```
class Point {
        // constructor
    public Point (int x, int y)

        // public accessible data fields
    public int x
    public int y

        // operations
    public void move (int x, int y) // move to given location
    public void translate (int x, int y) // change by offset
    public boolean equals (Object p) // compare two points
    public String toString () // convert to string
}
```

17.2 DIMENSION

A dimension is used to represent a rectangular size. Dimensions are characterized by a width and a height. Dimensions are used in many AWT methods and returned as the result of methods that need to characterize a size. The following summarizes the features of the class Dimension:

```
class Dimension {
      // constructors
   public Dimension ()
   public Dimension (int w, int h)
   public Dimension (Dimension d) // make copy

      // public accessible data fields
   public int width
   public int height

      // operations
   public String toString()
}
```

17.3 DATE

The class Date is used to represent both data and time values. Two dates can be compared to determine if one comes after the other. Once set, any of the fields in a date can be changed. The following summarizes the methods provided by the class Date:

```
class Date {
      // constructors
   public Date () // return current date and time
   public Date (int year, int month, int day)
   public Date (int year, int month, int day, int hours,
      int minutes)
   public Date (int year, int month, int day,
      int hours, int minutes, int seconds)

      // field access methods
   public int getDate () // returns day of month, 1-31
   public int getDay () // returns day of week, 0-6
   public int getHours () // returns hour, 0-23
   public int getMinutes () // returns minute of hour, 0-59
   public int getMonth () // returns month of year, 0-11
   public int getSeconds () // returns second of minute 0-59
```

```
         public int getYear ( ) // returns year number - 1900
         public int getTimezoneOffset ( ) // returns offset from GMT

            // epoch methods
         public long getTime ( ) // returns milliseconds since epoch
         public void setTime (long lval) // set time from epoch

            // field setting methods
         public void setDate (int date)
         public void setHours (int hour)
         public void setMinutes (int minutes)
         public void setMonth (int month)
         public void setSeconds (int seconds)
         public void setYear ( )

            // comparison methods
         public boolean after (Date day)
         public boolean before (Date day)
         public boolean equals (Object day)

            // output
         public String toString ( )
      }
```

When provided with no constructors, the class Date returns the current time and day. Otherwise, the date is set from the argument values given. The year value is given as the year minus 1900, that is, 97 represents 1997, and 112 represents 2012.

Notice that the method equals overrides the similarly named method inherited from class Object. Thus, the argument to this method must be simply Object. However, the methods after and before, which are defined here for the first time, can be restricted to working only with Date objects.

The recently released 1.2 revision of the Java language introduced a number of changes in the class Date. In order to reduce the connection between dates and the western style Gregorian calendar, a new class Calendar was added. Some functions formerly provided by class Date are now performed using a combination of Date and Calendar values. For example, the method getDate, which returns a day of the month, is now discouraged in favor of the following command:

```
Calendar.get(Calendar.DAY_OF_MONTH)
```

17.3.1 *After the Epoch*

Recent dates and times can be compactly represented by a single long value that represents the number of milliseconds since January 1, 1970, which is termed the start of the *epoch*. This quantity is returned by the method getTime. Most often these values are used in pairs, to obtain the amount of time used to perform a certain operation:

```
Date start = new Date( ); // starting time

int j = 0;
for (int i = 0; i < 100000; i++)
    j = j + 1;

Date end = new Date( ); // ending time
System.out.println("That took " + (end.getTime( )
    - start.getTime( )) + " milliseconds");
```

Epoch values for dates prior to January 1, 1970 are returned as negative numbers.

17.4 MATH

The class Math provides a number of constants, as well as useful mathematical functions. All values and methods are declared as static. Thus, these elements are accessible without creating an instance of the class. The class can be summarized as follows:

```
final class Math {
        // constants
    public static final double E  // 2.71828 ...
    public static final double PI // 3.1415926 ...

        // trigonometric operations, angles in radians
    public static double sin (double num)
    public static double cos (double num)
    public static double tan (double num)
    public static double asin (double num)
    public static double acos (double num)
    public static double atan (double num)
    public static double atan2 (double s, double c)

        // rounding operations
    public static double ceil (double num)
    public static double floor (double num)
    public static double rint (double num)
    public static int round (float num)
    public static long round (double num)
```

```
      // exponential and powers
public static double exp (double y) // e raised to x
public static double pow (double x, double y) // x raised to y
public static double log (double x) // log base e
public static double sqrt (double x) // x raised to 1/2

      // other operations
public static int abs (int num)
public static long abs (long num)
public static float abs (float num)
public static double abs (double num)
public static int max (int x, int y)
public static float max (float x, float y)
public static double max (double x, double y)
public static int min (int x, int y)
public static float min (float x, float y)
public static double min (double x, double y)
public static double random ( ) // value between 0 and 1
}
```

The method random() returns a value that is larger than or equal to 0.0, and strictly smaller than 1.0, uniformly distributed over the range. The following, for example, could be used to return a random number between 1 and 10 (inclusive of both endpoints):

```
int val = (int) Math.floor(Math.random( ) * 10 + 1);
```

More extensive random number operations are provided by class Random.

17.5   RANDOM

The method Math.random() can be used to generate random floating-point values larger than or equal to 0.0 and smaller than 1.0 with a uniform distribution. The class Random provides more general facilities, allowing not only the generation of random integers, but also the ability to reset the random number generator with a *seed* value. This latter feature provides a way to recreate the same random sequence of values many times, a property that is often useful in testing programs, as well as other situations. The facilities provided by Random can be summarized as follows:

```
class Random {
      // constructors
   public Random ( )
   public Random (long seed)
```

```
    // operations
public void setSeed (long seed)
public double nextDouble ( )
public float nextFloat ( )

    // integer value, can be either positive or negative
public int nextInt ( )
public long nextLong ( )

    // alternative distribution
public double nextGaussian ( )
}
```

All methods use a uniform distribution, with the exception of nextGaussian, which uses a Gaussian distribution. Other distributions can often be constructed from these. The following method, for example, takes as argument an integer array of weights and computes a random number with weighted distribution. It sums the array of weights, computes a random integer between 0 and the sum, then locates the integer in the array of weights:

```
static public int weightedDistribution (int [ ] weights) {
   int sum = 0; // compute sum of weights
   for (int i = 0; i < weights.length; i++)
      sum += weights[i];
      // compute random value less than sum
   int val = (int) Math.floor(Math.random( ) * sum + 1);
      // find point in distribution
   for (int i = 0; i < weights.length; i++) {
      val -= weights[i];
      if (val < 0)
         return i;
   }
   return 0; // should never happen
}
```

Given an array of weights (1, 3, 2), for example, the value 0 would be returned 1/6 of the time, the value 1 returned 1/2 of the time, and the value 2 returned 1/3 of the time.

17.6 TOOLKIT

The class Toolkit is mostly used to create the peer objects used in providing the device independent aspects of the AWT (see Section 15.11). However, in addition to creating the windows, buttons, menus, and other features of a graphical interface, the class also provides a few utilities useful to the programmer.

Toolkit is an abstract class, specialized for each type of platform on which a Java program can be executed. The implementation of Toolkit appropriate to the current environment is found by executing the method Toolkit.getDefaultToolkit( ).

The method getFontList( ) returns an array of string values, containing the names of the fonts available on the current system.

The method getImage( ) takes as argument either a string or a URL (see Section 21.4.1). If a string argument is used it should contain the name of a file. The image is loaded from the file or the URL address, and returned as a value of type Image.

The methods getScreenSize( ) and getScreenResolution( ) together return the size of the screen. The first returns the number of pixels in the screen, both height and width in a value of type Dimension. The second returns the number of dots per inch. Dividing one by the other will yield the physical size of the screen.

17.7 SYSTEM

The class System, and the instance data field of the same name provided by class Frame, give access to several systemwide resources. The most commonly used values are the input and output streams for the standard input, standard output, and error output. These are found at System.in, System.out, and System.err, respectively.

The method System.exit(int) immediately halts the currently running program, yielding to the operating system the integer status value given in the argument.

The method currentTimeMillis( ) returns the current time in milliseconds. The value is returned as a signed long value, representing the number of milliseconds since January 1, 1970 (see Section 17.3.1). Since the value is returned as a long, overflow will occur sometime in the year 292280995.

17.8 STRINGS AND RELATED CLASSES

The handling of strings in Java is similar enough to the handling of strings in other languages to seem natural to the programmer learning the language, yet sufficiently different in subtle points to be a potential source of trouble. In this chapter we will describe strings, string buffers, string tokenizers, and related classes.

The most important fact to remember is that in Java a String is an immutable value; it cannot be changed. One should think of a string as a constant, like a double-precision value. Just as a variable declared as holding a double can be assigned a new value, a variable assigned as holding a String can be assigned a new string, but this is not the same as changing the string value. A second class, StringBuffer, is closer, for example, to the C concept of a string as simply an array of character values. A string buffer can be subscripted, and individual elements modified. The following shows, for example, how to change *hope* into *cope* in both C and in Java.

C version	*Java version*

```
char * str = "hope";     String str = "hope";
str[0] = 'c';            StringBuffer strbuf(str);
                         strbuf.setCharAt(0, 'c');
```

17.8.1   *Operations on Strings*

The most common way to create a string is with a literal:

```
String name = "John Smith";
```

The various constructors for String also allow a string to be created from another string, from an array of characters or bytes, or from a string buffer:

```
char data[ ] = {'q','e','d'};
String quod = new String(data);
    // quod erat demonstrandum
```

The addition operator, +, is overloaded with a new meaning when either the left or the right argument is a string. In this case, the nonstring argument (if any) is converted into a string and a string catenation is performed. This is most often used to produce formatted output:

```
System.out.println(" The answer is: " + answer);
```

Note that the addition operator groups left to right, so that the meaning of the addition in the following two expressions is very different:

```
System.out.println("Catch-" + 2 + 2); // catch-22
System.out.println(2 + 2 + "warned"); // be forewarned
```

The String class defines a number of methods for returning portions of a string, converting values to a string, and comparing strings. These can be summarized as follows:

```
final class String { // declared final so it cannot be subclassed

    // constructors
  public String (String src)
  public String (char [ ] charArray)
  public String (byte [ ] byteArray)
  public String (StringBuffer buffer);
```

```
            // methods for creating new strings
            // catenate string with argument string
public String concat (String str)
            // replace old characters with new
public String replace (char oldChar, char newChar)
            // return subportion of string
public String substring (int offset)
public String substring (int offset, int endIndex)
            // convert case of all letters
public String toLowerCase ( )
public String toUpperCase ( )
            // return reference of current string
public String toString ( )
            // trim leading and trailing whitespace
public String trim ( )
            // create string from primitive data type
public static String valueOf (boolean bool)
public static String valueOf (char ch)
public static String valueOf (char [ ]  charArray)
public static String valueOf (int i)
public static String valueOf (long l)
public static String valueOf (float f)
public static String valueOf (double d)
public static String valueOf (Object obj)


            // comparison methods
            // compare ordering, return negative, zero or positive
public int compareTo (String str)
            // compare for equality
public boolean equals (Object obj)
public boolean equalsIgnoreCase (String str)
            // test front or end of string
public boolean endsWith (String str)
public boolean startsWith (String str)
            // find first occurrence of char or string
public int indexOf (char c)
public int indexOf (char c, int startingOffset)
public int indexOf (String str, int startingOffset)
public int lastIndexOf (char c)
public int lastIndexOf (char c, int startingOffset)
public int lastIndexOf (String str, int startingOffset)
}
```

There are a few subtle points that can trap the unwary programmer. Note that the identity operator, ==, tests whether two variables refer to exactly the same value. This is not the same as testing whether two string values have exactly the same character representation. In general, one should always use equals( ) to test the equality of objects, including strings, and not use the == operator. Because equals overrides the method inherited from Object, the argument must be an Object and not a String. A string value will always return false when compared to a nonstring. The method equalsIgnoreCase tests whether two values are the same, ignoring uppercase and lowercase distinctions.

The method compareTo( ) returns an integer result. This value is negative if the current string is lexicographically smaller than the argument, zero if they are equal, and positive if the string is larger than the argument. The exact integer value returned is implementation-dependent and should not be counted upon in any program.

The static method String.valueOf (Object obj) is a good example of a polymorphic method. The argument can be any type of object, including a null object. If it is not null, the method toString is used to convert the object into a string value:

```
final class String {
   .
   .
   .
   public static String valueOf (Object obj) {
      if (obj == null)
         return "null";
      else
         return obj.toString( );
   }
   .
   .
   .
}
```

The method toString is defined in class Object (where it returns the class name of the receiver as a string), and redefined in many classes. The value yielded by toString( ), and hence by valueOf( ), will be whatever method is appropriate for the dynamic, run-time type of the argument.

Because String.valueOf returns a legal result regardless whether or not the argument is null, it is a safer alternative to the use of toString directly:

```
Shape aShape = null;
   .
   .
   .
String a = String.valueOf(aShape); // will return "null" as string
String b = aShape.toString( ); // will generate null value exception
```

This property of the == operator can be used to demonstrate one subtle difference between creating a new string using the String constructor, and creating a string using the valueOf operator. One case generates a copy of the original string, while the other simply returns a reference to the original.

```
String one = "One";
String two = new String(one);
String three = String.valueOf(one);
System.out.println(" is one == two " + (one == two));
    // returns false
System.out.println(" is one == three " + (one == three));
    // returns true
```

17.8.2   *String Buffers*

A StringBuffer is similar to the C language concept of a string as an array of character values. A string buffer, like a vector, has a buffer of positions that may be larger than the number of character values it currently holds. This makes the representation useful when a sequence of insertion operations must be performed on the same string value. The methods provided by class StringBuffer can be described as follows:

```
final class StringBuffer {
        // constructors
    public StringBuffer (int capacity) // initially null string
    public StringBuffer (String str)

        // methods that change contents, return reference to ourselves
    public StringBuffer append (boolean bool)
        ... // and all other primitive data types
    public StringBuffer insert (int offset, boolean bool)
        ... // and all other primitive data types
    public StringBuffer reverse ()
    public void setCharAt (int index, char c)

        // methods to access values
    public char charAt (int index);

        // misc methods
    public int length ()
    public void setLength (int length)
    public void ensureCapacity ()
    public String toString ()
}
```

Note that the methods append, insert, and reverse both change the current string buffer and return a reference to the updated string buffer. This is different from the transformation methods in class String, which leave the receiver string unchanged but return a new string in which the transformations have been applied.

The append operator is used internally by the Java compiler to implement the + operator. A statement such as:

```
System.out.println("answer: " + answer);
```

is compiled as if it were written:

```
System.out.println(new StringBuffer("answer: ").append(answer)
    .toString());
```

17.8.3 *String Tokenizers*

The class StringTokenizer is useful for breaking a string into a sequence of *tokens*. Tokens are defined by a set of delimiter characters. Common delimiters include spaces, tabs, and punctuation such as periods or commas. The class StringTokenizer implements the Enumeration protocol (see Section 19.2), and can therefore be manipulated in an enumeration-style loop.

The methods provided by StringTokenizer can be described as follows:

```
class StringTokenizer implements Enumeration {
    // constructors
    public StringTokenizer (String str)
    public StringTokenizer (String str, String delims)
    public StringTokenizer (String str, String delims,
        boolean returnDelims)

    // enumeration protocol
    public boolean hasMoreElements ()
    public Object nextElement ()
    public String nextToken ()

    // return number of remaining tokens
    public int countTokens ()
}
```

The enumeration protocol requires that the method nextElement() return a value of type Object. In order to avoid the consequent casting of this value to a String, the equivalent method nextToken() can be used instead. The concordance program to be described in Section 19.7.1 will illustrate the use of a string tokenizer in breaking a line into a sequence of words:

```
class Concordance {
    public void readLines (DataInputStream input) throws IOException
    {
```

```
            String delims = " \t\n.,!?;:";
            for (int line = 1; true; line++ ) {
               String text = input.readLine( );
               if (text == null) return;
               text = text.toLowerCase( );
               Enumeration e = new StringTokenizer(text, delims);
               while (e.hasMoreElements( ))
                  enterWord ((String) e.nextElement( ), new Integer(line));
            }
         }
      }
```

The class StreamTokenizer (Section 14.3) provides a similar facility to breaking an input stream into tokens.

17.8.4   *Parsing String Values*

A StringTokenizer provides one method for breaking a string into component parts, resulting in a sequence of string tokens. If the string tokens represent primitive data values, the programmer requires a method to change the string representation into the primitive value. This functionality is provided by the wrapper classes, Boolean, Integer, Double, Float, and Long. One form of the constructor in each of these classes takes a String as argument and parses the string to ascertain the underlying value. The original value can then be obtained from the wrapper class, as shown in the following example:

```
String dstr = "23.7";
Double dwrap = new Double(dstr); // parse the string
double dval = dwrap.doubleValue( );
```

The wrapper classes also provide the reverse; that is, a way to change a primitive value into a string. Often there are a variety of different formats available. These facilities are summarized in Table 17.1.

Most of the conversion methods will throw a NumberFormatException if the characters do not represent a value in the correct format.

17.9   CHAPTER SUMMARY

The Java run-time system provides a number of useful utility classes. In this chapter we have explored several of these. A Point represents a location in a two-dimensional space, described by a pair of integer coordinates. A Dimension has the same representation—a pair of integer values—but is used to represent a two-dimensional size (height and width). A Date represents a calendar date and time value. The class Math provides access to a number of mathematical constants and useful functions. The Toolkit provides the means for accessing

Table 17.1 Wrapper class conversions to and from strings

Class	Conversion from string	Conversion to string
Boolean	new Boolean(str)	toString( )
	Boolean.valueOf(Boolean bval)	
Double	new Double(str)	toString( )
	Double.valueOf(double dval)	
Float	new Float(str)	toString( )
	Float.valueOf(Float fval)	
Integer	new Integer(str)	toString( )
	Integer.parseInt(String str, int radix)	toBinaryString( )
	Integer.valueOf(int ival)	toOctalString( )
		toHexString( )

fonts, and retrieving images over a network. The class System provides access to standard input and output areas.

A String in the Java language is an immutable (constant) value. The String data type provides a number of high-level operations. A related class, StringBuffer, permits changes to the individual fields in a string. The class StringTokenizer can be used to break a string into individual parts.

STUDY QUESTIONS

1. What type of values does a Point represent?

2. What type of values does a Dimension represent?

3. Both points and dimensions have the same internal representation; a pair of integer data values. What makes them different?

4. What type of values does a Date represent?

5. Write a Java expression that prints the current day of the month and hour.

6. What is the start of the epoch?

7. Why are data fields and constants in class Math declared as static?

8. How is a String different from a StringBuffer?

18 Understanding Graphics

The Java language provides one of the richest collections of graphical commands of any general purpose programming language. In this chapter we will explain some of the basic aspects of the classes associated with graphical operations in Java. Topics discussed include colors, fonts, images, and animation.

18.1 COLOR

The class Color is used to represent a color value. We know from optics that all colors can be formed by combinations of red, green, and blue. Color televisions use this principle, displaying colors as combinations of red, green, and blue dots. In order to represent colors in a computer more easily, each of the three amounts of red, green, and blue is represented by an integer value between 0 and 255. (There is nothing magic about the value 255; it was simply chosen so that each quantity could be stored in an eight-bit byte.) For each quantity, the larger the value, the brighter the component. A value of (0,0,0) is therefore black, while a value of (255, 255, 255) is white.[1] While in theory this encoding can represent 2^{24} different colors ($2^8 \times 2^8 \times 2^8$), in practice most display devices can handle only a limited range. When the exact color is unavailable, the actual color produced by a display device will usually be the closest matching color.

The Java library class Color allows colors to be specified using three integer values. The class also defines predefined constants for a number of commonly used colors. These are described in Table 18.1. The constructor for color takes as

---

[1] There is an alternative system that represents each color by a triple of floating-point values that represent the Hue, Saturation, and Brightness of the color. The HSB system is not used as much as the RGB system and will not be described here. The class Color provides methods for converting between the two systems.

Table 18.1   Methods for Class Color.

Predefined Colors

Color.black	Color.magenta
Color.blue	Color.orange
Color.cyan	Color.pink
Color.darkGray	Color.red
Color.gray	Color.white
Color.green	Color.yellow
Color.lightGray	

Description of Methods in Class Color

new Color (int, int, int)	constructor
brighter()	create brighter version of color
darker()	create darker version of color
getBlue()	return blue component of color
getGreen()	return green component of color
getRed()	return red component of color
toString()	return string representation of color

argument the three integer values representing the red, green, and blue components. These values can subsequently be retrieved from a color using the methods getRed, getGreen, and getBlue. The methods brighter and darker return brighter and darker versions of the current color. Finally, the method toString returns a string representation of the current color. A program that illustrates the use of many of the features of class Color is described in Section 13.5.

18.2   RECTANGLES

There are two classes in the Java library used for manipulating polygon shapes. The class Rectangle represents a rectangular area on a two-dimensional plane. The class Polygon represents more general polygon shapes.

We have used the class Rectangle already in the Cannon World program described in Chapter 6. In that program, every graphical object, each ball as well as each target, was placed on top of a rectangle that represented the location of the item. The application used the fact that a rectangle not only records a position on the two-dimensional surface but also can be easily moved to a new position and can tell whether or not it intersects with another rectangle.

A new rectangle can be created in a variety of ways. If no arguments are provided with the constructor, then an empty rectangle whose northwest corner is the origin is created. If two integers are specified, they are taken to be a width and height for a rectangle with the northwest corner at the origin. If four integer arguments are specified, the first two are the locations of the northwest corner, and the remaining arguments are the width and height.

```
Rectangle r = new Rectangle ();
Rectangle rTwo = new Rectangle (3, 4); \\ width 3, height 4
Rectangle rThree = new Rectangle (7, 6, 3, 4); \\ corner 7,6
```

Operations that test the state of a rectangle can be summarized as follows:

r.equals (rTwo)	Tell whether two rectangles are equal
r.inside (int, int)	Tell whether a point is inside the rectangle
r.intersects (rTwo)	Tell whether two rectangles intersect
r.isEmpty( )	Tell whether rectangle has nonempty extent

The size of a rectangle can be changed in a variety of ways. The add operation takes two integers that represent a point, and increases the size of the rectangle until it includes the point. The union operation does the same with another Rectangle argument, returning the smallest rectangle that encloses both. The grow operation takes two integer arguments and moves each of the horizontal sizes by the first argument amount and each of the vertical sides by the second, which can be either positive or negative. The method intersection calculates the intersection of two rectangles. The setLocation method moves a rectangle to a given location, while the translate method moves a rectangle by a given amount. The setSize method sets a rectangle size. Both the size and location of a rectangle can be changed by the method reshape, which takes four integer arguments in the same form as the constructor.

18.2.1   *Rectangle Sample Program*

A sample program, shown in Figure 18.1, illustrates the use of many Rectangle methods. Two rectangles are initially placed on the window. In each step all rectangles are either resized or moved, and a test is performed to see if any two rectangles intersect. If so, a new rectangle is generated with the same size as their intersection.

The method to move rectangles generates two random numbers. Using these, the rectangle is either changed in size or moved. Tests are performed to ensure the rectangle does not become negative in size or move off the board.

```
private void moveAllRectangles() {
    for (Enumeration e = rects.elements(); e.hasMoreElements(); ) {
        Rectangle r = (Rectangle) e.nextElement();
        int i = rand(5);
        int j = rand(5);
```

```
class RectTest extends Frame {
    public static void main (String [ ] args)
        { Frame window = new RectTest( ); window.show( ); }

    private Vector rects = new Vector( );
    private Random rnd = new Random( );
    private static int FrameWidth = 400;
    private static int FrameHeight = 400;

    public RectTest ( ) {
        setSize (400, 400);
        setTitle ("Rectangle test");
        rects.addElement (new Rectangle(4, 5));
        rects.addElement (new Rectangle(100, 100, 6, 7));
        }

    public void paint (Graphics g) {
        g.setColor(Color.green);
        for (Enumeration e = rects.elements( ); e.hasMoreElements( ); ) {
            Rectangle r = (Rectangle) e.nextElement( );
            g.fillRect (r.x, r.y, r.width, r.height);
            }
        moveAllRectangles( );
        spawnNewRectangles( );
        repaint( );
        }

    private int rand (int max) { return rnd.nextInt( ) % max; }

    private void moveAllRectangles() { ... }

    private void spawnNewRectangles() { ... }
}
```

Figure 18.1   The rectangle example program.

```
if ((i + j) % 5 == 0) {
    r.grow (i, j);
    if (r.height < 0)
        r.setSize (r.width, - r.height);
    if (r.width < 0)
        r.setSize (- r.width, r.height);
    }
else {
```

```
                    r.translate (i, j);
                    if (r.x < 0)
                        r.setLocation (r.x + FrameWidth, r.y);
                    if (r.y < 0)
                        r.setLocation (r.x, r.y + FrameWidth);
                    if (r.x > FrameWidth)
                        r.setLocation (r.x - FrameWidth, r.y);
                    if (r.y > FrameWidth)
                        r.setLocation (r.x, r.y - FrameWidth);
                }
            }
        }
```

The routine to test for intersections uses doubly-nested enumeration loops. If it locates two intersecting rectangles, a new rectangle is created and placed in the upper corner. Only one new rectangle is created in each move, in order to slow the process of filling the window.

```
private void spawnNewRectangles() {
    for (Enumeration e = rects.elements(); e.hasMoreElements(); ) {
        Rectangle r1 = (Rectangle) e.nextElement();
        for (Enumeration f = rects.elements(); f.hasMoreElements(); )
        {
            Rectangle r2 = (Rectangle) f.nextElement();
            if (r1.intersects(r2) && ! r1.equals(r2)) {
                Rectangle nr = r1.intersection(r2);
                nr.setLocation (0, 0);
                rects.addElement(nr);
                return;
            }
        }
    }
}
```

18.3   FONTS

A Font object describes the characteristics used to display printed text. Features of a font that the programmer can modify are the style, size, and font family (or logical name).

The logical font name describes the family of font styles being used. There are six recognized logical font names, Dialog, Helvetica, TimesRoman, Courier, DialogInput, and Symbol. The last is used to represent nonalphabetic symbols and is seldom used. Courier is a font with fixed-width characters, much like a typewriter. Helvetica and Times Roman are variable-width fonts, which are the type

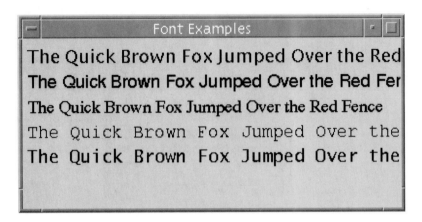

Figure 18.2   Example text printed in different fonts.

normally used for printed text. An example of text printed in each of the first five fonts is shown in Figure 18.2.

A font style describes the thickness and slant of the characters. In the Java library there are two characteristics that describe a style. These are the Bold attribute and the Italic attribute. Each is represented by an integer value, which can be combined. Thus, there are four different representations for each font family: plain (neither bold nor italic), bold, italic, and both bold and italic.

A font point size represents the size of the individual characters. Points are units used in typesetting. One point is approximately 1/72 of an inch.

The following chart describes the most commonly used methods recognized by instances of class Font.

Font(String name, int style, int size)	Construct new font
Font.PLAIN	Constant used to describe plain fonts
Font.BOLD	Constant used to describe bold fonts
Font.ITALIC	Constant used to describe italic fonts
getName( )	Return logical name
getSize( )	Return point size
getStyle( )	Return style characteristics
isBold( )	Determine if font is bold
isItalic( )	Determine if font is italic
isPlain( )	Determine if font is plain
toString( )	Return string representation of font

An instance of class Font can be created by providing the logical font name, a style, and a size. The name *must* be one of the six recognized family names (Dialog, Helvetica, TimesRoman, Courier, DialogInput, and Symbol). The style is formed using the class constants. A font that is both bold and italic can be created by adding the two values Font.BOLD and Font.ITALIC. The size can be any integer value, although not all sizes can be represented by all font families on any particular output device. In general, the size used in a display will be the closest available size to the one specified.

18.3.1 *Font Metrics*

A separate class, FontMetrics, is occasionally needed to get more detailed information about a font or about a string printed in a given font. For example, a font metric can be used to determine the width (in pixels) of a text that is to be printed in a particular font. Font metrics is an abstract class, and therefore you cannot directly construct instances of the class. The most common way to access a font metric object is by means of the method getFontMetrics provided by an object of type Graphics, as in the following example:

```
public void paint (Graphics g) {
   .
   .
   .
   g.setFont (aFont);
   FontMetric fm = g.getFontMetrics( );
   .
   .
   .
}
```

To determine the width of an individual character or a string, the methods fm.charWidth(char) or fm.stringWidth(String) can be used. The result is described in pixel units. Various other characteristics of a font are accessible using a font metric, for example fm.getHeight( ) will return the height (maximum character size) of the font. There are other methods. However these are rarely used.

18.3.2 *Font Example Program*

A small test program will illustrate both the use of methods in class Font and the way to program using checkboxes. The application will have a bank of six checkboxes on the bottom of the window, corresponding to the six logical font family names. Two buttons on the right (the east) will set either bold, or italic, or both, while a text edit field will allow the size to be set. An example text that illustrates the selected characteristics is then displayed in the middle of the application window. The main program is shown in Figure 18.3. The two banks of checkboxes are created by the two routines makeStyles and makeNames.

```
class FontTest extends Frame {
    static public void main (String [ ] args)
        { Frame window = new FontTest( ); window.show( ); }

    private int style = 0;
    private int size = 15;
    private String fontName = "Helvetica";

    public FontTest ( ) {
        setTitle("Font Test"); setSize(600, 150);
        add("East", makeStyles( ));
        add("South", makeNames( ));
    }

    private void display ( ) { repaint( ); }

    public void paint (Graphics g) {
        Font f = new Font(fontName, style, size);
        g.setFont(f);
        FontMetrics fm = g.getFontMetrics( );
        g.drawString(f.toString( ), 5, 10 + 2 * fm.getHeight( ));
    }

    private Panel makeStyles( ) { ... }

    private class StyleBox extends Checkbox implements ItemListener ...

    private class SizeBox extends TextField implements ActionListener ...

    private class NameBox extends Checkbox implements ItemListener ...

    private Panel makeNames( ) { ... }
}
```

Figure 18.3   The FontTest program.

The method makeStyles creates a grid layout of four horizontal panels. The first two are filled by instances of a class StyleBox that will allow a style to be set. The third is a SizeBox that will set the size of the example text. The final element is a quit button using the class ButtonAdapter defined earlier in Chapter 13.

```
private Panel makeStyles( ) {
    Panel p = new Panel( );
    p.setLayout(new GridLayout(4,1));
```

```
      p.add (new StyleBox(Font.ITALIC, "italic"));
      p.add (new StyleBox(Font.BOLD, "bold"));
      p.add (new SizeBox( ));
      p.add (new ButtonAdapter("Quit"){
         public void pressed( ){System.exit(0);}});
      return p;
   }
```

A StyleBox uses a technique we have seen earlier in Chapter 13. The class both extends the library class Checkbox and implements the class ItemListener. Thus, the class can encapsulate within itself both the creation of a Checkbox item and the task of listening when the Checkbox has been selected. When each box is selected it either turns on or off the given modifier bits, depending upon the state of the box. Notice that when checkboxes are created in this fashion, they are independent of each other, and can be set or unset individually. (For example, both the bold and italic checkbox can be set, in order to display bold italic output.)

```
private class StyleBox extends Checkbox implements ItemListener {
   private int modifiers;

   public StyleBox (int m, String name)
      { super (name);
      addItemListener (this); modifiers = m; }

   public void itemStateChanged (ItemEvent e) {
      if (getState( ))
         style |= modifiers; // turn on modifiers
      else
         style &= ~ modifiers; // turn off modifiers
      display( );
   }
}
```

A SizeBox is a type of TextField, that when edited changes the size value in the application class.

```
private class SizeBox extends TextField implements ActionListener {
   public SizeBox () { super ("" + size); addActionListener(this); }

   public void actionPerformed (ActionEvent e) {
      String sz = getText( );
      size = (new Integer(sz)).intValue( );
      display( );
   }
}
```

The method makeNames( ) illustrates the creation of a different type of checkbox. In this form, only one of the collection can be set at any one time. Setting one item will automatically unset all others. Such a group is sometimes referred to as *radio buttons*, as they operate in a fashion similar to the buttons on a car radio. To create a radio button collection, a CheckBoxGroup is created. This checkbox group is then passed with the constructor to each checkbox that will be part of the group.

```
private class NameBox extends Checkbox implements ItemListener {
    public NameBox (String name, CheckboxGroup cg)
        { super(name, cg, false); addItemListener(this); }

    public void itemStateChanged (ItemEvent e)
        { fontName = getLabel( ); display( ); }
}

private Panel makeNames( ) {
    Panel p = new Panel( );
    p.setLayout(new GridLayout(1,6));
    CheckboxGroup cg = new CheckboxGroup( );
    p.add (new NameBox("Courier", cg));
    p.add (new NameBox("Dialog", cg));
    p.add (new NameBox("DialogInput", cg));
    p.add (new NameBox("Helvetica", cg));
    p.add (new NameBox("TimesRoman", cg));
    p.add (new NameBox("Symbol", cg));
    return p;
}
```

When any button is pressed, the fontName field will be changed, and the display method activated.

18.4 IMAGES

An image is really nothing more than a two-dimensional collection of pixel values. Most commonly images are created by some video device, such as a digital camera, and stored in a file in a standard format, such as JPEG or GIF. A picture stored in such a format can be read into a Java program by first creating a URL (see Section 21.4.1), then using the toolbox routine getImage. The following program illustrates this technique. The first command-line argument is assumed to be a URL for a file stored in one of the standard formats. This image is read from the file and displayed as the value of the application window.

```
import java.awt.*;
import java.net.*;

class ImageTest extends Frame {
   public static void main (String [ ] args) {
      Frame world = new ImageTest (args[0]);
      world.show();
   }

   private Image image = null;

   public ImageTest (String fileName) {
      setSize (300, 300);
      setTitle ("Image Test");
      try { // read image from URL given in argument
         URL imageAddress = new URL (fileName);
         image = getToolkit().getImage(imageAddress);
      } catch (Exception e) { image = null; }
   }

   public void paint (Graphics g) {
      if (image != null)
         g.drawImage (image, 0, 0, this);
   }
}
```

18.4.1 *Animation*

Animation is simply the process of displaying a sequence of still pictures one after another. Just as with a movie, the eye is fooled into linking the pictures together, giving the appearance of smooth motion. The simplest animation program is shown below. Here a series of GIF files is read into an array of images. The paint routine selects one of these for display, then updates an index value so that the next image in sequence will be selected by the following display. Calling repaint ensures that the next image will then be displayed.

```
class AnimationTest extends Frame {

   public static void main (String [ ] args) {
      Frame world = new AnimationTest ();
      world.show();
   }

   private Image [ ] imageArray;
```

```
private int index = 0;

public AnimationTest ( ) {
    setSize(300, 300);
    setTitle("Simple Animation");
    imageArray = new Image [ 17 ];
    for (int i = 0; i < 17; i++) {
        String name = "T" + (i+1) + ".gif";
        try {
            URL address = new URL (name);
            imageArray[i] = getToolkit().getImage(address);
        } catch (Exception e) { imageArray[i] = null; }
    }
}

public void paint (Graphics g) {
    if (imageArray[index] != null)
        g.drawImage(imageArray[index++], 0, 0, this);
    if (index >= imageArray.length)
        index = 0;
    try {
        Thread.sleep(200);
    } catch (Exception e) { }
    repaint();
}
}
```

In order to slow down the animation, the paint routine will sleep for 200 milliseconds after drawing the image. On some platforms the animation will show an annoying flicker. This is because the method update, called by repaint, will redraw the screen in the background color before calling paint. This can sometimes be eliminated by simply overriding the method update to avoid redrawing the background:

```
// override update to simply paint window
public void update (Graphics g) {
    paint(g);
}
```

18.5   GRAPHICS CONTEXTS

As we have seen in almost all of our example programs, the majority of graphics in Java are generated using an object of class Graphics. Such an object is termed the *graphics context*. As we noted in Chapter 6, graphics contexts maintain a

Table 18.2 Operations Provided by Graphics Context.

clearRect	Clear a rectangular region
copyArea	Copy a rectangular region to another location
draw3DRect	Paint a three-dimensional rectangle
drawArc	Draw elliptical arc
drawBytes	Display bytes as text
drawChars	Display characters as text
drawImage	Display pixel image
drawLine	Draw a line from one point to another
drawOval	Draw oval outline
drawPolygon	Draw polygon outline
drawRect	Draw rectangle
drawRoundRect	Draw rounded rectangle
drawString	Draw string at given location
fillArc	Paint a filled elliptical arc
fillOval	Paint a filled oval shape
fillRect	Paint a filled rectangular area
fillRoundRect	Paint a filled rounded rectangular area
getColor	Retrieve the current foreground color
getFont	Retrieve the font used to print text
getFontMetrics	Retrieve font metrics object for current font
setColor	Set the current foreground color
setFont	Set the font for future printing operations
setPaintMode	Set drawing to paint mode
setXORMode	Set drawing to XOR mode

coordinate system in which the 0,0 location is the upper left corner, and values increase as they move down and to the right. Graphics contexts also maintain both a foreground and a background color, in a fashion we have already seen used with windows. Table 18.2 summarizes the most commonly used method provided by class Graphics. We have used many of these in our earlier case studies.

Drawing operations in graphics contexts can be performed in one of two different *modes*. The common mode is *paint* mode, established by calling the method setPaintMode. An alternative is XOR mode. The unique property of XOR mode is that if the same object is drawn twice, the second drawing command *erases* the object, restoring the image to the state it had prior to the first command. This property is similar to the logical exclusive-or (XOR) command, hence the name. The common use for this property is to draw cursors, or other graphics images that track the position of the mouse as it moves across a window. We will see an example of this in the program described in the next section.

18.6   A SIMPLE PAINTING PROGRAM

An example program will illustrate the use of many of the graphics context commands. The program will also show how one can create a static image that can be generated as a sequence of graphical commands, rather than all at one time.

The window for the application (Figure 18.4) has a row of buttons across the top. Pressing one of these buttons selects the type of figure to be drawn. Pressing the mouse in the canvas window then begins a drawing operation. As the mouse moves while still being pressed, a "ghost" image of the figure tracks the mouse location. When the mouse is released, the selected figure is drawn.

The source code for the painting application is shown in Figure 18.5. A Panel is used to hold the three buttons. The buttons themselves are defined as subclasses of an inner class Shape, which will do double duty as both a button listener class, and a recording of the currently selected shape. When pressed, the button will simply save its value in the variable currentShape. In addition to

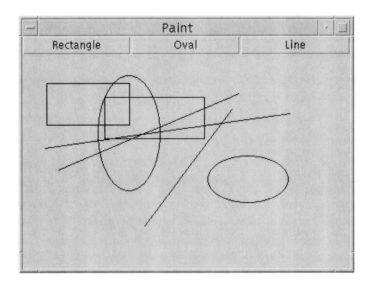

Figure 18.4   Window for painting application.

```
class Paint extends Frame {
   public static void main (String [ ] args)
      { Frame world = new Paint( ); world.show( ); }

   private Image image = null;
   private Shape currentShape = null;

   public Paint ( ) {
      setTitle("Paint");
      setSize(400, 300);

         // create panel of buttons
      Panel p = new Panel( );
      p.setLayout(new GridLayout(1,3));
      p.add(new Rectangle( ));
      p.add(new Oval( ));
      p.add(new Line( ));
      add("North", p);
         // add mouse event listener
      MouseKeeper k = new MouseKeeper( );
      addMouseListener(k);
      addMouseMotionListener(k);
   }

   public void paint (Graphics g) {
      if (image == null) // will happen only once
         image = createImage(400, 300);
      if (image != null)
         g.drawImage(image, 0, 0, this);
   }

   private abstract class Shape
      extends Button implements ActionListener { ... }
   private class Rectangle extends Shape { ... }
   private class Oval extends Shape { ... }
   private class Line extends Shape { ... }

   private class MouseKeeper
      extends MouseAdapter implements MouseMotionListener { ... }
}
```

Figure 18.5   Source for painting application.

representing a button, each shape will know how to draw itself in a rectangular region (Figure 18.6). The class Shape, as well as the drawing method, have been declared abstract. This means that it is not possible to create an instance of the class without first subclassing. Furthermore, each subclass *must* implement the method draw.

The first time the application is asked to draw its window, it copies the Image associated with the application component into a variable named image. Thereafter, to render the application window it is only necessary to draw the contents of this image.

Most applications that interact with the mouse need to recognize the mouse moving down. Of these, a few (such as the current application) need to differentiate between the mouse going down and the mouse going up. Fewer still need also to track the position of the mouse as it is moving. Because the latter action is relatively infrequent, the Java event library separates this task into a different listener. A MouseListener tracks only mouse presses and releases. A MouseMotion-Listener also tracks mouse movements, either while pressed or not. The mouse class we created for this class implements both interfaces, by extending the MouseAdapter, and implementing the MouseMotionListener interface (Figure 18.7, on page 308).

When the mouse is first pressed, the location of the mouse press is saved in a pair of local integer variables. A second pair of integer variables records the new location and is initially the same as the source location. As the mouse moves, the method mouseDragged is repeatedly executed. This method sets the graphical display mode to XOR, then repaints the current shape using the old coordinate locations. The effect will be the *erase* of the previous image. The end point locations are then set to the current mouse position and the shape redrawn. The effect is that the shape is continually erased and redrawn as the mouse is moved. When the mouse is finally released, the method mouseReleased is executed. This erases the old image one last time, changes the mode to paint, and draws the shape in its final location.

18.7 CHAPTER SUMMARY

A Java run-time library provides a rich collection of classes that can be used to manipulate graphical images. In this chapter we have investigated several of these. A Color represents a color value. Colors are specified by a trio of integer values, representing the amount of red, green and blue in the color. A Rectangle represents a rectangular region of the plane. A Font describes the characteristics of a printed letter. An Image is a picture composed of pixel values. A succession of images can be displayed one after the other in an animation. A Graphics object provides the tools necessary to perform simple graphical operations, such as drawing a line or oval.

```
private abstract class Shape
    extends Button implements ActionListener {

  public Shape (String name) {
    super(name);
    addActionListener (this);
  }

  public abstract void draw (Graphics g, int a, int b, int c, int d);

  public void actionPerformed (ActionEvent e)
    { currentShape = this; }
}

private class Rectangle extends Shape {

  public Rectangle () { super("Rectangle"); }

  public void draw (Graphics g, int a, int b, int c, int d) {
    int w = c - a; // width
    int h = d - b; // height
    g.drawRect(a, b, w, h);
  }
}

private class Oval extends Shape {
  public Oval () { super("Oval"); }

  public void draw (Graphics g, int a, int b, int c, int d) {
    int w = c - a; int h = d - b;
    g.drawOval(a, b, w, h);
  }
}

private class Line extends Shape {
  public Line () { super("Line"); }

  public void draw (Graphics g, int a, int b, int c, int d)
    { g.drawLine(a, b, c, d); }
}
```

Figure 18.6 Shape subclasses.

```
private class MouseKeeper
     extends MouseAdapter implements MouseMotionListener {
  private int startx, starty; // upper right corner
  private int lastx, lasty; // current position

  public void mousePressed (MouseEvent e) {
     lastx = startx = e.getX( );
     lasty = starty = e.getY( );
  }

  private void drawShape (Graphics g) {
     if (currentShape != null)
        currentShape.draw(g, startx, starty, lastx, lasty);
  }

  public void mouseDragged (MouseEvent e) {
     Graphics g = image.getGraphics( );
     g.setXORMode(Color.white);
        // erase old image
     drawShape(g);
        // draw new rectangle
     lastx = e.getX( ); lasty = e.getY( );
     drawShape(g); repaint( );
  }

  public void mouseReleased (MouseEvent e) {
     Graphics g = image.getGraphics( );
        // erase old image
     g.setXORMode(Color.white);
     drawShape(g);
        // now paint new image
     g.setPaintMode( );
     lastx = e.getX( ); lasty = e.getY( );
     drawShape(g); repaint( );
  }

  public void mouseMoved (MouseEvent e) { }
}
```

Figure 18.7   The mouse listener for the painting application.

STUDY QUESTIONS

1. What do the three integer values in a color represent?

2. What are the predefined colors available to the Java run-time system?

3. How does one tell whether or not a point is found inside a rectangle?

4. What are the style modifiers used with a value of type Font?

5. What is an animation? How can an animation be produced in Java?

6. How is a MouseMotionListener different from a MouseActionListener?

EXERCISES

1. Add buttons to the painting program described in Section 18.6 to create filled rectangles and ovals, as well as the outline rectangles and ovals it currently produces.

2. Add a panel with three sliders for selecting colors, similar to the panel described in Chapter 13. Use the colors selected by these sliders for the fill color in the figures you added in the previous question.

3. By adding a KeyListener object, add the ability to enter text and have it displayed at the current mouse location.

4. Add menu items to change the font and style of text values.

19 Collection Classes

Collections are classes designed for holding groups of objects. Almost all non-trivial programs need to maintain one or more collections of objects. Although the Java library provides only a few different forms of collection, the features provided by these classes are very general, making them applicable to a wide variety of problems. In this chapter we will first describe some of the basic concepts common to the collection classes, then summarize the basic collections provided by Java, and finally describe a few container types that are not provided by the standard library, but which can be easily constructed by the programmer.

19.1 ELEMENT TYPES AND PRIMITIVE VALUE WRAPPERS

With the exception of the array data type, all the collections provided by the Java library maintain their values in variables of type Object. There are two important consequences of this feature:

- Since primitive types, such as integers, Booleans, characters, and floating-point values, are not subclasses of Object, they cannot be directly stored in these collections.

- When values are removed from the collection, they must be cast back to their original type.

One way to circumvent the first restriction is through the use of *wrapper classes*. A wrapper class maintains a primitive data value but is itself an object and can thus be stored in a container. Methods are typically provided both to construct an instance of the wrapper class from a primitive value, and to recover the original value from the wrapper. The following, for example, stores two integers into instances of class Integer, then recovers the original values so that an arithmetic operation can be performed:

```
Integer a = new Integer(12);
Integer b = new Integer(3);
    // must recover the int values to do arithmetic
int c = a.intValue( ) * b.intValue( );
```

In addition, many wrapper classes provide other useful functionality, such as the ability to parse string values. A common way to convert a string containing an integer value literal into an int, for example, is to use an Integer as a middle step:

```
String text = "123"; // example string value
Integer val = new Integer(text); // first convert to Integer
int ival = val.intValue( ); // then convert Integer to int
```

Table 19.1 summarizes the most common wrapper classes and a few of their more useful behaviors.

Table 19.1   Wrapper Classes and Selected Behaviors.

Integer Wrapper

new Integer(int value)	Build Integer from int
Integer(String value)	Parse integer in String
intValue( )	Value of Integer as int
toString( )	Return decimal string representation of Integer
toBinaryString( )	Return binary representation
toOctalString( )	Return octal representation
toHexString( )	Return hex representation

Character Wrapper

new Character(char value)	Convert char to Character
charValue( )	Return char value of Character
isLetter( )	Determine if character is letter
isDigit( )	True if character is digit

Boolean Wrapper

new Boolean (boolean value)	Convert boolean to Boolean
booleanValue ( )	Retrieve boolean value from Boolean
toString( )	Generate string representation of boolean

Double Wrapper

new Double(double)	Convert double to Double
new Double(String)	Construct Double from string
doubleValue( )	Return double value of Double

19.2 ENUMERATORS

All collections can be envisioned as a linear sequence of elements. However, the particular means used to access each element differs from one collection type to another. For example, a vector is indexed using an integer position key, whereas a hash table can use any type of object as a key. It is frequently desirable to abstract away these differences and access the elements of the collection in sequence without regard to the technique used to obtain the underlying values. This facility is provided by the Enumeration interface and its various implementations. The Enumeration interface specifies two methods:

hasMoreElements( )	A Boolean value that indicates whether or not there are any more elements to be enumerated
nextElement( )	Retrieves the next element in the enumeration

These two operations are used together to form a loop. The following code, for example, shows how all the elements of a hash table could be printed:

```
for (Enumeration e = htab.elements( ); e.hasMoreElements( ); ) {
   System.out.println (e.nextElement( ));
   }
```

The methods hasMoreElements and nextElement should always be invoked in tandem. That is, nextElement should never be invoked unless hasMoreElements has first determined that there is another element, and nextElement should never be invoked twice without an intervening call on hasMoreElements. If it is necessary to refer more than once to the value returned by nextElement, the result of the nextElement call should be assigned to a local variable:

```
for (Enumeration e = htab.elements( ); e.hasMoreElements( ); ) {
   Object value = e.nextElement( );
   if (value.equals(Test))
      System.out.println ("found object " + value);
   }
```

With the exception of the array, all the collections provided by the Java library provide a method that generates an enumeration. In addition, several other classes that are not necessarily collections also support the enumeration protocol. For example, a StringTokenizer is used to extract words from a string value. The individual words are then accessed using enumeration methods. Section 19.6.1 describes how the programmer can create a new type of enumeration.

19.3 THE ARRAY

The most basic collection form in Java is the array. As noted in earlier chapters, the creation and manipulation of an array value is different in Java than in many other programming languages. The Java language makes a separation between (a) declaring a variable of array type, (b) defining the size of the array and allocating space, and (c) assigning values to the array. In many other languages the first and second tasks are merged. Combining these concepts makes it difficult to, for example, write functions that will operate on arrays of any size. These problems are largely eliminated in Java's approach to arrays.

An array variable is declared by indicating the type of elements the array will contain, and a pair of square brackets that indicate an array is being formed. The following, for example, is from the Solitaire game case study examined in Chapter 9.

```
static public CardPile allPiles [ ];
```

The brackets can be written either after the variable name or after the type. The following, for example, is an equivalent declaration:

```
static public CardPile [ ] allPiles;
```

Note that the array is the only collection in the Java library that requires the programmer to specify the type of elements that will be held by the container. An important consequence of this is that the array is the *only* collection that can maintain nonobject types, such as integers, Booleans, or characters. Other containers hold their values as instances of class Object, and can therefore only hold primitive values if they are surrounded by wrapper classes (Integer, Double, and so on).

An array *value* is created, as are all values, using the new operator. It is only when the array value is created that the size of the array is specified.

```
allPiles = new CardPile [ 13 ]; // create array of 13 card piles
```

Arrays can also be created as an initialization expression in the original declaration. The initialization expression provides the values for the array, as well as indicating the number of elements.

```
int primes [ ] = {2, 3, 5, 7, 11, 13, 17, 19};
```

Elements of an array are accessed using the subscript operator. This is used both to retrieve the current value held at a given position and to assign a position a new value:

```
primes[3] = primes[2] + 2;
```

Legal index values range from zero to one less than the number of elements held by the array. An attempt to access a value with an out-of-range index value results in an IndexOutOfBoundsException being thrown.

The integer field length describes the number of elements held by an array. The following loop shows this value being used to form a loop to print the elements in an array:

```
for (int i = 0; i < primes.length; i++)
    System.out.println("prime " + i + " is " + primes[i]);
```

Arrays are also *cloneable* (see Section 11.3.1). An array can be copied and assigned to another array value. The clone operation creates a shallow copy.

```
int numbers [ ];
numbers = primes.clone( ); // creates a new array of numbers
```

19.4 THE Vector COLLECTION

The Vector data abstraction is similar to an array of objects. However, it provides a number of high-level operations not supported by the array abstraction. Most importantly, a vector is *expandable*, meaning it grows as necessary as new elements are added to the collection. Thus, the programmer need not know the eventual collection size at the time the vector is created. To use this collection the Vector class must be imported from java.util.Vector. A new vector is created using the new operator.

```
import java.util.Vector;
    .
    .
    .
Vector numbers = new Vector ( );
```

Because objects held by a Vector must be subclasses of Object, a vector can not be used to hold primitive values, such as integers or floats. However, wrapper classes can be used to convert such values into objects.

Table 19.2 summarizes the most useful operations provided by the Vector data abstraction. The class has been carefully designed so that it can be used in a variety of different ways. The following sections describe some of the more common uses.

19.4.1 *Using a Vector as an Array*

Unlike an array, a vector is not created with a fixed size. A vector can be given a specific size either by adding the appropriate number of elements (using the

Table 19.2   Operations Provided by the Vector Data Type.

Size Determination	
size( )	Returns number of elements in collection as an int
isEmpty( )	Returns true if collection is empty
capacity( )	Return current capacity of vector as an int
setSize(int newSize)	Set size of vector, truncating or expanding as necessa
Element Access	
contains(Object elem)	Determines whether a value is in this vector
firstElement( )	Returns first element of collection
lastElement( )	Returns last element of collection
elementAt(int index)	Returns element stored at given position
Insertion and Modification	
addElement(Object value)	Add new value to end of collection
setElementAt(Object value, int index)	Change value at position
insertElementAt(Object value, int index)	Insert value at given index
Removal	
removeElementAt(int index)	Remove element at index, reducing size of vector
removeElement(Object value)	Remove all instances of value
removeAllElements( )	Delete all values from vector
Search	
indexOf(Object value)	Return index of first occurrence
lastIndexOf(Object value)	Return index of last occurrence
Miscellaneous	
clone( )	Return shallow copy of vector
toString( )	Return string representation of vector

addElement operation) or by using setSize. In the latter case, a null value will be stored in any index locations that have not previously been assigned a value.

```
Vector aVec = new Vector ();  // create a new vector
aVec.setSize (20);  // allocate 20 locations, initially undefined
```

Once sized, the value stored at any position can be accessed using the method elementAt, while positions can be modified using setElementAt. Note that in the latter, the index of the position being modified is the second parameter, while the value to be assigned to the location is the first parameter. The following illustrates how these methods could be used to swap the first and final elements of a vector:

```
Object first = aVec.elementAt(0); // store first position
aVec.setElementAt(aVec.lastElement( ), 0); // store last in location 0
aVec.setElementAt(first, aVec.size( )-1); // store first at end
```

19.4.2   *Using a* Vector *as a Stack*

A *stack* is a data structure that allows elements to be inserted and removed at one end, and it always removes the last element inserted. A stack of papers on a desk is a good intuitive picture of the stack abstraction.

Although the Java standard library includes a Stack data abstraction (see Section 19.5), it is easy to see how a Vector can be used as a stack. The characteristic operations of a stack are to insert or remove an item from the top of the stack, peek at (but do not remove) the topmost element, or/and test the stack for emptiness. The following shows how each of these can be performed using operations provided by the vector class:

aVec.addElement (value)	Push a value on the stack
aVec.lastElement( )	Peek at the topmost element of the stack
aVec.removeElementAt(aVec.size( ) - 1)	Remove the topmost element of the stack

As will be noted in Section 19.5, the Stack abstraction is slightly more robust, since it will throw more meaningful error indications if an attempt is made to remove an element from an empty stack.

19.4.3   *Using a* Vector *as a Queue*

A *queue* is a data structure that allows elements to be inserted at one end, and removed from the other. In this fashion, the element removed will be the *first* element that was inserted. Thinking about a line of people waiting to enter a theater provides a good intuition.

In a manner analogous to the way that the vector can be used as a stack, the vector operations can also be used to simulate a queue:

aVec.addElement (value)	Push a value on the queue
aVec.firstElement( )	Peek at the first element in the queue
aVec.removeElementAt(0)	Remove the first element of the queue

There is one important difference between this abstraction and the earlier simulation of the stack. In the stack abstraction, all the operations could be performed in constant time, independent of the number of elements being held by the stack.[1] Removing the first element from the queue, on the other hand, *always* results in all elements being moved and therefore always requires time proportional to the number of elements in the collection.

19.4.4   *Using a* Vector *as a Set*

A *set* is usually envisioned as an unordered collection of values. Characteristic operations on a set include testing to see if a value is being held in the set, and adding or removing values from the set. The following shows how these can be implemented using the operations provided by the Vector class:

aVec.contains(value)	See if value is held in set
aVec.addElement(value)	Add new element to set
aVec.removeElement(value)	Remove element from set

The equals method is used to perform comparisons. Comparisons are necessary to determine whether or not a value is held in the collection and whether a value is the element the user wishes to delete. For user-defined data values the equals method can be overridden to provide whatever meaning is appropriate (see Section 11.4).

Operations such as union and intersection of sets can be easily implemented using a loop. The following code, for example, places in setThree the union of the values from setOne and setTwo.

```
Vector setThree = new Vector( );
setThree = setOne.clone( ); // first copy all of set one
    // then add elements from set two not already in set one
for (Enumeration e = setTwo.elements( ); e.hasMoreElements( ); ) {
    Object value = e.nextElement( );
    if (! setThree.contains(value))
        setThree.addElement(value);
}
```

For sets consisting of positive integer values, the BitSet class (Section 19.6) is often a more efficient alternative.

---

[1] The assertion concerning constant time operation of stack operations is true with one small caveat. An insertion can, in rare occasions, result in a reallocation of the underlying vector buffer and thus require time proportional to the number of elements in the vector. This is usually, however, a rare occurrence.

19.4.5   *Using a* Vector *as a List*

Characteristic operations of a *list* data abstraction give the abilities to insert or remove elements at any location and the ability to find the location of any value.[2]

aVec.firstElement( )	First element
aVec.lastElement( )	Last element
aVec.insertElementAt(value, 0)	Insert to front of list
aVec.addElement(value)	Insert to end of list
aVec.contains(value)	See if value is in collection
aVec.removeElementAt(0)	Remove first element
aVec.removeElementAt(aVec.size( ) - 1)	Remove last element
aVec.indexOf(value)	Find location of element
aVec.removeElementAt(index)	Remove value from middle

Again, this use of the Vector abstraction to simulate a list differs from the classical description of the *list* abstraction in the algorithmic execution time of certain operations. In particular, the insertion or removal from the front of the collection may result in the entire set of values being moved, thereby requiring time proportional to the size of the collection. This is a critical concern only when the size of the collections is large or when this is a frequent operation. A more direct implementation of a list is described in Section 19.9.

19.5   THE Stack COLLECTION

Section 19.4.2 described how a stack could be simulated using a Vector. However, the Java standard library also provides the Stack as a data value. The names of the methods used to operate on this data type are slightly different from the Vector operations described in Section 19.4.2, and the structure is slightly more robust. Stack operations can be described as follows:

Stack aStack = new Stack( )	Create a new stack
aStack.push (value)	Push a value onto the stack
aStack.peek( )	Peek at the topmost element of the stack
aStack.pop( )	Remove the topmost element of the stack
aStack.size( )	Number of elements in the collection

---

[2] The list referred to here is the traditional data abstraction known by that name. The Java library unfortunately uses the class name List to refer to a graphical component that allows the user to select a value from a series of string items.

| aStack.empty( ) | Test for empty stack |
| aStack.search(value) | Position of element in stack |

The pop operation both removes and returns the topmost element of the stack. Both the pop and the peek operations will throw an EmptyStackException if they are applied to an empty stack.

The search method returns the index of the given element starting from the top of the stack; that is, if the element is found at the top of the stack, search will return 0, if found one element down in the stack, search will return 1, and so on. Because the Stack data structure is built using inheritance from the Vector class it is also possible to access the values of the stack using their index. However, the positions returned by the search operation do not correspond to the index position. To discover the index position of a value the Vector operation indexOf can be used.

In Chapter 10 we described some of the advantages and disadvantages of creating the stack using inheritance from class Vector.

19.6 THE BitSet COLLECTION

A BitSet is abstractly a set of positive integer values. The BitSet class differs from the other collection classes in that it can only be used to hold integer values. Like an array or a Vector, each element is given an index position. However, the only operations that can be performed on each element are to set, test, or clear the value. A BitSet is a compact way to encode either a collection of positive integer values or a collection of Boolean values (for example, on/off settings).

To create a BitSet, the user can specify the number of positions the set will represent. However, like the Vector, the bit set is extensible and will be enlarged automatically if a position outside the range is accessed.

```
// create a BitSet that initially contains 75 elements
BitSet bset = new BitSet(75);
```

The following list summarizes the operations used to set or test an individual position in the bit set:

bset.set (index)	Set a bit position
bset.get (index)	Test a bit position
bset.clear (index)	Clear a bit position

The get method returns a boolean value, which is true if the given bit is set, and false otherwise. Each of these operations will throw an IndexOutOfBoundsException if the index value is smaller than zero.

A BitSet can be combined with another BitSet in a variety of ways:

bset.or(setTwo)	Form bitwise union with argument set
bset.and(setTwo)	Form bitwise intersection with argument set
bset.xor(setTwo)	Form bitwise symmetric difference with argument set

The method toString returns the string representation of the collection. This consists of a comma-separated list of the indices of the bits in the collection that have been set.

19.6.1   *Example Program: Prime Sieve*

A program that will generate a list of prime numbers using the sieve of Eratosthenes can be used to illustrate the manipulation of a bit set. The constructor for the class Sieve (Figure 19.1) takes an integer argument *n*, and creates a bit set of *n* positions. These are initially all set to 1, using the member function set. The sieve algorithm then walks through the list, using get to find the next set value. A loop then walks through the remainder of the collection, throwing out (via the clear( ) member function) values that are multiples of the earlier value. When we are finished, any value not crossed out must be prime.

The remaining two functions illustrate how a new enumeration can be created. The value index will maintain the current "position" in the list, which will change as values are enumerated. The method hasMoreElements loops until a prime value is found, or until the size of the bit set is exceeded. The first results in a true value, the latter a false one. The method nextElement simply makes an object out of the integer value. A small test method is also included in the class, to illustrate how this class could be used.

19.7   THE Dictionary INTERFACE AND THE Hashtable COLLECTION

A *dictionary* is an indexed collection, similar to an array or a Vector. However, unlike array values, the index values need not be integer. Instead, any object type can be used as an index (called a *key*), and any object value can be stored as the element selected by the key. To place a new value into the collection, the user provides both the key and value. To access an element in the collection, the user provides a key, and the associated value is returned.

In the Java library, the class Dictionary is an abstract class that defines the behavior of the *dictionary* abstraction but does not provide an implementation. This interface can be described as follows:

dict.get(key)	Retrieve value associated with given key
dict.put(key, value)	Place value into collection with given key
dict.remove(key)	Remove value from collection

```
import java.util.*;

class Sieve implements Enumeration {
   private BitSet primes;
   private int index = 2;

   public Sieve (int n) {
      primes = new BitSet(n);
         // first set all the bits
      for (int i = 1; i < n; i++)
         primes.set(i);
         // then erase all the nonprimes
      for (int i = 2; i * i < n; i++)
         if (primes.get(i))
            for (int j = i + i; j <= n; j += i)
               primes.clear(j);
   }

   public boolean hasMoreElements () {
      index++;
      int n = primes.size();
      while (! primes.get(index))
         if (++index > n)
            return false;
      return true;
   }

   public Object nextElement() { return new Integer(index); }

      // test program for prime sieve algorithm
   public static void main (String [ ] args) {
      Sieve p = new Sieve(100);
      while (p.hasMoreElements())
         System.out.println(p.nextElement());
   }
}
```

Figure 19.1   Prime Sieve program.

dict.isEmpty( )   See if collection is empty

dict.size( )   Return number of elements in collection

dict.elements( )   Return enumeration for collection values

dict.keys( )   Return enumeration of collection keys

The get method will return null if the given value is not found in the collection. Otherwise, the value is returned as an Object, which must then be cast into the appropriate type. The remove method returns the value of the association being deleted, again returning null if the key is not a legal index element. There are two enumeration generating methods, one to return an enumeration of keys and one to return an enumeration of values.

The class Hashtable provides an implementation of the Dictionary operations. A hash table can be envisioned as an array of collections called *buckets*. To add an element to the collection, an integer value, called the *hash value*, is first computed for the given key. The method hashCode is used for this purpose. This method is defined in class Object and is therefore common to all object values. It is overridden in various classes to provide alternative algorithms. Using this integer, one of the buckets is selected and the key/value pair inserted into the corresponding collection.

In addition to the methods matching the Dictionary specification, the hash table provides the method clear( ), which removes all values from the container, contains(value), which determines whether an element is contained in the collection, and containsKey(key), which tests to see if a given key is in the collection.

The default implementation of the hashCode method, in class Object, should be applicable in almost all situations, just as the default implementation of equals is usually adequate. If a data type that is going to be used as a hash table key overrides the equals method, it is a good idea to override hashCode as well, so that two objects that test equal to each other will also have the same hash value.

19.7.1   *Example Program: A Concordance*

A concordance is a listing of words from a printed text, each word being followed by the lines on which the word appears. A class that will create a concordance will illustrate how the Dictionary data type is used, as well as how different collection classes can be combined with each other.

In the program shown in Figure 19.2, the primary data structure is a dictionary, implemented using the Hashtable class. The keys for this dictionary will be the individual words in the input text. The value associated with each key will be a set of integer values, representing the line numbers on which the word appears. A Vector will be used to represent the set, using the techniques described in Section 19.4.4.

```java
import java.util.*;
import java.io.*;

class Concordance {
   private Dictionary dict = new Hashtable( );

   public void readLines (DataInputStream input) throws IOException {
      String delims = " \t\n.,!?;:";
      for (int line = 1; true; line++ ) {
         String text = input.readLine( );
         if (text == null) return;
         text = text.toLowerCase( );
         Enumeration e = new StringTokenizer(text, delims);
         while (e.hasMoreElements( ))
            enterWord ((String) e.nextElement( ), new Integer(line));
      }
   }

   public void generateOutput (PrintStream output) {
      Enumeration e = dict.keys( );
      while (e.hasMoreElements( ) ) {
         String word = (String) e.nextElement( );
         Vector set = (Vector) dict.get(word);
         output.print (word + ": ");
         Enumeration f = set.elements( );
         while (f.hasMoreElements( ))
            output.print (f.nextElement( ) + " ");
         output.println (" ");
      }
   }

   private void enterWord (String word, Integer line) {
      Vector set = (Vector) dict.get(word);
      if (set == null) { // word not in collection
         set = new Vector( ); // make new set
         dict.put (word, set);
      }
      if (! set.contains(line)) set.addElement(line);
   }
}
```

Figure 19.2   The class Concordance.

The method readLines reads the input line by line, maintaining a counter to indicate the line number. The method readLine, provided by the class DataInput-Stream, returns a null value when end of input is encountered, at which time the method returns. (This method is also the potential source for the IOExcep-tion, which can be thrown if an error occurs during the read operation. In our program we simply pass this exception back to the caller.) Otherwise, the text is converted to lowercase, using the method toLowerCase provided by the String class; then a StringTokenizer is created to split the text into individual words. A StringTokenizer is a form of Enumeration, and so an enumeration loop is used to enter each word into the concordance.

The private method enterWord is used to place each new word in the concor-dance. First, the value associated with the key (the word) is determined. Here the program handles the first of two exceptional conditions that might arise. If this is the first time the word has been seen, there will be no entry in the dictionary, and so the result of calling get will be a null value. In this case a new and empty Vector is created and is inserted into the dictionary using the word as key. Using the Vector in the fashion of a set, the method contains is invoked to determine if the line has already been placed in the collection. (This is the second exceptional condition, which will occur if the same word appears two or more times on one line.) If not, the line is then added to the list.

Finally, once all the input has been processed, the method generateOutput is used to create the printed report. This method uses a doubly nested enumeration loop. The first loop enumerates the keys of the Dictionary, generated by the keys method. The value associated with each key is a set, represented by a Vector. A second loop, using the enumerator produced by the elements method, then prints the values held by the vector.

An easy way to test the program is to use the system resources System.in and System.out as the input and output containers, as in the following:

```
static public void main (String [ ] args) {
    Concordance c = new Concordance( );
    try {
        c.readLines(new DataInputStream(System.in));
    } catch (IOException e) { return; }
    c.generateOutput (System.out);
}
```

19.7.2   *Properties*

The Java run-time system maintains a special type of hash table, termed the *properties list*. The class Properties, a subclass of Hashtable, holds a collection of string key/value pairs. These represent values that describe the current executing environment, such as the user name, operating system name, home directory, and so on. The following program can be used to see the range of properties available to a running Java program:

```
public static void main (String [ ] args) {
    Dictionary props = System.getProperties( );
    Enumeration e = props.keys( );
    while (e.hasMoreElements( )) {
        Object key = e.nextElement( );
        Object value = props.get(key);
        System.out.println("property " + key + " value " + value);
    }
}
```

19.8 WHY ARE THERE NO ORDERED COLLECTIONS?

If one considers the "classic" data abstractions found in most data structures textbooks, a notable omission from the Java library are data structures that maintain values in sequence. Examples of such abstractions are ordered lists, ordered vectors, or binary trees. Indeed, there is not even any mechanism provided in the Java library to sort a vector of values. Rather than being caused by oversight, this omission reflects some fundamental properties of the Java language.

All of the Java collections maintain their values in variables of type Object. The class Object does not define any ordering relation. Indeed, the only elements that can be compared using the < operator are the primitive numeric types (integer, long, double, and so on). One could imagine defining in class Object a method lessThan(Object), similar to the method equals(Object). However, while there is a clear default interpretation for the equality operator (namely, object identity), it is difficult to imagine a similar meaning for the relational operator that would be applicable to all objects. Certainly it could not provide a total ordering on all objects. What, for example, would be the result of comparing the String "abc" and the integer 37? In short, ordered collections are not found in the Java library because there is no obvious general mechanism to define what it means to order two values.

One could imagine that an alternative to placing the method lessThan in class Object would be to create an Ordered interface, such as the following:

```
interface Ordered {
    public boolean compare (Ordered arg);
}
```

One could then create a collection in which all values need to implement the Ordered interface, rather than simply being Object. However, there are two major objections to this technique. The first is that since the argument is only known to be an object that implements the Ordered interface, one must still decide how to compare objects of different types (a Triangle and an Orange, for example). The second problem is that restricting the type of objects the collection can maintain to only those values that implement the Ordered relation severely limits the utility of the classes.

Another possibility is to imagine an interface for an object that is used to create comparisons. That is, the object takes both values as arguments, and returns their ordering. Such an interface could be written as follows:

```
interface ComparisonObject {
    public boolean Compare (Object one, Object two);
}
```

To manipulate an ordered collection, one would then create an implementation of this interface for the desired elements. The following, for example, would be a comparison class for Integer objects:

```
class IntegerComparison implements ComparisonObject {
    public boolean Compare (Object one, Object two) {
        if ((one instanceof Integer) && (two instanceof Integer)) {
            Integer ione = (Integer) one;
            Integer itwo = (Integer) two;
            return ione.intValue( ) < itwo.intValue( );
        }
        return false;
    }
}
```

The following program illustrates how such an object could be used. The static method sort is an implementation of the insertion sort algorithm. The main method creates a vector of integer values, then creates a comparison object to be passed as argument to the sort algorithm. The sorting algorithm orders the elements in place, using the comparison object to determine the relative placement of values.

```
class VectorSort {
    public static void sort (Vector v, ComparisonObject test) {
        // order a vector using insertion sort
        int n = v.size( );
        for (int top = 1; top < n; top++) {
            for (int j = top-1; j >= 0 &&
                test.Compare(v.elementAt(j+1), v.elementAt(j)); j--) {
                // swap the elements
                Object temp = v.elementAt(j+1);
                v.setElementAt(v.elementAt(j), j+1);
```

```
                v.setElementAt(temp, j);
            }
        }

    }

    public static void main (String [ ] args) {
        Vector v = new Vector( );
        Random r = new Random( );
        for (int i = 0; i < 10; i++)
            v.addElement(new Integer(r.nextInt( )));

            // sort the vector
        sort (v, new IntegerComparison( ));

        for (Enumeration e = v.elements( ); e.hasMoreElements( ); )
            System.out.println(e.nextElement( ));
    }
}
```

19.9   BUILDING YOUR OWN CONTAINERS

Even though the containers in the Java library are flexible, they cannot handle
all situations in which a collection class is needed. It is therefore sometimes
necessary to create new collection classes. To see how this can be done we will
create a class that implements the idea of a linked list. The major advantage of
the linked list over a vector is that insertions or removals to the beginning or the
middle of a linked list can be performed very rapidly (technically, in constant
time). In the vector these operations require the movement of all the elements in
the collection and can therefore be much more costly if the collection is large.

The LinkedList class abstraction is shown in Figure 19.3.[3] The actual values
are stored in instances of class Link, which is a nested inner class. In addition to
a value, links maintain references to the previous and next element in the list. A
private internal value firstLink will reference the first link. A link with an empty
value is used to mark the end of the list. The private internal value lastLink points
to this value.

Values can be inserted either to the front or the back of the list. An enumeration value can also be used to insert new elements into the middle of a list. The
value is inserted immediately before the element referred to by the enumeration.

---

[3] It would have been preferable to call this class List. However, as we noted in an earlier footnote, the
Java library already has a List class, which implements a graphical component used for selecting one string
item out of many alternatives.

```
class LinkedList {
   private Link firstLink;
   private Link lastLink;
   private int  count = 0;

   public LinkedList ()
      { firstLink = lastLink = new Link(null, null, null); }

   private class Link { ... }

   private class ListEnumeration implements Enumeration { ... }

   public boolean isEmpty () { return firstLink == lastLink; }

   public int size () { return count; }

   public Object firstElement () { return firstLink.value; }

   public Object lastElement () { return lastLink.prev.value; }

   public void addFront (Object newValue) { firstLink.insert(newValue); }

   public void addBack (Object newValue) { lastLink.insert(newValue); }

   public void addElement (Enumeration e, Object newValue) {
      ListEnumeration le = (ListEnumeration) e;
      le.link.insert (newValue);
   }

   public Object removeFront () { return firstLink.remove(); }

   public Object removeBack () { return lastLink.prev.remove(); }

   public Object removeElement (Enumeration e) {
      ListEnumeration le = (ListEnumeration) e;
      return le.link.remove ();
   }

   public Enumeration elements () { return new ListEnumeration(); }
}
```

Figure 19.3   The LinkedList class.

```
class LinkedList {
   private class Link {
      public Object value;
      public Link next;
      public Link prev;

      public Link (Object v, Link n, Link p)
         { value = v; next = n; prev = p; }

      public void insert (Object newValue) {
         Link newNode = new Link (newValue, this, prev);
         count++;
         if (prev == null) firstLink = newNode;
         else prev.next = newNode;
         prev = newNode;
      }

      public Object remove () {
         if (next == null)
            return null; // cannot remove last element
         count--;
         next.prev = prev;
         if (prev == null) firstLink = next;
         else prev.next = next;
         return value;
      }
   }

   private class ListEnumeration implements Enumeration {
      public Link link = null;

      public boolean hasMoreElements () {
         if (link == null) link = firstLink;
         else link = link.next;
         return link.next != null;
      }

      public Object nextElement () { return link.value; }
   }
      .
      .
      .
}
```

Figure 19.4   The inner classes in LinkedList.

All three methods make use of a common insertion routine provided by the inner class Link. This method is also used to maintain the count of the number of elements in the list. The classes Link and ListEnumeration are shown in Figure 19.4.

The class ListEnumeration implements the Enumeration protocol and is used for iterating over list elements. Note that the Enumeration protocol assumes that the methods hasMoreElements and nextElement will work in tandem and does not specify which of the two will actually advance the internal reference to the next element. Implementations of the Enumeration protocol use a variety of different schemes. This is why, for example, one should never invoke nextElement twice without an intervening call on hasMoreElements. In the LinkedList class, however, we assume that having examined the current value (the value yielded by nextElement), the programmer may wish to either insert a new value or remove the current value. Thus, in this case the task of advancing to the next value is given to the method hasMoreElements.

19.10 CHAPTER SUMMARY

In this chapter we have described the classes in the Java library that are used to hold collections of values. The simplest collection is the array. An array is a linear, indexed homogenous collection. A difficulty with the array is that the size of an array is fixed at the time the array is created. The Vector class overcomes this restriction, growing as necessary as new values are added to the collection. Vectors can be used to represent sets, queues, and lists of values. The Stack datatype is a specialization of the vector used when values are added and removed from the collection in a strict first-in, first-out fashion. A BitSet is a set of positive integer values. A Dictionary is an interface that describes a collection of key and value pairs. The HashTable is one possible implementation of the Dictionary interface.

The lack of any ordered collections is a reflection of the problem that there is, in general, no way to construct an ordering among all Java values.

The chapter concludes by showing how new collection classes can be created, using as an example a linked list container.

STUDY QUESTIONS

1. What are collection classes used for?

2. Because the standard library collection classes maintain their values as an Object, what must be done to a value when it is removed from a collection?

3. What is a wrapper class?

4. What is an enumerator?

5. What is the protocol for the class Enumerator? How are these methods combined to form a loop?

6. How is the Java array different from arrays in other languages?

7. What does it mean to say that the Vector data type is expandable?

8. How does the use of the Stack data type differ from the use of a Vector as a stack?

9. What concept does the class BitSet represent?

10. What is the relationship between the classes Dictionary and Hashtable?

11. Why are there no ordered collections in the Java library?

EXERCISES

1. Assume two sets are implemented using vectors, as described in Section 19.4.4. Write a loop that will place the intersection of the two sets into a third set.

2. Assume two sets are implemented using vectors, as described in Section 19.4.4. Write a loop that will place the symmetric difference of the two sets into a third set. (The symmetric difference is the set of elements that are in one or the other set, but not both.)

3. Add the following methods to the LinkedList class described in Section 19.9:

setElement(Enumeration e, Object v)	Change value at given location
includes(Object v)	Test whether value is in collection
find(Object v)	Return enumeration if value is in collection, or null

4. Modify the LinkedList class of Section 19.9 so that linked lists support the cloneable interface. (The cloneable interface is described in Section 11.3.1.)

5. Write an OrderedList class. This class will be like a linked list, but will maintain a comparison object, as described in Section 19.8. Using this object, elements will be placed in sequence as they are inserted into the container.

20 Multiple Threads of Execution

Most users of a computer are familiar with the idea of *multitasking*–for example, editing a spreadsheet at the same time that the computer is printing a report or receiving a fax. The computer appears to be doing more than one activity at the same time. Whether this is actually true depends upon the hardware involved. Unless you are using a machine with multiple processors, what is in fact occurring is that the operating system is rapidly cycling between the different activities, allowing each to execute for a small amount of time.

Multithreading is the same concept applied to an individual program. Each program has the ability to execute a number of tasks at the same time. Each of these computational tasks is called a *thread*. Unlike separate computer applications, multiple threads exist in the same executing environment (technically speaking, we say they have the same *context*). This means they share the same data variables, access the same methods, and so on. As with multitasking, this parallel behavior is usually just a charade; in fact the operating system is still executing only one thread at any one time and is cycling among all the different threads to give each an equal share.

20.1 CREATING THREADS

Recall the BallWorld application from Chapter 5 (Figure 5.2). This program created a bouncing ball, then moved the ball around on the window 2000 times before halting. You may recall that this is *all* the program did. It did not allow any sort of user interaction, and if you tried to stop the program before 2000 steps you could not.

In practice it is desirable to have programs that are more user friendly. Part of this is being able to interact with an application while it is running. One way to do this is to place the execution of the program in a separate thread, leaving the main program thread free to listen for user activity.

In Java, threads are created using the class Thread. There are two common ways that this class is used. One way is to subclass from Thread, and override the method run, which is the method that is executed to perform the task assigned to a thread. We could, for example, modify the BallWorld application (Figure 5.2) and create a bouncing ball thread as follows:

```
public class ThreadedBallWorld extends Frame {
    .
    .
    .
    private class BallThread extends Thread {
        public void run ( ) {
            while (true) {
                aBall.move( );
                if ((aBall.x( ) < 0) || (aBall.x( ) > FrameWidth))
                    aBall.setMotion (-aBall.xMotion( ), aBall.yMotion( ));
                if ((aBall.y( ) < 0) || (aBall.y( ) > FrameHeight))
                    aBall.setMotion (aBall.xMotion( ), -aBall.yMotion( ));
                repaint( );
                try {
                    sleep(50);
                } catch (InterruptedException e) { }
            }
        }
    }
    .
    .
    .
}
```

When started, the thread continually moves the ball, changing the direction of motion when the sides of the window are hit. Each time the ball moves the window is repainted, and the thread "sleeps" for 50 milliseconds.

The revised ball world application is shown in Figure 20.1. In the constructor for the application ThreadedBallWorld a Ball is created, and then a BallThread is produced to control the movement of the ball. Execution of the new thread is initiated by the call to start for the thread object. To illustrate that the user can now interact with the application as the ball moves, we have added a mouse listener object. When the mouse is clicked in the application window, the ball is moved to the mouse location. Notice how the paint method in Figure 20.1 needs only to call the paint method in Ball, since all the ball-moving code it carried in Figure 5.2 has been moved into the run method of BallThread.

Platforms differ on how they assign time to threads. On some systems threads are run until they sleep or until they yield to another thread. On other systems threads are given a fixed amount of time to execute, then halted automatically if they have not yet given up control when their time unit is finished. In order

```
public class ThreadedBallWorld extends Frame {

   public static void main (String [ ] args) {
      ThreadedBallWorld world = new ThreadedBallWorld (Color.red);
      world.show ( );
   }

   private static final int FrameWidth = 600;
   private static final int FrameHeight = 400;
   private Ball aBall;
   private int counter = 0;

   private ThreadedBallWorld (Color ballColor) {
      // constructor for new ball world
         // resize our frame
      setSize (FrameWidth, FrameHeight);
      setTitle ("Ball World");
      addMouseListener (new BallListener( ));

         // initialize object data field
      aBall = new Ball (10, 15, 5);
      aBall.setColor (ballColor);
      aBall.setMotion (3.0, 6.0);
      Thread ballThread = new BallThread( );
      ballThread.start( );
   }

   private class BallThread extends Thread { ... }

   private class BallListener extends MouseAdapter {
      public void mousePressed (MouseEvent e)
         { aBall.moveTo(e.getX( ), e.getY( )); }
   }

   public void paint (Graphics g) { aBall.paint (g); }
}
```

Figure 20.1   BallWorld application using threads.

to provide maximum portability, threads should either sleep occasionally (as is done here) or periodically invoke the method yield that is inherited from class Thread. Either of these actions will halt the current thread, allowing other threads a chance to perform their actions.

It is sometimes not convenient to create a thread class by subclassing from Thread. For example, it can happen that the thread class is already inheriting from some other class. Since in Java a class cannot extend from two classes, the designers of the language have provided an alternative technique. Instead of inheriting from Thread, the action portion of a thread can be declared as implementing the interface Runnable. The ball thread could be rewritten in this form as follows:

```java
public class ThreadedBallWorld extends Frame {
    .
    .
    .
    private class BallThread implements Runnable {
        public void run ( ) {
            while (true) {
                aBall.move( );
                if ((aBall.x( ) < 0) || (aBall.x( ) > FrameWidth))
                    aBall.setMotion (-aBall.xMotion( ), aBall.yMotion( ));
                if ((aBall.y( ) < 0) || (aBall.y( ) > FrameHeight))
                    aBall.setMotion (aBall.xMotion( ), -aBall.yMotion( ));
                repaint( );
                try {
                    Thread.sleep(50);
                } catch (InterruptedException e) { }
            }
        }
    }
    .
    .
    .
}
```

Note the format used for the call on sleep. Because the new class is not tied to Thread, the method sleep is not automatically inherited. Instead, the class name Thread must be explicitly provided in this case.

When a new thread class is defined by extending Thread, it inherits a start method from Thread and overrides the run method defined in the parent class. A thread belonging to such a class is started by applying start to it, which in turn will call run. However, when a new thread class, like BallThread, is defined by implementing Runnable, it has a run method but no start method. Consequently a different mechanism is required to start and run such a thread. This involves creating two objects. The first is the instance of Runnable (in this case a BallThread object). The second is an object of type Thread created using a constructor that takes the runnable object as argument:

```java
Thread ballThread = new Thread(new BallThread( ));
ballThread.start( );
```

The Thread object provides the start method that is necessary to schedule for execution the actions of the runnable object.

20.1.1   *Synchronizing Threads*

Two or more threads frequently need to share the same data fields. If two threads attempt to modify the same data area, it is possible for erroneous values to be produced. Assume we have two threads that share an integer data field, and assume that they each try to increment the value by 10. Internally an addition statement is divided into several separate steps. For example, the statement

```
a = a + 10
```

is executed as something similar to the following:

```
push the value of a on a stack
push the value 10 on the stack
add the two values on the stack
pop the top of stack, assign value to a
```

Assume that this same sequence of instructions is performed by two threads, and the original value of a is 50. Assume further that the thread that is running the first process is stopped immediately after the first push instruction above. The first thread will push the value 50 on its stack, then stop temporarily. The second thread will push the value 50 on its stack, increment by 10, then store the resulting value of 60 on its stack. Suppose now the first thread is restarted. It will continue with its actions, pushing 10 on the stack, adding the two values, and assigning the sum, 60, back to a. The end result will be that the value a will ultimately hold 60, not the value 70 that it should have held.

Although it might seem that a problem such as this might be rare, the speed with which computers execute means that a situation such as that described here, if possible at all, is not at all uncommon. Such errors are also exceedingly difficult to uncover, since they occur in such a rare situation. Fortunately, the designers of Java have foreseen this and provided a simple and elegant solution. A method that is declared as synchronized cannot be executed by more than one process at any time. In fact, if an object has more than one method declared as synchronized, then an attempt to execute any synchronized method will be delayed until the first synchronized method has been completed. If one thread is executing a synchronized method and a second thread tries to execute any other synchronized method with the same object, the second thread will be halted until the first thread completes. The solution to the problem just described is therefore to place the increment operation inside a method that is declared as synchronized:

```
public synchronized void increment ( ) {
      // only one thread can execute this
      // at any time
   a = a + 10;
   }
```

We will illustrate the use of a synchronized method in the case study presented in Section 20.2. There are many more advanced features of threads; however, they are generally not needed in most programs and will not be described here.

20.2 Case Study: A Tetris Game

A video game is a good illustration of the need for multiple threads of control. In a typical game, the user is constantly entering information, and the game itself is constantly moving. In a conventional single-thread programming language, one or the other of these tasks must be selected as the primary structure. Either the main program is a large loop that listens for the user's commands and every now and then moves the game forward, or it is a large loop that moves the elements of the game and every now and then listens for the user's instructions. Either form will end up being clumsy and difficult to debug.

A much more elegant solution is possible in the language Java. Each of these two tasks can be assigned its own process. Each thread is executed in parallel with other threads. One thread is simply listening for the user's commands, while the other thread is charged with moving the pieces (see Figure 20.2).

Of course, there must be some sort of communication between the two threads, and this is where most of the complexity in multithreaded programming occurs. In the Tetris game presented here, the communication consists only of one integer value, which maintains the next command to be performed.

In addition to demonstrating multiple threads of control, the Tetris game presented in this section will illustrate how to read keyboard events and an important technique for preventing flickering in graphical displays.

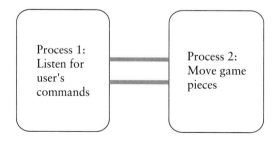

Figure 20.2 A double-thread program.

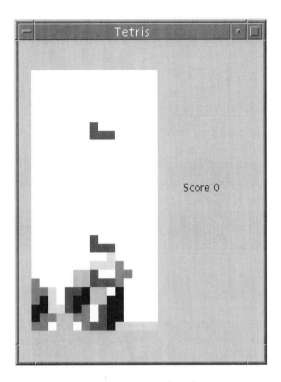

Figure 20.3   Application window for Tetris game.

20.2.1   *The Tetris Game Class*

Tetris is a popular video game. Playing pieces of several different forms fall from the sky and can merge together when they reach the ground. The player can move a piece left or right or rotate a piece as it falls to the ground. The player scores by arranging pieces as they fall so as to form a completely filled row in the ground. Figure 20.3 shows an example of a game in execution.

The primary class for the Tetris game is shown in Figure 20.4. As with all applications, execution begins with a static method named main. The main method creates an instance of the class Tetris, which is a type of Frame, and places this window on the display using the method show.

The constructor for the Tetris class sizes the application window, gives it a name, adds a listener for key presses, then creates and starts the second process. The game playing process will be an instance of a second class, named PieceMover. We will examine the structure of this class shortly. Once created, the thread of execution that will play the game is initiated by the issuing of the command start.

```
class Tetris extends Frame {

    public static void main(String [ ] args)
        { Tetris world = new Tetris( ); world.show( ); }

        // data fields
    public static final int FrameWidth = 300;
    public static final int FrameHeight = 400;
    private PieceMover player;

    public Tetris ( ) {
        setSize (FrameWidth, FrameHeight);
        setTitle("Tetris");

        addKeyListener (new keyDown( ));
        player = new PieceMover(this);
        player.start( );
    }

        // interface point between two threads
        // data shared by event handler and piece mover
    private int currentCommand = Piece.Down;

        // synchronized method for accessing shared data
    public synchronized int getCommand (int nextCommand) {
        int oldCommand = currentCommand;
        currentCommand = nextCommand;
        return oldCommand;
    }

    private class keyDown extends KeyAdapter { ... }

    public void update (Graphics g)
        { player.paint(sg); }
}
```

Figure 20.4   The Controller class for the Tetris game.

Communication Between Threads

Communication between the two threads of control is accomplished via a single integer variable (currentCommand). This value represents the next command to be executed. This variable is both set and accessed by means of the method getcommand. Note that this method is declared as synchronized. This means that only one of the two threads can be executing the method at any one time. If the other process attempts to execute the method, it will be held up until the first process completes. (In truth, the synchronization here is largely unnecessary, since the only penalty for simultaneous access will be that one process may receive an out-of-date value. Nevertheless, the use of the synchronized designation also helps to document the connection between the two threads.)

Handling Keyboard Events

Keyboard events are handled in a fashion similar to the mouse click events we have examined previously. A component maintains a collection of key listeners, which must each implement the KeyListener interface:

```
interface KeyListener extends EventListener {
    public void keyTyped (KeyEvent e);
    public void keyPressed (KeyEvent e);
    public void keyReleased (KeyEvent e);
}
```

As with mouse presses, the programmer can elect to either treat a key press and the key release as independent events, or simply examine one event for both actions. Implementing the KeyListener interface requires defining a body for all three methods. As normally one is interested in only one of these, an adapter class, named KeyAdapter, is provided that implements a null method for each of the three methods. To create a listener, one can inherit from this adapter and redefine the meaning of one of the methods. This is how key presses are handled in our application:

```
class Tetris extends Frame {
    .
    .
    .
    private class keyDown extends KeyAdapter {
        public void keyPressed (KeyEvent e) {
            char key = e.getKeyChar( );
            switch (key) {
                case 'g': player.newGame( ); break;
                case 'j': getCommand(Piece.Left); break;
                case 'k': getCommand(Piece.Rotate); break;
                case 'l': getCommand(Piece.Right); break;
                case 'q': System.exit(0);
            }
        }
    }
    .
    .
    .
}
```

Avoiding Flicker

As the game is being played, the screen is constantly being updated. This update process consists largely of drawing each individual square of the display. If this is done as separate graphical commands, the result can be an annoying flicker. There are several common ways to avoid this. Perhaps one of the easiest is the technique shown here. The method update( ) inherited from class Component normally first redraws the entire screen in the background color, then invokes paint to refresh the screen. If one overrides update rather than overriding paint, then the redrawing in the background color is avoided.

One often confusing feature to note is that although the update method invokes the paint method in the class of the player object (namely, the class Piece-Mover), the resulting actions are not performed by the piece mover thread. Updating the image is performed by the first thread, and it is independent of the piece mover thread, which continues to run on its own.

20.2.2   *The* PieceMover *Thread*

The class PieceMover is shown in Figure 20.5. The fact that the class extends class Thread and the presence of the method named run indicates that this class can potentially be executed as an independent thread.

The constructor for the class will be executed when the instance of PieceMover is created, as in Figure 20.4. The constructor sets the values of local variables, including creating an array of colors for the playing area. The playing area will be 15 elements wide by 30 elements deep. Because we think of the playing area as a graphical object, it will be easier to describe this by placing the horizontal movement first and the vertical movement second.

The thread starting point is a method named run. This method will be executed when the thread is started. Note that the method the programmer writes is called run, while the method used to initiate the thread is called start (the call on start in this case appears in Figure 20.4). The start method performs some other actions, such as setting up a schedule for thread execution, before invoking run. In our simple example, the run method will simply repeatedly create and drop playing pieces.

As the playing pieces move, they will indicate the change by altering the colors stored in the color table. Thus, the paint method simply cycles through the table, displaying each color in a small rectangle.

```
public void paint (Graphics g) {
    for (int i = 0; i < 30; i++)
        for (int j = 0; j < 15; j++) {
            g.setColor(table[j][i]);
            g.fillRect(20+10*j, 350-10*i, 10, 10);
        }
```

```
class PieceMover extends Thread {

    private Tetris controller;
    private Color table[ ][ ];
    private Piece currentPiece;
    private int score = 0;

    public PieceMover (Tetris t) {
        controller = t;
        table = new Color[15][30];
        currentPiece = null;
        newGame( );
    }

        // thread starting point
    public void run ( )
        { while (dropPiece( )) { } }

        // other methods
    public void newGame ( ) {
        for (int i = 0; i  < 30; i++)
            for (int j = 0; j < 15; j++)
                table[j][i] = Color.white;
    }

    public void paint (Graphics g) { ... }

    public boolean dropPiece ( ) { ... }

    private void moveDown (int start) { ... }

    private void checkScore( )  { ... }
}
```

Figure 20.5   The PieceMover class.

```
        g.setColor (Color.blue);
        g.drawString("Score " + score, 200, 200);
    }
```

The heart of the piece movement thread is the method dropPiece. This method creates a new piece, selecting the type of piece randomly from among the seven possibilities. If the piece cannot be moved downward once initially created at the top of the scene, the game is over, and the method returns false. Otherwise, a loop then reads the commands placed in the buffer shared with the controller, and acts on them, passing the command value to the individual piece for action. After every move the controller is asked to repaint, and control of the processor is yielded, allowing the other process time to execute. When control is returned, the piece movement process still sleeps for 100 milliseconds before reading the next command and moving once more.

```java
private boolean dropPiece () {
    int piecetype = 1 + (int) (7 * Math.random ());
    currentPiece = new Piece (piecetype);
    if (! currentPiece.move (Piece.Down, table))
        return false;
    int command = controller.getCommand (Piece.Down);
    while (currentPiece.move (command, table)) {
        controller.repaint ();
        yield ();
        try {
            sleep (100);
        } catch (InterruptedException e) { }
        command = controller.getCommand (Piece.Down);
    }
    // piece cannot move, check score
    checkScore();
    return true;
}
```

The while loop terminates when the piece can no longer move. At this point the method checkScore is called to determine if any points have been scored. Points are scored by completely filling a row. If such a row is found, the controller is notified that a score has been made, and the entire image is moved downward.

```java
private void checkScore()
{
    for (int i = 0; i < 30; i++) {
        boolean scored = true;
        for (int j = 0; j < 15; j++)
            if (table[j][i] == Color.white)
                scored = false;
        if (scored) {
            score += 10;
            moveDown(i);
            i = i - 1; // check row again
        }
    }
}
```

```
private void moveDown (int start) {
    for (int i = start; i < 30; i++)
        for (int j = 0; j < 15; j++)
            if (i < 29)
                table[j][i] = table[j][i+1];
            else
                table[j][i] = Color.white;
}
```

The method moveDown copies the colors from the row above into the current row, copying white values into the topmost row.

20.2.3 *The Game Piece Class*

An individual game piece is composed of a number of blocks. Each block is identified only by an x and y coordinate, maintained in a pair of parallel arrays. A piece also has its own color. The constructor for the class Piece (Figure 20.6) takes an integer that represents the piece type and initializes the locations appropriately. Only the initialization of the "S" shaped piece is shown; the others are all similar.

Other than the constructor, the only publicly accessible method for the game piece is the method named move. This method tries to move the piece according to the command given. The method returns false if the command is a move down and the piece cannot move, which indicates that no further actions are possible.

```
class Piece {
    .
    .
    .
    public boolean move (int command, Color [ ][ ] table)
    {
        erase(table);
        boolean canDoIt = false;
        switch (command) {
            case Down: canDoIt = testDown(table); break;
            case Right: canDoIt = testMoveRight(table); break;
            case Left: canDoIt = testMoveLeft(table); break;
            case Rotate: canDoIt = testRotate(table); break;
        }
        if (canDoIt)
            switch (command) {
                case Down: moveDown( ); break;
                case Right: moveRight( ); break;
                case Left: moveLeft( ); break;
                case Rotate: moveRotate( ); break;
            }
```

```
class Piece {
        // data fields
    private int x[ ];
    private int y[ ];
    private Color color;
        // moves
    public static final int Down = 1;
    public static final int Left = 2;
    public static final int Rotate = 3;
    public static final int Right = 4;

        // constructor
    public Piece (int type)
    {
        switch(type) {
            case 1: // s shaped piece
                x = new int[4];
                y = new int[4];
                x[0] = 7; y[0] = 29;
                x[1] = 7; y[1] = 28;
                x[2] = 8; y[2] = 28;
                x[3] = 8; y[3] = 27;
                color = Color.green;
                break;
                .
                .
                .
        }
    }
    .
    .
    .
}
```

Figure 20.6 The class Piece.

```
        draw(table);
        if (command == Down)
            return canDoIt;
        return true;
    }
}
```

Erasing and redrawing the piece are performed by transferring colors to the color table:

```
class Piece {
   .
   .
   .
   private void erase (Color [ ][ ] table) {
      for (int i = 0; i < x.length; i++)
         table[x[i]][y[i]] = Color.white;
   }

   private void draw (Color [ ][ ] table) {
      for (int i = 0; i < x.length; i++)
         table[x[i]][y[i]] = color;
   }
}
```

Before any command is performed, a test is conducted to see if the spaces the blocks will occupy subsequent to the command are open. The following demonstrates one of these routines; the others are similar. If the target locations are open, the corresponding move routine performs the actual transformation.

```
class Piece {
   .
   .
   .
   private boolean testPosition (int x, int y, Color[ ][ ] table)
   {
      if ((x < 0) || (x > 14))
         return false;
      if ((y < 0) || (y > 29))
         return false;
      if (table[x][y] != Color.white)
         return false;
      return true;
   }

   private boolean testDown (Color [ ][ ] table) {
      for (int i = 0; i < x.length; i++)
         if (! testPosition(x[i], y[i]-1, table))
            return false;
      return true;
   }

   private void moveDown () {
      for (int i = 0; i < x.length; i++)
         y[i] = y[i] - 1;
   }
}
```

The only tricky method is the rotation. One square, the square at position 1, is designated the square around which rotation will be performed. The differences in coordinates from this square are computed, and the updated coordinates determined.

```
class Piece {
   .
   .
   .

   private boolean testRotate (Color [ ][ ] table) {
      for (int i = 0; i < x.length; i++) {
         int dx = x[i] - x[1];
         int dy = y[i] - y[1];
         int nx = x[1] + dy;
         int ny = y[1] - dx;
         if (! testPosition(nx, ny, table))
            return false;
      }
      return true;
   }
}
```

20.3 CHAPTER SUMMARY

Java programs can have several independent sequences of execution, or threads. Each is represented by a different instance of class Thread. Threads share a common execution environment and can communicate with each other through the use of shared data values. Problems involving simultaneous access to these data values can be avoided by declaring methods to be synchronized. Only one thread is permitted to be executing a synchronized method at any one time.

In this chapter we have illustrated the use of threads by describing the implementation of a video game, similar to the game of Tetris.

CROSS REFERENCES

The BallWorld case study appears originally in Chapter 5. Placing balls in their own thread of control is also shown in the pinball game application described in Chapter 7.

STUDY QUESTIONS

1. What is the difference between multitasking and multithreading?

2. Describe the two ways to create a new thread.

3. What are the two ways described in this chapter to temporarily halt the execution of a thread?

4. When used in a method heading, what does the keyword synchronized mean?

EXERCISES

1. Add a keyboard listener to the BallWorld application shown in Figure 20.1. When the user types the keys u or d, change the ball direction to move upward or downward, respectively. When the user types q quit the application.

2. Change the mouse down method so that when the user presses the mouse a new ball is created and set in motion. To do this you will need to create a collection of ball objects (see Chapter 5). Each new object should execute in its own separate thread.

3. The Tetris game can be made to "speed up" by reducing the amount of time the piece mover sleeps between commands. Change the code so that this time is reduced by 5 milliseconds for every 100 points the user scores.

4. Change the program so that instead of scoring 10 points for each filled row, the player gets additional points for multiple rows scored with the same piece. For example, a second row will get 20 points, a third row 30 points, and a fourth row 40 points.

5. Change the program to score 50 extra points if an entirely filled row is all one color.

21 Applets and Web Programming

As noted in Chapter 2, although Java is a general purpose programming language that can be used to create almost any type of computer program, much of the excitement surrounding Java has been generated by its employment as a language for creating programs intended for execution across the World Wide Web. Programs written for this purpose must follow certain conventions, and they differ slightly from programs designed to be executed directly on a computer, such as the ones we have developed up to now. In this chapter we will examine these differences and see how to create programs for the Web.

21.1 Applets and HTML

Applications written for the World Wide Web are commonly referred to as *applets*. Applets are attached to documents distributed over the World Wide Web. These documents are written using the HyperText Markup Language (HTML) protocol. A Web browser that includes a Java processor will then automatically retrieve and execute the Java program. Two HTML tags are used to describe the applet as part of an HTML document. These are the <applet> tag and the <param> tag. A typical sequence of instructions would be the following:

```
<applet codebase="http://www.sun.com" code=Main width=300
    height=200>
<param name=name1 value="value1">
You do not have a Java enabled browser
</applet>
```

The <applet> tag indicates the address of the Java program. The codebase parameter gives the URL Web address where the Java program will be found, while the code parameter provides the name of the class. The height and width attributes tell the browser how much space to allocate to the applet.

Just as users can pass information into an application using command-line arguments, applets can have information passed into them using the <param> tags. Within an applet, the values associated with parameters can be accessed using the method getParameter( ).

Any code other than a <param> tag between the beginning and end of the <applet> tag is displayed only if the program cannot be loaded. Such text can be used to provide the user with alternate information.

21.2 SECURITY ISSUES

Applets are designed to be loaded from a remote computer (the server) and then executed locally. Because most users will execute the applet without examining the code, the potential exists for malicious programmers to develop applets that would do significant damage, for example erasing a hard drive. For this reason, applets are much more restricted than applications in the type of operations they can perform.

1. Applets are not permitted to run any local executable program.

2. Applets cannot read or write to the local computer's file system.

3. Applets can only communicate with the server from which they originate. They are not allowed to communicate with any other host machine.

4. Applets can learn only a very restricted set of facts about the local computer. For example, applets can determine the name and version of the operating system, but not the user's name or e-mail address.

In addition, dialog windows that an applet creates are normally labeled with a special text, so the user knows they were created by a Java applet and are not part of the browser application.

21.3 APPLETS AND APPLICATIONS

All the applications created prior to this chapter that made use of graphical resources have been formed as subclasses of class Frame. This class provided the necessary underpinnings for creating and managing windows, graphical operations, events, and the other aspects of a standalone application.

A program that is intended to run on the Web has a slightly different structure. Rather than subclassing from Frame, such a program is subclassed from Applet. Just as Frame provides the structure necessary to run a program as an application, the class Applet provides the necessary structure and resources needed to run a program on the Web. The class Applet is a subclass of Panel (see Section 13.4) and thus inherits all the graphical component attributes of that class.

Rather than starting execution with a static method named main, as applications do, applets start execution at a method named init, which is defined in class Applet but can be overridden by users. The method init is one of four routines defined in Applet that is available for overriding by users. These four can be described as follows:

init( )   Invoked when an applet is first loaded; for example, when a Web page containing the applet is first encountered. This method should be used for one-time initialization. This is similar to the code that would normally be found in the constructor for an application.

start( )   Called to begin execution of the applet. Called again each time the Web page containing the applet is exposed. This can be used for further initialization or for restarting the applet when the page on which it appears is made visible after being covered.

stop( )   Called when a Web page containing an applet is hidden. Applets that do extensive calculations should halt themselves when the page on which they are located becomes covered, so as to not occupy system resources.

destroy( )   Called when the applet is about to be terminated. Should halt the application and free any resources being used.

For example, suppose a Web page containing an applet as well as several other links is loaded. The applet will first invoke init( ), then start( ). If the user clicks on one of the links, the Web page holding the applet is overwritten, but it is still available for the user to return to. The method stop( ) will be invoked to temporarily halt the applet. When the user returns to the Web page, the method start( ), but not init( ), will once again be executed. This can happen many times before the user finally exits altogether the page containing the applet, at which time the method destroy( ) will be called.

Figure 21.1 shows portions of the painting application described in Section 18.6, now written as an applet rather than as an application. In place of the main method, the applet contains an init method. The init takes the place both of main and of the constructor for the application class. Other aspects of the applet are the same. Because an applet is a subclass of Panel, events are handled in exactly the same fashion as other graphical components. Similarly, an applet repaints the window in exactly the same fashion as an application. Because an applet is a panel, it is possible to embed components and construct a complex graphical interface (see Chapter 13). Note, however, that the default layout manager for an Applet is a flow layout rather than the border layout that is default to applications.

```
import java.applet.*;
import java.awt.*;
import java.awt.event.*;

public class PaintApplet extends Applet {

    private Image image = null;
    private Shape currentShape = null;

    public void init () {
            // change our layout manager
        setLayout(new BorderLayout( ));
            // create panel for buttons
        Panel p = new Panel( );
        p.setLayout(new GridLayout(1,3));
        p.add(new Rectangle( ));
        p.add(new Oval( ));
        p.add(new Line( ));
        add("North", p);
        MouseKeeper k = new MouseKeeper( );
        addMouseListener(k);
        addMouseMotionListener(k);
    }
        .
        .
        .
}
```

Figure 21.1   Painting program written as an applet.

21.4   OBTAINING RESOURCES USING AN APPLET

The class Applet provides a number of methods that can be used to load resources from the server machine. The method getImage(URL), for example, takes a URL and retrieves the image stored in the given location. The URL must specify a file in jpeg or gif format. The method getAudioClip(URL) similarly returns an audio object from the given location. The audioClip can subsequently be asked to play itself. A shorthand method play(URL) combines these two features.

The method getCodeBase( ) returns the URL for the codebase specified for the applet (see the earlier discussion on HTML tags). Since Java programs are often stored in the same location as associated documents, such as gif files, this can be useful in forming URL addresses for related resources.

The method getParameter( ) takes as argument a String, and returns the associated value (again, as a string) if the user provided a parameter of the given name using a <param> tag. A null value is returned if no such parameter was provided.

21.4.1   *Universal Resource Locators*

Resources, such as Java programs, gif files, or data files are specified using a universal resource locator, or URL. A URL consists of several parts, including a protocol, a host computer name, and a file name. The following example shows these parts:

```
ftp://ftp.cs.orst.edu/pub/budd/java/errata.html
```

This is the URL that points to the errata list for this book. The first part, ftp:, describes the protocol to be used in accessing the file. The letters stand for *File Transfer Protocol*, which is one common protocol. Another common protocol is http, which stands for *Hypertext Transfer Protocol*. The next part, ftp.cs.orst.edu, is the name of the machine on which the file resides. The remainder of the URL specifies a location for a specific file on this machine. File names are hierarchical. On this particular machine, the directory pub is the area open to the public, the subdirectory budd is my own part of this public area, java holds files related to the Java book, and finally errata.html is the name of the file containing the errata information.

URLs can be created using the class URL.[1] The address is formed using a string, or using a previous URL and a string. The latter form, for example, can be used to retrieve several files that reside in the same directory. The directory is first specified as a URL, then each file is specified as a URL with the file name added to the previous URL address. The constructor for the class URL will throw an exception called MalformedURLException if the associated object cannot be accessed across the Internet.

The class URL provides a method openStream, which returns an inputStream value (see Chapter 14). Once you have created a URL object, you can use this method to read from the URL using the normal InputStream methods, or convert it into a Reader in order to more easily handle character values. In this way, reading from a URL is as easy as reading from a file or any other type of input stream. The following program reads and displays the contents of a Web page. The URL for the Web page is taken from the command-line argument.

```
import java.net.*;
import java.io.*;

class ReadURL {
```

---

[1] It is important to distinguish the idea of a URL as a concept from the Java class of the same name. We will write URL in the normal font when we want to refer to a universal resource locator, and URL when we specifically wish to refer to the Java class.

```
public static void main (String [ ] args) {
   try {
      URL address = new URL(args[0]);
      InputStreamReader iread = new InputStreamReader(
         address.openStream( ));
      BufferedReader in = new BufferedReader(iread);

      String line = in.readLine( );
      while (line != null) {
         System.out.println(line);
         line = in.readLine( );
      }
      in.close( );
   } catch (MalformedURLException e) {
      System.out.println("URL exception " + e);
   } catch (IOException e) {
      System.out.println("I/O exception " + e);
   }
}
```

If you run the program, you should see the HTML commands and textual content displayed for the Web page given as argument. Since not all files are text files, the class URL also provides methods for reading various other formats, such as graphical images or audio files.

21.4.2 *Loading a New Web Page*

Applets used with Web browsers can instruct the browser to load a new page. This feature is frequently used to simulate links or buttons on a Web page, or to implement image maps. The method appletContext.showDocument(URL) takes a URL as argument, then instructs the Web browser to display the indicated page.

21.5 COMBINING APPLICATIONS AND APPLETS

The class Applet pays no attention to any static methods that may be contained within the class definition. We can use this fact to create a class that can be executed both as an applet and as an application. The key idea is that an Applet is a panel. We can nest within the applet class an inner class that creates the Frame necessary for an application. The only component of the window created for this frame will be the panel constructed by the applet. The main program, which is ignored by the applet, will, when executed as an application, create an instance of the applet. The applet can then create an instance of Frame for the application, placing itself in the center of the window. The constructor for the

Frame executes the methods init( ) and start( ) required to initialize the applet. The following shows this technique applied to the painting applet described earlier:

```
import java.applet.*;
import java.awt.*;
import java.awt.event.*;

public class PaintApplet extends Applet {

    // executed for applications
    // ignored by applet class
    public static void main (String [ ] args) {
        Frame world = new PaintApplet().application();
        world.show();
    }

    private Frame application()
        { return new AppletFrame (this); }

    private class AppletFrame extends Frame {
        public AppletFrame (Applet p) {
            setTitle("Paint Application");
            setSize (400, 300);
            p.init(); p.start();
            add("Center", p);
        }
    }
    .
    .   remainder as before
    .
}
```

Trace carefully the sequence of operations being performed here and the order in which objects are created. Since the Frame is nested within the Applet, it is only possible to create the frame (in the method application) after the applet has already been created.

21.6 CHAPTER SUMMARY

An *applet* is a Java application designed to be executed as part of a Web browser. Although much of the code for an applet is similar to that of an application, the two differ in some significant respects. Applets are created by subclassing from the class Applet, rather than from the class Frame. Applets begin execution with the method init, rather than main. Finally, applets can be halted and restarted, as the Web browser moves to a new page and returns.

Security over the Web is a major concern, and for this reason applets are restricted in the actions they can perform. For example, applets are not permitted to read or write files from the client system.

The chapter concludes by showing how it is possible to create a program that can be executed both as an application and as an applet.

STUDY QUESTIONS

1. What is an applet?

2. What is html?

3. How can a web page be made to point to an applet?

4. What is the purpose of the param tag? How is information described by this tag accessed within an applet?

5. What happens if a web browser cannot load and execute an applet described by an applet tag?

6. Why are applets restricted in the variety of activities they can perform?

7. What is the difference between the init and start methods in an applet? When will each be executed?

8. What is the function of a URL? What are the different parts of a URL?

9. How can one read the contents of a file addressed by a URL?

EXERCISES

1. Convert the pinball game described in Chapter 7 to run as an applet, rather than as an application.

2. Convert the Tetris game described in Chapter 20 to run as an applet rather than as an application.

3. Section 18.6 presented a simple painting program. Convert this program to run as an applet, rather than as an application.

22 Network Programming

In Chapter 2 we noted that much of the excitement being generated around Java is due to the potential use of the language in network programming–a process that deals with the task of connecting two or more computers together so that they, and the users working on them, can communicate and share resources.

Network programming is often described using the concepts of client and server (see again Figure 2.1). A *server* is an application that runs on one computer, called the *host computer*, and provides both a means of connection and useful information once a connection is established. Often we blur the lines between the computer and the application, and use the term server to mean both the application and the host computer on which it runs. A *client* is an application that runs on a different computer, and seeks to establish a connection to the server. Oftentimes there will be many clients for a single server (Figure 22.1).

Applets, such as those we examined in Chapter 21, are one form of client/server network computing. An applet, you will recall, is a program that is stored on a server computer, but when requested is transmitted across the network and executes on the client computer. However, applets are only a very simple example of a much more powerful concept. In general, we would like to perform computation on both the client and server sides of the network. In this chapter we will explore how this idea is realized in Java.

22.1 ADDRESSES, PORTS, AND SOCKETS

In order to communicate with each other, computers must first be connected. This connection can take various forms. Computers in a small area, such as a single office, might be connected over a *local area network*, or LAN. Computers connected over much longer distances, such as across a city or around the

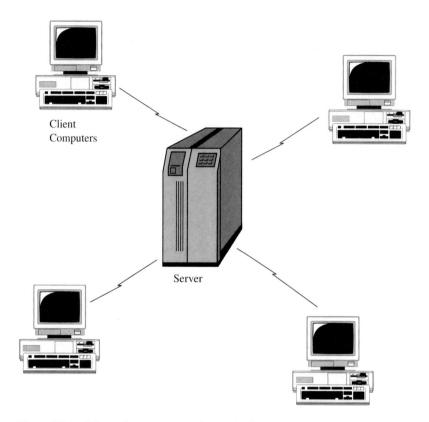

Figure 22.1   Many clients connected to a single server.

world, are typically connected by a *wide area network*, or WAN. The best-known WAN is the Internet, which is simply a loose connection of computers (really, a network of networks) that have agreed to communicate with each other following certain rules, or *protocols*.

For a computer to be able to select one application running on one computer out of the multitude of computers (tens of millions, in the case of the Internet) connected to a network, there must be an addressing scheme. On the Internet this address is known as an IP address, and is usually written in the form of four numbers, each between 0 and 255, separated by dots. An example might be 100.12.11.13. Humans are not very good at remembering or dealing with numbers of this form. Thus, computer names can also be written in an alternative, and more human-friendly representation.

A *domain name* address is another way to designate a specific computer. Like IP addresses, domain names are also written as a series of items separated by periods, although the connection between the two forms is not as direct as one might expect. Domain names denote a specific machine by means of a number of levels, the levels reading from more general on the right to more specific on the left. The computer this book is being written on, for example, is addressed as oops.cs.orst.edu. This address can be read as follows. oops (the name of my machine) on the network for cs (the computer science department at my university) at the institution orst (Oregon State University), which is in the highest level group edu (educational institutions in the United States). The series of names can be imagined as being analogous to the way that a physical address is often described as a building address, street address, city name, and country name.

In order to exchange data, clients and servers need more than just an address. Many servers, for example, can be running simultaneously on the same computer, and hence have the same IP address. Within a computer, the mechanism used to establish a rendezvous is termed a *port*. A port is a location where information can be exchanged between a client and a server. One can think of the term as analogous to a shipping port, where goods come in from abroad and are picked up for delivery to the interior, and vice versa. Ports are designated by integer numbers. Typically the values smaller than 1024 are reserved for predefined services (e-mail, file transfer, Web access), and user defined ports have larger numbers.

The combination of IP address and port number is used to create an abstraction termed a *socket*. Again, one can think of this as an analogy to a connection, such as an electrical socket. A client can "plug into" the server, creating a connection along which information can flow, and can subsequently "disconnect" leaving the socket free for another use. As we will see in the programming examples, a socket provides the facilities for creating input and output streams, which allow data to be exchanged between the client and server.

Finally, files that reside on a specific computer are described using the now ubiquitous URL, or *universal resource locator*. A URL consists of a number of parts. As we described in Section 21.4.1, three of these are the protocol that indicates the communication method used to obtain the item (for example, ftp for file transfer, or http for Web pages), a domain name address, and a file name within the computer. A fourth part, not mentioned in Section 21.4.1, is an optional port number. The port number is necessary only when the default port for the particular protocol is, for some reason, not being used.

22.2 A SIMPLE CLIENT/SERVER PROGRAM

In Section 21.4.1 we described how to open a stream and read the information stored at the location described by a URL. However, in general we would like to do more than simply read a file across the network. We would like to perform

```
import java.util.Date;
import java.net.*;
import java.io.*;

public class DateServer {
    static public void main (String [ ] args) {
        try {
            DateServer world = new DateServer();
        } catch (IOException e) {
            System.out.println("IO exception " + e);
        }
    }

    static final public int portNumber = 4291;

    public DateServer () throws IOException {
        ServerSocket server = new ServerSocket(portNumber);
        while (true) {
            System.out.println("Waiting for a client");
                // wait for a client
            Socket sock = server.accept();
            System.out.println("Got a client, send a message");
                // create an output stream
            OutputStreamWriter out =
                new OutputStreamWriter(sock.getOutputStream());
            String message =
                "Current date and time is " + new Date() + "\n";
                // write the message, then close the stream
            out.write(message);
            out.close();
        }
    }
}
```

Figure 22.2   The DateServer Application.

computation on both ends of a network connection. We earlier noted that this style of computing is generally known as client/server programming. We will illustrate the basic ideas of client/server programming using a pair of simple programs. The server is shown in Figure 22.2. In addition to the classes found in java.io and java.net, we use the class Date found in java.util. The application is named DateServer.

The port number is arbitrarily chosen as 4291. In fact any integer value larger than 1024 and not already in use on the server computer could have been selected.

The class ServerSocket is used to register the server with the port number on the underlying computer. Having registered itself, the server then sits and waits for a client.[1] The method accept will return when a client requests a connection. (An alternative form of accept allows the programmer to specify a time period for the wait, so the program can time out if no client ever comes by.)

The constructor for the ServerSocket, the accept method, and the write method for the output writer can all generate an IOException. We can simplify the program by declaring this exception as part of the constructor interface, and catching any such errors in the main method. By naming the exception in the method header for the constructor, any exceptions thrown by the library routines will pass through the constructor up to the calling procedure, where we catch them (in a try block) and simply print a message and halt.

The result returned by the accept message is a Socket, the connector that will allow a communication path to be established to the client. In particular, we can use the socket to create an OutputStream, which we here convert into a Output-StreamWriter (recall we discussed the various different forms of output streams in Chapter 14). Having made a connection, the server then sends whatever information has been requested back to the client. In this case, we simply write the current date and time as yielded by the Date class.

We explicitly close the output stream, since the program will thereafter go back to waiting for another client. Closing the stream will flush any pending output, and will free up certain system resources that are then available for use by this program or others. Oftentimes an explicit close will be omitted, since all such bookkeeping tasks will be performed automatically when a program terminates. However, if a program is finished with a resource and not yet ready to exit, as in this case, then it is considered good practice to explicitly release the resource.

On the other side, we need a client. The DateClient code is shown in Figure 22.3. The client requests a socket to be created to the given port on a specific computer. In this simple example, we are assuming the client and server run on the same computer. The IP address of the computer on which an application is run can be accessed using the method InetAddress.getLocalHost(). A more general facility is provided by InetAddress.getByName(domainName), which takes a string representation of a domain name and converts the name into an IP address.

Having created a socket, the socket can then be used to create an input stream, which we first convert into a Reader, and then to a BufferedReader (see

---

[1] Here the server is waiting in an infinite loop. On platforms where it is difficult to terminate programs running in the background, the reader may wish to replace the while loop with a finite loop, such as a for loop that will make three connections and then halt.

```
import java.io.*;
import java.net.*;

public class DateClient {
   public static void main (String [ ] args) {
      try {
         DateClient world = new DateClient();
      } catch (IOException e) {
         System.out.println("Received an IO exception " + e);
      }
   }

   static final public int portNumber = 4291;

   public DateClient () throws IOException {
         // open socket as a reader
      Socket sock = new Socket(InetAddress.getLocalHost(), portNumber);
      Reader isread = new InputStreamReader(sock.getInputStream());
      BufferedReader input = new BufferedReader(isread);

         // now read one line
      System.out.println("message is " + input.readLine());
   }
}
```

Figure 22.3   The DateClient Application.

Chapter 14). The buffered reader provides a method to read an entire line of input, which we simply print out.

If we run both programs on the same computer we will observe the expected outcome–namely, that the client will print the date and time given by the server.

22.3   MULTIPLE CLIENTS

There are many limitations to our first simple client/server system, but the two most important are that it only provided communication one way, from the server to the client, and it only permitted one client for one server. In our second example program we will address both of these points.

The Therapist program, Figure 22.4, is a rewriting of a classic and well-known computer game, originally called *Eliza* [Weizenbaum 1976]. The application simulates a Gestalt psychotherapist, and conducts a sort of question-and-answer session with the user. An example session might be the following:

```java
import java.net.*;
import java.io.*;

public class Therapist {
   static public void main (String [ ] args) {
      try {
         Therapist world = new Therapist();
      } catch (IOException e) {
         System.out.println("Received an IO Exception" + e);
      }
   }

   static final public int portNumber = 5321;

   public Therapist () throws IOException {
      ServerSocket server = new ServerSocket(portNumber);
      while (true) {
         Socket sock = server.accept();
            // start new thread to handle session
         Thread session = new TherapySession
            (sock.getInputStream(), sock.getOutputStream());
         session.start();
      }
   }
}
```

Figure 22.4   The Therapist Application.

```
Hello.  Welcome to therapy. What is your name?
Tim
Well Tim what can we do for you today?
I am writing a book on Java.
Tell me more
Do you know Java?
Why do you want to know?
Even my mother is learning how to program in Java.
Tell me more about your mother
   .
   .
   .
```

The therapist application is very similar to the date server described earlier. One important difference is that when a socket is requested by a client, a new *thread* is created to service this request. As we discussed in Chapter 20, this new thread then begins execution in parallel with the original task, which meanwhile completes the while loop and goes back to waiting for another client. In this fashion, many clients can be serviced simultaneously because each will be given their own thread of execution.

The servicing of the client is handled by an instance of TherapySession, shown in Figure 22.5. Note that the therapist passes both an input and output stream to the constructor for this class, permitting two-way communication between the client and the server. The class TherapySession is declared to be a subclass of Thread, which means that most of its processing will be performed by the run method, invoked when the therapist starts the thread.

For the moment, we have omitted some of the code used in the execution of this thread, so that the overall structure can be more easily seen. In order to simplify input and output processing, the constructor for the class converts the input and output streams into buffered readers and writers.

The run method begins by writing a generic greeting. The flush method is needed to transfer the output across the network, since otherwise the buffering of the writer will wait until more output has been generated. The next line is assumed to be a one-word name. Another generic response is then given, and the program moves into the loop which is the heart of the application.

The infinite while loop simply reads a line of text from the user, then determines and writes a response. We will return to the issue of how the response is generated after discussing the client side code.

The client program is named TherapyClient (Figure 22.6) and is again very similar to the Date client. The program creates readers and writers to handle the socket input and output, and it then simply reads lines of text from the standard input and passes them across the network to the server, printing the response on the standard output.

Although the therapy session application clearly has no innate intelligence, people are frequently fooled into thinking otherwise. This effect is achieved by a clever selection of simple rules for responding to what the user writes. Figure 22.7 shows the code that embodies these rules. If the user asks a question (a condition discovered by checking the final character), then the program will answer with a question. Otherwise the line of text is converted into lowercase, and broken into individual words. A StringTokenizer, which we discussed briefly in Chapter 14, is used in this process.

Once the line is broken into words, there are several simple rules that can be applied. If the user started a sentence with "I feel," then we can ask why they feel that way. Otherwise, we check every word to see if they mentioned a family member. If so, then we ask for more information on that relative. Finally, if nothing else has been applicable, we ask a general open-ended question. These are only a small sample of the rules that can be written—all to simulate intelligence when there is none.

```java
import java.io.*;
import java.util.Vector;
import java.util.StringTokenizer;

public class TherapySession extends Thread {
    public TherapySession (InputStream ins, OutputStream outs) {
        Reader isread = new InputStreamReader(ins);
        in = new BufferedReader(isread);
        out = new OutputStreamWriter(outs);
    }

    private String name = "";
    private BufferedReader in;
    private Writer out;

    private String response (String text) {
        .
        .
        .
    }

    public void run () {
        try {
                // get name
            out.write("Hello.  Welcome to therapy. What is your name?\n");
            out.flush();
            name = in.readLine();
            out.write("Well " + name + " what can we do for you today?\n");
            out.flush();

                // now read and respond
            while (true) {
                String text = in.readLine();
                out.write(response(text) + "\n");
                out.flush();
            }
        } catch (IOException e) { stop(); }
    }
}
```

Figure 22.5   The TherapySession class.

```java
import java.io.*;
import java.net.*;

public class TherapyClient {
   public static void main (String [ ] args) {
      try {
         TherapyClient world = new TherapyClient();
      } catch (IOException e) {
         System.out.println("Received an IO exception " + e);
      }
   }

   static final public int portNumber = 5321;
   private BufferedReader input, term;
   private Writer output;

   public TherapyClient () throws IOException {
         // open standard input as buffered reader
      term = new BufferedReader(new InputStreamReader(System.in));

         // open socket as a reader and a writer
      Socket sock = new Socket(InetAddress.getLocalHost(), portNumber);
      Reader isread = new InputStreamReader(sock.getInputStream());
      input = new BufferedReader(isread);
      output = new OutputStreamWriter(sock.getOutputStream());

         // now read and print
      while (true) {
            // read and print something from therapist
         String line = input.readLine();
         System.out.println(line);
            // get our response
         line = term.readLine();
         if (line.equals("Quit"))
            break;
         output.write(line + "\n");
         output.flush();
      }
   }
}
```

Figure 22.6   The TherapyClient class.

```
private String response (String text) {
    // answer a question with a question
  if (text.endsWith("?"))
    return "Why do you want to know?";
    // break up line
  Vector words = new Vector();
  StringTokenizer breaker =
    new StringTokenizer(text.toLowerCase(), " .,?!");
  while (breaker.hasMoreElements())
    words.addElement(breaker.nextElement());

    // look for "I feel"
  if ((words.size() > 1) &&
    words.elementAt(0).equals("i") &&
    words.elementAt(1).equals("feel"))
    return "Why do you feel that way?";

    // look for relatives
  for (int i = 0; i < words.size(); i++) {
    String relative = (String) words.elementAt(i);
    if (isRelative(relative))
       return "Tell me more about your " + relative;
  }

    // nothing else, generic response
  return "Tell me more";
}

private boolean isRelative (String name) {
  return name.equals("mother") || name.equals("father")
    || name.equals("brother") || name.equals("sister")
    || name.equals("uncle");
}
```

Figure 22.7   The response generator.

22.4   TRANSMITTING OBJECTS OVER A NETWORK

Objects can be transmitted over a network using the technique of *object serialization* described in Section 14.5. We illustrate this mechanism by presenting a portion of another client/server application. This application is an on-line pocket-change exchange calculator. The application will take a description of

```
import java.io.Serializable;

abstract public class PocketChange implements Serializable {
    public int penny = 0;
}

class BritishCoins extends PocketChange {
    public int twoPence = 0; // worth 2 pennies
    public int fivePence = 0; // worth 5 pennies
    public int tenPence = 0; // worth 10 pennies
    public int twentyPence = 0; // worth 20 pennies
    public int fiftyPence = 0; // worth 50 pennies
    public int pound = 0; // worth 100 pennies
    public int twoPound = 0; // worth 200 pennies
}

class AmericanCoins extends PocketChange {
    public int nickel = 0; // worth 5 pennies
    public int dime = 0; // worth 10 pennies
    public int quarter = 0; // worth 25 pennies
}
```

Figure 22.8   The Coin class hierarchy.

a collection of coins, either in British or American coinage, and calculate the equivalent in the other system.

To start, we need a class hierarchy to describe a collection of coins. This is provided by the three classes shown in Figure 22.8. The class PocketChange is an abstract class, parent to the two classes BritishCoins and AmericanCoins. Since both currencies share the concept of a penny, that is the only data field found in the parent class. Each subclass gives names for the various different types of coins in use in the country. (Fifty-cent pieces and dollar coins have actually been minted in the United States, but have never been widely popular.) This class description must be available on both the client and server sides of the network connection.

The class PocketChange has been declared as implementing the Serializable interface. This is all that is necessary to permit instances of the class to be written to and read from an object stream (see Section 14.5). It is not necessary to repeat the implements clause in the child classes BritishCoins and AmericanCoins, since they will inherit the Serializable characteristic from their parent class PocketChange.

We give only a portion of the server program (Figure 22.9), leaving the completion of the server program and the development of a client application as an exercise for the reader. The ChangeMaker application waits for a client to request a connection. When a connection is made, the program reads a

```
public class ChangeMaker {
    static final public int portNumber = 3347;
    static final public double exchangeBPenniestoAPennies = 1.615;

    public ChangeMaker () throws IOException {
        ServerSocket server = new ServerSocket(portNumber);
        while (true) {
            Socket sock = server.accept();
                // got a client, make the connections
            ObjectInputStream in =
                new ObjectInputStream(sock.getInputStream());
            ObjectOutputStream out =
                new ObjectOutputStream(sock.getOutputStream());

                // read the value
            PocketChange coins;
            try { coins = (PocketChange) in.readObject();
            } catch (ClassNotFoundException e) { continue; }

                // now convert the value
            if (coins instanceof BritishCoins) {
                    // convert British to American
                BritishCoins bc = (BritishCoins) coins;
                int bPennies = bc.penny + 2 * bc.twoPence +
                    5 * bc.fivePence + 10 * bc.tenPence +
                    20 * bc.twentyPence + 50 * bc.fiftyPence +
                    100 * bc.pound + 200 * bc.twoPound;
                int amPennies = (int) (bPennies
                    * exchangeBPenniestoAPennies);
                AmericanCoins ac = new AmericanCoins();
                ac.quarter = amPennies / 25; amPennies %= 25;
                ac.dime = amPennies / 10; amPennies %= 10;
                ac.nickel = amPennies / 5; amPennies %= 5;
                ac.penny = amPennies;
                    // write out american object
                out.writeObject(ac);
            } else {
                .
                .  convert American to British
                .
            }
            sock.close();
        }
    }
}
```

Figure 22.9   The ChangeMaker Server Application.

value from the input stream. Notice that the actual value read will be either an instance of AmericanCoins or an instance of BritishCoins, but the server has no idea which one. Instead, the server reads the value as an instance of the parent class PocketChange. Nevertheless, the *actual* value transferred will be an instance of one of the child classes.

The server determines which class has been transferred using the Java instanceof operator. The result of this test is used to determine which conversion should be performed, either from British to American coins, or the reverse. We show only the British to American conversion.

To calculate the correct amount, the value of the coins is first reduced to penny units, and then multiplied by the current exchange rate. (A more sophisticated program could, at this point, make another network connection to a server that would yield the current exchange rate.) Having determined the American penny equivalent to the British coins, a series of assignments are then used to convert this quantity into quarters, dimes, nickels, and pennies. The idiom

```
ap %= 25;
```

by the way, is a shorthand way of expressing the statement

```
ap = ap % 25;
```

that finds the remainder after dividing by 25. Any of the binary arithmetic operators can be written using the assignment-operator form.

Once the equivalent number of coins has been determined, the object representing the collection of coins is written to the output stream using the method writeObject. On the client side this quantity will be read using a corresponding readObject method. The server then closes the socket and goes back to waiting for the next connection.

22.5 PROVIDING MORE COMPLEXITY

We have only scratched the surface of the techniques that can be used in network programming. We will here describe some of the ways that further functionality can be added to our examples.

The *Remote Method Invocation* package (java.rmi) provides a framework for creating distributed applications (applications that run on two or more computers) in which the actual physical location of an object is transparent to the user. An object will support the same interface whether it is local to the machine, or on a remote machine connected by a socket.

A common type of network application involves a server providing access to a data base. The Java Database Connectivity (JDBC) library provides a simple and uniform interface that can be used to access a wide variety of different commercial database systems.

Servlets are an alternative to applets. While applets originate on the server computer but run on the client computer, servlets both originate and run on the server computer, and only transmit their results to the client. This technique is useful since programs running on the server are often permitted to perform tasks that are not allowed to be performed by applets. Just as the class Applet provides much of the mechanism for creating applets in a systematic and relatively easy fashion, the servlet library provides facilities for creating server software.

22.6 CHAPTER SUMMARY

Network programming involves applications running on two or more computers working in a cooperative fashion to solve a particular problem.

To work in tandem, applications must communicate. Computers establish connections by means of a series of different mechanisms. An *address* is used to designate a specific computer out of the many computers that may be connected to a network. A *port* is used to identify an individual application on a computer that is waiting to make a connection. Once the application is found, a *socket* is used to create the actual communication medium that links the two communicating applications.

The *streams* created by a socket can be used to transmit 8-bit byte values between the two communicating parties. By using the *stream* and *reader/writer* abstractions provided by the Java library, higher level objects can also be trasmitted easily across the network connection.

By processing requests in a separate thread of execution, a single server can be made to service many different clients simultaneously.

STUDY QUESTIONS

1. Explain what is meant by the terms *client* and *server*.

2. Explain how applets represent one form of client/server computing.

3. How are different machines in a network addressed?

4. What is a port? What is the difference between a port and a socket?

5. In what way is a URL object similar to a Socket object?

6. What is the difference between a Socket object and an object of type Server-Socket?

7. What information is needed in order to form a socket?

8. How does a client create a connection with a server? How does a server create a connection with a client?

9. Having established a socket connection, how is communication between client and server effected?

10. What is the benefit of having the Therapist server create separate threads to handle communiction with the client?

11. In the communication between the Therapist server and the client, why is it important for the writers to be flushed after a line of text has been output?

12. What Java facilities are required for transmitting objects over a network?

EXERCISES

1. Create an array of "fortune cookies," one-line comments offering advice or information. Then write a server program that will, when requested, return a randomly selected value from this list.

2. Many more rules can be added to the response generator for the therapist program. Examples include responding to "I want" or "I think" with a question that asks why the client wants or thinks that way (perhaps even including the text of the material that follows the first two words), a randomly generated generic response if nothing else is appropriate, searching for key words such as "computer" and making a response such as "Computers can be so annoying, can't they?" Think of some more question and answer patterns and implement them in your own version of the therapist.

3. Complete the ChangeMaker server, and write a client program that will interface with this server. Allow the user the ability to specify input as either American or British currency, using forms for the various numeric fields.

4. Unlike the Therapist program, the ChangeMaker does not service each client in a separate thread. Thus, each client must be completely serviced before the next client can be handled. Modify the ChangeMaker program to correct this, so that servicing a client is performed in a separate thread and can be performed in parallel with the main program waiting for a new connection to be established.

23 What's New in 1.2

Java is a language that continues to evolve and change, sometimes at an annoyingly rapid pace. This means that any book that tries to describe Java–and this one is no exception—can represent only an overview that captures a point in time. It is a certainty that some of the information described in this book will eventually become outdated and will have to be revised, replaced, modified or discarded. As a reader you can try to keep abreast of this process by by perusing articles in trade journals, by reading books that describe the latest versions of languages, by attending conferences or trade shows, by taking continuing education classes, and in general, by being aware of what is happening in the computing world.

In large part the evolution of Java involves not changes to the basic syntax of the language (although there have been some of those) but modifications to the library of packages that are included as part of most Java programs. This evolution involves both the basic libraries provided by Sun (the developers of the language), and third-party packages created and marketed by others.

To date (meaning, middle 1999) there have been three major stages in the life of Java as a language. The first version of the language to become widely popular was known as Java 1.0.2, after the version number assigned by Sun. This was replaced by Java 1.1, which was the reference version used in the writing of the first edition of this book. The major change between the earlier language and Java 1.1 was the introduction of the new and simpler event-handling model, based around listeners, that we have here been using since Chapter 6. Subsequent to the publication of the first edition of this book, Sun released Java 1.2. In this chapter we will discuss some of the more important changes and innovations that were included in that release.

23.1   COLLECTION CLASSES

The collection classes are a revision of the 1.1 (and earlier) container library described in Chapter 19. The collection API now includes linked lists and sets, in addition to the classes for vectors and hashtables found in the earlier library. Also many new operations have been added to the existing abstractions.

There has been some objection to the new classes because they include the concept of an *optional method*. An interface can claim to provide an operation, and a class can claim to implement the interface, and yet the class is permitted to throw an UnsupportedOperationException when the operation is invoked. This means that users need to be aware of this possibility, and check carefully which classes support which operations.

In Section 19.8 we explained why there were no ordered collections in the Java library, and discussed a technique that could be used to provide such data abstractions. The new 1.2 collection library now includes a number of ordered collections (SortedSet is the most useful example), and uses a technique almost identical to the one described in Chapter 19 to form the ordering between elements. Wrapper classes such as Integer and Double have been modified to make them integrate well with the ordered container abstractions.

23.2   SWING USER INTERFACE COMPONENTS

The *Swing* library is a significant extension to the AWT windowing toolkit described in Chapter 13. Many new graphical components have been added (such as split panes, and progress bars), and new abilities have been incorporated into existing components (such as the ability to put images on a button label). End users now have greater control over the appearance of graphical components and can change this appearance dynamically. Greater support is now provided for assistive technologies–for example, alternative input devices such as sound or braille output devices.

23.3   IMPROVEMENTS TO THE GRAPHICS LIBRARY

The Graphics class introduced in Chapter 5 has been greatly expanded to provide new operations for rendering two-dimensional graphics. The new class is called Graphics2D and provides tools for mixing overlapping images, transforming and clipping images, and alternative rendering techniques.

A new Graphics3D library has been added to assist in the transformation of three-dimensional images into a two-dimensional display.

23.4 INTERNATIONALIZATION

Building on the idea of *properties* described in Section 19.7.2, users can now create *Resource Bundles* that describe features that can be dynamically loaded. For example, rather than having a program print the text strings "Hello" and "Goodbye", a programmer can create resource bundles that describe the standard greetings in various different languages. After determining the correct language for a given user, a program can then dynamically load the appropriate resource bundle for the language and use the properties defined by the resource to print a greeting in the user's language.

Other support is provided for various currencies, descriptions of dates, times, measurements, and postal addresses. For example, the Date class may print a date in the United States as 14-Apr-98, and print the same date in France as 14 Avr 98. A time printed in the United States as 3:58:42 PM might be printed in Germany as 15:58:42.

23.5 JAVA BEANS

In the distributed computing world a *component* is a self-contained independent reusable software unit that can be dynamically loaded into memory. Collections of components are composed to create new applications. Components are higher-level abstractions than classes and may be written in many different languages.

Using the idea of *reflection* (the ability for a program to discover information about itself), the Java Beans API provides the tools to create and distribute reusable components in Java. Components examine themselves to discover what methods they support, and can automatically share this information with other components. Components then interact with each other by passing *events*, which are a more general form of messages.

23.6 SOUND

Java 1.2 now provides the ability to manipulate and play sounds recorded in a wide variety of formats and sampling rates.

23.7 DATABASES

The JDBC API provides a platform-independent way to connect with and perform operations on databases from a wide variety of different vendors.

23.8 REMOTE METHOD INVOCATION

The RMI API defines a simple way to hide much of the detail involved in client/server applications. Using RMI, a programmer can deal with a remote object, an object on another computer that is accessed across the network, in exactly the same way as if it were present on the local computer.

23.9 SERVLETS

As we described in Chapter 21, *applets* are programs that are downloaded across a network from a server computer to a client computer but run on the client machine. A *servlet* is similar, but it runs on the server side, not the client side. Thus servlets are typically permitted to perform operations that applets may not be allowed (and vice versa as well).

23.10 CHAPTER SUMMARY

Java 1.2 is the latest version of the Java programming language and associated libraries. The transition from Java 1.1 to Java 1.2 introduced many new libraries that provided significant functionality in a form that is easy for the programmer to use.

It is almost guaranteed that this will not be the last revision of the Java language or its libraries. The conscientious programmer should be aware of these changes and strive to understand the importance of developments as they occur in the programming field.

FURTHER READING

The most authoratative information is obtained directly from SUN, at their Web site http://java.sun.com/docs. Of the many Java 1.2 tutorials available, the one I like best is the addition to *The Java Tutorial*, called *The Java Tutorial Continued: The Rest of the JDK* [Campione 1999].

 **Java Syntax**

This appendix gives an overview of the Java language as it is used in this book. The method of description is informal, and it is not intended to replace a reference manual for the language. For example, statements that are legal in Java but are not used in the book are not described.

We will divide the presentation of the language into three major sections:

1. *Program structure*, where the overall organization of a Java program is defined; this includes packages, interfaces, classes, and methods.

2. *Statements*, where dicussion focuses on declaration statements, assignment statements, and statements that control the flow of execution within a method.

3. *Expressions*, where individual values are computed.

PROGRAM STRUCTURE

A Java program is written as a collection of files. Each file can contain an optional package name, an optional sequence of import declarations, and finally a sequence of class or interface declarations.

A.1.1 *Import Declaration*

An import declaration names an item from another package that will be used in the subsequent class or interface declarations. An asterisk can be used to include all the items in a package.

```
    // Example from program found in Chapter 22
import java.util.Date;
import java.net.*;
import java.io.*;
```

A.1.2   *Class Declaration*

A class declaration consists of an optional sequence of modifiers, the keyword
class, the class name, an optional parent class name, an optional sequence of
interfaces, and the class body. The class body is a sequence of class member or
constructor declarations, surrounded by a pair of curly brackets.

```
// Class definition from Chapter 4
public class FirstProgram {

    public static void main (String [ ] args ) {
        System.out.println ( "My first Java program!" );
    }
}
```

The modifiers discussed in this book have been public, abstract and final. A
public class can be used outside of the package in which it is declared. An abstract
class is one that cannot be instantiated, one that must be subclassed before
instances can be created. A final class is one that cannot be subclassed.

```
// Class definition from Section 8.4.2
public abstract class Number {
    .
    .
    .
}
```

The optional parent class name is used to denote that this class is being constructed using inheritance from an existing class. The keyword extends indicates
that inheritance is being performed.

```
// Class definition from Chapter 7
public class PinBall extends Ball {
    .
    .
    .
}
```

The optional sequence of interfaces is used to indicate that the class being
defined implements all the methods described in an interface declaration. Note
that a class can satisfy many different interfaces but can have only one parent
class.

```
// Class definition from Chapter 7
class Hole extends Ball implements PinBallTarget {
    .
    .
    .
}
```

A.1.3   *Interface Declaration*

An interface declaration substitutes the keyword interface for the keyword class. The body of an interface contains methods but no data fields. In addition, the methods specify only the function and argument names, but do not have a function body. In place of the method body, a semicolon is used to mark the end of a method declaration.

```
// Interface definition from Chapter 7
interface PinBallTarget {
   public boolean intersects (Ball aBall);
   public void moveTo (int x, int y);
   public void paint (Graphics g);
   public void hitBy (Ball aBall);
}
```

A.1.4   *Method Declaration*

A method declaration consists of an optional series of modifiers, a return type, a method name, an optional throws part, a list of arguments, and (in class declarations) a method body. A method body is a sequence of statements, surrounded by a pair of curly brackets.

```
// Class found in Chapter 8
class Stack extends Vector {

   public synchronized Object pop() {
      Object obj = peek();
      removeElementAt(size() - 1);
      return obj;
   }
}
```

The following modifiers have been used in the book:

public   The method can be invoked by messages sent to instances of this class. (Many examples occur, starting in Chapter 4.)

protected   The method can be invoked only within other methods associated with the class of the object, within other classes in the same package, or in methods defined as part of subclasses.

private   The method can be invoked only within other methods associated with this class.

final   The method cannot be overridden in subclasses. An example occurs in Chapter 9.

abstract   The method must be overriden in subclasses. (A semicolon replaces the method body when this modifier is used.) An example occurs in Chapter 8.

static   The method can be invoked without first creating an instance of the class. The main method must always be declared static.

synchronized   At any point in time only one thread can be executing this method. An example was presented in Chapter 8.

The return type for a method can be a primitive type, a class type, or void. The type void is used to indicate that the method does not return a value as a result.

A throws part indicates the exceptions this method might potentially throw. It is indicated by the keyword throws, followed by a list of exception names, separated by commas.

```
// Example from Chapter 14
class DataInputStream extends FilterInputStream {

    public byte readByte () throws IOException {
        .
        .
        .
    }
}
```

The optional sequence of formal arguments is a list of zero or more formal argument declarations, separated by commas. Each formal argument is a type (either a primitive type or a class name) followed by a variable name:

```
// From the concordance program in Chapter 19
private void enterWord (String word, Integer line) {
    .
    .
    .
}
```

A.1.5   Constructors

A syntax of a *constructor* is similar to a method but eliminates the return type, and the method name must match the class name. A constructor is invoked automatically when an instance of the class is created.

```
// Ball class from Chapter 5
public class Ball {

    public Ball (int x, int y, int r) {
        location = new Rectangle(x-r, y-r, 2*r, 2*r);
        dx = 0; dy = 0; // initially no motion
```

```
            color = Color.blue;
        }
          .
          .
          .
    }
```

A.1.6   *Data Field Declaration*

A data field declaration has an optional modifier part, a type, a variable name, and an optional initialization.

```
    // Ball class from Chapter 5
public class Ball { // a generic round colored object that moves
    protected Rectangle location; // position on graphic surface
    protected double dx, dy; // x and y components of motion vector
    protected Color color;   // color of ball
       .
       .
       .
    }
```

An initialization, if present, consists of an equals sign followed by a value:

```
    // From an example in Chapter 7
public class PinBallGame extends Frame {
    public static final int FrameWidth = 400;
    public static final int FrameHeight = 400;
       .
       .
       .
    }
```

A.2   STATEMENTS

The following describes only those statements that we have used in the book. The Java language also permits other statement forms that we will not describe.

A.2.1   *Declaration Statement*

A declaration statement consists of a type (either a primitive or a class type) and a variable name. It can have an optional initialization part, which provides an initial value for the variable.

```
    int size;
    double pi = 3.14159;
    Ball aBall;
```

A.2.2   *Assignment Statement*

An assignment statement is used to modify the value of a variable. The target variable (the value to the left of the equal sign) can be a simple variable, an array expresssion, or a field name. The right side can be any legal expression.

```
size = 3 + 4;
```

Binary operators can also be combined with an assignment statement. The effect is as if the target variable were used as the left argument with the binary operator, and the result assigned to the target:

```
i += 3; // same as i = i + 3
```

A.2.3   *Procedure Calls*

A method can be invoked as a statement. A method that is declared as void can be executed only in this fashion. If the method returns a non-void result, the value will be ignored.

```
aBall.move(12, 13);
```

The expression to the left of the period is known as the *receiver*. The class of the receiver will determine which method will be executed. If no receiver is specified, a method in the current class will be executed.

A.2.4   *If Statement*

If statements and switch statements are sometimes together termed *conditional statements*. They allow the programmer to select one alternative out of many. The if statement makes a decision based on a boolean-valued expression; if the expression is true, a statement is selected. The else portion of the statement is optional; if present and if the expression is false, the else statement will be executed.

```
    // From cannon ball game in Chapter 6
if ((cannonBall.x() > targetX) &&
    (cannonBall.x() < (targetX+50)))
    message = "You Hit It!";
else
    message = "Missed!";
```

Curly brackets can be used to group a series of statements together to form a *compound statement*. These statements will then be executed as a unit, either all together or (if the condition is not satisfied) not at all.

```
// From Figure 7.5
if (state == 1) { // draw compressed spring
    g.fillRect(x, y, pad.width, pad.height);
    g.drawLine(x, y+3, x+30, y+5);
    g.drawLine(x+30, y+5, x, y+7);
    g.drawLine(x, y+7, x+30, y+9);
    g.drawLine(x+30, y+9, x, y+11);
    }
else {  // draw extended spring
    g.fillRect(x, y-8, pad.width, pad.height);
    g.drawLine(x, y+5, x+30, y-1);
    g.drawLine(x+30, y-1, x, y+3);
    g.drawLine(x, y+3, x+30, y+7);
    g.drawLine(x+30, y+7, x, y+11);
    state = 1;
}
```

A.2.5   *Switch Statement*

A switch statement selects one alternative out of many. The selection is determined by the value of an expression. The result of the expression is compared against a list of constants, and when a match is found the associated statement is executed. One statement can be labelled as default, and will be executed if no other match is successful.

```
// From pinball game described in Chapter 7
switch (y / 40) {
    case 2: element = new Hole(0, 0); break;
    case 3: element = new Peg(0, 0, 100); break;
    case 4: element = new Peg(0, 0, 200); break;
    case 5: element = new ScorePad(0, 0, 100); break;
    case 6: element = new ScorePad(0, 0, 200); break;
    case 7: element = new Spring(0, 0); break;
    case 8: element = new Wall(0, 0, 2, 15); break;
}
```

The break statement is necessary in order to break out of the switch. If the break is omitted, then after execution of the case statements, control will drop into the next case statement. There are rare situations where this is useful; however, the normal situation is to break after each case statement.

A.2.6   *While Statement*

The while and for statements are often termed *looping statements*, since they have the effect of executing a statement repeatedly until a condition is satisfied. The statement can be executed zero times if the condition is false the first time the statement is encountered.

```
    // From pinball game described in Chapter 7
while (theBall.y() < FrameHeight) {
    theBall.move ();
        .
        .
        .
}
```

A.2.7   *For Statement*

A for statement consists of an initialization part, a test for completion, an update statement, and the body of the loop. The for statement is actually just a convenient shorthand for a while loop. That is, a statement such as the following:

```
for (int i = 0; i < 10; i++) {
    a[i] = 3 * i;
}
```

can be rewritten, and has the same effect, as the following:

```
int i = 0;
while (i < 10) {
    a[i] = 3 * i;
    i++;
}
```

A.2.8   *Return Statement*

A return statement is used to indicate the end of execution for a method. If an expression is provided, it will be the value returned as the result of the method execution. Otherwise, if no value is given in the result statement, the method must be declared as void.

```
return 3 + 4;
```

A.2.9   *Throw Statement*

A throw statement is used to raise an exception. Control will immediately halt in the current procedure, and the most recent matching catch block from a calling procedure will be invoked.

```
throw new StackUnderflowException();
```

A.2.10 *Try Statement*

Any code that can generate an exception should be invoked in a try block. The try statement is followed by an optional sequence of catch clauses. Each catch block specifies the type of exception it can handle. If the associated exception is thrown during the course of executing the statements in the try block, then the code in the matching catch statement will be executed. An optional finally block is executed at the end of the statement, whether or not an exception has occurred.

```
try {
   URL address = new URL(args[0]);
   .
   .
   .
} catch (MalformedURLException e) {
   System.out.println("URL exception " + e);
} catch (IOException e) {
   System.out.println("I/O exception " + e);
}
```

A.3   EXPRESSIONS

An expression is a programming construct that, when executed, will cause a value to be computed. Expressions are found in various types of statements, such as assignment statements, the conditional test in a while loop, or the selecting expression in a switch statement.

An expression can be placed in parentheses to form a new expression. This is often used to indicate grouping, or when the precedence of operators does not provide the desired value. For example, $2 + 3 * 4$ will be evaluated and produce the result 14, but $(2 + 3) * 4$ will yield the value 20.

A.3.1 *Literal*

The simplest type of expression is a literal. A literal (sometimes called a *constant*) has a self-evident type and value.

```
7 // integer literal
3.14159 // floating-point literal
true // boolean literal
'a' // character literal
"name" // string literal
null // object literal
```

The value null is a literal value that is used with variables of class type. This value is the initial value of all variables before they are assigned. Thus, the value null can be thought of as asserting that the variable does not refer to any object.

The following escape characters can be used in a character or string literal:

\b   backspace

\n   newline

\r   carriage return

\t   tab stop

For example, the following statement:

```
System.out.println("Hello\n\n\tWorld");
```

will produce the following output:

```
Hello

    World
```

A.3.2   *Variable*

A variable is a storage location that has been declared in a declaration statement. When used as an expression, the value currently stored in the variable is the value returned.

The name this is sometimes called a *pseudo-variable*. It is a variable that does not have to be declared. When used as an expression inside a method, it denotes the object executing the method (the object that was targeted as the *receiver* in the message expression that caused the method to be executed).

Data fields and methods declared within the class in which an expression occurs, and protected or public data fields or methods declared in parent classes, can be accessed simply by naming them as a variable. The meaning is the same as a data field access using this as the base expression, however the more complete form is seldom written:

```
public class Ball {
    protected Rectangle location;
    protected double dx, dy;
    protected Color color;

    public Ball (int x, int y, int r) {
        location = new Rectangle(x-r, y-r, 2*r, 2*r);
        dx = 0;
        dy = 0; // same as this.dy = 0;
        color = Color.blue;
    }
}
```

The name super is another pseudo-variable, one that can be used only as a receiver for a message, or in a constructor. The first form is used when a method defined in a parent class is overridden, and the programmer wishes to execute the parent method from inside the method appearing in the child class. In a constructor it is used to indicate the parameters to be passed to the parent class. Both forms are found in the following methods from Chapter 7.

```
public class PinBall extends Ball {

    public PinBall (int sx, int sy)
    {
        super(sx, sy, 10);
            // start out moving (roughly) vertically
        setMotion (-2 + Math.random()/4, -15);
    }

    public void move ()
    {
        dy = dy + gravityEffect;
        super.move();    // execute move method in class Ball
    }
}
```

A.3.3 Data Field and Method Access

Public fields within an object can be accessed by naming the object, followed by a period, followed by the field name:

```
aBall.location
```

Static fields can be accessed using a class name to the left of the period. As we noted earlier, data fields declared within the same class can be accessed without any base expression.

A method invocation uses the same notation as a data field access, but is followed by a parenthesis, an optional list of comma-separated parameter values, and a closing parenthesis.

```
aBall.setColor (ballColor);
```

A.3.4 Operators

A unary operator takes one expression as an argument. An example is the increment operator, ++, which is used to increment a variable. A binary operator takes two expressions as arguments. An example is the addition operator, +, which adds two numeric values. (The addition operator can also be used with

String values, in which case it means string catenation.) The list below gives the set of binary operators recognized by Java. They are shown in precedence order, with higher precedence operators appearing before lower precedence operators. Higher precedence operators will be performed before lower precedence operators; thus, $2 + 3 * 4 + 3$ will yield 17, not 23.

postfix operator	*expr++ expr--*
unary operator	*++expr --expr +expr -expr*
creation or cast	`new` *(type)expr*
multiplicative	`* / %`
additive	`+ -`
shift	`<< >> <<<`
relational	`< > <= >= instanceof`
equality	`== !=`
bitwise and	`&`
bitwise or	`|`
logical and	`&&`
logical or	`||`
assignment	`= += -=` etc.

A.3.5 *Object Creation*

An object is created using the new operator. As part of the creation process, a constructor may be executed to initialize the object. If any arguments are supplied with the call, they are passed to the constructor for the class, to be used in initializing the object.

```
aBall = new Ball (10, 15, 5);
```

A.3.6 *Arrays*

An array is a homogeneous (same-typed) collection of values that is declared using a pair of square brackets, without indicating the size.

```
Ball [] balls;
```

The number of elements in the array is determined when the array value is allocated, using a new statement:

```
balls = new Ball[20];  // create an array of 20 balls
```

An element in the array is accessed by an index position, which must be an integer value between larger than or equal to zero and smaller than the number of values in the array.

```
balls[8].moveTo(23, 17);
```

 **Packages in the Java API**

The table below lists the principle packages in the Java API. From time to time new libraries are added to the Java run-time system.

Package Name	Contents
java.applet	Applet classes
java.awt	User interface classes
java.awt.event	Event-processing and listener classes
java.beans	JavaBeans component model classes
java.io	Input and output classes
java.lang	Core classes
java.lang.reflect	Reflection classes
java.math	Arbitrary precision arithmetic classes
java.net	Network classes
java.rmi	Remote method invocation classes
java.security	Security classes
java.sql	Java database connectivity classes
java.text	Text manipulation classes for internationalization
java.util	Various utility classes

Glossary

abstract A keyword applied to either a **class** or a **method**. When applied to a class, the keyword indicates that no **instances** of the class can be created, and the class is used only as a **parent class** for subclassing. When applied to a method within an **abstract class**, it indicates that the method must be **overridden** in subclasses before any instance of the subclass can be created.

abstract class Syn. *deferred class*, *abstract superclass*. A class that has been declared using the abstract keyword. Classes can be declared to be abstract even if they do not contain any **abstract methods**.

abstract method A method that has been declared using the abstract keyword. Abstract methods can only appear in classes that have themselves been declared abstract.

abstract windowing toolkit A Java package which provides the graphical user interface facilities for a Java program. The AWT is an example of a **framework**.

abstraction A technique in problem solving in which details are grouped into a single common concept. This concept can then be viewed as a single entity and nonessential information ignored.

access specifier A keyword (private, protected, or public) that controls access to **data members** and **methods** within user-defined classes.

accessor function A function that is used to access the values of an **instance variable**. By restricting access through a function, the programmer can ensure that instance variables will be read but not modified. *See also* **mutator**.

ad hoc polymorphism Syn. *overloading*. A procedure or method identifier (or name) that denotes more than one procedure.

agent Syn. *object*, *instance*. A nontechnical term sometimes used to describe an object in order to emphasize its independence from other objects and the fact that it is providing a service to other objects.

anonymous class *See* unnamed class.

Application Programmers Interface (API)   The Java class library is generally referred to as the Java API. It is arranged in **packages** of related classes which can be accessed by a program using an import statement.

argument signature   An internal encoding of a list of argument types; the argument signature is used to disambiguate **overloaded** function invocations, selecting the **method body** that matches most closely the signature of the method call. *See also* **parametric overloading**.

ASCII ordering   A standard mapping between textual character values and an integer **internal representation**. The character value 'a', for example, is mapped on to the integer value 97, which can be stored in a single **byte** value. **Unicode** character values use 16 bits, or two bytes, and can thus represent a wider variety of symbols.

automatic storage management   A policy in which the underlying run-time system is responsible for the detection and reclamation of memory values no longer accessible, and hence of no further use to the computation. *See also* **garbage collection**.

AWT   See *Abstract Windowing Toolkit*.

base class   Syn. *ancestor type*, *superclass*, *parent class*. A class from which another class is derived.

binary representation   The encoded form of a value used at the machine level. For example, int values in Java are represented by a 4-**byte** machine word, short values by a 2-byte sequence, ASCII characters by a single byte, and **Unicode characters** by a two-byte sequence. Note that two different values may have the same internal binary representation, for example the short value 97 and the **Unicode** character 'a' are both represented by 00000000 01100001. *See also* **textual representation**.

binding   The process by which a name or an **expression** is associated with an attribute such as a variable and the type of value the variable can hold.

binding time   The time at which a binding takes place. *Early* or *static binding* generally refers to binding performed at compile time, whereas *late* or *dynamic binding* refers to binding performed at run time.

byte   The smallest grouping of binary bits used by the computer to represent data. A byte consists of 8 bits. Although a byte may have only one value, a byte can be *interpreted* in a number of different ways. The value 01100001, for example, can be interpreted as the number 97, or as the **character** value 'a'.

bytecode   The assembly language for an imaginary Java **virtual machine**. So-called because most instructions can be encoded in a form that is one or two **bytes** in length.

cast   A unary **expression** that converts a value from one type to another.

character   A value used to represent a single printed symbol. Historically characters were encoded as one-**byte** integer values, using the **ASCII** convention. However, this only permitted the representation of 256 different symbolic values. Java represents characters using a two-bit **Unicode** convention. The sixteen bits in a unicode character allow for the representation of most of the world's letters.

child class   Syn. *subclass, derived class*. A class defined as an extension of another class, which is called the *parent class*.

class   Syn. *object type*. An abstract description of the data and behavior of a collection of similar objects. The representatives of the collection are called **instances** of the class.

Class   The class that maintains behavior related to class instance and subclass creation.

class description protocol   The set of messages that an object understands.

class hierarchy   A hierarchy formed by listing classes according to their class-subclass relationship. *See also* **hierarchy**.

class member   *See* **member**.

client   An application running on one computer that wishes to obtain information from another application, the **server**, running on a different computer. The two computers must be connected over a **network**.

client-side computing   In a network environment, a program that is executed on the client side rather than on the server side of the network. The Java programming language is intended to perform client-side computing and so is more efficient than programs that must wait for execution on the (generally more overloaded) server machine.

cohesion   The degree to which components of a single software system (such as members of a single class) are tied together. Contrast with **coupling**.

collaborator   Two classes which depend upon each other for the execution of their behaviors are said to be collaborators.

collection classes   Classes used as data structures that can contain a number of elements. Examples include Vector, Stack, Hashtable and arrays.

command line argument   Arguments supplied to a program as part of the command that causes it to execute. The way these are written will depend upon your platform. These are transmitted to the Java program in an array of String values passed to the main program.

composition   The technique of including user-defined object types as part of a newly defined object, as opposed to using **inheritance**.

constant   A data field that is declared static and final, which is then guaranteed to exist in only one place and cannot change value. The identifier of such a data field is sometimes called a *symbolic name* and hence the constant is sometimes referred to as a *symbolic constant*.

constructor   A **method** used to create a new object. The constructor handles the dual tasks of allocating memory for the new object and ensuring that this memory is properly initialized. The programmer defines how this initialization is performed. In Java, a constructor has the same name as the class in which it appears.

contravariance   A form of overriding in which an argument associated with a method in the child class is restricted to a less general category than the corresponding argument in the parent class. Contrast with *covariance*. Neither covariant nor contravariant overriding is common in object-oriented languages.

coupling   The degree to which separate software components are tied together. Contrast with *cohesion*.

covariance   A form of overriding in which an argument associated with a method in the child class is enlarged to a more general category than the corresponding argument in the parent class. Contrast with *contravariance*. Neither covariant nor contravariant overriding is common in object-oriented languages.

CRC card   An index card that documents the name, responsibilities, and collaborators for a class, used during the process of system analysis and design.

data field   A class member in the form of a variable or constant that holds an instance of a primitive data type or a reference to an object.

data hiding   An encapsulation technique that seeks to abstract away the implementation details concerning what data values are maintained in order that an object may provide a particular service.

data member   *See* **instance variable**.

deferred class   *See* **abstract class**.

derived class   Syn. *descendant type, subclass, child class*. A class that is defined as an extension or a **subclass** of another class, which is called the **base class**.

descendant type   Syn. *subclass, child class*. *See also* **derived class**.

design pattern   A simple, elegant software design that captures, in generic terms, a solution that has been developed over time.

early binding   *See* **binding time.**

encapsulation   The technique of hiding information within a structure, such as the hiding of instance data within a class.

escape character   A multi-character sequence used to represent an otherwise unprintable character value. For example, the sequence \n represents a newline character. When printed, this character terminates a line of output and moves the current position back to the left margin.

event   An action, such as the user clicking on a button, pressing a key, selecting a menu item, or inserting a disk into a drive. The system will respond to such an event by carrying out certain actions, provided the program defines an appropriate **listener** for that event. *See also* **event listener** and **event handler.**

event-driven execution   A style of programming where the program largely responds to user-generated events, such as a mouse click or a keypress.

event handler   The part of the Java run-time system that enables events to be recognized and responded to.

event listener   A class that defines what will happen when a particular kind of event occurs. For example, a button object must be associated with a **listener** object that knows what to do when the button is "pressed". *See also* **event** and **event handler.**

exception   An unusual condition that prevents the normal sequence of instructions from going forward. An example would be attempting to use an uninitialized value (a null value) as the target of a message-passing expression.

exception handling   The portion of a Java program devoted to responding to the occurrence of an exception.

expression   A programming construct that returns a value. For example $1 + 2$ is an expression since it returns the value 3. A function is an expression because it returns a value that is an instance of its return type. *See also* **statement.**

extends   A keyword used in forming a new class as a subclass of an existing class, or a new interface as an extension of an existing interface.

final   A keyword used in forming either a final class or a final method within a class.

final class   A class declared using the keyword final. This keyword indicates that the class cannot be used as a base class for inheritance.

final method   A method declared using the keyword final. This keyword indicates that the method cannot be overridden in subclasses.

finalizer   A method with the name finalize, no arguments, and no return type. This method will be invoked automatically by the run-time system prior to the object in which it is declared being recycled by garbage collection.

Frame   A class in the Java library that defines behavior common to all application windows.

framework   A collection of classes that together provide the behavior common to a large variety of applications. The programmer creates a new application by specializing and extending the behavior of the classes contained in the framework, thereby providing the solution to a specific problem.

function   A method that has a return type other than void. A function is a form of **expression**. *See also* **procedure**.

function member   *See* **method**.

garbage collection   A memory-management technique whereby the run-time system determines which memory values are no longer necessary to the running program and automatically recovers and recycles the memory for different use.

Graphical User Interface   The graphical display for a program, through which the user interacts with a running application.

GUI   See *Graphical User Interface*.

***has-a* relation**   The relation that asserts that instances of a class possess fields of a given type. *See* ***is-a* relation**.

hierarchy   An organizational structure with components ranked into levels of subordination according to some set of rules. In object-oriented programming the most common hierarchy is that formed by the **class-subclass** relationship.

immediate superclass   The closest parent class from which a class inherits. The superclass relationship is a transitive closure of the immediate superclass relationship.

immutable value   A value that is not permitted to change once it has been set. Variables that hold such values are sometimes called **single-assignment variables,** or **symbolic constants**. In Java, immutable values can be identified via the keywords final and static.

implements   A keyword used to indicate that a class provides the behavior described by an **interface**.

information hiding   The principle that users of a software component (such as a class) need to know only the essential details of how to initialize and access the component, and do not need to know the details of the implementation. By reducing the degree of interconnectedness between separate elements of a software system, the principle of information hiding helps in the development of reliable software.

inheritance   The property of objects by which instances of a **class** can have access to **data fields** and **methods** contained in a previously defined class, without those definitions being restated. *See* **ancestor class.**

inheritance graph   An abstract structure that illustrates the inheritance relationships with a collection of classes.

inner class   A **class** definition that appears inside another class. Inner classes are allowed access to both the **data members** and **methods** of the surrounding class. Inner classes are used frequently in building **listener** objects for handling events.

instance   Syn. **object.**

instance variable   An internal variable maintained by an instance. Instance variables represent the state of an object.

interaction diagram   A diagram that documents the sequence of messages that flow between objects participating in a scenario.

interface   A description of behavior. Classes that claim to implement the interface must provide the services described by the interface.

Internet   A world-wide collection of machines that have agreed to communicate with each other using a common protocol.

is-a **relation**   The relation that asserts that instances of a subclass must be more specialized forms of the superclass. Thus, instances of a subclass can be used where quantities of the superclass type are required. *See* ***has-a* relation.**

interpreter   A computer program that simulates the actions of the imaginary Java **virtual machine.** The interpreter examines and executes the **bytecode** representation of a Java program.

iterator   A class that is used mainly to provide access to the values being held in another class, usually a container class. The iterator provides a uniform framework for accessing values, without compromising the encapsulation of the container.

Java API   *See* **Application Programmers Interface**

Java library   *See* **Application Programmers Interface**

JIT   *See* **just-in-time compiler.**

just-in-time (JIT) compiler   A technique whereby immediately before a program is to execute, the device-independent **bytecode** representation of a Java program is converted into machine code for a specific platform. The machine code representation will often execute much faster than will an **interpreter** running the bytecode representation.

late binding   *See* **binding time.**

layout manager   A component in the **AWT** that controls the layout of graphical components in a panel or window. Part of the graphical user interface system.

listener   An object that waits for an **event** to occur, then executes certain actions to respond to the event.

member   A **data field** or **method.** Sometimes referred to as a **class member.**

message   Syn. *message selector, method designator, method selector, selector.* The textual string that identifies a requested action is a **message-passing** expression. During message passing, this string is used to find a matching **method** as part of the method-lookup process.

message passing   The process of locating and executing a method in response to a message. *See also* **method lookup.**

message selector   Syn. *method designator, method selector, selector.* The textual string that identifies a **message** in a **message-passing** expression. During message passing, this string is used to find a matching **method** as part of the method-lookup process.

method   A class member which is an operation. A method has a **method header** and a **method body.** A method is invoked in a message passing style.

method body   The section of a **method** that specifies what operations will be invoked when the method is executed. The method body is written as a series of statements surrounded by a pair of curly brackets.

method invocation   *See* **message passing.**

method header   The portion of a **method** that describes the return type, the name, and the argument names and types. If the return type of a method is void it can only be used as a **procedure.** If it is not void it can be used as a **function** in an expression.

method declaration   The part of a **class** declaration specific to an individual method.

method designator   Syn. *message selector.* A method name identifier used as a **procedure** or **function** name in a **message-passing** expression. The method designator is used to search for the appropriate **method** during message sending. In general, you cannot determine from the program text which method a method designator will activate during execution.

method lookup   The process of locating a **method** matching a particular **message**, generally performed as part of the **message-passing** operation. Usually, the run-time system finds the method by examining the **class hierarchy** for the **receiver** of the message, searching from bottom to top until a method is found with the same name as the message.

method selector   *See* **message selector.**

mouse listener   A **listener** that sits and waits for mouse events (mouse press or mouse release) and then performs the appropriate action.

mutator   A **method** that is used to modify the value of an **instance variable.** By requiring such modifications to be mediated through a function, a class can have greater control over how its internal state is being modified.

native method   A **method** that is implemented in another language, such as C or assembly language. *See also* **primitive.**

network   The physical connections between two or more computers, plus the **protocol,** or message format and interpretation, that they use to communicate with each other. The Internet, for example, refers to both the physical connections and the fact that machines on the Internet agree to communicate using a standard called TCP/IP.

object   A value that can both maintain data fields and perform actions. The behavior of an object is characterized by the object **class.** *See also* **instance.**

object initialization   The process of ensuring that an object is in a proper state after it has been created. Usually this is the task of a **constructor.**

object-oriented programming   A style of design that is centered around the delegation of responsibilities to independent interacting **agents,** and a style of programming characterized by the use of **message passing** and **classes** organized into one or more **inheritance hierarchies.**

overload   Used to describe an identifier that denotes more than one object. Procedures, functions, methods, and operators can all be overloaded. A method that is overridden can also be said to be overloaded. *See* **parametric overloading.**

override   The action that occurs when a method in a **subclass** with the same name as a method in a **superclass** takes precedence over the method in the superclass. Normally, during the process of binding a method to a message (see **message passing**), the overriding method will be the method selected.

paradigm   An illustrative model or example, which by extension provides a way of organizing information. The object-oriented paradigm emphasizes organization based on behaviors and responsibilities.

parametric overloading   Overloading of method names in which two or more method bodies are known by the same name in a given context, and are disambiguated by the type and number of parameters supplied with the method invocation. (Overloading of functions, methods, and operators can also occur.)

parent class   Syn. *superclass*, *ancestor class*. An immediate superclass of a class.

Parnas's principles   Principles that describe the proper use of modules, originally developed by the computer scientist David Parnas.

pattern   *See* **design pattern**.

persistent object   An object that continues to exist outside of the execution time of programs that manipulate the object.

polymorphic   Literally, 'many shapes.' A feature of a variable that can take on values of several different types. The term is also used for a method name that denotes serveral different methods. *See* **pure polymorphism**.

polymorphic function (or **method**)   A function (or method) that has at least one argument that is a **polymorphic variable**.

polymorphic variable   A variable that can hold many different types of values. Object-oriented languages often restrict the types of values to being **subclasses** of the declared type of the variable.

primitive   An operation that cannot be performed in the programming language and must be accomplished with the aid of the underlying run-time system.

private method   A method that is not intended to be invoked from outside an object. More specifically, the receiver for the message that invokes a private method should always be the receiver for the method in which the invocation is taking place (see self). Contrast with *public method*.

procedure   A term sometimes used to describe a method that does not return a value (indicated by declaring the return type void). A procedure can only be used as a complete statement, it cannot be invoked as part of an expression.

procedure call   The transfer of control from the current point in execution to the code associated with a procedure. Procedure calling differs from **message passing** in that the selection of code to be transferred to is decided at compile time (or link time) rather than run time.

process   See *thread*.

protocol   A particular form that messages must adhere to when requesting a service or services from a server. For example, the HTTP internet protocol for accessing web pages. In an OO context, the term is also used in the description of a **class description protocol.**

pseudo-variable A variable that is never declared but can nevertheless be used within a method, although it cannot be directly modified (a pseudo-variable is therefore by definition read-only). The most common pseudo-variable is used to represent the receiver of a method. *See also* this *and* super.

public class A **class** that is global and can be accessed from other packages. One public class may be declared in each compilation unit.

public method A **method** that can be invoked at any time from outside an object.

pure polymorphism A feature of a single function that can be executed by arguments of a variety of types. *See also* **ad hoc polymorphism.**

rapid prototyping A style of software development in which less emphasis is placed on creation of a complete formal specification than on rapid construction of a prototype pilot system, with the understanding that users will experiment with the initial system and suggest modifications or changes, probably leading to a complete redevelopment of a subsequent system.

receiver The **object** to which a **message** is sent. The receiver is the object to the left of the field qualifier (period). Within a **method**, the current receiver is indicated by the variable this.

redefinition The process of changing an inherited operation to provide different or extended behavior.

refinement A style of overriding in which the inherited code is merged with the code defined in the child class.

replacement A style of overriding in which the inherited code is completely replaced by the code defined in the child class.

responsibility-driven design A design technique that emphasizes the identification and division of responsibilities within a collection of independent agents.

scope When applied to a variable identifier, the (textual) portion of a program in which references to the identifier denote the particular variable.

selector *See* **message selector.**

server An application running on one computer that will make information available to applications running on other computers. The computer making the request for information is known as a **client.** The two computers must be connected over a **network.**

shadowed name   A name that matches another name in a surrounding **scope**; the new name effectively makes the surrounding name inaccessible. An example is a local variable with the same name as that of a global or instance variable. Within the procedure, the local variable will be attached to all references of the name, making references to the surrounding name difficult. In Java, access to such values can be provided by a fully qualified name.

single-assignment variable   A variable the value of which is assigned once and cannot be redefined. In Java, single-assignment variables can be created using the keyword final.

socket   A network connection between two applications running on different computers. The socket permits information to be transmitted from one application to the other.

statement   A programming construct which carries out an action. A **method body** consists of a sequence of statements.

static   A declaration modifier that, when applied to instances variables and functions, means that the variables and functions are shared by all instances of a class and exist even when no instances have yet been created.

static method   A **method** that is declared static. Since such functions exist even when no instances have been created, they can be invoked using the class name as receiver.

stream   A programming abstraction that views a file, an array, or a network connection as a sequence of **byte** values. Operations are provided to read and write values to a stream. Higher level operations are then built on top of these stream abstractions to read and write more complex values.

strongly typed language   A language in which the type of any expression can be determined at compile time.

subclass   Syn. *descendant type, derived class, child class.*

subclass coupling   The connection formed between a parent and child class. Subclass coupling is a very weak form of coupling, since instances of the subclass can be treated as though they were simply instances of the parent class. *See also* **coupling** *and* **cohesion**.

substitutability, principle of   The principle that asserts one should be able to substitute an instance of a child class in a situation where an instance of the parent class is expected. The principle is valid if the two classes are subtypes of each other, but not necessarily in general.

subtype   A type A is said to be a subtype of a type B if an instance of type A can be substituted for an instance of type B with no observable effect. Subtypes can be formed through **inheritance**, although not all **subclasses** need be subtypes. Subtypes can also be formed using **interfaces**.

super   A keyword which is used in two ways: as a message inside a constructor to indicate that the constructor for the parent class should be invoked using the arguments which follow (if any); and as a pseudo-variable inside a method to show that the method after super is the method in the parent class and not the one from the child class which has been overridden.

superclass   Syn. *ancestor class*, *base class*. A class from which another class inherits attributes.

symbolic constant   *See* **constant**.

textual representation   A value that has been converted into characters in order to be more easily read by humans. Compare to **internal representation**. The internal value 00000000 0011001 would have a textual representation of 97 if it is a short integer, and a textual representation of 'a' if it is a character.

this   When used inside a method, a reference to the receiver for the message that caused the method to be invoked.

thread   A separate task or process that can proceed in parallel with other threads.

Unicode character   A 16-bit character value. Unicode characters can be used to represent a variety of non-roman alphabets.

unnamed class   Also known as an **anonymous class**. This is a Java device for defining a class (without a name) as a single expression, the value of which is a new object of that class. It is used in cases where only one object of the class is constructed.

URL   A *Universal Resource Locator*. A textual address that encodes the information necessary to obtain a resource across a **network**. This information includes a machine name, a file on the machine, the type of **server** that will provide the information, and the **port** through which connections to the server will be made.

virtual machine   An imaginary Java machine. Java programs are translated into assembly language instructions for this imaginary machine. To execute a Java program, an actual computer must simulate the working of the virtual machine.

void   A type name used to indicate a method returning no value—that is, a **procedure**.

World Wide Web   A collection of machines on the Internet that have agreed to distribute information according to a common protocol. This information is usually accessed with a *browser*.

yo-yo problem   Repeated movements up and down the class hierarchy that may be required when the execution of a particular method invocation is traced.

Bibliography

Actor Language Manual. 1987. Evanston, IL: The Whitewater Group, Inc.

Beck, Kent and Ward Cunningham. 1989. "A Laboratory for Teaching Object-Oriented Thinking." *Proceedings of the 1989 OOPSLA—Conference on Object-Oriented Programming Systems, Languages and Applications*. Reprinted in *Sigplan Notices* 24(10): 1–6.

Bellin, David and Susan Suchman Simone. 1997. *The CRC Card Book*. Reading, MA: Addison-Wesley.

Budd, Timothy A. 1997. *An Introduction to Object-Oriented Programming*, 2nd ed. Reading, MA: Addison-Wesley.

Campione, Mary, Kathy Walrath and Alison Huml. 1999. *The Java Tutorial Continued: The Rest of the JDK*. Reading, MA: Addison-Wesley.

Cardelli, Luca and Peter Wegner. 1985. "On Understanding Types, Data Abstraction, and Polymorphism." *Computing Surveys* 17(4): 471–523.

Chan, Patrick and Rosanna Lee. 1996. *The Java Class Libraries: An Annotated Reference*. Reading, MA: Addison-Wesley.

Cox, Brad J. 1986. *Object Oriented Programming: An Evolutionary Approach*. Reading, MA: Addison-Wesley.

Cox, Brad J. 1990. "Planning the Software Industrial Revolution." *IEEE Software* 7(6): 25–35, November.

Dahl, Ole-Johan and Kristen Nygaard. 1966. "Simula, An Algol-Based Simulation Language." *Communications of the ACM* 9(9): 671-678, September.

Danforth, Scott and Chris Tomlinson. 1988. "Type Theories and Object-Oriented Programming." *ACM Computing Surveys* 20(1): 29–72.

Gabriel, Richard P. 1996. *Patterns of Software*. New York: Oxford University Press.

Gamma, Erich, Richard Helm, Ralph Johnson, and John Vlissides. 1995. *Design Patterns: Elements of Reusable Object-Oriented Software*. Reading, MA: Addison-Wesley.

Gosling, James, Bill Joy, and Guy Steele. 1996. *The Java Language Specification*. Reading, MA: Addison-Wesley.

Horowitz, Ellis. 1984. *Fundamentals of Programming Languages*. Rockville, MD: Computer Science Press.

Ingalls, Daniel H. H. 1981. "Design Principles Behind Smalltalk." *Byte* 6(8): 286–298.

Kay, Alan. 1977. "Microelectronics and the Personal Computer." *Scientific American*. 237(3): 230–244.

Kay, Alan C. 1993. "The Early History of Smalltalk." The Second ACM SIGPLAN History of Programming Languages Conference (HOPL-II), *ACM SIGPLAN Notices* 28(3): 69–75, March.

Keller, Daniel. 1990. "A Guide to Natural Naming." *Sigplan Notices* 25(5): 95–102, May.

Kim, Won, and Frederick H. Lochovsky (Eds.). 1989. *Object-Oriented Concepts, Databases, and Applications*. Reading, MA: Addison-Wesley.

Lindholm, Tim, and Frank Yellin. 1997. *The Java Virtual Machine Specification*. Reading, MA: Addison-Wesley.

MacLennan, Bruce J. 1987. *Principles of Programming Languages*. New York: Holt, Rinehart & Winston.

Marcotty, Michael, and Henry Ledgard. 1987. *The World of Programming Languages*. New York: Springer-Verlag.

Meyer, Bertrand. 1988. *Object-Oriented Software Construction*. London: Prentice-Hall International.

Micallef, Josephine. 1988. "Encapsulation, Resuability and Extensibility in Object-Oriented Programming Languages." *Journal of Object-Oriented Programming Languages* 1(1): 12–35.

Milner, Robin, Mads Tofte, and Robert Harper. 1990. *The Definition of Standard ML*. Cambridge, MA: MIT Press.

Morehead, Albert H., and Geoffrey Mott-Smith. 1949. *The Complete Book of Solitaire and Patience Games*. New York: Grosset & Dunlap.

Nygaard, Kristen, and Ole-Johan Dahl. 1981. "The Development of the Simula Languages." In Richard L. Wexelblat (Ed.). *History of Programming Langauges*. New York: Academic Press.

Pinson, Lewis J., and Richard S. Wiener. 1988. *An Introduction to Object-Oriented Programming and Smalltalk*. Reading, MA: Addison-Wesley.

Sethi, Ravi. 1989. *Programming Languages: Concepts and Constructs*. Reading, MA: Addison-Wesley.

Stroustrup, Bjarne. 1982. "Classes: An Abstract Data Type Facility for the C Language." *ACM Sigplan Notices* 17(1):42–51, January.

Stroustrup, Bjarne. 1988. "What is 'Object-Oriented Programming?'" *IEEE Software* 5(3): 10–20, May.

Stroustrup, Bjarne. 1994. *The Design and Evolution of C++*. Reading, MA: Addison-Wesley.

Taenzer, David, Murthy Ganti, and Sunil Podar. 1989. "Object-Oriented Software Reuse: The Yoyo Problem." *Journal of Object-Oriented Programming* 2(3): 30–35.

Wegner, Peter. 1986. "Classification in Object-Oriented Systems." *Sigplan Notices* 21(10): 173–182, October.

Weizenbaum, Joseph. 1976. *Computer Power and Human Reason*. San Francisco: W. H. Freeman and Company.

Wikström, Åke. 1987. *Functional Programming Using Standard ML*. London: Prentice-Hall International.

Wirfs-Brock, Rebecca, and Brian Wilkerson. 1989. "Object-Oriented Design: A Responsibility-Driven Approach." *Proceedings of the 1989 OOPSLA—Conference on Object-Oriented Programming Systems, Languages and Applications*. Reprinted in *Sigplan Notices* 24(10): 71–76, October.

Wirfs-Brock, Rebecca, Brian Wilkerson, and Lauren Wiener. 1990. *Designing Object-Oriented Software*. Englewood Cliffs, NJ: Prentice-Hall.

Wulf, William A. 1972/1979. "A Case Against the GOTO." *Proceedings of the Twenty-Fifth National ACM Conference*. 1972; Reprinted in Edward Yourdon (Ed.). *Classics in Software Engineering*. Englewood Cliffs, NJ: Prentice-Hall.

Index

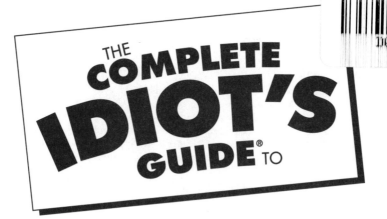

THE COMPLETE IDIOT'S GUIDE® TO

Communicating with Spirits

by Rita S. Berkowitz and Deborah S. Romaine

ALPHA

A member of Penguin Group (USA) Inc.

For Jess: Life is Life

International Standard Book Number: 0-02-864350-X
Library of Congress Catalog Card Number: 2002110185

05   04   8   7   6   5   4

Interpretation of the printing code: The rightmost number of the first series of numbers is the year of the book's printing; the rightmost number of the second series of numbers is the number of the book's printing. For example, a printing code of 03-1 shows that the first printing occurred in 2003.

Printed in the United States of America

Note: This publication contains the opinions and ideas of its authors. It is intended to provide helpful and informative material on the subject matter covered. It is sold with the understanding that the authors, book producer, and publisher are not engaged in rendering professional services in the book. If the reader requires personal assistance or advice, a competent professional should be consulted.

The authors, book producer, and publisher specifically disclaim any responsibility for any liability, loss, or risk, personal or otherwise, which is incurred as a consequence, directly or indirectly, of the use and application of any of the contents of this book.

Publisher: *Marie Butler-Knight*
Product Manager: *Phil Kitchel*
Managing Editor: *Jennifer Chisholm*
Senior Acquisitions Editor: *Randy Ladenheim-Gil*
Book Producer: *Lee Ann Chearney/Amaranth*
Development Editor: *Lynn Northrup*
Senior Production Editor: *Christy Wagner*
Copy Editor: *Anja Mutic*
Illustrator: *Chris Eliopoulos*
Cover/Book Designer: *Trina Wurst*
Indexer: *Angie Bess*
Layout/Proofreading: *Megan Douglass, Becky Harmon, Mary Hunt*

Contents at a Glance

Contents

Foreword

I admit I entered into my first reading with a genuine psychic medium on January 15, 1999, a bit skeptically. Though open-minded enough to try a medium, I really didn't believe that people could *see, hear,* and *talk* with spirits. In my late 30s at the time, I had never witnessed anything that led me to believe in such "nonsense." I went to see the medium because my brother-in-law, Derek, told me she gave him a reading full of details—including names, dates, and information a stranger could *never* know about him. Despite my skepticism, Derek's story intrigued me enough to risk the money it cost for the reading.

I ended up with much more than I expected that day. Rather than the normal one-hour reading, I had a three-hour reading that left me sobbing like a lost child for at least half of that time. I lost my psychic virginity and my manhood all in the same day! The names, dates, and secret details of my life came through exactly as Derek said his had. By the end of my reading, the medium had given me so much evidence, my skepticism shattered.

This single event altered the course of my life. I had recently had a book published about depression and bipolar disorder, and I had no idea what I would write about next. But after these three hours of spirit communication through a psychic medium with my deceased father and grandmother, I knew immediately that my next book had to be about spirit communication. So I began my research for *Medium Rare*.

The funny result, though, of being a skeptic for more than 30 years is that it doesn't prepare you for writing a book about spirit communication!

So I spent the next three years reading every book, magazine article, and website I could find on the subject. Because the reading material never satisfied my craving for a well-rounded education on spirit communication, I also immersed myself in three years of frequent readings with extraordinarily gifted mediums from around the world. Additionally, I interviewed these spirit messengers about their life, their gift, and the wisdom they had gained from their communication with spirits. And finally, I interviewed masses of people who had readings from psychic mediums.

A short time after I wrote *Medium Rare*, I learned about the impending publication of *The Complete Idiot's Guide to Communicating with Spirits:* the one book that could have saved me years of reading, interviews, and investigation. Well, thank you very much *Idiot's Guide* people! You couldn't have thought of this book a little sooner? I forgive the publishers, of course, because the author they chose to write this book, Rita Berkowitz, is both a dear friend and an incredible medium who helped me along my journey. In fact, the publisher discovered Rita by reading an article I had written about her on my holistic online magazine, OfSpirit.com.

In my spirit explorations, I kept hearing about this incredible psychic medium who could also draw the spirits she sees. The day I met Rita, my mind exploded into pieces when I saw her portfolio of spirit drawings. Each spirit drawing had a photo next to it of that person when he or she was still here on the earth plane. I found myself dumbfounded at Rita's ability to capture each spirit's distinct features: the eyes, the nose, the mouth, the ears, the hair—even the style of clothing or jewelry he or she normally wore. I knew immediately I had to have a reading from Rita and one of these stupefying spirit drawings.

Now a pro at getting psychic readings (or so I thought), I no longer got emotional during my readings. But when Rita drew my grandmother, seeing such a tangible display of evidence that Gram had survived death and was still around me caused some tears to leak out and run down my cheek. (I faked a yawn and wiped them off very quickly ….)

Elated with my spirit drawing and reading, I wrote about Rita on OfSpirit.com. Since that article became public, people from around the world have thanked me for introducing them to Rita Berkowitz. Rita is much more than a gifted medium and spirit artist; she is also a gifted teacher. This truth was never more obvious to me than when I received an advance copy of *The Complete Idiot's Guide to Communicating with Spirits*. Even with all I learned from my own research and experiences writing *Medium Rare*, Rita's book taught me insights about spirit communication, spiritualism, and activating my own spirit senses of which I was unaware.

Anyone interested in understanding the how and why of spirit communication or desiring to communicate with spirits on their own will gain a depth of insight from Rita's wonderful book that is invaluable for spiritual growth. If there is one thing I have learned in my three years of studying some of the most gifted mediums in the world, it is that we all have a unique potential for communicating with spirits—and we don't need a psychic medium to do it for us. I highly recommend you use the wisdom within this book to discover your own potential for spirit communication and enhance the wonder and amazement of your own, very personal, spiritual adventure.

Warmly,
Bob Olson

Bob Olson, editor of *OfSpirit.com Magazine*, is the author of *Medium Rare: A Skeptic's Journey into the World of Spirit Communication and the Afterlife* and *Win the Battle: The Three-Step Lifesaving Formula to Conquer Depression and Bipolar Disorder*. Bob writes and lectures on the subjects of spirit communication, life after death, and the spiritual principles of success and overcoming life's obstacles. Contact Bob through the OfSpirit.com website at www.ofspirit.com.

Introduction

Each of us has a different reason for wanting to communicate with loved ones who have passed to the higher side. Many of us have unresolved issues and concerns. Maybe you didn't get to say "good-bye" or "I love you" before your loved one passed. Perhaps the relationship was difficult. Maybe you just feel a need to maintain a connection. Or maybe you want to establish evidence of the continuity of life.

This book provides a foundation for you to explore your interest in spirit communication. Whether you've already experienced spirit contact (yourself or through a medium) or are just intrigued by the idea, you've come to the right place.

Co-author Rita Berkowitz is an ordained Spiritualist minister, certified medium, and commissioned healer. Throughout this book, we use stories and examples from her experiences. To protect the privacy of others, we've changed the names—but the stories are real.

Rita is also a talented artist. What she experiences as a medium, she can draw or paint for her clients. Although the veracity of the information she conveys during a reading is compelling enough by itself, seeing the image of a loved one arise from Rita's pencil and paper is irrefutable evidence of the continuity of life beyond physical boundaries.

Rita's spirit drawings appear throughout the book, along with photographs of the person from physical life. The names and stories of these people are real, and we thank them for being willing to share them with us—and with you.

About This Book

There are six parts to this book:

Part 1, "The Spirit World," looks at different perspectives on life, physical death, and the continuation of the spirit's existence. The four chapters in this section explore burial customs, the connection with the divine, the Spiritualist religion, and the answers we look to spirit communication to provide.

Part 2, "What's on the Other Side?" explores the differences between the earth plane and the spirit world. The four chapters in this section examine the various ways spirit contact happens and many reasons we welcome and seek it, look at why spirits choose to come through in communication, and why some spirits find it difficult to leave the earth plane.

Part 3, "Invoking the Spirits," investigates the validation and symbolism of spirit communication. The five chapters in this section provide information about, and exercises to develop, the psychic and psychical skills that facilitate spirit contact.

Part 4, "Activating Your Spirit Senses," looks at some of the more advanced skills that help mediums make spirit connections. The four chapters in this section include exercises to help you develop these skills.

Part 5, "Being: The Essence of Spirit," explores the healing aspects of spirit energy. The four chapters in this section look at the different ways spirit energy connects you to your past, your present, your future, and your environment.

Part 6, "Karmic Cycles and Soul Lessons," examines the ways you can use spirit energy in your life. These final three chapters give you ways to apply the lessons you learn to your individual life and to use spirit healing to influence the world community.

You'll also find two helpful appendixes. The glossary collects all the terms that we've defined throughout the book and adds a few more to provide a basic dictionary of words you need to know when reading and talking about the many aspects of spirit communication. The additional resources appendix lists other books that provide in-depth information about specific topics or that are just good sources for learning more about spirit communication. This appendix also includes contact information for websites, mediumship schools, and relevant organizations.

Extras

Each chapter contains boxes with interesting and useful information.

Spiritology _____
Check these boxes for terms and definitions so you'll know what we mean when we say …

Silver Cord _____
Here you'll find tips, information, and factoids that don't quite fit in the text but are too irresistibly interesting to leave out.

Premonition _____
These boxes contain cautions, because spirit communication is not a board game.

Mediums and Messages _____
Check these boxes for interesting anecdotes that provide insights and explanations about spirit communication.

Acknowledgments

It takes many people to turn a good idea into a good book, and we deeply appreciate the efforts of all those who worked to bring this book into existence. We give thanks to (and for) the wonderful team at Alpha Books, including publisher Marie Butler-Knight and our editors Randy Ladenheim-Gil, Lynn Northrup, Anja Mutic, and Christy Wagner. Special thanks go to Lee Ann Chearney of Amaranth, for her extraordinary vision, acceptance, guidance, and support.

Debbie thanks these people: Mike, Chris, and Cass for their love and patience. Dianne ("Dicycle"), for her observations and insights. Ava, for having the courage to speak the truth. Giuseppe, for the generosity of his amazing invitation. And Rita, for her insight, good humor, flexibility, and enthusiasm as we've shared the journey of writing this book.

Rita thanks these people: my husband David and daughters Deborah and Erica for all your love and support and not thinking it too strange that I spend so much time with "dead people." I want to thank Stephen O'Leary, Career Counseling Professor, for saying the right words, "Use your gifts." Thanks to Bob Miller, founder of the Silver Birch Healing Sanctuary, dear friend, and mentor for always teaching me that all spirit communication is for healing. And thanks especially to Bob Olson, who walked into church one morning and asked for a spirit drawing and changed both of our lives. Bob took on the awesome task of creating the online spiritual magazine, OfSpirit.com, that has helped to connect the people in the spiritual/holistic community around the globe. I can't begin to express the great appreciation I, as well as so many others, feel about his work. Thank you, Bob, for all that you do.

And last, we thank the many people who have been willing to share their stories, experiences, and spirit drawings with us to include in this book. These people and events are real, and they validate the continuity of life as nothing else can.

Trademarks

All terms mentioned in this book that are known to be or are suspected of being trademarks or service marks have been appropriately capitalized. Alpha Books and Penguin Group (USA) Inc. cannot attest to the accuracy of this information. Use of a term in this book should not be regarded as affecting the validity of any trademark or service mark.

Part 1

The Spirit World

Throughout history and across cultures, humankind has shared a common belief in the continuation of life after death. Although the physical body dies, the spirit lives on. These beliefs form the basis of numerous religions and faith systems.

The chapters in this part explore some of these common elements in beliefs and practices.

THE TRUTH AS TO WHY SPIRITS TRY TO CONTACT THE LIVING.

I See Dead People

In This Chapter

- ◆ Existence as a continuum
- ◆ Death, the journey continues
- ◆ Spirit communication is always about healing
- ◆ Are *you* in touch with spirits? A quiz
- ◆ Sharpening your mediumistic abilities
- ◆ Trust your intuition!

How often do you pick up the phone to call your sister, brother, parent, friend, or lover—someone near and dear to you—for no apparent reason and then find out that something significant has happened or is going on in the person's life? These bonds connect you in ways that transcend conscious communication. We welcome, and even expect, these connections as evidence of the depth of our relationships.

As these bonds connect us to others in our physical lives, they also extend beyond physical boundaries. Many people expect to stay in contact with loved ones even after they pass on. And we expect this contact to take place along the bonds formed in our physical lives. Spouses, parents, children, and dear friends—people connected through love in the physical world and separated by death—establish and maintain contact that transcends life and death.

Many people who want to communicate with spirits desire to make contact with loved ones who have passed on. (We're guessing that, because you're reading this book, you are among them.) And many spirits that initiate contact with the physical world have the same desire. This contact can be for comfort, to protect or shelter, to explain or forgive, or simply to continue a loving relationship.

The Continuity of Life

You might think of spirits as ghostly images that drift around just beyond the boundaries of physical experience. And in a sense, this perception isn't wrong … just incomplete. Spirits are all around us. Some we can see, hear, and touch—those who, like us, inhabit physical bodies. We may not recognize others that are present as *discarnate* spirits. They might be spirits that once lived or are yet to live in the *physical plane*, or spirits that exist solely in the *spirit plane*.

Spiritology

A **discarnate spirit** is one without a physical body. The **physical plane** is the level of existence at which spirits take physical form (our physical world). The **spirit plane** is the level of existence at which there are no boundaries of tangibility, time, or space.

The cycle of life and death has fascinated humankind for all of its existence. What, we ask through our spiritual and religious pursuits, defines the start and end of this cycle? This line of questioning finds itself limited by the boundaries of physical existence. But what if we reverse this thinking? Instead of looking at human beings as physical bodies that have spirits (or souls), what if we look at human existence as spirits inhabiting physical bodies? Then the cycle becomes a continuum.

The Greatest Journey Begins with Preparation

Many ancient cultures buried their dead as though they were leaving on grand, extended journeys. Excavated burial sites on nearly every continent show bodies carefully prepared and surrounded by valuables, food, and other items the departed might need in the afterlife. Scientists have dated some of these sites to be as old as the Neolithic period 10,000 years ago. Consistencies among sites in certain locations provide evidence that cultures often followed precise rituals in burying their dead. The ancient Egyptians meticulously removed the body's major organs, sealing them in clay jars placed around the body so the spirit would find them ready as it entered its next life.

The Healing Power of Love

While there are many reasons why people want to communicate with spirits, all paths lead to only one purpose: healing. Healing can take numerous forms, from emotional closure to physical health. It can be understanding, insight, knowledge, or acceptance. We speak of this healing as being "guided by the light"—undertaken with the protection of the Divine, however you define it within the framework of your belief system.

Comfort from the Other Side

Countless people, grieving the loss of loved ones, find comfort in contact with the other side. Sometimes it is loved ones who have passed who initiate the contact, reaching from beyond to comfort and even protect those on this side. Sometimes contact comes indirectly, from other spirits who want to reassure the living that those who have passed are at peace.

Often, relatives who have passed become regular visitors. In their communications, they have joyous stories to share. They want to be of comfort, to establish that existence continues beyond what we view as the boundary of death. As a result, many people live the remainder of their physical lives in regular communication with spouses, parents, grandparents, siblings, other relatives, friends, and associates who were close to them before passing. And they lose whatever fear of death they might have had, as they become confident that existence continues.

Unfinished Business

Communicating with those who have passed gives us an opportunity to wrap up loose ends. Family members are sometimes at odds with each other, lovers quarreling, siblings squabbling, friends bickering. It happens; it's a part of life. But we seldom know in advance when we've reached the end of our physical lives. Sometimes the physical part ends before the disagreement does, leaving the living steeped in grief and guilt.

Contact with the spirit that has passed can give both parties the chance to mend rifts. Sometimes the contact is direct, in which the spirit of the departed appears to the living loved one and there is a one-to-one communication. Sometimes the contact is indirect, as when a third-party spirit appears to say, "Robert is here. He wants you to know that he is fine and he's sorry for that argument right before his heart attack. It wasn't your fault, and his love for you will never die." There is great comfort in being able to apologize, explain, forgive, reconcile, say "good-bye" or "I love you"—whatever communication needs to take place.

What about spirits who are apparent strangers to us, and don't have a message from departed loved ones but instead just want to communicate with whatever physical entities they can reach and who will respond? Such spirits typically have their own reasons for making contact. In some way, they need help from you so they can continue their evolution on the higher, or other, side. Perhaps you're the contact point because you are in a space, such as a house, that belonged to or was familiar to the ghost in its physical existence. Maybe there is something about your life mission that intersects with the spirit's mission. Such a spirit has unfinished business, and you can help bring completion and resolution for the spirit. We talk more about this in later chapters.

Taking Familiar Form

Spirits often find it necessary to interact with us in ways that we, as physical beings, can experience. We like to see, hear, and touch our environment and all that is within it. After all, that's the essence of our physical existence. And especially if communication with the spirit world is new to us, we're more comfortable when we can experience such contact in familiar ways. You might see an image of the person, hear his or her voice, or even smell a favorite fragrance that the person used to wear.

Sometimes the contact might come through someone else, not necessarily a medium (a person who acts as a link, through his or her sensitivity, between the spirit and physical worlds) but perhaps a friend who might say, "I don't know where this is coming from because your mother has passed away, but I have this image of her in my head and she wants me to tell you that you should not go to the lake this weekend. Instead, you should stay close to home. And she's saying, for heaven's sake, paint the living room blue, not beige." If the words and tone sound just like your mother, don't panic: It's just your mother's spirit with a message for you, coming through in a way you recognize and through a source you trust. So for heaven's sake, stay home and paint the living room blue!

Personal Growth, Insight, and Empowerment

Communication with the other side might be common, but it is also special. Put it to good use! This is your opportunity to learn about yourself and your purpose in this life. Use the insights you gain to further your life purpose and to leave a positive imprint in this, our physical, world.

Knowledge empowers. It can help you to understand why you feel and act as you do, so you can direct your energy in positive ways. What you learn through your contacts with spirit entities can help you heal emotional wounds, physical ailments, and get your life on track.

Sometimes the insights that come to you through spirit communication are intense, or even disturbing. It can be helpful to have someone you can turn to, to discuss your feelings and concerns. There are professionals who combine psychic consultation with conventional therapeutic approaches. Chapters 13 and 24 provide more information about moving from insight to changes in your life.

Silver Cord

The venerable Gallup Organization surveys Americans on nearly any topic that could come up during dinner conversation. In a June 2001 poll, 38 percent of participants said they believed it is possible to have contact or communication with the spirits of people who have died. Fifty-four percent said they believed in psychic or spiritual healing, and 42 percent believed that houses could be haunted.

Do *You* See Dead People?

Rita Berkowitz, co-author of this book, is a certified medium and ordained minister in the Spiritualist Church. She began drawing faces when she was a child. At the time she thought these were of imaginary people and didn't recognize that this was what she was doing; she just drew what she saw. Now, as an adult with many years of education and experience that have broadened and deepened her knowledge, understanding, and skills, Rita receives spirit communication through drawing and other forms (we talk more about these in later chapters).

Do *you* receive spirit communication? Answer these questions to find out!

1. **Have you felt sudden changes of temperature?** If you're a woman in midlife, we're not talking hot flashes here! Often, spirit presence results in sudden and unexplainable temperature jumps up or down. Cold in particular is associated with the presence of a spirit. You might walk down a hallway and feel as though you've walked into a refrigerator. Less commonly, you might be sitting in your favorite chair when it feels like someone's cranked up the heat.

2. **Do you see sudden lights?** Spirits are energy, and light is an expression of energy. Floating or flickering lights often suggest the presence of spirits. Orbs (also called ghost orbs, ghost lights, or earth lights) are a particular form of presence, well documented and often photographed.

Premonition

Although we discuss seeing sudden lights here in the context of what this might suggest about the presence of spirits, it's important to recognize that this phenomenon can also suggest certain eye disorders. If you notice any interference with your vision, contact your eye-care professional.

In October 2001, Rita went to Arthur Findley College in Stansted, England, to spend a week studying mediumship. Earlier in the day Rita experienced an independent voice while walking through the beautiful gardens on the grounds. She decided to take a photograph of the gardens from the window of her room. When she got the developed photo back, the image of shimmering light appeared.

3. **Have you ever seen an image out of the corner of your eye? Can you identify that image?** Many people report seeing vaguely human shapes or shadows in their peripheral vision. Some can further report, if they don't give it too much thought or analysis, that the figure was a young girl in a nightgown or sure looked like Uncle Albert even though he's been gone for 15 years now. Yet turning your head to look directly at the image generally reveals nothing, which might cause you to doubt whether you actually did see anything.

4. **Have you had a discarnate spirit visit you in a dream?** It's often a source of comfort to those grieving the loss of loved ones to have their loved ones appear in dreams. Sometimes the dreams are reenactments of events that took place when the loved one was still in the physical plane. Other times the dreams appear to be messages from the loved one, attempting to reassure and convey love.

5. **Has your mind suddenly (and out of context) been brought back to a specific time and place, with a loved one who has passed?** Somewhat like a waking dream, this phenomenon could be the work of a spirit that wants you to know it is still with you and remains part of your everyday life. Activating the memory of an event that was meaningful to both of you is one way the spirit can validate its identity to you and demonstrate the continuity of life.

6. **Do you sometimes smell a specific scent that reminds you of a particular loved one?** It could be that this scent still lingers in places the two of you frequented, such as your home or car. And sure, it could be that someone else is

wearing the fragrance or has a similar smell. But smell is a sense that activates the emotions and memory, again creating validation. Many times it is a particular smell, such as of brewing coffee or breath mints, unique to the person who has passed, that provides clues that the person's spirit is still present.

7. **Have you ever felt a touch, or maybe the sensation that you're walking into a spider web?** Sometimes a spirit attempts to "reach out and touch"— which, of course, isn't especially practical for an intangible, discarnate entity! You might feel the energy of the spirit's presence making contact with your skin. Also, there is a phenomenon called *transfiguration* in which a spirit's *ectoplasm* flows around you.

8. **Do you ever hear voices when you know you are alone, or hear voices that no one else hears?** You might have the sense of "hearing" a particular word, phrase, sound, or even a song or piece of music. It might be obvious enough that you can connect it with a person who has passed, or it might puzzle you because it doesn't seem connected to anything in particular. This phenomenon is called clairaudience. With focus and concentration, you can often gain increasing clarity until you actually hear the message.

Spiritology

Transfiguration takes place when a spirit's physical characteristics superimpose over a medium's features, presenting an image of the spirit entity. **Ectoplasm** is a substance spirits produce to make themselves visible; comes from the Greek words *ecto*, meaning "outside," and *plasma*, meaning "a thing formed."

9. **Have you had a sense that something has happened to someone you love, and later found out that the person was in an accident or experienced some other traumatic event?** Not all spirit communication takes place across the border between the physical and spiritual planes. Spirits inhabiting bodies can make contact, too. The most common such contact is a phenomenon called crisis telepathy, in which you get an image of an event, or even just a sense that something has happened to a loved one.

10. **Have you been to a place or touched an object and gotten an image or sensory activation (sound, smell, taste) of a person or an event?** Perhaps you walk into the office and immediately *know* that a colleague is pregnant even before she's felt comfortable telling anyone in the office! She can't figure out how you know, but it's really just psychometry—the ability to "read" energy information given off by people and objects. You might be able to touch an antique table and instantly visualize the image of a pioneer woman in her white blouse and long, bustled skirt placing a letter on the table.

While in England studying at Arthur Findley College, Rita toured Bath and stopped for lunch at the Priory, a beautiful hotel and restaurant. Again, the shimmering light appeared. The Abbey in Bath proved quite magnificent, with an overwhelming feeling of spirit presence. When Rita's photo came back from the developer, a beautiful light radiated in the bottom of the photo with no explanation for its presence.

Experiences such as these are far more commonplace than most people realize. Other
people who are with you at the time might
also feel a spirit presence, as often happens in
a *circle*, although it is less likely because the
spirit making contact is not personal to them.

Spiritology

A **circle** is a group of
people, usually having mediumistic abilities, who gather to
connect with spirit entities.

Activating Your Mediumistic Abilities

Everyone has the ability to communicate with spirits. Many people simply don't use
this ability, just as they might not use other abilities that they have, such as singing or
writing. But spirits are always all around us. Discovering their presence and establishing connections just requires awareness and focus.

Sometimes this is as simple as sitting in a quiet room and allowing yourself to experience all of the energies in the room. From this is likely to emerge a sense of the
presence of others—spirits. With practice, you can focus on certain spiritual presences to the exclusion of others, gaining a clearer image or impression. And with
more practice, you can focus in such a way as to establish contact with a particular
spirit (provided the spirit is willing).

Just as it's important to learn the proper techniques for any activity that blends ability
and skill, you need to learn what to do and how to do it, so that your experiences
remain positive and provide knowledge and healing.

In Your Dreams

A common setting for communication between we mortals and those of the spirit
realm is the dream. In the dream state, the conscious filters of your brain are turned
off. As a result, dreams often teem with vivid and otherworldly images that seem as
natural and real as the world we inhabit when awake. We don't doubt or question
these images; at best, we look at them as insights or lessons, and at worst, we simply
dismiss them as "just dreams." This makes dreams a natural environment for spirit
contacts that we might otherwise reject or ignore.

Spirit contact in the dreamscape can take any number of forms. Sometimes departed
loved ones appear as living, tangible beings—often younger and more vibrant than in
life as we remember them. (This is often how the spirits of loved ones in other visitations appear, too; more on this in later chapters.) We might engage with these images,
in our dreams, much as we used to in real life. We might play out the life we wanted
to have. Or the dream may have no correlation to real events and circumstances. This
is the beauty and the power of dreams: Anything goes.

Mediums and Messages

One of the themes in spirit contact dreams relates to travel. For example, the dreamer might be driving along a familiar road and stop to pick up a hitchhiker that he or she recognizes as a loved one, or go to the airport to meet a loved one's incoming flight. These settings make sense; after all, the visiting spirits are on a cosmic journey of sorts, traveling through time and space to call on us.

Occasionally, a dream visit from a spirit brings a message or even a warning. This could be about anything. Some of the most common and dramatic messages relate to health issues. A departed loved one might appear in a dream to tell you to schedule an appointment to have the doctor check out that mole on your neck. You do, and it turns out to be skin cancer, caught in the earliest stages so it ends up being nothing more than a minor inconvenience. Ignoring these messages causes the dreams to become more persistent and perhaps more graphic or startling, until finally you "get" it and see the doctor.

Premonition

Sometimes spirit visitation dreams are more symbolic than practical, and it takes some detective work to figure them out. If such dreams puzzle you, don't just dismiss them as nonsense. There are many good books on dream interpretation (see Appendix B for some to get you started) that can help you understand the meanings of the symbols and images that occur in your dreams.

The tone of most spirit visitation dreams is one of comfort and reassurance. The loved one might feel your sadness and sense of loss, and want you to know that the connection remains strong despite the physical separation. The spirit typically appears as whole, happy, and healthy; we know instantly that all is well. And this is the point. The visit is to reassure you, through images and experiences that make sense in the context of your physical world, that everything is okay. The message is clear: "Feel happy for me, because I am at peace."

Calling All Spirits

Spirits aren't just sitting around on the other side, waiting for opportunities for contact with you. (Well, most aren't, anyway.) Often, you need to ask them to make themselves available for communication.

In the chapters that follow, we help you identify and clarify your interests and reasons for contacting the spirit world, and give you methods and approaches to help you make the contact you desire. And in Chapter 10 we talk about how to find a qualified, competent, and honest psychic professional who can guide you in your efforts.

Tell Me What You Want, and I'll Give You What You Need

When you're new to the processes of consciously communicating with spirits, you might feel disappointed and even skeptical when the contact or information that you receive isn't what you wanted. Relax. This is fairly common. As beings more knowledgeable than we physical entities, discarnate spirits tell us what we are ready to hear.

As physical beings, we have a tendency to want The Answer. What is the meaning of life? Is there a God? When am I going to die? We aren't always seeking, or willing to accept, just answers or, less definitive still, just information. Yet just as it is the small stuff that matters in physical life, it's the little things that matter in the bigger picture. And sometimes we—physical and spirit entities—have differences of opinion about *what* matters.

On the verge of separating from her husband of 20 years, Caroline came to Rita for a reading. In the sitting, Rita got an image of the Braintree Split, a local landmark that was a fork in the road. In this image, Rita saw the skies open up and the vision of Caroline's grandparents, whose identities were clear to Caroline. They said, "Stay with him, work this through." Caroline didn't really want to hear this message, but decided to give it a try. She's now been happily married 33 years!

If you've made contact with the spirit world and you're not getting the information you want or you don't understand the information you're receiving, take a look at what you're asking. Does your question match up with what you really want to know? Sometimes we ask one question, yet actually want information of a different sort than the answer will produce.

The more specific your question, the more clear your focus and the more likely you are to receive the response you seek. You might ask, "What is it like on the other side?" when really what you want to know is, "Do you still love me, even though you've passed on and now exist in a realm I can't share with you?" Your loved one's contact with you is, in itself, evidence that the answer to your real, even if unasked question, is a resounding "Yes!"

With experience, you'll gain understanding and confidence that will help you ask the right questions and make sense of the answers that you receive. Chapter 4 provides more information about this. There's really no great mystery to getting useful information from the spirit world!

When You Just *Know:* Trust Your Intuition

Sometimes we speak of intuition as the sixth sense (the other five being those of tangibility: seeing, hearing, smelling, touching, and tasting). Intuition makes use of the other senses, and can also enhance them. Typically when we talk about intuitive messages, we say things like, "I feel" or "I sense." A person who is in tune with this sixth sense might say, "I intuit."

One dictionary defines intuition as "immediate cognition." You just *know*, instantly and unequivocally—and often act accordingly. You might suddenly turn left when your usual commute route turns right, then hear on the radio that there was a horrible accident just beyond the intersection at which you would've turned right had you followed your regular route. Chance or coincidence? We don't think so!

When it comes to contact with spirits, intuition becomes your most powerful tool and your most reliable guide. Your other five senses aren't of much value when it comes to evaluating experiences that are not tangible. But your intuition can tell you whether you're right on ... or whether it's time to move on. However illogical it might seem at times, your intuition will never lead you astray.

Premonition

Allowing your conscious mind to override your intuition can make your intuition appear faulty when it's really right on target. Intuition is immediate; anything longer is intervention from your conscious mind.

How do you know when it truly is your intuition, and not just your feelings of grief, sorrow, or longing? This isn't always easy, particularly if your feelings are intense. If you are concerned about whether an apparent contact or communication is authentic, consider consulting a medium. This brings in a "third party" who doesn't have knowledge of your past or the many little details only someone who was close to you would know.

A medium certified with the Spiritualist Church, such as co-author Rita, has extensive training and skill in validating a spirit's identity before sharing the contact with the person who is requesting it. Spirits typically offer authenticating information in the form of knowledge no one else—at least not the medium—would have. This might be a nickname or recollection of an event, or mention of a favorite fragrance or food—whatever can conclusively establish that the spirit is who he or she says ... or you believe. If a medium cannot authenticate a spirit's identity, then you can be fairly certain other factors are at play, such as your feelings.

Bringing Us Goodness and Light

The most important thing to remember about communicating with spirits is that such communication is a gift through which you can do good for yourself and for others. Spirits allow or initiate contact so they can help us ... and many times we can help them.

Is there a dark element to the other side? Inasmuch as there is a dark element in our physical world, probably. There are always those who seem capable of distorting good to do bad. Horror movies make the most of this potential. But what they're really doing is exploiting our fears, especially the fear of the unknown and unprovable. And judging by the popularity of these films, there's plenty of fear to exploit!

But communicating with spirits is not about fear, evil, or darkness. Rather, spirit communication is about love, goodness, and light. If you believe that goodness guides existence, as your authors do, then you know that the spirits of loved ones who have passed on, guardian spirits, and other spirit entities want to help us, not hurt us. (And sometimes they want us to help them, too.) The pursuit of goodness frames our existence and purpose, physical and spiritual.

That is the focus of this book: to help you communicate with your spirit guides, spirit guardians, and loved ones to find comfort, reassurance, and answers. You might be seeking closure, reconciliation, or guidance on the passage through your physical life. Your reasons for wanting to communicate across the boundary of physical existence are as unique as anything else about you. This book seeks to provide you with the understanding and tools you need to make the contact you desire.

Let your journey begin!

The Least You Need to Know

- Love is the energy that connects our physical world with the spirit world.
- There are many ways to experience contact and communication with spirits.
- Dreams are familiar settings for spirit contacts.
- Everyone has the ability to communicate with spirits, but many people don't use it.
- Spirits want to help us, and to bring goodness into our lives.
- Sometimes spirit contact gives us the opportunity to help the spirit move onward in its evolution.

2

Divine Purpose

In This Chapter

- Customs of ancient cultures
- The mythology of "crossing over"
- Completing the soul's journey
- Spirits among us
- Celebrating the continuity of spirit

There is a divine purpose in spirit communication, and its history throughout humanity stands as incontrovertible evidence. Nearly every religion or faith system in the world today, and indeed throughout history, incorporates some element of belief in an existence beyond life in the physical world. These beliefs transcend the boundaries of religion to demonstrate a nearly universal acceptance of the soul's ongoing existence.

Such beliefs do not contradict religious frameworks that support reincarnation, the promise of heaven, a unity of spirit, or other tenets that define a particular faith or religion. Beliefs in the soul's continuation beyond the death of the physical body are part of many faith systems, supported by and supporting a diverse and vast number of faiths. And they share in common the fundamental principle that knowledge and light lead the way to communication that is for goodness and healing.

Preparing for the Afterlife

Through the ages, there have been many diverse customs and practices related to the passage of the spirit from the physical world to the spirit world—death. However, they are consistent in their reflection that human beings have probably always believed in the continuation of the soul's existence after the physical body dies. Throughout history, most cultures have viewed death as a passage to another level of being. Burial traditions remain as tangible evidence of this view.

> ### Silver Cord
>
> It wasn't until the advent of Buddhism in India around the sixth century B.C.E. that historical documents reflected the concept that life might not end with the death of the physical body. Few faith systems picked this up, however, and today it is a view that remains restricted to just a few faiths.

> ### Spiritology
>
> The **Paleolithic** period began two and a half million years ago and is considered the dawn of modern humankind. Often referred to as the Stone Age, it was the time when humans began creating tools and implements out of stone and other natural materials. This was the point of development at which humans became clearly distinct from other animals.

The most staid and venerable of reference resources, *Encyclopedia Britannica, Fifteenth Edition*, says: "Death rites and customs stem from an instinctive inability or refusal on the part of man to accept death as the definitive end of human life; they thus reflect the belief that human beings survive death in some form and represent the practical measures taken to assist the dead to achieve their destiny …."

As the earliest archaeological evidence dating to about 50000 B.C.E. (the time of *Paleolithic*, or Stone Age, humans) demonstrates, human beings have always viewed the end of this life as a preparation for the next. Many of these preparations involve the physical body, from dressing it in the finest attire to embalming it to prevent its deterioration. Although in modern times we might think of these procedures as simply part of the funeral preparation, they are in fact persistent evidence of our conviction that there is, so to speak, life after life. Even the tradition of cremation that has emerged in some cultural traditions such as Native American and Hindu reflects a releasing of the spirit from its physical body so that it can be free to exist as a spirit.

Will we need these physical bodies we now inhabit when we move beyond our current lives? Nearly all prevailing belief systems say no. Rather, they hold that there is a discarnate (without a physical body) existence beyond the physical existence, in which a body is not necessary. Earlier cultures, however, were less certain of this and often buried loved ones with a supply of food, water, and sometimes even furnishings, jewelry, and other accoutrements that might be necessary or useful for survival in the next world.

Awaiting Rebirth

If you're about to enter a new existence, it makes sense that you should be in the proper position. This seems to have been the belief of the Paleolithic peoples who once roamed the plains of what is now Europe. Archaeologists have uncovered numerous skeletons curled into fetal positions, apparently in readiness for "birth" into their next lives. Uncovered burial sites also contained food and stone implements such as hammers and knives.

We don't have any way of knowing conclusively what these early humans actually believed about life or death. There are no written records or even drawings to document these prehistoric times. But the archaeological findings strongly suggest that Paleolithic humans viewed death as a transition, not an end. They greatly anticipated and eagerly welcomed the birth of each new child; it seems reasonable to conclude that they would also celebrate and honor the passing into the next life.

Just as they communicated among each other in the physical world, perhaps they communicated with those in the spirit world. We do know, from archaeological evidence, such as drawings and etchings on rocks and in caves, that later humans did have such beliefs. And we know that the few cultures living in a relatively Stone Age manner today, also appear to have such beliefs.

With the inner eye of your imagination, it's easy to see a small group gathered around a fresh mound of earth that marks the place where a group member has been returned to the womb of Mother Earth, singing and dancing in celebration of this transition, just as the group might gather in joy and happiness to welcome an infant's birth.

Crossing the River

By the time ancient Greek and Roman civilization dominated much of the Western world, the "other side" had become a tangible place. This perception grew from the *mythology* of the time and became a crucial element of the era's *philosophy*. Mythology gave the ancient Greeks and Romans their gods, which then framed their beliefs and social customs.

In this ancient mythology, Hades was the god who ruled the souls of those who passed from physical life. Because the living resided on the ground and the gods inhabited the heavens, the kingdom of Hades was underground, or the Underworld. Its location within the earth established it as a place the living could not go, and provided for a physical separation between the world of the living and the world of the dead.

There was no judgment of good or evil involved, and Hades was not the counterpart to the "devil" of later belief systems. Hades was not a place, even though the word became a handy substitute in seventeenth-century England for what had become a vulgar term, "Hell," which was a most unpleasant location indeed!

Spiritology

Mythology is a collection of a culture's popular beliefs used to explain the unknown, such as the origin of life, to define acceptable behavior, and to teach moral lessons. **Philosophy** is a formal system or structure for studying and applying a society's beliefs and standards.

Because the Underworld was a place from which no one returned, mythology evolved a barrier to separate the world of the living from the final home of the eternal soul, the river Styx. Upon the body's death, the soul had to make what could be a treacherous crossing to get to the other side, where happiness and loved ones who had already passed awaited. The boatman who ferried souls across the river Styx was a monstrous creature named Charon who demanded advance payment from his passengers in exchange for the labor of his services.

Of course, these souls were no longer of the physical world and could not make payment themselves, so it was up to their living relatives or friends to buy safe passage for them. They did this by placing a coin in the mouth of the departed. Charon extracted the coin and allowed the soul to board his boat, which he then steered through the roiling waters of the Styx to the other side.

Making it to the other side wasn't quite the end of the journey for the soul, however. Once across the river, there was a gate that blocked passage to the world of eternity. Cerberus, the three-headed dog with a voracious appetite, guarded the gate and could only be distracted from his duties by being fed. So the living relatives of the departed put a cake of honey with the body as payment to Cerberus for entry into the Underworld. Only then could the soul pass through the gate to be reunited for all eternity with the loved ones who had already made their passages.

Only Charon could navigate the perilous river and because there was no way to pay the fare for the return passage, he never brought anyone back. Although the physical person couldn't return to the world of the living, the spirit, however, could. Ghosts, visible images of the departed, often appeared to the living, and engaged freely in communication with those in the physical world. After taking up residence in the Underworld, the soul could appear as a vision and speak with the living. Soldiers often called on the souls of great warriors who had passed on, to be by their sides in battle and help them to great victory. If that was not to be, they guided them to the shores of the river Styx for their own journeys to the palace of Hades and to eternal life.

Ancient Roman beliefs and practices were similar to those of the Greeks. Some of the names were different—the river the Romans crossed was the Acheron, for example.

Premonition

Determining death in ancient times was less than precise. It was so common for a person to "come back to life," in fact, that Greek law required a waiting period of three days between the declaration of death and the burial of the body. The many "awakenings" that took place during the three-day waiting period no doubt reinforced the belief in the continuation of life.

Embalming and the Circle of Necessity

The ancient Egyptians were the first to systematically preserve the physical body after death to prevent its decay and deterioration by using the process of embalming. The term originally meant "to apply balm," a reference to the early practice of covering a dead body in fragrant oils and spices. The ancient Egyptians believed that once the soul left the body it embarked on a long spiritual journey, called the "circle of necessity," after which it would seek to return to the body it had left behind in the physical world. This made it necessary to preserve the body for the duration of the soul's expedition, typically identified as 3,000 years, so the soul would be able to return to its body and live again.

Because a properly prepared and preserved body was so essential for the soul to complete its journey through the circle of necessity, only priests could perform embalming. In fact, this preparation for the soul's journey was so important that it took place behind the walls of the Necropolis … "death city."

The typical embalming procedure involved removing and carefully storing the body's organs, including the brain, in special urns called canopic jars. Resin was then poured into the jars to prevent the organs from deteriorating. After soaking in a salt solution called natron for as long as 70 days, the body was dried and wrapped in long, resin-soaked strips of cloth—creating what we call a mummy.

What we think of as traditional mummification was actually a service available only to ancient Egyptians who could afford it. The poor received a much less sophisticated embalming process, which involved soaking the body in the salt solution and then placing it in a common burial chamber.

The mummified body was then placed in a coffin or crypt of some sort, with the urns containing its organs surrounding it. The crypt was then carefully sealed; after all, it had to preserve its contents for 3,000 years so the soul could return to claim its body when the journey was complete. Without a body to return to, the soul was destined to travel endlessly, unable to come full circle into its new life.

While the soul was on its 3,000-year journey, it was not possible to communicate with it. It was common, however, to offer prayers for its safe travels and happy return. And of course, only through legend was there any "evidence" of a spirit returning to claim its well-preserved body. No one lived long enough to provide eyewitness proof!

The concept of the circle of necessity was common in other ancient cultures as well, such as the Celts and some tribes in Peru. And today it is an element of belief systems, such as some forms of Hinduism, although preservation of the body is no longer essential. The soul's journey is one of spiritual growth and enlightenment that leads to a higher spiritual existence rather than a return to a physical life.

Spirits Among the Living

You might feel, see, and hear the presence of loved ones who have passed. This might happen during times of crisis, or it might be a normal part of your everyday life. If you're accustomed to these visitors you probably find them comforting, as did the ancient Japanese. They believed that when the spirit left the body at death, it entered into existence as a *kami*, a spirit entity or supernatural being. Death was not a process of leaving but rather a transition into another form.

Spiritology

A **kami** is the spirit of a departed family member that remains among the family and community. It comes from the Japanese word for "divine." As an element of the Shintō religion, kamis can also be the spirits of deities and of things from nature.

A kami remained a part of the family and the community, participating in important decisions and offering guidance. People who in life were good and helpful become benefactors and protectors as kamis; people who in life were not so good become troublesome kamis. Just as in physical life, the good and the bad were simply part of the mix. Kamis who had been leaders and heroes in physical life were more powerful spirit entities than those who had been ordinary citizens. A few, like kings and rulers, became god-like as kamis.

The belief in kamis became the foundation for Shintō, Japan's indigenous, or native, religion. Within Shintō, kamis could be deities (gods and goddesses), ancestral spirits (family members), animals, and even other natural things such as trees. Despite their presence in everyday life, kamis remained unseen and unheard except to those with special powers to communicate with them. Today we would call such people mediums—those who could intervene to halt a disruptive kami's actions or to encourage help from a benevolent kami. Many of these interventions, according to legend, had to do with healing, either to rid a family or village of illness or to bring health to an individual.

Otherwise, communication with kamis came in the guise of actions and events. Fortune, good or bad, was considered the work of kamis. Every family's home had a shrine to honor its kamis, and throughout the countryside there were (and in many places still are) shrines to honor important kamis, typically deities and heroes. Through these shrines, people could share messages with kamis. Buddhism eventually incorporated some elements of Shintō, among them the concept of kamis, which spread the belief into other cultures and societies, including China and India.

Contemporary Belief in the Continuity of Spirit

Nearly every contemporary faith incorporates some degree of belief in the continuity of spirit. We'll just touch on some of the key concepts here; Appendix B contains references for those who want to know more about specific religious beliefs.

Celebrations of spirit exist in many cultures. Most had their roots in belief systems of some sort, and now have migrated into popular culture. There must be something about the end of autumn as it transitions into winter that makes it an apparent window between the physical world and the spirit world. Celebrations and festivals had their origins in pagan religious practices that have made their way into various faith systems. (Pagan beliefs allow worship of multiple deities, gods, goddesses, and natural events such as the changing of the seasons. They are typically contrasted to belief systems based on worship of a single, omnipotent God, such as in Christianity and Judaism.) The Festival of Samhain, for example, has become the Christian celebrations All Hallow's Eve (falling on October 31) and All Saint's Day (falling on November 1).

Awaken, Spirits!

October 31 was the last day of the ancient Celtic year and the Festival of Samhain, the Celtic god of the dead. As one year became another, the Celts believed, the spirits of the dead could return from the beyond to share joy and happiness with their living loved ones. Feasting, dancing, and singing celebrated this opportunity. Enormous bonfires lit the night sky, welcoming revelers and spirits alike.

But fearing that some of the returning spirits might have less than honorable intentions, people often donned masks and costumes to hide their true identities. The good spirits of departed friends and relatives of course knew those behind the masks and could make contact for a joyous reunion. The light of dawn, marking the start of the Celtic New Year, recalled the spirits to the spirit world.

Today we know this festival as Halloween, and its modern celebration has little to do with its Celtic origins. For most people, it is nothing more than an excuse to dress up in costumes (and perhaps behave in ways that cause them to be grateful their identities are hidden)—and for children, to acquire enough candy to keep dentists very busy for yet another year!

> ### Mediums and Messages
>
> Do you feel a little extra energy in the air on All Hallow's Eve? Do you have a sense that there is a presence around you that you don't ordinarily feel? Perhaps it is the spirits of your loved ones, taking the opportunity of heightened awareness to attempt a connection with you. Many people experience such contacts around this time of the year as well as throughout the year.

A Communion of Spirits

In 835, Pope Gregory IV proclaimed that the last day in October was to be known within the Catholic Church as All Hallow's Eve, or "All Holy Evening." On this date, he decreed, Catholics everywhere were to gather and remember those who had given their lives in the name of their faith. The next day, November 1, became All Saint's Day (also called All Soul's Day), a time to remember all who had passed on.

The Catholic Church views this "communion of spirits" as a reminder that there is a continuous link between the souls of the living and the souls of the dead. Says the Catechism of the Catholic Church, the Church's official teachings, "Between them there is an abundant exchange of all good things." Various Protestant religions also observe these celebrations.

Day of the Dead

This doesn't sound like a very joyous celebration, but in fact the Day of the Dead is quite festive. The tradition started long ago with the Aztecs, who once inhabited the land we now know as Mexico, to honor the Aztec goddess Mictecacihuatl, who ruled the dead. Even in Aztec times this was a happy celebration, praising Mictecacihuatl for watching over the souls of those who had passed into her realm. There were several days of dancing, singing, and feasting, during which the spirits of the departed also joined in the festivities.

Through the centuries, the influences of other cultures and belief systems realigned the Day of the Dead to take place during Christian celebrations of All Saint's Day during the last days of October and first days of November. Today, the official celebration of the Mexican Day of the Dead takes place on November 2. Families and friends gather at the gravesites of loved ones, or establish shrines in their homes, to tell stories and remember those who have passed.

It is said that you can feel the spirits reveling right alongside their living relatives! There is also much feasting and drinking, with small offerings of the departed's favorite foods and drinks (and even tobacco if the person was a smoker) at the graveside or on the shrine's altar.

Finding Your Own Divine Purpose

We all have our reasons for wanting to establish and maintain a personal "communion of spirits." Yours might be linked to your faith system or religious practices, or the result of an independent belief in the continuity of the spirit. Traditions through the history of humankind and formalized celebrations within organized religions today affirm that such desires are nearly universal. And these desires are positive. They are rooted in love and in goodness—truly what we would consider divine purpose, connections for a greater good. This is the essence of communicating with spirits.

The Least You Need to Know

- ◆ Cultures throughout all of human history have had some sort of belief in the soul's existence beyond physical death.

- ◆ The belief that the spirits of those who have passed on return to visit or even "hang around" in the physical world is common throughout the world.

- ◆ Many faiths and religions incorporate belief in the eternal spirit into their practices.

- ◆ Divine purpose is both universal and personal, and defines spirit communication as connection for a greater good.

Chapter 3

Spiritualism: Continuity of the Spirit

In This Chapter

- ◆ Humble beginnings in Hydesville, New York
- ◆ The clairvoyant writings of Andrew Jackson Davis
- ◆ Beyond Sherlock Holmes: Sir Arthur Conan Doyle's interest in Spiritualism
- ◆ Doubters and frauds
- ◆ The role of the medium in Spiritualism
- ◆ Spiritualism's link to the divine

Many of the world's faith systems incorporate some concept of a soul's continuing existence after the death of the physical body. But just one, Spiritualism, is actually founded on these concepts. Spiritualism accepts that spirit communication is a natural and common occurrence in the physical world that has been taking place throughout the history of human existence, and that much healing and good can come from it.

Like all belief systems, Spiritualism comes with its own traditions—the stories and experiences that make up its history and heritage. Some are entertaining, while some are inspiring. Collectively, they reflect the evolution of Spiritualist thinking from random communication with spirits to the purposeful connections modern Spiritualist mediums make. Spiritualism today has much to offer to those seeking to understand our human spiritual resources, and the many ways in which spirits, in and out of the human body, interact and evolve.

But before we get into that, let's time-travel through the evolution of Spiritualism. Sit back and put up your feet ... it's time to meet the characters and circumstances that have taken Spiritualism through its rise, near-fall, and revival in the world today.

Two Sisters and a Ghost

Modern *Spiritualism* came into popular practice in 1848 when two sisters—Catherine and Margaretta Fox—moved with their parents into a small house in Hydesville, New York. Their story is well documented through an affidavit Mrs. Fox wrote about the family's experiences, as well as through numerous anecdotes from those who heard about the strange communication that the Fox sisters established with a ghost who already resided—unwillingly and unhappily—in the house.

On December 11, 1847, the Fox family moved into its Hydesville home, which was to be a temporary residence while the family's new house was being built. Almost immediately, they heard noises in the night. Not being familiar with the history of the house, they tried to ignore the strange sounds that kept them awake. But on March 4, 1848, the bangs and rappings became particularly loud. Catherine and Margaretta were very frightened and ran to their parents' bedroom. The parents, too, were awake and listening, and walked through the rest of the house to try to find the cause of all the racket.

Spiritology

Spiritualism is a faith system based on belief in the continuity of life beyond physical death.

There were knocks on the pantry door and footsteps in the hallway. Windows and doors were closed tight; nothing appeared out of the ordinary. Yet the rapping, banging, and thumping continued even as the Foxes searched the house. "I then concluded that the house must be haunted by some unhappy restless spirit," Mrs. Fox later wrote in her affidavit about the family's experiences.

The frightened sisters decided they were going to sleep in their parents' room until the noises ceased. After a week or so, they began to feel more comfortable. One night, Catherine, feeling brave in the safety of her parents' bed, said, "Mr. Splitfoot, do as I do!" and she clapped her hands. To her amazement, she heard clapping in response. Then Margaretta clapped one, two, three, four … and heard back one, two, three four raps!

The girls called for their mother. Mrs. Fox took over the questioning, determined to get to the bottom of the situation. She tested the visitor's knowledge by asking it to rap the number of children she had. Seven raps. She asked again; she had just six children. Seven raps again. Puzzled at first, Mrs. Fox then asked how many of those children were living. Six raps. No one outside the family knew that the youngest Fox child, little Emily, had passed as an infant some years earlier.

With a simple code—two raps for "yes"—and more counting, Mrs. Fox extracted the information that this was indeed a ghost, a man who had been murdered in the house by a man who had once lived there. Not knowing the history of the house's residents, Mrs. Fox asked her neighbors, the Redfields, who had lived in the area all of their lives, to come over. As it turned out, the Redfields had once lived in the house and knew of the other families who had also called it home. Again, there was an exchange of names and raps. Mr. Redfield went through the list of names of the house's former residents until one name—Bell—returned two raps, the signal for "yes." Frustratingly, however, the neighbor wasn't able to identify the ghost. Finally, Mrs. Fox hit upon the solution. She worked out a code to identify the letters of the alphabet, and instructed the spirit to rap once for each letter of his name. The questioning eventually elicited the name of one Charles Rosna, who, other neighbors later recalled, had been a traveling peddler who had disappeared six years earlier.

Further questioning brought forth the claim that Rosna's body was buried in the cellar. Neighbors who rushed to dig for the body were unable to locate anything, because a high water table just a few feet beneath the basement's earthen floor flooded into the basement as soon as they dug into it, leaving Rosna's fate unproven. Or was it? In the summer of 1848, when the weather became dry, the Foxes and some of their curious neighbors went back into the basement. This time they were able to dig deeper, unearthing bone fragments and a peddler's bag.

It was evidence enough to launch the Fox sisters into careers as mediums. They soon discovered that it wasn't only their resident spirit with whom they could communicate. It seemed they could summon spirits of all sorts, spirits eager to make contact with loved ones in the physical world.

The sisters quickly became well known even beyond their local community. Hundreds of people flocked to their home for spirit communication. In 1849, Margaretta Fox gave a demonstration of her mediumship abilities in New York City, which sealed her fame. Much of the time, the famous were among those who came to her during her career as a medium, including author James Fennimore Cooper (who penned *The Last of the Mohicans*, among other stories) and William Cullen Bryant, poet, attorney, and editor of New York's *Evening Post*. The media dubbed the sisters and those who believed in their abilities "Spiritualists"—and a movement was born.

Mediums and Messages

The November 23, 1904, edition of the Boston *Journal* carried an article that claimed a skeleton had finally been discovered in the basement of the old Fox house. Children playing in the basement discovered a false wall, behind which the bones apparently belonging to Charles Rosna rested. The wall had been constructed directly beneath the kitchen and pantry, the location where the Foxes had heard all the knocking, rapping, and footsteps.

The Poughkeepsie Seer

The events that catapulted the Fox sisters to fame as mediums and established Spiritualism as a movement did not just happen out of the blue, of course. Others had been exploring the relationship between body and spirit, some from within the context of religion and others from the framework of science. Just before the Foxes moved to Hydesville, another New Yorker, Andrew Jackson Davis (1826–1910) published what was to become a breakthrough work for him and for Spiritualism: *The Principles of Nature, Her Divine Revelations, and a Voice to Mankind.*

As a young child, Davis showed strong psychic abilities. When the family moved to Poughkeepsie, Davis encountered a tailor who detected these abilities and discovered that Davis could use them for medical diagnosis. At the age of 18, Davis had a *metaphysical* experience that changed the course of his life. In what was either a *trance* state or a *visitation*, Davis met the spirit of famed theologian and scientist Emanuel Swedenborg (1688–1722) who had died more than 100 years before Davis was born.

It was this visit that produced the book *The Principles of Nature, Her Divine Revelations, and a Voice to Mankind*, which Davis dictated over the course of more than a year. In the book, he predicted the discovery of the eighth and ninth planets (Neptune and Pluto, respectively), at the direction of Swedenborg. Under Swedenborg's direction, Davis also wrote *Univericoelum (The Spiritual Philosopher)*. Himself an uneducated man, Davis wrote these and other manuscripts in a ponderous, scholarly, and complex style similar to that of Swedenborg.

When published in 1847, *The Principles of Nature* met with intense interest among those already interested in the concept of the continuing life of the spirit. It wasn't until after the events of Hydesville, however, that Davis's book gained popular attention. Although somewhat cumbersome to comprehend, *The Principles of Nature* outlined in great detail the interrelationships among human physical existence, the mind, and the spirit (personal as well as divine). The language was complex and technical, making it difficult for the average person to read but affirming its connection to Swedenborg, who wrote in the same style.

Spiritology

Metaphysical means "around the physical" and is a term generally used to describe experiences and events that have no apparent physical explanations. A **trance** is a state of altered consciousness in which the medium allows a spirit to speak through him or her. A **visitation** is when a spirit speaks *to* you rather than *through* you.

Spiritualism's Most Famous Advocate: No Mystery Here

In its relatively short existence, Spiritualism has drawn interest and support from a number of famous people. Few were better known than Sir Arthur Conan Doyle (1859–1930). You might know of him as creator of the great fictional detective Sherlock Holmes. But did you know this renowned writer was also a physician … and a prominent investigator of psychic phenomena, as well as one of Spiritualism's most zealous supporters? Although better known as a writer of mystery novels and stories, Doyle was trained and practiced as a physician. In fact, he was knighted in 1902 for his work with military field hospitals in South Africa during the Boer War.

As it turns out, 1902 was a fortuitous year for the good doctor. That was also when he met Sir Oliver Lodge, a renowned physicist of the time who was intrigued by the relationship between the physical world and the realm of human consciousness. He was particularly fascinated with the concept of thought transference—the process of being able to communicate one's thoughts without physical means such as speaking or writing. Doyle was also interested in this area, and had engaged in some informal research of his own. He respected Lodge and his studies, and found the other scientist's methods compelling.

After establishing a literary career writing detective and romance novels, Doyle's interest in thought transference led him to the logical next level, communication between spirits in this world and in the spirit world. He turned his full attention to that and joined the Society for Psychical Research, a prominent and well-respected organization of the time. He also attended mediumistic readings at his friends' homes, which so intrigued him that he began his own studies with a medium.

In midlife, Doyle published a number of books that were a considerable departure from the fiction that had made him famous: *The New Revelation, The Vital Message, Wanderings of a Spiritualist,* and the two-volume *The History of Spiritualism.* These books discussed his research, his conclusions, and his beliefs, all of which strongly advocated Spiritualism.

In his own spirit communication through mediums, Doyle was able to make contact with his son, who was wounded and died during World War I, his mother, and other relatives. These experiences were both comforting and validating for him, and gave a depth to his insights that could only come from such deeply personal contacts. Unfortunately, they also gave rise to criticism from skeptics who felt that Doyle's grief dulled his scientific senses. But they only strengthened Doyle's commitment to Spiritualism.

Doyle concluded his literary career in 1930 not with a final Sherlock Holmes adventure but with what he considered a work of enlightenment, *The Edge of the Unknown.* This book, his last, presented Doyle's observations and insights about 15 famous mysterious events, such as magician Harry Houdini's apparent dematerializations and writings from the other side by a number of authors, including Charles Dickens and Jack London.

> ### Silver Cord
>
> Despite their opposing beliefs about Spiritualism, Sir Arthur Conan Doyle and magician Harry Houdini (whose real name was Erich Wiess) were good friends. In his book *The Edge of the Unknown,* Doyle writes of his belief that Houdini had significant psychic abilities, which Houdini denied. Houdini believed mediums were, as he was, simply masters of deception. However, when Houdini's mother died, he went to a medium who was able to bring her through and convey what she and Houdini had established as the secret message they would use as evidence that life continued beyond death of the physical body.

Doubters, Challengers, and, Sadly, Frauds

Of course, there have always been—and always will be—those who doubt the authenticity of spirit contact and spirit communication. On the one hand, it's perfectly natural to expect proof or evidence that a spirit communication is authentic (we discuss this in more detail later in this chapter). But there are those who are never satisfied with the evidence as proof.

In the late decades of the nineteenth century, the Spiritualist Church became a formal entity with congregations throughout the Western world. This organization gave a level of credibility to Spiritualism, and established it as a process inextricably linked to the divine (more on this later in this chapter). Spirit contacts were not late-night parlor games, but rather integral elements of a religious institution. This gave increased credibility to Spiritualism, and many of the movement's early detractors became its most ardent supporters (including Sir Arthur Conan Doyle, who started his explorations of psychic phenomena from the scientific platform of evidentiary proof).

Spiritualism as an institution has endured its share of scandal through the years, typically the result of fraudulent actions on the part of people acting as mediums. Tragically, those seeking insight and understanding, particularly when driven by grief and desperation, are vulnerable to manipulation. By the 1930s, England had passed the Fraudulent Medium Act and other legislation intended to protect the public from cheats and hoaxsters, which of course didn't prevent them from scamming the unsuspecting. Over the next few decades, Spiritualism lost popular favor and entered into a period of decline. Although this did nothing to diminish the authenticity of spirit communication, it did leave people somewhat floundering for other ways to address their spiritual needs.

Since the 1970s, however, interest in spirit communication and Spiritualism has been on the rise. This is partly the result of a more open environment with regard to personal freedom and expression and partly the re-emergence of interest in self-healing. The surge of interest in "New Age" concepts that swept through the United States and other parts of the Western world in the 1980s broadened the appeal and acceptance of spirit contact and communication. Although the exact numbers are hard to come by, it's safe to say that more people practice Spiritualism today than ever in its history.

Mediumship and Spiritualism

Mediumship is an integral part of Spiritualism. Through mediums, spirits communicate with those in the physical world. Mediums who are certified in the Spiritualist Church (as is co-author Rita) undergo extensive training and must pass a series of qualifying examinations (including doing a complete church service with spirit communication to the satisfaction of a board of ordained spiritualist ministers and certified mediums).

> **Premonition** _____
>
> Before your first visit with a medium, or at least before the reading begins, ask about the medium's qualifications and training. Expect to hear where the medium received training and certification, how long the medium has been practicing, what kind of mediumship he or she practices, and what other background he or she has. Even though it is the mediumistic abilities that make spirit communication possible, it is his or her life experiences that filter the information coming through.

All mediums have psychic abilities, but not all psychics have mediumistic abilities. (There's more on this in Chapter 14.) It takes time, focus, and training to develop skill as a medium. It is a Spiritualist medium's responsibility to prove the continuity of life beyond a shadow of a doubt. This means that when the Spiritualist medium finally begins talking to you with messages from spirits that are present, he or she has a clear sense of what the spirit looks or sounds like, why the spirit is present, and even who the spirit is. This doesn't mean the medium knows all of this for certain, only that he or she has a good idea about it.

Spiritualism holds that every human being has at least limited mediumistic capacity. Each of us has the ability to communicate with spirits on the other side, if we pay attention to the signals we receive. As is the case with any other ability, some people are more skilled than others.

Mental Phenomena

Do you ever think something, then have a friend call and say it? Must be *telepathy!* Such events happen often, yet we usually don't give them a second thought. But do you ever struggle with a dilemma, then "hear" a voice (sounding, to the ear of your mind, suspiciously like your grandmother who passed away five years ago) telling you what to do? If you're tuned into your psychic senses, you might notice and acknowledge this message. If you're oblivious to your psychic senses, you might act on the message without understanding its origin or dismiss it from your mind because it isn't logical.

> **Spiritology** _____
>
> **Telepathy** is a process of thought transference in which one person receives information from another without using any physical means.

Such experiences are often mental mediumistic phenomena; that is, a spirit has activated your mediumistic abilities in an attempt to convey a message to you. Of course that was your grandmother's voice speaking to you from beyond the physical world! You know, as she does, that only she would call you by the childhood nickname she gave you when you spent the summer with her way back when.

When a trained medium receives mental phenomena, they can be quite spectacular. There is countless documentation of mediums delivering messages of detailed instruction for carrying out tasks that the medium knows nothing about. Even writing a book, preparing a seven-course meal, or creating an invention!

Physical Phenomena

Physical mediumship is more advanced and more complex. Not everyone has the mediumistic abilities necessary to receive physical phenomena. Such phenomena might include levitation, materialization, transfiguration—all of which involve the spirit using the medium's energy to convey its message. Rapping and table-tipping are also physical phenomena (see Chapter 11).

Carolyn came for a sitting and drawing, and a great uncle who was a minister came through. Carolyn said she knew she had a great uncle in the family who wore a clerical collar, but she didn't know what he looked like. Three months later, her husband was looking through a box of old photos and called out, "I think I found a photo of the man Rita drew for you." Indeed, it was a match.

Sometimes physical phenomena are quite specialized, putting to use the medium's special talents. Rita receives physical phenomena in the form of spirit drawing or spirit painting; you'll see her artwork throughout this book. Other mediums might receive spirit communication through spirit photography or automatic writing (which we'll talk more about in Chapter 10).

Spiritualism and the Divine

Key to Spiritualism is the conviction that human existence consists of the body, mind, and spirit. The body, made of matter, is the outer, physical shell that contains both the mind and the spirit. The mind, also made of matter but of a different sort, houses the spirit, made of energy. This energy is what links spirits across the border of the physical world and makes spirit communication possible.

Also key to Spiritualism is the conviction that this energy is Light, in that it represents the presence and the power of the divine. As a result, it is good and it is for help and healing. Spirit communication, likewise, is for good and for healing. Spiritualist mediums always begin their readings with a prayer to welcome the Light (the divine) and request its guidance in keeping the reading focused on its intent—which is always to heal in some way.

Although its details change with each reading to be specific to the circumstances, purpose, and person, this is the general prayer Rita uses: "Infinite Spirit God, I ask that you be with me during this reading. I ask that you surround us with white light. I ask that this be healing, helpful, evidential and to prove the continuity of life. I ask that this reading be blessed and that it help this person on his or her path. I give thanks for what we are about to receive. Amen."

The Power of Intent

To have a mediumistic reading without purpose is like driving without a destination. You certainly *could* end up someplace interesting and enjoyable, especially if you travel by car a lot and instinctively make the right choices about which direction to go. When the journey is spiritual rather than physical, most people have specific reasons for seeking spirit contact. Many desire contact with specific loved ones in the spirit world. This is one part of intent. It doesn't always turn out that you get who you want; calling on the divine places the communication in a higher power. In seeking, the divine will give you what you need but not always what you request. People sometimes make promises before they pass, but they can't always keep them because the choice might not be theirs.

Help and Healing

We've emphasized that the primary purpose of spirit communication is help and healing. What this means for you is unique and personal. Perhaps healing is closure following a loved one's sudden and unexpected passing, to help you move on in your life.
You could desire understanding of someone's behaviors that have affected you in some
way. Or you might just want proof that the spirit does continue after physical death,
to give meaning and direction to your life.

Prove It!

It is human nature to want "proof," especially of things that are deeply important to
us on a personal level. For the Spiritualist medium, establishing "proof" of the continuity of life is essential with any spirit contact. This is usually not the kind of tangible
proof in terms of something you can see or touch. Rather, it is evidence in the form
of knowledge that only you and the spirit could share. Perhaps this is the spirit referring to you by a childhood nickname only one person would know. Or reminding you
of a long-forgotten event, or giving the answer to a question you didn't know you
were asking. Understanding and insight become clearer, which is how spirits are able
to help those of us on this side.

The Appeal of Spiritualism

Spiritualism encourages self-exploration and learning. It fits within just about any
religious framework, and perhaps as importantly as any other function, it dispels fear.
It is, in fact, nothing more than the function of being spiritual—which we all are,
regardless of our belief systems, simply because we are human beings with physical
and spiritual selves.

Many of those attracted to the Spiritualist movement as it rose to prominence in the
fifty years or so following the Fox sisters were people who challenged and probed the
"meaning of life" from various contexts—they were physicians, scientists, writers and
poets, artists. But they were also just ordinary people seeking answers to questions
everyone has. Spirit communication puts the quest for information into *your* hands.
You determine what to ask, and what to do with the answers you receive. It's quite
empowering, as upcoming chapters will show you!

The Least You Need to Know

♦ Spiritualism was boosted into popularity after the Fox sisters established communication with a ghost inhabiting the house they moved into in Hydesville, New York.

♦ The Poughkeepsie Seer, Andrew Jackson Davis, published his breakthrough books on Spiritualism with the help of the spirit of Emanuel Swedenborg, who died more than 100 years before Davis was born.

♦ There have been many famous supporters of Spiritualism through the years, including the creator of Sherlock Holmes, Sir Arthur Conan Doyle.

♦ Proof of the continuity of life is at the core of Spiritualist beliefs and practices.

♦ Spiritualism as a religion is appealing because people are encouraged to seek answers to the questions they have.

♦ Spiritualism holds that connections to the spirit world take place through the divine.

Chapter 4

Why Make Contact?

In This Chapter

- ◆ Figuring out what you want to know
- ◆ Authenticating the continuity of life
- ◆ Understanding your reasons for wanting to make contact: a self-exploration
- ◆ Interpreting spirit messages

What interests you about communicating with spirits? What do you want to learn? Whom do you want to contact? The reasons people pick up a book like this one are as different as the people themselves. But you all have one thing in common: You are seeking answers.

Although mostly it's those of us in the physical world who wish to contact the spirits of loved ones who have passed on, sometimes it's a spirit on the other side that initiates communication. What could a spirit possibly need from us on this side of life? You might be surprised!

Inquiring Minds Just Want to Know!

Let's face it: You're curious. You want to know that there *is* something beyond this physical life. And you wouldn't mind knowing a bit about what that something might be like. This desire to prove the continuity of life is normal and it is among the most basic of human curiosities. In fact, it is one of the most significant factors that make us human beings. We think, therefore we anticipate and we question.

Phenomena come in many forms—voices, visions, sensations. Being able to validate or authenticate these messages is what establishes them as intentional. This happens when all of the bits and pieces of information that you gather build images that are familiar to you. Sometimes the images aren't what you expect, or even recognizable until you do a little digging.

The very first spirit message that Rita received in a reading was from a great-aunt she didn't know she had. After the reading Rita called her mother, who was able not only to verify the spirit's message but also to tell Rita about this great-aunt who had passed to the other side quite a few years before. The experience was compelling enough to demonstrate the continuity of life and it also convinced Rita to investigate communication with spirits.

Spirit contact is not random. This is not a party game (more on the hazards of treating it as such in Chapter 11). The spirits who come through have some connection to you. You might not be aware of the connection at first; they could be spirits who passed over long ago, people you don't remember or didn't even know about. You might need to go away from a reading and do some research, as Rita did after "meeting" a great-aunt she didn't know existed until her mother was able to confirm the information.

Premonition

Don't let your curiosity suppress your normal good judgment. Unfortunately, wherever there is need there is someone waiting to take advantage of it. Spirit contact is certainly no exception. Let the details speak for themselves. Take what you experience with a great grain of salt; information that comes through a medium can be colored by the medium's perceptions, which aren't always accurate. Also, someone who wasn't especially insightful in physical life doesn't become all-knowing in the spirit world. If the experience doesn't feel right to you, don't feel compelled to continue or to stay.

But somehow the spirits who come through are important to you. They are willing to establish contact and they have something to say to you. Make a mental appointment to meet with the spirit, ask your guides and loved ones to be with you before meeting with the medium, and be open to what comes through.

A Time for Healing

Every spirit communication should be a healing experience, and should always be looked at in that way. You might not know, when you first embark on a spirit contact experience, what healing you need. You might need closure, or help getting through a difficult time. Much of the hurt people carry around is buried so deep within that they are no longer consciously aware of it. Communication with a spirit who knows exactly what the wound is and what caused it can bring that hurt to the surface, at which point the healing process can begin.

If it seems that we keep stressing the point about healing, you're right. Spirit contact always comes in healing and light, which is so important that we can't stress it enough. Even when the messages you receive aren't what you expected or what you want to get, they should be positive and helpful. If you have any sense that the situation is dark or negative, end it immediately. This is not spirit contact. It might be manipulation (from this side, not the other side!), it might be your fears, or it might be a matter for which you should seek psychological counseling. But it is not the spirit if it's not happening with goodness and light.

Mission: Unknown

Your life—your existence in this physical world—has purpose. You, particularly and uniquely you, are here for a reason. Your soul has a mission to complete during its time here. One of the most exciting and at the same time most frustrating, aspects of this is the mystery of it all. You don't know what your soul's mission is; you don't know the grander scheme of why you are living your life. You just have to make the choices that you hope and believe take you in the right direction. Each soul's lessons are unique. The path of your life, the journey of your soul, matters to, as well as beyond your individual existence.

The freedom and the opportunity this mystery offers means that you are not compelled to follow any particular path. Your life is not predetermined; your destiny is not a stationary target but is instead a dynamic and ever-changing journey. *You* make the choices and decisions that become your life's—and your soul's—path. With this freedom comes accountability, of course. You, and you alone, are responsible for the choices you make and the outcomes that are the consequences of your decisions.

This is the "growth" element of your spirit's journey through physical life. As we all know, growth is not easy. It often involves starts and stops, and sometimes even backsliding to repeat the lessons we didn't quite get the first time around. It might seem that your decisions always end up leading you in directions you don't want to follow, but find yourself headed. Rather than making choices, you are following patterns. And rather than spiraling upward, so to speak, to higher levels of understanding and insight, you end up running in circles!

Silver Cord

Many people believe that their fates are absolutely predetermined. An in-depth study of religions, however, will show that free choice is always given to us. We make our own decisions about how we live. Spiritualism preaches personal responsibility, that each of us is responsible for our own decisions in life and that we create our happiness and our inner peace by living according to natural law.

Many of us want to know more about why we are here, what lessons we need to learn during our physical lives, and how we can leave the earth plane a better place, however slightly, than it was when we arrived. With knowledge comes increased ability to make appropriate, and directed, choices and decisions.

And wouldn't it be nice if you could get a little help and guidance, to bump you off the familiar but doomed track and onto the path to the life you want to live, the life you feel could or should be yours, the life that will make a difference? Well, you can. Although your life is yours and yours alone to shape and direct, there's no "rule" that you have to go it alone. Those who have passed this way before you and moved on are more than willing to reach out a helping hand ... figuratively speaking.

Your Personal Reasons: A Self-Exploration

Why do *you* seek spirit contact? The more clearly you can establish your intent for seeking contact, the more likely it is you'll obtain specific, and useful, information. This is not to say that you'll then get the answers you want. But you will receive the answers you need. The following questions can help you clarify what contact you are seeking and what you hope to find out. This is not a test; there are no right or wrong answers. This is just a process to get you thinking about how communication with spirits can help you.

1. Are you presently grieving the loss of a loved one? If so, whom, and what were the circumstances of his or her passing?

   _____

   _____

   _____

2. What unresolved issues have been left hanging in your life by the passing of a loved one?

   _____

   _____

   _____

3. Are there particular people you want to contact? What are your reasons?

   _____

   _____

   _____

4. What changes would you like to see happen in your life as a result of spirit communication?

   _____

   _____

   _____

5. Do you have a message to convey to a loved one who has passed on? If so, what is it?

   _____

   _____

   _____

6. If you had a particular moment or experience to relive with a loved one who has passed, what would it be?

   _____

   _____

   _____

7. What expectations do you have about working with a medium?

_____

_____

_____

8. Who might come through that would be a surprise for you?

_____

_____

_____

9. What fears or apprehensions do you have about spirit contact?

_____

_____

_____

10. What do you most want to know, or to have happen, through a spirit contact?

_____

_____

_____

If other questions occur to you, jot them down as well. The idea is to help prepare yourself. It is sometimes helpful to compile a brief family history before having a medium do a spirit reading. This gives you a broader sense of who might come through. And remember that spirit contact is not limited to relatives. Friends or friends of the family who have passed to the other side also have connections with you, and are just as likely to come through for you depending on the messages they are bringing.

Identifying Spirit Contact

How do you locate a loved one in a crowd? Do you look for someone who is six-foot-two, has brown hair and hazel eyes, and wears a New York Yankees cap? It's a good place to start. Do you listen for that laugh that quickens your pulse, try to smell the essence of a familiar fragrance, watch for certain movements and gestures? Details help!

We tend to identify people who are important to us by the characteristics that matter to us. This is how we establish a sense of familiarity and recognition. Physical traits alone, although they are helpful in making preliminary assessments, are often too general to make conclusive identification. While you might think of those gorgeous hazel eyes when you think of your loved one, it is your loved one's unique personality traits that make the case.

Recognizing a spirit's identity is a similar process, of connecting to familiar personality traits. After all, you don't get a set of wings and a gold harp when you pass over, and then instantly become something you never were in physical life! The personality that was the essence of your identity as a physical being survives to remain the essence of your identity as a spirit being. Just as in our physical world, it is the minutiae of the person that let you know it is that person.

Mediums and Messages

When Rita was doing spirit contact during a church service, a young man came through for a woman in the congregation. Rita gave his physical description, and then said, "and he's extremely strong in personality." Rita stood up and demonstrated the young man's walk, and shared some of the colorful language he was using. The woman for whom this spirit was coming through laughed; these details let her know exactly who it was!

Physical characteristics, although helpful, are sometimes too vague or general, depending on the depth of the description, to provide conclusive identification. A spirit can come through at any age, even older than at passing. This is particularly true for those who pass from their physical lives as children or young adults whose bodies haven't yet reached their physical prime. Generally, there are some features that make the spirit identifiable, but they might not be what you expect.

The character traits that come through during a spirit contact make it possible for you to establish a spirit's identity. These traits comprise the evidence that proves the continuity of life, because they are the bits and pieces of life. Sometimes the confirmation of identity happens almost immediately; there is something the spirit does or says that lets you know without a doubt that this is your Aunt Margaret or your great-grandfather. Sometimes the clues are subtle, and the spirit's identity remains uncertain until you have time to think about the messages.

It's important to separate spirit communicating from what could be psychic. Sometimes what you don't know turns out to be more evidential than what you do know. This happens when relatives you didn't know you had come through, or you receive information about them that you didn't know. And sometimes it takes some digging to uncover their stories.

When Rita was doing spirit contact during a church service, a man came through who kept showing an amazing array of Italian pastries. Sitting in the congregation was his daughter, who recognized him but was puzzled by the Italian pastries. Her father, she said, had been a baker by profession but he baked only bread. The woman went home and talked with her uncle, her father's brother. Her uncle said that although his brother had established his career baking bread, he had originally trained as a pastry chef. This is how doing your research, exploring the information you receive, gives you the full message.

The Communication Challenge

Communication certainly ranks right at the top of the list when it comes to human challenges. Even among those of us on the earth plane, communication problems have made "I'm sorry" our most common words! Even when we can see each other, make eye contact, and observe body language, we can misunderstand one another. We confuse meanings and intent, say things we don't mean, and misinterpret the words of others. Add differences in language and culture to the mix, and a translator becomes necessary.

Imagine the challenges, then, of communicating across the planes of spirit existence! The most amazing aspect of the Fox sisters' contact with the spirit of Charles Rosna in their Hydesville home was not the contact itself but that they worked out a code through which they were able to exchange information (see Chapter 3).

Just as existence on the spirit plane transcends the physical body, so does communication transcend speech. Spirit beings don't require language as we know it to communicate with each other. So in contact with us, it is sometimes difficult to find ways to communicate their messages … particularly when those messages are about learning that has happened for them on the other side.

Spiritology

A **psychical vocabulary of symbolism** is the "dictionary" of symbols and representations that a medium acquires to make communication with spirits possible.

What Does *That* Mean?

A medium's consciousness interprets the messages that come through, translating them into concepts and words that those of us on the earth plane can understand. A spirit must work within the capabilities of the medium's interpretations. Most mediums acquire a *psychical vocabulary of symbolism* that allows them to have consistent communication with spirit entities. It's another language of sorts, related to the medium's level of development, and becomes the standard that spirits use in working with the medium.

Colors, feelings, numbers, and an array of sensory experiences (representations of sight, hearing, taste, touch) often become part of a medium's psychical vocabulary of symbolism. A medium might typically see the color blue, for example, when a spirit is attempting to communicate about an event that caused sadness. The logic of the connection might not be apparent to the medium; what matters is that the medium knows the connection and uses it to clarify and express the spirit's message.

We'll come back to this in greater detail in Chapters 9 and 10.

CAUTION

Premonition

If you hear voices that are dark or negative, or that are telling you to do things you know are wrong, these are not the voices of spirits. Spirits always come through in goodness. They will not come through to approach you in a negative way. If the voices that are coming through are negative, you need to seek guidance from a medium or a mental health professional.

Janice came to Rita for a spirit drawing. As Rita began to draw the spirit image that presented, she felt an overwhelming desire to draw the knot of her hair on the top of her head, rather than on back of the head or at the nape of the neck as was the style of the time. Rita tried several times to move the knot to a more conventional placement, but kept redrawing it on the top. Janice recognized the woman as her beloved great-grandmother. She came back a week later to show Rita two photos, each showing the knot centered on the top of her great-grandmother's head just as Rita had been guided to draw it.

Like a Good Book ...

In fact, this is why we call spirit communication a "reading." The medium "reads" all of the fragments of information—all of the signs—and organizes them into a presentation that makes sense to the person desiring contact. As with books, there are varying degrees of complexity in such a presentation. Sometimes it's simple and straightforward, with the key points clear and unmistakable. Other times, the medium must work with the spirit and with you to get the translation right. And sometimes you need to take the information and go away with it, to think about it and try to understand its multiple layers and meanings.

When a Spirit Reaches Out to You

Many times spirits initiate contact to be helpful, to make amends, to say, "I love you and I'm still with you," or even, "I'll be waiting for you, to reach out to you when it's your time to cross." Remember, the essence of an individual's personality as it was here on the earth plane extends into the spirit's existence on the higher side. Someone who was compassionate and helpful in the physical world will still want to reach out to help others. And those who were maybe not quite so understanding and interested in others often become so as they move forward on their spiritual journeys.

As one illustration of the soul's evolution and progression after passing, Rita shares an experience from her own life. Rita and her father had a difficult relationship. The medium who first brought him through said, "He's saying he's sorry because someone told him he had to." Rita made a joke about there being a 12-step program on the other side, and the medium said that, in fact, for many spirits it was something quite like that. A year later, a different medium brought him through and that medium said, "He's saying he wants to say he's sorry but he says that you wouldn't recognize him as saying that."

Can I Help You?

Spirits don't suddenly know everything, see everything, and hear everything. Passing to the other side doesn't make a spirit omniscient or all-knowing! Although many spirits do acquire heightened insight, understanding, and knowledge, this results from the growth and evolving that take place as the spirit continues its mission.

The spirit that has learned a lesson sometimes wants to share the learning with others who are struggling with the same issues. Perhaps the situation doesn't need to be as difficult as you are making it, or you are overlooking an important piece of information. Maybe the answer is right there in front of you, but you just can't see it. Just as family and friends on the earth plane might try to help you with such matters, those who have passed to the spirit plane might want to reach back and offer a helping hand. Accept, use, and enjoy this help! It comes to you in goodness and healing.

Making Amends

One of the most common reasons spirits seek contact with their loved ones on the earth plane is to make amends for mistakes they made in their physical lives. This can be as healing for the spirit as for the person on the earth plane. Mary, a woman at the start of her middle years, came to Rita desperately wanting to contact the spirit of her stepfather who had raised her. The stepfather had been a tall, slender man during the prime of his life, but in old age had developed Alzheimer's disease that ultimately resulted in his death.

What came through to Rita, however, was the image of a husky, short man who had died of a heart attack. Rita drew the image that came through, and when Mary saw the drawing she gasped in disbelief: The spirit visitor was Mary's natural father who had abandoned the family when Mary was a child! Mary had spent most of her life hating this man for what he did to her family, and now here he was, reappearing from beyond the physical world. To do what? More damage?

> **Silver Cord**
>
> Sometimes a spirit comes through with a message that is important for the spirit to give to you, often a recognition of how actions on the earth plane might have affected you and your life. The circumstances could even be ones you didn't know about before receiving the message. Healing goes both ways!

As Rita continued the reading, it became clear that Mary's father had come through to say he was sorry for having deserted the family so many years before his death. There were circumstances Mary didn't know about, but the bottom line was that her father made decisions that hurt his family, and he wanted Mary to know he understood how hard her life had been as a result. Although this was not the contact Mary wanted, it provided the answers to many questions she had and ended up being a tremendous healing experience for Mary, as well as for her father's spirit.

When Crisis Strikes

It's common for spirit contacts to come through in times of crisis, either personal or large-scale. People who become critically ill and spend days or weeks in the hospital hovering between life and death often report, when they recover, that loved ones who had passed were with them the whole time. These contacts are comforting, letting you know that no matter what the situation, you are not alone.

Easing the Pain of Grief

No matter how strongly you believe that you and your loved ones will reunite on the other side, there is grief when a loved one passes before you do. The emptiness that you feel can be overwhelming. Sometimes a spirit can reach back from the other side to offer comfort and solace, to say, "I'll always be with you." These contacts can come through a medium, or through direct experiences. A familiar fragrance that floats seemingly from nowhere. The sense of a laugh, distant and not quite audible, over something your loved one would have found hilarious. A dream in which your loved one appears. In reality, these contacts are probably much more commonplace than most of us recognize. Because they are often so subtle, and because grief is such an overwhelming emotion, we just don't pick up on the gentle signals. But they are there, and they can be a source of great comfort.

When It's Your Time to Make the Crossing

If there is only one message you get from this book, let it be this: You are not alone! When it is time for your spirit to cross from the earth plane to the spirit plane, there will be a gathering of spirits waiting to welcome you. This can be a great source of comfort for those who know passing is imminent, such as people who are terminally ill, as well as for family and friends who remain on the earth plane and are grieving.

Even Spirits Have Needs

The spirit plane is a busy and dynamic existence. Spirits are not just floating around. The soul's mission continues, and the spirit often experiences significant understanding and insight as its mission continues to unfold. A loved one who has passed to the higher side might need help from you for this to happen, or might want to let you know that you are providing help even though you don't know it. When you accept the amends a spirit offers from the higher side, it allows that spirit to move forward.

Keeping the Connection

You might experience a range of emotions and feelings as you begin thinking about spirit communication and all that it might mean in your life. The opportunities are nearly endless, and what you make of them can change your life in ways you can't now imagine. Yes, there is often sadness, regret, hurt, or loneliness when a loved one passes. But the connections are still there; the existence continues. You don't ever really lose someone you love.

The Least You Need to Know

- It is natural and normal to want to explore the continuity of life.

- The same personality characteristics that existed on the earth plane will remain in the spirit plane.

- Spirit contact always comes in goodness and healing.

- Spirit communication, like all communication, sometimes requires digging below the surface of the messages to determine their true meanings.

- Sometimes spirits make contact because we can help them as they evolve.

Part 2

What's on the Other Side?

From Hollywood movies to religious writings, there are many expressions of the higher side and what it is like to be there. Is it heaven? Is it a void? Is it another dimension of existence?

Let's take a look at what existence on the higher side might be like, and investigate some of the ways spirits communicate across the border to bring messages of love and healing.

Spirit Geography: Planes of Existence

In This Chapter

- ◆ Hollywood's vision of the hereafter
- ◆ Religion's views
- ◆ Using energy to connect with spirit
- ◆ Akashic records: the story of your soul
- ◆ Ways to connect with your divine energy
- ◆ How spirits evolve

In this physical world, we define nearly everything in terms of time and space. We measure our opportunities and limitations in those terms. It takes 45 minutes to drive 20 miles to work. It takes 35 minutes for a cake to bake. Once a year, we celebrate the anniversaries of our births, which we count in years and which define life itself. When you are two years old, someone else takes care of your every need. If you are 16 years old, you can drive (to your birthday party to enjoy cake, if you like!). When you are

85 years old, you know you are reaching the end of your physical life. Time and space are our boundaries, and there is just so much of either.

The first time Rita's father showed himself to Rita, he presented himself at the age of 27 with a full head of golden hair, a pier 49 T-shirt, and a muscular physique. When Rita first saw him, she questioned who he was. He had been 41 when she was born, and she never had seen him as a young man. Other times after that, he showed himself at age 50 or so, although he was almost 81 when he passed to the world of spirit.

On the other side, there is no time and space. There are different levels of existence but there is no sense of linear time or structured space as we know those limitations here in the physical world. Spirits do not age chronologically. When they come through in communication with us, they might appear at any age from before or after their physical lives ended. The spirit "embodies" its image of ideal, whatever that might be, which might change as the spirit evolves.

Lights, Camera, Action!

As humans, we spend a lot of time and energy trying to understand, define, and explain life beyond death. From the spooky to the sentimental, we've created views of the hereafter in books and movies. Here are just a few examples:

- *Hamlet*, William Shakespeare's sixteenth-century play, is one of the earliest works in which the plot revolves entirely around interaction between a spirit and a person in the physical world. Hamlet, the young prince of Denmark, receives visits from the spirit of his recently murdered father, the king, who tells Hamlet that the murderer was none other than Claudius, the king's brother who has since assumed the throne. To authenticate the spirit's claims, Hamlet has his father's murder re-enacted according to the spirit's description of the events, and finds Claudius's reactions convincing proof of guilt. Four hundred years after it was originally written, Shakespeare's play still appears on stages across the world each year. In 1997, it was released as a movie featuring Kenneth Branagh in the starring role.

- *Ghostbusters* (1984) and *Ghostbusters II* (1989) combine surprising compassion with comedy and action as these films follow the adventures of a team of "scientists" who capture ghosts and release them to the higher existence they can't seem to find on their own. The cast includes Bill Murray, Dan Ackroyd, Sigourney Weaver, and Annie Potts.

- In the 1990 romantic thriller *Ghost* (Patrick Swayze, Demi Moore, Whoopi Goldberg), a husband refuses to move on to the other side until he saves his wife from the unscrupulous "friends" who murdered him. The film won Goldberg a Best Supporting Actress Oscar for her role as Rita, the reluctant medium who connected Sam (Swayze) and Molly (Moore).

♦ While inattentively fiddling with the radio, Daniel Miller (Albert Brooks) drives his sports car into the path of a bus in the 1991 movie *Defending Your Life*. He finds himself in Judgment City, where a panel reviews the key points of his life to determine where Daniel goes next.

♦ In the 1998 film *What Dreams May Come*, comic Robin Williams plays it straight as Chris Nielsen in an imaginative and ultimately touching story that explores the heavy concepts of tragedy, loss, suicide, heaven, purgatory, and hell.

♦ Young actor Haley Joel Osment captivated audiences in the 1999 film *The Sixth Sense*, with his character Cole's somber assertion "I see dead people." Among them was child psychologist Malcolm Crowe (Bruce Willis), not yet aware that he no longer inhabits the earth plane.

♦ In the 2002 thriller *Dragonfly*, Kevin Costner plays Dr. Joe Darrow, an emergency room physician who believes his wife, killed in a bus accident, is attempting to contact him through his critically ill patients (especially those who have near-death experiences).

Mediums and Messages

The dead people young Cole sees in *The Sixth Sense* are somewhat frightening, conveying a sense of desperation. One unequivocal assertion we can make is: Spirit contact is not like this! When you "see dead people" they will not be gruesome, scary, or in any other way unpleasant. If what you experience scares you, your fears are in control, not spirits. Even spirits in need don't make contact or come through in ways that we might find frightening. If they did, why would we continue the contact?

These, of course, are but a very few of the movies that deal with the "Is there life after death?" question. Feel free to add your favorites to the list, which truly is so extensive that it could be the topic of a book itself! Indeed, it seems that Hollywood works overtime to bring us new and varied versions of life beyond physical death each year. How close to the truth are these presentations? Well, how close are Hollywood presentations of *anything* to their real counterparts? Entertainment, after all, is the mainstay of Hollywood. That's what sells tickets and keeps people in their seats. When we watch movies, we want to get our money's worth in terms of entertainment value.

Spirits come through as they want us to perceive them, and in ways that affirm their identities to prove the continuity of life. Spirit communication, we say again, *is always about goodness and healing*. When we seek genuine spirit communication, the drama of the connection is what keeps our attention—often for long after the experience of the connection draws to a close.

Heaven and Hell, Reward and Punishment

Many Western faith systems present a view of life, death, and what happens beyond death as a structure of good and bad, reward and punishment, heaven and hell. You live a good life here on the earth plane, and then, as a reward, your soul goes to heaven when your body dies. There is a process of judgment by an all-powerful God, with an immediate result. In some belief systems the decision is final, while in others there are ways the spirit can "earn" its way to a better place in the hierarchy of the hereafter, either through its own actions (penitence) or through the prayers and penitence of those on the earth plane.

The soul's destination after physical death—heaven, hell, or *purgatory*—is a place described by physical attributes. Heaven is generally portrayed as a location in the sky that exists above the physical earth, far beyond the ability of sight to perceive it. In many Christian faiths, heaven is the home of God and the ultimate destination for "good" souls. Hell, by contrast, is generally portrayed as deep within the earth's core, a place of fire and eternal burning. It is the domain of the devil, the ultimate evil, and the ultimate destination for "bad" souls. The concept of judging a life to determine the soul's destination and journey beyond physical death did not come into existence until the Middle Ages (800 C.E. or so).

Spiritology

Purgatory is a station of transition where the soul goes to await judgment following death of the physical body. Within the Roman Catholic belief system, a soul in purgatory may atone for the sins committed during its physical life to then qualify for eternal existence in heaven.

The role of such representations is often more to enforce codes of morality and behavior than to advance an understanding of the soul's continuing existence. Rewards encourage one set of behaviors, while punishments discourage another. Strict reward and punishment structures leave little room for learning or changing. An action receives a judgment, for which there is then either a reward or a punishment. A more acceptable, and certainly more positive, approach for many people is one that requires accountability within the context of learning, growing, and evolving.

Eternal Existence with the Gods

The premise of heaven and hell predates Christianity and other modern faith systems, existing in the mythology of many ancient cultures whose faith systems embraced multiple gods, including the Greeks, Romans, Egyptians, Celts, and Mayans. In these systems, heaven was the home of the gods from whom came the light and warmth that made life on earth possible. This heaven arched through the sky above the earth, with the movements of the sun the visual evidence of its existence. In Greek and Roman mythology, Hades ruled the underworld from his palace within the underworld and various other gods did so in other cultures (see Chapter 2).

Neither heaven nor the underworld in these ancient cultures were exclusively good or bad; in fact, the gods and goddesses who inhabited them had both good and bad characteristics. And everyone who died went to the underworld, because this was where the dead "lived" after death. They didn't endure eternal suffering; to the contrary, theirs was an existence free from the pains and problems of physical life. There was no judgment to determine who ended up where; it seems that "life" pretty much went on as before death, but without the physical trappings.

Transcendence, Nirvana, and Beyond

The faith systems of the world are varied and diverse, and each has its own perspectives on life, death, and beyond. Here's what some of them are:

◆ Olam Ha-Ba, the "World to Come," the belief in afterlife, as in some Jewish sects

◆ Reincarnation, the belief that the soul returns to another physical life, integral to faiths such as Hindu

◆ Resurrection, the belief that the soul returns to its physical body in a whole and pure state

◆ Nirvana, the belief in transcendence of the self, as in Buddhism

It's All About Energy

It is through energy that spirits are able to communicate across the boundary between the earth and spirit planes. Understanding different approaches to energy systems gives us insights into how spirit communication takes place.

Energy both separates and links the physical and spirit worlds. It is the essence of all existence, although it takes many different forms. You are energy, the chair in which you are sitting is energy, the book you are holding is energy. The principles of science—physics, specifically—substantiate this. All objects, tangible and intangible, visible and invisible, audible and inaudible, are matter. And all matter is comprised of energy structures—atoms, molecules, electrons—that vibrate at certain frequencies. The rate, or speed, of the frequency determines the matter's tangibility.

The energy of matter that forms an object we consider solid, such as a chair or a book, vibrates so slowly that we are able to physically perceive its matter. The energy of matter we cannot see, such as the air we breathe, vibrates very fast. Your physical body vibrates slowly enough to have tangibility, while your spirit vibrates so fast that you cannot perceive its presence through your five physical senses. And energy on the spirit plane vibrates so fast that it doesn't have an appearance or presence at all, as we might define that, unless a spirit chooses to represent itself in a tangible form.

Silver Cord

Few people think of Albert Einstein (1879–1955) as a mystic. But it was this famous physicist who, in his watershed work in physics, *Relativity: The Special and the General Theory* (first published in 1918), described, defined, and quantified all existence as energy that vibrates at different frequencies. Low-frequency vibrations produce tangible or visible representations such as the objects of our everyday lives, Einstein said, and high-frequency vibrations produce energy we can't quantify with our physical senses. It was a very New Age concept from a scientist who lived three quarters of a century ago!

The energy of the physical body is not capable of vibrating at a high enough rate to exist solely on the spirit plane. So when there is a spirit contact, the spirit comes through to the earth plane. To make its presence known, the spirit must slow its vibration as the medium raises his or her vibration so they can meet and communicate.

Your Body's Energy Centers: Chakras

As a structure comprised of energy, your body has energy centers called *chakras*. Life energy, called *prana*, flows through them. Your *aura* is a final, outer layer of energy that surrounds the body. There are seven chakras, which roughly align with your body's physical nervous system:

♦ The first chakra, often called the root chakra, resides at the base of your spine. Its energy is the energy of survival, which relates to your security and well-being. Your root chakra connects you to your physical life. The color associated with this chakra is red.

♦ The second, or sacral, chakra resides in your lower pelvis, and is the energy of sexuality, relationships, creativity, and emotions. The color associated with this chakra is orange.

Spiritology

A **chakra** is a center of energy within your body. The word means "wheel" in ancient Sanskrit. **Prana** is a Sanskrit word meaning "life energy." Your **aura** is an outer layer of energy that contains your body's prana and keeps it circulating through your chakras.

♦ The third, or solar plexus, chakra resides in your solar plexus or "gut"—the center of your abdomen just above your navel. Its energy relates to personal power and self-esteem. The color associated with this chakra is yellow.

♦ The fourth, or heart, chakra resides at the level of your heart and is the energy of emotional love, affection, and partnership. The color associated with this chakra is green.

♦ The fifth chakra resides at the base of your throat and is the energy of expression and truth. The color associated with this chakra is blue.

♦ The sixth chakra, often called your "third eye," resides in the center of your forehead. Its energy is the energy of inner vision and psychic perception. The color associated with this chakra is indigo.

♦ The seventh, or crown, chakra resides at the crown of your head. It is the energy portal that connects you to the divine and the collective spirit that exists beyond your individual being. The color associated with this chakra is violet.

The prana that flows through your chakras connects your physical body with your spirit. Increasing the flow of prana to a particular chakra activates and enhances it. Yoga and meditation are two ways to awaken your chakras (more about these practices later in this chapter).

In yoga, the seven chakras are the centers of energy that flow through the body.

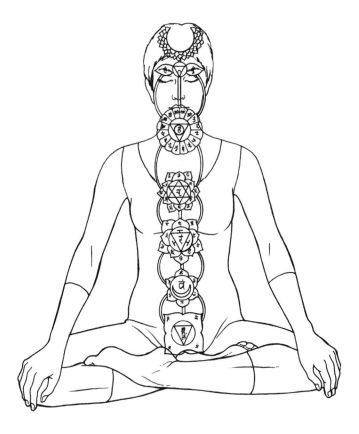

The Human Energy Field: Your Subtle Body

Your physical body is more than a container that carries you through your life. In fact, your existence is a composite of seven layers of energy known as the *human energy field*. These layers are called *subtle bodies*. They are simultaneously independent and interrelated, and correlate to your chakras:

◆ Your etheric subtle body is like an energy shadow of your physical body. It is the energy element that connects you to physical life, and it correlates to your first, or root, chakra.

Spiritology

The **human energy field** is the composite structure that contains your physical existence. The **subtle bodies** are the seven layers of the human energy field.

◆ Your emotional subtle body is the energy of your feelings and emotions. It correlates to your second and third chakras.

◆ Your astral subtle body functions as a conduit between the physical energies and the spiritual energies of your existence. It correlates to your fourth, or heart, chakra.

- Your mental or intellectual subtle body is the energy of your thoughts and intellect. It correlates to your fifth and sixth chakras.

- Your causal subtle body is your connection to the divine. It correlates to your seventh, or crown, chakra. It is the most highly developed of your energy structures, and through it you are connected to a greater cosmic or spiritual existence.

Remember our discussion of energy vibration earlier in this chapter? The varying vibrational levels of these different energy layers, or subtle bodies, allows them to co-exist with what you perceive to be your physical existence. They just vibrate at higher rates, so you are mostly unaware of them.

Energy flows between the human energy field that is beyond your individual existence and the chakras that are your personal existence. In this way, you are separate from yet integrated with the overall energy of all existence. It's as though your body "plugs in." Even though you reside on the earth plane because your existence is physical, you remain connected to the spirit plane because, after all, the essence of your existence is the energy that is your spirit.

Your Soul's Story: Your Akashic Record

An *Akashic record* is a cosmic collection of all that ever was, is, and will be, as documentation, so to speak, of the soul's existence, mission, and journey. It's not an actual document or book or even record as we might think of these, but rather exists in the realm of spirit as a divine record. The content of the Akashic record is said to be deeply symbolic. It is possible to connect with your Akashic record through meditation or through a good psychic counselor.

Psychic counselors who do past-life regressions believe this is made possible by accessing your Akashic record (see Chapters 21 and 22). And some people believe that your spirit guides draw from your Akashic record as they provide you with guidance and assistance (see Chapter 7).

There are references or parallels to the concept of Akashic records in many faith systems, including the following:

- The Bible's Book of Revelation (the Book of Life) and recording angels, who document the soul's thoughts and deeds for God to review on Judgment Day

Spiritology

An **Akashic record** is the collection of all of your soul's actions and travels, past, present, and future. The term comes from the ancient Sanskrit word *Akasha*, which means "primary or primordial substance."

- Buddhism's Akasha or Akasa, the life essence that is present as a space around the physical and spirit worlds and that contains all existence

- Psychoanalyst Carl Jung's collective unconscious, the premise that all people share certain symbolisms, thoughts, and beliefs through a connected unconsciousness (see Chapter 22)

- The cosmic consciousness or collective mind of metaphysics, which holds that all spirits, on the earth plane and on the spirit plane, are united on a deep level of consciousness

Connecting with Your Divine Energy

There are a number of ways that you can connect with your divine energy. Among the most common are prayer, meditation, and yoga. All combine the physical, mental, and spiritual dimensions of existence. (And there are *Complete Idiot's Guides* for all three: prayer, meditation, and yoga! See Appendix B for details.)

Prayer

Through prayer, we communicate directly with the divine, however it is that we perceive it. This can be as God, as god or goddess, as the Universe, or the collective spirit. Although it is a communication between an individual and his or her divine, prayer can take place in groups. The collective power can be amazing, particularly when directed toward healing or releasing a spirit to continue on its journey.

Rita was once called to a house where a spirit, whose physical life had been ended by murder, was unable to complete its transition from the earth plane to the spirit plane. The house was filled with great sadness, and its new owners often saw moving objects and heard noises. They realized that this was an opportunity, and wanted to help the spirit. Rita gathered a small group at the house to pray for and with the spirit, encouraging the spirit to accept the welcoming contact from friends and family already on the other side and asking for divine assistance with the transition. Finally the connection was made, and the spirit moved on. All who were praying could feel the sadness suddenly lift.

Prayer connects you with the divine by activating your causal body and the energy of your seventh, or crown, chakra.

Meditation

Meditation connects you with the divine by activating your mental subtle body and your sixth, or "third eye," chakra. A common meditative practice is to focus on a single thought until all other thoughts leave your mind. You then explore this single thought in total completeness. Through this process, you can gain relaxation and clarity.

Silver Cord

Charles Darwin (1809–1882) was a physician, minister, and naturalist who studied the survival of plant and animal species in their natural habitats. Darwin observed that natural selection meant the strongest and most adaptive representatives of a species were the ones that survived and reproduced. He published his findings in 1859, in what would become his defining work and most famous book, *On the Origin of Species by Means of Natural Selection, or the Preservation of Favoured Races in the Struggle for Life.*

Yoga

Yoga postures, or asanas, activate various chakras, which in turn access their correlating subtle bodies. Yoga combines activities of the physical body with meditation, providing a range of connections that can be quite basic, as with breathing exercises, or complex, as with postures that access the causal subtle body.

Spirit Evolution

Even though they don't age as we think of aging, spirits evolve as they acquire wisdom and insight. Here on the earth plane, we tend to think of evolution as a scientific process defining the changes that a species of animal or plant experiences over the course of its known existence. This is the means by which the species adapts to changes in its environment, and in a Darwinian view—which refers to the theories of evolution put forth by naturalist Charles Darwin—the means by which the species extends its life. In theory, a species can perpetuate its existence for as long as it is capable of changes that remain compatible with its environment.

When a species exceeds its capacity to adapt, it dies out—one by one—until finally there are no members of the species left. Prehistoric creatures, such as the dinosaur and the wooly mammoth, are now extinct; they were unable, as a species, to adapt to the changes in their environments. Scientists theorize that every species will ultimately reach the limits of its abilities to adapt, or evolve, and will become extinct. But even in the finality of one ending is the beginning of a different existence. New species arrive, with new capabilities for change and adaptation, and the cycle of life continues.

Remember, though, that time and space define the cycle of life here on the earth plane. These borders contain and define the spirit's physical existence here, as they do all living things. But on the spirit plane, there are no such boundaries. Evolution is endless. A less common definition of evolution seems more applicable to the concept as it applies to spiritual growth: "unfolding; the action or instance of forming and giving something off; emission" (*Merriam-Webster's Collegiate Dictionary, Tenth Edition*, Merriam-Webster, Inc., 1993).

The instant the physical body's death releases the spirit, the spirit's experience of its existence changes. (Think of a butterfly emerging from a cocoon.) The higher side consists of many different levels of evolution, although these are not hierarchical or judgmental. The spirit, of course, evolves during its physical existence on the earth plane, too. Your physical life is a dimension of your soul's mission, and is a necessary (and, we hope, a most pleasant) journey.

The Least You Need to Know

- ◆ The representations of Hollywood offer a sensationalized—and inaccurate— view of life beyond the physical world, often playing on our fears.

- ◆ Most religions and belief systems incorporate some sense of the soul's existence beyond the physical body's death.

- ◆ Energy is the common force that connects the earth plane with the spirit plane, and it is through energy that connection between the two planes can take place.

- ◆ Your soul has a mission that extends through and beyond your physical life.

- ◆ Prayer, meditation, and yoga are some of the ways in which you can connect with the divine.

- ◆ There are no boundaries of time and space on the spirit plane, so a spirit's evolution is endless.

Chapter 6

Birth, Death, and Passing Over

In This Chapter

- ◆ Theories and beliefs about the spirit's beginnings
- ◆ Helping spirits pass over
- ◆ Are we disturbing those on the other side?
- ◆ A different, but continuing, relationship

Physical life has two defining transitions: birth and death. When giving birth a woman and her partner usher a new life into this world. This is a wondrous event, a glorious time. Even complete strangers smile and offer congratulations at the news of a baby's arrival. But what does the spirit experience as it transitions from the spirit plane to the earth plane and to the confines of a physical body? Does the spirit welcome the journey as much as we welcome its arrival?

And what about the transition on the other end of life? We know from communicating with those who have passed over that there are varying experiences of the transition, although crossings seem to share several common characteristics. Is this a solitary journey? Or do the spirits of those gathered around us on the earth plane somehow send us off to a welcoming contingent waiting on the other side? Spirit communications and near-death experiences suggest that the spirit is never alone, even in its transitions between one world of existence to another.

The Spirit Before Birth

We all think and talk about what might happen *after* death parts us from our physical bodies. As soon as we become aware of our mortality, we begin to worry about its inevitable conclusion. But what about *before* our entry into this physical world? Where, and what, are we? When it comes to the soul's beginnings, we have far more questions than answers!

The Soul's Beginnings: A Theological Perspective

Through the ages, *theologians* and religious scholars have debated the matter of the soul's beginnings, putting forth various theories. Some of these theories are decidedly Christian, while others either predate Christianity or appear in numerous faith systems, Christian and non-Christian. These are, of course, very complex concepts. We'll just briefly touch on a few of them to give a sense of their diversity and variation.

The prevailing, or at least most widely held, view of the soul's origin dodges the question of origin altogether by simply saying that the soul has always existed. This view shows up in various Western and Eastern faith systems, including certain Christian sects, Judaism, Hinduism, and Buddhism. It also exists in secular, or nonreligious, views, such as the discourses of the ancient Greek philosopher Plato.

Spiritology

Theology is the study of God and God's relationship with humankind within the context of a structured religion or faith system. A **theologian** is someone who studies theology.

Many Christian faiths, including Catholicism, hold the view that God creates a new soul each time a child is conceived. If for some reason that child is not born into a physical life, its soul goes directly to a spirit existence—in this context, to live in heaven. Other faith systems believe that just as a child's parents create a new physical body from the joining of their bodies, so, too, do their united spirits contribute equal parts to creating the new spirit that will inhabit that physical body.

And still other faith systems blend various theories and beliefs to come up with approaches that take a little of this and a little of that.

The Soul's Beginnings: A Metaphysical Perspective

Within the framework of the metaphysical arts such as numerology (the study of energy as expressed through numbers) and astrology (the study of energy as expressed through the movements and relationships of stars, planets, and other celestial bodies), the soul chooses the moment and circumstances of its birth. This choice helps to define the soul's mission in its physical life, and defines the energies of the Universe that will support the soul as it moves toward achieving its mission. This framework is not one of destiny, but rather of the choices of free will that lead the soul either toward or away from its mission. The soul travels toward its mission for as long as that takes and regardless of whatever detours it encounters along the way. There is no predetermined path; the path unfolds according to the decisions and choices a person makes.

Charting the Soul's Course

Astrology is a blueprint of your personal energy. It fits within the context of the Universe's energy as a whole, much as the blueprint for a house fits within a neighborhood or community. At your birth, your astrological chart shows just the basic structure of your life and the energies within the Universe that will support your spirit's journey through its physical life. You retain the free will to make decisions contrary to the flow of this supportive energy. Such choices often result in a life filled with challenges and disappointments.

Rather than pinpointing your soul's origin, astrology shows your spirit's travels. This is, of course, far beyond the traditional sun-sign astrology most people know from the daily horoscope! This level of astrology is quite complex. Although in theory astrology shows the future as well as past journeys of your spirit, in practice it is virtually impossible to interpret the information with complete accuracy. Doing so relies on a level of understanding that appears unlikely on the earth plane (although there are some extraordinary astrologers out there who are able to make amazingly accurate interpretations).

Always remember the importance and role of free will. Every choice you make affects the course of your physical life on the earth plane and your spirit's journey through its existence. Even if you could look ahead, what you would see would be a future dependent on precisely the state of your existence at this very moment—which, just in the process of looking ahead, would change!

The Universe Has Your Number

Numerology assigns numeric values to all aspects of your existence. You already know some of these—your date and time of birth, your age, the current date. Other dimensions of your life have numeric values as well, such as the names of people and places. Every number has a particular symbolic representation. Certain numbers are master numbers; that is, they are more powerful than other numbers.

> **Silver Cord** _____
>
> Want to know more about astrology or numerology? *The Complete Idiot's Guide* series has you covered! Pick up *The Complete Idiot's Guide to Astrology*, by Madeline Gerwick-Brodeur and Lisa Lenard (Alpha Books, 1997) and *The Complete Idiot's Guide to Numerology*, by Kay Lagerquist and Lisa Lenard (Alpha Books, 1999).

The Greek mathematician Pythagoras, who lived in the sixth century B.C.E., established a correlation between mathematics and energy. He determined that certain numbers reflect a higher vibration of energy than others, leading to their interpretation as master numbers.

In numerology, the numbers associated with your physical life represent various characteristics of your spirit, from its mission to its challenges. Understanding your personal numerology can give you additional insights into your spirit's journey.

The Soul's Beginnings: A Spiritualist Perspective

Spiritualism teaches that the origin of the Universe and all that exists within it is unknown, and really doesn't matter! What does matter is that we *do* exist, and that our spirits continue across the spectrum of physical life and the spirit world. The focus in Spiritualism is on advancing the spirit's mission as the spirit travels through the physical world.

Passing Assistance

At birth, we know there is a considerable contingent waiting on this side to welcome the new life. Doctors, nurses, partners, siblings, grandparents, and friends all gather to participate in the birth, in some way or another. What we can't see is the contingent gathered on the other side, assisting the spirit in its transition into the physical world—although we must presume it is there. It is said, in spirit contacts, that those in the spirit world cry when a baby is born to the earth plane, just as we cry when a person leaves his or her physical existence to enter the realm of spirit.

The situation repeats itself at physical life's other transition, death. Loved ones, and often health care professionals, gather around the dying person to offer whatever comfort is possible. And although you cannot see them, the welcoming contingent has gathered on the other side, waiting to greet the spirit in its return.

What's different, typically, is the mood and tone of these two events. A baby's birth inspires a great sense of joy and wonder. A person's impending death often fills us with sadness, loss, and even despair. This is of course normal. We mourn the loss of those we love, even when we know they aren't really lost to us but are just moving into a different existence. Our point of focus is on the "different," and we know we will miss what we had. Knowing that there is life beyond the death of the physical body helps relieve some of the hurt. You know the life of the spirit continues, and this knowledge brings comfort and peace.

Silver Cord

Today we think of a wake as an often rowdy celebration of the life of a person who has just passed on. But originally the term identified the tradition of having someone sit awake all night beside the body of the one believed to have died, to make sure the person didn't in fact "wake up." Before modern technology made it possible to determine unquestionably that the physical body's functions had ceased, it was often difficult to know whether the person was in fact dead or had slipped into a coma.

If you are with a loved one who is dying, let the person know you are there even if he or she appears to be unaware of what's happening. Touch, talk, cry, laugh, pray—do whatever comes naturally. The mind and body might be shutting down, but the spirit is expanding. As it often happens in spirit contact, the spirit wants loved ones to know that those final words and caresses were both noticed and helpful. And as your loved one's spirit achieves release, open yourself to feeling its joy and liberation.

Although you will feel loss and grief when you realize the passing has taken place, you will also have the comfort of knowing that you shared in the passage and that your loved one made the transition. This is one of the most intimate sharings you can have with someone. As a medium, Rita has been with those who are about to pass and has seen the gathering of those, the family members and friends on the higher side, reaching to welcome the one who is about to pass.

The experience is amazingly powerful, and is often the resounding "Yes!" that you seek when asking the question (aloud or whispered in your mind), "Is there really life beyond death?"

Releasing Fear

Letting go is as important for the departing spirit as it is for those left on the earth plane. The transition from physical life to spirit existence is both natural and inevitable. We on the earth plane can assist a spirit to complete its transition, through spirit contact and prayer. This can provide the comfort and the encouragement the spirit needs to release its bonds with the earth plane and allow those in the spirit plane to welcome their loved one.

Releasing Love

Love is our most powerful emotion. It can enable us to do things that should be beyond our abilities, such as when a woman lifts a car to free a loved one trapped beneath in an accident. Love, we say poetically, transcends all. Because of this, we long for love; it is what makes our human existence meaningful. And when love enters our lives, we don't want to let it go.

Sometimes, the power of love can be strong enough that a loved one's spirit is unwilling to pass over after death releases it from its physical body. The spirit might want to stay as close to the earth plane as possible to remain near the loved one who is still there. Or the spirit might feel unable to move away because the pull of love from the one remaining on the earth plane is too strong to let it go.

There are ways for those in the physical world to help the spirit's transition between the earth plane and the spirit plane. For example, spirit contact and prayer can help both the person remaining on the earth plane and the spirit that needs to pass over. Love is like an incredibly fluid and flexible band of energy. It will always flow between and around the spirits at either end, maintaining the connection between them.

Completing Unfinished Business

Sometimes a person's passing happens before the spirit feels it has finished its business on the earth plane. This is especially the case if death is sudden, leaving behind tangible loose ends such as financial matters. Spirits might not become all-knowing once they pass over to the higher side, but they do know that loved ones who remain on the earth plane often need help with these loose ends. So the departing spirit stays close to the earth plane to try to communicate the message offering guidance and help from the higher side.

Sometimes the loved one on the earth plane can feel this presence. There might be a sense of being directed about what to do with certain bills, to look in the upper left-hand desk drawer for the check ledger, to contact the bank about joint accounts, to send letters to creditors. Sometimes another person comes in to handle the matter, and seems to know just what to do even without any previous experience. Once these tasks are accomplished, the spirit is satisfied and moves on.

Rita was doing some *message work* during a church service and came to a woman whose significant other, the man with whom she shared her home, possessions, and life, had passed. After providing a full description of himself that the woman joyously recognized, the man said he wanted to talk to her about some papers that needed to be signed. "Tell her," he communicated to Rita, "to make her own decisions and not pay any attention to all the others who feel they have her best interests at heart, because only she knows the right thing to do."

Spiritology

Message work is what those in the Spiritualist Church sometimes call the portion of the church service that presents spirit communication.

The woman nodded and said nothing, and Rita concluded the service. Afterward, the woman came up to Rita and asked if they could talk for a moment. It had taken some time for the woman to absorb the communication and all that it implied, she said, but she wanted Rita to know how important and timely the message was. "I'm selling some property that we had owned together," she said. "Everybody has advice, but this is what I want to do. I'm signing the papers next week!"

Unfinished business is not always task-oriented, of course. Because the timing of death is more likely to be unexpected than anticipated, there are often dangling issues that get cut off before resolution. A father and a daughter might never quite acknowledge to each other that they respect and admire the other's achievements. Spouses or partners might not have the opportunity to apologize and make up after an argument. Siblings might not reach the point of maturity in their physical lives where they can move beyond the rivalries of youth.

Loved ones remaining on the earth plane, as well as the spirits who have passed, need to bring these matters to resolution. Sometimes the experience of this happens through a dream or visitation immediately following the death. Other times it takes place months or years down the road, and might require intervention from someone else, such as a medium.

People sometimes worry that reaching a level of completion has taken too long, and that it has interfered with the spirit's existence to the same extent it has disrupted theirs. Although here in the physical world a significant amount of time might have passed since the loved one's death, remember that on the higher side there is no time or space. What feels like a long time to you is really no time at all for the loved one on the other side. All that matters is that the healing takes place, so both the incarnate and discarnate spirits can move on.

Reaching Across the Border

Spirits are busy on the other side. There are no spirit communications that suggest spirits are lolling around out in the ethereal heavens somewhere, plucking at stars and watching the Universe unfold before them. To the contrary, it appears that existence on the higher side is quite active, and even intense. The difficulty for us on the earth plane is trying to understand how this can be when the framework we use to measure it—time and space—does not exist.

So what do they do on the higher side of life? To be sure, There is much learning and developing as each soul embarks on the next segment of its journey. But all is not serious! In fact, part of the evolution for most spirits is having fun and enjoying things that perhaps they didn't get to do on the earth plane.

Rita was doing a reading for a woman whose fiancé had passed. "I have someone here who is playing the trumpet," Rita said. "In fact, he's quite resoundingly playing 'When the Saints Go Marching In!'"

Mediums and Messages

Spirit contact sometimes comes without being summoned. Rita was at a wake for a friend's father who had passed, when the father's spirit grabbed her by the psychic coattails and communicated that he wanted to convey a message to his daughter. Rita walked over to her friend, took her hand, and said, "Your father wants me to tell you he's dancing with your mother again!"

The woman burst into tears of joy. Her fiancé, she told Rita, had always wanted to learn to play the trumpet but had never had the time or the resources. Clearly, once those factors didn't matter, he was free to pursue this dream … and pursue it with vigor! Many, many spirits share with us the fun and wonderful experiences they are having.

It's hard for us to imagine being busy when there are no time and space constraints, because these are the factors that define "busy" for us here on the earth plane. But spirits certainly have plenty to do on the higher side, and in fact are likely "busier" than we can comprehend!

Do (Not) Disturb

We've been saying that the spirit has a mission. Part of this mission unfolds during the spirit's existence on the earth plane, and part of it on the spirit plane. When we attempt to make contact with the spirit of a loved one who has passed, are we interrupting anything?

It's important to always keep in mind that a spirit who does not want to make contact will not make contact. You cannot force spirit contact or communication. You cannot demand that a spirit make itself available to you. (Well, you can demand all you want, but nothing compels the spirit to respond!) A spirit comes through because it wants to, because it desires to share a message with you. Your efforts to make contact will not disturb a spirit, or keep it from what it needs to do. Just as you won't answer your doorbell if it rings when you are in the shower (if you even hear it), a spirit will not respond to communication attempts if it is otherwise occupied.

When a spirit chooses not to come through, it is likely because it is involved in something it does not want to interrupt. Just as there are activities here on the earth plane that require intense concentration and participation from start to finish, there are such events on the spirit plane. After all, insight and enlightenment don't just happen! Spirits must work to understand and complete the lessons that are crucial to their missions on the higher side, just as you must do the same during your existence in the physical world.

Death by Choice: Suicide

Suicide is a great moral and spiritual dilemma for us on the earth plane. Nearly every faith system views suicide as an act contrary to the normal order of things, whether as an interference with the role of God in determining physical life and death or as a rift in the energy flow of the Universe. After a loved one takes his or her own life, those who remain on the earth plane are left not only with tremendous grief, pain, and guilt, but also to wonder what consequences await their loved one on the higher side.

Those remaining on the earth plane worry tremendously about what happens to those who pass by taking their own lives. What spirits tell us is that when someone passes through suicide, the higher side is a classroom of sorts where the spirit gets help thinking about and handling the issues that led to the suicide. Some souls, whether in their physical lives or on the spirit plane, are just not able to work through their problems and issues. On the higher side, there is help. There is always learning, and there is always a positive outcome somewhere.

> **Premonition**
>
> If you or someone you know are thinking about committing suicide, please seek professional help without delay. Suicide is *not* the answer to any question or problem. Nearly every community has a suicide hotline you can telephone for information and referral to an appropriate health-care provider.

Violent Death

We know that the spirits of those whose lives are taken through violence are more likely to remain earthbound than spirits that don't experience such abrupt transitions. It is this circumstance, indeed, that resulted in the birth of modern Spiritualism, when the spirit of a man murdered in their house inspired the Fox sisters to attempt communication with him (see Chapter 3). Such traumatic and unexpected death moves the spirit from its physical body so abruptly that it sometimes cannot complete the transition.

When this happens, we on the earth plane can help, again through spirit contact and prayer. We can help send them to the light! Visualize the person moving toward the light, helping them see the hands that are reaching out to them so they can make the transition. It is sometimes necessary to convince the spirit that his or her physical body is gone, and there is no choice now but to move on. When done with love and compassion, this is greatly healing for the spirit and allows it to continue its transition.

Silver Cord

The soul's inability or refusal to recognize that its physical body no longer exists was the theme of the 1999 silver screen hit *The Sixth Sense*. In this movie starring Haley Joel Osment and Bruce Willis, the main character was murdered but carried through the motions of his physical life as though he was still living them.

In many ways, the violent trauma is just as disruptive for loved ones who remain on the earth plane. They are left with many loose ends and much unfinished business. The process of helping the loved one come to grips with the reality of the situation and complete his or her crossing can also aid those on the earth plane in reaching similar acceptance. Establishing a spirit connection can also offer those on both sides the opportunity to say good-bye and bring closure.

Is This All Just Wishful Thinking?

No one likes to think of continuing in this life without the loved ones who bring so much joy and meaning to the journey. Yet inevitably, some loved ones will pass to the other side before us, and we will feel the separation as loss and pain. This is natural and normal, part of the experience of being human and of our existence in the physical world. (Many believe this is a core element of the soul's mission on the earth plane, as loss and pain can be paths to enlightenment and insight.) So is the desire to make contact with those who have passed just wishful thinking, a means of easing hurt and grief?

To some extent, it certainly is. The sense of loss that comes with a loved one's passing validates the spiritual existence for both the one who has passed and the one who remains on the earth plane. But beyond the pain, there is still the sense of connection.

You never really lose touch with those who are important to you (notice we said "are," in the present tense, and not "were," in the past tense), regardless of where in the Universe each of you is.

That your spirits are now on different planes changes your relationship, just as a friendship will change when one friend moves from Boston to San Francisco. The move doesn't mean the end of your friendship. It just means the courses of your respective lives have changed and your relationship is changing as a result. Instead of meeting for coffee twice a week, you might send daily e-mail messages, weekly letters, and telephone each other late at night when the chaos of your busy daily lives finally quiets enough for you to enjoy uninterrupted conversation. Will you miss each other and the relationship you had when you both lived in Boston? Indeed! But will you still remain friends? Certainly, if that is what you both desire.

Spirit contact is of course more complex than managing a long-distance friendship. Your two spirits are now on journeys that are no longer contiguous. The separation is momentous for each, and allows each to move toward achieving its mission. And communication across this separation is momentous, too, because in addition to keeping you in touch with someone greatly important to you, it affirms (you know this as well as we do by now, so say it with us) the continuity of life. Once this happens, there is nothing wishful about it!

The Least You Need to Know

- There are many concepts about the soul's beginnings, but no one really knows how or when a soul comes into existence.

- Astrology and numerology are among the metaphysical systems that explore and express the spirit's journey, in its physical life as well as its spiritual existence.

- A spirit's transition from the earth plane to the higher side is not always easy, and can be affected by events on this side.

- Those of us on the earth plane can offer assistance, through spirit contact and prayer, to an earthbound spirit completing its passage to the other side.

- Spirit contact is more than just wishful thinking. It is indisputable evidence that the life of the spirit extends beyond the life of the physical body.

Chapter 7

Spirit Guides

In This Chapter

- ◆ Your ever-present spirit guides
- ◆ An exercise for identifying your spirit guides
- ◆ An exercise for asking your spirit guides for help
- ◆ What's in it for your spirit guides

Wouldn't it be nice if you could share in the wisdom and learning the other side has to offer … from this side? You can, and probably already do, even though you might not know it! Spirit guides are with each of us all the time. Some people are very aware of their guides, and can even tell which guides are present. Some people only sense a spirit guide's presence in times of need or stress, while others sense the presence of their guides a good deal of the time.

Spirit guides are here to watch out for us, help us understand life lessons, and help us find joy and wonder as we journey through our earth plane existence. And often, contact serves for the spirit guide's progression as well. Spirits can learn by helping us through our experiences, too.

You and Your (Spirit) Shadow

Although your spirit guides are with you all the time you aren't always aware of their presence, any more than you're aware of the presence of your shadow. Just as familiarity blurs the details of your regular commute route or daily activities, the continuous presence of your spirit guides sometimes makes them just part of the psychic scenery.

Whether or not you know it, your spirit guides are always with you. They communicate with you on a higher level. Some of the information they have to share is instructional, helping you to discover the learnings of your lessons in this life. You might "hear" or "see" this communication, and be as consciously aware of it as you would be of a dialogue with an earth plane friend. Other times you simply take an action or make a decision that turns out right, and you might marvel at having done so. Do you feel as though someone is smiling at you then, giving you a pat on the back? Thank your spirit guides!

A key concept with spirit guides is "guidance." Guidance is something that is optional. It is additional information, a different perspective, that you can use or not use, as you choose. You are not required to follow a spirit guide's advice. What you do with the information your spirit guides provide is entirely up to you.

Spirit guides aren't with us to live our lives for us, or to keep us from making poor choices and mistakes. Ultimately, you are responsible for your own life and the path it takes. Spirit guides are extra resources for you to tap into, and to draw from in considering the many elements of information that go into the decisions you make. It's up to you to use or discard that advice, according to how it fits with other advice and information. You, and you alone, are accountable for the course of your life.

CAUTION

Premonition

Your safety always remains your responsibility! Don't rely on spirit guides, however protected they make you feel, to keep you safe when you put yourself in hazardous situations. Remember that spirit guides are with us to help with the lessons of our lives, not to keep us from the consequences of potentially risky decisions.

Someone to Watch over You

Do you sometimes feel that your spirit guide is some sort of a heavenly protector who watches over you and keeps you from getting into harm's way or into trouble? You might even refer to this protector as a guardian angel (although technically speaking, a guardian angel is an entirely different entity). You might have spirit guides that function in this way. They stay with you, surround you with light and energy, and help you find your way safely through the day and to your destination.

A Little Help from Beyond

During your existence on the earth plane, you develop a certain expertise. (If you're truly talented, you might have several areas of expertise.) You might be an artist, a banker, an accountant, an engineer, a carpenter, an attorney, a doctor, a writer. When you pass to the other side, this expertise goes with you. As you evolve on the higher side, your first order of business is to complete whatever personal matters need attention. After that, you can use your expertise to guide people on the earth plane.

This is the help that comes to you through your spirit guides. They have expertise in areas that are important in your life, and come to offer guidance in those areas. Often, your spirit guides help you to move toward achieving your life's mission.

Cast of Thousands

Most spirit guides were once people who walked the earth plane and now have an expertise that they can share with you. They can offer help with just about any need you might have, from the mundane to the spiritual. You might have one spirit guide who offers advice about matters relating to your professional life, and another that gives you a boost when you're involved in physical activities. You might even have shopping guides!

Rita has a particular spirit guide that has been with her for a long time and is with her when she paints, yet when she does spirit drawings she can feel that other spirit guides come in to guide the process. She can see the shift in the style of her drawings, and then she knows a different guide is at work. When she paints her own spirit guides, she can feel them guiding her work to create the images that unfold on her canvases.

A spirit guide might have a heritage that is very different from yours. Yet if you look closely, you'll find that there is some sort of connection. Perhaps there are elements of the spirit guide's heritage that allow you to look at things differently than your own heritage and culture permit. Our spirit guides help us through the processes we need to complete so we can make the changes and experience the growth needed to make our own life paths unfold. Each of us is so unique! Some people don't want to go any further than their neighborhood, while others want to travel around the world. Spirit guides give us inspiration for journeys that we want—or need—to take.

Friend, Family, Stranger?

A spirit guide has a particular skill or expertise to offer you, which is why you have different spirit guides at different times of your life, and even during different activities.

Occasionally a spirit guide might be a friend or a family member who has passed to the higher side. But most of the time, your spirit guides are not the folks you'll find in your family album. The only time a spirit guide might be a relative is when this person has an expertise that you need. If you're a painter and your grandfather was a plumber, your grandfather doesn't have much to offer you about painting—even though you might very much enjoy his spirit visits. A spirit guide comes to teach or assist you. A loved one comes to fuss over you, to tell you to eat your oatmeal and button your coat!

Sometimes you might believe a relative has come through to give you some help. Think this through carefully before accepting it. Did this relative have expertise in the area he or she is now offering assistance with? If Aunt Martha couldn't balance a checkbook on the earth plane, she's not going to become a financial whiz when she passes to the higher side! If you have someone coming through, whether directly or through a medium, who says she's Aunt Martha, coming to give you financial planning advice from the other side, don't feel that you have to accept the advice. Sometimes the signal isn't quite clear; this either isn't Aunt Martha, or it is but she hasn't come to help you plan your financial future. Sometimes a visit is just a visit. Ask the spirit to clarify his or her identity and purpose.

> **Premonition**
>
> If a spirit guide's apparent message doesn't make sense to you, explore it further. Never make changes in your life solely on the basis of information that comes to you through spirit communication. As with all advice, explore all the possibilities and consequences before choosing a course of action.

Who Are Your Spirit Guides?

It's fun and exciting to meet your spirit guides. Most of them are just as eager to meet you. Even though they've been a part of your life for who knows how long, they've operated in the shadows. Everyone enjoys recognition, and spirit guides are no exception. In fact, many spirit guides will go out of their way to help you figure out who they are.

Rita was painting a picture of her spirit guide when a friend came in and asked, "What's his name?" Rita struggled with fragments of words and kept coming up with "Frangelico, Angelico, friar," with words going back and forth, until finally "Fra Angelico" came to her. But this didn't mean anything to Rita or her friend, so Rita just pushed it to the back of her mind.

Three weeks later, Rita heard her father's voice say "Look it up!" This had been his constant message during his presence on the earth plane, so it came as no surprise that it was his message from the other side. So Rita went to the encyclopedia and found an entry for a Fra Angelico, a painter who lived in the fifteenth century. All the information that she had told her friend about this painting monk was verified in the encyclopedia.

End of the Day, *November 1989, oil on canvas. Rita's painting of her spirit guide Fra Angelico.*

Being the skeptic that she is, Rita dug deeper for more information about Fra Angelico. At the Worcester Art Museum's research room, Rita found an article written in approximately 1850, critiquing Fra Angelico in the same way that Rita's work had been reviewed just a few months earlier! In both cases, the critiques stated, "Master of hands and faces but not enough painterly quality. Too interested in telling the story." For Rita, this verified that Fra Angelico was indeed her spirit guide; the chances of something like this happening at random are pretty incredible.

Silver Cord

The Italian painter Fra Angelico (ca. 1400–1455), whose given name was Guido di Pietro, lived on the early side of the famous Italian Renaissance period in art that produced Leonardo da Vinci and Michelangelo. One of his famous paintings, a fresco called *The Annunciation,* is in a church in Florence, the monastery of S. Marco. According to the "standard of standards" in art history basic texts, *History of Art,* art historian H. W. Janson writes Fra Angelico preserves "dignity, directness, and spatial order … but his figures, much as we may admire their lyrical tenderness, never achieve the physical and psychological self-assurance that characterizes the Early Renaissance image of man."

Most people have a dominant guide who is present nearly all of the time. When Debbie (Rita's co-author of this book) and Rita talked on the telephone for the first time, Rita immediately "met" Debbie's spirit guide, even though Debbie was unaware of his presence. An energetic and powerful presence, this guide is a Native American in full, colorful dance attire. He dances with great energy, and it is this energy that gives Debbie her "Never say die!" approach to life. Now that she is aware of her spirit guide, Debbie feels his energy and his presence—especially when flying downhill on her bicycle! Debbie looks forward to getting to know her "Feather Dancer" and to learning what lessons he is here to help her learn.

Silver Cord

Guided meditation, or directed communication, is a common method of helping your conscious self to step aside. This opens and frees your mind, body, and spirit to be receptive to spirit contact.

You might, like Debbie, become aware of your spirit guides when a medium introduces you to them. Or you might already have a sense that a presence accompanies you through the activities of your daily life, or even a clear vision that you can already identify as a spirit guide. Whatever the case, your guides are with you to help you get the most from your life. Your guides are your spirit friends, and you can initiate communication with them just as you might pick up the telephone to call your earth plane friends.

Meet Your Spirit Guides: A Directed Communication Exercise

Who are *your* spirit guides? Here is an exercise that can help the guides disclose themselves to you. You might want to read through it several times. In that way, you can go through the steps without interrupting them to see what comes next. It's not important that you follow each step exactly. What matters most is that you are comfortable, relaxed, and open to the experience and whatever information it reveals to you.

1. Make yourself comfortable in a location where you won't have any distractions or interruptions.

2. Take three slow, deep breaths, in through your nose and out through your mouth. Let the first breath clear your body, let the second breath open your mind, and let the third breath free your spirit.

3. Consciously form the thought: "This is my time to be one with God and for God to be one with me." (God, of course, being the divine of your belief system or choice.) Set an intent to meet your spirit guide.

4. In your mind's eye, see yourself sitting on a bench in an open, beautiful garden. There are flowers and trees, and the air smells fresh and clean. It is peaceful and calm.

5. Open your mind and your heart to welcome the visitor you know is approaching, with the same delight and excitement you might feel when a friend or a relative comes to visit.

6. Watch your visitor, your spirit guide, approach. Notice it, but don't shift your focus to looking at the guide's appearance, attire, and demeanor. Invite your guide to join you.

7. Open your spiritual senses to allow communication with your guide. Listen with your inner hearing, observe with your inner vision. Ask your guide to share with you whatever information he or she wishes to share.

8. When your spirit visitor appears ready to leave, thank him or her for coming to visit. Say good-bye in comfort and in joy, knowing that you can and will meet again.

9. Smell the clean, fresh air, and gaze at the beautiful flowers and trees in your garden. Gradually feel yourself rise from your bench. Step back, and feel yourself leaving the garden and returning to your physical location.

10. Become conscious of your breathing. Feel yourself back in your body, become conscious of your breathing. Wiggle your fingers and your toes, open your eyes.

> **Silver Cord**
>
> Among your spirit guides, there is generally one that is a dominant presence. He or she serves as the guardian who decides what other spirit contact to permit. In this gatekeeper role, your primary spirit guide "screens" your spirit visitors to keep you from being overwhelmed by contacts from spirit guests eager to visit with you. As you get to know your dominant spirit guide and become aware of his or her presence and interactions in your life, you'll know when your gatekeeper steps aside to allow other communication to come through. Mediums like Rita often observe this when doing readings.

Identifying Your Spirit Guide

Now it's time to put on your analytical thinking cap. Who is your spirit guide? What is his or her link to you, and what lessons is this guide in your life here to teach you? What information did your spirit guide share with you? Get your pen or pencil, and write down your impressions while they're still fresh in your mind. If you need more space than we've provided here, write your responses on a separate sheet of paper.

1. Did you get a clear image of your spirit guide? Describe the image.

   _____

   _____

   _____

2. Does your spirit guide seem familiar? Did you get a sense of a name or a place that might help to identify this spirit guide? Write down any words or images that came to you.

   _____

   _____

   _____

3. Did your spirit guide appear to be male or female? What physical characteristics could you sense? Write the most complete description that you can.

   _____

   _____

   _____

4. What kind of clothing was your spirit guide wearing? Did his or her clothes appear to be historical or contemporary?

   _____

   _____

   _____

5. What cultural heritage did your spirit guide appear to embody? Is this a culture similar to, or very different from, your own?

   _____

   _____

   _____

6. Did your spirit guide seem familiar, as though you've met before? Describe aspects that feel familiar.

   _____

   _____

   _____

7. Did your spirit guide speak to you? What did your guide say? Describe the guide's voice and what your guide said.

_____

_____

_____

8. Did your spirit guide tell you his or her name, or provide you with clues? Did you have a sense of a name or a word floating in your thoughts? Write down your impressions.

_____

_____

_____

9. What mannerisms did your spirit guide have? Did he or she make gestures, sit with legs crossed, or stand during the visit? Write down all that you can remember.

_____

_____

_____

10. Write down any other details about the visit.

_____

_____

_____

Cosmic Counsel

Rita's spirit guide Fra Angelico is an ever-present teacher who helps Rita refine and improve her technique and skill as a painter. She can ask Fra Angelico for help, or he can come through with inspiration. Spirit guides are with us to teach and help us learn. Your spirit guides can help you enhance the abilities and talents that you have, and even discover those that you didn't realize you had, but they cannot give you what you don't have. It is always your role and responsibility to develop your gifts and aptitudes and make the most of them.

Mediums and Messages

When Rita did a second exercise to meet her spirit guide, Fra Angelico appeared again. Rita expected the room that the monk created for their second meeting would look like the cell in a monastery, but instead it looked like a large, elegant dining room. In the center of the dining table was a bowl of fruit. When Fra Angelico walked into the room, Rita waited, extremely excited to talk with him, but the monk stopped to eat a pear. She said to him, "I am a painter." He smiled back and said, "I know." Rita said, "I paint with much larger brushes than you did." He chuckled and said, "I know that, too." Then in the meditation they walked over to one of Rita's paintings. She picked up a paint brush and his hand slipped over hers like a surgical glove, and their two hands painted together.

Life Lessons: A Directed Communication Exercise

You, too, can seek the counsel of your spirit guides. In the mediumship classes that she teaches, Rita uses the following exercise to help her students learn more about their spirit guides and the lessons they have come to teach. (The first three steps are the same ones you followed to establish contact with your spirit guides.)

1. Make yourself comfortable in a location where you won't have any distractions or interruptions.

2. Take three slow, deep breaths, in through your nose and out through your mouth. Let the first breath clear your body, let the second breath open your mind, and let the third breath free your spirit.

3. Consciously form the thought: "This is my time to be one with God and for God to be one with me." Set an intent to meet your spirit guide or teacher.

4. With your eyes closed, see yourself on a magnificent university campus. There are beautiful gardens and buildings made of white marble all around you. (You can close your eyes if this helps you concentrate, or focus your sight on a specific point.)

5. As you stand on this campus, you see many paths of white, crushed stone. You know that one of these paths is yours, and you start to walk it.

6. Walk your path until it takes you to a beautiful building with a grand staircase leading inside. Climb the staircase and enter the building.

7. Stand quietly in the building's entrance, waiting for instructions about where to go next. You will be directed to the room where you will meet your teacher, one who is guiding you from the higher side.

8. Go to this room, and enter it with an open mind. Have no expectations, no pre-conceived ideas about whom or what you will find in the room. Allow the room to unfold, and wait until someone else enters the room.

9. The person who joins you is your spirit guide, your teacher. Ask the guide what lesson you need to learn. A lesson will appear before you. Be still, stay in the quiet, and let the lesson become part of you.

10. When the lesson is complete, thank your spirit teacher, say good-bye, and know that you can and will meet again.

11. Walk back to the building's entry, go through the door to the outside, and walk down the beautiful staircase to the path that brought you here. Follow the path back to the edge of the campus. Look around you, see that the sun is high and the sky is blue, and all is well.

12. Become conscious of your breathing. Feel yourself back in your body, become conscious of your breathing. Wiggle your fingers and your toes, open your eyes.

Silver Cord

Cleansing breaths help to clear your energy so that you are refreshed and receptive to whatever experiences and messages await you in spirit communication. They also help re-ground you when the communication ends, so that you are once again fully and completely in the here and now.

Understanding the Lesson

Now, while your lesson is fresh in your mind, write down the images that came to you. This is often very much like interpreting your dreams. Images and concepts might be symbolic and representative rather than literal and direct.

1. Were you able to determine right away which path was yours to follow?

_____

_____

_____

2. What thoughts, emotions, or feelings did you experience when your spirit guide arrived and the lesson got underway?

_____

_____

_____

3. Did you get a clear image of who your spirit teacher was? Describe the image. If you completed the "Meet Your Spirit Guides" exercise earlier in this chapter, was this the same spirit guide that came to you then?

_____

_____

_____

4. Describe the lesson as it unfolded.

_____

_____

_____

5. Did the lesson make sense to you? Did it relate to something that you do in your life, such as your profession, a talent that you have, or a hobby or special interest?

_____

_____

_____

6. What images appeared in the lesson? Were there certain colors, sounds, or words?

_____

_____

_____

7. How did you participate in the lesson?

_____

_____

_____

8. Did you have questions during the lesson? Did you ask questions? Did you get answers? Did the answers make sense to you?

_____

_____

_____

9. What meaning does the lesson have for you right now?

_____

_____

_____

10. What aspects of the lesson will you want to explore further (such as through meditation, focused thinking, or writing in a journal) to try to understand their meanings or purposes?

_____

_____

_____

The Path of Spirit Progression

The help that spirit guides give us is invaluable. It can take us to levels of understanding, skill, and ability that would take much, much longer for us to achieve without their help. Often, this interaction is a two-way street; that is, spirit guides benefit, too. They are progressing and evolving on the higher side, moving along the paths of their soul-missions just as we are doing the same in the paths of our physical lives. Teaching and learning are flip sides of the same coin; it is impossible to separate one from the other. In teaching us, our spirit guides are also learning for themselves.

Feel the Energy!

Your spirit guides bring much positive energy into your life. All you have to do is plug into it, and its many advantages are yours for the taking. Keep your heart, mind, and spirit open to the energy, and it can be the ground swell that carries you to new heights. Their lessons and advice can be enlightening. And they can be fun, bringing you much joy. Let the energy be with you!

The Least You Need to Know

◆ Often, you are unaware of the presence of your spirit guides. But they are there, helping you in many ways.

◆ Most people have multiple spirit guides, with different guides taking the lead depending on what you're doing or what kind of help you need.

◆ You can invite your spirit guides to show themselves to you, so that you can meet them and know who they are.

◆ You can ask your spirit guides for specific help, and you can choose to decline advice and suggestions.

◆ Just as you learn from your spirit guides, your spirit guides can learn from you. This helps them evolve on the higher side.

Chapter 8

Earthbound Spirits

In This Chapter

- ◆ The mysteries of the Winchester mansion
- ◆ Recognizing earthbound spirits
- ◆ Identifying visiting spirits
- ◆ Why spirits visit and what messages they bring

In the decades framing the turn of the twentieth century, the heiress to the Winchester rifle fortune built an elaborately confusing mansion to hide from and fool the ghosts she was convinced were haunting her. But what some consider ghosts, we refer to as earthbound spirits. Often, they remain on the earth plane because they have unfinished business. In a location where people observe phenomena happening, there's always a reason the spirit has been unable to make its transition. Releasing the spirit is not a matter of "ghost-busting" to rid a house of an unwanted guest; it is a process of encouraging the spirit to move on and join loved ones on the higher side.

Most spirits that appear on the earth plane, however, come to us just for a visit, often to provide comfort and even to share in earthly joys such as the birth of a child, a wedding, or other life milestones. If you "feel" that someone you love who has passed over is with you, he or she probably is—and it is all about love, comfort, and healing.

A Perfect Life That Wasn't to Be

Most ghost stories have an element of tragedy to them. The spirits of people whose deaths were in some way untimely are unable to complete their transitions, and remain sadly and often noisily stuck in the middle. Such tales are told around campfires and at slumber parties. One such story is that of the Winchester mansion.

In 1860, the American Civil War was just getting underway when a small company that was soon to become the Winchester Repeating Arms Company developed the weapon that would forever change the hazards of the battlefield. The Henry rifle had a magazine that could load and fire a bullet every three seconds. The North's Union Army soon equipped its soldiers with this devastating weapon, and the man at the helm of Winchester Arms, Oliver Winchester, became instantly and phenomenally wealthy. Two years after the Henry rifle made its debut, Oliver's son William took a bride: Sarah Pardee.

William and Sarah seemed to have the perfect life ahead of them when Sarah gave birth to a daughter four years later. But even wealth and social status couldn't protect the fledgling family from the dangers of illness, and their baby Annie died not long after birth. The loss was more than Sarah could bear, and she slipped into the dark depths of depression where she remained for nearly 10 years. Sadly, it wasn't long after her return to normal life that tragedy struck again. Tuberculosis claimed William's life in 1881, leaving Sarah a widow and alone at age 42.

Sins of the Family

According to the lore surrounding Sarah Winchester's story, after several years of grieving that took her to the brink of depression again, Sarah consulted a medium. Although Sarah hoped to be reunited with her husband and daughter, the reunion wasn't quite what she anticipated. The medium claimed to make contact with William, but she brought the dire message from him that Sarah must use the vast fortune she inherited to atone for the sins of the Winchester family.

Sarah was to use her money to build a house where all of the spirits of those who died because of Winchester rifles could live for all eternity. She was to go West, the medium told her, until she found the location for this home. Because the Winchester fortune had accrued at a cost of countless lives, the medium said, Sarah was to dedicate the rest of her life to this endeavor.

Premonition _____

Although the message and instructions the medium gave to Sarah make for interesting storytelling, they should set off warning bells in your head. As we will caution you time and time again, spirit contact comes in goodness and healing, not for vengeance. There are many people (perhaps including Sarah herself, who reportedly was distressed to hear the wild tales people told about her) who believe that Sarah's eccentric construction project was the result of a mind and an imagination overwhelmed by grief and loss. When Sarah's safe was opened after her death, all it contained were the obituaries of her husband and daughter, and a locket of her daughter's hair.

Sarah packed her things and moved West in 1892, where she found and purchased a small farmhouse on 160 acres on the outskirts of San Jose, California, about 40 miles south of San Francisco. The house didn't stay small for long. With a $20 million inheritance and an income of $1,000 a day, Sarah began a building project that continued day in and day out, until her death in 1922. She even had a private railroad constructed to bring building materials and furnishings to the property. At that time, the house sprawled over 6 acres and had 160 rooms, some finished and some still under construction. Through the years that Sarah lived in it, the house was reported to have had more than 600 rooms built and then torn apart to make way for other rooms!

Dead-End Doorways and Stairways to Nowhere

The most important room in Sarah's mansion was the séance room, where she went every day to commune with the spirits who told her what to build next. The Winchester mansion's séance room was hidden deep in the center of the sprawling house. It had just one entrance but three ways out. One exit was through the door leading into the room, one through a closet and then a door with a knob only on the side of the séance room, and another that opened to a 10-foot drop into the kitchen below.

At some point, Sarah's focus shifted from constructing a spirit sanctuary to building a safe haven for herself, apparently for protection from the ire of spirits angry at her and her husband's family for designing and producing the instruments of their deaths.

The house was filled with stairways—40, by one count—that often went nowhere. One contained 42 steps that only rose 9 feet because each step was just 2 inches tall. Another stairway climbed to the ceiling, with no door at the top. There were doors that opened to walls or to drop-offs either to other rooms or to the outside. Chimneys rose to within feet of ceilings and then stopped, or extended beyond the roof but connected to nothing within the house. Sarah reportedly slept in a different bedroom every night, choosing—apparently at random—from among 25 or so bedrooms in the house.

Thirteen ... Everywhere!

Many structures within the Winchester mansion reflected Sarah's fascination with the number 13. There were 13 hooks in the séance room, upon which hung the 13 robes of different colors that Sarah wore while communing with the spirits. Windows inside and out contained 13 panes of glass; stairways had 13 steps. Sink drains had 13 holes, and chandeliers held 13 lights. The house had 13 bathrooms. Even Sarah's will continued the pattern, containing 13 pages.

No one really knows why the number 13, traditionally viewed as unlucky, captivated Sarah to such an extent. It remains, along with the many other oddities of the mansion she built, a mystery. Today, the Winchester house is registered as a California historical landmark and is open for tours. Appendix B provides contact information.

For all of her eccentricities, Sarah Winchester had a generous and giving spirit. In 1909, Sarah donated half a million dollars to the Connecticut General Hospital Society to build a tuberculosis hospital in memory of her husband, who died of the disease. The facility Sarah's ongoing donations built, a tuberculosis sanitarium called the William Wirt Winchester Hospital, outlived the disease it was designed to treat. Today, nearly a century later, the New Winchester Chest Clinic continues as an affiliation with Yale University's School of Medicine to provide medical care for patients with a wide variety of lung and chest ailments.

Paranormal Phenomena: Is It a Haunting?

Paranormal phenomena are amazingly common. Among the people you count as your friends and even family, we'd bet that more of them than not have experienced what they believe to be ghosts. "I was walking through the hallway when suddenly there was a young girl standing there, just standing there looking at me!" says Aunt Sue at dinner one evening. Or your friend Jonathan confides, "It was eerie, man, but there was this guy standing in the hallway and when I said 'hey' to him, he just faded away!"

Are such experiences hauntings? It is possible that they are contacts with *earthbound spirits*. And that's all that a haunting is: The presence of earthbound spirits. The phenomena that manifest as a result could be the spirit's attempt to gain attention. It might be because the spirit is angry about something, such as having passed before feeling ready, or angry at a particular person about events that took place before the spirit's physical death. It could also be the spirit's attempt to ask for help in completing its transition. A spirit that feels trapped isn't necessarily going to have the best communication skills! Think about it: When you are confused, angry, or hurt, you also don't think, speak, or act with great clarity.

Spiritology

Paranormal phenomena are the events and sensations people attribute to the presence of "ghosts," such as unusual sounds and sights for which there are no obvious explanations. An **earthbound spirit** is a spirit existing between the earth plane and the higher side, commonly referred to as a ghost.

As a Spiritualist medium, Rita is often called upon to visit houses where people feel there are hauntings. In one house she was asked to visit, Rita and the others with her could feel a heaviness as soon as they entered. It was as though the air itself was heavy, and it was difficult to breathe. The house's new owner had a similar response and had become afraid to go into certain rooms where the sensation was particularly strong.

Rita and her group sensed the presence of a man, a woman, and two children. They felt that the man was very angry and abusive, and that he had locked the woman and the children in the attic—the room in the house where the unpleasant energy was the strongest. Rita and her group prayed and felt they released the earthbound spirits in the house to move on to the light. The house's owner felt an immediate shift in the energy throughout the house, and was vastly relieved.

Six months later, the owner called Rita and her group back, saying that the earthbound spirit had returned, as a threatening presence. To the group's surprise, the negative energy was indeed back—and much stronger. Rita and her colleagues finally realized that this negative energy surged when the homeowner, a woman, was home alone, with her husband away. It became clear that the earthbound spirit was very strong and defiant, and could hide at will. An abuser in his physical life, this spirit had developed a pattern of behavior that made him extraordinarily abusive when he was alone with his wife and children, yet outwardly ordinary when others were present. It took three visits for Rita's group to finally release the damaged spirit, so he could complete his transition to the higher side—where, presumably, he had a lot of work to do.

Apparitions and Visions

You've probably experienced visual manifestations of spirit presence—a flash that you see out of the corner of your eye, a shadowy figure that appears and then disappears, perhaps even a clear image of a loved one who has passed. *Apparitions* are among the most common experiences people have among paranormal phenomena. Sometimes apparitions just appear and then disappear, while other times the spirit's image remains to engage in communication of some sort. Often, making a visual appearance is a spirit's way of saying, "See! It's really me!" to validate or authenticate its identity.

Did You Hear That?

From footsteps to moans and cries, the sounds of spirits tend to frighten people more than visual images because there is more of a mystery to them. When you can see something, it takes on a level of tangibility regardless of whether you can actually reach out to touch it. When you hear something that doesn't seem real, you find yourself questioning it. What is it? Is it harmful?

Sounds and noises are simply other ways in which energy becomes tangible. They activate a physical sense in you—hearing—that gets your attention. Sometimes this is the only means by which a spirit chooses to communicate with you, while other times the spirit might subsequently appear as a visual image as well.

I Didn't Touch It!

One of Rita's friends was among the early casualties of the AIDS epidemic. A fun-loving prankster in physical life, Richard wasn't about to let his friends mope about his passing—or celebrate the joys in their lives without him. He wanted to make sure they knew he was still with them. At a dinner party, he filled the air with the fragrance and sensation of rich Godiva chocolate—his favorite indulgence. Rita returned to her painting studio one evening to find a doll sitting on the top of a canvas that was hanging nine feet above the floor, posed exactly as the figure in the portrait! Spirits often move objects around to let you know they're there, and to let you know who they are.

Why a Spirit Stays

Spirits generally remain earthbound when they have not accepted their passings. Perhaps the spirit's physical life came to a sudden end as the result of an accident or an act of violence, leaving the spirit confused about where it belongs. Sometimes the spirit cannot let go of its earth plane existence, either afraid to complete passage to the higher side or unwilling to release its connection to a loved one still on the earth plane. While we tend to think of earthbound spirits as "trapped," they're really just in need of help to make the transition from the physical world to the spirit world.

This doesn't do much to advance the spirit's progression and evolution, of course. It's as though the spirit is treading water, so to speak. An earthbound spirit doesn't necessarily choose to resist passage (although some spirits do); it just doesn't realize it has the choice to continue the passage. There are circumstances and events in your life that leave you feeling confused and unsure of what to do next; imagine the confusion and uncertainty you might feel if you were suddenly uprooted from the existence that's become familiar!

Sometimes a spirit has unfinished business on the earth plane, especially if physical death came unexpectedly. A spirit might want to guide a surviving spouse or partner through the difficult decisions that accompany physical death, such as making funeral arrangements or wrapping up financial loose ends. We don't usually think of such a spirit as earthbound in the traditional sense; once the unfinished business is completed, the spirit will feel free to move on in its transition.

Just Visiting

Sometimes spirits just like to visit, to let you know they are fine and to stay in touch with you, like your earth plane friends and family do. At first, this kind of contact can be disconcerting, as it was for one family whose son Jeff passed tragically and unexpectedly as a young adult. Although the family was stunned and grieving, they also remembered with great joy the happiness and delight the fun-loving young man had brought into their lives. They often reminisced about his kind and generous nature.

Not long after Jeff's passing, family members started noticing phenomena. The flowers on the dining room table seemed to be in a different place every time someone came into the room. Sometimes, there were voices and noises that sounded like Jeff and his friends had come over for an afternoon of socializing, as had often been the case during his life. The family called Rita and planned a time for her to come to their house to verify whether these phenomena were indeed communications from Jeff.

When Rita entered the home, she anticipated that she would encounter the energy of an earthbound spirit, the young man's spirit. She did her opening prayers, and then began walking through the house. Much to her surprise, joyous spirits filled the house. Many, many relatives and friends were there, strong presences that felt like they were gathered to celebrate a momentous occasion.

Rita shared her perceptions with the family, who was overjoyed. They all began talking about Jeff, when suddenly something caught Rita's attention and she pointed to the dining room table. "Do you see the flowers moving?" she asked. The family members nodded. This was one of the phenomena they saw frequently.

At the family's invitation, Rita opened herself to contact with the spirits who were present. The first to come through was Jeff's grandfather who gave such a full description of himself that his identity was undeniable. Over the course of the next few hours, no fewer than a dozen of the young man's relatives and friends came through with messages of love and thanks.

Later in the evening, as Rita sat talking with the family, each time she mentioned the grandfather she would hear the sound of tinkling glass, like wind blowing through a chandelier. After this happened a few times, the mother asked Rita if she could hear the sound and Rita realized that everyone in the room could hear it. Everyone was very excited; this was yet another validation. The tinkling sounds continued through the evening, as if in response to the conversation.

As Rita was getting ready to leave, the young man's mother gently touched her arm. "Can you tell me who held Jeff's hand when he made the crossing?" she asked. Rita put the question out. To everyone's surprise, the spirit who came through was a woman, the mother of a friend. The woman had been very ill in the months before her death, and Jeff had visited her most afternoons. When Jeff passed, it was this woman's spirit who reached out to take his hand, to ease and guide his passage to the higher side.

Silver Cord

Spirits sometimes visit to offer comfort in times of sadness, encouragement when times are tough, and healing energy when you are injured or ill (physically or emotionally). You might feel this contact as a gentle touch, a breeze, or even a surge of energy. It is for you; it is to help you. Welcome these contacts, and give thanks to those who bring them to you.

Advice and Warning

"Don't step off the curb!" shouts a voice in your head, and, startled, you hesitate, one foot floating just above the street. The crosswalk light is green for pedestrians; why shouldn't you cross? Then, from nowhere, a car screams into the intersection, running the red light. Had you started across the street, you'd now be a hood ornament. Give thanks to your spirit guides and spirit visitors!

Advice and caution from those on the higher side can take many forms, and often influences your actions without your awareness. You might "just have a bad feeling" about someone who smiles at you in the coffee shop and leave without getting your morning latte, then read the next day in the newspaper that the person held the shop's customers hostage at gunpoint for four hours. Or you might decide to buy a newspaper from a street-corner vendor, even though there's one waiting on your doorstep at home, then open it to find an ad for an apartment that's just what you're looking for ... and you get it because you're the first one to call. Coincidence? We don't think so!

Helping an Earthbound Spirit Find Release

Movies have made millions, even billions, of dollars from the "ghost-busters" theme, crafting stories around every imaginable twist and turn. But the real issue isn't "busting" wandering spirits so they're no longer nuisances in the physical world. It is helping them to complete their transitions, so they can move on to the next phase of their evolution and growth as spirits.

When an earthbound spirit is present, you often feel a sense of heaviness in the air. You might get goose bumps, and feel like you need to leave right away—the "uh-oh" feeling. It's important to pay attention to these messages; they are warnings. Earthbound spirits are troubled and confused, and need help to cross to the other side, where they should be.

We on the earth plane can help earthbound spirits break free from whatever is holding them. Just as with all spirit contact, it is important to do this with the highest intent and with divine protection. Do not embark on this alone; even experienced mediums go in groups when called upon to help earthbound spirits find release. Instead, seek help from a professional who is consistent with your belief system—clergy, shaman, medium.

And remember, many so-called hauntings are nothing more than visits from spirit friends and relatives who just want to stay in touch with you! They might have messages of advice or comfort for you, or might simply want to let you know that they are well and still connected with your life, even though they are no longer in physical forms.

Enjoying the Company of Spirits

Your loved ones who enjoyed sharing the adventures of your life when they were on the earth plane want to continue enjoying that sharing, even though they can't be with you physically. They come in and out of your life at will, free to move between the spirit world and the earth plane. They are not earthbound, but simply come to visit you and to remain a part of your daily life—even if you're not aware of their presence. And if you do sense that the spirit of great-grandmother Maria or Uncle Sylvester is admiring your new baby or your new house, smile!

The Least You Need to Know

- ◆ The Winchester mansion remains a great and entertaining mystery. No one really knows why Sarah Winchester built this convoluted and sprawling structure.

- ◆ Many "hauntings" are simply visiting spirits who bring messages of love and comfort. It is never their intent to frighten you.

- ◆ A spirit might become earthbound when its physical life ended with significant unfinished business.

- ◆ Visiting spirits come and go freely. They are not bound to the earth plane but visit as they please.

Part  3

Invoking the Spirits

Spirit communication often is highly symbolic, as are dreams. This can make it challenging to figure out the true meaning of the connection. Often, it isn't what it seems—but it is always something that you need to hear or receive.

The chapters in this part explore the symbolism of spirit communication and provide information about the skills it takes to allow spirit communication to take place. Exercises give you opportunities to practice your abilities.

Incoming Messages

In This Chapter

- ◆ Recognizing spirit contact
- ◆ Confirming spirit identity
- ◆ Defining your intent and limits
- ◆ Clarifying confusing messages

It's an important day in your life—could be a graduation, a wedding, the birth of a child, or any event of significance. You retreat to a favorite quiet space to regroup and prepare yourself, and suddenly you feel like the room is full of people, even though clearly you are alone. You might even experience the sensation of hearing voices or seeing people sitting or standing around, even though you know no one else is there. What gives?

Don't worry … you're not hallucinating or losing your mind. It's just your spirit support team, here to give you loving advice! Significant life events require great energy—physical, emotional, and psychical. Just as your earth plane friends might rally around to give you strength and support, so, too, might spirit visitors from the higher side.

Picking Up the Signals

When you perceive a spirit presence, it's no accident. It might be just the spirit of a loved one who wants to drop by to say hi, taking joy in your new, heightened awareness of existence beyond the earth plane. Often, spirits have been around you for much longer than you recognize, just waiting for you to reach a point of openness that permits you to know of their presence.

It's for You!

Just as your friends and family here on the earth plane drop in or telephone, the spirits of loved ones on the other side like to come by for a visit now and then. You might sense a loved one's spirit presence when you are engaged in an activity that you and your loved one enjoyed together when you were both on the earth plane, such as hiking or riding a motorcycle or working in the garden. Or you might have the feeling of a loved one patting you on the back for a job well done, or giving you a hug of comfort during a difficult time.

How do you know that this is a loved one and not a spirit guide (which we discussed in Chapter 7)? Sometimes it might be hard for you to tell, but generally your spirit guide is present to provide specific expertise and a loved one's spirit comes to give loving advice. Of course, if a loved one had a particular expertise that you happen to need, you could end up with the loved one's spirit serving as a spirit guide! By and large, the spirits of friends and family visit just as friends and family might visit on the earth plane.

Robin brought her young daughter Lilly to the Angel's Loft to have her spirit guide drawn. A drawing started to appear on the paper of a youngish woman, about 30. Robin recognized the woman from photographs she'd seen of her mother-in-law, who indeed had passed to spirit at a young age. When she brought the spirit drawing home her husband Richard gasped, speechless. He truly felt his mother present, guiding their daughter Lilly.

Many people find that their relationships with friends and family in spirit become deeper and more connected as spirit contact continues. Perhaps you were unable to form the kind of relationship that you wanted to have with your father or your sister in the physical world. As a spirit evolves on the higher side, he or she learns lessons that, for whatever reasons, couldn't be completed during physical life. On the higher side these lessons become apparent, and the spirit progresses in understanding and knowledge.

Silver Cord

Part of the healing that can take place through spirit contact is a mending of rifts that existed on the earth plane, allowing the relationship to evolve. You might also gain knowledge and understanding, and feel closer to your father or your sister in this spirit relationship than you did in your physical world relationship.

Who's There?

How do you know who is trying to make contact? This can be a great challenge. When you are working with a medium, the spirit will convey images and impressions intended to give you indisputable evidence of his or her identity. Many spirits that come through to Rita begin by sharing the experiences of their passings. These details are generally easy to verify. The spirit might then offer pieces of information that only you, the loved one on the earth plane, could know or would understand.

Rita once held a circle to communicate with spirit loved ones of a group of friends. Because Rita knew each of these people quite well, when she opened the circle with a prayer and established intent, she asked that each spirit give some piece of information that she couldn't already know. One by one, spirit visitors came through to greet the friends in the circle. When it came to Rita's husband David, it was his father who came through and showed himself sitting in a canoe. Rita immediately told her husband, "But this isn't the canoe we used to use," referring to family canoe trips they used to take.

David asked what the canoe looked like, and Rita said it was green with wood trim. David then asked what color of green, and Rita replied, "God-awful house paint green." David was stunned. When he was 16, he'd brought a canoe home from camp. The first thing his father said to him was, "Where did you get that God-awful house paint green canoe?"

This single detail became the validating comment for David, who until that time had been quite a skeptic about spirit communication. It is this level of detail that you should expect when a spirit claims to be coming through for you. Irrefutable identification is just that: There is no mistaking the message as something else!

Making a correct spirit identification isn't always this easy or straightforward. It's important to accept, at first, the information that comes to you without attempting to pin down an identity or shape the information to meet an assumption or expectation. Sometimes the spirit coming through is a distant relative that you might not recognize at first, or a person outside your family. You might need to look through photos, search your memory, and even talk with other people before you are able to figure out the visiting spirit's identity. When you do finally make the connection, however, there will be no question in your mind about the spirit's identity!

Establishing Intent

Establishing intent is about making it clear why you are seeking spirit contact. You are asking for divine assistance and protection. And you are agreeing to proceed with an open mind, heart, and spirit, receptive to the spirits that choose to communicate with you and to the messages that they bring.

Establishing intent is not, as people sometimes misunderstand, about asking for contact with specific spirits or for specific information. You can do either of these, of course. But you may or may not get what you ask for. Only when you free yourself from the limitations of expectations will you be able to receive what the spirits are showing or bringing you.

Mediums and Messages

Rita, like most mediums, begins every spirit contact with a prayer to establish intent, welcome the divine, and invite the light. This reminds those on the earth plane who are participating in the spirit communication of the special and divine nature of the contact, and puts out positive energy signals to the higher side to attract positive energy in response.

Fear Not ... These Are Friendly Forces

It's natural to be afraid in unfamiliar circumstances. It might scare you to realize that you have visitors from the higher side, if you're not accustomed to being aware of their presence. But these visitors are in fact familiar to you—just not in the ways you might be expecting. Your spirit guests show up to give you support, encouragement, and sometimes just company. There is no reason to be fearful.

If you continue to feel afraid, you need to look for the reason. Are you in a strange location? Is there something about the circumstances that is activating a psychical alarm within you? Is this an intuition alert that something isn't quite right? It's important to pay attention to these signals, and to respond appropriately. Always remember: Spirit visitors don't come through to scare you.

Physical Phenomena

Spirits might choose to use physical phenomena to make their presence known to you. You might see shadows, flashes of light, objects moving (or objects having been moved). You might hear voices or other sounds, or feel a touch. Spirits love to work with electrical appliances, and they will sometimes turn them on and off with only the use of "spiritual remote" or spirit energy. Spirits choose the means of contact that is most likely to be effective. If you are by nature skeptical, the contact is likely to be bold and unmistakable so it catches and keeps your attention. A visiting spirit might appear as a full and complete image standing in your hallway or sitting at your kitchen table, knowing that you will immediately recognize his or her image and identity.

If you are accustomed to spirit contact and familiar with the spirits who visit you, the physical phenomena might be subtle. You might wake up in the morning to the smell of coffee brewing when you don't own a coffeepot, and instantly think of your grandmother who used to drink a dozen cups a day. You might come home from work and automatically throw your jacket over the back of a kitchen chair, only to have it land on the floor because the chair has been neatly pushed against the table—not where you expected it to be.

Some forms of physical phenomena are quite sophisticated or specialized, such as spirit drawing and automatic writing. These are typically phenomena that manifest to mediums (and can manifest to you when your mediumistic abilities are activated), or may come to you because you have an ability that allows you to use them. We discuss these phenomena in Chapter 10.

Mental Phenomena

Mental phenomena make use of your psychical, or spiritual, senses: clairvoyance (inner vision), clairaudience (inner hearing), and clairsentience (inner sensing or knowing). It is sometimes harder to recognize mental phenomena as spirit contact because your mind is the screen upon which so many of the interactions of your life play out. These phenomena can be extraordinarily lucid, and yet you know full well they are not "real"—that is, that they are not happening in the realm of the tangible world. It's more about you sensing them, even as they play out in such vivid detail that they feel real.

You might worry that these experiences are nothing more than the products of your (active) imagination, or even dismiss them as such. At first, spirit communication does feel like imagination! Rita tells her mediumship students to think of it like learning to play the piano. When you first start, you hit a lot of wrong notes. Maybe even more wrong notes than the right ones! But as you play more, you get better. You hit fewer wrong notes, and those that you do hit are more obvious. You correct them immediately, and the next time you play them right.

The same process unfolds with spirit contact. At first, it all seems like imagination or like wishful thinking. Of course the image of your close friend Connie is in your head; you love her and miss her now that she's passed to the higher side. And it makes sense to have this little internal dialogue going with her. After all, the two of you could talk for hours. You must be just remembering conversations that once took place. But then it occurs to you that the dialogue is actually about something that occurred *after* Connie's passing, something current. It feels, in fact, as though you and Connie are having a real-time conversation.

Silver Cord

It's the minutiae, the detail, that makes this real, that makes it clear that this is spirit contact and communication. Not, "Your mother used to bake cakes," but, "Your mother always used Duncan Hines cake mixes."

This is the point at which you begin to realize that this goes beyond your imagination. Could it be that you truly are communicating with Connie? "Yes, of course, dearie!" comes the response, in Connie's unmistakable tone and with the nickname for you that only she could get away with using. Yes, you could've imagined the whole thing. But you know you didn't. This is not just your imagination.

Setting Limits

You don't have to accept spirit contact just because it's there, any more than you have to answer the telephone because it's ringing. (Likewise, spirits don't have to accept your "calls" when you want to make contact.) But how often will you let a telephone ring? Most of us jump to answer, no matter what we're doing! Learning to just let it ring is a key lesson in taking control of your life. And so it is with spirit contact. Just because Connie wants to chat doesn't mean you have to let her in. You can refuse spirit contact by gently and kindly asking that she come back when you're finished with whatever is keeping you busy at the time. You might even want to say this out loud. If the message is important, such as a warning of some sort, the spirit will persist and you'll have little choice but to notice. But for most other communication, your spirit visitors will simply call again.

When it is you who is initiating spirit contact, a good opportunity to set your limits is when you establish intent. As you invite divine light, request the limits that you desire. Rita establishes limits around how much she is willing to physically feel through spirit. She will allow a tingling sensation in the affected part of the body that took the spirit to the higher side, but she will not accept any sensations that go deep enough to cause discomfort or pain. This arises from her first experience as a medium, in which she so strongly felt the spirit's passing from a heart attack that she felt like her own heart was about to explode. Her teacher immediately intervened, and from that time on Rita established limits with her spirit helpers as to what she was willing to accept.

Your limit range might be "please respect the time I've set aside for family" or "let's communicate after I finish my work." Sometimes spirits want to come to you at night when you are sleeping, because people are more receptive in the dream state or in the altered state of sleep. Setting limits helps define and shape the spirit signals that come to you. A spirit cannot make or continue contact unless you allow it, although you might need to articulate your desires to make them clear.

Sometimes spirit messages come in fast and furious, and you might want to shelter your receptiveness. Or there are times when you don't want to be disturbed. You can establish a boundary of protection—what Rita calls "closing the door but not locking it." This lets your spirit guides know that if there is an urgent message, they can still reach you. But otherwise, you don't want to be disturbed for the defined time. Begin by saying prayers of your understanding and surrounding yourself with white light. Some people see this as a tower, others see it as a globe, and still others see it as a pyramid.

> **CAUTION**
>
> **Premonition** ___
>
> If ever you feel uncomfortable during a spirit contact, break off the contact immediately. Say out loud, "This contact is over!" Just as you wouldn't continue an interaction with a physical entity if it made you uncomfortable, don't do so with a spirit entity. If you are in a class, ask the teacher for help rather than disrupting the circle.

Many times, spirit communication is brief and self-limiting. A spirit breezes in for a chat and breezes right back out again. When you've had a more extended spirit visit, you can end the contact by saying good-bye, just as you might end a visit with any friend. It's nice to thank the spirit for visiting and sharing with you. Sometimes the spirit just leaves, and you know he or she is gone even though neither of you brought the visit to a formal end.

Cosmic Clutter and Spirit Static

When you think about it, there's really a lot of communication taking place between the earth plane and the higher side. How do you know how much of it is relevant to you? At first, signals from the higher side can be confusing. This newly awakened receptiveness in you is eager to accept whatever comes its way. But like a radio that receives a dozen signals on the same frequency, there can be so many signals coming through that they overwhelm your ability to sort and understand them.

Often, your lead spirit guide will screen these signals on your behalf. Your spirit guide might block the irrelevant signals and restrict the relevant ones to times and settings in which you can be receptive. A medium can function in a similar way, accepting one spirit at a time to come through with his or her message.

Psychic Confusion

It is possible to confuse psychic contact with mediumistic contact, particularly if a medium is making contact on your behalf. This is why it is so important for you to establish your intent to be open to whatever will be, and to try to clear your mind of expectations. A good psychic (and all good mediums are good psychics) will receive the psychical signals of your expectations, which can cloud mediumistic signals. Instead of allowing Uncle Jack to come through because that's who's there with a message, the medium might get the image of your husband Joe because that's who's on your mind.

Does the message or communication from the spirit seem oddly jumbled or not quite right? When you experience confusion, you need to step back and sort things out. You might end the spirit contact for the time being and think things through in your mind. Try writing down your impressions. Put them away for a day or two, and then look at them again. Consider these questions:

- Are there inconsistencies that jump out at you?
- Can you detect fragments of identifying characteristics that point to different people?
- Who's been on your mind lately?
- Are you truly open to receiving whomever comes through, or do you have your heart set on making contact with someone in particular?
- What do you want to have happen or what do you desire from this contact?

When you try again to establish a connection, speak your intent out loud. If you truly want to make contact with a specific spirit, make that part of your intent. It may or may not happen, depending on whether the spirit wants to make contact with you, but at least your desire for the contact is out there and the focus of your mind is now consistent with your intent.

Resolving Fear and Apprehension

A little apprehension is normal whenever you are doing something that is important to you or that you are unsure about. But you should also feel excited and happy about establishing communication with spirits on the higher side. Doing so gives you wonderful opportunities to feel the love and healing that those on the higher side want to extend to you.

If you are fearful about spirit contact, try to identify what worries or frightens you. Write it down or speak it out loud, so it is out there in a tangible way. Then you can explore why you feel the way you do. Seek the services of a professional medium who can make contact on your behalf and help you understand the messages that come through for you.

The Gift That Keeps Giving

Spirit communication is the ultimate gift of love. It establishes that there is in fact life beyond physical death, and that what matters to us in our physical lives has value in the bigger picture of existence. It gives us comfort, healing and knowledge, enriching our lives on the earth plane. Spirit communication also shows us that the connections that bring pleasure and joy to our souls continue, unlimited by the borders of physical existence.

The Least You Need to Know

- ◆ Spirits use various methods to make themselves known to you.
- ◆ Physical phenomena take place in tangible ways, such as objects that move.
- ◆ Mental phenomena take place in your mind, without outward manifestations.
- ◆ At first, it's natural to be uncertain whether your experiences are imagination or spirit communication.
- ◆ You are always in control of spirit contact.

Chapter **10**

A Little Help from the Pros

In This Chapter

◆ Determining a medium's qualifications

◆ The medium's view of spirit communication

◆ What it's like to have a reading

◆ How to steer clear of fakes and frauds

◆ Healing through spirit contact

If this is *your* loved one, why would you need an intermediary—a medium—for communication between the two of you to take place? You don't, always; many people enjoy regular and ongoing communication with loved ones who have passed to the other side. But spirit contact is often subtle. Communication on the spirit plane is much different than here on the earth plane, and it often requires the assistance of an "interpreter" to get messages through—going both directions.

Just as it isn't always easy for us to get a good connection with those on the other side, it's sometimes challenging for spirits to communicate with us in ways that make sense in our physical world. Mediums have highly developed abilities in these areas, and put their skills to use to help those of us on the earth plane make contact with loved ones on the other side.

Medium, Well Done

From accountants to writers, most professionals complete some sort of specialized education and training that gives them the core qualifications they need to work in their fields. This establishes a certain level of consistency, at least in theory, about the professional's capabilities and proficiency. When you go to a doctor or a lawyer, you can assume that there is a certain baseline of education and expertise in place. Doctors, lawyers, and many other professionals must pass certain certification or licensing tests before the law allows them to be in practice.

Being a good medium requires a blend of psychical skill, book knowledge, and practice. There is much more to spirit contact than simply putting yourself out there as a conduit for spirit energy! A medium must know how to handle situations that might arise from the spirit world as well as from the physical world. Spirit communication is often intense for those involved—you, the spirit visitor, and the medium. Many mediums have some background in counseling or psychology, which gives them additional skills for helping people deal with the information that comes through as well as grief.

When considering the services of a medium, ask about the medium's education and experience (more about choosing a medium a little later in this chapter). Both are important; it is through their blending that a medium acquires expertise.

Training and Experience

Good mediums spend considerable time learning and refining their skills and abilities. There are a number of schools and organizations throughout the world that provide teaching for mediums. (Appendix B lists some of them.) Such programs teach not only mediumistic skills but also knowledge, concepts, and theories about matters of the spirit and existence. Some programs are structured to take a certain amount of time, while others are self-paced and designed to accommodate people who also have other activities in their lives.

> **CAUTION**
> **Premonition** _____
>
> In most locations in the United States, there are no laws that regulate the qualifications of mediums (beyond the general laws that apply to anyone in any kind of business, of course). It doesn't hurt to check with your local Better Business Bureau and your state's Office of the Attorney General to see whether there are complaints about the medium you are choosing.

Many mediums also teach mediumship classes (as Rita does). Not only does this extend their expertise to those new to mediumship, but it also helps them to keep their own skills sharp. In so many ways, the best way to learn is to teach!

Finding the Medium Who Is Right for You

The best way to find a good medium is to work through a source that you trust. If you have friends in metaphysical fields, start by asking for their recommendations. Schedule appointments to meet with several mediums, either by phone or in person, so you can understand the medium's training, experience, and expertise. Ask questions such as:

◆ Have you received formal training in mediumship? If so, where?

◆ Are you affiliated with any organizations or groups, such as the Spiritualist Church, Church of the Divine Man, a metaphysical center or college, or other faith-based structures?

◆ How long have you been a practicing medium?

◆ How many readings do you do in a week or a month?

◆ How would you describe your mediumistic approach?

◆ What other education, experience, and background do you have?

◆ What do you charge for your services?

Often, the answers you get will lead you to other questions and discussion. And pay attention to your intuition! Are you feeling that this is someone you want to work with? Keep in mind that this person could connect you with very powerful and personal messages. Do you have a sense of trust when you talk to this person?

You might feel that you just know this is the right medium for you, and that is good. But if you are new to this, it's to your advantage to at least go through the same conversation with other mediums recommended to you. It's also smart to ask for the names of references that you can contact. This gives you a broader base of information from which to make your decision.

> **Silver Cord**
>
> At the end of your interview with a prospective medium, ask for three professional references that you can contact. Then contact them! Ask very generally about the medium's skills, and let the person talk.

What a Medium Experiences During Spirit Communication

Spirits manifest themselves to mediums in different ways, and each medium has a different way of experiencing spirit contacts. Most mediums have a dominant mode—clairvoyant (psychic sight), clairsentient (psychic intuition), or clairaudient (psychic hearing)—through which they experience spirit contact. This is the psychical, or spiritual, sense through which a spirit first makes contact.

For Rita, spirit contact often begins as a blend of clairvoyance and clairsentience. The first information to come through is usually an awareness of how the person appeared in physical life, such as whether it was a man or a woman, and how the person passed to the other side. She often can feel how tall the person was in physical life, and she feels the person's weight as though her body is growing larger or smaller. Then she typically feels the condition of passing, which expresses itself as a twinge in the related part of her body. Finally, all of Rita's inner, or psychic, senses become activated to provide full information about the person.

Other mediums might work differently based on what gifts they have. Spirits will use whatever abilities and talents the medium has, and use them in ways that are comparable to the medium in terms of intellectual and emotional development. It's important to remember that the medium's abilities, interests, and biases all influence the messages that the medium brings through. A good medium will tell you this up front and again and again, reminding you to put the information you receive into the framework of *your* life.

The medium should not ask a lot of questions about you before doing a reading. The less the medium knows about you, the more confident you can be that the information coming through is genuine.

Special Forms of Spirit Communication

Spirits can be quite creative when it comes to finding ways to communicate. Activating psychical senses sometimes isn't enough; the spirit desires a more tangible impression. These techniques require practice, practice, practice for the medium to become truly skilled.

Automatic Writing

In automatic writing, the spirit takes control of the medium's hand to move a pen or a pencil across paper. (Some modern mediums even use computers—automatic typing!)

The message might be in a language other than those the medium speaks. The handwriting is often strikingly different from the medium's handwriting, and might be difficult to read or even illegible. It takes great patience for a medium to develop adeptness with automatic writing. Compared to psychical abilities such as clairsentience, automatic writing is quite slow and tedious. But some spirits prefer this means of communication.

Sometimes, automatic writing is your first clue that you have mediumistic abilities. You might be sitting there doodling when suddenly the pen takes off on what seems to be its own accord and begins forming symbols or words. Go with the flow! With much practice, automatic writing can become a tool of communication for you. Those who are skilled in automatic writing often blend it with other psychical skills, and develop a system of asking questions and receiving answers. More typically, automatic writing conveys messages that the spirit simply wants to deliver.

Spirit Drawing

Spirit drawing is Rita's special expertise. A spirit comes through to her, and her spirit guides use her artistic talent to draw the spirit's image. A spirit drawing presents a visual likeness of the spirit as he or she is showing at the time, which can be younger or even older than the person was at the time of passing. Spirits tend to show themselves either as they know you will recognize them, or as they want you to see them.

The latter was the case when Rita did a spirit drawing of her co-author Debbie's father. When Debbie first saw the drawing, she felt disappointment. Some of the features looked like her father, but overall the drawing wasn't what she remembered. So Debbie started going through the pictures she had of her father, from his childhood through the year of his passing. Nothing really matched up.

Disappointed, Debbie started putting everything back. She picked up a stack of pictures and papers, and a newspaper clipping fell out and landed in her lap: a faded photograph of Debbie's father, exactly the image in Rita's spirit drawing! Debbie's father directed Rita to produce an image of himself that he preferred, and that he wanted to convey to Debbie. He wanted Debbie to see him not only as her father, but in the larger context of his experience of life.

For many people, spirit drawings are the ultimate evidence of the continuity of life. There is nothing quite like the feeling that rushes through you when you see the image of a loved one appear at the hands of someone who could not possibly know what this person looked like. As the cliché goes, sometimes a picture is worth a thousand words.

Rita and Debbie live on opposite coasts, so Rita did Debbie's reading by telephone and then mailed the spirit drawing to her. Debbie's father chose to present himself in a way that was at first unfamiliar to Debbie but as he was familiar to his friends. The drawing didn't match any of Debbie's photos, but turned out to be an amazing likeness of a photo from an old newspaper clipping.

Psychometry

Although we have an entire chapter about psychometry later in this book (see Chapter 16), since it is a psychical skill with widespread applications, we want to touch on this important mediumistic form here. Psychometry is the ability to read the energy imprints of objects that can act as springboards for the medium to connect with the spirits to whom the energy belongs. A medium might hold a set of keys, for example, and sense the energy of the person who once carried them. This can generate an energy message, so to speak, that travels into the universe like a beckoning wave. When the spirit responds, the medium can establish connection and communication.

Transfiguration

During transfiguration, the medium's features take on the image of the spirit that is coming through. The spirit uses ectoplasm, a tangible substance created from the energy field that surrounds the spirit, to superimpose its image over the medium's. Transfiguration typically occurs when spirit contact takes place in a circle (see Chapter 11).

Spirit Photography

Photographs that end up including spirits generally happen by accident, although some people do set out to take pictures of locations where they know spirits to be present. Unfortunately, photography is a medium (no pun intended) that is easy to manipulate, and spirit photography has lost much credibility as a result of fraud.

CAUTION **Premonition** _____

With the increasing popularity of spirit photography in the 1920s came an increase in fraud. Anyone with a basic knowledge of film developing and printing techniques, a darkroom, and a little imagination could create amazing images—and even more so today when you consider digital photography and computer manipulation of images. The resulting lack of credibility causes spirit photography to fall out of favor as a legitimate means of representing spirit presence.

What You Can Expect During a Reading with a Medium

You've found a medium you trust, and you're ready for some spirit contact. Now what? Well, odds are high that this is more than just a random adventure for you. Most people want to make contact with specific loved ones who have passed to the higher side. It might be feelings of loss, grief, love, worry, and even curiosity that drive your desire for communication. You might have some unfinished business with the person who passed—maybe you didn't have a chance to say good-bye, or there were some uncertainties about feelings or actions on either side that were left hanging when the person passed. Perhaps you made a pact to communicate across the great divide, and you are now curious to find out what it's really like on the other side.

Don't worry about what the medium might think of your reasons for wanting to contact a loved one on the higher side. First of all, an experienced medium, like a good doctor, has seen and heard it all. Second, a professional medium isn't really interested in making judgments about your interests and needs. A good medium simply wants to help you find whatever information and answers you are seeking, and present them to you for the highest good and in light.

Your reading should take place in an environment in which both you and the medium feel comfortable. If you are meeting with the medium in person, the surroundings should be inviting and make you feel welcome. If you are doing a reading by telephone, you should be somewhere free from distractions and you should have the sense that the same is the case for the medium. Before the reading begins, ask the medium what he or she expects from you. Can you talk to the medium during the reading? Can you ask questions of the spirits who come through? Consciously clear your mind of expectations and anticipation, and focus on being open and receptive to whatever happens. Sit in an open posture, with your legs and arms uncrossed. You can close your eyes or leave them open, whichever you prefer. Let the medium know when you are ready to start.

For the Highest Good and with Light

The medium should always begin the reading with a prayer or a blessing that asks for divine light and goodness to guide the communication. It is very important to establish your intent in this way; through spirit communication you are opening a doorway, but you don't want just anyone to come through.

Evidence of the Continuity of Life

Validation is the most crucial aspect of spirit communication, and should be the first thing that takes place. You must know, beyond a shadow of a doubt, that the spirit the medium says is your father is indeed your father. The medium should present you with information that is undeniable—straight up, without having to ask you confirming questions along the way.

Often, as we've mentioned in earlier chapters, the first information to come through from a spirit is about his or her passing. It might be because this is the last earth plane memory the spirit has, or because it is the detail likely to be most vivid in your memory. Rita often experiences sensations in her body that correlate to the cause of death. The sensations are often vivid and mimic the physical ailment. She might feel a headache when someone passed from a stroke, central chest pain in the case of a heart attack, or a wider chest pain in the case lung disease.

The medium should have more to offer than, "I have a woman here who passed of a heart attack." The medium should be able to give a description of the person, of certain physical or personality characteristics that at least hint at the person's identity. When Rita did a reading for Debbie, she didn't know anything about Debbie or her family members and friends who had passed. When Rita said, "I have a gentleman here who is showing at about 60 years, with salt and pepper hair brushed back and to the side in a soft part, with a full face and a broad nose," Debbie immediately suspected this to be her father who had passed several years ago. When Rita said, "On the earth plane, he was quite set in his ways and didn't like it when people disagreed with him—and neither did they!" Debbie was certain (and delighted) that this spirit visitor was indeed her father.

> **Silver Cord**
>
> Mediums certified in the Spiritualist Church are trained to identify a spirit totally so the person knows it can be no one else. Even among talented mediums, this skill requires a high level of consistency that typically takes a number of years to achieve.

The Message

Spirits do come through just to say "hi!" and to let you know that they are there and still in contact with you. They take as much delight in this contact as you do. But the spirits who make contact for extended communication typically have specific reasons for the contact and specific messages to convey. Messages might be directly from the spirit to you, or from a spirit serving as an intermediary.

> **Mediums and Messages**
>
> Rita had a man come to her for a spirit drawing. She described two spirits who came through, the man's mother and uncle, and then did a spirit drawing of the uncle. When Rita showed him the spirit drawing, the man said, "Yes, that's my uncle but I wanted my father!" So Rita went back to the spirit to see if the father would come through. He would not. Rita shared with the man what the spirits communicated: "Your father was a very shy man, while his brother, your uncle, always took center stage. So he came through first, and wanted to be drawn!" The man confirmed that in fact his father had been extremely shy.

Steering Clear of Fakes and Frauds

Times of struggle and challenge are opportunities for personal growth and insight. Sadly, they are also openings for the unscrupulous to become opportunistic. As with anything else in life, if it seems too good to be true then it probably isn't either good or true. Put away those rose-tinted glasses ... you need to see clearly when you reach out to the other side.

Fakes and frauds, we're sorry to say, lurk wherever sorrow and sadness co-exist with the inability to "prove" anything and the potential for money to exchange hands. A fake is someone who pretends to make the desired contact, sometimes with the best of intentions (to help you feel better). A fraud is an intentional fake motivated by self-interest, which is almost always financial. These folks, sometimes well intentioned but often simply unscrupulous, are willing to offer you what you want because there's something in it for them.

Misguided Intentions

The well-intentioned fake sincerely feels your pain and wants to make it go away. Such a person might enhance, or outright pretend to make, the contact you desire, leading you to experience what you (desperately) want to believe. This might be a person you know who has psychic abilities, a stranger you've gone to for help in making contact with a loved one who has passed on, or even a professional medium. This person doesn't intend to hurt you in any way, and sees his or her actions as kind and good. And what you don't know, after all, won't hurt you if it's in your best interests.

Who knows what's in your best interests? Not this person! And you're bound to find out at some point, either because you make a genuine connection at another time or because you eventually figure it out. In the end, the well-intentioned fake can cause even more pain than the outright fraud because you *trusted* this person.

Check, Please

The only intention the fraud has is to take your money. This person is nearly always a stranger to you, someone you've selected to help you contact the other side. Perhaps you came across this person's business card somewhere, or you found the name in the phone book. The first question that this person asks you is your best clue whether he or she is legitimate. "How will you be paying for your services today?" is surely a tip-off about this person's interests!

Tricks of the Trade

Frauds are so effective in their trade because it's impossible to prove their actions. But there are some common tricks to put you on the alert. Your fraud warning alarm should go off if the medium …

- Discusses money before asking what you need. Yes, a good medium is worth the price he or she asks, and needs to discuss charges up front. But the medium's first questions should be about your interests, needs, and expectations.

- Requires your credit card information or cash payment before doing a reading. Of course, payment should not depend on whether you like the reading. But you should receive the service before you're expected to pay.

- Is on the other end of a psychic hotline. Yes, the advertising is tempting; you can call any time, and you don't have to leave the comfort of your own home. But what do you know about that voice on the other end of the line? It's better to steer clear.

- Asks a lot of personal questions before beginning your reading. Those who are particularly adept make this questioning appear as though it is casual conversation, while the medium is actually *fishing* for the details that will become part of your "reading."

♦ Promises connection with a specific spirit or loved one, or promises specific information or results. There is no way to guarantee anything with a reading.

♦ Makes specific predictions about your future. Your future is the outcome of the choices and decisions you make on your way, and it is ever-changing. Although there are likely signs that point to probable outcomes, we have two important words for you: free will. Nothing about your future is carved in stone.

Spiritology

Fishing is when the medium gives small bits of information and then asks questions to fill in the picture. It is generally the hallmark of someone who at best is inadequately trained and at worst is an outright fraud.

♦ Tells you to take specific actions. No medium has the knowledge to tell you what to do, or what events will result from your actions. This is your life, and only you can make the decisions that direct it.

Desperate Illusions

It is possible for you yourself to be the fake, so to speak. Not that you intentionally set out to delude yourself or others, of course. It's just that sometimes you can want to hook up with that special someone on the other side so badly that you see signs of connection everywhere that aren't genuine or aren't really there.

This is where it's particularly important to pay attention to authentication messages. What clues are you getting that suggest this is your brother or your mother or your best friend from college? The evidence of identity should be irrefutable, and it should be evidence that is not especially common. If it's not, then the identity of the spirit contact remains uncertain. (Sorry.)

If you are desperate to make contact with someone specific, all that you know about that person is highlighted in your conscious thoughts as well as in parts of your memory that are just below the surface of your recall ability. A medium might pick up these psychical signals, misinterpret them as mediumistic signals, and convey them to you as messages from the higher side when they are in fact just a reflection of the signals your subconscious mind is sending out. The medium is in essence "reading" your mind. The energy that you are putting out there is so powerful that it creates images the medium can't help but pick up. And it isn't always possible for the medium to be aware of this happening. Only you can know.

Keep your mind as open as possible. You can make it more difficult for the medium to connect with spirit if you are sitting there concentrating on what it is that you want to have happen. That energy can block the communication.

Energy Healing

A special form of spirit contact is energy healing, which usually takes place in a circle or other group setting (more about circles in Chapter 11 and about healing in Chapter 18).

In a healing, the medium calls on spirit physicians and chemists—spirit healers— to send healing energy through the medium, or *healer*, to the person in need.

While mediums can transfer healing energy, there are many people who are not mediums but who are healers. Some are even able to use spirit contact to diagnose or identify illness (more in Chapter 18). Spirit healing can be very powerful, and can relieve physical, emotional, and spiritual pain. People sometimes feel the effects immediately, or they feel them over a period of hours, or even days.

Spiritology

A **healer** is a person (who may or may not be a medium) who has the ability to receive healing energy from the higher side and direct it to people on the earth plane who are ill or injured physically, emotionally, or spiritually. In Spiritualism, a healer is always referred to as a healing medium.

The Least You Need to Know

- A medium's qualifications should include a combination of education and experience.

- Interview a prospective medium as you would interview any professional whom you want to entrust with important information.

- Special forms of spirit communication, such as spirit painting, require unique talents in the mediums who use them.

- One of the first things that should happen in a reading is for the medium to convey clear and irrefutable evidence of the continuity of life and the identity of the spirit who is coming through.

- Never make a change in your life because a medium, or a spirit, tells you to. Carefully evaluate everything that comes to you through a reading before taking any action as a result.

Chapter 11

Tipping Tables and Blowing Horns: It Must Be a Séance!

In This Chapter

◆ The show-biz séances of days past

◆ Modern spirit circles

◆ Making sense of spirit signals

◆ What you can expect when you participate in a spirit circle

◆ There really are trumpet circles

Candlelit rooms and movielike effects certainly make for grand shows that can at once bedazzle and confound. But this is Hollywood's version of a séance—an antiquated term that modern mediums no longer use.

When a group gathers to communicate with spirits, the event is a respectful circle inviting physical phenomena from present spirits. It takes a lot of practice and skill to accomplish this advanced level of mediumship. Circles are no Halloween tricks or party-game larks, but profound and powerful vehicles for sacred spirit contact.

Once Upon a Séance

The word *séance* is of French origin and means "to sit." Although certain Taoist sects conducted séances—spiritual retreats at which sect leaders received divine counsel—as long ago as the third century, it was with the emergence of the Fox sisters and modern Spiritualism in the mid-1800s (see Chapter 3) that the term became synonymous with sitting in communication with spirits.

Through their history, séances have ranged from the subdued to the outrageous, from close-knit gatherings of people intent on making contact with loved ones to groups whose members shared only the desire to meet someone famous, or even notorious, from the other side. Some skeptics have made careers from debunking séances, and unfortunately they've not found a shortage of work. During their heyday in the early decades of the 1900s, séances were favorite events across the United States.

While many were authentic spirit communication experiences for participants, many were simply intended to amuse and amaze those in attendance. The inclination toward sensationalism made it difficult, if not impossible, to separate the valid from the contrived. Although the phenomena that occur at séances can be authentic spirit communication, the image of the séance is so closely connected with the perception that a séance is all about entertainment that mediums today shy away from the very term.

Mediums and Messages

Legend has it that before his death on October 31, 1926, famed magician Harry Houdini promised he would conduct the ultimate feat: He would escape death itself. Every year on Halloween, in locations around the world, "Houdini societies" conduct séances to attempt to contact the master of escapism. So far, none have succeeded.

Let the Show Begin!

The séances of the late 1880s often took place in a private home, sometimes following a dinner party. Guests seated themselves around a table, often in the parlor because this was a room that could be closed off, sitting close enough to hold hands. The medium sat among them. As the séance was to begin, the host dimmed the lights in the room. A hush fell over the gathering, and the medium instructed all the participants to take the hands of those sitting next to them, forming a chain of energy around the table.

"We call upon our spirit guests to come forward and to make their presence known," the medium would intone. Those around the table watched each other and the room, eagerly anticipating the first arrivals. They were seldom disappointed. Shadows, flashes of light, bumps and raps, and moving objects (including the table) soon gave evidence of spirit presence.

When a *trance medium* presided, visiting spirits presented themselves through the medium's body. The medium's demeanor and voice often changed to reflect the spirit's mannerisms. Someone in the group might call out, "Spirit that has joined us, identify yourself!" (In modern circles, participants just offer a greeting: "Good evening!") Under the guidance of a *materialist medium*, such presence might even take the form of a human image with clothing and features clear to those in attendance.

Spiritology

A **trance medium** enters a state of altered consciousness that allows spirits to communicate through his or her body. A **materialist medium** receives spirit messages that manifest themselves in physical appearances, such as images visible to others who are present.

Some spirits cooperated nicely. One might be the departed mother of a person in attendance, another the brother of someone else. Some mediums had specific spirit guides that "took over" the séance, giving messages and teaching lessons. At other times, according to reports from the era, the summoned spirits were obstreperous, causing objects to fly about the room, mussing up hair and clothing, and creating a nuisance in general. Other spirits came and went without providing any clues as to their identity and the purpose of their visit, leaving guests to try and figure it out later.

This isn't to say that all of this was just entertainment. There were many people who were making authentic contact, such as one-time skeptic Sir Arthur Conan Doyle. But those who used legitimate activities for fraudulent purposes grabbed media attention and public interest, which overwhelmed the genuine work that was going on. Physical mediums became leery of using physical mediumship except in small, private gatherings, causing public interest in spiritualism to diminish through the middle decades of the twentieth century.

Silver Cord

A rare and amazing kind of séance is the cabinet séance, in which the medium sits in a small cabinet. One at a time, spirits emerge from the cabinet, seemingly as tangible as the people in the room. They form these images using ectoplasm, an energy-based substance drawn from the cabinet medium. Few mediums have this extraordinary level of ability. Cabinet séances are amazing events to attend!

Phenomena or Fiction?

The phenomena manifested at many séances were authentic. Whenever people gather and focus their energy on making a connection between the earth plane and the spirit world, they are likely to succeed. Many séances conducted under the guidance of talented and capable mediums certainly made the kind of contact that provided proof of the continuity of life, bringing comfort and closure for those seeking it.

Unfortunately, the temptation to create a memorable experience (and perhaps personal fame and fortune) led a good many séance organizers to contrive the events that took place. Skeptical guests exposed numerous acts of fraud, from strings attached to objects that the medium tugged and moved to elaborately constructed platforms creating the illusion of levitation—the action of a physical object, sometimes a person, lifting into the air.

The séances that were fabrications and fictions made for great entertainment, as was really their intent, but at the same time discredited the séance as a legitimate venue for genuine spirit contact. Imagine the distress of believing that you've connected with the spirit of a loved one and then discovering it was all a setup! Such séances are not the efforts of those seeking the highest and the best; they are the manipulations of those driven by selfish motivations.

The Real Deal: Modern Circles

Gathering together for spirit communication can be a powerful and amazing experience. Modern circles present good opportunities for beginning mediums to use and refine their skills, and for those who want to experience spirit communication to do so in a sheltered, controlled setting. Often, there are several mediums participating in the circle, giving a range of experience and expertise.

Ideally, a modern circle gathers in a room that is used only for the purpose of holding circles, or at least remains unused for a few hours before the circle is held. This reduces interference from extraneous energy. A circle generally begins by clearing the room's energy, which prepares the environment to be as receptive and supportive as possible.

Some circles prefer subdued lighting because it helps set a mood of relaxation and focus, while some sit in total darkness, and others meet in regular daylight. There is no reason to hold a circle in near or complete darkness; a room's lighting is a matter of concern only for those of us on the earth plane, not for spirits. Like a one-on-one reading with a medium, a circle begins with a prayer to welcome the divine, to ask for openness and guidance, and to establish intent.

There are many kinds of circles—they can be either *open* or *closed*. Open circles welcome participants at a wide range of mediumistic abilities, from those who just want to experience a circle to those who are developing their skills as mediums. There is one medium who takes the lead, although several mediums might participate in spirit communication. Generally, the spirits who come through have connections to and messages for people in the circle, and a number of spirits make contact during the circle. These messages come through the mediums, and sometimes through participants who don't realize that they have mediumistic abilities.

Spiritology

In an **open** circle, anyone can attend and there is a wide range of mediumistic ability. A **closed** circle is a group that meets regularly with the same members. The circle is closed because the members are working to build a constant group vibration that facilitates easier communication to spirit guides who are also working together from the higher side.

Those who are part of a closed circle are often mediums, and there is a high level of mediumistic ability in the circle. Mediums sometimes call these medium circles or working circles. The level of intensity is often higher because the level of mediumistic ability is higher, and spirit communication can take place along a broad continuum of methods—from clairsentience to transfiguration. Closed circles sometimes become teaching environments for spirit guides, who come through with generalized information rather than messages for specific participants.

Who Should Be in a Circle

Just about anyone can enjoy the experience of being in an open circle. To find a circle that you might join, contact a Spiritualist Church in your area or ask your metaphysical friends about circles they might know of or participate in. Many of the guidelines for finding a qualified medium that we recommend in Chapter 10 also apply to finding a legitimate circle.

It's important to set aside any expectations or preconceived ideas about what will happen during a circle, and just be open and receptive. Typically, there is a lead medium for the circle who will talk with you before you attend, to be sure you understand how the circle functions and what is expected of you.

What happens in a circle is not secret, but it is private. Spirit communication is often intense and deeply personal. While you are free, of course, to share your own experiences with spirit contact, please respect the experiences of others in the circle as confidential.

What if a spirit contact comes through for you? Enjoy! Be open to the experience, and welcome the information from the communicator—the spirit that is bringing you the message. As we've said throughout this book, spirit communication is about goodness and healing. The energy of the circle shelters you, and you can feel safe within it. If you feel uncomfortable at any time, ask for help from the mediumistic leader.

Who Should *Not* Be in a Circle

Participants should come to the circle with positive energy and positive intent. There are people who believe they can use the circle and its psychical energy to control other people or to manipulate aspects of their own lives. They may try to use spiritual energy to control a relationship, for example, or to influence personal prosperity or fame. If you are not coming into a circle for the highest and best good, you can be certain your efforts will backfire. You can call it the law of cause and effect, the law of karma, or you get what you give. No matter what you call it, negative intent ultimately brings negative results.

> **CAUTION**
>
> **Premonition**
>
> Because mental health affects perception, thought patterns, and behavior, mental illness interferes with a person's ability to establish intent. Conditions such as depression, anxiety, schizophrenia, and addiction alter perception and make it unwise for a person who has any of these or other mental conditions to participate in a circle.

In an open circle, you can't be sure of everyone's intent despite the care and effort of the circle's lead medium to screen participants. The very nature of an open circle—anyone can attend—makes this virtually impossible. This is yet another reason why it's important to start the circle by asking for divine protection.

We Are Gathered Here Today ...

So the big day is here and you're going to your first circle! What should you wear, what should you expect, how should you act? The circle's leader should have given you some guidelines about these things already. In general, you'll get the most from your experience when you ...

- Wear comfortable, clean clothing.

- Avoid perfumes and fragrances (which can be disturbing to others in the confines of a closed room as well as have an effect on a room's energy).

- Leave your expectations or doubts at the door, and enter the circle with an open and receptive mind and spirit.

In most circles, you can ask questions and request information or a specific spirit contact, although there is no guarantee that you'll get what you ask for.

Setting an Open and Positive Attitude

Of course you have your reasons for wanting to participate in a circle. No doubt there is at least one loved one who has passed whom you would like to contact. This is natural and good. Keep in mind, however, that the universe has its own intentions! There might be no contact that comes through for you, or what does come through might not be what you hoped for or expected. Nonetheless, it is the communication you are intended to experience. So get the most from it! If the circle permits you to ask questions, feel free to do so. You should feel comfortable with the others who are present, and confident that they will respect your privacy with regard to what information comes through, as you will respect theirs.

For the Highest Good: Establishing Intent

Establishing intent is not about deciding whom you want to contact and what information you want to receive. Rather, establishing intent is a process of opening yourself to whatever it is that a spirit wishes to communicate, and establishing that you desire your communications to take place for the highest good.

Inviting Spirit Presence

The lead medium typically invites, or invokes, spirit presence to join the circle through prayer or a formal greeting. This is called an invocation. Depending on the medium's primary method of contact, this might happen within the medium or through external manifestations that are apparent to everyone in the circle. Others in the circle might also receive spirit contact, depending on their mediumistic abilities.

Identify Yourself, Please

The first responsibility of someone who is receiving spirit contact is to establish the spirit's identity. An experienced medium does this before sharing the contact with the circle, so he or she is able to say, "I have a gentleman here who always wore a New York Mets baseball cap, who wants to tell Marie that she shouldn't be angry with him for not saying good-bye before he passed because he's still here with her, and she should celebrate her birthday next week with a lemon meringue pie from Martha's Bakery."

Now, if that message doesn't convince Marie and everybody else in the circle of the continuity of life and the authenticity of spirit communication, nothing will! Of course, not all contact is that complete or specific. Sometimes, the details are very small, and you might not fully recognize the spirit until some time after the circle. Just as you are new to this, the spirits who want to contact you might be, too. It can take a little time to settle into a pattern that works for both of you.

Mediums and Messages

A common and fun exercise that mediums sometimes do in spirit circles is bending spoons. You hold a spoon by the bowl and rest one finger on the handle very lightly. You invite Spirit to come, and then let go of the thought. When Rita has done this exercise, the circle starts singing. Suddenly, you can feel the spoon moving, then watch the handle begin to bend. It is the energy of Spirit that causes this to happen, and Rita says the spoon really heats up in your hands! As an exercise, this proves that Spirit can come and work through us rather than just giving us answers. And, we suspect, it's as much fun for spirits as it is for us!

Sometimes it takes a while to figure out who is coming through and why. Rita has taught art for many years. She had a student once who, 10 weeks into a 12-week course, had to leave for medical reasons. The young man had diabetes that was difficult to control, and as a result lost circulation to parts of his foot. He went into the hospital to have a toe amputated, and a few weeks later ended up having his leg amputated from the knee down. Rita sent cards to him and included him in her healing prayers over the course of a year or so, but eventually lost touch with him. A few years later, Rita heard that he had passed.

A number of years later, Rita was in a medium's circle and one of the other mediums said to her, "I have a young man named Greg who is showing as an amputee, and he wants to say 'thank you.'" Rita accepted the message but she was perplexed; she didn't remember a young man named Greg or anyone with an amputated leg. A few weeks later, she was driving past a restaurant, one that had been a favorite of hers for quite a few years. She felt as though her head was "snapped" to look at the restaurant, and suddenly she remembered who Greg was! He had been the chef at the restaurant and the art student who lost his leg to diabetes. At the next medium's circle, Rita gave thanks in return to Greg and to the medium who had brought his message through.

Recognizing and Interpreting Manifestations

Spirit contact can come through in an almost infinite variety of ways. The more people there are in the circle, in fact, the more variety there is! A spirit might choose to come through to someone other than the lead medium—even to you!

As we discussed in Chapter 10, at first these experiences might feel like your imagination has gone into overdrive. This is normal, and others in the circle will give you support and encouragement. Just let the experience unfold; there will be plenty of time afterward to analyze and understand it.

Common manifestations of spirit contact include the following:

◆ Hearing words or phrases, often in your head rather than out loud

◆ Seeing flashes of a person's face, clothing, or other characteristics

◆ Images or references to certain colors, numbers, or symbols

◆ Flashes of scenarios that appear like memories

If you have any of these experiences, share them with the circle even if they seem to have little context. Messages from the higher side aren't always presented in ways that make logical sense to us. Even if the messages are for you, it might take input from others in the circle for the messages to make sense to you. And if the messages are not for you, you want to get them out there so they reach the right person.

In Goodness and in Healing

When Rita holds circles, she views every circle (and every spirit contact) as a request for healing—emotional, physical, spiritual. Her opening prayers always ask that healing love and light surround the circle. She asks infinite spirit God to send the spirit guides and loved ones of all who are present to come close, and that the people participating in the circle are open to receive.

Those on the receiving end of healing energy have experiences that range from feeling very calm to feeling better, either immediately or after some time has passed. Spirit energy cannot, and is not meant to, make everything better; it is always simply for the highest and the best. Why do we have to suffer? Why do we suffer? We don't know! There are spiritual lessons in illness, and many things that we don't understand. We are sometimes volunteers for people around us to learn their lessons. We don't always know the divine purpose of a particular situation; it is beyond our capacity to have such knowledge.

Through prayer, meditation, and spirit communication we can ask for, and receive, help. Although we don't have to be hurt to learn, it seems that most of the time we humans don't want to learn and we get stuck in our egos, and it takes a hurt of some kind to kick us into action. Look at how many times people get stuck in dysfunctional relationships but won't leave, or do destructive things to themselves but won't stop. Sometimes we do things to ourselves that amount to slow suicide. If you can change your life, if you can do what you need to do, your life will change. Spirit energy can help you gain the insights you need to make changes. This is what spirit healing is all about—physical, emotional, and spiritual.

Mediums and Messages

Table tipping is a form of spirit communication in which spirit energy comes through your hands and causes a special three-legged table to tip on its legs, or even move across the room with your hands very lightly on it. Usually, two people have their hands together on the table. One asks a question, and the table taps the response—either yes or no, or a sequence of taps that stop at letters of the alphabet. Sometimes the table can really get moving, almost like it's walking up steps. Although table tipping is fun and people enjoy it, it can be a long, tedious way to get answers!

Let the Trumpet Blow!

Reality can sometimes be stranger than fiction. There truly are "trumpet circles." These unique events represent a high level of development in the medium, and they concentrate spirit energy in special ways. In fact, it is likely that this "real deal" became the model for the frauds who became so popular for their show-biz séances. A trumpet circle is an amazing experience.

In a trumpet circle, a special, long metal horn is placed in the center of the circle. The room is made totally dark, and those in the circle concentrate on welcoming spirit energy. If a spirit accepts the invitation, the trumpet then rises and becomes the mouthpiece for the spirit. In audio recordings of trumpet circles, you can clearly hear different voices coming through the trumpet. Although Rita has been to several trumpet circles, she has not yet experienced the trumpet rising. Several of her teachers have, however, and found the experience remarkable.

The Least You Need to Know

- The infamous séances of the late 1800s and early 1900s were often more entertainment than genuine spirit communication, and typically produced sensational effects.

- Today's spirit circles are usually valid, genuine settings in which spirit contact is authentic.

- There are many kinds of modern circles that are either open or closed. Open circles generally welcome anyone to participate.

- It is important to maintain an open mind and spirit when attending a circle.

- If anything makes you uncomfortable in a circle, ask for help from the circle's mediumistic leader.

- Sometimes, the messages conveyed to you during a spirit circle don't become clear until later, when you have a chance to think about them and connect them to events and people in your life.

Chapter 12

Uncovering the Medium Within

In This Chapter

- ◆ Discovering your psychical abilities: a directed communication exercise
- ◆ Learning how to focus
- ◆ Refining and developing your mediumistic skills
- ◆ Using your mediumistic skills for the highest good

Most people (and you are probably among them) have had some kind of contact with the spirit world, from just the sense that someone is present to direct messages and advice from loved ones who have passed to the higher side. Perhaps you want to make contact for yourself, or to use your mediumistic abilities to make contact for others.

Mediumistic skills are like any other skills: You start with a basic or inherent ability (that everyone has to some degree), and through education and experience you develop and refine that ability into a reliable, consistent set of skills. With practice and guidance, you can learn to communicate with the spirit world. Whether you want to contact someone you know in spirit or someone who simply knows more than you do, like a spirit guide, there are many techniques that just about anyone can learn.

So You Wanna Be a Medium!

While everyone has the ability to connect with those in the spirit world, some people are more open to such connections than others, and are more aware of the connections that take place. As an element of the universe, you are already linked to its energy—you're already plugged in!

Developing and refining your mediumistic skills will lead to experiences that are amazing, amusing, entertaining, and profound. You will certainly experience growth in your personal life, and will also help others to grow in their lives and understanding. Even if you choose not to develop your own mediumistic abilities, becoming aware of them will let you become more receptive to spirit communication through others.

Your Innate Psychical Talents

You've no doubt noticed that we use both the term "psychic" and "psychical" throughout this book. (And no, the latter is not a misspelling of "physical"!) While they are interchangeable on a certain level, they actually define a somewhat different set of skills.

Spiritology

Psychic skills are those through which unspoken communication takes place between people on the earth plane.
Psychical skills are those through which communication takes place between people on the earth plane and entities in the spirit world.

Psychic skills are those abilities that you use to communicate in unspoken ways with other people on the earth plane. A psychic (someone who is using psychic skills) reads from earth energy; he or she reads the vibrations of what is going on here on earth.

Psychical skills are those abilities that you use to communicate across the earth/spirit divide. The skills are similar to those that a psychic uses—remember, all mediums are psychics (although not all psychics are mediums; more on this later). A medium (someone who is using psychical skills) communicates with deceased beings through his or her own sensitivities.

Freeing the Medium Within

Becoming a medium is more often than not a process of being the medium you already are! As a child, you were likely in touch with your spirit far more intimately than you are now as an adult. Part of what we view as "growing up" is learning to suppress this spontaneous and unconstrained piece of ourselves. Reconnecting with this piece is just a matter of allowing it back into our lives.

An Exercise to Activate Your Mediumistic Abilities

What are your mediumistic abilities? This directed communication exercise can help you identify and activate your psychical skills. Read through these steps until they are familiar enough that you can follow them without reading through each one.

1. Make yourself comfortable in a location where you won't have any distractions or interruptions.

2. Take three slow, deep breaths, in through your nose and out through your mouth. Let the first breath clear your body, let the second breath open your mind, and let the third breath free your spirit.

3. Consciously form the thought: "This is my time to be one with God and for God to be one with me." (God, of course, being the divine of your belief system or choice.) Set an intent to explore a spirit contact using all of your psychical senses.

4. Envision yourself sitting on a bench in an open, beautiful garden. There are flowers and trees, and the air smells fresh and clean. It is peaceful and calm, and you are open to receive whatever spirit visitor arrives.

5. As your spirit visitor approaches, notice but do not attempt to control the psychical sense that is first activated. Do you hear a voice or a sound? Do you see an image? Do you "sense" a presence?

6. Welcome your spirit guest, and communicate to him or her using the psychical sense that feels most natural. Make a note in your conscious mind of which sense this is, but don't let your consciousness intervene with its use.

7. Push this psychical sense to use it to the fullest capacity you are capable of at this point. If you begin to feel frustrated, you are pushing too hard and your conscious mind is becoming involved. Back off until you feel comfortable again.

8. Now choose a different psychical sense. If your initial sense was clairaudience, choose clairvoyance. Concentrate on perceiving visual images using your inner vision. Acknowledge, but don't shift your focus to, these images. If they are just fragments, that's okay. Sometimes images come in bits and pieces (the term mediums use to express the fragmented way in which information sometimes comes to them, especially beginning mediums). They will become clearer. Let the images take shape and form.

9. When you begin to feel complete with the messages, gently release the concentration you are using to activate these psychical senses. Return to the sense that was first activated, and use this sense to communicate thank you and good-bye to the spirit who came through.

10. Take three slow, deep breaths, in through your nose and out through your mouth. Feel yourself back in your body, become conscious of your breathing. Wiggle your fingers and your toes, and when you are ready, open your eyes.

When you feel ready to do so after completing the exercise, write down your experiences.

1. Which psychical sense was first activated? What was your initial experience of it?

_____

_____

_____

2. Whom did you meet? What sense of identity did this psychical sense provide about your spirit visitor?

_____

_____

_____

3. How did you experience this psychical sense?

_____

_____

_____

4. What was the second psychical sense that you attempted to activate, and what was your initial experience of it? What added information did you get about your spirit visitor?

_____

_____

_____

5. What happened with the initial psychical sense as you brought this second psychical sense into play?

_____

_____

_____

6. What interactions did you have with your spirit visitor through your psychical senses?

_____

_____

_____

As your mediumistic skills develop, use variations on this exercise to further explore your psychical senses. You might find that your abilities include advanced skills such as automatic writing and drawing spirit-inspired images.

Learning Focus

The most challenging aspect of using your mediumistic abilities is learning to focus them. Think of this like entering a room crowded with people who are talking, laughing, eating, drinking, and even dancing to the music that plays in the background. A cacophony of "input," to use a term from our computer-driven culture, assaults your senses. Yet within seconds, you locate the friends you are to join, and make your way to them. How are you able to do this?

Focus. All of your senses align toward identifying and locating your friends. Your eyes scan the room for images of clothing and other physical characteristics. Your ears tune in to frequencies of sound that are closest to what you know signals their voices. Your sense of smell seeks the fragrances your friends typically wear. You search for other details that narrow the scope of your quest to find your friends—foods, drinks, or dance moves. All of this transpires without much conscious participation from your mind, of course, and in fractions of time barely measurable. Then click! You're locked in on your target, and in moments you're sharing in the revelry with your friends.

Learning to focus your mediumistic skills is very similar to singling out individuals in a crowded room. In fact, you undoubtedly used some of these skills—your psychical abilities—in locating your friends at a party. (One way to further develop these abilities is to consciously concentrate on using them in such ways; but more on that later!) With practice, you become both skilled and comfortable using your core psychical skills—clairvoyance, clairaudience, and clairsentience—to receive mediumistic messages.

Mediums and Messages

One evening in Rita's circle a student came to her describing a young man dancing with a top hat and cane. He was tall and handsome with brown hair, and was quite the character. Rita could immediately identify him as her friend Tom, a choreographer who danced with a top hat and cane many times, and who danced with Rita at parties. He came through with a message that Rita needed to do more dancing and not work so hard, which is definitely something Tom would've said to Rita here on the earth plane.

Filtering Signals

When you search for someone in a crowd, you simultaneously receive and reject signals. Looking for a male friend? Automatically your focus shifts … men in, women out. Short? You glance right past those who stand head and shoulders above the crowd. Always in vogue when it comes to attire? Your attention migrates to those wearing the latest styles—and overlooks those who are not. Drinks Pepsi … or nothing? Loves those little cocktail wienies? Laugh sounds like a cross between a choking lion and a giggling little girl? You filter all of these signals and countless others, consciously and subconsciously.

When receiving spirit signals, the filtering process is sometimes more challenging (particularly when you are just beginning to develop your mediumistic skills) because the signals are less tangible to your conscious mind. You might *think* you heard a voice or saw an image. Did you really? Or was it just your imagination? This kind of conscious questioning is actually a sign of progress in your development. As we said earlier, spirit communication feels like imagination at the beginning!

Intent and Limits

Mediumistic signals sometimes come to you unbidden. Rather than you attempting to invoke spirit connection, a spirit comes to you and wishes to make contact. The spirit might desire to convey a message to you or to someone else. As we discussed in Chapter 9, it's important for you to establish intent and set limits. Otherwise, you'll feel like a giant antenna, picking up lots of static but not getting any clear channels!

Establishing intent makes it clear that you always desire spirit communication for the highest good and with light. Whether you initiate contact or spirits contact you, take time to consciously establish intent. Setting limits reminds visitors from the boundary-less spirit world that your world has structure and constraints, and that you can't always be available when spirits want you to be.

We Worked So Hard, *December 1989, oil on canvas. Rita often works with troubled inner-city youths and one young man seemed to attach himself to her. Not an easy person to counsel, Rita decided to ask in meditation, "Who dropped this boy into my lap?" A man showed himself to Rita and told her he had been a migrant tobacco farmer. When Rita showed the boy this painting, he told her that his family had been tobacco farmers and that he thought he recognized the man it portrayed. Rita feels this spirit guided her to work with these youths.*

This is a good opportunity to call on your spirit guides for assistance. Use the "Meet Your Spirit Guides" guided communication exercise in Chapter 7 to ask for communication with your spirit guide. Then ask your spirit guide to help you maintain the limits you wish to set. Rita has established with her spirit guides, for example, that she does not want spirit contact to disturb her sleep unless absolutely necessary—the sleep state is a favorite time for spirits to attempt contact because your mind is very receptive. Instead, she makes herself available for spirit communication during her waking hours. She does permit spirit messages to come to her in the dream state, which is okay because it doesn't wake her up.

Your Circle of Safety

The best place to practice your mediumistic skills is in a circle. There is strength in numbers, as the cliché goes, and the others in the circle can help and guide you as you are learning. They also learn from you, even though you might feel that as a novice you have little to offer them. You might find one circle and stay with it for a long time as participants grow together in their mediumistic skills and maintain a group vibration that those in spirit will come to recognize, or you might participate in several circles that have different members.

Check with the Spiritualist Churches and metaphysical groups in your area to find out what opportunities there are for learning mediumship. Appendix B also provides some general resources to get you started.

> **Premonition**
>
> Beware the scams and the unsophisticated! Some people recognize that they have mediumistic abilities, but don't work to develop them before using them for financial gain. This leaves them—and you—open to random spirit contact that may or may not be beneficial. As much as we'd like to believe that everyone offering mediumistic services is doing so for the highest good, the sad reality is that this is not the case. Always check references and qualifications. If you have any doubts, go somewhere else.

If you are not able to find an organized mediumistic circle, consider forming one of your own. You might be surprised and delighted with how many people (many of whom are likely already among your circle of friends and acquaintances) are interested in, or already have some level of participation with, mediumistic abilities and spirit communication. Where there is one, there are usually many—it's just a matter of finding each other. (Chapter 11 offers advice and suggestions for choosing circles and circle participants.)

Developing Your Psychical and Mediumistic Skills

Realizing that you have mediumistic abilities is often exhilarating—like recognizing that you can sing, paint or dance when you've always wanted to do those things but thought they were beyond your reach. You are opening yourself to a whole new world—literally and figuratively. But after the novelty of discovery wears off, what's next? You want to learn more, of course, and to explore your talents and see where they lead you.

Is this a calling to a career change? You might indeed decide that you want to be a professional medium. But that's really a very personal decision that requires you to consider all aspects of your life. Regardless of how far you think you might want to take your development as a medium, start with the basics.

To some extent, your learning curve as a medium begins with the abilities that seem most prominent. Do you experience voices and sounds? Your predominant psychical ability might be clairaudience, and is a good place for you to start your development process. As is the case with your physical senses, your psychical senses are intertwined. (Do you taste or smell that freshly baked cinnamon roll?) As you develop one, you'll discover and develop others.

Medium or Psychic?

You probably already use your psychic abilities in your communications among friends and family here on the earth plane. You pick up the telephone right before it rings, and it's your sister calling. You impulsively turn left instead of right, and find a parking space. You stop by to see a friend, just in time to see him before he dashes off on an unexpected business trip.

Take these abilities to the next level, to communicate with spirit entities on the higher side, and now you're talking medium!

Finding a Mentor

As with any other skill that you want to develop, finding a mentor who can guide and assist you is a great boost. You can learn from your mentor's experience and expertise as well as from your own experiences and any courses that you are taking. You might even think of this as an apprenticeship of sorts. It might be a teacher from your mediumship courses who becomes your mentor, or another medium that you meet through a circle.

Seek a mentor whose skills are significantly more advanced than yours, someone who is a leader of sorts in the spiritual or metaphysical community. Look for someone whose abilities and integrity you respect and trust, and ask if he or she is willing to mentor you. Because learning and teaching are so intimately integrated, those who want to learn are often also eager to teach.

> **Silver Cord**
>
> The difference between teaching and learning is subtle but important. Teaching is what comes to you via another; learning is what you do with that information after you receive it. The greater part of developing any skill is learning.

Honing Your Skills: The Cycle of Learning

Practice makes perfect, no matter what you're doing. (Well, maybe not perfect, but certainly better!) The more you use your mediumistic abilities, the more competent you will become. Even when you reach the point of producing consistent results, practice leads to continuing improvement. Like playing the piano or riding a bicycle, you meet new challenges, reach new heights of achievement, and rest on plateaus of proficiency until it's time to repeat the cycle of learning. And in time, your skills become second nature, simply part of what defines you and how you function in your life.

Should You Go to School?

The short answer is, of course! If you want to learn more about *anything*, the most logical route is to go to school or take some classes. If there is a Spiritualist Church in your area, that is a good place to start. Spiritualist Churches offer instruction and classes in mediumship. They can also refer you to legitimate, qualified programs that offer more extensive study, if this interests you. One such program is the Spiritualist Course of Study for Mediumship, part of the Morris Pratt Institute's Course of Study for Spiritualism. (See Appendix B for more information about MPI and other educational resources for mediums.)

Local universities and colleges, community colleges, and other educational institutions sometimes offer what they might call "extended learning" programs. (Sometimes these are called "life experience" or "adult continuing education" programs.) These are courses, generally not for college credit and often taught when regular credit classes are not in session, conducted by local experts. Such programs run the gamut from computer skills to tarot reading. You might find a course in psychic abilities, or even mediumship.

As with most learning experiences, the value of such courses depends on the expertise of the teacher. Always check the credentials of both the program and the teacher! Talk with the teacher before enrolling in the class, and ask about his or her training, experience, and orientation. Is he or she a Spiritualist? Or just a fan of the Ouija board? Does he or she view spirit communication as learning and healing, or just see it as entertainment? What if educational opportunities are in short supply in your area? Some programs offer distance learning courses (also called correspondence courses). A key benefit with such courses is that you can learn at your own pace, and within the constraints of other demands placed on your life and your schedule. Not everyone can drop everything to go to school, or even squeeze enough time from a busy day to take night classes!

Premonition

There are no universal accreditation procedures for courses and programs that teach mediumship, so choosing one is indeed a process of "buyer beware." The best way to find a reputable program is to ask sources you trust, such as mediums you might know or organizations that you know to be reliable.

The disadvantage of distance learning programs, of course, is that you're pretty much on your own. There's no opportunity for structured practice because you won't have an instructor working with you to help you receive and give messages. If you're considering a distance learning program, make sure you have adequate access to a medium. Lessons should be structured and detailed, and should include specific advice for addressing various scenarios that might arise during a spirit communication experience.

Realistic Expectations

We talk a lot about establishing intent, and always try to make clear that this means asking for divine light to guide spirit communication for the highest good and for the greatest healing or learning. A piece of this inevitably becomes, "So what do you want to accomplish with this communication?"

At times, you might desire contact with a specific spirit entity—your mother, father, sister, brother, spouse, or friend who has passed to the other side. Often, this spirit is willing to oblige, and responds to the energy signals that you send out. This is always gratifying and comforting; it reestablishes your sense of the continuity of life in very direct and obvious ways.

But spirits aren't always willing or able to respond when we want to call on them. Spirits are active and learning on the higher side, too! Spirits have free will, too. It's important to remain open to the spirits and to messages that do come through, even when they don't appear to be what you want. There is a grander scheme to the universe than we, as physical beings, are capable of understanding, and we often simply need to accept that.

Your Expectations for Yourself

If you are using your mediumistic abilities to communicate with spirits for yourself, remain open to whatever the experience turns out to be. The questions that you have, and the contacts that you desire, might not be the matters that are relevant in a particular communication, or even in general. Always keep as your conscious intent that spirit communication is for the highest good. Be still, and just let the information come through. You'll have plenty of time afterward to think and analyze.

Ask questions of your spirit connections if you are unclear about a message, but realize that the meaning of the message might not become clear to you until quite some time later. A message that appears enigmatic might be just a piece of a much larger message that will come to you over multiple spirit connections, or that contains information you aren't ready to receive yet. Be patient; the meaning will come!

Expectations When Using Your Abilities for Others

When you use your mediumistic abilities on behalf of other people, remember that you are just the messenger. It is not your role to interpret the messages that you receive, or to judge them (although certainly your consciousness filters them; more on this in Chapter 13). Let the images and concepts come through. Always remember that you are in charge; deliver them responsibly.

Sometimes, information comes in bits and pieces. If you are patient, the fragments will take shape and make sense to the sitter who is receiving them.

Lessons and Healing

Your mediumistic abilities are a great gift, and with them comes the responsibility to use them wisely and always for the greatest good (we keep emphasizing this because it is such an essential point). Indeed, spirit contact can be, and often is, joyous and fun. Not many of us would be drawn to it if it wasn't! Spirit communication can bring much insight, understanding, comfort, and delight into your life. In the end, it's all about you!

Handling Challenges

Messages that come through spirits are sometimes unexpected or intense, and can surface issues that you need to confront, address, and resolve. If your intent is pure (meaning that you've established that this spirit communication is for the highest good), tremendous healing and learning will come as a result.

Silver Cord

Many mediums, like Rita, are trained in psychology, ministry, or related fields. This gives them the ability to provide more "earthly" guidance in response to the effects messages have for the people receiving them.

When these messages are for you, take time afterward to sort through your emotions and thoughts. Keep a journal about your experience, if this helps you. Talk with a friend who understands. Talk with a medium, if you know one whom you trust. And if the issues that arise feel overwhelming, seek professional help from a therapist. It doesn't matter what initiates the process of healing; what counts is that you follow through so that healing can take place.

Using Your Abilities to Help Others

There is great receiving in giving. It can be tremendously satisfying to use your abilities and skills to help others, and to bring messages of comfort and love from loved ones who have passed. Imagine what our world could be like if we all used our talents, mediumistic and otherwise, to help and nurture each other!

The Least You Need to Know

- Everyone has some level of mediumistic ability.

- Developing your mediumistic skills requires a combination of education and practice.

- Your psychical senses connect you to the spirit world in the same way that your psychic senses connect you to others on the earth plane.

- You can use your mediumistic abilities to help yourself and to help others.

Chapter 13

Understanding the Message

In This Chapter

♦ The symbolism of spirit communication

♦ The affirmation of detail

♦ The emotions that spirit messages can evoke

♦ Whether spirit communication should change your life

Spirit communication brings you messages that you need to know—some that you've always wanted to know, and some that you didn't realize you wanted to know. Sometimes the meanings are obvious. "I get it!" you exclaim.

Other times the meanings are obscure, even enigmatic. They can be like puzzles for you to solve to reveal the pictures they present, or like the children's games in which you move squares around in slots, horizontally and vertically within a frame, until you get them all into just the right position and then a recognizable scene or image emerges. To make sense of spirit messages, you have to "get" the picture, even when it comes to you in fragments.

Interpreting Information

Spirit communication can be like going to a therapist … only more. It can be like an all-night, depths-of-your-souls conversation with a best friend … only deeper. It can be like waking from a dream and knowing exactly what its symbolism means … or knowing the dream was important but not being able to figure out its meaning.

Often, your spirit contacts will be with those you knew on the earth plane who have passed to the higher side. They are familiar to you, and this familiarity makes you more receptive to communication from them. Just keep in mind that people don't change that much just because they pass to the higher side! If someone was, shall we say, less than brilliant in his or her earth plane existence, don't expect to receive great insights from this spirit on the higher side to rival the thinking of Elizabeth Tudor or Albert Einstein. If Uncle Fred couldn't keep track of his money during his life on the earth plane, he's not going to become a Rockefeller on the higher side. But Uncle Fred might have other insights and knowledge to share with you—and you may just find the information he gives you astonishing and profound.

My Filters or Yours?

Interpretation of spirit communication starts, of course, with the medium who is receiving the messages. It is through his or her filters—belief system, level of development as a medium, other talents and knowledge—that spirit messages must pass first. On the one hand, this is a clear limitation: You can only receive information that is within the scope of the medium's background and knowledge to deliver. On the other hand, however, this is a benefit in that it focuses the information in ways that make sense to the medium and to you.

> **Silver Cord**
>
> Modern Spiritualism holds that the psychosocial aspects of the medium attract spirits who are at the same level, to convey messages that are within the medium's scope to understand and communicate.

At a church service, Rita was doing message work and had come through a rather stiff-standing older gentleman who, in his physical existence, had been quite critical and conservative. He always stood in a military stance and didn't have a supportive word to say to anyone. Everything had to be proven to him; he redefined the word skeptic. In this service, the man was coming through for his nephew, a young man in the congregation who was a developing healer. The uncle described a location in the young man's backyard where the young man was establishing his healing work, and then said to his nephew, "Well done!"

The image the uncle described was of the healing light coming into the place where the young man, a *dowser*, did much of his healing work. The experience was particularly moving because such healing would have been totally foreign to the uncle in his physical life, as would have any praise or recognition.

Spiritology

A **dowser** is someone who uses divining rods or a pendulum to search for water or to check energy fields. In healing, dowsing is also used to balance the chakras (bodily energy centers).

Like a Dream

In many respects, making sense of spirit messages is like interpreting dreams. Spirit messages are often very symbolic; symbolism is one of the most primal and at the same time most powerful means of communication. Symbolism transcends the boundaries (such as language, culture, and belief systems) that divide people on the earth plane as well as the barriers between the earth plane and the spirit plane.

Each medium has a structure of symbols that spirits use in communication through that medium. Gold might represent riches and wealth in the symbolism dictionary of one medium, while for another it represents opportunities as yet unfolded. A good medium knows his or her symbols, and can present to you its meaning rather than the symbol itself. Always evaluate and assess the information you receive within the context of your life and its realities. Sometimes you need to reinterpret the message from the medium so that it fits your life.

If you are receiving spirit communication directly, just let the information come to you rather than try to interpret it as it's coming through. Remember that sometimes spirits struggle, too, to make sense when they communicate! The limitations of the earth plane can cause a spirit to fumble for just the right images and presentations. Once spirits find the best bridge of communication that links to you, messages can have astounding clarity.

As you explore and develop your own mediumistic abilities and psychical skills, it's a good idea to keep a journal of the symbols that appear to you consistently. They might include certain sounds, smells, or sights. Or they might include numbers, words, colors, or objects. Write down the symbol, and then a brief description of its context. Over time, this will become your personal dictionary of symbols.

It's in the Details

As we say throughout this book, it's the details that make the difference. It's easy enough for a medium (or a spirit contact) to say, "Your father liked to watch football on Sunday afternoons." Not much of a stretch to make that fit many people's lives! But it's another thing entirely to say, "Your dad loved those Green Bay Packers! He never missed a home game at Lambeau Field, and God help anybody who moved his 'cheesehead' from the rabbit ears antenna when the away game was on television!"

Jim is a member of the Greater Boston Church of Spiritualism where Rita worked on a recent Medium's Day. Jim wanted a spirit drawing done for his mother, Cleo, but he did not reveal this to Rita at the time, so as not to influence the spirit connection. Cleo's father appeared on the paper, and Jim recognized him instantly. As Rita drew, her spirit guides showed Rita her own Uncle Tom's hairstyle so Rita would know exactly how to render Jim's grandfather's hair in the picture. Spirit guides sometimes trigger information accessible to mediums, to stimulate what needs to be given out. Rita always felt this drawing couldn't have been more exact if Jim's grandfather had been posing for a portrait while here on the earth plane.

It is the details that give our lives meaning, and it is the details that provide evidence of the continuity of life beyond physical existence. It is the details that prove, beyond a doubt, that you are communicating with Uncle Jordan or Aunt Ruth or your cousin Stephen who drowned when he fell through an air pocket in the ice on Lake Michigan. And it is the details that let you know that these are valid experiences, these are authentic messages, and these are feelings you can trust as true.

Digging Deeper

Sometimes the message comes through loud and clear, but you can't recognize the spirit communicator. It might be someone in your distant family, or it might not be whom you expected. Dig a little to find out how this message is relevant to you!

Early in her spirit communication experiences, Rita was sitting in a circle with a British medium who did not know her or anything about her. He said to Rita, "I have an uncle here for you, his name is Yekah."

The medium gave a lot of detailed information about this uncle, but it wasn't anyone Rita recognized. Because many members of her mother's family had not come to this country, Rita called her mother to see who this spirit visitor might have been. She started by asking her mother to name her brothers.

"There's Morris and Mosha," her mother said, and then asked Rita, "What are you trying to find out?"

Rita told her mother of the experience with the medium, and gave the information that the medium had provided. "Yes, Uncle Yekah. He was *my* uncle!" Rita's mother said.

Even though it took some research to understand the message, it was a message that had great meaning for Rita on multiple levels. It gave her information about her life, and it absolutely affirmed the continuity of life. The only way this medium could've received this information was through spirit, as Rita hadn't even known this uncle existed.

When the Message Is for You to Deliver

Sometimes during your reading with a medium, a message will come through for you to deliver to someone else. This is usually because you are willing to listen and are open to the communication, while the intended recipient is not. Many times, it is to say "I'm sorry, it's not your fault," to make amends, and sometimes just to say "I love you."

A woman in Rita's congregation was sitting with a medium when a message came through for a childhood friend, Martin. It was from a mutual friend, Carl, who had committed suicide after being arrested for drinking in public. Carl went to jail, while Martin ran away and escaped arrest. Carl hung himself in jail, and Martin had carried the burden of guilt ever since, over not being there to prevent it.

The message was from Carl to Martin, telling Martin it wasn't his fault. Carl had been depressed for a long time, and had committed suicide because of his depression, not because he'd been arrested or because of any sense that Martin had abandoned him. "It's not your fault," Carl wanted to say to Martin. He chose their mutual friend for expressing this, because she was open to the communication and Martin would accept the message coming from her.

Transforming Negative Energy

Sometimes messages that come through from the spirit world seem confused, unhappy, or even dark. Remember, though, that we want all spirit communication to come to us for the highest good. Messages might be painful because they stir old resentments and hurts. But this is the path to healing such wounds, for you and probably for the spirit bringing the messages to you.

Mediums and Messages

Spirits sometimes come through to make amends for negative energy that they spread in their physical lives. During message work in a church, Rita had a gentleman come through who was heavyset and scant of hair, and who made it clear that in his physical life he had been an angry and argumentative personality. He never had a kind word for anybody, and often left people in tears. He was coming through at this church service to say to those people in the congregation that day, "I'm sorry, I'm sorry, I didn't mean to be so hurtful."

Rita had a man come to her for a reading, hoping to find guidance from the higher side. His mother was getting ready to pass, and he and his brother were having heated arguments about how to handle all of the arrangements. It was his grandmother who came through, a kind and gentle woman. She wanted to communicate directly to her grandson, and she said, "You have many good and right things to say, but you need to learn how to present yourself differently, so people will listen and take you seriously."

Emotionally Powerful Messages

Many messages that come through spirit communication are deeply emotional. They are messages that convey apology, forgiveness, comfort, and most importantly, love. They touch us in the deepest cores of our beings, sometimes uncovering both pain and joy we didn't know were there. This is one way we know that these messages are authentic. They're so personal that there's no way anyone could fake them!

But once stirred, these emotions are powerful and intense, and can make you feel quite unsettled until you are able come to grips with them (especially if you are one who keeps your emotions to yourself). Deeply emotional experiences on the earth plane tend to be clearly defined by time: a wedding, a funeral, a birth of a child. Deeply emotional experiences activated from the spirit plane often extend across conventional borders of time and place, touching many dimensions of your life simultaneously. It can be overwhelming to feel such intensity.

If you are planning a reading with a medium, schedule it for a time when you will be able to deal with the emotions that might arise. Try not to do it on your lunch break from work, if possible! Although the intensity of your feelings might startle you, it's perfectly normal. And it's what allows healing to begin.

After a reading (or any spirit contact), take some time for yourself, to think about the messages you received and begin to understand their meanings. You might want to:

- ◆ Take a long walk or go for a bicycle ride. Physical activity occupies your body, and being in nature connects you with a reality that is larger than yourself. This frees your mind to explore the new information it's received.

- ◆ Write in your journal. This activity takes you intentionally within yourself, giving focus to contemplation and understanding (see the journaling exercise in the next section).

- ◆ Talk with a trusted friend. Someone who knows you well can help you connect seemingly disparate messages to situations and experiences in your life. Within the context of love and kindness, this friend can gently show you things about yourself that you can't see.

- ◆ Explore and resolve intense emotions, such as anger and hurt, through counseling or psychotherapy. A mental health professional can help you accept past hurts and use them to strengthen and shape your life as it moves forward.

> **CAUTION**
>
> **Premonition** _____
>
> Don't fall into the trap of going to a medium to have someone else make your hard decisions. A good medium (an experienced and ethical medium) will not tell you what to do but instead will present you with information to help you choose appropriately. *Never* make changes just because a medium tells you to or gives you information that tells you to do so. Spirit communication is for you to learn, not for you to avoid responsibility for your life and your decisions! Spiritualists stress personal responsibility.

A Journaling Exercise

Keeping a journal is a good way to explore your experiences and feelings about spirit communications. It's just for you, so you don't have to worry about spelling or grammar or any of that. Writing with a pen or a pencil on paper causes you to use different parts of your brain than other forms of communication do, which helps you see things from a different perspective. The following exercise lets you explore a message you might have received from a spirit contact:

1. Find a comfortable, quiet place where you can write in your journal without interruption. Put on music and light candles if you like.

2. Write with a pen or pencil on paper.

3. First, write down the message that you received. Write it in as much detail as you can recall.

4. Next, write about how it felt to receive the message. How did you respond or react? What feelings did you experience? How old did the message make you feel?

5. Write some memories of times in your life when the information of this message would have been helpful.

6. Finally, write about what changes you might make in your life to make use of this information. What can you do differently? How can you do it?

White Cake with White Frosting

Judy came to Rita a week before her birthday for a reading. This was Judy's first birthday since her mother's passing the summer before. Her mother, a baker, had always created elaborate birthday cakes to celebrate family birthdays. Because this was just a part of who her mother was, Judy had never appreciated these cakes, which were truly works of art. So now Judy wanted to contact her mother to say "I miss you so much, and I want to thank you."

Rita started the reading, and quite quickly established a connection with Judy's mother. After presenting Judy with the identifying information that confirmed this was indeed her mother, Rita said to Judy, "Your mother is presenting you with a white cake and white frosting for your birthday."

Judy smiled and said, "That's very sweet, but you must be mistaken. My mother would never have made me a plain white cake with plain white frosting while she was alive, and I can't imagine that would be the message she would choose to send now."

So Rita continued with the reading, presenting Judy with a variety of messages from her mother that ranged from "I'm glad you married Jed, he's a good man," to "I like your new hairstyle, it really accentuates your eyes." Judy was delighted with this communication from her mother, and told Rita it was just like sitting in a room having a chat.

But Rita kept getting the message about the white cake with the white frosting. Finally, Rita said to Judy, "Your mother is very insistent about this white cake with the white frosting! She wants to present this to you in honor of your birthday." Rita didn't know that Judy's birthday was coming up.

At first, Judy just sat there. Then her face turned pale and she burst into tears. Judy's mother had really liked to bake, and always insisted on making gourmet cakes for family celebrations, but Judy had always begged for just a white cake with white frosting! The experience was very affirming and comforting to Judy because she knew her mother was really there and finally hearing her.

Seeking Clarification

Communication, spirit or earthbound, is not always clear or consistent. When in doubt, ask! Spirits aren't intentionally mysterious or enigmatic; they want you to understand the messages they are bringing. Sometimes, however, they just aren't able to communicate in ways that make sense to you. Of course, communication on the earth plane has its challenges, too—so much so that we might think of each other as being from different planets!

From the Spirit World

Is the confusion coming from the spirit? A spirit who was not especially articulate while on the earth plane, or who has been on the higher side for a long time (measured in earth plane time, of course), might struggle to find the right images and symbols. Sometimes, the symbolic language is different between the communicator and the medium. It's fine to say, "I don't understand. Can you put it another way?"

Is it the case that the medium seems to understand the message, but is having trouble conveying it to you? The message might be clear to the medium on a clairsentient

level, but difficult to translate into language that communicates the message to you. It's like trying to squeeze a baseball-size orange through a one-inch tube. You might succeed, but although what comes out the other end might smell and taste like an orange, it isn't going to look anything like the orange it started as! Again, ask for clarification. Rita always tells people to let her know if there is anything they can't relate to, and explains that she will ask her guides for clarification.

Silver Cord

When messages seem unclear, write down exactly what the message is as it's coming through, to the best of your ability to capture it. Put this aside for a few days, and then come back to it. Sometimes things will make more sense when you give them a little distance.

From Yourself

Sometimes it's us who don't get the message, or we interpret it in ways that are different than the spirit bringing the message seemed to intend. This is especially likely to be the case when the message is counter to a long-held belief or resistance. If all of your life you viewed your father as distant and uninterested, you're naturally going to resist messages from the other side that are attempting to communicate his love for you.

It could be that the message isn't authentic; perhaps this isn't really your father but another loved one who might have looked or sounded like your father—a grandfather, brother, or uncle. Or it could be that your father's spirit has evolved enough on the other side to want to reach out to you to make amends. You should be able to get enough identifying information to determine which is the case. (See also "Desperate Illusions" in Chapter 10.)

Life-Changing Experiences

Sometimes spirit messages are so revelatory that they become turning points in your life. When you gain new understanding and insights, great. Let these insights guide the changes you make to restructure your life, and you have truly learned through spirit communication.

Just remember, however, that spirits don't usually come through to say, "Invest in Microsoft and move to Denver." Before you make a major life change, consider all of the ramifications, all of the pros and cons. Then make your decision based on all of the circumstances of your life. If you hate your job, have no one depending on you for support and sustenance, don't like the weather in Phoenix, and just inherited $100,000 from Great Aunt Delia, then you might want to buy some Microsoft stock, quit your job, pack your things, and move to Denver. Don't make a major change in your lifestyle, though, just because a medium or a spirit tells you to. This is *your* life, and only you should make the decisions that shape its direction.

The Peace of Understanding

Welcome the messages that come to you through spirit communication for the understanding and comfort they can bring to you. Accept the learning and the healing that comes to you from the higher side. Through spirit communication, you often can find answers that have otherwise eluded you.

The Least You Need to Know

♦ Spirit communication comes through for understanding and healing.

♦ The details are what confirms the spirit's identity.

♦ Be prepared for spirit communication to bring powerful emotions to the surface.

♦ If a spirit message doesn't make sense to you, seek clarification.

Part 4

Activating Your Spirit Senses

Do you follow your intuition even when it appears to be leading you in directions contrary to logic or common sense? Do you experience spirit contact? Many people have strong psychic and mediumistic abilities but don't recognize it.

The chapters in this part discuss some of the advanced abilities that mediums use to communicate with spirits. More exercises let you test your own skills.

Chapter 14

Mediumistic Sight, Hearing, and Knowledge

In This Chapter

- ◆ Your physical senses and the tangible world
- ◆ Your psychic senses and the energy world
- ◆ Your psychical senses and the spirit world
- ◆ Enhancing your senses and expanding your perceptions

Among the fictional alien races the starship *Enterprise* encountered on TV's popular science-fiction series *Star Trek: The Next Generation* were the Betazoids. On the outside, these peaceful beings looked just as human as, well, humans. But on the inside … that was a different story. Advanced brain development and heightened function gave these aliens a unique ability: They were empaths. They could communicate without speaking, sensing each other's thoughts as well as the thoughts of non-Betazoids. And even though Betazoids started life with their empathic powers, they had to practice to develop their skills.

Sometimes science fiction isn't so far removed from reality! Although we've yet to send crews on spaceships to explore distant galaxies, the *Hubble* telescope speeds through space to orbit the earth about 15 times every 24 hours, sending back amazing images of faraway star systems. Human footprints trail across the lunar dust of the moon's surface. Space shuttle flights and assignments to the orbiting space station have become almost routine for NASA astronauts and other scientists. And many ordinary human beings right here in the real world of everyday life—your friends, your colleagues, your relatives, and maybe even you!—have the psychical abilities that would make them feel right at home on Betazed, fictional home planet of the Betazoids.

Exploring Your Physical Senses

Yes, we do mean *physical* senses. These are the senses you first learned about in grade school science class and through which you experience the tangible world—sight, hearing, smell, taste, and touch. These senses connect you to your physical world, allowing you to gather the information that becomes your perceptions.

Learning to use your physical senses to their fullest extent increases your awareness of your surroundings. Look up from your reading right now. What is the first thing that you see? Describe everything about it that you can perceive through vision—colors, shapes, textures (as dimensional perceptions). When you've exhausted your visual perceptions, find one more visual detail. Repeat this exercise, calling on each of your physical senses. Make this a daily activity and you'll be amazed at how quickly your sensory capabilities expand.

It's a Tangible World

The energy that gives our physical world its form and context presents itself in many tangibilities. The frequency of an energy's vibration determines our sensory experience of it. We see colors and shapes, smell fragrances, touch textures, taste flavors, hear sounds. The energies of these experiences are distinct and discreet most of the time. Most of us don't taste colors, for example, or see sounds. (Although many mediums do.)

Nonetheless, our physical senses work in a sort of synchronous way. This is most obvious with the senses of taste and smell. Ever notice how the flavor goes flat in favorite foods when you have a cold that plugs your nose? That's because much of what you perceive as flavor is actually smell rather than taste. The receptor cells for these two senses—technically known as *olfaction* and *gustation*, respectively—reside fairly close to each other and their signals travel to the same section in your brain for interpretation.

Other physical senses complement each other, too, although their interrelationships are often not as obvious. Typically you hear more clearly, and in greater detail, when you can also see the source of the sound. This allows you to combine visual signals with audio signals, expanding the range of information that reaches your brain. Similarly, sight enhances touch. Seeing an object's size, consistency, color, and texture gives a framework for the perceptions of that object that come through touch.

Spiritology

Olfaction is the technical term for the sense of smell. **Gustation** is the technical term for the sense of taste (and the basis for the concept of "eating with gusto").

Expanding Your Physical Senses: An Exercise

One way to expand your physical senses is to focus on one sense, gathering as much information as possible. Here is an exercise to help you do this:

1. Get a notepad and pen or pencil so you can write down your experiences. Then go to a location where there is a lot of activity, such as a park, a shopping mall, or a busy restaurant.

2. First, look around you. What do you see? Write down at least 10 sights.

3. Next, what do you hear? Write down at least 10 sounds.

4. Now, what can you touch with your hands, feet, and other parts of your body? (Consider the floor you walk on, the bench you sit on, even the pen and paper in your hands.) What do you feel, and with what part of your body? Write down at least 10 sensations.

5. What do you smell? Describe at least 10 fragrances and odors.

6. Taste is sometimes a difficult sense to integrate into an exercise such as this, unless you go to a restaurant or other location where you can drink and eat. If you are in such a location, write down your descriptions of the tastes you experience.

How often do you find yourself using more than one sense to form a perception? Think first about the primary sense that you're using, and then any other senses that come into play. You might receive visual perceptions about a person, then add to the information you are gathering when you hear the person's voice and smell any perfumes or fragrances (or other odors). Although the point of this exercise is to focus on what each sense can contribute to your perceptions, in practical use your sensory experiences combine to form impressions that are more complete.

Spiritology

Extrasensory perception (ESP) uses your nonphysical senses to gather impressions and perceptions about physical and nonphysical experiences.

Exploring Your Psychic Senses

Your psychic senses are your senses, sometimes called *extrasensory perception* (*ESP*). They allow you to take your physical senses to the next level, and also to gather information that your physical senses alone cannot detect.

Intuition: More Than Just a Feeling

Just about everyone has had "gut feelings"—about people, events, places, circumstances. You meet someone at a business luncheon and instantly know, without tangible information, that this person is someone to avoid. Maybe it's that every hair on your body is standing on edge or that you can't suppress the shudder that goes through you when you shake hands with this person. But you *know*. Your "gut feeling" is telling you something isn't right.

Take this to the next level, and now you're talking intuition. What images does the handshake evoke? What is your sense of this person? What other psychic senses does this person activate in you? What, precisely, is the message your intuition is giving you about this person? Some people experience vague intuitive messages, while others experience intuition that provides considerable detail.

You might have intuitive feelings about friends and family, or about such mundane events in daily life as what song will play next on the radio (a fairly common manifestation of intuition). You can cultivate this psychic sense by practicing it.

Telepathy: Reach Out and Connect

Telepathy is the communication that takes place without using your physical senses. It's not really mind reading, although that's a common perception. Rather, telepathy is a process of sending and receiving messages. You might, however, "pick up" on messages that others don't realize they're sending to you.

Telepathy, like initial mediumistic experiences, can feel more like imagination than ability when you are new to your awareness of it. After all, how can you really know what's in someone else's head? You can, of course, but proof can be elusive. But with practice, you will soon learn to distinguish between what you think or imagine and what you receive and send. Chapter 15 discusses telepathy in detail.

Premonition

No one, not even the most talented psychic or medium, can "read" your mind and receive information that you don't wish to share. Your private thoughts and feelings are always yours; your spirit guides help assure this. Sometimes you do send messages about your thoughts and feelings without consciously realizing that you are doing so. This happens because you are willing, on a spirit level, to share them, which is how it might seem that a psychic has tapped into your innermost thoughts.

Precognition: Sensing the Future

Do you ever sense something, an event or occurrence, and then find that later it happens? This is precognition, a psychic ability to perceive experiences beyond the boundaries of time. This psychic sense taps into the universal energy field, the energy of all existence, encompassing the physical and nonphysical worlds. A common form of precognition is crisis precognition, in which we sense impending difficulties or disaster involving loved ones here on the earth plane.

You might think of precognition as predicting the future. Certainly when events unfold as you sensed them (especially when there was no way you could have known of their details), this appears to be the case. But remember that precognition transcends the borders of time that define the events and reality of our physical world. This definition construes time as a linear continuum. Time really isn't linear; it's coexistent. That is, all time exists simultaneously. There is no past, present, or future—there are only our perceptions of these conceptual dividing points.

Most people aren't aware of precognitive experiences until after the events they perceived unfold. This gives the appearance that the events were destined to occur. You read a newspaper report about an assassination attempt on a world leader, and suddenly realize, "I knew

Silver Cord

Is it possible to change the future? Certainly! Could you prevent the assassination of a world leader because you had a premonition that it would happen? Probably not, unless you are a member of the leader's security detail and can intervene with physical events as they unfold. Many, many choices and decisions determine the course of events.

this was going to happen!" But there are myriad circumstances that also unfold, countless events that are the result of choices and decisions—the all-important function of free will.

Psychometry: Reading the Energy

Many psychics have trouble going into antique stores. The residual energy stored in their furnishings and objects can rush out at the psychically sensitive just as the smell of baking cinnamon rolls floods through a shopping mall with a bakery. Touching an object connects you with the energy it has stored from others who have touched or owned it. You might experience this energy through any of your psychic senses. Chapter 16 discusses psychometry in detail.

Exercises for Expanding Your Psychic Senses

You can expand the capabilities of your psychic senses by practicing them. Let's use intuition as an example (we'll give you exercises to build your telepathic and psychometric abilities in later chapters). Spontaneous intuition often comes to people during everyday activities. Here are some ways to "tune in" to your intuition, making it a more conscious function.

- ◆ **Listening to the radio.** Do you listen to the radio in the car and at work? Try to intuit what song will play next. When you get good at this (or tired of it), try to intuit what commercial will come on next.

- ◆ **Answering the telephone.** How often do you reach for the ringing telephone and "know" who's calling? Or pick up the phone *before* it rings to find someone on the other end who has just dialed your number? When the phone rings, take a moment to try and sense who's on the other end of the line. Quickly jot the name on a piece of paper, then answer the phone. Were you right?

- ◆ **Listening to your inner voice.** What inner messages do you receive when meeting people for the first time? When you have the opportunity, write down these perceptions (most people will be quite unnerved if you whip out a notepad and say, "Just a minute! Let me get this down!"). Make sure that you keep these notes in a secure place where others aren't likely to come across them. Later, go back to your notes and see how accurate your perceptions were.

- ◆ **Rolling the dice.** Take a set of dice in your hand. Predict the number, and then roll the dice. How often does your number come up?

◆ **Cutting a deck of cards.** Get a deck of cards that you use for nothing else but this exercise (so you don't pick up any other energies). Decide that you want to turn up two cards, such as a jack and a queen. Cut the deck; see if you cut it on that card, or that card is the next card above or below. How close are you?

These are only starting points. There are endless ways to use intuition in your life, and the more you use it the better at it you will become.

Exploring Your Psychical Senses

Your psychical senses are closely related to your psychic senses. But rather than using them to explore earth plane experiences, you use them to connect with the spirit world. The three key psychical senses—clairaudience, clairvoyance, and clairsentience—correspond to key physical senses (hearing and sight) and psychic senses (intuition).

Clairaudience: Hearing the Unspoken

Clairaudience is the inner sense of psychical hearing, the ability to hear voices and sounds from beyond the earth plane. A spirit contact might begin with the sense that someone is talking to you. You don't actually hear these words in the same way you hear the words of someone who is talking right in front of you. Instead, you hear them within your head. You might even feel that you're imagining them!

Because spirit contact usually comes for a purpose, to deliver a message, the spirit might persist with the message until you finally "get" it. You may or may not know the spirit communicator, and the message could be for you or for someone else. You might hear the words over and over, or perceive the message as a directive: "Tell Robert not to worry. His job will change, but it will be for the better and he'll do fine."

It's important to first just receive the message, without attempting to filter or interpret it. This is especially important if the message is for you to deliver to someone else; let that person decide what the message actually means.

Early in her mediumistic experiences, Rita was doing a church service and had had few clear clairaudient experiences. She was receiving a lot of information for a woman in the congregation, and the woman was nodding and agreeing. Then Rita kept hearing "Frenchie" without much context, so after a few moments she just put the word out there for the woman. The woman was very excited; this was the nickname of a woman who had been a close friend and mentor!

Another time, Rita had a set of parents coming through for two sisters. The father was an accomplished musician, and the music was coming through. Rita was talking about how magnificent the music was, and then said: "Now your mother is here." Then Rita heard someone just banging out a tune, like a marching band. She shared this with the daughters, who started laughing. "Yes, mother sure could bang out a tune!" one of them said.

When you receive clairaudience, use the opportunity to refine and develop this sense. Determine the following:

- What does the voice sound like?

- Is the voice male or female, old or young, soft or harsh?

- Do you know whose voice it is?

- What is the message?

- Is the message for you or for you to deliver to someone else?

Messages that are for you might also come through the clairaudience of a medium. When this is the case, remember that the medium's consciousness filters this message; it's unavoidable. If the message is clear and makes perfect sense to you, great! If it seems vague or perhaps even unrelated to you, ask the medium for clarification. There might be symbolism in the words the spirit communicator chooses to use, or the spirit just might not be expressing the message clearly. Verbal communication on the earth plane can be challenging enough!

Mediums and Messages

During a reading, a grandfather came through. He started out talking about his personality, which was sometimes very sweet but sometimes very strong. Rita kept seeing a newspaper being held in front of his face. Rita told the woman she was doing the reading for, "He sits there with the newspaper in front of his face, almost as though he's hiding because he doesn't want to talk to people." Three or four times Rita mentioned this, and the woman finally said, "You never said he was *reading* the paper. Yes, this is my grandfather. I didn't find out until after he died that he actually couldn't read!"

Clairvoyance: Seeing Visions

Clairvoyance is the inner sense of psychical vision, the ability to see images from beyond the earth plane. Such visions might be explicit, showing you facial details and clothing, for example. More often, clairvoyant images are less specific and might be shadowy or incomplete. You might see, in your mind's eye, the image of a person's head and upper body, but not the arms and legs. Or you might see a steering wheel, but not the car. Even when incomplete, clairvoyant images can be quite vivid—they seem real and tangible even as you know they are not.

At other times, clairvoyant images are more dreamlike. The images might be symbolic or representative rather than literal. You might repeatedly see the color blue, the shape of a triangle, a marigold in full bloom. Every medium has a "dictionary" of symbols; certain objects and images that have specific meanings whenever they appear. This symbolism may or may not make sense in terms of earth plane experiences.

When you receive clairvoyant messages, try to experience as much of the images as possible. If you are alone or in a circle, describe out loud what you're seeing. If this is not practical (the images come to you when others are there or you just can't speak out loud), explore the images as much as your mind's eye will permit, and when the clairvoyant experience is over write down as much as you can recall.

- What exactly do you see? Describe shapes, colors, features.

- Is the image clear and complete, or foggy and incomplete?

- Do you recognize the image? If so, what is it? If not, what does it remind you of or make you think of?

- Does the image relate to your life?

- What seems to be the message of the image?

If a medium brings through clairvoyant images, ask for clarification about anything that doesn't quite make sense. If the medium describes someone that sounds very much like your father who has passed but this spirit is showing with a full beard and wearing a hat, two things never associated with your father, this might seem inconsistent and therefore incorrect. Don't be so quick to jump to such a conclusion!

Rita begins every sitting with, "I am seeing …" because she is predominantly clairvoyant and sees images all the time. In one sitting, she was clearly tasting all of the father's favorite foods and talking about it. Then Rita received an image of the father with a huge bowl of salad in front of him and then pushing it away as if he didn't want it. The woman laughed; her father had always refused to eat salad!

Spirits present themselves as they want to be seen. Maybe there's a joke in this image for you—did your dad try to grow a beard but was unsuccessful or people made fun of him? Did he have a favorite hat that you hated or found embarrassing? Spirits love humor! Even if your father never wanted a beard or wore a hat on the earth plane, he might want to present himself in this way to you now as a message that he's perhaps loosened up or is enjoying a carefree existence. And of course, there is always the possibility that the medium has misinterpreted the image, which is why you should ask for clarification when the descriptions seem off.

Clairsentience: Experiential Knowledge

Clairsentience is like intuition to the tenth degree. It is the psychical sense of just knowing, and the psychical sense mediums experience all the time. Mediums feel the presence of spirits, feel the size and bulk of their bodies, the stance of the person, just like they are standing inside of them. They feel the condition that caused the person's passing, can smell or taste—as if actually within the person.

> **Premonition**
>
> Spirit messages come to us for good and for healing, not to do harm. If you are hearing voices or seeing images that are instructing you to hurt yourself or others, this is not spirit communication. Please seek help from a psychologist or therapist.

Some mediums view clairsentience as a discreet psychical sense, while others perceive it as the combination of multiple psychical senses. In some regards, this is like trying to separate the physical senses of smell and taste. Yes, each is a discreet and individual sense that responds to particular sensations. Yet one does not function completely without the other.

Clairsentience is an experience of the whole. You might get the sensation of hearing a voice, seeing an image, and even smelling a fragrance or odor—all at the same time, just as your physical senses experience a person who walks into the room. Or you might not have any tangible perceptions, but just an overall sense of a place or an event.

To get the most from clairsentient experiences, open yourself fully to the experience. Let all of the information come through. After the experience concludes, try to answer these questions:

- Do you recognize the person, place, or event?

- How are you experiencing these perceptions? Can you identify specific psychical senses?

- What seems to be the nature or purpose of this clairsentient experience? Is the message for you or for you to deliver to someone else?

◆ How do you feel as this experience is unfolding? Are you aware of external activities and sensations, or has the clairsentient experience completely enveloped you?

Clairsentient perceptions might feel intangible, unreal, and even more mysterious than dreams or imagination, especially when you are new to exploring your psychical senses. With practice and focus, clairsentient experiences can be quite amazing and profound.

Setting Aside Consciousness

Sometimes your conscious mind gets in the way of, or limits, your psychical senses. There are a number of ways that you can set aside your consciousness to enhance the perceptions of your psychical senses.

Meditation

Meditation is the process of preparing your mind for openness. It is not, as those unfamiliar with it sometimes assume, a process of emptying your mind. That would be impossible! Meditation is rather a means of refining your focus so that you gradually exclude disruptions and interruptions. There are many ways to meditate and many purposes for meditating; here, we'll just look at meditation as a means of connecting with spirits.

Remember the "Meet Your Spirit Guides" exercise from Chapter 7? That is a form of meditation. In that exercise, you used your mind to place yourself in a receptive mode. You did this by focusing on specific details: sitting on a bench, looking at and smelling flowers, watching your spirit guide approach. The more you focused on these details, the more specific they became and the less aware you were of the endless other activities of your thoughts, memories, and brain and body functions. You were able to go within yourself, to use your inner senses (your psychical senses) to experience energy perceptions from beyond the earth plane.

Trance

A trance is a state of suspended consciousness into which a medium enters to allow spirits to communicate through him or her. When this happens, the medium's spirit steps aside to let the visiting spirit "borrow" some of the medium's physical abilities, such as speech. A medium in trance state might also take on the physical mannerisms and gestures of the visiting spirit, seeming to become the spirit's personification.

Silver Cord _____

An experienced medium can control both entering and emerging from the trance state. An inexperienced medium might find that a visiting spirit wants to stay a little longer, like a child who doesn't want to leave an amusement park even though it's closing time. After all, visiting spirits enjoy their contacts with us, and some are reluctant to give up center stage! This, again, is why it's so essential to establish your intent for spirit communication to come through in light and for the highest good. Experienced mediums have made their limits clear, which sets the boundaries for the visiting spirit's stay.

This is a shared experience between the medium's spirit and the visiting spirit. The visiting spirit cannot make the medium do or say anything he or she does not want to do or say, nor has the spirit any interest in trying to do so. Visiting spirits come through with messages that they want to convey to us here on the earth plane—scaring the bejesus out of us isn't going to do much for their credibility!

Dreams

"To sleep, perchance to dream ...." The immortal words of William Shakespeare capture the delight and escape that dreaming offers. In the dream state, your conscious mind retreats and releases its control and censorship of the activities of your brain. This frees the mind to experience perceptions that would otherwise be blocked.

The brain, as the physical organ that interprets the vast range of perceptions you experience, is particularly receptive to mediumistic messages during the dream state. Rita often finds that spirit messages come to her in the dream state. Although she has established a restriction around spirits waking her from sleep unless absolutely necessary, she frequently awakens with the realization that she's received spirit messages.

Sometimes spirit messages have the appearance of dreams. You might wake up with images of visiting with your mother who has passed, for example, and feel as though you "lived" the scenario in your dream. The dreamscape might be a presentation of an actual setting or event from when your mother was alive on the earth plane and the two of you went somewhere or did something together. This might feel to you like a dream-memory—reliving in your dreams a favorite memory from your life. Or your dreamscape might be someplace fantastical, magical, mystical—clearly not a setting you've ever experienced in your tangible life.

Keeping a journal is an effective way to explore your dreams and spirit messages that come to you through dreams or in the dream state. Keep a pad and pencil next to your bed, and write down the images and feelings that are present when you wake up. Later, when you have the time and the opportunity to explore these impressions, write about what you think they mean.

One helpful technique is *free association*. From the notes you wrote about your dream experiences, make a list of what appear to be key words or concepts. Beside each word, write the first thoughts that come to you. Don't let your conscious mind censor this process! Just let the thoughts and images flow. Give yourself 30 seconds to a minute for each, and then move to the next. You don't want to be thinking and analyzing, just reacting.

See Chapter 17 for more about dreams, including special dream states such as lucid dreaming and astral travel.

> **Spiritology**
>
> **Free association** is the practice of saying or writing the first thing that comes to mind in response to a particular word or image.

Transcending Boundaries

One of the most exciting aspects of developing your physical, psychic, and psychical senses is that it expands your awareness of the experiences that are your life. This brings a fullness and richness to your life, like seeing a black-and-white photograph become full color. It can put you in touch with your mission in this life, make you laugh (and make you cry), help you understand why certain things happen, and connect you with loved ones who are important to you in a continuing affirmation of the continuity of life.

The Least You Need to Know

- ◆ Your physical, psychic, and psychical senses present you with the information that shapes your perceptions of your existence.

- ◆ With practice, you can enhance any and all of these senses.

- ◆ Energy is the connecting force that links all of your senses.

- ◆ Using your senses to their fullest expands your perceptions and heightens your awareness, enriching your life.

Chapter **15**

Telepathic Bridges

In This Chapter

- ◆ What telepathy is ... and isn't
- ◆ Studies of telepathy
- ◆ An exercise to sharpen your telepathic skills
- ◆ Putting telepathy to work
- ◆ Let your spirit do the visiting
- ◆ Two exercises in astral projection

Your mind is a powerful tool. As a bridge between your thoughts and your spirit, it converts energy into images, memories, and articulations. You can't see your mind, although certainly you can show it! Scientists have explored the workings of the mind for decades. Some now believe there are chemicals called polypeptides that conduct the energy impulses we identify as the mind's functions, activating the brain cells that translate the impulses into perceptions.

Telepathy comes from Greek words meaning "far feeling." Sometimes called thought transference, it is a process of exchanging energy to communicate, rather than using physical senses. When telepathy takes place between mortals, it's a psychic skill.

Just as children are sensitive to spirit presence, they have strong telepathic capabilities. The unspoken communication between mother and child can be remarkable to observe. Even more amazing is a mother's sudden recognition, without physical evidence and often when her child is nowhere in sight, that something is wrong. Every family has its collection of in-the-nick-of-time rescue stories.

Read My Mind!

Scientists tell us that, at most, we use about 10 percent of our mental capacity. That leaves quite a lot of ability untapped! Surely all those gray cells aren't just hanging around waiting for electrical impulses to stimulate them. In fact, they might already be hard at work, and you just don't know it.

How often does something like this happen to you:

♦ You're having lunch with a friend, and you both start to say the same thing.

♦ You're talking on the phone with your brother and you say what he is thinking.

♦ You stop by your sister's house to drop off the jacket you borrowed just as she's calling to tell you she needs it back.

♦ Your spouse stops at the grocery store on the way home from work and buys the items on the list you just wrote out.

♦ You pick up the phone to call your mother just as she was about to call you.

♦ You and a stranger walk toward each other on the sidewalk. You both step to the right, then to the left, then to the right again as you unsuccessfully try to let the other pass. Finally you each step to the side and gesture for the other to go past.

All these situations could be examples of telepathy. Telepathy often occurs between two people who are emotionally connected to each other. The deeper the emotional bond, the more likely and frequent telepathic communication is. You think about an event or object, which intensifies its energy in your mind. Someone who is emotionally close to you picks up the signal because it's a change in the normal balance of energy between the two of you.

What about the last example in the list? This truly is a random event, because you and the stranger don't know each other. But you're likely sending messages to each other that arise from the small but nonetheless present anxiety about who should step aside. Each of you picks up the energy signal the other sends—and the signals happen to carry the same message.

Was It a Dream?

The dream state is an environment in which you are particularly receptive to telepathic communication, from other mortals as well as from spirit entities. The filters of your conscious mind are asleep, so to speak. The dream state serves as a telepathic bridge, a communication connection that bypasses the physical senses.

You might awaken from a dream in which you've experienced telepathic communication confused about whether you dreamed it or whether it was real. It can be hard for you to tell, but is often easy to confirm if the communication was with someone you know. Ask the other person who was in your dream if he or she had a similar dream. Sometimes it takes several days, weeks, or even months before you recognize the telepathic nature of a particular dream. Telepathic dreams can involve either incarnate (physical) or discarnate (spirit) beings. If your dream involves communication with a spirit being, you can ask the spirit to visit you again (more on this later in this chapter).

Spirits like to visit during your dream state for much the same reason: You're open to it. It's common to dream of a visit with a loved one who has passed, and for you to share favorite experiences. If your mother loved flowers, she might come to you in your dreams and stroll with you through elaborate gardens. (See Chapter 17 for more about dreams.)

Silver Cord

Keeping a dream journal is an excellent way to learn how to understand your personal dream symbolism. The symbolic elements that show up in your dreams are likely the same ones that emerge when there is spirit contact for you. Dreams can provide insights and information that wouldn't come to you in any other way. You might even discover that your dreams are also the venues for spirit visits.

Psychic Prying: Stay Out!

So is your mind an open book? Are your thoughts available to anyone who chooses to peek at them? Certain thoughts are openly available, if you are not taking any measures to protect them. These are the things that are moving through your consciousness. If someone said, "What are you thinking right now?" these are the thoughts you would mention.

It is unethical to attempt to perceive another person's thoughts without that person's knowledge and permission. It's like walking into someone's house without knocking or announcing yourself. This kind of "mind reading" is intrusive and is seldom done in goodness.

You can protect yourself from being on the receiving end of psychic prying. Just establish a protection of light around your being. Envision this as a dome that covers you. Establish the intent that only those with whom you wish to communicate on a telepathic level can have access. This creates a shield around your thoughts.

It's Your Mind, and Only You Can Control It

Some people believe that they can use their thoughts to control others. No one can control your thoughts or "will" you to do something you don't want to do. What a dangerous weapon this could be, were it possible! But even extensive government experiments during the Cold War era proved that it's not possible.

Various agencies of the United States and the former Soviet Union conducted tests of telepathic communication and control in the 1960s and 1970s. Although psychically gifted test subjects scored high in ESP tests such as perceiving the symbols on cards, they did no better than the odds of chance in using telepathy to "will" other subjects to some sort of action. Mind control is a tantalizing concept of science fiction, and so far it remains safely contained in the realm of fiction rather than exposed in the arena of science.

Crisis Contact

Many people experience telepathic communication in times of crisis. One friend suddenly perceives that another friend has been in a car accident. A sister living on the West Coast gets a sense of panic about her brother living in the Southeast, then hears on the news that a tornado swept through the town where he lives.

Energy intensifies in times of crisis. When bonds already exist between people, rapid spikes in energy intensity send a psychic alert. Sometimes more than two people are involved in the telepathic communication, as when a crisis involves a parent and the children and all of them experience some form of a connection as a result. Each person's experience can be different.

Sometimes crisis telepathy presents itself as a warning, a connection of intuition that is sent directly from one person to another without conscious intervention of the mind. You might not even realize that you've sent a telepathic warning to someone until that person calls or otherwise contacts you.

Validating Telepathy

The first formal efforts to analyze telepathic experiences and understand the processes of telepathy took place in the 1880s, when the Society for Psychical

Research in London began publishing reports about the phenomenon in its journals. As the circulation for those journals grew, so did interest around the world. In these early explorations, researchers used the term extrasensory perception, or ESP, to describe the ability to communicate without using the physical senses.

Sir Arthur Explores Thought Transference

Sir Arthur Conan Doyle, author of the Sherlock Holmes detective novels and an early member of the Spiritualist movement (see Chapter 3), was fascinated with what was at the time called thought transference. He and an architect friend in another location decided to see how well and how much faster they could communicate architectural ideas and drawings than through the process of writing and mailing their ideas to each other. They agreed that at a specified time every week, each would sit down and sketch his ideas, then concentrate on sending the images to the other. They would then switch and focus on receiving the images the other was sending, and sketch those.

They were on target with each other far more frequently than the odds of chance, and Doyle became convinced of the scientific validity of telepathic communication. He later continued some of his studies through the Society for Psychical Research, and published many of his writings on the topic.

J. B. Rhine and Zener Cards

In 1930, an American *parapsychologist*, J. B. (Joseph Banks) Rhine (1895–1980), at Duke University began conducting experiments following scientific research conventions. At first, Rhine used common items to test the ability of subjects to telepathically send and receive messages. Among them was an ordinary deck of playing cards.

Then a colleague and fellow parapsychologist, Karl Zener, developed the set of special cards, known today as Zener cards, with five symbols: circle, square, star, wavy lines, and plus sign. The deck contains 25 cards, 5 of each symbol. The odds of randomly guessing the correct symbol are one in five.

In early tests, subjects sat across a table from each other. One subject turned up a card, holding it so the other subject couldn't see it, and concentrated on sending a mental image of the card's symbol to the other subject. The other subject then said what he or she thought the symbol was.

Spiritology

A **parapsychologist** is a scientist who studies psychic phenomena. The word parapsychology means "study of what is around the mind."

A score of 20 percent right is the baseline, because this is the number of right answers likely just on the basis of the odds. Scores higher than 20 percent suggest telepathic ability on the part of one or both subjects. More important, high scores validate that telepathy is in fact a real, observable phenomenon. Because of their simplicity and consistency, Zener cards have become a standard for telepathic training as well as testing.

Later experiments put the two subjects in separate rooms so they couldn't see or hear each other, or in any other way use their physical senses to communicate. This came in response to criticism that subjects could give each other subtle signals that tipped off which cards were being turned over. Separation didn't change the results.

You can use Zener cards to improve your personal telepathic abilities. They are available at many metaphysical shops and bookstores. Practice working with a friend to send as well as receive card images. Telepathy is like any other skill. The more you use it, the more proficient you become.

> **Silver Cord** _____
>
> Parapsychologist J. B. Rhine was inspired to study psychic phenomena by Sir Arthur Conan Doyle's studies in thought transference. Ironically, Rhine earned Doyle's ire later in his life for exposing as a fraud a medium that Doyle respected.

Early in Rita's psychic development, her friend Judy became convinced of Rita's telepathic abilities but Rita still felt unsure. So Judy and Rita agreed that, as a test, they would both meditate at 10 P.M. on a Friday to see if they could communicate telepathically. Rita would then call Judy at 10:20 P.M.

At 10 P.M., Rita began to meditate and set her intent on visiting her friend Judy. When she went into meditation, she could clearly see Judy's apartment. She saw Judy sitting on the left corner of the couch, wearing a geometric print caftan. Rita saw an incredible white glow around Judy.

When Rita called Judy at 10:20 P.M. and described to Judy what she had seen, Judy was delighted. In fact, she was sitting in the corner of the couch wearing that geometric caftan. "I'm glad you could see the glow around me as I was meditating," Judy told Rita. Rita "visited" Judy telepathically just as vividly as if they'd been physically sitting in the room together.

Sharpening Your Telepathic Skills: An Exercise

Do you have a friend who is as interested in telepathy as you are? Here's an exercise that the two of you can do together to practice and sharpen your telepathic skills.

1. Determine a time at which you will, each in your separate locations, sit down to meditate. Determine how long your meditation will last (10 minutes is good). Use one half of this time to send, and one half to receive a message. (Make sure your times are opposite, so that one of you receives when the other sends!) Use a timer to signal the end of each time period.

2. At the agreed-upon time, begin your meditation. Ask for the meditation to proceed in goodness and light. Start with three deep, cleansing breaths.

3. Concentrate on sending a message to your friend. Perceive the message in whatever way feels comfortable to you, but stick with a single representation.

4. When the sending time is up, take three cleansing breaths and shift to receive mode. Concentrate on opening your mind to the message your friend is sending.

5. When the meditation time is up, bring yourself back to the context of your physical environment.

6. Write down everything you can remember about the experience. On one side of a piece of paper, write the messages you were trying to send to your friend. On the other side, write the messages you think you received from your friend.

7. Phone or visit each other to compare experiences. How often were you right? When you were wrong, were you off in consistent ways, such as perceiving yellow when your friend sent you the color orange?

Generally speaking, if you are on target more often than not, you've exceeded the odds of chance. The greater the gap between on and off, the more intense the telepathic experience. Don't be discouraged if at first you barely hit the odds of chance (or even are below them). You will improve with practice! As you become more proficient, make your messages more complex.

Telekinesis: Using Telepathy to Move Objects

Telekinesis (also called psychokinesis) is the phenomenon of using the mind's energy to move objects without physical intervention. Perhaps the most famous demonstrations of telekinesis came in the 1970s when a young psychic from Russia named Uri Geller came to prominence for his ability to bend spoons and other metal objects without any physical contact.

How does this work? One theory is that the concentration of energy from your mind alters the energy structure of the object you're focusing on. At the point when you release your mind's stream of energy, the object re-forms itself according to the energy pattern you've been sending. If you've sent bending, the spoon bends. If you've sent twisting, it twists.

You can practice telekinesis in a kinder, gentler way. All you need is a quarter. If you toss a quarter ten times, your odds of calling whether it lands heads or tails are about 50-50. There are only two choices, which keep the experiment simple. Calling heads or tails correctly more times than not demonstrates telepathic ability—you are "reading" the energy of the coin to identify which side is up.

Directing the coin to land either heads or tails demonstrates telekinetic ability. You are using the energy of your mind to guide the coin's fall in a determined way. Go ahead, practice! When you get good with the coin, move on to a pair of dice; or one die, to keep it a little less complicated. Just be sure that you focus on sending energy to direct the number at which the roll will stop rather than trying to determine what the number will be. A fine point, but it's the point of distinction between telepathy and telekinesis in this context.

Astral Projection

Astral projection is the phenomenon of your spirit leaving your body to travel beyond it. You might call this psychic visiting. Sometimes it happens spontaneously. You might have a flash image of a friend working at her desk, and then call and tell her what she's wearing or what she's doing. You also can cultivate this psychic skill through practice.

Silver Cord

Astral projection is a conscious form of telepathic visitation. You are deciding to "visit" another person or place. Telepathic communication can happen without a conscious effort, such as crisis telepathy.

Here are two exercises that you can use to practice astral projection. As always when working with spirit phenomena, start each exercise by asking for goodness and light. Even though with astral projection you're not asking for spirit contact, you are connecting your spirit with other spirit energy when your spirit leaves your physical body.

How is it that your soul can travel about, and then know to return to your physical body? Doesn't it seem that the freedom of *not* having a body would be quite enticing? You have an energy umbilical cord, so to speak, that links your spirit with your body for as long as your body lives. It's called the silver cord.

This is not a tangible or physical connection, but a link of energy. Your silver cord keeps your body and your spirit connected, no matter what your state of consciousness. It is said that your silver cord appears at physical birth and disappears at physical death.

Astral Projection Exercise: Two People

This exercise requires two people. Choose someone you trust who shares your interest in astral projection. As in the telepathy exercise, be in different physical locations.

1. Determine a time at which you will each meditate, and for how long (five minutes is good). Use a timer so you know when your time is up.

2. At the agreed-upon time, begin your meditation. Ask for the meditation to proceed in goodness and light. Start with three deep, cleansing breaths.

3. Concentrate on your friend. Release your mind to travel to him or her.

4. What can you hear? What can you see? What can you feel? What is your friend doing? What is your friend wearing?

5. When the meditation time is up, bring yourself back to the context of your physical environment.

6. Write down everything you can remember about what you experienced—sights, sounds, smells, even tastes.

7. Call or visit your friend to share experiences.

Astral Projection Exercise: Solo

This is an exercise you can do by yourself.

1. Sit where you are comfortable and there are no distractions. Determine the length of time you want to meditate (or let the meditation run its own course, which you can do because you are alone in this exercise).

2. Begin your meditation. Ask for the meditation to proceed in goodness and light. Start with three deep, cleansing breaths.

3. Focus on letting your spirit go to sit across from you, so you can see it.

4. Through your spirit, see your physical self.

5. What do you see? Is the experience similar to looking in a mirror? If not, how is it different?

6. When your meditation is over, bring yourself gently back to your physical environment.

How completely were you able to leave your body? How did you feel during the experience? How do you feel about it now?

Mediums and Messages

The first time Rita tried the solo astral projection exercise, she chose to sit outside on her deck. Because the day felt a bit chilly, she wore a vest. She projected out okay, but then all she could see was the color yellow. So she went back into her body and asked, "What am I doing wrong?" The response came back: "Sitting too close!" Rita had projected her spirit from her body, but only slightly—all she could see was the yellow of her vest! She did the exercise again, and this time sat across the deck from herself.

What's Spirit Have to Do with It?

When telepathic communication takes place between a physical being (like you) and a spirit entity, it becomes spirit communication. Most mediums don't use the term telepathy in reference to spirit communication, because usually spirit communication takes place using more specific and sophisticated methods, such as clairaudience and clairvoyance. These methods give more extensive information.

The Least You Need to Know

◆ Telepathy lets you communicate without using your physical senses.

◆ Only you—no one else—can control your thoughts and mind.

◆ Telepathy often happens during dreams, although it can be confusing to separate the communication from dream elements.

◆ Telekinesis lets you use telepathy to influence the physical actions of objects.

◆ With practice, you can improve your telepathic skills.

Chapter 16

Psychometry: The Power of Places and Objects

In This Chapter

◆ The energy trail you leave in your wake

◆ What objects are most likely to retain energy

◆ How to "read" energy imprints

◆ Exercises to improve your psychometry skills

◆ Psychometry as a bridge to spirit contact

Places and objects hold residual energy from the souls that come in contact with them as energy imprints. Sometimes the sense of this is strong, as when you touch a lamp in an antique store and the image of a pioneer woman reading beneath its light flashes through your mind. Sometimes the sense is weak, as when you feel a slight tingle at holding your grandmother's favorite button tin in your hands. Psychometric ability can turn places and objects into links between this world and the hereafter.

When you take a photograph, fragments of light interact with the molecules that form the surface of the film to take shape as visual images. The film—or the negatives processed from it—contain those fragments, those bits and pieces of energy, virtually indefinitely (well, at least as long as the film remains intact and undamaged). As many times as you want, you can develop pictures from that film. You can look at these pictures again and again, the representations of energy that you've captured on paper.

Spirit energy is like light energy in that it alters surfaces that it contacts. It interacts with the molecules that form those surfaces, leaving virtually indelible fragments. These fragments, when "developed" through psychic expression, present images. Rather than taking visual shape, like pictures, these energy imprints can take many forms. But unlike pictures, these energy imprints are dynamic. That is to say, every new energy contact with them (such as you picking up the object that holds them) can evoke something different. You get something like a metaphysical slide show (although the images are not always visual).

Energy Imprints

Whatever you touch, you leave a little of yourself behind. From a physical perspective, you leave molecules of scent and skin oils. These are the substances that tracking dogs can detect. (A dog's nose is so sensitive to smell, it can "read" just a few molecules.) You might also leave fingerprints, skin cells, and DNA (microscopic fragments of your genetic coding). These are the substances that high-tech detective methods can retrieve and use to identify you. Solid surfaces such as desktops, doorknobs, and windows are likely to collect more of these physical tracings from your touch.

You also leave energy molecules. These are intangible and undetectable by physical means. Energy imprints are often micro-vignettes that capture and store representations based in emotion. In touching the object, you might feel a flash of joy or of sadness. You might see, fleetingly in your mind's eye, the image of a baby's birth or the gathering at a funeral. The stronger the emotional connection, the more intense the energy imprint … and the more vivid the energy "replay" that occurs.

The more often you touch an object, the more of your energy it retains. Items worn often and close to the body, such as wedding rings and favorite clothing, retain high levels of energy. Items you touch infrequently, such as silverware or jewelry you wear just once a year, typically retain low levels of energy.

An object you touch infrequently can hold a lot of residual energy if the only times you touch it are emotionally intense. If the jewelry you wear once a year is the necklace and earrings you wore at your wedding and now wear it when you celebrate your anniversary, it's going to hold much more energy than if it's a bracelet you bought on a whim and wear only occasionally because you feel guilty about leaving it sit in your jewelry box. Because people pray with them, rosary beads often contain strong personal energy.

Capturing Energy Imprints on Film

In 1939, Seymon Kirlian, a Russian electrician by trade and inventor by avocation, discovered that when he took pictures of his hand, the developed photographs often showed a glow around his fingers—his hand's energy field. One of the most famous examples of *Kirlian photography* came from the University of California Center for Health Science, showing the glowing photographic image of a full leaf although the leaf in the picture had a piece ripped off. The leaf's energy field completed its image, even though the leaf was no longer intact.

Since its inception Kirlian photography has evolved in various technological directions, some of which use electrical equipment rather than cameras to capture images of energy. Currently, researchers are exploring ways to apply Kirlian photography to medical diagnosis and treatment. Doctors have long known that the body's energy composition changes in illness. Whether you look at these changes as physiological—the outcome of biochemical changes within the body—or spiritual, they are verifiable. Researchers hope that some day Kirlian technology will present energy images that can monitor the progress of treatment for serious diseases like cancer and heart disease.

> **Spiritology**
> **Kirlian photography** is a process of taking pictures in which the photo shows the object and its energy field.

What Kinds of Objects Retain Energy?

Any object that you touch holds at least a little of your energy. Some objects hold energy longer than others. Generally, the more solid or dense the object, the longer it retains energy imprints. Metals, jewelry, and even items such as pottery or crystal can hold a person's energy over generations of time. But even fabric, books, papers, and other more fragile objects can retain energy for surprisingly long periods of time—perhaps however long is necessary for the object to convey its energy messages to the person who needs to receive them.

Metals

The physical structure of any metal is very dense. As a result, it holds energy for a long, long time. Ann's grandfather, a firefighter, died in the line of duty fighting a fire when Ann was just four years old. Ann had been the last person in the family, other than her grandmother, of course, to speak to him that fateful day. Many years later, as Ann prepared to sell the house where her grandparents had lived, she came across an envelope pushed to the back of a bureau drawer. Inside the envelope she found the belongings her grandfather had carried on his person the day he died.

When Ann picked up her grandfather's keys, she felt a tingling, almost like an electrical charge, and remembered herself as a four-year-old, sitting on her grandfather's lap. Image after image of her grandfather and his life flashed through Ann's inner vision, including his last moments in the fire. All these years, these keys retained his energy … and now, 40 years after his death, that energy surged as a gift connecting Ann with her grandfather.

Objects like keys and jewelry retain great amounts of energy not only because they're metal but also because they're usually in daily contact with whomever uses or wears them. Every morning after putting on his firefighter's uniform, Ann's grandfather took his ring of keys from the top of the bureau and put them in his pants pocket. He carried the keys there, close against his body, reaching for them occasionally, his thumb and forefinger rubbing the medal of the Virgin Mary he hung on the ring for protection, until he came home again after his shift and put them on the bureau.

Those keys collected energy from every experience he had all through each day, compiling a virtual energy record of his life. They recorded the energy trail of his life, and of his passing. At his death, the keys were sealed in an envelope by Ann's father and stored away by Ann's grandmother, where they stayed until Ann found them. The envelope helped to contain the energy imprints the keys held. And each time Ann touched the keys, she experienced a different perception of her grandfather. Ann carries the keys with her now, and her grandfather's energy walks with her.

Jewelry of emotional significance, particularly wedding rings, also stores significant energy. Part of this comes from the intensity of emotion of the jewelry's first use, and part of it comes from the everyday contact the jewelry experiences. All the joy and sadness, success and disappointment, calm and outburst … these emotions that are the expressions of life become attached to possessions such as jewelry in the same way that electromagnetic energy becomes attached to an audiotape or a CD.

To replay a tape or a CD, you need a compatible machine. But to "replay" energy imprints, all you need is to tune into your psychic sensitivities! Holding your dad's watch or your great-grandmother's ring could bring forth a flood of energy experiences.

When Rita was in her first psychic development class, another student, a young man,
brought a bottle cap. It was a simple, plain,
Coors beer bottle cap. He asked for someone
to psychometrize this. Two students tried and
couldn't get anything, and then the teacher
handed the bottle cap to Rita. As she held the
bottle cap in her hands, Rita saw a vision of
being in the woods and then saw a very, very
dark place with a pool of water in it. Although
it embarrassed her to say the words out loud,
she said to the young man and the class, "I see
funny-looking men in yellow suits!"

 Premonition

Many people with
highly refined psychic or mediumistic abilities find it difficult to
be around antiques. Antiques are
often treasured family heirlooms,
passed down through generations of family members. They
can retain many energy imprints,
which can present a flood of
images and information to someone who is receptive.

The young man laughed. He had been up in the New Hampshire woods and had
gone caving with his friends. They had gone into a cave that had a big pool of water
inside. In the pool, left behind by other cavers, was a bottle of Coors chilling in the
frigid water. The four young men shared the bottle and brought back the bottle cap.
They were all wearing yellow neoprene suits!

Furnishings

Where do you spend the most time when you are in your home? You might say the
living room or the kitchen or even the bedroom (as we spend a third of our lives
sleeping). And none of these answers is wrong. But in truth, the most extensive interaction you have with your home is actually with your furnishings.

A good number of furnishings are nothing more than functional, of course. You use
them and then put them at the curb for recycling or disposal after they wear out.
Some furnishings, however, become family heirlooms. Through the years, they take
on emotional and historical significance. The delicate china tea set a distant cousin
carried home from a trip to the Far East ... by sailing ship. The marble-top dressers
that Great-Great-Grandfather Pete carved as a 14-year-old apprentice the year the
American Civil War ended. And even the handprint of your daughter, from when she
was three years old, now frozen in plaster of Paris and hanging in a frame on the wall.

The objects of our daily lives pick up considerable energy. How long and to what
extent they hold depends on the object's use and the number of people who use it.
Debbie was in an antique store when she rested her hand lightly on top of a small
table. Like a flash, she saw the image of a Victorian-era woman, dressed in a long,
dark skirt and a white blouse with a high, buttoned collar and long sleeves. The
woman's dark hair was pulled back and wrapped around her head.

At first Debbie thought the vision was a spirit, but it remained still, like a photograph. When Debbie lifted her hand from the table, the image disappeared. When she touched the table again, this time in a slightly different place, the woman's image reappeared. But this time she sat in a chair beside the table, holding some sewing or embroidery in her hands. Each time Debbie touched a different place on the table, a different image of the same woman appeared.

The shop's proprietor noticed Debbie's apparent interest in the table and told Debbie it had just come into the store earlier that week. The woman who had owned it had recently died. The family held an estate sale, and the table had been among the items that didn't sell. It was a lovely piece that had been in the family for several generations, the proprietor said. The woman would sit for hours at the table, which was in front of her living room window, sewing or reading.

Fabric and Clothing

When a tracking dog is about to set out on a track, its handlers try to have it smell an item belonging to the missing person. An item of clothing, not washed since the person last wore it, is ideal, because it captures and holds the person's scent. The more contact with the cloth, the stronger the scent signals that the dog can read. The dog then searches for matching signals, following them until the trail runs out or the dog finds the person.

Fabric can hold energy imprints for long periods of time, too, and for much longer than it holds a scent. Dresses, scarves, hats, and similar items that end up stored in trunks in attics for years and even decades hold tight to the energy imprints they've collected. Pull such an item from its sanctuary, and those imprints might seem to float out, just like dust.

In one of Rita's classes that she teaches at the church, she asked her students to bring items to practice psychometry readings. One student brought his most treasured possession, a woolen New York Yankees baseball cap. He handed it to Rita and said, "Here, see what you get from this."

Rita held the cap in her hands and felt the most incredible adrenaline rush of her life! She had the impression of being on the baseball diamond, looking out at the pitcher. Her heart was pounding and her hands were sweating. She described these responses to the student, who was tickled. The cap, he said, had belonged to a former New York Yankees catcher! What Rita "read" from the cap was the experience of the catcher, crouched behind the batter during the high excitement of a baseball game.

Bonnie came to see Rita at the First Spiritualist Church of Quincy in September 1995. During the sitting a drawing came through of her grandmother, Margaret. Bonnie recognized the face immediately, with delight. Two years later, in April 1997, Bonnie's daughter Aileen came to Rita for a spirit drawing and the same woman wearing the same housedress appeared on the paper.

Picking Up the Trail

Psychics who work with police to find missing people read the energy imprints of objects connected to the missing person. These energy vibrations become a trail the psychic can follow, providing details about the person's fate that police have been unable to determine based on physical evidence. Often, a psychic working in this capacity can hold an object from a crime scene and describe information about the person who committed the crime.

Silver Cord

Psychics have been involved in many famous crime investigations, including a 1940 case involving the murders of three civil rights workers in Mississippi, and the disappearance of Patty Hearst and the search for victims of mass murderer John Wayne Gacy in the late 1970s.

Rita has been involved in a number of missing persons situations. In one, a 14-year-old girl had disappeared. A friend of the girl's mother knew of Rita's work and called Rita to see if she could help. The girl had been missing since Friday evening, and it was Sunday afternoon when Rita got the call.

The family feared the girl had been abducted. Her hairbrush was still on her dresser, and the girl never went anywhere without it. So Rita asked if she could hold the brush. As soon as she took the brush into her hands, Rita knew the girl was safe and fine. "She's at a house just south of route 37, the house of somebody she knows," Rita said. "I'm seeing three brick steps going up to the front door and a storm door with the initial 'K' or 'R' on it."

Later that evening, Rita got a phone call. The girl had been found, safe and a little embarrassed, at the house of a friend—you guessed it—just south of route 37, with three brick steps going up to the front door and a "K" on the storm door! The girl had gone to spend the weekend with her friend, thinking her mother knew of the plans.

Pick Up the Vibes: Exercises to Develop Your Psychometry Skills

You have countless opportunities to practice and develop your psychometry skills. Here are two exercises to get you started. The first is a structured meditation; the second is an exercise of opportunity.

Exercise One: Reading Familiar Energy

For this exercise, you need the help of a friend. Ask the friend to bring a small object that he or she wears frequently, such as a watch, a piece of jewelry, or a scarf. Also ask your friend for permission to do an energy reading from this object. Don't look at the object. Make yourself comfortable where you aren't going to have interruptions, and ask your friend to join you.

1. Take three cleansing breaths, and ask that your energy meditation proceed in goodness and light, for the best intent.

2. Close your eyes and ask your friend to place the object in your palm. Feel its weight, its pressure against your skin. Feel whether the object is light or heavy, cool or warm, dense or soft. Is it metal? Is it wood? Is it fabric?

3. Without trying to create a mental picture of the object, let its image form in your mind. Be open to any perceptions that occur, including visual images, sounds, smells, or tastes.

4. If you know what the object is, set that knowledge aside. Focus on receiving the object's energy. It might come to you in vignettes or flashes.

5. Describe to your friend what you're receiving. Don't attempt to filter or interpret the information in any way, just convey it.

6. If something about the energy imprint is unclear, form a question about it in your mind and wait for an answer. (It will come!)

7. When you feel the energy exchange is over, gently return to your normal state of consciousness. Become aware of your toes, your legs, your fingers, and your arms.

It's most helpful to you in developing your psychometry skills if your friend is willing to discuss the possible meanings of the energy messages that you received through the object. But understand that he or she might not want to do this, if these messages have evoked unexpected emotions. Psychometry, like other energy reading, can reveal deep meanings. As you become more comfortable with reading energy in this way, you can try reading objects from people you don't know quite as well.

Exercise Two: Reading Random Energy

As you go about the many activities of your daily life, look for opportunities to experience the energy imprints of objects around you. Although you won't get much feedback to confirm the accuracy of your perceptions, this exercise helps you make psychometric skills part of your everyday life. Here are some examples:

◆ Hold an apple in your hand. What does it taste like?

◆ Go into an antique store. Touch the first object that catches your attention. What do you feel?

◆ In a music store, touch or hold an old instrument (if the proprietor allows you to). Can you hear music, or see the musician who once played it?

◆ Go to a used bookstore. Walk until you reach a shelf that compels you to stop. Pass your hand slowly in front of the books on the shelf. Take down the one that seems to draw your hand to it. What is the title? Who is the author? What is the topic? Do these have any significance for you? Open the book. What is the copyright? Is there anything about the book that has special meaning?

◆ Walk slowly through the exhibits at a history museum. Stop at the first display that compels you to look closer. What is the exhibit? What do you feel, hear, see, sense?

As you can see, the opportunities this exercise offers truly are unlimited!

Linking to Spirit Contact

Psychometry certainly has many applications in psychic contexts. But what about in spirit contact? Many mediums use psychometry to establish a link to a loved one on the higher side. Handling an object imbued with the loved one's energy instantly signals other holders of the same energy—the loved one—to connect. It's like a cosmic directory assistance!

The contact established using psychometry as its bridge can be especially powerful, and is very helpful when you want to contact a particular spirit entity. Often, this approach quickly establishes evidence of the continuity of life, because it transitions from the tangible world to the spirit world in a way that appears logical to us.

Sometimes the energy readings the medium gets from the object help direct questions the medium can ask of the spirit entity. This might provide direct information that you are seeking, or the information that you need to have (even if you don't yet know that you need it).

> ### Mediums and Messages
>
> When Jeanette came to Rita for a spirit sitting, she brought a wedding ring with her. Rita took the ring and held it in her hands, and within moments a man came through. Rita described the man in full detail, including physical characteristics and personality. "That's my father!" Jeanette said. Then Rita very clearly tasted chocolate-covered coconut and heard the father singing the commercial jingle, "Sometimes I feel like a nut, sometimes I don't!" Rita asked the woman, "Did your father ever bring you Mounds candy bars?" The woman laughed. "Absolutely!" she said. Spirit will always trigger information that's stored in your mind.

Spirit Presence or Residual Energy?

Places retain energy, too. Locations are just collections of objects; a house is walls, floors, stairs, and other surfaces that people contact all the time. In fact, much of what people perceive as "haunting" is really not spirit presence at all, but rather an energy imprint, also called residual energy, which captures and replays a significant event. Because such events typically have intense emotional connections, they are generally connected to a person (or people) and might have to do with some sort of trauma or tragedy.

It isn't always easy to determine whether spirit presence is genuine or residual, because the same kinds of events can connect either to the physical world. Generally, an energy imprint doesn't involve any kind of interaction. Its presentation might change so that you have a different perception of the energy experiences that are retained. An experienced medium can tell whether the energy is active or residual.

Rita was asked to visit a home that its owners, two adult sisters, believed was haunted. The sisters had not had pleasant childhoods in the house, and for many years as adults had been estranged from their parents. The women inherited the house after their mother and then father passed away, and they wanted to sell it. But every time they went into the house they were overcome with fear, and left without venturing much further than the vestibule.

As Rita walked into the house, all seemed calm enough with no evidence that the father's spirit was present. Rita did detect distinctive energies. Among them was the energy of a mentally disabled great-aunt who had lived with the family for a time. Hers was a confused but benevolent presence. Rita and the sisters prayed to help the great-aunt find her way to the higher side, and her presence was gone.

As Rita continued walking through the house, she could feel the energy, sometimes intense, of childhood traumas the sisters had experienced at the hands of their abusive father. These traumas lingered as energy imprints that activated memories in the sisters. As soon as Rita explained this to the women, they immediately felt better. Knowing that there were no spirits remaining in the house, they were able to clean it out and sell it, and move on with their lives.

Trauma, of course, leaves intense energy behind. But not all intense energy is traumatic. Many homes are filled with energy imprints of the moments of joy and laughter that marked the lives of the families who lived there. You might step onto the lawn of an old home and suddenly hear shouts and giggles of children playing hide and seek, or see in your mind's eye a yardful of tents made from bed sheets. Happiness leaves its imprints, too.

The Least You Need to Know

- Just about all objects have the capacity to retain energy.
- Objects with strong emotional meaning retain the most intense energy.
- "Reading" an object is a process of allowing its energy imprints to "replay" their messages for you.
- Places and locations can store energy imprints, which can sometimes be misinterpreted as spirit presence.
- Psychometry can be a powerful tool for establishing spirit contact.

Chapter 17

Dream Weaver

In This Chapter

- ◆ Your body's need to dream
- ◆ Using dreams to understand your emotions and feelings
- ◆ Archetypes and the collective unconsciousness
- ◆ Keeping a dream journal
- ◆ Interacting with your dreams
- ◆ Asking spirits to visit your dreams

"I had the weirdest dream last night …." This must be one of the most common morning greetings in the English language! It sets the stage for what you know is going to be a presentation of events that defy logical understanding. And yet it's a phrase that intrigues us all, because we all have "weird" dreams. By listening to the dreams of others, we hope to learn more about what our dreams might mean—or at least to feel secure in knowing that everybody has dreams that don't seem to make sense.

The dream state is a mysterious existence. Some say it is one that allows the soul to roam freely, unconfined by the parameters of reality as they define consciousness. When you dream about a loved one who has crossed over, could this in fact be a spirit visitation? The dream state also offers a natural doorway for spirit communication. The filters of your conscious mind are at rest, unable to block signals they otherwise would restrict or reinterpret. This leaves you receptive to the messages these signals might bring.

The Dream State

We talk about the dream state as if it's a place we can go to, like we might think of going to California or New York. The journey holds the promise of exciting adventures that will take us beyond the realm of our everyday lives. It's a little scary, sometimes, but we can calm our fears by reminding ourselves, "It's just a dream …."

What happens during the dream state? The earliest written records speak of dreams and their mysteries. In many cultures, ancient and modern, dreams sometimes represent visitations from the divine of your belief system. Some cultures believe that the soul leaves the body during dreaming to visit a special world in which it actually lives in dreams; to wake someone during a dream, according to this belief, is to risk severing the soul's connection to the body. Modern psychology looks to dreams as providing insights into your concerns, worries, and fears.

From your body's perspective, the dream state is as essential as sleep itself. There are two clear stages of sleep, *REM* and *NREM*, that cycle throughout the time you are asleep. Your body starts a sleep cycle by drifting off into NREM sleep, during which all physical functions become quiet and still. Not even your eyes move, which is why this is called the "no rapid eye movement" stage of sleep. About 90 minutes into NREM sleep, your brain suddenly wakes up—you are dreaming!

Spiritology

REM (rapid eye movement) sleep is the stage of sleep during which the eyes move rapidly and dreams take place.
NREM (no rapid eye movement) is the stage of sleep during which there is little dreaming and no rapid eye movements.

During REM (rapid eye movement) sleep, your eyes move rapidly behind your closed eyelids, as though watching a movie. Although your body generally is still, your brain is as busy as when you are awake. Over the course of an eight-hour sleep, most people cycle through four or five REM stages. Each tends to be longer than the one preceding it. The first REM stage might last five to 10 minutes, while the last one can last an hour or longer. This is partly why you are more likely to remember the last dream of your sleep—it's usually the longest, most detailed, and most vivid.

Sleep studies show that the REM stage of sleep is essential for your body to feel rested. This suggests that dreaming has a physiological importance; that is, your body needs not only to sleep but also to dream so that it can restore itself.

Clearing Your Brain: Data Dump

One theory about the importance of dreaming views dreams as "data dumps" for your brain. During your waking hours, your brain collects and processes a seemingly endless volume of information—stimuli from your physical senses, your thoughts, your emotions, the functions of your body. Your brain somehow processes everything you encounter while you are awake, even if you are unaware.

Because the vast majority of this collected content has no context, it doesn't really qualify even as information. Your brain has no idea what to do with it, quite literally, and so it stores it away. When you begin to dream, the conscious parts of your brain that keep this data "behind the scenes" ease their control, and these fragments begin to float, as it were, into the parts of your brain that process thought. As you sleep, your brain then shapes these floating fragments into images that you perceive as dreams.

Within the framework of this theory, or viewpoint, there is nothing more to dreams than a discharge of electrical energy. Dreaming is a "clearing" of your brain's circuitry, preparing it for the next day's data collection. Rather like a computer's hard drive, your brain collects and then discards data in a cycle tied to waking and sleeping.

Silver Cord

Studies in which researchers deprive volunteers of sleep, or interrupt sleep when EEG signals show the brain has entered the dream state, show the clear importance of dreaming to sleep. When sleep interruptions, disturbances, and deprivation that prevent dreaming continue over a period of days or weeks, the chemical balances of the brain change. This affects just about every function in your body, from heart rate to mood. When study volunteers are permitted to return to normal sleep and dream patterns, the chemical levels return to normal.

Working Out Your "Stuff"

From the framework of psychology, dreams allow you to experience and understand emotions and feelings that you don't address during your waking hours. Within this context, the content of dreams takes on symbolism that is personal to you. By writing down your dreams or talking about them, you can begin to see the patterns of your personal symbols and relate them to events and emotions taking place in your life. In this framework of interpretation, dreams seldom mean what their images suggest.

What a Nightmare!

We've all had bad dreams, nightmares from which we wake up scared and shaking, sometimes not certain if we're still dreaming. The content and images of nightmares also are symbolic, generally representing major fears or worries. Some cultures believe that dreams are an altered state of reality, and if you can work out your lessons in the dream state, you don't need to work them out in the waking state. If you are afraid of an issue or person and can face your fears in the dream state, you don't have to work them out when you are awake.

You might think of nightmares as the ultimate "working through." We can interact with our dreams, making contact with the visions that appear there. Whenever something disturbing happens in a dream, you can immediately surround yourself with a "safety zone," and remind your dreaming self that you are safe. Then you can question your "dream" actors as to their purpose in your nightmare and confront them if necessary. "I don't want this to happen anymore. Stop! Tell me why you're here!" You might be surprised at how effectively this ends the nightmare (and what answer you receive to your question!). If you can do this, you are working through your concerns. Rita's husband has strict instructions not to wake her if she appears to be having a nightmare! If you aren't used to interacting with your dreams, think about the issues upon waking, and the fearfulness of the dream will dissipate as you begin to analyze what happened in the dream. See more on interacting with your dreams later in this chapter.

Sigmund Freud and the "Royal Road to the Unconscious"

The father of psychoanalysis, Sigmund Freud (1856–1939), held that dreams revealed repressed desires (often sexual), and that dreams were the "royal road" to the inner sanctum of the unconscious mind. His book, *The Interpretation of Dreams*, published in 1899, was a groundbreaking work that attempted to explain dreams in the context of waking experiences and unexpressed thoughts and wishes. Analyzing and interpreting one's dreams, Freud believed, was the route to understanding one's needs.

Carl Jung and the Archetype

Psychotherapist Carl Jung (1875–1961), initially a student of Freud, viewed dreams as the unconscious mind's efforts to convey messages to the conscious mind, often by tapping into what Jung termed the *collective unconscious*. The collective unconscious, Jung said, is a vast repository of shared human experiences—*all* shared human experiences. Because of its vastness, we connect to it through universal symbols Jung called *archetypes*. Archetypes represent a range of interpretations; the key is identifying those that are relevant to you within the context of your life experiences.

Dreams, according to Jung, are a direct link to the collective unconscious. What we remember from the connection, upon waking, we perceive in the form of archetypes. As author James R. Lewis succinctly defines in his book *The Dream Encyclopedia* (Visible Ink Press, 1995), "archetypes … predispose us to unconsciously organize our personal experiences in certain ways. Archetypes are not concrete images in the collective unconscious. They are more like invisible magnetic fields that cause iron filings to arrange themselves according to certain patterns."

Spiritology

The **collective unconscious** is the combined shared experiences of all humankind. An **archetype** is a pattern of images that represents a specific and universal realm of experience, such as the hero or the victim.

Archetypes are icons of human experience that you must then apply to the specifics of your life experiences. They might appear in dreams to explain past or current events, or to provide glimpses of the broader context of your life mission and your soul's journey. Common archetypes and their representations include the following:

- ◆ Actor or acting a role, representing the parts of yourself that you present to others

- ◆ Anima/animus, representing the elements of the opposite sex that are present in you (feminine qualities in men, masculine qualities in women) and also how you view the opposite sex

- ◆ Four of anything including the number itself, representing stability, completion (such as in the cycle of the four seasons), wholeness

- ◆ Father, representing power, authority, responsibility, tradition, procreation

- ◆ Mother, representing life, love, caring, nurturing, creativity

- ◆ Old man, representing wisdom and forgiveness

◆ Old woman, representing the energy of life (through birth) and death

◆ Rebirth, representing repressed issues that are resurfacing or another chance to do or receive something you thought was lost

◆ Shadow, representing the dark side of your personality or the parts of yourself that you keep hidden (sometimes even from yourself)

Jung further connected dreams to mythology, observing that despite the many and varied mythologies of world cultures from ancient to modern times, common themes—in the form of archetypes—emerge that link them. He speculated that mythology represents the efforts of the conscious mind to organize the information received through dreams into structures (stories and belief systems). As universal symbols, archetypes permeate nearly all aspects of our modern culture, from character representations in movies, books, and even the comics to the symbolisms of astrology and Tarot.

Esmirelda, *December 1989, oil on canvas. Rita asked to see the spirit guide who works with her when she reads Tarot cards. An old Gypsy woman revealed herself as Rita's inspiration.*

Archetypes in Spirit Communication

As symbolic representations, archetypes appear in spirit communication. Remember from earlier chapters that we've talked about developing your personal dictionary of symbols. Archetypes can help you understand the deeper meanings of some of these symbols by giving them a universal context.

Understanding Your Archetypes: An Exercise

Archetypes are useful only to the extent that you can connect the universal knowledge and understanding they represent with the events and circumstances of your own life. This representation can by physical, emotional, and spiritual. A technique called *free association* is a good method for gaining understanding about the archetypes and symbols that appear in your dreams as well as in spirit messages that you receive (directly or through a medium).

Spiritology

Free association is a process of saying or writing the first things that enter your mind when you think of a particular word or symbol.

Free association is easy to do. Get some paper and a pen or pencil. Find a comfortable place to sit, where it is easy for you to write and where you won't be distracted.

1. Choose one image from a dream. Write it at the top of a piece of paper.

2. Set a timer to give yourself a time limit—one to three minutes. This encourages you to work quickly, without giving your intellect an opportunity to interfere.

3. Write every word that the image you selected evokes. Do this without thinking about what you're writing. The faster you do this, the more intuitive your responses. It doesn't matter whether the words seem to be related to the image; just write them.

4. When the timer goes off, stop writing.

5. Look at the words that have put themselves on the paper. Do any of them instantly relate to the image? Do any of them seem so unrelated as to be far-fetched?

6. On another piece of paper, write some of the archetypes these words seem to represent. Under each archetype, list the words that relate.

7. What pattern do you see emerging? Sometimes this isn't immediately obvious to you. You might need to journal, meditate, or otherwise ponder the archetypes, words, and images to make the connection.

8. If a pattern doesn't appear, set the exercise—the word list and the archetype organization—aside for two weeks. Then come back to it, and see if you can recognize a pattern.

Do this exercise regularly to build a foundation of understanding about what archetypes mean to you. Not every dream element has extended symbolic meaning, of course. Over time and with practice, you'll come to easily identify those that do.

A Doorway to the Higher Side

The dream state is particularly conducive to spirit contact and spirit visitation. When you dream, your conscious mind eases its control over what you think and perceive, allowing you to be more open. This happens because the dream state is the closest to an altered state from waking consciousness that most of us achieve on a regular (daily!) basis. So it's the easiest way for a spirit loved one to contact you. You might not know whether you're dreaming; the dream may feel more real, more vivid than usual—as if it has actually happened. It's common to see deceased loved ones and to receive messages from them in the dream state.

There are many times that a spirit will visit you in the dream state. There is a very different feeling when this happens than when you just dream about the person. It feels real, and it makes sense. Six months after Rita's father passed, her daughter came running into her bedroom one night and said, "I was dreaming but I know I wasn't dreaming, and Poppa was in my room."

Silver Cord

Some people believe that the dream state is actually the soul's opportunity to leave the physical body and travel as a spirit. It reconnects with cosmic energy, and exists in a discarnate state for the duration of its travels. Where does your spirit go? It's hard to say, although meditation might reveal this to you.

Rita held her daughter, and asked her how Poppa was. Her daughter said he was fine. Rita asked, "Were you worried about him?" Her daughter replied that she was. Rita told her daughter, "You know, he probably just came to visit you to let you know he was okay, because you were so worried." Her daughter smiled, gave Rita a hug, and went back to bed.

Inviting Spirit Visitation in Your Dreams

You can intentionally invite spirit entities to visit you in your dreams. If you have situations that you didn't resolve with someone who has now passed to spirit, you can resolve them through visiting in spirit in the dream state. Or you can just reconnect with a loved one, for the joy of experiencing the connection again! The following exercise can help you initiate a dream visit with Spirit:

1. As you are beginning to fall asleep, set the intent that you are going to meet with a specific person in the dream state, in which a dream will play out the unresolved situation.

2. Permit yourself to go to sleep.

3. When you wake up, don't worry about whether you remember the dream. Instead, focus on how you feel. Do you feel you've achieved resolution?

4. Ask a question about the situation and see how you feel. Your dream journal can help with this. If you still feel the situation is unresolved, try again the next night.

Joseph had problems with his father throughout his life. When his father passed to spirit, Joseph was afraid these problems would never be resolved and he was left with a feeling of need because there was unfinished business between them. So Joseph did this exercise. The first night he felt nothing. The next night he tried again, and this time was a little forceful in his intent.

Joseph said, "Dad, I've waited 39 years to speak to you. I want to speak to you tonight in the dream state." The next morning, to Joseph's surprise, when he tuned into the situation with his father he felt total peace. He didn't remember the dream, but every time he thinks of his father now, he feels content.

When you wake up in the morning (or if you wake up during the night after a dream), write as much as you can remember about your dreams in your dream journal. Did you dream of the person you were thinking about when you fell asleep? Did it feel like you and this person were enjoying each other's company?

Don't be discouraged if you wake up and remember dreams that have nothing to do with the spirit loved one you hoped to contact, or if you remember nothing at all. Spirits, you recall, are not always willing or able to respond when we want them to. Just be patient, and keep trying.

Past Life Dreams

Your past lives are always part of you, and sometimes your dreams give you the opportunity to connect with them. Famed American psychic Edgar Cayce (1877–1945) taught that when you are looking at a past life dream, the way you recognize it as such is that everything in it is in context. If you are dreaming that you're walking down the street in 1840 in Kansas, you are not seeing a red Corvette drive by! The roads are dirt, not pavement. Clothes and surroundings are appropriate for the period; nothing is out of context.

Keeping a Dream Journal

Do you wake up from an intense dream and know, just *know*, its message is vitally important ... then fall back asleep and remember very little in the morning? How frustrating! If you're interested in exploring the meanings and messages of your dreams, you can't rely on memory. You need to keep a dream journal.

A dream journal doesn't have to be anything fancy, although many bookstores sell very nice dream journals and blank journals that you can use to record your dreams and your thoughts about them. A plain old spiral-bound notebook will do. You might want to keep a notepad and pen at your bedside so you can jot down dreams when you awaken from them, and later transfer the information to your dream journal. Use your dream journal to record ...

♦ The details of your dreams as you remember them, without interpretation or filtering. Just describe the dream as it occurred, as best you can remember it.

♦ Your free association exercises for each dream. You can do these on separate paper and then transfer the information to your dream journal, or do them right in the journal.

♦ What is going on in your waking life—what's happening at work, with your family, with your significant other.

♦ Your thoughts and ideas about what the archetypes and symbols of your dreams might mean in a common or universal context as well as in the context of your personal life.

♦ Any learnings or "ahas!" that you get as you work through a dream's interpretation.

Keeping a dream journal gives you documentation of your dreams so that you can go back to look for common themes and symbols.

Silver Cord

Where do premonitionary dreams come from? Some believe your soul can read your Akashic record (see Chapter 5) during dreams, which gives access to all past and future information of your soul's travels and experiences. When you return to a waking state, remnants of this access remain. When these fragments involve events that have not yet occurred in your physical existence, you interpret them as precognitive or premonitionary. This access is also how some people explain past life memories.

What Dreams Mean

Can a dream be, well, just a dream? Do all dreams have hidden meanings and messages? What about dreams that seem so literal they are like replays of the events of your day? Dreams often have multiple layers of meaning that extend from the literal to the symbolic. Sometimes a dream is just the events of your day, bubbling through your subconscious mind so they can break free and disperse. Other times, a dream brings you a specific message or insight.

Interpreting Symbolism

Symbolism is the language of dreams. Dreams, like thoughts, move in fluid images. There is no sense of time or the structure that time imposes. There are many books available on the subject of dream interpretation (Appendix B lists a few that can get you started).

Some symbols have common meanings (that may or may not be archetypes). Water, for example, often represents the emotions. It can also suggest significant change and transition ("sea change"). Dreams of death, dying, and being killed are common and frightening, but generally represent transformation and "letting go" of something that has been part of you or your life for a long time. Other times, dream symbols have particular meaning for you. You might always dream about driving on a highway that never turns, goes up, or goes down whenever you find yourself in a rut in your work or your life. The best way to identify your personal dream symbols is to keep a dream journal in which you record elements of your dreams and your thoughts about what they could represent or mean. Over time, patterns will emerge that will help you identify your unique dream symbols. Personal dream symbols often fit within archetypes or common dream symbols.

Here are some common dream symbols:

- Anchor—staying in one place
- Automobile—the means by which you move through life
- Baby—something new in your life
- Bed—intimacy
- Blanket—cover, hiding
- Bridge—connection, link, transition
- Climbing—struggle to overcome an obstacle

- Clothing—your persona (what you project to others), the physical body
- Death—renewal, end of one thing and beginning of another, transformation
- Elevator—change, ups and downs
- Flying—freedom and joy, rising above
- Gate—exit from one place or circumstance and entrance to another
- House—your spirit, your mind, your inner self
- Key—solution, answer
- Losing teeth—loss of control
- Naked—uncovered or exposed
- Trash—disorder and confusion in your life
- Wall—obstacle

Premonitions and Warnings

It's unnerving to wake from a dream that a friend was in a car accident or that a fire swept through the apartment complex where your sister lives. Such events are within the realm of possibility, and indeed often appear as news stories. How do you know if these kinds of dreams reflect your fears and worries or are foretelling disaster?

The first step is to write about the dream and any surrounding circumstances that you can recall. Did you fall asleep with the television or radio on, perhaps listening to a news report of a car accident or an apartment building fire? Did you read about one in a newspaper or magazine earlier in the day, or even a few days ago? If so, it could be your worries at work that manipulate your dreams. Writing about why these events worry you can help you reach insight about them.

So many people dream of a disaster in the family and then it happens. It's common to be afraid that the dream caused the disaster in some way or to just be frightened when you recognize that you've had a precognitive dream. Don't be afraid! Spirit is trying to give you information so you can be strong for other family members, to make sure there is someone who will not be in shock and can take on the position of strength and leadership that coping with disaster requires.

If there don't seem to be external influences, pull out your dream journal and look for other dreams like this, either in subject matter or symbolism. What were they? How are they similar and how are they different? Have you had premonitionary dreams before? If so, what does this dream have in common with those dreams?

In the end, it doesn't hurt to call your friend and ask him to be especially careful when driving today, or to phone your sister to remind her to check the batteries in her smoke detectors. You might never know whether you helped avert a disaster, but you will feel better that you acted on a potential warning.

Interacting with Spirits in Your Dreams

Whether in spirit communication or situations you are trying to work through, you can consciously interact with your dreams to get more information from the dreams or to work out events, trauma, or situations with other people. Did you ever wake yourself up from a dream? Most people have. Earlier, we talked about working through issues in nightmares by surrounding yourself with a "safety zone" and then confronting the situation or person creating anxiety for you in the dream. You can do this with any dream that you're curious about.

If you can wake yourself from dreams, then you can learn to consciously interact with the dream. Work up to this level of participation in your dreams by first writing your dreams down in your dream journal. Then, when you have a dream you are curious about, invite a "clarification" the next night when you go to sleep and see what dreams come to you. Eventually, you'll be able to interact with the dream while it is occurring.

In a dream that is a spirit communication, allow yourself to interact with the visiting spirit as though you were in the same room—which, really, you are. If you have questions or seek information, ask. This is an ideal opportunity to try to work through lingering concerns or issues that you still might have with the person. You don't always remember these interactions, although you will usually feel more calm about the issues after the dream takes place.

The Least You Need to Know

- Dreams rely on a language of symbolism, some of which is archetypal and some of which is personal.

- To interpret your dreams, you need to consider them in the broad context of what's going on in your life.

- The dream state is an ideal environment for spirit visitation and communication.

- You can interact with your dreams to gain understanding and insight.

- When you receive a spirit visitation in the dream state the experience feels real and logical, unlike most dreams.

Part 5

Being: The Essence of Spirit

Even as you exist on the earth plane in a physical life, inhabiting a physical body, you remain connected to the energy of the spirit plane. This energy sustains you, is full of love, and is available to you whenever you need it.

Spirit energy is divine energy. As such, it links us all—on the earth plane and on the higher side—with the God of our understanding. Making connections across the border of physical existence gives you insights into your thoughts, feelings, behaviors, and actions.

Chapter **18**

The Healing Power of Spirit Energy

In This Chapter

- ◆ How you give and receive energy
- ◆ What your aura shows about you
- ◆ The energy healing of Reiki
- ◆ The energy healing of Spiritualism
- ◆ An exercise for self-healing

Life is a constant exchange of energy. You acquire energy from, and give energy to, others in your life—both on the earth plane and on the higher side. Sometimes this is intentional, as when you focus on sending healing energy to a loved one who is ill, or aiding someone you love in crossing over to the other side, or when you call on a friend to support you in a time of need.

But sometimes these energy exchanges are unintentional and unbalanced. You might give too much of yourself, literally, to others, leaving little for your own needs and growth. In such situations, energy healers can help restore your personal balance of energy.

Life as an Exchange of Energy

Every contact you have with other people, with other living things, is an exchange of energy. Sometimes this exchange is palpable. You feel a surge, almost like an electrical charge, when you shake the hand of a person who has an outgoing personality and great vigor, or the warmth of love surround you when you hug a loved one.

We "read" these energy exchanges, and use them both to communicate with and make assessments about each other. What do you notice about a couple that tells you they are deeply in love? They might walk along or sit together, holding hands, touching and sharing each other's physical space so they appear to be more as one than as two. As you get near, you can feel the energy of their togetherness like you might feel the charged air beneath a high-tension power line. This is such wonderful energy that you might feel like walking past this couple again, just to connect with it!

Energy You Give to Others

You give energy to others nearly every moment of the day, in each interaction you have with someone else. When this process stays a fairly balanced give-and-take situation, you don't notice much about it. You give and you receive, and your energy stays supportive of you physically, emotionally, and spiritually.

When the balance shifts to giving more than to receiving, you might feel tired, run-down, and edgy. Everyone around you wants, wants, wants. No one seems to care what *you* might want or need. This constant demand drains your energy, and it's no longer sufficient to support your body, mind, and spirit.

Premonition

Beware the psychic vampires! These are the people—and everyone knows at least one—who draw energy from you the instant you are in contact. In person, over the phone, even by e-mail, the psychic vampire seems to "plug in" to you and drain you dry. You can protect yourself from these psychic suckers by visualizing yourself surrounded with white light.

You might start to see indications of this in your health and attitude. You could become more susceptible to the "office bug" and assorted minor ailments. You might find yourself clumsier than usual, and prone to small injuries as a result. It's not that these problems are your fault. Rather, you're not able to resist them.

You might even feel like your energy is being taken away from you, withdrawn from you, instead of you willingly giving it. We speak, sometimes, of people who "suck us dry." These people have such intense needs that they draw energy from those around them but have little to give back to make the process an exchange.

Have you ever said, "I just can't deal with this relationship anymore. It takes too much energy." You might be thinking in terms of the work you put out to sustain the relationship, the amount of time you spend trying to manage your behaviors and emotions. But you're also sensing a loss of energy, literally. It's like the other person is a magnet, and every time you go near, it feels like little fragments of you go flying toward it.

Energy You Acquire from Others

Exchange is a process of giving and receiving. Just as you give your energy to others, you receive energy from others. The strongest, most positive, most supportive energy is love. When love thrives in any of its multiple dimensions, energy blossoms. It's almost as though you can feel and watch your energy intensify.

Sometimes it sounds trite to talk of "the power of love." From sonnets to rock songs, the phrase is everywhere. So much so, in fact, that the spell checker in your word processing program might identify it as a cliché and ask you if you want to change it! But love is the foundation of the universe's energy, and its power is very real.

When you feel happy and good in the presence of someone else, you're drawing from an energy based in love. It is this energy base, the energy of love, that heals. When you feel it, you know it. It recharges and replenishes you. It restores your sense of well-being and happiness. It makes you whole and unites all parts of your being.

Can you receive "bad" or negative energy from others? Certainly. This is the hallmark of what psychologists call dysfunctional relationships. No one really understands why, if we *can* choose the energy of love that we don't. There are as many explanations for this as there are people. Sometimes this is baggage carried from other lives. Perhaps it's related to your soul's lesson in this life.

What's more important than the "why" of such choices is the recognition that they are choices. You don't have to accept negative energy from others! Not from anyone! Change is not always easy, but it is possible. And there's plenty of positive energy— the power of love—out there to support you in choosing to refuse negative energy.

Bioenergy: Your Aura

Your aura is the energy field that surrounds your body. All living beings have auras— plants, animals, humans. Auras contain the energy of biological life. When spirit energy connects with yours, it does so through your aura. This is how spirit energy heals—it flows into your aura, replenishing and strengthening your personal energy. Your aura also acts to protect you. When you pray or meditate to connect with the God of your understanding, your aura enlarges. People who can see auras can see this happen.

Your True Colors

Auras appear as colors. If this seems odd to you, think about electrical storms. They often produce lightning of different colors depending on what other substances are in the air at the time they strike. Energy, when it takes a form that the human eye can detect, is quite colorful.

Silver Cord

During illness, there sometimes seems to be a hole in the aura or darkness in that area, or the aura can become weak in color and density. The aura's color changes and may become muddy, but there is no particular color associated with illness. Aura can display manifestations of both physical and mental health problems.

The color of your aura provides clues about your physical, emotional, and spiritual states. The vibrancy of the color—whether it's bold and vivid or subdued and flat—and the thickness of its layer influence the meaning of it. Color interpretations, like the symbolism of dreams, are general. What particular colors mean to you can vary.

The energy emission of your aura is very low range, beyond the range of normal vision. But with practice, you can learn to extend the reach of visual detection. (We have an exercise for you in the next section.) Here are common colors and their general meanings:

♦ **Yellow.** When vibrant, yellow represents success, intelligence, wisdom, and creativity. Dull yellow suggests selfishness and negativity.

♦ **Red.** When vibrant, red suggests sensuality and passion. Dull red suggests anger, fear, and anxiety. If you become angry during a conversation, your aura might show a spike of red, reflecting the intensity of emotion you're feeling.

♦ **Green.** Green is related to healing and suggests balance and health.

♦ **Blue.** A blue aura says that you're searching for spiritual information and answers. Light blue indicates that your quest is just beginning; dark blue suggests you've chosen the path you want to follow and you are now seeking enlightenment. Dull blue (dark or light) indicates self-righteousness.

♦ **Purple.** A purple aura suggests that you have high spiritual awareness and are broadly accepting of others. Purple indicates balance, patience, and helpfulness.

♦ **Orange.** You are likely friendly and open toward others when your aura is orange. Vivid, dark orange suggests ambition and drive.

♦ **Pink.** As you might suspect, pink relates to affection and love. A pink aura also suggests that you are calm, and have the ability to soothe and calm others.

- **Brown.** When your aura is brown, you are likely confused, discouraged, or frustrated. Brown tends to be a stress color, suggesting that things are out of balance in your life.

- **Black.** A black aura says your energy is being blocked. Some people do this intentionally, to protect themselves from energy vampires. Other times, a black or a very dark aura suggests negativity and depression.

- **White.** A white aura indicates intense energy and protection. Your aura might be white when you are meditating, praying, or intentionally giving energy to others.

Because your life is constantly changing, so is your aura. It changes with the physical and emotional changes that occur during your daily life. An aura that's bright and vivid indicates that your health is good and your energy is strong. An aura that's gray or neutralized shows someone in need. You can send healing energy to someone you know is in need. However, that person's spirit (sometimes called higher being in the context of energy healing) decides whether to accept it. Although this is a process of choice, it's not one that you participate in consciously. Similarly, if someone sends you healing energy, your spirit determines whether to accept it. This is another way that your energy protects you.

Silver Cord

An aura camera doesn't really capture your energy, although the images it produces can be stunning. Rather, it uses infrared film to record the heat you are generating. The more heat is present, the more vivid the colors.

Explore Your Aura: An Exercise

Do you want to see your own aura? It's easy to do, and you can do it alone! All you need is a white or black (preferred) nonreflective surface, such as a piece of poster board, a darkened room, and a candle.

1. Put the candle in the center of the room and light it. It should be the only light in the room.

2. Standing with the candlelight behind you, hold your hand in front of the nonreflective surface, about 10 to 12 inches away. Focus on your hand. You'll soon see energy appear around it, like a halo.

3. Now, prop the nonreflective surface against the wall so that you can hold both hands together. Hold your hands as if you're holding a ball of energy and sending healing between them. You can actually see energy move back and forth between your two hands.

If another person is present, you can have that person stand in front of the nonreflective surface (which must be large enough to function as a screen). What colors do you see around this person?

The Aura and Healing

Seymon Kirlian, the Russian electrician and inventor now famous for the form of photography that bears his name (we introduced Kirlian and his work in Chapter 16), discovered that the auras of health and illness have distinct illuminations. Diseased leaves projected differently when photographed than healthy leaves of the same species. Even though the leaf itself appeared healthy, the leaf's aura showed that it had already been infected.

Although Kirlian was certainly not the first person to explore the correlation between energy and illness, he was the first to provide evidence of it. This was a significant discovery step in understanding as well as validating energy healing.

A predecessor of Kirlian, Walter J. Kilner, invented a special lens through which the aura becomes visible. Called a dicyanin screen, the device filters light rays to make the very low spectrum rays of the aura more easily visible to the human eye.

Energy Healing

Energy healing works through spirit chemists, spirit physicians, and other healers to heal someone on the earth plane physically, emotionally, and spiritually. A spirit chemist is a spirit guide that works through healing to change the biochemistry within the body. A spirit physician is a spirit guide that works like a physician on the earth plane might. Certain people who do healing have "specialist" spirit guides. A healer might have a "bone specialist" spirit guide, and so the healing related to bone problems is especially effective.

Energy healing makes a profound difference in people. The changes are physical, emotional, and spiritual—you need all three for healing to happen. It's also essential to release any anger that you're holding. Holding onto anger creates a constant cause and effect—you send out negative energy and so it returns to you. The result is dysfunction of some sort.

Energy healing is not about making everything better; it is about reaching your highest and best. Sometimes the outcome isn't quite what you might expect. Rita once worked as a psychologist with troubled adolescents. A boy told her something he was going to do to break the law and asked her to pray for him. She told him if she did so, he would be caught and arrested, because this would be the highest and best outcome for him. He did go out to do it, and he did get arrested! He ended up going to jail, but then managed to turn his life around and is now doing fine.

Although there are numerous specialized forms of energy healing, all people have the ability to do energy healing. As always, it's essential to begin with setting your intent for the highest good for the other person, and to conclude with thanks to your spirit guides and the God of your understanding.

Hands-On Focus: Reiki

Reiki is an ancient system of hands-on energy healing. The word means "universal energy." Reiki originated in Buddhist practices in ancient India, then was lost for several centuries. It resurfaced in Japan in the 1800s. In contemporary Reiki practice, there are four levels of practitioner identified as level 1, level 2, level 3, and master.

Reiki treatment involves having a Reiki practitioner place his or her hands on your body so that the energy passing through them activates the energy in the body part that is hurt or diseased. The premise is similar to that of acupuncture: to restore the flow of energy. As you feel the energy that the Reiki practitioner is guiding through your body, you talk about the images that appear in your head. This releases trapped energy, and allows the natural flow to resume.

In the United States, Reiki therapy is often combined with psychotherapy. The Reiki practitioner is also a trained psychologist or therapist. As with all forms of energy healing, the outcome can be quite profound.

> **Premonition**
> Energy healing is not a substitute for conventional medical care! If you are sick or injured, always see the appropriate health care practitioner for diagnosis and treatment. Energy healing works to supplement all other forms of healing, not replace them.

Spiritualist Healing

Energy healing is a fundamental element of Spiritualism, which believes that healing is part of all spirit contact and communication. Each service includes healing, as do most circles. During healing, the medium or leader asks healing spirit guides to come close. Each healer also asks his or her specific spirit guide healers to come close.

In the Spiritualist church service, members of the church who are known to have strong healing abilities are invited to stand behind chairs designated as healing chairs, to direct energy to people in need. The person who comes up to sit in the chair receives the directed healing.

The healer lightly touches the head and shoulders of the person in the chair, to let the healing energy flow into them. The prevailing thought about this is that the energy is "intelligent" and will go to where the person needs it. The person receiving healing should relax, and release anything that he or she is holding onto that is no longer needed. When the healing session is finished, the healer gently brushes the shoulders to clear the space.

Mediums and Messages

Intent matters! There was a man in Rita's congregation who was told by a medium (not Rita) that he would be taking a healing chair and meet the love of his life by standing behind the chair. So every Sunday he would stand behind the chair hoping he would meet the love of his life. Although he was a good healer, he did not fulfill the promised message. He came to Rita in frustration, and she explained to him that his intent should be to heal, not to meet a partner. The intent of healing is to help the other person. And who knows, maybe the love of this man's life *is* healing!

Rita knows what it's like to be on both sides of the healing chair. As a Spiritualist minister, she regularly conducts healings. In the fall of 1996, Rita neared completion of chemotherapy for breast cancer. The chemotherapy left her feeling very sick and drained. She felt so sick during the church service that she asked someone else to drive her home after the service. Rita came to a healing chair and her friend and mentor, Bob Miller, stood behind it.

Bob lightly touched Rita's shoulders, and then raised his hands above her. She felt like an enormous vacuum was sucking everything out of her. Then another member of the church came forward and added healing energy … and then other healers did the same, one after the other, adding the energies and resources of their spirit guides to the healing.

"I felt like all of the love in the universe came into me," Rita says about the experience. At the end of the service, Rita's nausea and tiredness disappeared. She no longer felt weakened from her cancer treatments. In fact, the following day she put in a full day's work. (Rita is now cancer-free.)

What people experience during spirit healing ranges from feeling very calm to feeling better either immediately or after some time. Spirit healing can't and isn't meant to heal everything; the purpose is always for the highest and the best. There are spiritual lessons in illness, and many things that we don't understand. We are sometimes volunteers for people around us to learn their lessons. We don't always know the divine purpose of a particular situation; this is beyond our capacity.

Lorie came to Rita for a sitting and drawing at the First Spiritualist Church of Quincy. Her stepmother, Janice, came through. Lorie had been close to her stepmother and Janice kept reporting herself to Rita as mother vibration. Janice has come through in spirit drawings for different family members, appearing for each person at different stages of her life. For Lorie, the image is of Janice when she was already ill and the resemblance is striking.

Joey was his mother's favorite, so there was no surprise when she came through wearing the flowered dress she wore to his wedding.

Absent Healing

Absent healing is healing energy you send to someone who doesn't necessarily know that you're sending healing to them. You might offer healing prayers for a friend who's sick. You might do a healing meditation for the cashier at the grocery store or the mail carrier after hearing that the person is having surgery. There are dozens of times every day that you learn of or encounter people who need healing.

Rita had many powerful experiences in her work as a counselor to troubled adolescent boys. One evening, someone broke into her office and stole, among other things, her leather jacket. It was a cold night, and Rita had to walk to her car without a coat. She was aggravated, and on the drive home she vented to her spirit guides.

"What do I do about this?" she asked. "How do I deal with these boys?" In answer she heard, "Send them healing." She said, "You've got to be kidding!" But she got the message again, so that's what she did. When Rita got to work the next morning, her jacket had been returned! It was the first time in the facility's history that stolen property had been returned, although thefts were quite common. There's no doubt in Rita's mind that the reason it came back was because she sent the healing. Take a look back to Chapter 12 and take another look at Rita's painting, *We Worked So Hard*, which depicts the spirit she believes led her to this challenging but fulfilling work with troubled youth.

Maintaining Energy Balance

When you use your own energy for healing, you're using magnetic energy. This is a powerful source, but it quickly depletes. When you send healing to others, learn to use universal energy rather than your own energy. Here's how a Native American healer taught Rita to draw energy *through*, rather than *from* herself:

- ◆ Visualize the opening of your crown chakra and invite in energy from Father God.

- ◆ Visualize the energy from Mother Earth coming in through the soles of your feet.

- ◆ Allow these energies in your heart chakra—Father God, Mother Earth—and send the energy out through the palms of your hands.

Remember, healing is always about love, with the highest and best intent. You can recharge depleted energy by raising your left hand, which is the receiving hand, palm upward. Concentrate on allowing the energy of the universe to flow into you through your palm, letting it recharge and revitalize you.

Grief is very real. Inasmuch as we know that life continues on, the feeling of loss can be overwhelming. Even for mediums who can stay in touch with their loved ones quite easily, the loss of a loved one brings tangible pain. This pain needs to be healed. Give yourself the time and the space to feel your emotions. Allow yourself to go through the full process of grieving. If you're having difficulty coping with your grief, seek professional help from a grief counselor or psychotherapist.

The Lessons of Healing

Rita prepared to display some of her paintings in a studio show. She rushed around the gallery space, trying to make sure everything hung in its place. She still needed to place some of her art, and time was running short. Hurrying down the stairs, she missed a step and twisted her ankle. Ow! She crumpled in a heap on the stairs. Her ankle hurt, but more than anything she felt somewhat panicked. This was not a time she could afford to be hobbled by an injury—she had work to do!

She lay there for a few minutes, mentally crying, "Why me? Why now?" This, of course, did little to make her ankle feel better. Finally she said to herself, "What's going on here? Why have I created this in my life?" She put her hands on her ankle and directed energy to it, just as if she were healing someone else. Then she said, "What do I need to learn from this? To stop rushing around so much?!" She forgave herself for creating the situation that allowed her to injure herself, and continued directing energy to her ankle. After about 20 minutes, Rita stood up and walked slowly down the rest of the steps. Within two hours all of the swelling was gone and she could walk easily.

> **CAUTION**
>
> **Premonition**
>
> People sometimes want to separate medical and spiritual, but really they remain connected. Doctors are spirits, too, and medicine is spiritual. It's important to see it as a whole experience. Healing is only part of the process; seeing a medical doctor and getting treatment is also part of the process, and the two must be combined.

This isn't to say that injury and illness are consequences of your doing. They are not. This is not a process of placing blame. Rather, it's a process of looking at the events that happen and trying to figure out what lessons they hold and how to make the best of them. No one wishes for cancer or a heart attack. But when these situations of crisis occur, they can become pivotal points in your life. You are the creator of your path through this life, and part of your mission is to find your way around the obstacles that are blocking your way.

As actor Michael J. Fox explains on the flap copy of his best-selling memoir, *Lucky Man* (Hyperion, 2002), he would not trade his experience with Parkinson's disease even if given the opportunity to wave a magic wand and erase it all. Living and coping daily with the tough challenges of Parkinson's, for Michael J. Fox and for millions of others, can be transformed into a life path of spiritual growth and rich experience.

Self-Healing: An Exercise

One of the most powerful aspects of energy healing is that you can do it for yourself. Try this exercise:

1. Begin by setting your intent and asking for light and love to surround the healing.

2. If you can touch the part of your body that needs healing, lay your hands on it. If you can't reach it, visualize it. You can also focus on an emotional or relationship problem.

3. Ask the God of your understanding to send love and light to the part of your body or to the situation. Ask what you need to learn from this problem.

4. Forgive yourself, forgive others, and bless the process you've just gone through (including the problem for which you've asked for healing).

You don't have to like whatever problem it is that you have, but blessing it is important because this says that you understand its purpose in your life and that you accept it. Self-healing can be very profound.

Drawing Energy from Beyond

The universe is a generous, abundant, giving source. All that you need is yours for the asking. The trouble is, most of the time we either don't know what we need or forget that we need to ask for it. The energy of the universe is always available to help you, in many and diverse ways. If you want to make changes in your life, put your intent out to the universe. What comes back might surprise and delight you.

As Rita says, "Ask, and the universe will provide!"

The Least You Need to Know

◆ Energy is a very powerful healing force.

◆ Energy healing works with and complements conventional medical treatment, but isn't intended to replace it.

◆ You have the ability to send healing energy to others and to yourself.

◆ Healing takes place on the physical, emotional, and spiritual levels.

◆ The energy of the universe is yours for the asking!

Chapter **19**

Everything Is Spirit, Spirit Is Everywhere

In This Chapter

♦ Indigenous cultures and their spirit connections

♦ The value of ritual and ceremony

♦ Exploring the spirit energy of the earth

♦ Meeting your power animals: a guided meditation

♦ The healing power of plant energy

♦ Keeping spirit strong

Many cultures around the world infuse their physical environments with the life and animation of the spirit world. Spirit is energy, spirit is everywhere, and spirit energy is supportive and healing. These cultures honor not only the spirits of those who have passed on, but also the spirit of the earth itself.

A number of the practices and rituals of these cultures are finding their way into everyday life for many people. Aromatherapy and flower essences use the energy and spirit of plants for healing. Crystals carry the energy of the earth itself, a powerful and supportive force alone as well as in combination with other energy forms.

Of the Land: Indigenous Beliefs

In the beginning of human existence, everyone had a close and intimate relationship with the environment. The land supported life. Survival meant connecting with the cycles of nature: day and night, the four seasons, planting and harvest, birth and death.

Early cultures moved to follow the cycles, trying to keep pace with those that meant life and those that spelled certain doom. Over time and as tribes grew in numbers, moving every few months became impractical. Large groups became easy targets for predators, and made it difficult for the group to respond quickly to environmental changes.

To keep up with the changing bounty of the earth, some tribe members continued in nomadic ways while the rest settled in a location where the land provided fairly steady support—shelter, water, limited food. Those who stayed behind learned to harvest and lay in crops, saving for the lean times when darkness exceeded light and the earth showed few signs of life.

The hunters—those who left the group to follow their food sources—shadowed migratory herds for hundreds of miles. They learned that the further from home the kill was, the harder they had to work to get the meat, bones, and hides back to the tribe. So they learned to direct the migratory flow, keeping it closer to the home tribe.

For centuries, people lived according to these patterns. They learned to appreciate, as their forebears had, and to be thankful for the earth's riches. They identified the energy of the focal points of their celebrations as spirits representing Mother Earth, Father Sky, the birds, the trees, the grasses, the water. Every element had its energy, and every element had its spirit. And they began to formalize their gratitude through song, dance, and ceremony.

These celebrations became the mythology of humankind that carries forward to modern times in many forms and practices.

Native American Spirit Traditions

As the indigenous culture of North America, Native Americans have always honored the spirit energy of the world around them. Rather than controlling the physical environment, the Native American belief is that we are here to take care of the environment, to take care of the earth and the bounty it supplies to make life possible.

Within most Native American belief systems, life is seamless, existing across time and space. Those who have passed to spirit simply exist in a different form than those who have physical bodies. Rituals and ceremonies emphasize the connections between the earth plane and the spirit world, and communication between the two is ongoing.

> **Silver Cord**
>
> Native American cultures honor the grandfather spirit, and many times even refer to God as Grandfather Spirit. Grandfather Spirit is wisdom, strength, and courage. Grandmother Spirit is also wisdom, but as the wise nurturer.

Mayan Spirit Traditions

Many ancient Mayan cultures believed that the dead descended into the Underworld. There was no death, really, just a relocation to this setting. There, they inhabited one of nine Underworld levels. This was similar to the belief systems of other cultures of the same time period, such as the ancient Greeks and Romans.

One Mayan tribe, la Candones, held a belief system that was somewhat different and closer, at least in context, to the Western concept of heaven. The la Candones people believed that rather than descending to the Underworld the dead ascended to a place, similar to the land they inhabited on earth, where they then lived forever without wanting for anything. There was no need to work; everything necessary for a pleasant and worry-free existence was provided. The distinction between this belief and heaven is that there was no concept of needing to "earn" passage to this ethereal land. Everyone went there after death, not just those deemed deserving.

African Spirit Traditions

The indigenous cultures of Africa are varied and diverse. However, their belief systems share a number of common characteristics. These include the following:

◆ Belief in a higher being or God that exists beyond the realm of humankind's understanding, who is nonetheless able to appear to the people as a visible entity.

♦ A God that is genderless, although often appears as both male and female.

♦ Spiritual powers associated with objects and beings (animals, plants, other people) of daily life.

> **Spiritology**
>
> A **cosmology** is a culture-specific description of the origin and structure of the universe. It typically includes explanations of creation, the nature and roles of men and women, and concepts related to death and the dead.

♦ Many levels of spirits linked to elements of the natural environment, such as spirits of the river, spirits of the air, and spirits of the earth itself.

♦ Spirit visitors were often those spirit entities, usually ancestors, who acquired divine energy upon passing and can help their relatives on the earth plane.

♦ A *cosmology* that documents a tribe's origins and path to its current existence, presented in the context of myths, legends, and riddles.

Ritual, Ceremony, and Tradition

Rituals are formalized actions that we repeat, with certain significance, in conjunction with specific events or situations. Ceremonies incorporate rituals into celebrations. A ceremony often contains multiple rituals. The wedding ceremony, for example, includes the rituals of exchanging vows and rings.

When these celebrations become ingrained in the community culture, they become tradition. We inherit them, and participate in them sometimes without fully understanding why but just because they're how we do things. At weddings, we toss rice at the bride and groom as they leave the church. Why? You get 10 points if you know! No? Rice is showered upon newlyweds as a symbol of fertility.

Such symbolic practices fill our lives. They connect the small events of our daily lives with the bigger picture of how we fit in the universe. Tradition dictates how we honor passages from birth through death. Birthdays celebrate the day of entry into physical life, and the countdown to the day of departure, as yet unknown. They remind us that we are all connected to a greater energy, the energy from which we come, in which we exist, and to which we return.

Ritual and ceremony can also establish energy connections, such as for spirit contact. When you set your intent for spirit communication to come for the highest and the best, you're "tuning" the energy of your connection to support this. Prayer, meditation, and other focused practices accomplish similar purpose.

Rites of Passage

The vision quest is integral to many cultures that hold a deep connection to the earth. In such cultures, like many aboriginal tribes of Australia and Native American tribes, spirit guidance is an essential part of the rite of passage to adulthood.

In Western cultures, external events such as obtaining a driver's license and reaching legal age of consent (or drinking alcohol) are the hallmarks of the transition from child to adult. In many indigenous cultures, however, becoming an adult means demonstrating that you have reached maturity physically, emotionally, and spiritually.

Physical maturation is apparent. Emotional maturation reflects in attitudes and behaviors. Spiritual maturation occurs when the young person has the adult experience of connecting with his or her spirit heritage and with the spirit energy of the earth. Only when young people connect with their spirit origins and ancestors are they fully able to take their places as adults within their communities.

On the typical vision quest, one goal is for you to meet and identify your power animal—an animal spirit with special traits or characteristics that represent attributes or qualities that you have or need. Power animals are deeply symbolic. As the quest gets underway, you begin to see signs and indications that, as they accumulate, point toward a particular animal. As you start out, you might see a crow fly across your path, a squirrel run up a pine tree at the edge of the woods, and a rabbit bound off into the underbrush. Which might be your power animal? At this point, any ... or none.

Over the span of your vision quest, other animals or representations of them appear. After a time, one stands out and your attention focuses on this animal. And at some point, there's an encounter—such as through a vision or a dream—in which you know that this is your power animal, and the animal's spirit tells you why. (See the later "Power Animal Journey: A Guided Meditation" section for another way to identify and meet your power animal.)

Shaman Soul Release

Shamanism is an earth-based religion, meaning that it's integrated with its environment. It's quite complex, and we're just going to briefly talk about a small portion of Shamanism, soul release (also called soul retrieval). Shamanistic belief systems hold that as we go through our lives and are traumatized in various ways, we lose little bits of ourselves. This depletes personal energy, causing physical, emotional, and spiritual problems.

Shamans, through guided meditation, help you to identify what those missing parts are and bring them back. This lets you experience the healing that takes place when that essence of you comes back. In some ways, the process is similar to Western psychology's inner child work, or therapy to reconnect with and bring back your inner child, the parts of you that you've lost. Most of us have been told throughout our lives that there are things we can't do, which is trauma. So we lose those parts—creativity, musical ability, whatever. Through psychotherapy that sometimes includes hypnosis, you reconnect with these parts of yourself to restore your sense of wholeness and balance.

Shaman soul release helps you find and bring back missing spirit, or energy, elements. The shaman leads you in a very light meditative state, from which you can then identify what's bothering you. You make this identification, not the shaman. Say that you have pain in your neck. In this light, altered state, you go inside of yourself, so to speak, to look at this pain. You might touch it or determine who or what it is. Then you ask your spirit guides to take it away and replace it with healing light. This last part is very important for restoring the balance of your energy; you can't just take away some energy without putting some back to fill the void.

Earth Energy

The earth itself is a tremendous source of energy. Magnets, gemstones, and crystals carry the earth's energy, which has many applications in conventional as well as spirit healing. And of course, earth energy supports all other energy on the earth plane.

Silver Cord

Because of their capability to store, amplify, and transfer energy, crystals have many applications in modern science. Crystals made the first radio transmissions possible, for example. Today crystals appear in everything from the liquid crystal display on your watch to sophisticated medical imaging technology.

Animal Energy

Animals contain great spirit energy. In many indigenous cultures, animal spirits represent the connection between the earth and the divine. The spirits of certain animals have special significance. Native American tribes had animal spirit guides that helped them in nearly all functions of daily life.

These beliefs carry over into modern life in many ways. The United States has the bald eagle as its official symbol, which represents power and grace. Golfing fans know the great American golfer Jack Nicklaus as the golden bear. Fast cars are mustangs, jaguars, and cougars.

Power Animals

Like spirit guides, power animals bring special energy connections to your life. And like spirit guides from the higher side, your power animals change according to your needs (physical, emotional, and spiritual) and what is going on in your life. Power animals are also called totem animals or just totems. A totem is an emblem or a symbol that has spiritual significance.

Any animal can be a power animal; each animal has particular traits and characteristics. When this animal is your power animal, it shares these attributes with you to give you the energy they provide. When you are learning something, such as when you are in school, your power animal might be an owl for wisdom. If you feel someone is threatening your child or your family, perhaps you draw from the energy of the bear. When you are working creatively, such as writing or painting, the power animal supporting you might be a spider or a crow.

You don't choose your power animals. They choose you. Familiar power animals such as bears, wolves, and owls have become almost archetypal in their representations of certain attributes:

- ◆ Ant—teamwork, patience, focused action

- ◆ Armadillo—safety, protection

- ◆ Bear—power, strength, healing, protectiveness

- ◆ Beaver—determination, productivity, persistence

- ◆ Buffalo—abundance, the natural order of things

- ◆ Butterfly—change, metamorphosis, transformation, joy, freedom

- ◆ Crow—spiritual strength, creativity

- ◆ Dove—peace, calmness, unity

- ◆ Dragonfly—carefree, good luck

- ◆ Eagle—vision, strength, flight, divine

- ◆ Elephant—strength, power, royalty, family

- ◆ Frog—cleansing, rebirth, transformation

- ◆ Hawk—guide, vision

- ◆ Lion—intuition, imagination, family, courage

Silver Cord

A totem pole is a tradition specific to the Native American tribes of the Pacific Northwest. Carved from a cedar tree, a totem pole contains the images or representations of the power animals important to a family group or clan. It serves to identify the group's history and heritage, told through the symbolism of the totems carved into the pole.

- Owl—wisdom, seeing what others can't

- Peacock—immortality, pride

- Salmon—pride, intensity

- Snake—rebirth, change, healing, shrewdness

- Spider—creativity, fate

- Turtle—steady, loyal, protected

Power Animal Journey: A Guided Meditation

Rita's good friend Martha Tierney wrote the following guided meditation for meeting your power animals especially for this book. A certified metaphysical hypnotherapist and spirit-trained shamanic facilitator, Martha maintains a private practice in Boston, Massachusetts. For more information about Martha and her practice, you can go to her website at www.marthatierney.com. Thanks, Martha!

We recommend that you read this guided meditation into a tape recorder, so you can listen and follow its suggestions. If you don't want to listen to your own voice, ask someone whose voice you find soothing and calming to record it for you.

To prepare for listening to your tape and the journey it will take you on, follow these tips:

- Be sure that you will not be disturbed during this process (turn the phone ringer down or off, or unplug the phone).

- Dim the lights.

Premonition

Do not listen to your "Power Animal Journey" tape while driving a car, operating heavy equipment, or doing anything else that requires your full attention. This guided meditation will affect and alter your perceptions.

- Put on some background music: Soothing or patterned drumming music (for journeying) can assist in altering your state of consciousness/ awareness.

- Begin to slow your breathing.

- Choose a sitting position; this will likely keep you more focused and awake.

- Make sure your posture is straight and that you're not feeling restricted in any way—get comfortable.

Here is the guided meditation. Read it through a couple times, so it's familiar and you can read it smoothly. Where you see *<pause>*, pause for two or three seconds and then continue. This might seem awkward while you're doing the reading, but when you're listening to the tape it gives you time to follow the suggestion. Read in a steady, calm voice.

Continue to focus upon your slow *<pause>*

comfortable *<pause>*

breathing *<pause>*

allowing yourself to drop your shoulders *<pause>*

and warmly relax your back *<pause>*

you may begin to relax your body starting at the top of your head *<pause>*

relaxing your scalp *<pause>*

forehead, eyes, nose, and mouth *<pause>*

letting your cheeks and jaw relax and drop your jaw slightly

resting your tongue naturally, at the top of your mouth, and behind your front teeth *<pause>*

Feel how relaxed you are from your throat, up through your head, to the top of your scalp *<pause>*

so relaxed *<pause>*

and continue on down *<pause>*

relaxing the throat *<pause>*

warming and relaxing your shoulders, arms, and hands *<pause>*

noticing how wonderful you feel as you continue to release all inner tension from the top of your head, right down through to your shoulders and arms *<pause>*

bring your attention to your chest *<pause>*

allow yourself to let go of all of today's stress, simply let it melt away *<pause>*

freeing you to relax so much more than before *<pause>*

and with every breath *<pause>*

you are able to release *all* of today's unhealthy tension that you may have held within your body *<pause>*

as you relax your waist, your organs, colon and genitals *<pause>*

warming and relaxing your pelvis *<pause>* your hips *<pause>*

and as you move down through your thighs *<pause>*

the front *and* the back of your knees feel so much more relaxed *<pause>*

as you continue to release the day's tension *<pause>*

relaxing your calves, the muscles supporting your chins *<pause>*

your ankles are relaxed, you may rotate them if you wish *<pause>*

and the warmth of relaxation

continues on down through the arches of your feet *<pause>*

the soles of your feet, and on down into each toe.

Check your body and see if there is any tension still left,

and if there is, simply release it by warming it with your intention. That's right, let it go *<long pause>*

Now try to imagine your relaxed energy growing out from of the bottoms of your feet, like a tree growing roots, into Mother Earth *<pause>*

your roots can be as straight or windy as you wish *<pause>*

and as deep or shallow as you wish *<pause>*

allow yourself a moment to feel the energy of love and balance *<pause>*

touching *<pause>* nourishing *<pause>* your lovely roots *<pause>*

Bringing your attention to the top of your head, allow your relaxed energy to reach toward Father Sky *<pause>* feeling the warmth of the sun relaxing you *<pause>* nourishing you *<pause>*

and when you feel you have touched upon the right area of Father Sky bring that wonderful loving feeling down into the crown of your head down through your body *<pause>* washing away any worry *<pause>* any tension or discomfort *<pause>*

if you wish you may allow Father Sky to meet and blend with Mother Earth within you *<pause>*

and as you do *<pause>*

feel how radiant and beautiful you feel *<pause>*

let this energy of healing love continue to feed and nourish your body, mind, and spirit *<pause>*

as you allow yourself to imagine yourself in a calm sacred space *<pause>*

it can be somewhere you've been before *<pause>*

or somewhere you discover here today *<pause>*

that's right, allow yourself to travel anywhere you wish *<pause>*

as you begin to get comfortable in your nice safe *<pause>* calm *<pause>* sacred space. A space that is all yours right now *<pause>* a place where no one will interrupt you.

Relax in your nice spot and feel the beauty that surrounds you *<pause>*

take a moment to smell the air *<pause>*

feel the warm gentle winds upon your face *<pause>*

there may be sounds of nature around you *<pause>*

maybe there is a babbling brook nearby that you can hear,

or a bird singing its song to his mate *<pause>*

whatever you wish here is fine *<pause>*

for this is your sacred spot in the universe.

As you continue to feel the energy of nature all around you, supporting you *<pause>*

this is your time to journey to meet with your Power Animal *<pause>*

He or she will come to you to guide you *<pause>*

and protect you *<pause>*

he or she will become a companion to you and you a companion to him or her *<pause>*

It can be any animal you feel comfortable with at this time *<pause>*

off in the distance you see an animal moving slowly toward you *<pause>*

if you wish you may move forward to meet them on their way *<pause>*

If, for any reason *<pause>*

you do not feel right with the first animal you see *<pause>*

there will be another one who comes along *<pause>*

to greet you *<pause>*

as the two of you meet, just take a moment to sense one another *<long pause>*

you may communicate with one another simply with your thoughts *<long pause>*

you will and do understand one another easily *<pause>*

if you feel ready and you would like to extend yourself in friendship at this time,

you may *<long pause>*

perhaps you would like to walk, or fly, or swim with your new friend, to get to know how he or she lives, go ahead *<long pause>*

you may relax with your friend *<pause>*

or play with your friend *<pause>*

or explore with your friend *<pause>*

take the time you wish together, for a few moments *<pause>*

when it is time, I will call you back *<pause>*

<three-minute pause>

The two of you will have a uniquely personal relationship together *<pause>*

a relationship of reciprocity *<pause>*

you may visit one another at any time you wish simply by calling to one another
<pause>

<one-minute pause>

It is time to take your leave now *<pause>*

give thanks to your new friend *<pause>*

give thanks to Great Spirit for this wonderful experience with your Power Animal.

Remember that your Power Animal can change into any size, larger or smaller, when you need protection.

He or she can and will work in any way that the situation calls for to protect you *<pause>*

you may ask if your Power Animal would like to return with you to your sacred space so that he or she will know where to meet you the next time *<pause>*

if you are comfortable with that *<pause>*

return now to the point where the two of you met *<long pause>*

going back to your journeying point *<pause>*

and return now to your sacred space *<pause>*

If your Power Animal is with you take a moment to exchange good-byes for now *<pause>*

Until you meet again *<pause>*

alone now, return to the room in your home where you started this special journey *<pause>*

feel the room around you *<pause>*

feel the energy of Mother Earth and Father Sky *<pause>*

Join them *<pause>*

thank them for healing you and for holding your place during your journey *<pause>*

Release Father Sky with love and pull down your relaxed energy *<pause>*

that's right, pull it all back, right back to the crown of your head where it started from *<pause>*

feel your relaxed energy strengthening again *<pause>* tightening *<pause>*

like a loose mesh weave closing up *<pause>*

Release Mother Earth with love and gratitude *<pause>*

and as she releases, call back your roots *<pause>* all your roots *<pause>*

and bring your relaxed energy right back into your feet again where it started from *<pause>*

feel your relaxed energy strengthening again *<pause>* tightening *<pause>*

like a loose mesh weave closing up *<pause>*

(Read the remaining lines more quickly.)

Feel your feet now *<pause>* your chins, calves, and knees *<pause>*

your thighs, hips, and pelvis *<pause>*

your colon, genitals, and organs *<pause>* your chest and back *<pause>*

your shoulders, arms, and hands *<pause>*

your throat and tongue *<pause>*

your cheeks and jaw *<pause>*

mouth, nose, eyes, and forehead *<pause>*

the top of your head and your scalp *<pause>*

I am going to count to three, and when I do,

you will open your eyes and feel confident, loved, fresh, and revitalized,

ready to continue on with your day.

You will remember the experience with your Power Animal in full detail.

That's right, you will remember in detail your experience with your Power Animal.

1 *<pause>* feeling alert and aware *<pause>*

2 *<pause>* feeling happy and vital *<pause>*

3 *<pause>* open your eyes now *<pause>* and you are feeling alert and refreshed *<pause>*

happy to continue on with your day.

You can repeat this guided meditation as often as you like. After a while, you'll see certain patterns begin to emerge. You might have an owl as your power animal for as long as several years, and then have the ant. Your power animals change according to your needs, so that their energy fulfills where yours is lacking.

When Animals Pass to Spirit

Pets are loyal and loving companions. Like all living things, they have vital energy. Often when Rita does readings, spirits come through with their favorite pets accompanying them. Pets do follow us to the higher side.

Often, a pet is so identifiable that it becomes a key piece of identifying the person who's coming through when that's not clear. Pets show themselves by species (dog, cat), size, and personality. It's wonderful to know that our beloved pets, like human loved ones, are still around us, even when they pass to the higher side.

Rita met with Kim via the telephone. She called after the passing of her dear friend John and asked for a spirit drawing of him. Rita always tells clients that she cannot promise that a specific spirit will come through, but John was there and very willing to communicate. John chose to show himself as a younger man although he had been much more mature when he passed to spirit. John talked about the month of March and showed the number eight. Kim confirmed that John celebrated a very special eighth anniversary in March. Rita identified lungs filled with smoke and Kim confirmed that John had been a heavy smoker. John also appeared with his beloved beige cat. Yes, animals go to spirit, too!

> **Mediums and Messages**
>
> At an evening church service, Rita came to a woman in the congregation and started to chuckle. She said, "I don't know how to tell you this, but I have a dog here that's coming through for you. It's a wire-haired terrier." Then Rita said, "He behaves as if he has springs attached to the bottoms of his feet! He's jumping straight up, it's as if I can hear the word *boing!*" The woman was overjoyed and burst into tears. Her beloved dog had passed to spirit a month earlier … a wire-haired terrier that she always told people behaved as though he had springs on the bottoms of his feet.

Plant Energy

Many times a spirit will show a particular plant as a symbol; roses as love, daisies as new beginnings, for example. As with all symbols, each medium will create his or her own dictionary.

Plants give us all life-sustaining energy, every day. The whole-wheat bread you drop in the toaster in the morning … plant energy. The salad you eat for lunch … plant energy. The sautéed mushrooms and green bean casserole you enjoy for dinner … plant energy. Plants—grains, fruits, vegetables—are the fuels that give your body the energy it needs to carry out the functions of living.

Many plants have additional energies that often are not apparent, unless you are tuned in and know about these special qualities. Some of these qualities can be explained through biochemistry. We can look at the plant's chemical composition and know the effect it will have on the body. But all plants have healing energy properties on the energy level. You can't see, taste, or smell these properties. They act on your aura to influence your personal energy.

Medicinal Plants

Medicinal herbs and botanicals, for example, contain chemicals that function as drugs. The plant foxglove contains digitalis, which is the chemical now used in the drug digoxin, prescribed to strengthen and regulate the heartbeat. There are thousands of such plants, many of which are the basis for the drugs of modern medicine as well as ancient medical systems such as traditional Chinese medicine (TCM).

Plants with medicinal qualities act on your physical body to influence physical functions. The changes that result can affect emotional and spiritual aspects of your health as well.

Flower Essences

Flower essences use water to capture the energy imprints of plants. In most plants, the flower is the most potent energy source because it is the plant's structure of regeneration. Flower essences come in liquid form, and have no taste or smell. They work by interacting with your personal energy field through your aura. Flower essences influence your spiritual and emotional dimensions.

Dr. Edward Bach, a British bacteriologist, discovered flower essences in the 1930s while he was doing research in the then-new field of vaccines. He began to find evidence that the plants he was using in his culture mediums actually influenced health by themselves, by interacting on an energy level.

Each plant has specific qualities that act on certain issues. Essence of pine, for example, influences self-acceptance. Roses, so familiar as symbols of romance, not surprisingly influence compassion and love.

Aromatherapy

Aromatherapy has become popular in Western cultures because it smells good. You can enjoy aromatherapy whether or not you understand its energy foundation. Many people enjoy the fragrances associated with aromatherapy. From a scientific perspective, the smells of various substances elicit responses in the brain that cause biochemical changes. From an energy perspective, aromatherapy acts on the body's energy field in the same ways as flower essences.

Honoring Spirit

You *are* spirit, and you are *of* spirit. The essence of your being is spirit energy in its own right. Your energy also connects with the spirit of the physical world around you, and the universe at large. Spirit and energy are inseparable. They exist contiguously, across the earth plane and the spirit world. Spirit energy links us to the natural environment that supports our physical needs, to each other, and to loved ones who no longer walk the earth plane.

This is the foundation of belief for many indigenous cultures, and it is the foundation that supports spirit contact and communication. Honoring this foundation, in yourself and in others, makes it possible for it to continue supporting you—in your everyday life as well as during times of special need.

The Least You Need to Know

♦ There is a continuous energy that supports all life on earth. All the world's religions speak of a higher being, an omnipotent supply of energy, that puts life force into all things. Everything is spirit, spirit is everything.

♦ Ritual and ceremony provide constant reaffirmation of our connection to all that is spirit.

♦ You don't choose your power animals. Your power animals choose you, depending on what your needs are at the time. Your power animals change as your physical, emotional, and spiritual needs change.

♦ Plant energy heals in ways we can observe and in ways that only our spirits recognize.

♦ All energy is connected. There are no boundaries between the energy of the earth plane, the energy of the higher side, and the energy of the universe.

Chapter 20

Near-Death Experiences

In This Chapter

- ◆ What happens during a near-death experience
- ◆ Common characteristics of near-death experiences
- ◆ Why you come back
- ◆ Lessons, collective and personal

A bright, beckoning light. A welcoming circle of family and friends. Peace, tranquility, and joy. These are common elements many people report when their souls travel to the brink of the other side and then return.

We call this experience "near death" because you return from it. What makes it "near" instead of permanent? What happens to send you back when it's not quite your time to leave your physical life? Why would you be allowed to go, or be summoned to, the very brink and then be sent back?

Stepping to the Edge

Each *near-death experience* (also called an *NDE*) is unique, yet most near-death experiences share common characteristics. These typically include the following:

◆ Sudden trauma that precipitates the experience.

◆ The sensation of rising out of your body and observing it, and the activity going on around you, as an entity separate from your body.

◆ An end to any pain you might have been experiencing in your physical body, and an overwhelming sense of peace.

◆ The experience of floating through a dark tunnel or corridor.

◆ A bright light that draws you to it like metal to a magnet.

◆ The presence of loved ones gathered to greet and welcome you, just on the other side of the bright white light.

By definition, a near-death experience takes place when you reach the point of clinical death. Your heart stops, your breathing stops, your brain stops. All signs of physical life cease … and then return. Although the medical view is that brain cells begin to die after three minutes without oxygen, people have existed in a state of clinical death for as long as 90 minutes.

Spiritology

A **near-death experience (NDE)** occurs when the physical body experiences clinical death and the spirit leaves, and then life returns to the body and the spirit returns.

How is this possible? From the earth plane perspective, doctors have lots of ideas, but no conclusive explanations. From the higher side perspective, when it's not your time, it's not your time.

The Shock That Separates

Most of the time, a physical trauma precipitates a near-death experience. This might be a life-threatening injury, a crisis during surgery, a heart attack, a severe allergic reaction—any number of circumstances that strike suddenly and without warning. Such trauma shocks or jolts your being, separating it into its components. The physical and the emotional, as inherent elements of your tangible body, remain as your body. Your spirit, perhaps doing what it's "programmed" to do, leaves.

But the higher side is not prepared for your arrival because, despite the events unfolding on the earth plane, it's not your time to leave your physical existence. Of course your spirit always exists with one foot (so to speak!) in the spirit world and the other on the earth plane. This is the essence of physical life as we've discussed it throughout this book. Your physical body encases your spirit for its travels on the earth plane, but your spirit is still part of, and connected to, the bigger energy of the universe.

Although your spirit might freely travel during your dream state (many spirits do; see Chapter 17), it does so with intent. Not that you know your spirit is about to take off to go visiting, but your *spirit* (your higher being) knows. It disengages carefully from your physical and emotional dimensions—and returns in similar fashion.

During a near-death experience, your spirit is lifted from your physical body. There is no intent; it just happens. Little wonder you find the experience bewildering at first! Many people report that one of the first sensations they become aware of is that the pain they were feeling in their bodies, usually intense because of the trauma, is suddenly gone.

Mediums and Messages

A near-death experience is a spirit communication of the most direct kind. One of the first spirit drawings Rita did was for a woman who had been critically injured in a car accident. When Rita took Harriet's hand in hers, both of them expected a loved one of Harriet's would come through. Much to their surprise, however, the contact involved Harriet herself. "What I'm seeing is an angel come and lift you out of your body in your accident," Rita said. "This was to protect you from feeling the pain from your many injuries, which would have been overwhelming to you." "Yes," said Harriet. "I remember. I came back to my body in the hospital."

I See ME!

There you are, just looking around, and suddenly what you see is … you! No mirrors, no tricks. It's really you in the flesh, as seen from the spirit. This is a consistent part of near-death experiences. Some people feel themselves lifting from their bodies and floating toward the ceiling, then looking down to see themselves as the focal points of desperate efforts to cut the journey short. For many people, this is quite a jolt. One moment everything is as it should be, and the next moment nothing is as it was. And there you are, looking at yourself from a view you've never had before!

Some people report that they are able to look down on their physical bodies during near-death experiences, watching the flurry of activity taking place in the efforts to revive them. A person who has had a near-death experience often can describe, in considerable detail, events that, if still within the physical body, he or she would not be able to see or hear. These events might include watching the doctors and nurses prepare and give injections, shock the heart, and place breathing tubes. The disembodied spirit can often hear conversations taking place in hallways and other places distant from the body's location. When they return to physical life, people report these conversations.

The events of near-death experiences that take place in the physical world are easy to verify, because other people participate in them and can recall them. Some of the most intriguing insights we have into existence beyond the earth plane come from people who experience physical death and then come back. This is yet further evidence of the continuity of life.

The Goodness and Love of the Higher Side

A body that has experienced severe trauma—injury, heart attack, shock from illness, and the like—is nearly always in great pain. These are assaults on the integrity of the body, and they leave damage in their wake. When their spirits withdraw from these damaged bodies, people who have near-death experiences report, the pain goes away. They can look at their bodies and wonder if they really want to return, especially when so much goodness and love beckons from the higher side.

This is the "good" that we request when we ask that spirit contact and spirit healing come through for the greatest good and the highest intent. It is a welcoming, benevolent sense of absolute love—which makes sense as it is a representation of the divine.

This goodness is pure; it is the energy of pure love. It exists only for learning and healing. It is this goodness that manifests when spirits come through with messages. And it is the goodness that welcomes spirits that are passing over.

Tunnel Travel

Many people describe a distinctive tunnel or corridor, usually darkened, that they find themselves in when their spirits leave their bodies. At the end of this tunnel they can see a bright, white light, and they know that this is the portal to the higher side.

Some people report feeling fearful or frightened while in this tunnel, while others experience it as nothing more than a passageway that links the earth plane with the spirit world. No one really knows what this tunnel is or represents, but it is common to many near-death experiences.

Silver Cord _____

When it is time for your spirit to join your loved ones on the higher side, there is also sense of transition. Spirit communicators tell us that there is a sense of moving from one place to another and a sense of moving into the light. The spirits waiting to greet you on the higher side differ with the passing person's desires, needs (on the higher side), and soul's mission. You could cross over to an old-fashioned, backyard Italian picnic ... or find your dearly departed lover offering you a dance.

Into the Light

In near-death experiences, people often report seeing a bright light with friends and family who have passed to the higher side already gathered around its edges. This is the light of divine energy. This is the light that reassures you that God is near and all is well. There is love, warmth, peace, and joy, and a strong feeling of desire to move into the light to complete the passage. Most people report feeling an overwhelming sense of pure love.

Of course, because it is not yet your time, you cannot complete the passage no matter how enticing the light and the love. And this is clear to your spirit, however much it might want to make the crossing. Spirits on the other side know, too. And as much as they want to communicate joy and goodness, they are there just to let you know that they are there … and that they'll be waiting for you when it is your time to pass.

For many people who have near-death experiences, the light fosters a resurgence of faith in their God of understanding and a renewed commitment to following a spiritual path for the rest of their earth plane journey. It is an amazing and powerful thing to connect with such goodness and love!

So Many Welcoming Spirits!

Typically in a near-death experience, the spirits gathered on the other side of this light are smiling and happy to see their loved one, but they aren't beckoning for you to join them. They know it's not quite your time. But they want you to know that all is well with them. This is like a spirit communication of the most wondrous and direct sort!

Seeing the loved ones that have already passed is joyous, but this is often where the sadness comes in: You want to stay. It's been a long time since you've seen many of them, perhaps, and you want to visit at least.

Here and There ... at the Same Time

During a near-death experience, you're not really in this world or the next. You're sort of in between, existing a little in each but in neither completely. You aren't aware of this to any great extent. It's your spirit that appears to have the recall of events that happen during the near-death experience, which is how you return with a memory of events you couldn't possibly have witnessed or experienced.

Connie brought her brother to Rita for a spirit drawing, and a drawing of their grandmother came through for him. He saw her eyes and began to cry. It is sometimes overwhelming when one can see the eyes of a deceased loved one appear on a sheet of paper. A year later, Connie, owner of the New Age gift shop Magick Mirror in Bristol, Rhode Island, came to see Rita, and the matching picture of her grandfather came through for her. The connection to a loved one who has passed to spirit, even in a spirit drawing here on the earth plane, is profound, powerful, and full of love. It's no wonder that it is the loved ones who are there to greet us when indeed it is our time to pass to spirit.

Often, a person can relate, in verbatim detail, conversations taking place among others in hallways and physical locations outside the room where his or her body lies. The people engaged in these conversations might be different groups discussing the situation—doctors and nurses in one group in one location, family and friends in another.

The spirit has a simultaneous experience of all events related to the "death." It witnesses the frantic activity to bring the body back to life, and sees events and overhears discussions that aren't possible to experience from the body's location. At the same time, the spirit is moving through the tunnel toward the bright light and the spirit entities that are at the other end. There is no time, there is no space. There is just energy and existence.

Not Quite Time to Go

With continuing advances in medical technology, near-death experiences are becoming increasingly common. People who just 10 years ago would have been declared dead from their conditions are now "brought back" to life. Many then go on to full recovery from their physical injuries and enjoy long, full lives.

Are they truly "brought back" or is it the divine order of the universe that their spirits are communing with the higher side? Of course, this is difficult to answer with certainty. But it seems that if it was your time to go, you would go—no matter what technology was being used to prevent such an outcome. And conversely, if it's *not* your time to go, you won't—not because technology saves your life, even if that's how it looks, but simply because it's not your time to go.

When it becomes clear that rather than completing the passage their spirits are instead returning to their physical bodies, people often report a sense of sadness and even resistance. They have "seen the light" and want to become one with it, to move into the warmth, peace, and joy that they feel.

Other people feel a sense of relief. Their lives on the earth plane are unfinished, and they know this. They are eager to return to complete those lives, and comforted in knowing what lies ahead for them when their time to make the crossing does come.

Divine Order ... or Accident?

If there is a divine order, how can "accidents" such as near-death experiences happen? This is a valid question, and one that many people ask in trying to understand or explain the phenomenon of near-death experience. Remember, however, the critically important role of free will. Your actions determine your movement along your path. Your destiny is a journey, not an end point.

We could engage in debate about whether anything happens by accident. Perhaps your near-death experience is as much a part of the divine order of the universe as was your birth. Perhaps there are lessons for you that you can only learn by coming so close to making the crossing.

The Edge of Death

So what, exactly, happens when your body dies but the higher side says you're not ready to make the crossing? There are biological phenomena, of course. Once your heart stops beating, blood stops circulating through your body. Vital organs feel the oxygen shortage immediately, and your body's shock response leaps into action. This response sends *epinephrine* coursing to your heart, with the intent of jolting it into action, and simultaneously shuts down all body functions not necessary to support life.

Spiritology

Epinephrine is a natural chemical your body makes that stimulates heartbeat and breathing. Its release is part of your body's "fight or flight" survival response.

It seems odd to think that so much of this intricate design that is your body could have so many dispensable functions. But the core functions necessary to just keep your body alive are few: heart, lungs, circulation, brain. Everything else can wait—because if these core functions go, nothing else matters.

This is what we think of as the edge of death—one more shutdown function, and it's all over. In a near-death experience, that "one more" happens. The physical body dies, at least briefly. It's at this point, it seems, that the spirit makes its exit.

For many years, the medical explanation for the experiences people have during the time they're "dead" has focused on the various chemical and electrical changes taking place in the brain as it attempts to cope with catastrophic oxygen loss. Nonessential parts of the brain begin to shut down almost immediately when oxygen levels reach a certain point. Among them are the parts of the brain responsible for cognition—thought and memory.

The rapid chemical and electrical changes that occur during this process cause brain cells to flare and die, activating memory and thought fragments. These flares account for the images of loved ones that people believe they see during near-death experiences, according to this explanation model.

You don't actually see anyone; you just experience the activation of memory of that person. This is the same process that causes you to "see" your entire life flash before your eyes when facing what you believe is imminent death.

It's an intriguing concept, and until research in the late 1990s and early part of the twenty-first century, it was widely accepted by medical personnel as the physiological explanation for near-death experiences. But this recent research shows that the brain's shutdown is more rapid and more complete than previously thought. Once oxygen levels fall below critical levels, brain function virtually ceases. It doesn't appear that even these chemical and electrical actions take place; there's no fuel source (oxygen) to make them happen.

Another clinical theory puts forth the idea that it's the brain's return to function following a near-death experience that causes the activations that trigger memories and thoughts. As brain cells fire back up, they initially over-respond, like the flare of throwing straw on a fire, before they settle back into normal function.

Coming Back

Coming back to physical life is often quite a shock. Suddenly you're reunited with the pain your physical body is experiencing, and that's not pleasant. It's a clear indication that you are still alive.

Many people report a sense of joy and exhilaration at being reunited with their physical bodies despite the pain, because it means they will continue in their physical lives. At this point, people often think of loved ones on the earth plane, such as children, and feel grateful that they can remain with them.

There is sometimes sadness at leaving, once again, the loved ones who have passed to the higher side. Seeing them again is joyous, and even though it tells you that they'll still be waiting for you when it is your turn to make the crossing, it's not easy to leave them.

Often, spirit loved ones maintain their contact from the higher side, appearing in visitations. It's not that they weren't willing to do this before the near-death experience, it's rather that the NDE makes people more receptive to spirit contact.

A Transforming Experience

Just as a near-death experience gives a person who has one a new lease on life, it also provides a glimpse across what we've always perceived to be an impenetrable barrier. A near-death experience is profoundly moving, and often life-changing, for someone who has one. Many people who experience them find that they return to existence on the earth plane with awakened psychic and spiritual sensitivities. They see firsthand that death is a gateway, not an end.

Some people return to physical existence a bit reluctantly, in fact, not especially willing to leave the joy and peace that they've experienced as they've stood in the portal that links the earth plane and the higher side. Others return with a renewed sense of mission and destiny, confident in the continuity of life and certain of their places in the divine order of existence.

Heightened Spiritual Sensitivity

Spirit communication of any sort often heightens spiritual sensitivity. Evidence of the continuity of life is awe-inspiring. Not only does it affirm that life continues beyond physical death, but also that there is a divine energy that is the source of all existence. This represents the God of your understanding. As it becomes irrefutable that existence continues, so, too, does it become undeniable that God exists (again, this is the God of your understanding; there is one divine being but there are many presentations and perspectives of its existence).

> **Mediums and Messages**
>
> Doris stopped in to see Rita on a lark, thinking it would be fun and funny to get a spirit drawing. She thought she would get a drawing of some Native American guide that couldn't be proven and would have no meaning. Both Doris and her husband considered themselves atheists, and purported to practice no religion. When Rita began to draw, the face of an older woman came through. Doris was stunned: It was in fact her mother-in-law! Doris came back to see Rita quite a few times afterwards, saying that she and her husband could no longer deny an afterlife.

Heightened or New Psychic Senses

Your psychic senses are how you link to, experience, and understand communication that takes place on an energy level. The intensified energy of a near-death experience often makes permanent changes in the abilities of your psychic senses.

It's as though there's been an electrical current surge through your energy field, rearranging its alignment and strengthening its charge. Your psychic senses, as part of this energy field, pick this up.

Even your physical senses can demonstrate how this might work. Think back to the last time you had an intestinal virus. Not a pleasant recollection, for sure! Do you still remember the last food you ate before you became ill? Can you taste it, see it, smell it? When something becomes associated with a strong experience, we remember it long after the experience ends!

Near-Death Lessons

Why do we have near-death experiences? No doubt one answer is to prove the continuity of life. Nothing is more compelling than going beyond the boundaries of physical life yourself and returning to remember and talk about it!

Every near-death experience has a unique lesson for the person who experiences it. It is a personal and intimate communication between you and the spirit world. The lessons of near-death experience are many and varied; the only lesson that matters to you, however, is the one of *your* near-death experience.

Although most people who survive to tell of their experiences seem to recover completely, nearly everyone is changed. It's an extraordinarily profound experience. Some people do find themselves confronting physical changes as a result of the events that caused the near-death experience. There might be partial paralysis from a stroke or the injuries suffered in a car accident. There could be loss of limb or function.

But even in these situations, people tend to feel very positive about the experience. The physical reminders are also about learning and healing. No one wishes for such changes, of course. But when they happen, they tend to strengthen the conviction that life continues beyond physical death, and that life—everyone's life—has value and purpose.

> **Silver Cord**
>
> Because near-death experience is a form of spirit communication, it is also about healing. Lessons are intended to reconnect you with spirit, with God, with love—however it is that you need to reestablish these connections in your life and existence. Only you will know, in the end, the lesson of your near-death experience.

Using a Near-Death Experience for Growth on the Earth Plane

It seems virtually impossible to go through a near-death experience and not grow from it. As difficult as the circumstances might be, this is a gift to you from the universe, from the higher side, from the God of your understanding. You could turn away from the opportunities it offers you. But why would you? You've already had the experience … let it fulfill its intent!

Millions of people walking the earth plane today have had near-death experiences. The collective lessons of their experiences have the potential to change the world, to make the world a better place. These are the lessons of love, compassion and support for one another. Imagine the possibilities!

The Least You Need to Know

◆ Millions of people have had near-death experiences.

◆ As unique as each near-death experience is, there are also consistent common qualities that link all near-death experiences.

◆ The bright light that so many people see is the light of divine energy, the light of the God of your understanding.

◆ A near-death experience happens for a reason, but it's up to you to figure it out and learn from it.

◆ Going through a near-death experience often leaves you with a profound sense of connectedness to spirit and a renewed sense of mission in your life.

Chapter 21

Time, Space, and the Soul's Life

In This Chapter

- ◆ Looking at reincarnation
- ◆ Your soul's journey
- ◆ Identifying your soul group
- ◆ Exploring a past life: a guided meditation
- ◆ Using what you learn to better understand your soul's mission

Just how old is your soul, and how many lives has it experienced before this one? The idea that the spirit lives indefinitely is intriguing enough. It's comforting to know that there is more to our existence than the physical life we now live, however much we enjoy it. But to think of living multiple physical lives … that's fascinated humans for centuries.

What happens when a spirit enters a new "life"? Is it possible to contact spirits that have "passed on" in this way, that is, reincarnated? For example, if your father has reincarnated, can you still contact him as your father in the spirit world? Do you, in your present life, remember your past lives? Do the experiences of those past lives extend in some way into this life—can you contact one of your own past (or future) selves? Do certain souls travel together? This chapter examines the concepts of past lives and reincarnation, and relates them to communicating with the dead and to past life therapy.

The Cycle of Existence

Cycles are the natural order of existence—day and night, planting and harvest, birth and death. As early cultures observed these cycles, they noticed that they repeat. Spring follows winter, autumn follows summer, light follows darkness. Over and over again, the pattern repeats. Why, then, would this not be the pattern or cycle of human life?

The concept of *reincarnation* dates back to earliest recorded history, and extends across various cultures. The Greek philosopher Plato believed—and taught—that the soul was separate from the body. While the body clearly was mortal—it lived and died—the soul was not. The soul, according to Plato, was immortal and continually reincarnated.

Reincarnation is a fundamental tenet of many Eastern religions. Hinduism believes that the soul returns to physical existence in various forms, depending on the lessons it still needs to learn. Such forms might be animal, plant, or human. A key element of reincarnation in many Eastern belief systems is *karma*. The principle of karma is simple: What you give is what you get!

> **Spiritology**
>
> **Reincarnation** is the return of the spirit to a physical body and physical existence. The word "incarnate" means "in the flesh." **Karma** is the energy of cause and effect that you put out into the universe that comes back to you in this and other lifetimes, and it's always about learning.

In its religious context, karma shapes reincarnation and defines the lessons of the next incarnation. In a broader context, karma is energy. Your thoughts as well as your actions are patterns of energy. Everything you think, everything you do, affects the universe in infinitesimal ways. Karma, as energy, has a ripple effect that extends far beyond logical comprehension.

Your Soul's Journeys

Your spirit has a divine mission, a way it fits in the grand scheme of the universe. To fulfill its mission, your spirit chooses paths and journeys. It chooses its time of entry into this life, and the circumstances into which it will make its entrance. Your soul chose your parents to be the physical entities responsible for giving you physical life.

These are choices and decisions that take place well beyond the realm of your conscious mind. In fact, they often take place before what you identify as your conscious mind actually exists! In a way, it's like your spirit sits with God, co-creates your path with God, and plans the next phase of your existence. Continued existence on the higher side? Life on the earth plane? It depends on what lessons your spirit needs to learn. These determinations take place not only before you enter your current physical life, but throughout your existence as a physical being even though you have no conscious awareness of them.

Past life regression, which we talk about later in this chapter, is one way that you can gain a sense for the travels of your spirit. Experiences that you chalk up to déjà vu (the sense that you've been to a particular place or met a certain person before) could well be connections that you had in previous lives.

> ### Silver Cord
>
> What about "bad" lives? Of course, no one would choose a life of pain and suffering! So why, if the soul has choice, does so much suffering exist in our physical world? For reasons that we can't comprehend, this is somehow part of the divine order and the soul's lessons. What we do know, through spirit communication, is that the learning that occurs as a result of life's hard lessons becomes part of the spirit's evolution.

You come to this lifetime to learn, and you decide on the lessons of this lifetime before you arrive. This doesn't mean these lessons happen automatically. Every choice you make, every decision you make, determines the next path you take along your journey. This is free will: You choose the direction of your life. Even if it doesn't seem that your life is one of choice at all, your spirit has made decisions about how it will learn the lessons of this lifetime.

The really great thing is that you don't have to go it alone! Each morning when you get up, say out loud, "God, show me the pebbles I need to step over, show me the boulders I need to walk around." You don't have to bang your head against the wall to "get" it! When we ask for help and guidance, we can more easily learn the lessons that we came here to learn.

Soul Companions

Are there people in your life that you feel you're just destined to be with? Friends, lovers, even your siblings and your children, might feel like they are intended to be a part of your life. You know each other at a level of intimacy that seems to transcend your relationship. You have intuitive and even psychic connections. You finish each other's sentences, you call or stop by when one is thinking about the other. You are connected to each other in ways that even other people notice. You are likely members of the same soul group—a cosmic family of sorts, spirits that travel together through existence.

Even if you don't consciously know your connections to the physical lives of others in your soul group, you eventually encounter them during your life. This might be a stranger you meet in a coffee shop who seems so familiar that you begin talking as though you've known each other forever—which might indeed be the case! It's usually a great delight to connect with the members of your soul group. You're all traveling together on your spirit journeys for a reason—you have lessons to share with each other or a shared mission.

Relationships are not always the same. The characteristics of physical life that we consider important—such as gender and family lines—are just outer trappings. You are man or woman in this life, and you likely were woman and man in other lives. You and a soul partner might have been husband and wife in one life, and brother and sister in another. As awkward as this might feel when you think about it, remember that spirit existence doesn't have the constraints of our physical world. Details like gender and relationship have little bearing, in the context of spirit growth and evolution, beyond their roles in bringing together the spirits who need to learn together.

Lessons of the Spirit

What are these lessons your spirit needs to learn? Each of us has different lessons; each soul has a unique mission. The more highly evolved your spirit, the more likely it is that your mission involves helping others with the lessons of their missions. Those who leave their legacies in history as great people—from religious leaders like Gandhi, Jesus, and Buddha to political leaders who direct the lives of millions of people—are highly evolved. Their spirits choose to return to physical lives to help direct the lives of others toward the highest and the best.

Highly evolved spirits are not just the famous and the powerful in their earthly lives, however. Who do you know in your life who seems to have wisdom and insight beyond his or her years? We sometimes say of such a person, "she has an old soul." Intuitively we understand that, on a spirit level, this person has traveled many lives.

We believe that the ultimate goal of spirit evolution—and by extension, the lessons our spirits learn—is to work toward becoming one with the divine. A lofty ideal, to be sure! But if existence is about the spirit's evolution, it is the only ideal that is possible. All lessons move toward increasing understanding and compassion—for ourselves and for others.

The Continuity of Time

It's hard for us to conceptualize timelessness. Yet this is the paradox of the continuity of time: When time is endless, it isn't time. Time, by definition, is a limitation. We ascribe characteristics to it that make it seem finite, but these are artificial. Minutes, days, months, years—methods of measuring time were made for the linear human mind.

Silver Cord _____

Our familiar calendar is called the Julian calendar. The Romans developed it during the rule of Julius Caesar (around 46 B.C.E.). It divides the year into 365 days (except every fourth year, when there are 366 days) and organizes those days into 12 months. As the Romans conquered much of what was then the Western world, they imposed this system of structured time on other cultures.

Even as we think of the cycles of life, we think of time as a linear element. We speak of past lives and future lives, lives that exist along a linear continuum. This implies that time has a beginning and an end. Again, this reflects the limitations of our physical existence, as spirits tell us there is no time on the higher side! Only in the physical world does time frame existence.

Connecting with Your Past ... and Your Future

The connections of your past continue in the present. They also link you to your future, even though as yet you have no perception of it. The experiences and lessons of the past shape both the present and the future.

The idea of connecting with future lives is quite intriguing. Wouldn't it be wonderful to know the future? The problem is, because it hasn't happened yet, you can't verify it. With past life experiences, there's often a way to affirm what you sense were your experiences. Through spirit contact, you might receive information that validates perceptions that you have about a past life. You can connect this information and your perceptions to events and circumstances in your current life.

With future lives, this validation process is not in place. You can't verify what you haven't yet experienced. Further, these are glimpses of *possible* futures. Remember, free will determines the paths of your life. You choose the directions you take ... in this life and in other lives. This makes your future lives moving targets. Each decision you make (consciously or on the spirit level) influences the path of this life and subsequently the paths of future lives.

Sometimes in your current life you find yourself in a situation with someone that is difficult. When Rita worked with troubled youth, she found one young man particularly difficult. Tony seemed to seek her out, yet continually challenged whatever she told him. For reasons Rita didn't understand, she was especially tolerant of Tony—which she found frustrating because he took far more of her time and effort than it seemed she should give him.

Asking her spirit guides, "Why is this kid in my life?" Rita did a meditation to explore a possible past life relationship with Tony. The connection came to her quickly: In a past life, he had saved her life.

In this past life that took place in the mid 1800s, Rita's father was a wealthy plantation owner. Rita had married an apparently gracious Southern gentleman, only to discover too late that a wicked temper dispelled any qualities of grace. In this life, Tony was a slave on the plantation, and he happened by the house one day when Rita's abusive husband was beating her. Tony hid until Rita was alone, and then helped her to flee from the house.

After this meditation, Rita knew that in her current lifetime, no matter how difficult Tony was she would never send him away. The images from the meditation played on Rita's mind, however, and she decided to paint them. When the painting was finished, she hung it in her studio. The next time Tony came in, he walked over and stood in front of it.

"I've been there," he said. "Where is it? It's not around here, but I know I've been there." The painting he recognized was of the vision of himself in a past life, helping Rita in a past life escape from an abusive husband!

Past Life Therapy

Exploring your past lives can have great therapeutic value. Often, we carry around much guilt, anxiousness, and fear that we can't pin to specific causes. Sometimes these feelings link back to past life experiences. Finding the connection can help you understand and resolve the issues responsible for the feelings.

Past life therapy, or past life regression, is a recognized form of therapeutic counseling. Many professionals of diverse backgrounds—physicians, psychologists, psychoanalysts, hypnotherapists, among others—offer past life regression as part of an overall counseling approach.

In past life therapy, the therapist puts you into a light hypnotic state. The therapist talks to you. Although you are deeply relaxed, you are not beyond consciousness. You are just at the level where your conscious mind is not intruding into the process.

During the session, you might see yourself in a different time and place with people who look similar to, but are not the same as, people in your current life. The therapist might ask you questions about what you see. When the therapist brings you out of the hypnotic state, you usually still remember the past life information that surfaced.

Past life therapy is often very profound. You might be amazed by how quickly you understand the connections between things that happened in past lives and things that are happening in your present life. You gain understanding and insight into why you behave in certain ways, even when your behavior doesn't seem to make "logical" sense.

> **CAUTION** **Premonition** _____
>
> If you have an overwhelming romantic attraction to someone you meet, it doesn't necessarily mean you're a match made in heaven! It might mean there are still lessons for you to work out with this person. Karmic connections aren't necessarily romantic. If you feel a sudden, intense attraction, go into meditation and see if you can connect to a past life relationship to understand what you returned to teach each other.

Connecting with Your Past: A Guided Meditation

Past life therapy is only one way to connect with your past. You can call on your spirit guide to help you explore this dimension of your soul's existence. This guided meditation can get you started. It is similar to the guided meditations in Chapter 7.

1. Make yourself comfortable in a location where you won't have any distractions or interruptions.

2. Take three slow, deep breaths, in through your nose and out through your mouth. Let the first breath clear your body, let the second breath open your mind, and let the third breath free your spirit.

3. Consciously form the thought: "This is my time to be one with God and for God to be one with me." Set an intent that your spirit guide will help you to explore a past life.

4. In your mind's eye, see yourself sitting on a bench in an open, beautiful garden. There are flowers and trees, and the air smells fresh and clean. It is peaceful and calm. Across from your bench is another bench, also inviting and peaceful.

5. Watch as your spirit guide approaches. Welcome your guide, and thank him or her for coming. Invite your spirit guide to sit on the bench across from you.

6. Open your mind and your heart. Open your psychic and spiritual senses to allow communication with your guide.

7. Ask your spirit guide to introduce you to a past life. Listen to your guide with your inner hearing, and watch with your inner vision what your spirit guide shows you.

8. Observe yourself. Look at what you are wearing. Observe other people who are around you. Observe what events are taking place. Just observe … understanding the meanings and connections will come.

9. Ask what lessons you brought from that past life that you are working on in this life.

10. When your past life experience seems finished, thank your spirit guide.

11. Take three slow, deep breaths, in through your nose and out through your mouth. Feel yourself back in your body, become conscious of your breathing. Wiggle your fingers and your toes, open your eyes.

After you are fully aware, pull out your journal and write about your meditation and the past life experiences it showed to you. Some people prefer to think about the experience for a while before writing in their journal about it; do what's comfortable for you. Here are some questions to help you understand your experience.

1. What did you look like? What clothes were you wearing? How were you wearing your hair? Do you have a sense for what period of time it is? Is everything in context for the time? To make sure this is really a past life, everything needs to be in the correct context. Describe what you see.

   _____

   _____

   _____

2. Who else was present in the experience? Did any of these people look familiar? Describe each person in as much detail as you can recall. Include clothing, hairstyles, and other characteristics.

   _____

   _____

   _____

3. Now that you've written detailed descriptions of the other people in the past life that you linked to, do any of them seem familiar? Disregard factors such as gender and relationship; focus instead on what seems familiar.

_____

_____

_____

4. What were you doing in this past life? Did you get a sense of your occupation? Write down all that comes to your mind about your job or daily activities in the past life.

_____

_____

_____

5. What cultural heritage did you have in this past life? Is this a culture similar to, or very different from, the one you have in your current life?

_____

_____

_____

6. What was your family like? How many children did you have? Do these people seem familiar?

_____

_____

_____

7. Did anybody speak? Did they have accents? What language did they speak? If other than a language you speak, could you understand them?

_____

_____

_____

8. How did you interact with the others in this past life connection? What seemed to be your relationships to them?

_____

_____

_____

9. Did you get any sense for your name or any other identifying characteristics about yourself? How old did it seem that you were?

_____

_____

_____

10. What did your surroundings look like? Could you hear any sounds or noises? Did you smell anything?

_____

_____

_____

11. Write down any other details about the experience.

_____

_____

_____

Often it takes time to fully understand the connections between your current life and your past lives. Recalling past life details doesn't always paint a complete picture; you might have to wait for some of the pieces to settle into place for you.

After you've connected with a past life, you can do additional meditations that focus on the connections you've discovered. With each exploration, you'll learn more about your spirit's travels and you'll understand more about your journey through this life.

Understanding Your Soul's Mission

Each physical life that your spirit inhabits has a purpose and a role in your soul's mission. Exploring past lives gives you additional pieces to add to the picture. Eventually patterns will emerge that will help you to get a better sense for what your spirit's mission is, in this life as well as beyond.

In this life, as in at least one previous life, Rita is an artist. Through exploring her past life connections, Rita has come to understand that part of her spirit's mission—and her mission in this life—is to prove, through art, the continuity of life. Her spirit drawings have touched countless lives, affirming her sense that this is the reason for this life's journey. What's your soul's mission?

Hilda had arranged for a spirit drawing for her husband Arthur as a gift. When Arthur arrived, Rita began to draw and a beautiful mature woman appeared on the paper. Arthur wasn't sure who this could be, so he brought it home to show to his wife. Hilda looked at it, showed the portrait to her mother, who immediately took a photo out from her wallet, which matched exactly, including the woman's dress. Rita had drawn Hilda's grandmother, Maria. Yes, in-laws come also!

The Least You Need to Know

◆ The concept of reincarnation has been part of belief systems in many cultures for thousands of years.

◆ Your soul experiences different physical lives so that it can carry out its mission and learn its lessons.

◆ In a past life dream or meditation, everything needs to be in context of the particular era.

◆ The people that you feel especially connected to in this life might be part of your soul group, spirits that travel together through different lives.

◆ Past life therapy is a way to understand how the events of past lives influence your behaviors in your current life.

◆ You can use guided meditation to connect with your past lives.

Part 6

Karmic Cycles and Soul Lessons

Do you feel like you've been this way before? Quite possibly you have! Your spirit's mission might take you through numerous lifetimes. The lessons you need to learn in this lifetime might be matters left unresolved in previous lifetimes.

These chapters look at how you can bring together your psychic and mediumistic abilities to draw healing energy for yourself and to send healing energy to others—both those on the earth plane *and* those who have passed to spirit.

Chapter 22

Mastering Your Spirit Gifts

In This Chapter

- Finding out what your psychic gifts are
- Using your abilities to consciously shape your future
- Asking questions—and being open to the answers
- Why do you want to explore these abilities?—an exercise
- Keeping yourself open to the possibilities

Everyone has the mediumistic abilities that can bridge the veil between the physical and spirit worlds. Using these gifts is simply a matter of opening yourself to the possibilities. You'll find that you are naturally stronger in some abilities than in others. Focusing to develop these skills leads to improvements in all parts of life. Everything is energy, and it is all connected.

Your spirit gifts open new vistas to you, which are often quite profound. Certainly it's entertaining to develop some gifts, such as telepathy. But it's also a process of discovery, of learning, of helping yourself and others. These are gifts of love and of healing, and using them in these ways leads only to good.

When you start to open up through meditation and feel what attracts you, you start to put the pieces together. We get different pieces to master in this or other lives. As we work on understanding each gift that comes to us through psychic or spirit connection, we bring them together in a whole picture. This picture unfolds over many lifetimes and in concert with many other fellow journeyers (both on the earth and on the spirit planes). This is not a process to fear; it is a process to welcome and cherish. It is part of the divine order of the universe.

Identifying Your Spirit Gifts

Although you likely excel in certain spirit gifts and lack interest or refinement in others, they exist in unity. Also, there is an integration between what you might view as your tangible gifts and your spirit gifts. Rita, for example, is blessed with artistic talent. Combining that with her mediumistic abilities provides an avenue for development in both areas. We all have roles in spreading the message that life is continuous.

What are your particular spirit gifts? Even now, you probably have some idea of the areas in which you seem to have inherent ability. These are good areas to start your spiritual unfoldment, and there is an exercise later in this chapter to help you identify your starting points.

Using Your Spirit Gifts

First and foremost, your spirit gifts exist for goodness and healing. No matter what those gifts are or to what extent you choose to develop them, they are your link to an energy that is much larger than you are. They connect you to the divine, and to all existence. Self-exploration is very important. As you travel this path, you will discover yourself.

Perhaps you feel you really don't want to expand your own mediumistic senses, but instead want to explore the ways someone else's abilities—a psychic's or a medium's—can bring new information into your life. This is a wonderful start. Of course you can experience spirit contact through readings. But this changes you and your abilities, too, because everything is energy and everything is connected.

Think of all the many ways that you use your physical senses during the course of a day—or even an hour. In fact, that's a good exercise: For one hour, write down every time you use a particular physical sense. Start with taste, because we tend to think of this as an isolated, intermittent sense. After all, you don't go through your day tasting everything; you use your sense of taste only when you eat. Or do you? You might be surprised! Then move to your sense of smell, your sense of sight, your sense of hearing. When you walk past a bakery, the smell invites you in. You are driving down the highway and you see a hawk fly, and it gives you a sense of freedom. You taste cinnamon and think of your mother's apple pie.

Silver Cord _____

Cats offer good observation of the integration of physical sense. They have heightened sensory perception in their mouths through which they smell what they taste. Have you ever watched the breathing of a cat that is in a new experience or environment? It crouches with its mouth slightly open, giving the appearance of panting. This isn't just to bring more oxygen into its system to accommodate its "fight or flight" response. All of those extra air molecules bring information to the cat's sensory systems, expanding what it collects about this new challenge.

What happens to you when you enter a new environment or situation? Do you feel like all of your senses are heightened and on edge? People who engage in high-risk adventures such as skydiving often report intensified sensory experiences. When such an adventure takes you close to what you perceive is the brink of death (though not a near death experience), you might indeed feel that you can taste the air! You also might feel like you can hear colors and see sounds. The energy of the experience is so strong that it crosses conventional borders.

The same happens with your psychic senses. As you explore and develop them, they become more integrated with each other as well as with your physical senses. This increases the amount of information you can gather about your environment, your experiences, and, really, your life. If you're paying attention, this is all information that increases your understanding.

Naturally Curious

The expression might be, "curious as a cat," but in reality, no creature on this earth is more curious than the one who stares back at you in the mirror. We humans want to know *everything*. How does that work? Why does it do that? What happens if …?

In childhood, we ask just these questions. By the time we become adults, we have learned *not* to ask these questions because they don't always have apparent answers. But often, it is the question that matters more than the answer, because asking the question honors the quest—the journey—for knowledge and understanding.

Reclaim your natural curiosity! This is how you grow and develop as a human being, and evolve as a spirit being. Life is a dynamic adventure, an exploration. Your psychic abilities are additional tools available for you to use and appreciate.

Shaping Your Future

You hold your future in your hands, regardless of the extent to which you choose to develop and use your psychic gifts. Each choice you have, every decision you make, influences the next step you take along the path of your soul's mission. You don't consciously think about this the vast majority of the time. Your higher being—your spirit in interaction with the thought energy of your subconscious mind—makes many of the choices and decisions that guide your direction.

When you become aware of some of these decisions, you can make them with intent. This is powerful indeed! It's a good thing to move toward your spirit's mission even when you are unaware that you're doing so; life seems easy and smooth when this happens. When it doesn't, you might find challenge and frustration along your path. Nothing seems to quite work out for you. You feel a half step off—and maybe you are, because you can't see the path. Imagine how different your journey would be if you could see each step and where it takes you! You can, once you start looking.

Peter came for a sitting and drawing in 1996 at the First Spiritualist Church of Quincy. He immediately recognized the drawing, but laughed and said that his Uncle Walter would never be caught in a suit and tie. When Peter searched for a photo, the only one he could find was a picture where Walter, in fact, wore a suit and tie! Rita finds that certain people, when appearing from spirit for a portrait, dress accordingly.

A New "World" View

We seek because we sense that there is more to our lives, this existence, than we detect. We know, at some level, that growth and development are important spiritually as well as physically and emotionally. We know that ours is a dynamic, not a static, existence. We see evidence of this all around, from the physical signs we see in the mirror—the changes of aging—to the spiritual changes we feel as we encounter situations such as the passing of loved ones. Your psychic senses help you "make sense" of all of these experiences.

What concerns you the most about the progress of living? For most people, it is worry about what lies at the end of the road. All life moves inexorably toward this end; we see this every minute of every day. Once, people were terrified to venture very far from their homes, convinced that the earth disappeared beyond the horizon. There was nothingness, a vast void, on the other side of where the sky meets the earth. Traveling there was … well, beyond comprehension.

But then Christopher Columbus sailed the ocean blue—and changed the world view for everyone else. (As did dozens of other courageous and curious explorers.) Of course the earth continued beyond what the human eye could see. Today we laugh at the perception of a flat earth; we've seen the view from space, and we know better.

You are an explorer, too. And you might fear that your world disappears or ends beyond what you see as its physical boundaries. Spirit contact tells us, as did Columbus's reports back to his sponsors, that there is no end. It's just different. Columbus and his fellow explorers found exotic new lands, with new species of plant and animal life and physical surroundings like nothing they'd ever seen. This is where your spirit explorations will take you.

> **Silver Cord**
>
> Of course, Christopher Columbus was not the first explorer to expand the view of the world. The Vikings traveled to what is now the northeast United States more than 2,000 years ago. Explorers came from many countries to settle what was referred to as the New World, including the earlier ones who were to become the Native American settlers.

What you learn, whether about geography of the physical world or evidence of the spirit world, changes your world view. Knowledge changes how you perceive the events in your life. Knowledge changes *you* and the way you live your life.

Helping Others

What do you do in life? Think about how you use your tangible abilities and talents. Inevitably, you use them in the service of others. You might do this because it's your job and someone pays you to. But odds are, you do what you do because you enjoy how it helps someone else. Whether you build bridges, perform surgery, sweep sidewalks, sell newspapers … no matter what you do, it somehow helps others.

Your spirit gifts expand your ability to help, in different ways. At the very least, they give you increased insight, empathy, and compassion. You see a bigger picture, which gives you the ability to view the actions of others in a different context. When you know that there is more to life than meets the physical senses, you can be more kind, tolerant, and forgiving. Learning to forgive yourself first, and then to forgive others in your life is a cherished gift; and, yes, forgiveness is *always* possible.

Is there a relationship to someone important in your life—a child, parent, sibling, spouse—that you feel is drifting, or is impossible to repair? Nothing is impossible with time, love, and effort. If you can spend two hours a day in front of the television, you can decide instead to set aside a portion of that time for improving your relationship. Be tenacious and steadfast, even if your efforts are rebuffed at first. After all, you've got endless time across many lives to get it right. And what better time to start than now.

Remember, spirit contact is about healing, learning, and love.

Ask the Right Questions and Keep an Open Mind

What do you want to know? Sometimes asking the right questions is the hardest part of seeking answers. The more specific the question, the more directed the answer—and also the more limited. Everyone has unresolved issues. Relationships of any kind are complex and often confusing. Human behavior is even more so! Your questions are personal to you, and their answers are likely to bring about significant change in your life.

Are you ready to know the answers you seek? It seems obvious that you are, if you're asking the questions. But sometimes the questions take us in unexpected directions. The answers often aren't what you anticipate, although they provide the information that you ultimately need.

We talk a lot about proving the continuity of life. This is something that interests most people who want to make spirit contact. We miss loved ones who have passed to the higher side, and want more than anything, at times, to have just one more contact.

Love is an all-powerful energy that connects us through space and time, but the sense of loss that accompanies a loved one's passing can be overwhelming.

Receiving contact from the spirit world is a blessing. It is also a life-altering experience for many people. Seeing is believing ... and believing isn't always easy. Even when your faith incorporates belief in the continuity of life, you might not be prepared for how evidence of it affects you. Again, remember that spirit communication is for good and for healing. And it comes of love, the most powerful energy of all.

Premonition

If you are interested in furthering your abilities, take the time and effort to properly develop your mediumistic skills. As with any other skills, knowledge and practice bring improvement and expertise. Appendix B gives some resources for furthering your mediumistic education.

Where Do You Want Your Skills to Take You? A Self-Exploration

What skills do you want to develop? Do you want to become more in tune with your intuition? Explore personal issues? Facilitate spirit contact for others? Do you want to connect with earth energy, spirit energy, or both? The following self-exploration can help you determine where, and how to start your psychic development.

1. What psychic or mediumistic abilities do you feel that you have? Circle those that apply.

    Clairaudience

    Clairsentience

    Clairvoyance

    Intuition

    Premonition

    Psychometry

    Spirit contact (loved ones or spirit guides)

    Telepathy

2. What psychic or mediumistic abilities do others tell you that you have? Circle those that apply.

   Clairaudience

   Clairsentience

   Clairvoyance

   Intuition

   Premonition

   Psychometry

   Spirit contact (loved ones or spirit guides)

   Telepathy

3. Is this statement true or false for you: Psychic senses are as much a part of my daily life as are my physical senses.

   Yes   No

4. If there was just one question you could ask the God of your understanding, what would it be?

   _____

   _____

   _____

5. How do you communicate with the God of your understanding? Check all that apply.

   _____ I pray in times of need

   _____ I pray at certain times

   _____ I meditate at certain times

   _____ I meditate regularly

   _____ I feel that I'm in continual communication with God

   _____ I don't communicate with God

   _____ I don't believe in a divine being

6. What is your faith or belief system? Has it been consistent throughout your life?

    _____

    _____

    _____

7. Have you had a near death experience? If so, what was it like? How did it affect your life?

    _____

    _____

    _____

8. Have you ever experienced a miraculous healing?

    _____

    _____

    _____

9. Have you ever received healing energy and prayers from others? If so, did it seem to have an effect?

    _____

    _____

    _____

10. Have you ever sent healing energy and prayers to someone else? How did you feel about doing it, and did it seem to have an effect?

    _____

    _____

    _____

11. This life is a journey for your soul. What do you want it to experience?

    _____

    _____

    _____

12. Do you feel that your life has a sense of mission or purpose beyond the activities of everyday living? Describe it.

_____

_____

_____

13. Are there people in your life right now that you feel you have psychic or intuitive connections with? How do you use these connections?

_____

_____

_____

14. What comes to your mind when you think of your own passing?

_____

_____

_____

15. Do you have spirit guides or guardian angels? How do you know, and how do they help you? Have you ever seen them?

_____

_____

_____

16. Do you have dreams that involve visits or communications from loved ones who have passed to the higher side? Describe the most recent such dream.

_____

_____

_____

17. If you could have any psychic or mediumistic skill, what would it be and why?

_____

_____

_____

Obviously, there are no right or wrong answers here; this is an exercise to help you explore what interests you and how you might develop your abilities to aid that exploration. You can revisit the exercise in Chapter 12 to further identify and develop your psychic skills.

Shaping and Enhancing Your Skills

The best way to develop your psychic and mediumistic skills is to find a good teacher! Start with sources that you trust, and see where they lead you. You might feel there aren't many options in your local area, but keep looking. Eventually you will find the right opportunities. You might have to drive or travel to find the teachers you need. Don't just wait until something comes to you! If you don't connect, just keep looking. Don't give up, and don't settle for what you know isn't quite right.

If spirit learning opportunities are abundant in your local area, great! But don't limit yourself to them. Remain receptive to new doors that open. Try to have many different teachers, so you learn more than just the one teacher's way. Each teacher has different abilities and will bring out different abilities in you. Be sure that, under any circumstances, you trust the teacher. Don't idealize the teacher, though—teachers are just human, just like you. They're just more aware of their skills!

Oh, the Possibilities!

The possibilities that your psychic abilities open to you are endless! If you find yourself being inspired along a healing path, try different modalities. Experience them, see whether you relate to them or whether they really don't make any sense. It could be that it's not your path, or that you're not ready for it yet.

Remain an explorer. Self-exploration especially is very important. As you travel this path, you will discover yourself, and you will learn more about your purpose in this life and how you can use your gifts to help others and make this world a better place. In the end, that's really what this is all about!

The Least You Need to Know

◆ Each of us has mediumistic abilities. The extent to which you develop and use yours is up to you.

◆ Remember to ask your question, set an intent, and then go into meditation.

- Your life is a mission for your spirit. Your psychic senses help you to understand what this mission might be, so that you can shape your life for the learning your spirit needs.

- Psychic abilities and mediumistic skills are available to you to use for helping yourself and others. Always use them in love and for the highest intent.

- Learn from those you trust whose level of expertise is higher than yours. Seek opportunities to learn and expand your knowledge.

Chapter 23

Soul Patterns and Life Lessons

In This Chapter

- ◆ Exploring your patterns
- ◆ An exercise to ask your spirit guide for help
- ◆ Changing negative thoughts to positive energy
- ◆ An exercise to create an affirmation
- ◆ You can change your soul's path

Is it so hard to make certain changes in your life because the changes are difficult, or could it be because your soul is resisting your efforts to derail it from its pattern? Whether you believe you have many lives, or just this one, the awakening of spirituality leads to many questions … and, if you are willing to accept guidance from beyond yourself, many answers.

It's fun to play around with your psychic abilities, to see how many times you're right about the next song on the radio or to call a friend right when she's about to pick up the phone and call you. It's entertaining to look at people's auras and to see what you "read" from objects you touch and places you go. And this is all well and good.

But there is much more beyond fun and entertainment. We all have serious issues and concerns that drain our energy and keep us from finding the joy and happiness that our lives can and should contain. Gaining insights into the circumstances that create negative energy in your life gives you the means to turn that energy around.

Awakening to the Possibilities

Patterns are behaviors we slip into, almost without realizing that we have done so. Certain events or situations act as triggers that activate a pattern. You don't consciously think, "Louise is home two hours late *again*. I'm going to yell at her, she'll get mad and yell at me, and then we'll have a big fight and not speak to each other for the next three days." But that's what happens.

What is behind this reaction for you? Does it come from Louise's patterns, your patterns from earlier in your life, or patterns from previous lives that represent learning still necessary for your spirit? No matter the source, gaining an understanding of the bigger picture can help you change your patterns so they support a more loving and joyful life.

The Energy of Intent

Many good and right things happen to you in your life without your conscious awareness or efforts to structure or plan them. Through no efforts of your own, you end up in the right place at the right time. You might not even notice that this happens! Once you become aware of the connections, however, you can begin to use them in conscious ways.

Using Your Psychic Abilities for Insight and Learning

College professors joke (or complain) that students seem to think they can learn by osmosis. Put the textbook under your pillow when you go to sleep at night, and when you wake up you will have absorbed the book's contents. Wouldn't it be wonderful if this could happen? But the reality is that you won't know anything about the contents of that book until you look between the covers. You must read the book to understand its message. And you might even need to read additional books and go back to original sources to get enough information to qualify as learning about the subject.

But learning doesn't happen by osmosis. It requires effort, work and focus. A hammer doesn't build a house; intuition doesn't fix a struggling relationship. It's up to you to use the tools available to you, in ways that allow you to build the life that lets you develop and grow.

Calling on Your Spirit Guides: A Guided Meditation

Your spirit guides are always available to help you. Often they are at work when you don't realize that they are there, or even that you need their help. Invite your spirit guide to give you specific guidance about a particular problem, challenge, or concern. Use this guided meditation to structure your lesson.

1. Make yourself comfortable in a location where you won't have any distractions or interruptions. Prepare yourself for meditation. Take three slow, deep breaths, in through your nose and out through your mouth. Let the first breath clear your body, let the second breath open your mind, and let the third breath free your spirit.

2. Consciously ask your spirit guide to join you, to help you with your concern or your question.

3. Envision a place of peace and calm. There are two comfortable chairs. You are sitting in one of them. Your spirit guide enters the room and sits in the other.

4. Focus your thoughts on what it is that you want your spirit guide to help you understand. Be specific. Complete the request, "I want you to help me understand …"

5. Open yourself to receiving your spirit guide's response, in whatever form it takes. Listen with your inner hearing, observe with your inner vision.

6. If anything is unclear to you, ask more questions. Ask how you can use this information to resolve your problem. Remain calm and open, even if your spirit guide's response seems to be missing the point of what you asked.

7. Ask your spirit guide how to use the information he or she has just provided.

8. Thank your spirit guide for coming, and say good-bye.

9. Feel yourself back in your body, become conscious of your breathing. Wiggle your fingers and your toes, open your eyes.

 Silver Cord

No matter what change you want to make in your life, you can always ask to be guided by a higher power, your higher self, your loved ones, your spirit guides. They can't make the changes for you, but they can lead you to the lessons you need to learn so that you can acquire the insight and information to make changes.

As with any spirit communication, it's important to stay open to whatever information comes through for you. You might feel that the information your spirit guide gave you was interesting but not especially relevant; insight and advice that comes through symbolic interaction is not always clear. Writing in your journal about your spirit guide lesson can help you to explore the many meanings that the message has.

Are You Doomed to Repeat It Until You Finally Get It?

Throughout history, leaders and philosophers have warned us that unless we learn the lessons of history, we are doomed to repeat them. We turn to this as explanation for the cycles of challenge, strife, and even war, which define human existence. If only we could "get" it, then we could end this cycle of doom!

This lifetime we're living right now may be just one piece of our soul's progression. This is not about being doomed to repeat the lessons we don't get. It's about the journey of "getting" it. It's about having the privilege to keep learning, so that we can continue to evolve and grow.

Each of us comes to this physical life to learn. Our lessons are not just behavior-oriented lessons like being kind to one another, although certainly these acts of compassion are elements. Rather, they are lessons of insight and understanding to allow us to make *paradigm* shifts.

Spiritology

A **paradigm** is a model or framework of collective beliefs and behaviors.

Your beliefs and behaviors form your personal paradigm. This is the pattern of your life. What you do represents what you believe, whether or not you are aware of it. In some ways, paradigms are similar to the symbolism that shows up in dreams, and in the symbolic messages that come through spirit communication.

The Energy of Your Thoughts

The most important thing in your life that you can change is the way you think! In reality, this is the only thing you can control and change, and yet it's the thing we spend the least amount of our time and effort doing.

Your thoughts are energy. Your thoughts are as tangible as your words and your speech. When you change the way you think, you change the way you move your life—just as when you change your pace when walking you change the way your body moves. When you choose to live your life in the flow of goodness and love, then you change your own energy vibration, which has an amazing ripple effect on every person you touch.

The Negative Energy of Worry

Many of life's challenges come from worrying about the actions and behaviors of other people. You might think that you change your energy, but so what? If the energy of all the people around you stays stuck, how does that help you in the end?

You may find that you create your life by worrying about what you don't have. All of this worrying sends out negative thoughts. When you change your thoughts, you change your energy. This is the "self-fulfilling prophecy" trap: You worry so much about something that it comes to pass, at which point you can say "See? I told you this would happen!"

Angie spent a lot of time worrying about having enough money to pay her bills. No matter how hard she and her husband worked, there never seemed to be quite enough. They argued about money; their money concerns seemed to rule their lives. Finally Angie realized she couldn't continue this way, and made the determination that every time such a thought came into her head she was going to replace it with a positive thought about the good things the money they did have made possible. Instead of thinking, "I don't have enough money for this," Angie consciously changed her thought to "I have just enough money to meet this need."

This worked fine for Angie. She immediately felt as though a tremendous burden lifted from her. She found that although not worrying about money didn't change how much of it she and her husband had, it relieved the stress of always feeling like she had to fix things. And oddly enough, it made it seem as though the money they did have was adequate—barely—to meet their minimum needs even if it wasn't as much as they wanted.

As Angie became more attuned to the energy of her thoughts, she realized that even though she had changed her thoughts about money, her husband still had many negative actions and thoughts. She worried for a while about how to change that, and suddenly it dawned on her: She *couldn't* change him! She could only change the way she thought about him. She had to change her perceptions.

Accomplishing that shift in perceptions became her next focus. Every time she found herself thinking, "All Richard does is complain about not having enough money," she made the conscious effort to think instead, "Richard is financially comfortable." Eventually, this caused Angie to change the way she reacted toward Richard. Instead of snapping at him, she was able to empathize with his concerns and say things that contained heartfelt support. It wasn't long before Richard also relaxed, and between them they were able to find ways to be economical and efficient. Feeling more confident, Richard found a new job with a better salary. Their financial situation improved considerably.

Changing Negative Thinking to Positive Thoughts

Negative thinking is insidious. Sometimes, even when your actions are positive, the thoughts that drive them come from a negative perspective. This spills out into everyday life in ways you often don't recognize.

We tend to focus on what we don't want to have happen. I don't want to get cancer, I don't want to be in an accident, I don't want to lose my job, I don't want to get lost when I'm driving through San Francisco, I don't want to fail my biology test, I really hope there are no delays at the airport when I fly to Baltimore next month. Feel how the energy of these concerns shifts when you instead say or think:

- ◆ My body is healthy and strong, and I take good care of it to keep it that way. My cells, my tissues, my organs, my systems are all working together.

- ◆ I will drive with attention and focus, and I will arrive at my destination safely.

- ◆ I like my job, and I want to stay in it as long as it continues to meet my needs and my company's needs. I have good skills and abilities that, combined with the learning of this job, make it possible for me to always have a good job.

- ◆ San Francisco is a beautiful city. Even though this is my first time here, I have a map and good directions, and I know I will find my destination.

- ◆ I've been looking forward to this trip since I planned it three months ago. The people who work for the airline are just as interested as I am in making sure that my flight is as smooth and uneventful as possible.

> **Silver Cord**
>
> Athletes, musicians, dancers, and other performers often use positive visualization to prepare for events. They focus on envisioning themselves moving perfectly through the event, from start to finish, experiencing every move. When they get to the actual event, they've already gone through it so many times that the pattern for success is well established and all they have to do is follow it. There is no room for worry about "what if …."

When you find yourself worrying about what you *don't* have, make a conscious choice to instead think about what you *do* have. When you change your perceptions, you change your reality. The key is to change your thinking from focusing on what you want but don't have to wanting what you have. Hope in the positive and avoid composing your hopes as negatives. If you find that you conceive your hopes in negative terms, you may be surprised to find that, in some way, you are hoping for the worst—for something that is unlikely to happen, for your fears! Instead hope for what *will* happen. Thoughts are energy, and they are creative force—positive, hopeful thoughts create your *positive, hopeful* reality.

The Challenges of Change

Change is not easy. Although this might seem the epitome of understatement, it's necessary to say this. *Change is not easy*. One of the ironies of insight is that for as wonderful as it is to know why you do something, there isn't a direct link to making changes in your life to support your newfound learning. Insight leads to decisions about actions, but it doesn't directly result in actions.

The connection between insight and action (change) requires conscious attention and continual effort from you. You can decide to make a change, but then you must continue making choices that support this decision. Tuning into the energy of the universe, through your psychic senses and through spirit contact, connects you to endless support. We say, when we talk about this support, that it is yours for the asking and that it is there to help you carry out your spirit's mission in this life.

It's important to remember that this is true in the context of the bigger picture. There is a grand scheme to existence that none of us have the ability to comprehend—in physical life. It is beyond your power to change everything. Many recovery programs and support groups begin their meetings with a simple prayer: "God grant me the serenity to accept the things I cannot change, the courage to change the things I can, and the wisdom to know the difference."

Breaking Free from Negative Patterns

Negative patterns often develop as a result of inaction rather than action. You slide into habits based on can't, don't, won't. You *can't* get a good job because you *don't* have a college degree and you *won't* be able to do all the other things that you like doing if you quit your current job to go back to school.

When you read such a statement in a book, it's easy to see the elements of choice that are present. In real life, "can't" and "don't" situations are those over which you truly have no control. If you are paralyzed from the waist down, your legs don't work as they did before and you can't walk as you did before. No matter how much you want to change this situation, you are not able to do so. These are facts of reality, and there is little that you can do about them.

You can, however, choose the ways you deal with these constraints. You can decide to work out regularly to strengthen and condition your upper body, so that you can become fully mobile using a wheelchair. You can choose to use weights, stretching, massage, and other physical therapy techniques to tone, as much as possible, the muscles and structures in your legs that no longer work as intended. You can determine that you will find ways to transcend your physical limitations that will then allow you to keep doing anything you want to do—albeit maybe in a new way!

Negative pattern is anything that's causing you difficulty in your life, a pattern of repetition, one that you realize you fail to understand. Why do you keep doing this, you wonder? Somehow, you miss the connections between your actions, past and present. You recognize the events or circumstances that puzzle you, but you struggle to perceive the connection these have to your current behaviors and situations. You remember, but you just don't understand the relevance all this has to your life path.

Negative patterns get the attention because they are often destructive. When things are going well, it seems that we have the tendency to coast along, not really noticing the details. It's only when relationships, jobs, health, and other aspects of your life begin to fall apart that you might look for the patterns that establish the problems. And "if" is a key word here; noticing patterns requires mindful awareness—conscious intent.

Any time you can substitute the word "won't" you are clearly in a circumstance of choice. This is the case most of the time! Changing your thought processes and your energy to think in terms of "will" is very powerful. You can choose to recast your thinking in the positive and fully "choose your choices," reinforcing behaviors of strength, confidence, and love. When you want a child to be careful with a drink, you say to the child, "Hold the glass straight" rather than, "Don't spill the milk!"

> **CAUTION**
>
> **Premonition**
>
> When you have a painful relationship to resolve that involves someone who has passed to the other side, it's important to first release the despair, to let it go. The situation, no matter what it was, was not your fault. This moves both you and your spirit loved one toward healing.

When we say things in the negative, we open the door for our greatest fears to manifest. Negatives are about fears. Expressing hope in the negative reinforces the fear, however subtly. When you express your hopes in the positive, then you move in a positive direction. And maybe others will be encouraged, both on the earth plane and the spirit plane, to move with you!

Establishing and Maintaining Positive Patterns

One reason that negative patterns are so difficult to change is that we focus on putting an end to them but are sometimes thoughtless about replacing them with positive patterns. Behaviors and thoughts are energy; when you take energy away, it leaves a void. Without intentional replacement, that void will fill with whatever energy is readily available. More often than not, this will be the same energy that you just sent away, because it's right there. It's the flow of least resistance.

When you dig a hole in the yard and just leave it, what happens? Most of the time, it fills back up with dirt, rocks, weeds—whatever is handy. The only way to keep this from happening is to intentionally put something in the hole to replace the dirt that you remove. Energy is the same way. It's great to remove negative energy, but to keep it from returning you need to replace it with positive energy.

Leonard came to Rita for a reading because he was having extreme relationship difficulties. Now in his 40s, he had never had a relationship longer than three or four months. The person who came through to Rita was a man that Leonard identified as his father. "Was your father a doctor?" Rita asked. "He's showing me a doctor's bag."

Puzzled, Leonard said that no, his father had been a jeweler. Rita went back to the spirit visitor, who again showed her a doctor's bag. This time there was also a message. "There was something with your mother and a doctor when you were about four years old," Rita said. "Do you remember that?"

Leonard was quiet. He did indeed remember his family talking about the matter. His mother was having an affair with the family doctor, he told Rita, and all the family gossiped about it. Leonard immediately recognized that this was the source of his distrust of women, and the reason none of his relationships lasted. He was able to release the negative energy of the mistrust and move forward with his life. He's been in a loving relationship with the same woman for seven years.

Silver Cord

Absent healing is a wonderful and powerful use of energy. It's important to see the person well, see the part of the body that's injured as repaired, to see the person as healthy, whole, and complete.

Spiritualists believe in reformation of the human spirit at any time, here or hereafter. What this means is that at any time, we have the opportunity to change our lives and move in a positive direction. Our life paths are fluid. Life can always be turned around. If spirit is telling you the bridge is out, are you going to just drive off the cliff? You can take a detour! If any psychic or medium tells you something is carved in stone, run the other way. If spirit gives you a warning, it means that you have an opportunity to make changes.

Your Personal Action Plan: An Exercise

Positive energy is powerful. You can use it to shape and focus your life in ways that allow your dreams and hopes to become your reality. What about your life would you like to change? Let this exercise show you just how effective this can be!

1. Choose a hope or an aspiration, something that you'd like to have as a part of your life that is not a part of it right now.

2. Articulate this hope as an affirmation. Be as specific as possible (see Rita's example following the exercise).

3. Write this affirmation in the first person ("I am ..."), then in the second person ("he/she is ..."), and then in the third person ("Rita is ..."). This is important because it makes the affirmation both internal and external, and gives you different perspectives of the same vision. Write each version of your affirmation five times.

4. After writing them, read your affirmations out loud, one in each person. How do you feel when you hear the words? Allow yourself to feel where it feels awkward to you, and then change your affirmation until it becomes entirely comfortable to you. (It's important to release your affirmation to God for the highest and best intent. Sometimes what you hope for is not for your highest and best; if it were to materialize, it would cause problems for you, such as an affirmation to marry the current love of your life when there are serious issues that make it unlikely the relationship would work.)

5. First thing in the morning, write (or say, if you don't have time to write) your affirmations five times in each person. After you complete the affirmations, consciously release the hope to the highest and the best.

6. Continue this process until your affirmation begins to manifest for the highest and best. Each time, be sure to release your affirmation to the God of your understanding.

The first time Rita did this exercise, she knew her affirmation would be about her painting. So she went into her studio and wrote, "I show my paintings. She shows her paintings. Rita Berkowitz shows her paintings."

She wrote this affirmation for a few days, and then realized it needed something more. So she revised: "I show and sell my paintings. She shows and sells her paintings. Rita Berkowitz shows and sells her paintings." But this still wasn't enough. So Rita revised the affirmation a third time, coming to, "I show and sell excellent paintings. She shows and sells excellent paintings. Rita Berkowitz shows and sells excellent paintings."

Rita wrote her affirmation five times a day for several weeks. Then she got the idea for a series called "City Folks." In the ordinary scheme of the art world, a painter does 10 or so paintings, takes slides of them, and then contacts gallery owners to view the slides and try to land shows. It's a challenging, sometimes grueling, process Rita had been through a number of times already. Although it's very important for an artist, it was something Rita had trouble looking forward to!

Rita wrote her affirmations every morning and started working on the paintings in the series. She had just completed the third painting when gallery owners began stopping by her studio, seemingly for no apparent reason related to Rita's current cycle of work. They saw the paintings she was working on, and started asking when the series would be finished, and whether she wanted to show the paintings. This spontaneous offer to show is almost unheard of in the art business, and Rita was astonished. The series turned out to be Rita's most successful, and the paintings sold all over the United States. Rita's affirmation came to pass!

Changing Your Soul's Path

Your soul negotiates with the divine (God) to establish its mission, and to choose the life paths that will support this mission. This is the element of existence you might think of as destiny—it is the cosmic course of your spirit, something that is determined as the course of events that will unfold no matter what.

Destiny comes from the Latin word *destare*, which means "to take a stand." This is what destiny is from your soul's perspective—taking a stand for what it needs to accomplish during this lifetime. Taking a stand requires conviction and action. You'll see that it is hard to take a stand by passively allowing life to flow around you. You act with firm conviction to take a stand—to put your destiny in motion—through the thoughts and actions you choose.

 Mediums and Messages

In Greek mythology, the Fates were three goddesses whose role was to spin the threads of life for each person born. One, Klotho, spun fibers into the thread (birth). Another, Lachesis, controlled the length of the thread (life). The third, Atropos, wielded the scissors that cut the thread off (death). Mortals remained powerless to influence the actions of the Fates; they alone determined the dimensions of life.

Your soul's path is the means by which it takes a stand. Because your actions determine its course, it is dynamic and ever changing. Each decision you make advances your soul toward its mission. Some choices change the direction of your path and the length of time it takes to achieve what is necessary.

When Rita's husband David came home from work in December 1996 and said that he had a new perk at his job, tuition reimbursement for spouses, Rita felt great excitement. She had long wanted to go back to school for her master's degree in painting, and this looked like the perfect opportunity, dropped right in her lap.

She did a meditation about it, and instead got a very different and unmistakably clear message from her spirit guides: "Go back to school, get your master's degree in psychology." The message was emphatic and powerful. Rita did two more meditations and got the same message, which affirmed for her that it was the right choice. So she went to graduate school and earned her master's degree in psychology. She now finds that what she learned is a crucial part of the work she's doing.

It's important to confirm or verify any message that tells you to make changes in your life. Ask three times, as Rita did. If you get different answers, back off. If this is genuinely an opportunity that has your name on it, it will still be waiting for you whenever you're ready to accept it. Always make sure you are 100 percent comfortable with the message before making any changes or taking any actions based on it.

Finding Fulfillment in This Life

Inasmuch as your life on the earth plane is a piece of the bigger whole and but a passage in your soul's journey, it is itself a mission. It's wonderful to be aware of the ways in which your life fits into other facets of existence. But your life is the here and now of your current existence, and the only way to make this part of your journey worthwhile is to make it the best experience possible.

You live in the here and now. Infinite decisions, choices, and actions shape the future, some of which are within your control and many beyond it. Keep your mind open! Remain unattached to outcomes, and allow process to happen.

Sheree works in Women of Wisdom and has seen many spirit drawings produced for others. In her drawing, Sheree immediately recognized her grandmother Delia and the description of Delia's home. Delia reported everything, including her favorite color, insisting as well on being drawn with her hair in a 1970s-style frizz perm. Sheree didn't remember her grandmother with this hairstyle, but upon asking her father, he could produce photos with Delia wearing the frizz perm and the same color dress she had insisted upon in the drawing.

The Least You Need to Know

◆ Your thoughts project powerful energy.

◆ Expressing a hope or a dream in a negative way puts out negative energy, turning your hope into a fear.

◆ Through affirmations, you can shape your thoughts to help your hopes and dreams become your reality.

◆ You can always make changes; there is always time.

◆ Your soul's path is dynamic and ever changing.

Chapter 24

Using Spirit Energy to Heal the World

In This Chapter

- ◆ Seeing the bigger picture
- ◆ What your life's journey means to you and to others
- ◆ Healing yourself and others
- ◆ Healing the world
- ◆ Change starts with you
- ◆ How sending healing energy can bring about change

Each life, each spirit entity, is unique, with its own set of experiences, challenges, and learnings. Yet each life and spirit entity is also a piece of the journey that is the world's existence. We can shape the world's future—our future—through the efforts of our spirits, whether they are working to the good from this side, or from the higher side.

When we evolve to a certain level we become one with the higher, one with the collective energy. As individual evolution becomes higher, individual personalities become less important. We move from "mine" to "ours," from "I" to "we." Our physical lives give us the opportunities that our spirits need to make these transitions. And through these transitions, we influence and shape the world's energy.

The Bigger Picture

Each of us has an absolutely different mission, and each mission has infinitely many paths that can take you to it. The people who enter our lives (on the earth or spirit planes) all have reasons for doing so, regardless of how long they stay or what it seems we accomplish as a result of their presence.

It is an amazing choreography. Even though it doesn't always feel that way, the people who come into your life come together for good purposes. Even when you think this is not the case, or that the outcome is less than you hoped for, we are all working toward a positive end. Sometimes the people who have the greatest roles in revealing lessons and leading to progress are the people who are the most challenging. Challenge is a form of questioning, of problems that present opportunities.

At one point in her life, Rita worked for a company that was incredibly difficult because the owner liked to play mind games with people. If you were on his good side it wasn't so bad, but when you were on his bad side, he made your work life nearly impossible.

After Rita had been at the company for some time, the owner offered her an astonishing promotion. But it immediately became clear that there were many strings attached to the offer. Ultimately, Rita felt the only choice that she had was to leave the company, so she did. She went to a new job, where her interactions with clients resulted in a series of paintings that she otherwise would never have thought to do.

The people who push you in these ways are often pushing you toward where you are supposed to be in the bigger picture, even when it seems that all they're doing is pushing your buttons, or forcing you toward difficult situations.

Your Journey's Meaning

Spirit communication provides validation that the journey that is your life has value, purpose, and meaning. Those who have passed to the higher side can reach back to you to show you there is more to existence than physical life. Your passage through this physical life is an opportunity for your spirit to grow and evolve and for the events of your life to contribute to growth and evolution for others.

For You

Your spirit is here on the earth plane, living as a physical entity, because there are lessons for you to learn. These lessons often come in the form of challenges. You face problems, adversity, even crises. You wouldn't consciously choose these circumstances because they are often hard and painful and involve loss and suffering.

Silver Cord

Astrology is a way to confirm the information that you receive through meditation. Because astrology is the blueprint of your life, it shows the path of your spirit's evolution.

But these are the experiences that are your soul's lessons. They are what you point to as defining moments in your life. From them you make changes—sometimes forced—in the outward ways of your life. You see and experience these changes. The inward changes that accompany them are not so obvious or visible. They reflect the personal growth that results from confronting the challenge.

It's not that this is the only way your soul can evolve, through the lessons of problems and difficulty. Rather, it's that the problems and difficulties are the events that force you to pay attention to your soul's mission. You learn just as much (if not more) from situations of loving kindness, of goodness for the highest intent. One goal of healing is to increase the learning that comes from good.

The Hierophant, *August 1991, oil on canvas. Rita worked on a series of paintings based on the Tarot in the early 1990s. In the Tarot deck, the Hierophant card is the symbol of all that is spiritual coming together. Recently a teacher of Rita's sat in trance and told her of a rabbi in full regalia who was her guide. When Rita showed him the painting, he smiled and said, "That's him."*

For Others

Your life touches the lives of countless others. This is most obvious in your immediate circle of contact—your family, friends, neighbors, co-workers. You form bonds and connections with these people through which you send and receive energy.

Sometimes people enter your life, or you enter someone else's life, for a specific purpose and this is clear from the moment you meet. The purpose might be limited and defined. A mechanic who opens a shop on your commute route just when your car needs repair. A woman ahead of you in line at the grocery store who tells the clerk that a position has become available in her company just when you're looking for a job. A security officer who happens to drive by when you're walking through a nearly deserted parking garage after working late. Circumstances such as these are constant reminders that the energy of the universe is there to help you in times of need, small and large.

Sometimes the contact is amazingly brief. A woman who profoundly changed Rita's life was someone she spent just five minutes with at a holiday party in 1995. Grace was studying art, and wanted to meet Rita because Rita was a professional artist. Grace was 92 years old, a tiny woman who walked a mile and a half from her house to the School of Fine Arts in Boston, where she studied figure drawing.

After talking with Grace, Rita thought to herself, "If she's not too old to learn, I'm not too old to learn!" Rita then made the decision to return to college for her graduate degree, setting aside her worries about possibly being the oldest person in her class (she wasn't).

Other times, your life becomes entwined with the life of someone else for reasons that aren't very clear. This is particularly true for mediums whose role is to bring people into contact with messages and information that will be profoundly moving, and then to drop from the picture. From a Spiritualist perspective, this is the key purpose of mediumistic abilities.

Sometimes you think people come into your life for you to help them, and they end up helping you instead, in ways you didn't know you needed help. When Susan met Alan, he had some substance abuse problems. Susan thought she could help him, and before long she became involved in an extramarital affair with him. Her marriage was difficult, and she found comfort in helping Alan.

But Alan's substance abuse problem was significant, and as he slid into decline he became less comforting and more challenging. In a flash of insight born of Alan's problems, Susan realized she needed to redirect her energy toward working on the problems in her marriage.

Working Toward a Common Good

As much as we like to focus on the positives of psychic and mediumistic abilities, it's a reality that they occasionally reveal challenges and problems. When this happens, surround the situation with as much white light as you can. You probably can't stop the situation from unfolding; it clearly is necessary for those who will experience learning as a result.

Also send healing prayers, to help those who are caught in the situation to pull from it the information and insight that moves them in the direction of what is for their highest intent.

> **Premonition**
>
> When your psychic or mediumistic abilities show you a negative situation or a disaster, send healing energy immediately. Don't wait to see if your prediction is right, and don't worry if it doesn't come to pass. You might never know that you made a difference. Always send healing that is for the highest and the best.

The World's Energy

Spirit connection is so amazingly powerful that you might be tempted to look at it as the heal-all for our planet, the world environment that supports us. This is a pretty good temptation, as temptations go! As with all tools, you must learn how to use your psychical (mediumistic) gifts to bring spirit connection into your life and to apply its insights for your good and growth as well as for the common good and growth.

The world—our world community—doubled in size from the 1960s to the 1990s. In the space of a single generation, twice as many spirits entered earth plane existences. We see the consequences of this population growth as an incredible drain on resources, environmental as well as social. Although the energy of the universe is endless in its capacity to support life, boundaries and limits define the Earth's ability to do the same. As we draw from the Earth to sustain our physical lives, it becomes increasingly important for us to replenish and restore its environment.

Energy is an endless flow, a continuous exchange. The universe gives to us, we give to the universe. There is no loss, only exchange. Resources don't really become depleted; they just change form. There is an abundance of all that we need out there—we just have to remember to ask.

What Can You Change?

Change, all change, starts with you. You probably could argue that it stays with you, too, because in reality all you can change is yourself. You can change your thoughts and actions, your beliefs and behaviors. The differences might sometimes seem so small as to be inconsequential, but they have significant ramifications nonetheless.

The Power of Free Will

We've talked a lot about your free will and how it shapes your path through this life. Students frequently ask Rita, "What happens when someone else sends you healing and you don't want to accept it?" Perhaps you sense your time of passing is near and you don't want to delay it, or you just don't want this healing energy that's being sent to you.

Your higher self, in conjunction with your gatekeeper (main spirit guide), guard access to your spirit. Your higher self decides whether to let the healing in. This is often related to the journey you've agreed to embark upon in this lifetime. You agree, before you enter this life, to what you will do and accept. This agreement frames the choices you make.

If healing comes to you for your highest and best, it's not intended to make everything better. It's simply there for you to use if you choose. It won't interfere with your soul's path. If it's your time to make your transition to the higher side, then you will, no matter what energy those on the earth plane try to send to you. And if it's not, then you won't.

The Power of Love and Goodness

All healing comes in love and goodness. It's sometimes hard to believe that this is the core of our existence, the basis of the universe, when so much of what we see and hear in our everyday lives seems far removed from either love or goodness.

When we talk about the higher vibration of the higher side of life, we are talking about a place of light, a place of love and goodness. We come from there! Even in our physical forms we remain part of this love and light. You come to this earth plane existence to learn, but you are always connected to the source of your origin. Before, during, and after incarnation, we are always spirit.

Teresa, *March 1991, oil on canvas. Rita sat with some friends doing readings, when above her friend Teresa's head she saw a vision of a young nun praying. She mentioned it to Teresa and did a quick sketch, which was later to become a painting.* Teresa *stayed in storage for about nine years when Rita met an astrologer Terese, who was to become a good friend and who was fascinated by Rita's spirit artwork. Rita told her she painted a painting of a young nun named Teresa and Terese asked Rita if the nun was actually St. Theresa, "The Little Flower." Being of a different religious origin, Rita had not heard the story, so she showed her friend the painting. Terese became quite excited and brought a book that showed an actual photo of St. Theresa; they seemed to match.*

Connecting Beyond Yourself for the Greater Good

We are all connected. Some connections are closer than others, but we are all connected as one. If one person hurts, it affects every one of us. Alone, your energy is powerful enough to shape the flow and direction of your personal life. But in combination with the energy of others, you become part of a whole that is far greater than the sum of its parts. Imagine what could happen if everyone would …

- ◆ Send healing to the earth.

- ◆ Send healing to the parts of the world where there are problems.

- ◆ Send healing not only to the people they love but the people they don't.

- ◆ Send healing to the people they care about as well as those who cause them problems.

- ◆ Send healing to those challenged by disaster and tragedy.

There are no limits to the good that we can accomplish when we pool our individual energies! Make your own list of healing prayers to further focus your energy for the highest intent. You might send healing when you …

Silver Cord

It just takes a moment to send healing energy to transmute the energy of problems that you see. It doesn't have to be anything big. Just send healing!

- ◆ Drive past an accident on the highway.

- ◆ See a police chase.

- ◆ See aid units on their way to a rescue.

- ◆ Hear of a family left homeless by a fire.

- ◆ Hear that a child is missing.

- ◆ Learn that a neighbor lost his job.

- ◆ Hear that a local business is closing.

Add your own reasons to send healing:

_____

_____

_____

_____

_____

Many of us spend a lot of our time worrying about things we believe we cannot change. We don't have to feel helpless in these situations. We can send out healing, do what we can on a spiritual level and on a psychic level and connect with the energy to transmute it to work toward the positive.

There is much strife and discord in our world, and it often seems so overwhelming that there is little hope for change. But change takes place one person at a time. And over time, this adds up to an amazing collective energy capable of changing—and that does in fact change—the vibrational pattern of energy throughout the world and the universe.

As insignificant as it might seem for you, as one person, to change the way you think, it is impossible for such a change to exist in isolation. Every thought, every action, affects the flow of energy in ways both obvious and obscure. More often than not, you don't see the full and multiple outcomes of these changes.

We often use the metaphor of tossing a pebble into a pond and watching the shift in energy ripple outward from the point of impact, until ever so faintly those ripples reach the shore and echo back toward their center again. Even when you can no longer see them, the ripples are still moving through the water.

On the Earth Plane

From our lives here on the earth plane, we cannot always see the outcome as being for the highest good. We have to trust that when we are working in light and for the higher good, the energy and the healing will go in that direction.

Avoid attachment to outcomes; that's "I" energy, or ego energy, not healing. Send healing, send love. The body has an intelligence (as does the earth); the healing will go where it needs to go.

To the Spirit Plane

The same holds for those on the spirit side. They can send healing and love to the earth plane. You can also send healing and love to the higher side to help a spirit entity evolve to a higher place.

Many times, those on the higher side can see the bigger picture. In turning to the higher side for assistance and guidance, you can go to the master teachers, to the spirit guides, and to the infinite source (the God of your understanding) and ask them to send healing to the earth plane.

Mediums and Messages

Rita's friend and mentor Bob Miller uses every opportunity to send healing energy to people. When walking down the street, if he sees somebody looking very distraught, he goes to them, shakes hands like he knows them, and sends spiritual healing to them! Then he pretends to have confused the person with someone else, and gracefully disengages. This gives him the opportunity to make the physical contact to send the healing.

Using Universal Energy to Help Others

The energy of the universe belongs to all of us. It is ours. We can tap into this energy at any time to be of service. When you are sending healing to a disaster or to someone who is fixing a flat tire at the side of the road, you send positive energy out there. No matter how small, it matters—and it only takes a moment. All too often, we are so caught up in our own busy worlds that we don't see the needs of others. We need to help those who are hurting. We need to take care of ourselves.

Fly high, and see the big picture!

The Least You Need to Know

- Look beyond your own life to help take care of the needs of others who might be hurting.

- The energy available for healing and to help others is endless.

- The power of one is significant; the power of many is awesome.

- It only takes a moment to send healing energy, yet the effort can change someone's life. It's all about goodness and love!

Glossary

Akashic record   A pictoral record of all of your soul's actions and travels, past, present, and future that occurred since the beginning of time, imprinted in the astral light.

apparition   A visual manifestation of spirit energy.

archetype   A pattern of images that represents a specific and universal realm of experience, such as the hero or the victim.

aura   A final, outer layer of energy that surrounds the body.

bits and pieces   The term for the way mediums express the fragmented way in which information sometimes comes to mediums, especially at the beginning of their development.

cerebrum   The largest and most highly developed component of the brain.

chakra   One of the seven centers of energy within your body.

circle   A group of people, usually having mediumistic abilities, who gather to connect with spirit entities.

clairaudience   The psychic sense of inner hearing.

clairsentience   The psychic sense of inner knowing.

clairvoyance   The psychic sense of inner vision.

closed circle   A group that meets regularly with the same members.

collective unconscious   The combined shared experiences of all humankind.

communicator   The spirit that is bringing you the message.

cosmology   A culture-specific description of the origin and structure of the universe.

discarnate spirit   A spirit without a physical body.

dowser   A person who uses divining rods or a pendulum to search for water or to check energy fields. In healing, dowsing is also used to balance the chakras (bodily energy centers).

earthbound spirit   A spirit existing between the earth plane and the higher side, commonly referred to as a ghost.

ectoplasm   A substance spirits produce to make themselves visible; comes from the Greek words *ecto*, meaning "outside," and *plasma*, meaning "a thing formed."

embalming   The process of preserving the physical body after death to prevent its decay and deterioration.

epinephrine   A natural chemical your body makes that stimulates heartbeat and breathing.

extrasensory perception (ESP)   The nonphysical senses that gather impressions and perceptions about physical and nonphysical experiences.

fake   A person who pretends to make the desired contact, sometimes with the best of intentions (to help you feel better).

fishing   The medium gives out small bits of information and then asks questions to fill in the picture.

fraud   An intentional fake motivated by self-interest that is almost always financial.

free association   The practice of saying or writing the first thing that comes to mind in response to a particular word or image.

gustation   The technical term for the sense of taste.

healer   A person (who may or may not be a medium) who has the ability to receive healing energy from the higher side and direct it to people on the earth plane who are ill or injured physically, emotionally, or spiritually.

human energy field   The composite structure that contains your physical existence.

hypnosis   A sleeplike state in which behavioral patterns can be changed to create healing.

invocation   A prayer or formal greeting that invites spirit presence.

kami   The spirit of a departed family member that remains among the family and community.

karma   The energy of cause and effect that you put out into the universe that comes back to you in this and other lifetimes.

Kirlian photography   A process of taking pictures in which the photo shows the object and its energy field.

levitation   The action of a physical object, sometimes a person, lifting into the air through spirit energy.

materialist medium   A medium who receives spirit messages that manifest themselves in physical appearances, such as images visible to others who are present.

message work   The portion of the service that presents spirit communication in the Spiritualist Church.

metaphysical   A term generally used to describe experiences and events that have no apparent physical explanations.

mythology   A collection of a culture's popular beliefs used to explain the unknown, such as the origin of life, to define acceptable behavior, and to teach moral lessons.

near-death experience   A phenomenon that occurs when the physical body experiences clinical death and the spirit leaves, and then life returns to the body.

olfaction   The technical term for the sense of smell.

open circle   A circle for spirit contact that anyone can attend, with a wide range of mediumistic ability present.

pagan beliefs   Worship of multiple deities, gods, goddesses, and natural events such as the changing of the seasons.

Paleolithic period   Period of time in history that began two and a half million years ago and that is considered the dawn of modern humankind.

paradigm   A model or framework of collective beliefs and behaviors.

paranormal phenomena   The events and sensations people attribute to the presence of "ghosts," such as unusual sounds and sights for which there are no obvious explanations.

parapsychologist   A scientist who studies psychic phenomena.

past life regression therapy   The process of exploring past life connections to present issues and concerns.

philosophy   A formal system or structure for studying and applying a society's beliefs and standards.

physical plane   The level of existence at which spirits take physical form (our physical world).

power animal   An animal spirit with special traits or characteristics that represent attributes or qualities that you have or need.

prana   A Sanskrit word meaning life energy.

precognition   The psychic sense that permits you to perceive experiences across the boundaries of time, into the future, seeing them before they happen.

psychic skills   The skills through which unspoken communication takes place between people on the earth plane.

psychical skills   The skills through which communication takes place between people on the earth plane and entities in the spirit world.

psychical vocabulary of symbolism   The "dictionary" of symbols and representations that a medium acquires to make communication with spirits possible.

psychometry   The ability to sense a person's residual energy on objects and in locations.

purgatory   A station of transition, in certain religions, where the soul goes to await judgment following death of the physical body.

Reiki   An ancient system of hands-on energy healing.

reincarnation   The return of the spirit to a physical body and physical existence.

spirit chemist   A spirit guide that works through healing to change the biochemistry within the body.

spirit physician   A spirit guide that works like a physician on the earth plane might.

spirit plane   The level of existence at which there are no boundaries of tangibility, time, or space.

Spiritualism   A faith system based on belief in the continuity of life beyond physical death.

subtle bodies   The seven layers of the human energy field.

telepathy   A process of thought transference in which one person receives information from another without using any physical means.

theology   The study of God and God's relationship with humankind within the context of a structured religion or faith system.

thought transference   The process of being able to communicate one's thoughts without physical means such as speaking or writing.

totem   An emblem or symbol that has spiritual significance.

trance   A state of altered consciousness in which the medium allows a spirit to speak through him or her.

trance medium   A form of spirit communication in which the medium enters a state of altered consciousness that allows spirits to communicate through his or her body.

transfiguration   A spirit's physical characteristics superimposed over a medium's features, presenting an image of the spirit entity.

universal energy field   The energy of all existence, encompassing the physical and nonphysical worlds.

vision quest   A ritualistic spiritual exploration seeking contact with power animals, spirit guides, and the spirits of loved ones who have passed to the higher side. Many times it is used as a rite of passage.

visitation   A phenomenon when a spirit speaks *to* you rather than *through* you.

Zener cards   A deck of 25 cards, with 5 cards each of 5 symbols, that researchers use to measure telepathic ability.

Appendix B

Additional Resources

Browse through these additional resources to find more information about topics that interest you.

Books

Andrews, Ted. *Animal Speaks*. St. Paul, Minnesota: Llewellyn Publishers, 1952.

Atwater, P.M.H., with David H. Morgan. *The Complete Idiot's Guide to Near-Death Experiences*. Indianapolis: Alpha Books, 2000.

Budilovsky, Joan, and Eve Adamson. *The Complete Idiot's Guide to Meditation*. Indianapolis: Alpha Books, 1999.

Campbell, Joseph, with Bill Moyers. *The Power of Myth*. New York: Doubleday, 1988.

Cayce, Edgar. *You Can Remember Your Past Lives*. New York: Warner, 1989.

Denning, Hazel. *True Hauntings: Spirits with a Purpose*. St. Paul, Minnesota: Llewellyn Publications, 1996.

Finkelstein, Arthur, M.D. *Your Past Lives and the Healing Process*. Malibu, California: 50 Gates Publishing Company, 1997.

Hammerman, David, Ed.D., and Lisa Lenard. *The Complete Idiot's Guide to Reincarnation*. Indianapolis: Alpha Books, 2000.

Hay, Louise. *Heal Your Body*, 4th ed. Carson, California: Hay House, Inc., 1993.

Ingerman, Sandra. *Soul Retrieval: Mending the Fragmented Self.* San Francisco: Harper, 1991.

Lewis, James R. *The Dream Encyclopedia.* Detroit: Visible Ink Press, 1995.

Moore, Thomas. *Care of the Soul.* New York: HarperCollins Publishers, 1992.

———. *Soulmates.* New York: HarperCollins Publishers, 1994.

Pliskin, Marci, CSW, ACSW, and Shari L. Just, Ph.D. *The Complete Idiot's Guide to Interpreting Your Dreams.* Indianapolis: Alpha Books, 1999.

Prophet, Mark A. *Kuthumi Studies of the Human Aura.* Los Angeles: Summit University Press, 1997.

Robinson, Lynn, and LaVonne Carlson-Finnerty. *The Complete Idiot's Guide to Being Psychic.* Indianapolis: Alpha Books, 1998.

Tart, Charles T. *Body, Mind, and Spirit: Exploring the Parapsychology of Spirituality.* Charlottesville, Virginia: Hampton Roads, 1997.

Weiss, Brian L. *Many Lives, Many Masters.* New York: Simon & Schuster, 1988.

———. *Through Time into Healing.* New York: Simon & Schuster, 1992.

Websites and Organizations

www.OfSpirit.com

This website hosts a weekly online magazine that presents articles, information, and resources for learning more about energy healing, spirits and angels, principles for attracting prosperity, and methods for maintaining good health. The site also features many links to other useful websites and resources.

www.SoulStirring.org

This website features information and examples of spirit-related art by many diverse artists working in all media (including the spirit drawings of co-author Rita Berkowitz).

www.snu.org.uk (Spiritualists' National Union)

This is the website of the nationally recognized Spiritualism organization in the United Kingdom. The site offers information about qualified mediums, the religion of Spiritualism, special events involving Spiritualism, and general articles. It also features links to related websites and resources.

International Association for Near-Death Studies
PO Box 502
East Windsor, CT 06028
www.iands.org

This organization coordinates and sponsors studies of near-death experiences.

Schools for Mediumship

Arthur Findlay College
Stansted Hall
Stansted
CM24 8UD, England
Phone: 01279 813636
Fax: 01279 816025
E-mail: afc@snu.org.uk

The Arthur Findlay College is the world's most renowned educational institute for Spiritualist mediumship. Students study Spiritualist philosophy and religious practice, Spiritualist healing and awareness, and spiritual and psychic unfoldment. Link to the college's page from the Spiritualists' National Union website, www.snu.org.uk.

Lily Dale Assembly
5 Melrose Park
Lily Dale, NY 14752
716-595-8721
www.lilydale.org

The Lily Dale Assembly is a Spiritualist community that offers daily lectures, demonstrations, and healings in July and August of each year. Classes feature a broad range of subjects related to human spiritual development.

Morris Pratt Institute
11811 Watertown Plank Road
Milwaukee, WI 53226-3342
Phone: 414-774-2994
Fax: 414-774-2964
www.morrispratt.org

Founded in 1889, the Morris Pratt Institute provides a comprehensive course of instruction to prepare an individual for the ministry of Spiritualism as a Spiritualist teacher, licentiate, or ordained minister, healer, and medium. The course is a self-paced program of distance learning. The Morris Pratt Institute is well respected in the international Spiritualist community.

Index